Teaching as Decision Making

Successful Practices for the Secondary Teacher

Second Edition

Georgea M. Sparks-Langer
Eastern Michigan University

Alane J. Starko
Eastern Michigan University

Marvin Pasch
Eastern Michigan University

Wendy Burke
Eastern Michigan University

Christella D. Moody
Ann Arbor Public Schools

Trevor G. Gardner
Northern Caribbean University

PEARSON

Merrill
Prentice Hall

Upper Saddle River, New Jersey
Columbus, Ohio

Library of Congress Cataloging-in-Publication Data

Teaching as decision making: successful practices for the secondary
teacher / Georgea M. Sparks-Langer . . . [et al.].—2nd ed.
    p. cm.
Includes bibliographical references and Index.
    ISBN 0-13-047478-9
    1. High school teaching—United States—Decision making. 2. Effective
teaching. I. Sparks-Langer, Georgea M.
    LB1607.5.T43 2004
    373.1102—dc21

                                                    2003008593

Vice President and Executive Publisher: Jeffery W. Johnston
Executive Editor: Debra A. Stollenwerk
Associate Editor: Ben Stephen
Editorial Assistant: Mary Morrill
Production Editor: Kris Robinson
Production Coordination: Carlisle Publishers Services
Photo Coordinator: Valerie Schultz
Design Coordinator: Diane C. Lorenzo
Cover Designer: Jeff Vanik
Cover image: Superstock
Production Manager: Pamela D. Bennett
Director of Marketing: Ann Castel Davis
Marketing Manager: Darcy Betts Prybella
Marketing Coordinator: Tyra Poole

This book was set in Minion by Carlisle Communications, Ltd. It was printed and bound by R.R. Donnelley
& Sons Company. The cover was printed by Phoenix Color Corp.

Photo Credits: Irene Springer/PH College, 1; Tom Watson/Merrill, 8, 133, 172, 406; Anthony Magnacca/Merrill,
16, 51, 96, 348; Anne Vega/Merrill, 39, 108, 214, 304; Todd Yarrington/Merrill, 71; KS Studios/Merrill, 118; Scott
Cunningham/Merrill, 146, 177, 194, 203, 230, 279, 330, 362, 389; Ken Karp/Prentice Hall School Division, 260;
Courtesy of Christella Moody, 399, 405.

Pearson Education Ltd.
Pearson Education Singapore Pte Ltd.
Pearson Education Canada, Ltd.
Pearson Education—Japan

Pearson Education Australia Pty. Limited
Pearson Education North Asia Ltd.
Pearson Educación de Mexico, S.A. de C.V.
Pearson Education Malaysia Pte. Ltd.

10 9 8 7 6 5 4 3 2
ISBN: 0-13-047478-9

To our families and spouses for their continuing support and encouragement. Special thanks to Peter, Bob, Judy, Patricia, Christopher, and Charles.

Educator Learning Center: An Invaluable Online Resource

Merrill Education and the Association for Supervision and Curriculum Development (ASCD) invite you to take advantage of a new online resource, one that provides access to the top research and proven strategies associated with ASCD and Merrill—the Educator Learning Center. At **www.EducatorLearningCenter.com** you will find resources that will enhance your students' understanding of course topics and of current educational issues, in addition to being invaluable for further research.

HOW THE EDUCATOR LEARNING CENTER WILL HELP YOUR STUDENTS BECOME BETTER TEACHERS

With the combined resources of Merrill Education and ASCD, you and your students will find a wealth of tools and materials to better prepare them for the classroom.

Research

- More than 600 articles from the ASCD journal *Educational Leadership* discuss everyday issues faced by practicing teachers.
- A direct link on the site to Research Navigator™ gives students access to many of the leading education journals, as well as extensive content detailing the research process.
- Excerpts from Merrill Education texts give your students insights on important topics of instructional methods, diverse populations, assessment, classroom management, technology, and refining classroom practice.

Classroom Practice

- Hundreds of lesson plans and teaching strategies are categorized by content area and age range.
- Case studies and classroom video footage provide virtual field experience for student reflection.
- Computer simulations and other electronic tools keep your students abreast of today's classrooms and current technologies.

LOOK INTO THE VALUE OF EDUCATOR LEARNING CENTER YOURSELF

Preview the value of this educational environment by visiting **www.EducatorLearningCenter.com** and clicking on "Demo." For a free 4-month subscription to the Educator Learning Center in conjunction with this text, simply contact your Merrill/Prentice Hall sales representative.

Preface

THEORETICAL/CONCEPTUAL FRAMEWORK

Teaching as Decision Making: Successful Practices for the Secondary Teacher is the work of teacher educators with deep roots in schools. The book attempts to bridge the theoretical with the practical, recognizing the import of theory and skill development, carefully planned lessons and teachable moments, and the intangible but all important magic of the teacher/student relationship. Careful decision making, which is necessary to plan lessons that address the needs of specific students, is stressed along with understanding the broader issues and context at hand. The text encourages readers to reflect upon five key factors involved in making and implementing ethical and effective decisions about teaching and learning:

- Students (culture, styles, needs, interests, development)
- Content (key concepts, outcomes and standards, required thinking)
- Pedagogy (methods, approaches, strategies, assessments)
- Philosophy (moral aspects, beliefs, aims, values)
- Context (physical environment, political conditions, social aspects)

A sample middle-level interdisciplinary unit on Zimbabwe is included in the appendix and referenced throughout the text to develop future teachers' skills in unit and lesson planning within the context of local and state standards. Additional examples are drawn from high schools and a multitude of individual lessons. With every strategy learned, students are invited to critique:

- its strengths and weaknesses
- where, when, and with whom it might be most effective
- how it might need to be modified for special student needs
- what values or social relationships it might promote

Thus the reader learns **technical reflection** (e.g., How do I use this technique and improve upon it?) as well as **critical reflection** (e.g., What long-range values are being promoted?). Teachers need to ask themselves both kinds of questions, and new teachers need information on the technical aspects of the job. Therefore, practical, concrete skill development and models for instruction are provided, and deep reflection on their use is prompted through reflection journals, Reflecting on the Ideas activities, and Practice Activities.

The teaching approaches and strategies presented in this text are grounded in contemporary learning theory and **constructivist practice**. The authors' view of constructivism centers on students actively engaged in building understanding, whatever the strategy or lesson design. Engaged learners construct meaning across a range of strategies such as direct and inductive approaches, cooperative learning and independent learning, learning centers, and role-play.

v

Any approach that purports to be constructivist must start with students first. This edition of *Teaching as Decision Making* makes that process explicit by rearranging chapters so that information on learning, student characteristics, cultural differences, and authentic learning appears before information on learning outcomes, assessments, or lesson plans.

The text emphasizes understanding the students as well as the results of teaching—the students' learning. Future teachers learn to continuously inquire into the meaning students are making of the ideas, skills, and dispositions being taught through both formal and informal **assessment** (e.g., preassessment).

Finally, the text uses a bridge metaphor to describe the process of building connections between students and content. One of the key aspects of the metaphor is that students must trust teachers enough to come across the bridge with them. The process of relationship building, both with individual students and across a learning community, is a thread through our discussion of instruction and the approaches to classroom management presented at the end of the book.

ORGANIZATION OF TOPICS

Chapter 1 provides a model of teachers' reflective decision making and introduces the metaphor of bridge building for considering the many aspects of teacher reflection. It also considers the teacher/student relationships that are at the heart of teaching.

Chapters 2 through 12 are organized into three themes: Planning for Instruction, Implementation, and Creating a Positive Learning Environment.

Topic 1. Planning for Instruction: Setting the Stage
- Understanding students and learning (Chapter 2)
- Teaching for understanding and authentic learning (Chapter 2)
- Choosing and analyzing classroom goals (Chapter 3)
- Teaching to content standards (Chapter 3)
- Planning for educational outcomes/objectives (Chapter 4)
- Assessing learning performances (Chapter 5)

Topic 2. Implementation: Hands-on Teaching
- Reflective lesson design and constructivist theory (Chapter 6)
- Designing and teaching lessons and assessments
  - Direct approaches (Chapter 7)
  - Inductive approaches (Chapter 8)
  - Facilitating structures and strategies (Chapter 9)
- Differentiation and diversity (Chapter 10)

Topic 3. Creating a Positive Learning Environment
- Building the classroom community (Chapter 11)
- Dealing with classroom disruptions (Chapter 12)
- Managing classroom discipline (Chapter 12)

The book concludes with an Afterword, which leads future teachers to envision their future as continual learners and to accept the importance of commitment and hope in shaping a career.

FEATURES OF THE TEXT
Strengths

Teaching as Decision Making:

- emphasizes developing skills in classroom curriculum design; specifically, planning, teaching, and assessment skills. Readers are prepared to create teaching units based on state or local curriculum standards.
- emphasizes both technical and critical reflective decision making. Readers learn technique and how to critique it for its long-range effects and ethical implications.
- stresses conceptual understanding, rather than fact-centered planning, through its analysis of content and outcomes.
- uses backward design principles in its curriculum design process, beginning with substantial goals, planning assessment strategies, and then creating lessons to lead toward the goals.
- emphasizes authentic, real-life tasks for learning and assessment (e.g., student-led research, problem-based learning, alternative assessment, and inductive models of teaching).
- recognizes both formal and informal modes of teaching and the role of teachable moments alongside carefully planned lessons.
- summarizes contemporary research on learning, memory, and brain functioning.
- develops, through its detailed explanations and concrete models, the ability to design, teach, and reflect upon the results of a variety of approaches to learning:
  - direct approaches (storytelling, minilectures)
  - inductive approaches (inquiry, problem-based learning, student research, role-play and simulation)
- presents strategies and structures to support teaching approaches
  - questioning
  - group learning activities and cooperative learning
  - academic service learning
  - integrating technology in instruction
  - centers and contracts
- describes short- and long-term planning strategies.
- focuses on the importance of differentiated instruction, including meeting the diverse needs of multicultural, gifted, special education, bilingual, and urban students.
- presents in two chapters a practical and balanced approach to classroom management. Concrete strategies in behavioral, humanistic, and research-based traditions provide a base for developing a philosophy of classroom management and creating a learning community.

Pedagogical Features

The pedagogical features of this text are:

- *Chapter Overview:* A short section highlights the key ideas that follow.
- *Opening Activity:* Each chapter begins with an activity that prompts the reader to reflect upon the topic to come, usually a case or situation.
- *Chapter and Section Objectives:* Each chapter or each section within a chapter has a list of learning outcomes that will be developed.
- *Check Your Understanding:* After a presentation of important ideas, readers are invited to check their understanding of the content.
- *Reflecting on the Ideas:* Throughout each chapter, readers are asked to consider their response to the ideas or to take an alternate point of view.
- *Chapter Summary:* At the end of each chapter, key ideas are summarized.
- *Practice Activities:* At the end of sections and chapters, readers are asked to complete skill-building activities or reflection exercises.
- *Unit Preparation:* At the end of each chapter students are asked to complete activities that will lead to the creation of a curriculum unit. Students who complete each of these activities will have a complete unit by the end of the book.
- *Portfolio Activities:* Each chapter contains suggestions for items based on chapter content that may be included in a professional portfolio.
- *Search the Web:* When applicable, chapters contain references from the World Wide Web.

Special Features

Special features in this text include:

- *Reflective Teacher Decision-Making Model:* The model is presented in Chapter 1 and is referred to throughout the book.
- *Sample Unit:* A sample unit on Zimbabwe (in the appendix) provides an example of each unit component, including various types of lessons.
- *Reflection Journal:* The journal prompts readers to consider the technical aspects (e.g., What worked? Why? What would you do differently? Who learned what?) and to reflect critically on the ethical and moral aspects (e.g., What values were promoted today?) of the lessons they teach.

Improvements

The following items are improvements in this second edition:
- The reflective decision-making model includes the role of relationships and the community in learning.
- The chapter on understanding students and learning appears earlier (moved from Chapter 4 to Chapter 2) to emphasize the central role of the learner.

- The section on constructivist learning has been expanded.
- The role of standards and alternative assessments is emphasized.
- Concepts and practices of differentiation (adaptations) for student needs are provided throughout the text.
- Academic service learning and teaching with technology are expanded.
- Each chapter ends with unit preparation assignments, portfolio activities, and Web resources.
- Reflection journals encourage analysis of student learning results and critical pedagogy after teaching specific lessons.
- The management chapters emphasize the development of a positive classroom community.

ACKNOWLEDGMENTS

The authors wish to acknowledge the many instructors and hundreds of students at Eastern Michigan University who have helped us test and revise this textbook. They provided much valuable feedback and numerous insights. We are grateful for such individuals entering the field of teaching. We extend special thanks to Deborah Harmon, whose careful feedback on differentiation and diversity made this a more insightful book.

We would like to offer special thanks to our colleagues who served as reviewers: Jane Boyle, Metropolitan School District of Wayne Township, Indianapolis; Barbara Kacer, Western Kentucky University; Mary Clement, Berry College; Harriett B. Arnold, University of the Pacific; and Sara Dallman, Colorado Christian University.

Finally, thanks to Debbie Stollenwerk, Ben Stephen, Kris Robinson, and all the people at Merrill/Prentice Hall for helping to make this long process more manageable. We particularly appreciate Valerie Schultz's selection of photographs. They remind us of the students at the heart of our efforts.

ABOUT THE AUTHORS

Georgea M. Sparks-Langer   is a professor in the Department of Teacher Education at Eastern Michigan University and coordinator of a grant to improve teacher quality through a student teaching performance assessment that documents K–12 student learning gains. A former foreign language teacher, she has presented workshops nationally and internationally for the Association for Supervision and Curriculum Development (ASCD), Phi Delta Kappa, and numerous states, countries, districts, and schools. She has published extensively in the areas of staff development (as Georgea M. Sparks), teacher education, and teachers' reflective decision making in journals such as *Journal of Educational Psychology, Educational Leadership, Journal of Teacher Education,* and *Journal of Staff Development.* She is coauthor (with Amy Colton and Loretta Goff) of *Collaborative Analysis of Student Work to Improve Teaching and Learning* (ascd.org).

Alane J. Starko   is Department Head and professor in the Department of Teacher Education at Eastern Michigan University. A former elementary classroom teacher and teacher of the gifted, she has been an active consultant in the areas of classroom differentiation, creativity, and education of the gifted and talented. Alane has been a board member and service publications editor for the National Association for Gifted Children. In addition to her work on both editions of *Teaching as Decision Making,* she is author of *Creativity in the Classroom: Schools of Curious Delight, It's About Time,* and a variety of articles, and she is coauthor (with Gina Schack) of two books on authentic research with young people.

Marvin Pasch   recently retired from his role as a professor in the Department of Teacher Education at Eastern Michigan University and is now the Senior Editor for Social Studies for the State of Michigan Merit Award Program's Sample Curriculum and Plans for Education (SCoPE) project. During his higher education career, he was a college administrator at EMU and Cleveland State University for 16 years and a faculty member for almost 30 years. He taught junior and senior high school social studies for 11 years. He has a 35-year interest in instructional planning and program evaluation and has published articles in the *Journal of Staff Development, Journal of Teacher Education, Social Education, Science Teacher,* and *Educational Leadership.*

Wendy Burke   is an Assistant Professor in the Department of Teacher Education at Eastern Michigan University. A former high school English teacher, she has been an active consultant in the areas of novice teacher induction and mentoring, professional development, and school reform. Wendy is on the Editorial Review Board of *The Teacher Educator.*

Christella D. Moody   was a public school teacher in Chicago Public Schools for 11 years and then spent 15 years in the Ann Arbor (Michigan) Public Schools as a teacher, school administrator, coordinator of multiethnic instruction, and coordinator of staff development. She has consulted in more than 10 states on effective teaching and multicultural education. She is the historian of the National Alliance of Black School Educators and the developer of the Young Educators Society for the State of Michigan. She is currently president of Current Directions Publishing Co. and executive director of the C. D. Moody Educational Foundation.

Trevor G. Gardner   is Vice President for Academic Administration at Northern Caribbean University in Mandeville, Jamaica. A former professor in the Department of Teacher Education at Eastern Michigan University, he was also an elementary and secondary teacher, a high school principal, and a school board member. He is an international consultant in school discipline and positive parent participation, having created the Rational Approach to Practical School Discipline (RAPSD), which is featured in Chapter 12, as well as the Participating Parents for Progress (PPP). Over the past 19 years he has consulted with more than 100 schools and colleges on discipline, multicultural education, and desegregation.

Brief Contents

Contents

Note: Every effort has been made to provide accurate and current Internet information in this book. However, the Internet and information posted on it are constantly changing. It is ineveitable that some of the Internet addresses listed in this textbook will change.

Teaching and Reflective Decision Making

CHAPTER OVERVIEW

In this book we explore how decision making contributes to the effectiveness and empowerment of teachers. Empowerment involves a feeling of self-efficacy—the knowledge that you make a difference in your work environment and that what you do as a teacher affects how students learn. An empowered teacher has assumed the responsibility to be a reflective decision maker, an active designer of instruction who reflects on teaching practices and student learning. We consider how reflective teaching is like bridge building and examine the power and importance of relationships in teaching.

Where are we heading?

Consider two alternative styles of teaching: the consumer versus the reflective decision maker. The **teacher-consumer**, through preference or circumstance, permits the curriculum—the content and methods of what is taught—to be determined and organized by others. Typically, the teacher-consumer has surrendered to the textbook the responsibility to define, analyze, and develop the curriculum. As consumers, they may follow the teacher's manual verbatim, without considering the worth of each topic or activity to the students in a particular school or classroom. They may not consult other teachers and experts to explore alternative methods and resources. Thus they do not participate in the creative process that brings curriculum to life.

Delegating all decisions about curriculum to a textbook poses significant risks. Textbooks present a wide variety of topics and often include an abundant assortment of important and unimportant, relevant and irrelevant information (Erickson, 1998). That information includes the concepts, skills, and phenomena that should be emphasized, with the addition of "details, embellishments, redundancies, illustrations, examples, facts, and names" (Dempster, 1993, p. 434). Too often, the student loses the point of the lesson in the midst of the profusion of information. Furthermore, the teacher may teach too many topics superficially, without sufficient depth for learning to take place. Similarly, teachers can become overwhelmed by the profusion of content standards that 21st-century students are required to master. Without careful attention to priorities and thoughtful planning, both teachers and students can be buried in ineffectively applied requirements (Carr & Harris, 2001).

Contrast the teacher-consumer with the reflective decision maker or with the **teacher-designer**, who uses content standards to develop district and/or grade-level goals, clarifies the outcomes to be learned and ways of assessing them, creates units of study, and only then decides what instructional materials, activities, and assessments are appropriate. Textbooks may be used, but the teacher (or team of teachers), not the textbook, is the major decision maker. Key topics are taught in sufficient depth to develop understanding; topics of little importance are eliminated.

Teacher decision makers have the fullest opportunity to flex and stretch their reflective thinking. They make *planning* decisions by choosing and analyzing content, clarifying outcomes, selecting learning activities, and assessing student performance. They make *implementation* decisions as they design and teach units and lessons, assess learning, make adjustments for individual student needs, and enhance their students' thinking skills. Finally, they make decisions about *classroom management*, applying their beliefs and principles about individual human beings and communities to create and maintain a positive learning environment.

After completing instruction, reflective teachers analyze student success and revise their teaching plans accordingly. Yet these teachers are interested in more than just what goes on in their classrooms. They participate actively with others in professional development activities, and constant learning (Beerens, 2000). They also take an active interest in the growth of their profession and the recurring need for educational change and improvement (National Board for Professional Teaching Standards, 1991; Darling-Hammond & Sykes, 1999).

This text explores a wide range of issues, strategies, and topics that teachers must consider in the 21st century. Further, it reflects on the characteristics of an effective decision maker.

A number of teacher-educators have used the term *teacher reflection* to describe a teacher's instructional decision making (Schon, 1987, 1991; Spring, 1985; Zeichner, 1996; Zeichner & Liston, 1996). The many views of teacher reflection (Grimmett & Erickson, 1988; Valli, 1997) range from the *technical view* (e.g., How well are the techniques I'm using working?) to the *critical* ethical/moral view (e.g., What are the long-term effects on society of this content or this technique?) (Colton & Sparks-Langer, 1993). A common definition consistent with the approach taken in this book is "the teacher's ability to make rational educational choices and to assume responsibility for one's choices" (Ross, 1987, p. 2), in other words, to make thoughtful instructional decisions. A key aspect of such decision making is to consider multiple points of view rather than acting on the first idea that comes to mind.

Our work has focused on the question, What do teachers need to think about when making a teaching decision? Good teaching decisions are based on much more complicated questions than these: What shall I do on Monday? What works? Decisions that appear to be straightforward are related to multiple variables. Each must be weighed according to its impact on students, both short and long term. Reflecting on these variables is a complex process, and not every educator engages in it. In fact, we have observed that frequently a person who attempts to tell you there is one right way to teach hasn't taught very many students—or is trying to sell you something!

Reflective teachers ask themselves, Is this an effective technique for this type of lesson? They also ask: Is it suited to this group of students? Do I have the necessary skills to use it? Does it model ethics I believe in? Is it fair? Is it important? Will I be able to look back on this day and feel I have done what students needed most? We cannot answer these questions for you, although teaching would be much easier if we could.

Rather than describing a single methodology, we have attempted to provide a broad range of options. We have our preferred strategies, which you'll probably be able to discern, but it is most important that you thoughtfully identify and follow your own process and beliefs. Reflective teachers carefully weigh knowledge of how students learn and develop with knowledge of the best practices in pedagogy and a host of other variables. This book will help give you the tools you need in order to consider a wide variety of factors in making wise educational decisions.

SECTION 1. TEACHING RESEMBLES BRIDGE BUILDING

Section 1 Objective

After you have completed this section, you will be able to describe how bridge building resembles teaching and learning

This is a book about teaching and even about bridge building, metaphorically speaking. It will help you learn a lot about the things teachers do and the ways they help students learn. It will help you begin to understand the way teachers think when they plan lessons, teach, and consider whether their lessons are successful.

Two Ends of the Bridge—Students and Content

Teachers build many kinds of bridges. We can imagine teachers building bridges to connect them to their students or to connect students. Similarly, we can imagine building bridges between subjects or between one idea and another. Perhaps the most basic bridge a teacher must build is the bridge between a student and the content the teacher hopes the student will learn (see Figure 1.1).

Metaphors, like this metaphor of a bridge, can be powerful tools in learning. They provide us with another view of important topics, in this case the process of reflective teaching. Stop for a minute and think how teaching is like building a bridge between a student and the content and what you would need in order to build a good bridge. Jot a few ideas on paper before you continue reading.

In order to build a bridge between a student and the content, you need to know a lot about your students. You must know what the students already understand about the topic, their interests, and their current and needed skills. You also should know how the students

Figure 1.1   Five Factors Contributing to Teaching Decisions

From *Teaching as Decision Making: Successful Practices for the Elementary Teacher* (p. 6), by A. J. Starko, et al., 2003, Upper Saddle River, NJ: Merrill/Prentice Hall. Copyright 2003 by Pearson Education, Inc. Reprinted with permission.

learn best and how their background can help in the learning process. Your end of the bridge will have to be wide, reflecting your full understanding of your many students. This will be a challenge, since you will have many students, each needing to cross the bridge.

The other end of the bridge is equally important. In order to build an effective bridge between students and content, you need to know the content well. Again, your end of the structure must be wide, reflecting your in-depth understanding of the subject to be learned. It is not enough to know *some information*. As a teacher, you need to know how to find the *most important information*, the ideas that will help students learn and grow for years to come. Time in school is too precious to waste on ideas that are trivial. You must anchor this end of the bridge to powerful ideas that will help students understand new content, solve problems, and ask important questions.

The Middle of the Bridge—Teaching

Once the two ends of the bridge are firmly anchored, you must actually build it. This is the part of the process we most commonly associate with teaching. When we build the bridge, we plan lessons and activities for students that will help them understand the content, moving them from what they know to what they do not know. It is ideal to build a bridge that is strong enough to support students on their journeys *and* scenic, so they may cross with joy and interest. To do so, you will need lessons that are clear, well-structured, and interesting. The lessons will need to be familiar enough to make students comfortable, challenging enough to move them forward, and novel enough to interest them. This is no small challenge!

It is also important to understand the conditions under which the bridge is built. Just as bridge building needs to be appropriate for the climate and geography of the area, so will your teaching need to be suitable for the **context** in which you teach. Activities or goals that may be appropriate for one group may be unsuitable in another political, cultural, economic, or social environment. It would be interesting to consider what kinds of contexts might be analogous to sunny days, swampy ground, or earthquakes. Think about the elements of this bridge-building metaphor as you consider the teacher decision-making model below.

SECTION 2. REFLECTIVE TEACHER DECISION MAKING

Section 2 Objectives

After you have completed this section, you will be able to:

1. consider a variety of factors when planning and reflecting on teaching results; and
2. develop a vision of the kind of caring relationships you will establish in your classroom learning community.

Teaching is a complex endeavor. No one learning activity will work with all students, in all circumstances, or for all types of content and objectives. The teacher must make a conscious decision every moment about what to do. Such decisions are based on a great deal of information and must often be made in a split second. At other times, you will be able to take more time to reflect on the complexities of teaching and learning, for example, when you are making lesson plans and redesigning lessons. The decision-making model attempts to clarify the factors to be considered when making teaching decisions.

REFLECTING ON THE IDEAS

Reflective teachers make a full range of decisions about planning, implementation, and management. Imagine yourself sitting at your desk planning a lesson for a class you will teach. Make a list of all the factors, issues, and knowledge a teacher needs to consider when making such teaching decisions.

In Figure 1.1 our bridge shows five factors that contribute to successful and responsible teaching decisions: the students, the subject matter (content), pedagogy (knowledge about teaching), the learning context, and the teacher (Richardson, 1996; Shulman, 1986).

Let's consider each factor in greater detail. The first factor influencing teaching decisions is **student needs and characteristics**. This is the first end of the bridge in Figure 1.1. The teacher needs to consider students' home background and culture when trying to relate new ideas to their prior experiences. For example, referring to curling to illustrate a point in a science lesson may totally confuse a student who has never seen that sport. In contrast, a teacher who utilizes students' knowledge of seesaws when teaching the concept of fulcrum makes a connection that facilitates learning. Students' developmental levels and learning styles may also influence the choice of activities. Teachers need to include multiple pathways for learning that include all senses and appeal to all students' interests and talents.

Considering teaching situations from the perspective of students' needs can make the difference between technical and critical reflective thinking (Zeichner & Liston, 1996). For example, if a student is disruptive in class, a teacher who is thinking only about the technical aspects of "How will I complete this lesson?" will approach the situation differently than one who considers, "What might be causing the student to act this way?" In the first instance, the teacher is likely to look for the quickest way to quiet the disruptive student—probably some type of disciplinary consequence. In the second case, the teacher might think of multiple possibilities, ranging from lack of sufficient challenge in the lesson to lesson content that conflicts with values taught in the student's home. Those needs would result in different strategies for addressing the problem.

The **subject matter**, or content (at the other end of the bridge), also influences teaching decisions. Each subject will have standards set by the state or district that specify key student learning outcomes for the different grade levels. Teaching science may call for certain activities, whereas teaching literature may require different strategies. Understanding content is important, but it is not sufficient. A good teacher must be able to "translate" ideas so that students understand them. It may take several attempts before a teacher discovers how to represent a complex idea so it makes sense to students.

A significant influence on decision making is how much the teacher knows about **pedagogy**: teaching, learning, assessment, and classroom management. The teacher needs a professional knowledge base of concepts, theories, and techniques to draw upon. These ideas include knowledge of human development, learning theory, multicultural education, assessment strategies, and teaching methods, to name a few. They are important tools for bridge building.

Another very important aspect of a teacher's thinking is the **context**, the conditions that influence everyday classroom life. The social, cultural, and political forces in the school, district, and community help determine what is taught and sometimes how it is taught. For example, many state departments of education are holding educators accountable for their students' learning of state standards.

Finally, **teacher characteristics and beliefs** have an important impact on decision making. Teacher traits such as self-confidence, enthusiasm, cultural background, intelligence, and commitment affect what a teacher will do on a particular day. Personal beliefs, or philosophy, about students' ability to learn, the purposes of school, and social values will also influence a teacher's choice of actions.

Teachers are shaped by their culture's assumptions about truth, learning, intelligence, and work. Often a teacher's beliefs about teaching can be expressed in metaphors used to describe their work, like the metaphor of the bridge cited here. Think about the ways two teachers' classrooms might differ if one viewed teaching as planting seeds and waiting for harvest, while the other viewed it as parallel to athletic coaching. Reflective teachers are aware of the beliefs, values, and assumptions that underlie their teaching and are able to reexamine those beliefs when appropriate (Langer, Colton, & Goff, 2003).

 It is important to consider all five factors (students, subject matter, pedagogy, context, and teacher beliefs) before, during, and after teaching. For example, when designing curriculum and lessons before teaching, the teacher may consider the following questions: What do I know about the students' backgrounds and interests? What do students know or believe about this topic? What objective do I want students to achieve? Which concepts are most important? What types of activities will I need for students to learn the necessary content? What problems may arise during the lesson? What strategies have I planned in order to confront problems if they arise?

During teaching, the teacher observes how well the ideas are being understood by students and reflects on all five factors as possible explanations for why the lesson seems to be going well or not. For example, if students seem confused by the lesson, the teacher might reflect upon the following questions: Is this lesson out of sync with students' cultural experiences? Are the students distracted by something that happened at lunch? Am I continuing with the same activity too long? Do I need to get students actively involved? Using this information, the teacher makes adjustments as needed in the pace, depth, and complexity of the lesson. Such decisions may even require shifting to a different activity or, in unusual circumstances, changing to a different lesson and objective(s).

After teaching, the reflective teacher evaluates the success of the lesson by asking: What do the students' work and responses tell me about how well they attained the objective(s)? Why was the lesson successful or unsuccessful? What could I have done differently? What have I learned about my students or about this topic? The five factors can help answer these questions. The teacher can then use this information to revise the lessons as necessary and to plan future ones more intelligently.

In your field experiences and early years of teaching, you will begin to see how these ideas can be woven together into the wonderful complexity of teaching.

Relationships and the Caring Community

Another important idea is the way two of our factors—the students and the teacher—come together. Consider once more our metaphorical bridge. Even if the bridge is built well, with strong ties to the students' world and strong links to the content, it is of little use unless the students cross over willingly with the teacher. One of the great truths about teaching is hard to learn from a book: *Teaching is about relationships.* In the end, students must trust you enough to come across the bridge with you. Going to new places can be frightening. A caring relationship allows students to find the courage to try new things, risk failure, and learn to grow. These relationships are at the heart of teaching. Caring relationships sometimes mean being gentle and other times being stern. At all times they require us to view each student as one of our planet's most priceless treasures.

In a caring community, we build students' skills and their hope. Students who enter our door must understand that we know they can learn. They must know that we expect them to learn, we care whether or not they learn, and we intend to help them so that they do learn. The concept of caring is an essential element of effective teaching (Noddings, 1992, 1995; Pang, 2001).

Goleman (1995) makes the argument that emotional intelligence (EQ) is a set of patterns, behaviors, and kinds of thought that are essential for success both in learning and in the workplace. He believes that effective educators must both teach and model appropriate affective and cognitive development. These include such components as

Caring is at the Center of Good Teaching.

self-awareness, independence, optimism, accountability, empathy, and the ability to manage one's feelings. Goleman (2000) suggests that school curricula must include a more complete "emotional literacy curriculum" that addresses issues such as handling stress, conflict resolution, decision making, and group dynamics.

Given the many other demands on busy teachers' time and school schedules, teachers may question whether we can assume responsibility for emotional development that has been traditionally centered in the home. Goleman and others would argue that we have no choice. In a culture in which school violence is often part of the headlines, one of the most important things we do may be taking time to teach emotional skills. Still others suggest that the links between emotional intelligence and life success are more complex, and that it is important to attend to the emerging body of research before making whole-scale changes in curriculum (see, for example, Cobb & Mayer, 2000, Mayer & Cobb, 2000). However the research emerges, it seems reasonable to assume that teaching to support healthy emotional development is most likely to occur in a climate of healthy relationships between students and teachers, with teachers modeling the kinds of affect and the kinds of intellect to which their students should aspire.

Still another way to focus on the types of relationships that are needed in classrooms is the increasing interest in the idea of linking spirituality and education, both as a means of fostering relationships and as a vehicle for developing character. Many teachers are uncomfortable with the thought that spirituality may have a place in public education. The important division between church and state makes any practice that could be interpreted as promoting specific religious beliefs inappropriate. Yet writing in this area has increased to the point that a major publication, *Educational Leadership*, devoted an entire issue (December 1998/January 1999) to exploring "The Spirit of Education." The interest in this issue was so great that it sold out more rapidly than any issue in the history of the publication.

Palmer (1998, 1998/1999) describes spirituality as "the ancient and abiding human quest for connectedness with something larger and more trustworthy than our egos— with our own soul, with one another, with the worlds of history and nature, with the invisible winds of the spirit, with the mystery of being alive" (1998/1999, p. 6). From Palmer's perspective, the courage to teach is the courage required to open our hearts and ourselves to the relationships required to teach. It requires asking the important questions that are embedded in all disciplines: Does life have meaning? What can I trust? How do we deal with suffering? How do we appreciate beauty? These are not questions we can answer for our students. They are questions that can be explored together while studying a myriad of academic subjects, building and requiring relationships of trust in safe communities.

Renard and Rogers (1999) have developed a more complex model of relationship-driven teaching. Their model centers on fulfilling students' fundamental emotional needs so that learning can take place. If students' emotional needs are being met in school, they are more likely to engage in learning (Rogers, Graham, & Ludington, 1998). When students believe teachers care about them, they are more motivated to learn and more likely to cross the metaphorical bridges we are building. Renard and Rogers describe two underlying principles and six standards that strengthen relationship-driven teaching. They can be useful as we consider ways to build communities in a variety of classrooms.

The first principle is based on the work of Covey (1989), "seeking first to understand" (Renard & Rogers, 1999, p. 35). Our first goal in building relationships with students is to seek to understand them. We must understand the knowledge, beliefs, experiences, and interests of our students as they are—not as we would like them to be. The second principle involves managing the learning context, not the learners. It requires establishing school situations likely to foster **intrinsic motivation**, motivation that comes from within the students, so that teachers do not attempt to dominate or control students from the outside. Teachers who are able to manage conditions, rather than students, are more likely to motivate students.

The six standards described below (Renard & Rogers, 1999) are designed to build a motivating teaching context.

1. *Safe.* Safety in school must include not just physical safety (although that certainly is important), but emotional safety as well. Students must know that they will be safe from threats, intimidation, or embarrassment. In a safe classroom, students are free to take risks and try new things.
2. *Valuable.* Students are more likely to engage and persist in learning if they perceive that what they are doing is valuable. Valuable content fills a need, solves a problem, and can be interesting and enjoyable.
3. *Successful.* Students need evidence of their success to maintain motivation. They need activities which are challenging enough that they recognize their growth while still allowing for success.
4. *Involving.* Students are more motivated to learn when they feel they have a stake in what is going on around them. Students who take part in planning an activity or other decisions about their learning are more motivated to continue.
5. *Caring.* Everyone wants to be liked. Students want to feel that their teachers accept, value, and care about them. The harder some children are to like, the more they probably need to know you care. Caring can be very hard work.
6. *Enabling.* Good teachers constantly seek out the best practices that help their students learn. They continue to learn and grow in search of teaching methods that will be effective with all students, rather than relying on "tried and true" methods that work with many students but leave some behind.

The Responsive Classroom model (Charney, 1992; Horsch, Chen, & Nelson, 1999) briefly described in Chapter 11 is another example of a model of teaching and management focused specifically on the development of self-management and motivation in classroom communities.

REFLECTING ON THE IDEAS

Observe a teacher you consider to be effective. Be particularly attuned to the things the teacher does to develop positive relationships with students and foster intrinsic motivation. It may be helpful to divide a paper into the six areas listed above and make notes of behaviors that appear to fit each category. Share your observations with a colleague, and look for similarities and differences.

As you study this text and learn about teacher reflection and planning, consider how the activities you plan for your classroom may facilitate strong relationships and student motivation. Fortunately, there are many times in education when an instructional choice can serve more than one goal. For example, in Chapter 2 you will learn that some scholars believe that an emotionally safe classroom atmosphere is more compatible with brain development than one that is highly competitive or negative. Other scholars would recommend the same type of atmosphere but for different reasons: perhaps to develop the relationships of trust necessary for student motivation. Be alert to other parallel recommendations. In many cases the strategies that are recommended for optimum cognitive growth also will serve important affective functions and vice versa. In the end, whatever strategies you choose for teaching will form the structure of the bridge you cross with your students. It will be the heart of your teaching—the community of relationships you build in your classes—that will determine whether you cross successfully.

Practice Activity

Practice Point

Choose a metaphor and relate to it a brief reflection describing your view of the core role of a teacher. You may wish to develop this metaphor into a more formal description of your philosophy of teaching. It can be helpful to examine your metaphor and your philosophy periodically and see if they have changed as you have developed in experience and expertise.

CHAPTER SUMMARY

We have provided a model for reflective teacher decision making, a metaphor for thinking about teaching, and information on the importance of relationships in teaching. The rest of the book develops your ability to design instructional units and manage your classroom. As you explore the chapters that follow, examine the information in a careful and systematic way and respond to the exercises provided. We have written this book because we believe the information can help you to be the best teacher possible. We hope that you will find the information both practical and thought provoking. It is our vision for you to become a reflective teacher "designer," capable of making thoughtful and appropriate instructional decisions. We wish you well on the journey.

Unit Preparation

As you read this text, we will describe a process for creating a teaching unit. If you complete each "Unit Preparation" section in turn, you will develop an original teaching unit by the time you complete this text. To begin, it is important that you determine the audience for your unit. Ideally, you should prepare a unit for a real classroom, preferably one in which you are currently doing a variety of field experiences.

Identify that class now. Begin talking to the teacher about content areas that would be appropriate for unit planning and special class needs you should consider. Find out whether content in that class is typically organized in single-subject or interdisciplinary units. You probably will find the unit planning process easier to use in content that is organized around key concepts rather than skills. For example, a unit on types of poetry or habitats will fit this planning model more readily than a unit on how to read a map, although map reading could be embedded in many units. More detailed information on selecting unit content will be found in Chapter 3.

For now, it is most important to make a decision about the class for which you will be preparing materials and the general areas you might address. *Begin reading in that area now.* It is essential that you have a solid understanding of the content yourself before trying to teach it to others. Do not make the mistake of thinking that because you are teaching adolescents your content knowledge can be limited. Selecting the most important content for secondary school students requires teachers to know far more than they teach. Only by knowing the content well can you make good decisions about content emphases and organization. Be sure to keep all relevant bibliographic information for your reference list. Keep track of any commercial materials or materials that you use in the unit and reference them appropriately.

 ## *Portfolio Activity*

The Portfolio Activities in this text are designed to help you compile a collection of materials that can be helpful in demonstrating your knowledge and reflection about teaching and learning. In some cases the Unit Preparation activities also can serve as parts of your portfolio. In other cases we will suggest additional activities. For example, one of the most powerful means of describing our beliefs about teaching is through the metaphors we use. The metaphor you wrote for the last practice activity could be polished and placed at the front of your portfolio to illustrate your educational philosophy.

 ## *Search the Web*

The World Wide Web can be a valuable resource for reflective teachers seeking information on content, research on teaching, or even lesson ideas. A strength of web publishing is that it is accessible to many individuals; many teachers and organizations throughout the world are able to post information for others to share. Of course, it is a challenge to carefully review and determine the credibility of the source and accuracy of the information on the web. Further, many web addresses are unstable; if you visit a website today (or we print one in this text), there is no guarantee it will exist next year. The teacher who created it may have taken another position with a different address, the organization may have lost its web-savvy organizer, or any number of other scenarios may exist.

We will cite web resources that appear to be stable and will probably continue to be useful for many years. One of the most important of these resources is the Educational

Resources Information Center (ERIC) system. It provides links to virtually any type of document about education and a variety of search services. To find the ERIC Clearing-house for middle-level resources, go to: ericeece.org/midlink.html

Use the following addresses for ERIC resources on the teaching of the subjects indicated:

Science and Math: www.ericse.org
Social Studies/Social Science: ericso.Indiana.edu
Reading, English, and Communication: eric.Indiana.edu
Languages and Linguistics: www.cal.org/ericcll

REFERENCES

Beerens, D. (2000). *Evaluating teachers for professional growth: Creating a culture of motivation and learning.* Thousand Oaks, CA: Corwin Press.

Carr, J. F., & Harris, D. E. (2001). *Succeeding with standards: Linking curriculum, assessment, and action planning.* Alexandria, VA: Association for Supervision and Curriculum Development.

Charney, R. S. (1992). *Teaching children to care: Management in the responsive classroom.* Greenfield, MA: Northeast Foundation for Children.

Cobb, C. D., & Mayer, J. D. (2000). Emotional intelligence: What the research says. *Educational Leadership, 58*(3), 14–18.

Colton, A., & Sparks-Langer, G. (1993). A conceptual framework to guide the development of teacher reflection and decision making. *Journal of Teacher Education, 44*(1), 45–54.

Covey, S. (1989). *The seven habits of highly effective people.* New York: Simon & Schuster.

Darling-Hammond, L., & Sykes, G. (Eds.). (1999). *Teaching as the learning profession: Handbook of policy and practice.* San Francisco: Jossey-Bass.

Dempster, F. N. (1993). Exposing our students to less should help them learn more. *Phi Delta Kappan, 74*(6), 433–437.

Erickson, L. (1998). *Concept-based curriculum and instruction: Teaching beyond the facts.* Thousand Oaks, CA: Corwin Press.

Goleman, D. (1995). *Emotional intelligence.* New York: Bantam.

Goleman, D. (2000). Toward a model emotional literacy curriculum. www.eq.org/articles/goelman.html

Grimmett, P. P., & Erickson, G. L. (Eds.). (1988). *Reflection in teacher education.* New York: Teachers College Press.

Horsch, P., Chen, J., & Nelson, D. (1999). Rules and rituals: Tools for creating a respectful, caring, learning community. *Phi Delta Kappan, 81*(3), 223–227.

Langer, G. M., Colton, A. B., & Goff, L. (2003). *Collaborative Analysis of Student Learning.* Alexandria, VA: ASCD.

Mayer, J. D., & Cobb, D. R. (2000). Educational policy on emotional intelligence: Does it make sense? *Educational Psychology Review, 12*(2), 163–183.

National Board for Professional Teaching Standards (1991). Toward high and rigorous standards for the teaching profession. 1525 Wilson Blvd., Ste 500, Arlington, VA 22209 (www.NBPTS.org).

Noddings, N. (1992). *The challenge to care in schools.* New York: Teachers College Press.

Noddings, N. (1995). *Philosophy of education.* Boulder, CO: Westview Press.

Palmer, P. (1998). *The courage to teach: Exploring the inner landscape of a teacher's life.* NY: Jossey-Bass.

Palmer, P. (1998/1999). Evoking the spirit in public education. *Educational Leadership, 56*(4), 6–11.

Pang, V. O. (2001). *Multicultural education: A caring-centered, reflective approach.* New York: McGraw-Hill.

Renard, L. & Rogers, S. (1999). Relationship-driven teaching. *Educational Leadership, 57*(1), 34–37.

Richardson, V. (1996). Teacher thinking. In J. Sikula (Ed.), *Handbook of research on teacher education,* 2nd ed. New York: Macmillan.

Rogers, S., Graham, S., & Ludington, J. (1998). *Motivation & learning.* Evergreen, CO: Peak Learning Systems.

Ross, D. R. (1987). *Teaching teacher effectiveness research to students: First steps in developing a reflective approach to teaching.* Paper presented at the annual meeting of the American Educational Research Association, Washington, D.C.

Schon, D. A. (1987). *Educating the reflective practitioner.* San Francisco: Jossey-Bass.

Schon, D. A. (1991). *The reflective turn: Case studies in and on educational practice.* New York: Teachers College Press.

Shulman, L. S. (1986). Those who understand: Knowledge growth in teachers. *Educational Researcher, 15*(7), 4–14.

Spring, H. T. (1985). Teacher decision-making: A meta-cognitive approach. *The Reading Teacher, 39,* 290–295.

Valli, L. (1997). Listening to other voices: A description of teacher reflection in the United States. *Peabody Journal of Education, 72*(1), 67–88.

Zeichner, K. M. (Ed.). (1996). *Currents of reform in preservice teacher education.* New York: Teachers College Press.

Zeichner, K. M., & Liston, D. P. (1996). *Reflective teaching: An introduction.* Mahwah, NJ: Lawrence Erlbaum.

Planning for Instruction: Setting the Stage

Understanding Students and Learning

CHAPTER OVERVIEW

Our understanding of our responsibilities as teachers is best reflected in how we tend to our commitments to our students. Only when we are successful in helping them to further develop as active learners are we really teaching. Said another way, a primary factor for improving student achievement is to raise teachers' expectations for students' learning. Understanding our students—what they know, what they care about, how they learn best, and how their knowledge relates to our content—is key to this process. It is equally important to understand our own experiences as students and to reflect on the ways they influence how we think about our students.

This chapter focuses on students, the ways they differ as individuals, and the factors that affect their learning. It also provides activities that encourage you to reflect on your assumptions about students, how they learn, and how you might best approach working with them as their teacher. By considering the ways in which students' characteristics impact their responses to learning activities, teachers can plan lessons around the needs of the most important people in the classroom: the students.

Opening Activity

Throughout this chapter we will follow an imaginary middle school teacher, Ken Cowan, as he develops a unit on life in Zimbabwe: A World's View from Africa. Assume for a moment that Ken has decided to use a textbook reading and a lecture to inform his eighth-grade students about life in Zimbabwe. While he is teaching, he is getting little response from his students. They seem to be bored. Sue is staring out the window, and three students in the back are whispering. Ken has planned his lecture carefully and provided much detail about the events, but the students seem uninterested.

Practice Point

What is going on here? Consider some of the factors that might be contributing to the students' lack of attention. Think about what influences your own learning. List as many factors as you can.

You may have thought of some of the following possibilities: The teacher never got the students' attention at the beginning of the lesson, he did not make the material relevant to their everyday lives, or the material was too abstract and complex for the students. Perhaps they were sleepy because it was right after lunch, or perhaps the content was presented in a disorganized and confusing way, the lecture lasted too long, no visual aids were used, students were not directly involved through interaction with the teacher or with others, or the presentation lacked variety.

 ## REFLECTING ON THE IDEAS

Think about what motivated you to want to learn in the classroom, specifically when you were a middle or high school student. What factors were important to you?

Many reasons might explain why students are inattentive during a learning activity. If Ken wants to redesign this activity so that it will be more effective the next time he uses it, he will need to know why it did not work very well. This chapter presents information about students and the ways they learn that can help you with such decisions.

Teacher Reflection and Decision Making

Reconsider the theme of this book: teachers' decision making. In order to plan learning experiences, make modifications while teaching, and redesign activities so they are more effective in the future, teachers need to do some very complex thinking. Recall the discussion of the five factors involved in reflective teaching decisions in Chapter 1. Figure 2.1 shows how teachers reflect on instructional decisions by taking into account student needs; content (ideas) to be learned; teachers' knowledge of learning theories, methods, and assessment (pedagogy); the conditions (context) surrounding the learning; and teacher characteristics. These same factors are considered in selecting and implementing learning activities.

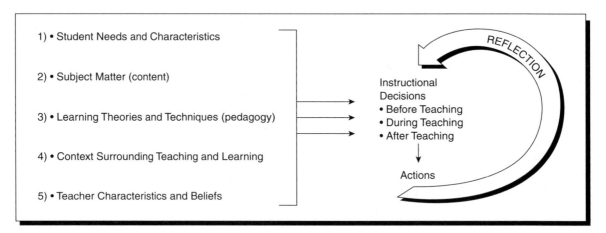

Figure 2.1   Factors Influencing Teaching Decisions

From *Teaching as Decision Making: Successful Practices for the Elementary Teacher* (p. 22), by A. J. Starko, et al., 2003, Upper Saddle River, NJ: Merrill/Prentice Hall. Copyright 2003 by Pearson Education, Inc. Reprinted with permission.

To decide which method to use with which content and with which students, you need to understand quite a bit about student characteristics and how students learn. The first section of this chapter examines the types of information you will want to consider about individual students. The second section explores various learning theories and their practical applications more generally, as they may affect any student in your classroom.

SECTION 1. THE LEARNER: STUDENTS' PERSONAL CHARACTERISTICS

Section 1 Objective

After you have completed this section, you will be able to describe characteristics of students that may influence teaching decisions.

All instructional decisions involve students. The most carefully conceived objectives or well-designed lessons have meaning only when they affect particular students. You will have to consider the ways the students' strengths, weaknesses, needs, desires, and interests will affect the teaching and learning process. The more you know about the individual differences among your students, the more effectively you can adapt instruction to your particular class and to each new group of students you encounter throughout your teaching career. It will also be helpful for you to be continually reflective about your own assumptions about students, their abilities and interests, and your communication style as you work with them.

Gathering Information

In many ways, a good teacher's information gathering about students parallels the diagnostic skills we expect in physicians. A good physician is a careful observer, using a variety of skills to understand what is happening in a patient's body, but knowing the immediate symptoms is not enough. The physician must know a great deal about a patient's history, allergies, and lifestyle in order to determine the best course of action. Teachers have a similar challenge in understanding students' intellectual and emotional growth. You must understand what students know and how they are learning, both immediately and in a broader context, to make good decisions about instruction.

Probably your most vital skill as a teacher is the ability to gather, understand, and use information about your students. Information will come in many forms. Some information about students' families, health, and past educational experiences will come with students' records. If, for example, you are a math teacher and you noticed that Peter was having trouble with math, it would be helpful to know that until last year his math grades were above average. With that knowledge you would need to consider what might have occurred last year and how that knowledge should affect your planning. Certainly you will need to make sure Peter learns the math skills he did not learn last year. You may find that by concentrating on the specific skills taught during that time you can bring Peter up to speed more quickly than with a general review of last year's material.

Information about your students will come from a variety of sources including:

- **standardized tests**, particularly if the test is aligned with your curriculum and if test results are broken down into specific areas, skills, or knowledge
- observations of your students' behavior both within and outside of the classroom
- analysis of their work, tests, and presentations
- individual conversations with students
- communication with parents, guardians, and community members

Gathering this information can be invaluable in understanding the community and cultures within which your students learn. All these types of information will be important as you assess what students know before teaching and strive to understand their responses during learning activities.

Gathering this information is only part of the process of understanding students. It is also important to reflect on it and analyze how it might influence your decision making as a teacher. Teachers must use care and caution when creating profiles of students' characteristics, needs, and abilities, realizing that such profiles are never fixed, static, or unchanging. A teacher who understands her students realizes that they are in a perpetual stage of development, growth, and maturation. Finally, teachers should use discretion when speaking about their students with others.

Culture

One of the most fundamental ways in which students may differ from one another is in their culture (Banks, 1987, 1999). **Culture** has been defined as "the ideation, symbols, values, and beliefs that are shared by a human group" and include the "... institutions, or other components of human societies that are created . . . to meet their survival needs" (Banks, 1999, p. 115).

Each of us has been raised in a particular culture. We have spoken at least one common language; celebrated particular holidays; understood specific family structures; appreciated certain kinds of food, music, art, and literature; and shared values with people around us.

Students' cultures influence their way of perceiving, evaluating, behaving, and doing, just as teachers' cultures impact their decision making in the classroom. Cultures affect the way students communicate, the structure of their family, the art and music they value, their social relationships, and many other important factors in their lives. Cultural influences have multiple layers, some more easily visible than others (Pang, 2001). Cultures vary in their means of communication (language, symbols, artifacts), means of interaction (customs, practices, interactional patterns) and values (values, norms, beliefs, expectations). It is much easier to observe differences in dress and dialect than it is to understand the value orientations that impact your students' lives. Such cultural differences make students' school lives unique and affect their lifestyles, values, attitudes, and school performance.

The dominant culture (**macroculture**) in the United States is Anglo–Western European. The formal institutions, official language, dominant social values, and other aspects of life in this society were shaped by the experiences of early settlers from Western Europe. For example, the individualism that has been a traditional American value has its roots in Judeo-Christian ethics, and our government was modeled on the English parliamentary system. Yet, the United States is, in actuality, a multicultural society and consists of many microcultures.

A **microculture** may be defined as a smaller culture within a macroculture that has its own unique cultural patterns. As this nation has grown, many groups of immigrants have arrived, each bringing its own cultural traditions. Some groups who joined our society came voluntarily in search of a better life. Other groups were involuntary immigrants brought against their will; for example, many African Americans (Ogbu, 1983). All of these groups have made valuable contributions to the United States. In fact, one of the greatest riches of our country is the diversity of its people and the strengths and influences each culture has contributed to the whole. The "melting pot" metaphor of the United States poorly represents our multicultural perspective, because it does not adequately address many groups' interest in and practice of maintaining their cultural identity within and outside of their homes.

At various times in our history, specific cultural groups have been deemed less desirable, less intelligent, or less valued because of their differences from the larger culture. For example, during the late 19th century, the Chinese and the Irish were considered undesirable and were subject to social and economic prejudice. Shops seeking employees sometimes posted signs reading, "No Irish need apply." Such exclusionary practices, while different in form, still persist today. It is still true that African American, Hispanic, and students for whom English is not their first language are more likely to be placed in lower ability classes than white students (Oakes & Lipton, 1999). Schools can have an influence in reversing this trend. If educators increase their knowledge of the differences among and within cultures, the schools can better serve the diverse needs of students and affirm their many cultural heritages.

Culturally relevant teaching (Ladson-Billings, 1994, 1995; Pang, 2001; Wlodowski & Ginsberg, 1995) requires that teachers be knowledgeable about and responsive to the cultural differences among their students. It recognizes that teaching for varied cultures is not as simple as using diverse pictures on the bulletin board or presenting units on different countries, although it would include both of those practices. Note that students' responses to learning tasks are affected by their culture's understandings of importance, opportunity, novelty, and value. Culturally competent teachers (Ford, 1996; Ladson-Billings, 1994, 1995) learn from their students what the students value, how they feel, and how they interact most comfortably. Such teachers recognize the ways in which their own culture, language, background, and experiences impact their relationships with students in the classroom. Only by knowing students well and by providing students the opportunities to learn from every person in that classroom can teachers plan activities that will allow them to learn effectively and create a learning community that respects diversity.

Some students come not only from a culture whose traditions and values differ from those of the mainstream, but from homes in which Standard English is not the primary language or is not spoken at all. According to one report, one out of every seven students grows up speaking a language other than Standard English (Oakes & Lipton, 1999). Some students are truly bilingual, that is, they speak English and a second language. Others speak little or no English. In fact, some "bilingual" students have had such limited or confusing language experiences that they are not proficient in either language. Although many districts provide support for large bilingual populations in the form of special classes or tutoring, many students for whom Standard English is not the preferred language may be in your classes with little or no additional support. In order to serve the needs of this special population, it is important to consider both the characteristics of bilingual students and the strategies that help them succeed in English-language schools.

No single profile exists for bilingual students. Their behaviors and achievements may vary enormously, depending on their previous educational experiences, familiarity with English, and cultural background. Some bilingual students display low academic achievement because of the difficulties in learning created by language barriers. Others have difficulties conveying in an unfamiliar language information they have learned in school, in their native country, or at home. Still other students feign lack of knowledge in order to avoid embarrassment or questions that they may not understand.

The insecurities that accompany this striving to communicate in a new language may be expressed in multiple ways. Imagine yourself in a foreign country, unable to speak the language in which others are communicating. People around you think you are ignorant because you express your ideas so poorly or do not express them at all. How might you react? Some students react to such situations by acting out, sometimes even creating their own cultural stereotypes: "We are tough in my country. We do not mix with weaker people." It is much easier to reject first than to feel rejected. Others respond by withdrawing, avoiding any circumstance that might demand communication.

Some students, especially as they gain experience in the mainstream culture, can become confused or uncertain about their identity. These students may be unwilling to speak their native language and reluctant to invite non-English-speaking relatives to school functions or to provide the necessary translation. The struggle to define a personal identity can be particularly acute for students who come from underrepresented groups within their native countries or from countries in which the media are suppressed. Such students have difficulty defining their identity or role in either country.

Culturally diverse and bilingual students find themselves in the often uncomfortable position of straddling two or more cultures: the dominant culture and their own culture. Their cultural identity is directly influenced by their level of acculturation or acceptance of the dominant culture (Cross, 1995). Some students find strength in their home cultures, perhaps by wearing their traditional clothing and bringing lunches containing their native foods. Other students may exaggerate behaviors they associate with the United States; they hide their home culture by imitating the dominant culture in food choices, clothing choices, or other areas. Students from culturally diverse backgrounds also can indicate their feelings about the macroculture and their native culture through their choice of hairstyle and preferences in music and dance. Teachers of students from diverse cultures or whose primary language is not English will be most successful when they work to get to know the individual students and their learning needs and experiences, rather than making decisions based on assumptions, stereotypes, or prior experiences.

All cultures have clearly defined gender roles that affect students' performance or behavior in schools (Cline, 1998). In some cultures, a young girl's honor requires that she remain apart from young men, often beginning at an early age. In others, girls are expected to marry, or at least leave school and wait to marry, in their early teens. Such values create conflict for young women whose identities span two cultures and for the young men who might feel obligated to protect them. Tensions can also occur when female school personnel interact with students or parents whose traditions preclude women from occupying positions of authority.

Other, less obvious differences in cultures can also cause misunderstandings. How might a student whose culture sees owls as symbols of bad luck view a Halloween decoration? How might a teacher for whom eye contact is a sign of integrity respond to a student whose culture requires lowered eyes in the presence of authority? Clearly, both language and cultural differences can affect students' interaction in school and, hence, their achievement. More information on teaching culturally diverse students is presented in Chapter 10.

REFLECTING ON THE IDEAS

Create a "culture box" to share with your peers: Think about your own culture. Choose one to three items that would best reflect who you are and what you value. Bring these items to class, and share them with your peers as you discuss how they reflect you and your culture.

Prior Knowledge and Experience

Students' prior experiences at home, at school, and in the community affect their interpretations, responses, and performance in many areas. Cognitive psychology has informed us that learning is not a passive event, like filling a cup, but an active process in which each individual builds knowledge, linking new bits of information or experience to internal circuits (or structures) called **schemata**. Students and teachers are able to make sense of and interpret what they are experiencing and learning through the use of schemas (Borko & Putnam, 1996).

In what ways might students' prior experiences affect their learning? If, for example, students have never seen the ocean or a movie of the ocean, they may have difficulty understanding lessons on wave motions, tide pools, or *Moby Dick*. Students who have never traveled outside their hometown have fewer schemata available to provide the basis for a discussion of variation in climates.

It is important to assess your students' familiarity with major concepts that underlie your instruction. For example, students who have not experienced segregation or seen or heard about its effects are less prepared for meaningful learning regarding civil rights than those whose experiences provide ties to the subject. You might begin a lesson on the civil rights movement by asking students to interview someone who was somehow involved in or influenced by the movement. For another example, you might begin a lesson on the digestive system by beginning with an exercise that asks students to work with a partner and explain the process by drawing it on a sheet of paper.

Some students' prior experiences, either at home or in school, have not provided them with the expected concepts or skills for their grade level. Effective instructional planning must include careful diagnosis of prior knowledge, experience, and skills related to your topic.

If some students lack important knowledge and skills, you must decide whether remediation or compensation would be more appropriate. A **remedial approach**, or **remediation**, entails teaching prerequisite knowledge and skills before proceeding with planned instruction. For example, before teaching a lesson on solving problems using area and perimeter, one teacher identified several students who were unable to solve equations with two variables. Based on this finding, she divided the class into two groups and allowed one group to concentrate further on single-variable equations before introducing additional variables. Since solving for two variables is dependent on skills developed in solving single-variable equations, she believed that further instruction in these skills was necessary before that group could go on successfully to the more advanced material. If the necessary knowledge and skills can be attained in a reasonable length of time, remediation is the logical choice.

Sometimes, however, remediation is not possible or would represent an unreasonable use of class time. In such cases, a teacher may choose **compensatory instruction** instead. Compensation involves choosing an instructional approach that circumvents areas of weakness. For example, a teacher in an urban school might choose to alter a lesson on ecosystems to focus on systems found in parks and vacant lots, rather than the woodland communities emphasized in the text. This would allow the teacher to proceed with the content (ecosystems) without spending time elaborately developing concepts about woodlands. If a student is strong in math but has weak reading skills, the teacher might provide reading assistance to the student in interpreting a math story problem rather than delaying instruction in problem solving until the student's reading skills can be remediated. In each case, a compensatory approach would allow meaningful instruction to take place, despite weaknesses in prerequisite experiences or skills.

In addition to experiences, knowledge, and skills, students bring attitudes, values, and social patterns that have been shaped by prior experiences. Some students come from homes in which school success is highly valued. In other home environments, students may be encouraged to value street smarts, athletic success, or social status. Some families reward problem solving or independent thinking, whereas some emphasize conformity and the memorization of facts. Some homes are language-rich and encourage a variety of expression; other homes prefer children to be seen and not heard.

Students who come from homes that support the types of learning emphasized in school have intellectual and emotional advantages. Some do not. Careful observation and attention to student and parent comments can help you identify students who need extra support in balancing values from home and school. High expectations for all students, rewards for varied accomplishments, ties to personal experiences, and family involvement all set a classroom tone that balances recognition of the variety of values students bring to school with the encouragement of attitudes likely to promote achievement. Being aware of such student values and interests will allow you to tap those interests through lesson planning or individualized activities.

Interests

Understanding students' interests is perhaps one of the least considered aspects of preparing to teach. Certainly most teachers would agree that students are more likely to learn material if they are interested in it. Interests affect what we learn, how we pay attention, how much we persist in the face of difficulty, and how extensively we study particular subjects. However, using students' interests in teaching does not necessarily mean we will plan units solely around the latest pop culture phenomenon or current event, although such studies may sometimes be appropriate. It may mean using examples from students' interests to explain key ideas or practice essential skills. Understanding students' interests can help teachers tie curriculum to students' needs, identify fruitful areas for enrichment or independent study, and design powerful application projects.

Some of the interests and concerns of students at a given age are predictable. Strong, Silver, and Robinson (1995) referred to a "curiosity connection," in which teachers tie curriculum to key adolescent issues. For example, a study of the American Revolution is more interesting if the key question "When is rebellion justified?" is tied to students' concerns about personal independence and separation. However, other student interests may be idiosyncratic to a particular place, time, or individual(s). Identifying such interests can make the difference between students who are engaged in the lesson and those whose thoughts and concerns are anywhere but in the classroom.

Teachers have many informal ways of identifying students' interests. Certainly it would be difficult to miss the latest media/marketing craze attached to every fast-food meal, the hot issues in the school paper, or the fact that everybody teases Juanita about studying plants rather than wanting to go to the movies. However, there may be times when you want to assess student interests in a more systematic manner.

In this type of formal data gathering, you may use **open-ended questions, closed-ended questions**, or a combination of the two. In an open-ended response inventory you might ask questions such as these:

If I were stuck alone on a desert island and could have only three items for recreation, they would be _____.

When the news comes on, I usually listen to stories about _____.

If I could invite anyone, living or dead, to visit our classroom, I would invite

_____.

By examining the responses to several such questions, it is possible to identify themes and trends in students' concerns. Such analysis can provide a wealth of information and insight into the worlds of individual students. The parallel disadvantage is, of course, that open-ended questions are not easily tallied and may be time consuming to analyze for large groups.

Another alternative is to present students with a closed-ended set of responses. One way to do this is to use a list of possible topics and interests and ask students to circle the ones they find most interesting. Also consider allowing students to decide how they might best share their interests, hobbies, or talents with you and the class. Students who have been studying dance may want to perform for the class, or students who are interested in working with computers may design a web page for the class. Others might use their knowledge of video by creating a "movie" of the class, using video clips—set to music—of their peers as they present their interests to the class.

The **KWL** strategy is a helpful means for gathering information on students' interests in a topic. To use KWL, you introduce a topic of an upcoming lesson or unit and record on a three-column chart what students know (K), what they want to know (W), and later what they have learned (L) about that subject. The KWL strategy provides reflective teachers with a rich source of useful information. It serves as an informal **preassessment** of students' prior knowledge and gives them a chance to share their interests. It is important to use this information in planning later activities; otherwise, students will not continue to raise questions or share their interests if they never have a chance to investigate them.

Students' responses to class assignments may indicate areas of interest. Students who are asked to list names, birth dates, and death dates for two generations of a family tree and respond with six generations including maiden names, occupations, and places of birth may have an interest in genealogy. Likewise, students whose five-page essays turn into a twelve-page treatise, or who constantly turn class discussions toward a favorite topic, give you clues to areas of interest.

Sometimes identifying student interests leads students to independent investigations. For example, a tenth-grade student became interested in the high school greenhouse, which had not been used in many years. Through an individual contract with the biology teacher, the student was allowed to complete some class assignments at her own pace and eliminate others while she investigated the operation of greenhouses and the possibilities for making the facility operational. As a result of her project, the student became the resident expert on greenhouses, the greenhouse became operational, and the student learned that her interests were valued by her teacher.

Other times student interests can form the basis for short- or long-term class activities. A teacher who knows that many students are preparing to get their driver's license may use car loans, insurance rates, and gas mileage to study mathematical or marketing principles. If students are involved in a school or community controversy, a history teacher may use the opportunity to draw parallels to important historical events. Students fascinated with motion pictures may hone their writing skills developing (and possibly filming) a screenplay. You might consider asking students about their hobbies, community volunteering, or part-time jobs to determine how you might incorporate them into your curriculum and classroom assignments. In each case, the ties to students' interests would facilitate their involvement in content.

Intellectual Abilities

In every class you will find a range of general and specific intellectual abilities. General intellectual ability is traditionally indicated by IQ scores derived from a test originally developed to predict success in school. Although IQ tests frequently provide information on the ease with which individuals approach school tasks, they have been called into question as measures of total intellectual potential. Since the early 20th century, psychologists have debated the importance of general intelligence versus sets of specific academic abilities. Are individuals generally either "smart" or "less smart," or do they differ in more complex ways? Might a person be intelligent in math and less intelligent in literature? What kinds of important intellectual abilities might not be measured by paper-and-pencil tests or a test given in one day?

Contemporary learning theorists continue to debate the nature of intelligence itself. Two examples will suffice, as a complete description of theories of intelligence is beyond the scope of this book.

Sternberg (1985, 1997) developed a theory of intelligence that includes three basic components: the componential system, or workings, of the mind in processing information; the response to novelty; and the ability of the individual to react to the environment, an ability we might call practical intelligence, or street smarts. Individuals who have strengths in one of these three areas might show very different abilities. Persons whose componential systems are particularly strong might be a whiz at taking in and processing information. They might have little trouble analyzing a complicated math formula or remembering factual information for a test. Individuals who deal well with novelty might come up with original ideas or be excellent problem solvers. They might write unique stories, invent interesting experiments in chemistry class, or constantly suggest alternatives to class assignments. You have probably known someone with particular ability to interact with the social environment, someone who always knows the way to get things done—someone with practical intelligence. When students were taught in ways that emphasize all three types of intelligence, student achievement improved (Sternberg, Grigorenko, & Jarvin, 2000; Sternberg, Torff, & Grigorenko, 1998).

Gardner (1983, 1991, 1993) believes that we all have **multiple intelligences**. His original work identified seven independent intelligences: linguistic, musical, logical-mathematical, spatial, bodily-kinesthetic, interpersonal, and intrapersonal. According to this theory, each person has a unique profile of intelligences, strong in some, weaker in others. Fine dancers might have exceptional bodily-kinesthetic intelligence but not necessarily be outstanding in mathematics or music. Persons with unusual interpersonal intelligence might make particularly fine counselors, teachers, or friends. More than ten years after the original model was developed, Gardner identified an eighth intelligence: naturalist intelligence (Checkley, 1997). Gardner believes that as he continues his work,

Figure 2.2   Gardner's Eight Intelligences

From *Teaching as Decision Making: Successful Practices for the Elementary Teacher* (p. 31), by A. J. Starko, et al., 2003, Upper Saddle River, NJ: Merrill/Prentice Hall. Copyright 2003 by Pearson Education, Inc. Reprinted with permission.

other intelligences will be identified. Schools traditionally have focused their attention on only two of Gardner's seven intelligences: linguistic and logical-mathematical. Some educators now are trying to identify the intelligences through which individual students learn best; they are also working to develop all types of intelligence in classroom settings (Armstrong, 1994; Gardner, 1993) (see Figure 2.2).

The roles of general and specific ability or the validity of test scores will continue to be debated. Yet, several things are clear from a practical standpoint. Students' intellectual abilities differ in complex ways. They can be thought of as having profiles of intelligence, with strengths in some types of thinking and relative weaknesses in others. Some students learn traditional school tasks quickly and easily. They can solve problems, think abstractly, and remember information more readily than others. Other students may have other intellectual strengths, but have not had many successes in school. These students need more assistance in learning, extended opportunities for practice, and a careful linking of new and prior experiences.

Most students demonstrate strengths in some areas and weaknesses in others. It is important to provide appropriate instruction for such students, challenging their abilities with a depth and pace of instruction that would not be appropriate for all students. If students show advanced ability in language but difficulty in mathematics, it is important to investigate such patterns and vary instruction to meet them. Teachers may also wish to consider how to nurture less traditional forms of intelligence and become more aware of students' strengths and weaknesses in spatial, kinesthetic, or interpersonal learning. It is much more important to match instruction to students' needs than to worry about whether students' particular patterns of abilities mean the students are or are not "intelligent."

Finally, teachers must be cautious about interpreting any test that attempts to assess intellectual ability. A test score represents performance on a particular day. The score may be influenced by factors as diverse as illness on the day of the test, familiarity with the language of the test, and prior experience with the vocabulary and materials of testing. Cultural and language differences have a significant impact on traditional test performance. Students who have been exposed to key test vocabulary words clearly have an advantage over those who have not or those for whom the English language is unfamiliar. Students who have worked with computers before are likely to be more comfortable in a testing task involving computers than those for whom using computers is a new experience. Are those students less "smart" than students whose previous experiences have enabled them to be more successful test takers? To provide instruction that is appropriate to student needs and abilities, teachers must take into account IQ and standardized test information as well as observations of performance under a wide range of circumstances.

 ## REFLECTING ON THE IDEAS

List at least four ways in which students in an eighth-grade class might differ from one another. How might each of these differences affect how you might teach a curriculum unit in your content area?

Learning Styles

In addition to intellectual strengths and weaknesses, students vary in the ways they learn best, or their **learning styles**. Hunt (1979) said that learning style "describes a student in terms of those educational conditions under which he is most likely to learn. Learning style describes how a student learns, not what he has learned" (p. 27).

One principle underlies the many theories of learning styles: All individuals do not learn best in the same way. Circumstances or methods that may promote learning for one individual may not be helpful for others. Some learning styles are not better or stronger than others, merely different. An approach may seem logical to a teacher and work well for some students—the students whose styles are similar to that of the teacher—but not be effective for other equally intelligent students whose styles are different.

Perhaps the simplest variation in learning styles may be found along sensory channels. Some individuals learn most effectively through visual information; they process information best if they acquire it through their eyes. Others learn best auditorily, processing information most efficiently if they acquire it through their ears. Still others benefit most from information presented kinesthetically, involving the sense of touch or whole-body movement. These differences do not reflect the relative acuity of eyes, ears, or other senses. Although students with poor eyesight certainly would have trouble with information presented to them only visually, persons with 20/20 eyesight may still not process visual information well. The connection between the eyes and the brain simply may not function as well as the connection between the ears and the brain. For example, students who are strong auditory learners may best experience the civil rights movement by listening to the teacher or other speakers talk about people, events, and issues. Strong visual learners would absorb the lesson most successfully through a combination of pictures, video, and text. Kinesthetic learners would benefit from opportunities to role-play a dramatization of key events.

Some learning styles theories are based on other ways individuals absorb and process information (Guild & Garger, 1998). For example, Gregorc (1982) derived a theory of learning styles based on the ways individuals organize and process information from all the senses together. His model is based on two opposing dimensions of learning processes: perception and organization. *Perception* refers to the means by which an individual acquires information. Most people have the ability to perceive both concrete information (accessible to the senses) and abstract information (ideas, feelings), although one way or the other may be more comfortable for them.

Individuals also vary in how they *organize* information. Some individuals organize information best in a sequential or linear way, with each bit of information leading to the next in a straight-line manner. Others are more comfortable with an organization Gregorc calls *random*, a nonlinear, holistic approach characterized by leaps of logic and the processing of several bits of information simultaneously. Each individual can have preferences somewhere on the continuum between the two extremes.

Gregorc combines the perceptual and organizational abilities into four learning styles associated with particular behaviors and characteristics; concrete sequential, abstract sequential, abstract random, concrete random. Each style has a unique and organized view of the world and operates from a particular point of view. Although no individual operates in only one style, many people have strong preferences for one or more channels. Such preferences can be identified through a learning styles inventory or more informal observations of behavior, language, and habits.

Individuals with a dominant *concrete sequential* (CS) style prefer to work with concrete information processed in a sequential manner. Such individuals might be characterized as practical, structured, down-to-earth, and organized. CS adults balance the checkbook carefully, organize closets, and rarely forget appointments. CS teachers are naturals at keeping complete records, arranging classroom materials, and developing logical units of study. CS students learn best when information is presented in a systematic fashion, with practical applications and hands-on activity.

Persons with a dominant *abstract sequential* (AS) style prefer learning abstract information and organizing it sequentially. Such persons may be seen as studious and intellectual. Adults with AS style are happiest when searching for new knowledge, analyzing problems, or evaluating issues through logic and reason. They may not be concerned with such concrete issues as whether two socks match or the outdoor temperature. Further, AS teachers may present brilliant lectures or carefully structured research projects, and AS students may debate logically, analyze literature critically, and forget their lunch.

Individuals with an *abstract random* (AR) style prefer abstract information, but process it in a holistic, nonlinear fashion. These persons may be seen as sensitive, emotional, and artistic. AR individuals may write poetry, counsel friends, and be expert at relationships, whether between individuals or academic disciplines. They may have moments of personal or professional insight without being able to explain them. AR teachers love interdisciplinary teaching, thematic units, and a classroom full of art (including on the ceilings). AR students may be the life of the class, have an eye for beauty, and possess a wonderful imagination, but have little idea how to transfer ideas into concrete reality.

Finally, *concrete random* (CR) individuals process concrete information in nonlinear ways. CR individuals are natural problem solvers, explorers, and inventors. CR individuals love to tinker with gadgets, appliances, or ideas. Their garages and cupboards may overflow with spare parts and unusual tools for future experimentation. As teachers, they have classrooms full of experiments and emphasize creative problem solving and independence, and CR students flourish in such an atmosphere, often finding solutions to problems through intuitive leaps they cannot explain. Like AR learners, CR students have trouble when asked to show their work (Butler, 1986; Gregorc, 1982).

In this brief overview, you may have caught a glimpse of yourself or someone you know. In examining how these characteristics might affect teaching and learning, you might consider what would happen if teachers of one style taught students of another style, or vice versa. The mismatch between teaching style and learning style could create difficulties for both student and teacher. None of the styles are "right"; they are just different.

Schools should not try to match teachers' and students' styles in assigning classrooms. Aside from the logistical difficulties of such a proposal, it would be a disservice to allow students to function in only their preferred mode. Students need to learn to adapt to different situations, taking on various styles as needed. However, teachers can make sure that at least some of the activities for each topic or unit allow students to function in preferred ways. In addition, teachers can provide special support to students assigned work outside their preferred styles.

Kathleen Butler (1995, 1996) has developed materials to teach adolescents about their learning styles. She believes that helping students understand their personal style can help them study more effectively and interact more productively with teachers and peers. You may want to consider whether teaching your students about style difference may be an effective way to enhance their learning. You may also want to examine your own experiences as a learner and reflect on how these experiences have caused you to feel more comfortable, successful, or capable in the learning of some subject areas or classrooms than others. Knowing this information about yourself will help you when reflecting on how to approach the different styles of your future students.

Dunn and Dunn (1975; Dunn, 1996, 1997) have a different approach. They describe learning styles as "the manner in which 18 different elements of four basic stimuli affect a person's ability to absorb and to retain information, values, facts or concepts" (1975, p. 74). The four types of stimuli are environmental, emotional, sociological, and physical. For example, under environmental stimuli, students may prefer bright or dim places, warm or cool places, a specific noise level, or a particular physical arrangement. Emotional stimuli include variation in motivation, persistence, responsibility, and amount of structure preferred. Sociological variables include preferences for working individually, in pairs, in teams, or in groups. Physical variables include perceptual (sensory modalities) differences and preferences for food and time of day. Each variable interacts with culture and prior experiences in complex ways. The fact that students vary in their responses to such a large number of variables helps to explain the number of individual differences found in each classroom. Dunn and others (1995) found that despite these limitations, matching individual style preferences can have a positive impact on student learning.

One of the more interesting questions in learning styles research is whether styles vary along one or more dimensions across cultural groups (Dunn & Griggs, 1995; Shade, 1997; Smith, 1998). Gay (1994) notes that culture and ethnicity have a strong impact on shaping learning styles, but that it is essential to use caution in interpreting research. An emerging research base suggests that patterns of learning styles differ across cultures. Boykin (1994), for example, examines learning styles in African American students; Swisher and Doyle (1992) review style patterns among Native Americans; and Shade (1997) provides a helpful summary across populations. As you learn about the cultural groups you teach, it may be helpful to consult literature on style differences. The gender and socioeconomic background of your students also may have an impact on their learning styles. However, it is essential to remember that generalizations across an entire population are of limited value when applied to a specific individual. Each student in your classroom must be considered as an individual, not as a representative of a particular group.

 ## REFLECTING ON THE IDEAS

Imagine you are teaching a unit on fractions. List three activities that would appeal to varying learning styles. You may use any of the learning style frameworks presented above. Label each with the learning style(s) to which it would appeal. For example, "Create a model that represents the following fractions: 1/3, 5/6, and 17/15—visual."

Which of the activities listed are most appealing to you? Think about how your own learning style may affect your teaching. In what ways might it be helpful? In what ways might it cause difficulties for your students?

SECTION 2. LEARNING: HOW DOES LEARNING OCCUR?

Section 2 Objective

After you have completed this section, you will be able to explain how the mind constructs meaning and its implications for teaching.

As we prepare to think about teaching in ways that help students learn, it can be help-ful to briefly review some of the things we know about how learning occurs. Although you probably learned these principles in more detail in your classwork in educational psychology, we will review a few key principles. You may want to consult a textbook in educational psychology (for example, Ormrod, 2000) for more details.

Students Learn Only What They Are Ready to Learn

One of the most commonly used phrases in education is "developmentally appropriate practice." Tomlinson (1999) refers to the fact that students learn best when instruction is matched to their development and readiness. With some basic understanding of de-velopment, learning, and possible teaching strategies, you can begin to identify the cru-cial ways in which you will need to vary your activities to match the unique needs of your students. Sometimes it is the role of the teacher to assess and dignify students' prior experiences, perspectives, and problem-solving abilities before the students will become ready for acquiring any other knowledge or skills.

Your students will display varying levels of physical, cognitive, emotional, and moral development. Students at the middle and high school level are transitioning between preadolescence, adolescence, and young adulthood (Lipsitz, Mizell, Jackson, & Austin, 1997; Manning, 1994). Such students may appear to be fully in control of their emotions one day and seemingly out of control the next. Frequently, students at this age desire to be viewed as adults and are in the process of trying new roles and identities (Stevenson, 2002). Some of these identities may cause students to posture, act out against others, engage in bullying behavior, or withdraw socially from you and other students. Providing safe places for students to express themselves, their fears and anxieties, and their newly forming ideas about the world will help to support them emotionally, cognitively, and morally. If, how-ever, students' behavior leads you to believe they may cause themselves or others harm, it is your legal and moral responsibility to seek the support and guidance of counselors in your school building or district. In the early years of teaching, theory and experienced teachers can be helpful to you in identifying what constitutes problems that must be ad-dressed immediately and what is normal for students in this developmental range.

Students develop from concrete to abstract thinking over time. You may remember Jean Piaget (1970), the Swiss psychologist who studied his children and discovered dis-tinct stages of cognitive growth. Even at the middle and high school level, students may demonstrate little logical thought (at least from an adult perspective). Some of these stu-dents will need concrete experiences on which to base their learning. They will need mul-tiple hands-on experiences, including the exploration and manipulation of physical objects, in order to grasp abstract concepts, especially if they have had negative or mise-ducative experiences in prior learning activities. *Miseducative learning experiences* is a term Dewey (1902) used to describe those learning experiences that caused students to learn information incorrectly. Ideally, students should be invited to explain their reason-ing and to challenge others' explanations that seem illogical. In this way, teachers can bet-ter understand why a student thinks in a particular manner. Later in the chapter, we will discuss this idea of **metacognition**, the process of having students think about their thinking.

Students with multiple experiences in any area will show greater development and more sophisticated thinking than those who have not had similar experiences. It will be important to identify students who lack developmental experiences shared by most of your students. For example, students who come from homes in which they have had few opportunities to converse with adults will need extra practice in presenting ideas, learning to listen, and perhaps explicit teaching of vocabulary.

An appropriate level of challenge also is an important part of readiness. You may have noticed that you are most successful and most motivated in learning a new skill if you move forward in ways that are challenging but allow for feelings of success. The same is true for students. Vygotsky (1997) used the term **zone of proximal development** to describe the zone in which the learning is beyond students' current understanding but close enough to be reachable with careful scaffolding—support and direction—by the teacher. The best learning is neither so easy that it is obvious nor so difficult that it is overly frustrating.

Adolescents often have well-shaped identities as learners within the school context. Some may believe they are destined to be low achievers. It can be a challenge for the teacher to find the level of instruction at which students have feelings of both challenge and success, but assessing students' readiness is one useful way for knowing where to begin your instruction with them.

Students Construct Their Own Understanding

Piaget and Vygotsky contributed to our understanding of how knowledge is obtained. It is not transmitted intact from one individual to another—teaching would be much easier if that were the case! Rather, knowledge is constructed by individuals as they interact with the world and with other human beings. For example, imagine students who have a conversation with a person from another race for the first time. The students will try to fit this experience with other previous experiences and information collected from such influential sources as the media, friends, and family. The students may voice some erroneous assumptions about this individual based on their prior knowledge of other people of the same race. If an adult is nearby, the adult is likely to challenge the students' understanding, probably emphatically, by insisting that the individual should not be stereotyped in this way. If the students meeting the individual have the opportunity to get to know him or her better, they may likely see the value of the other student, recognize commonalities, and appreciate any differences.

Modeling also can create powerful learning experiences. In this last case, the adult could demonstrate and explain what to do when meeting someone for the first time. In this way the concept of acceptance and tolerance is taught directly through experiences, not through a ten-minute lecture on the nature and characteristics of diversity. When a reflective teacher understands that students' concepts have been constructed over time through interactions with those around them, he or she has another reason to learn more about the cultures within which those ideas have been built.

A parallel principle is that students' existing concepts—built into their cognitive structure through experience—are not easily dislodged by simple explanations. Some of these are powerful cultural learnings. For example, a teacher cannot reverse a cultural norm of quiet respect for adults simply because she hopes her students will ask many questions. Other misconceptions are based on experience. For example, students who have had many experiences in which individuals from a specific cultural group have a certain talent, such as being able to sing or dance, often believe that every person of that culture has those abilities. Explanations to the contrary may not be powerful enough to dislodge these associations. New learning can occur, however, when multiple new experiences challenge the misconception. These experiences are discussed in the next section.

Constructivism or constructivist teaching is based on the assumption that students build their own understanding. A wide range of definitions for constructivism (Perkins, 1999; Philips, 1995) have led to considerable disagreement over what does and does not constitute constructivist teaching. All definitions, however, center around strategies that allow students to actively interact with ideas that provide maximum opportunities for concept development. For some, constructivism means "objects and events have no absolute meaning, rather, the individual interprets each and constructs meaning based on individual experience" (Brooks & Brooks, 1993). Constructivists tend to eschew the breaking down of context into component parts in favor of environments wherein knowledge, skill, and complexity coexist naturally (Hannafin, Hannafin, Land & Oliver, 1997, p. 109). Some individuals interpret this to mean that direct teaching must necessarily be ineffective or that shared knowledge is elusive, at best. Brandt and Perkins (2000) state:

> Perkins (1992) distinguishes between without-the-information-given (WIG) constructivism and beyond-the-information-given (BIG) constructivism. Ardent WIG constructivists argue that for real learning, students must virtually reconstruct knowledge for themselves, with appropriate support. BIG constructivists believe that giving learners information directly is fine and often preferable; but to learn it, they must then apply it actively and creatively. (pp. 167–218)

This book is designed to support a constructivist approach to teaching from a position more closely aligned with BIG constructivists. From our perspective, the key to constructivism is not whether learning takes place in a complex environment or whether objects do or do not have absolute meaning. The important idea for teaching is that while we can present information, we cannot give knowledge to students; they must construct it themselves. All of our teaching decisions must be designed to help them do so effectively. More information on constructivist teaching can be found in Chapter 6.

It can be helpful to understand the way information enters memory in order to build new concepts. The theory that describes this procedure is called **information processing**. Three elements of an information-processing model are illustrated in Figure 2.3: the sensory memory, short-term (working) memory (STM), and long-term memory (LTM.) A teacher's ability to tap into students' long-term memory will help to create further connections between activities in the classroom and student learning.

The meaningful extent of something to us is determined by the amount of experience we have had with it: the more experience, the more connections; the more connections, the more meaning. It is the teacher's job to help students see relationships between new and old information and to help them organize the new information they learn. Sometimes teachers try to make a comparison with something they think is a

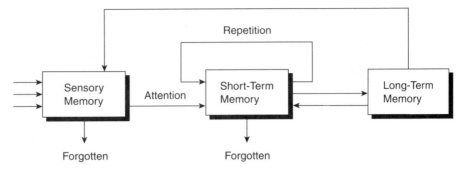

Figure 2.3   The Information-Processing Model

From *Teaching as Decision Making: Successful Practices for the Elementary Teacher* (p. 39), by A. J. Starko, et al., 2003, Upper Saddle River, NJ: Merrill/Prentice Hall. Copyright 2003 by Pearson Education, Inc. Reprinted with permission.

common experience. Yet the students do not share that experience, and so the analogy falls on closed ears. One teacher tried to introduce a lesson on *Romeo and Juliet* to a group of tenth-graders by comparing it with *West Side Story*. Unfortunately, few of the students had seen the movie or the play. The teacher had failed to link to the students' prior knowledge.

The following ideas from information-processing theory can provide important assistance in teaching (Wolfe, 2001).

- *Attention is a gatekeeper.* If something is not noticed, it will not be learned. Human attention is limited: If your students are attending to something outside the window, something inside their desks, or even something inside their heads, they will not be able to attend to your lesson. It is important to keep students actively involved in lessons in order to keep their attention focused. Boredom and distractions are enemies of attention.
- *Short-term memory is of short duration (5–20 seconds) and limited capacity.* Once students are paying attention, they can think about only a few new ideas at a time. It is best to concentrate on a few key ideas at one time and use multiple and varied experiences to reinforce them. It is also helpful to tell students directly which ideas are the most important and to write them on the board.
- *Long-term memory and short-term memory work together.* The prior knowledge in long-term memory provides the base to which new ideas are connected. Prior knowledge in long-term memory also helps determine which information enters the short-term memory at all. With no prior experiences with skunks and no adult to intervene, a child may not even notice that a skunk is anything new or interesting. The skunk could pass out of sight labeled as a cat—furry and black and white—without the child learning anything. It is important for teachers to provide the scaffolding that helps students find ties between the new concepts to be learned and their prior experiences in long-term memory.
- *The types of experiences we provide for students have a direct impact on how effectively new concepts are processed.* More diverse experiences with a concept by

students (multiple contexts) will create more powerful meaning. For example, students learning about civil liberties will build more powerful concepts if they read about civil rights leaders, engage in conversations with people whose work concerns challenging or defending the law, attend a political demonstration, watch videos of historical events that relate to the civil rights movement, and engage in some kind of community activism concerning issues they have selected. Students who have compared the issues that concern their community with those that impact others are actively involved in building the bases for concepts about civil rights, leadership, citizenship, and community involvement. More opportunities for active processing of information—activities that require students to do something with the information rather than just absorb it—build more ties in long-term memory and more powerful understandings.

• *Well-organized information is easier to remember.* When teaching, it is important to help students understand how ideas are related and which ideas are most important. This can entail the use of **graphic organizers**, lists of steps, and explicit ties to prior knowledge. When information does not have a logical structure, it can be helpful to create one. For example, many students have learned the names of the Great Lakes (a relatively random list) by remembering the mnemonic device HOMES. Repetition can be helpful for remembering less meaningful information that needs to be accessed quickly. Think about how much easier it is to remember phone numbers that you use frequently as opposed to those you call rarely. Similarly, drill and practice activities can be helpful in memorizing certain facts or learning to spell nonphonetic words.

• *Finally, because learning is built through experience, the ways information is processed will vary across cultures.* The relevant prior knowledge will be different, and even the models of effective teaching and learning may vary by culture. For example, many Native American tribes' traditional means of learning and teaching relies heavily on observation and modeling. Other contemporary American groups dive into new experiences and learn by doing. A thoughtful teacher will analyze her students' prior learning experiences when planning new learning activities.

Researchers in the area of **situated cognition** emphasize the importance of context in building understanding (Brown, Collins & Duguid, 1989.) New knowledge is not acquired in a vacuum. It develops through interactions within a specific context. From this perspective, learning is facilitated when the circumstances of learning more closely resemble the context in which the information is needed or used. For example, solving word problems in math would be less powerful than solving actual problems for which mathematical information is necessary: for example, figuring out how to build a big enough water treatment plant to support a 20% population increase in the community for which it provides service.

Advocates of this model emphasize the importance of authentic learning activities, described in the next section. To design instruction based on situated learning, teachers must select a meaningful context, or situation, that will allow students to acquire the desired learning. They also need to provide "scaffolding" or supportive activities that help students succeed in the complex situation (Young, 1993).

Brain-Based Education

One of the more interesting trends in education today is the effort to link new information coming from neurology and neural psychology to classroom practice. If we understand more about how the brain functions, it seems logical that such knowledge would help us plan better for student learning. This perspective highlights the need for brain-compatible or **brain-based education** (Wolfe, 2001).

Although brain research will bring important information to educators, as with any research, it must be read analytically. Any time you are told "research says you should. . . ." it is important to ask these questions: What research? Under what conditions? With what populations? When we ask these questions about the recommendations being made for brain-based education, we find mixed results. In some cases, the conclusions and generalizations, particularly those drawn from animal research, seem a bit premature for the amount of data. For example, some writers have claimed that brain research proves that early development is so important that the most critical learning occurs before students enter school. In fact, while early learning is important, the brain continues to develop in important ways throughout a healthy life (Bruer, 1999).

Despite this caution, research surrounding brain-based learning promises to bring more important information with each passing year (Wolfe, 2001). In the meantime, it is interesting to note that many recommendations made by writers in this area are consistent with the constructivist approaches rooted in cognitive psychology: Engage students actively in learning, organize content clearly, and involve students in complex activities (see, for example, Caine & Caine, 1997; Jensen, 2000; Scherer, 2000).

Both psychologists and brain researchers also study memory. Different types of information are stored differently in the brain (Sprenger, 1999). Most of what we teach in schools will be recorded as **semantic memory**, or information learned from words. The descriptions of long-term memory given in this chapter describe processes for semantic memory. **Episodic memory**, or spatial memory, is the memory associated with places. If you have ever walked back to the place where you lost something in an effort to reconstruct your actions, you were hoping to trigger episodic memory. **Procedural memory**, or "muscle memory," records the actions of your body. Because it operates outside the realm of conscious thought (unlike semantic memory), procedural memory can allow human beings to do two things at once; for example, drive a car while having a conversation. **Automatic memory** is described as "conditioned reflex memory" (p. 53). It stores information that has been memorized through repetition, perhaps multiplication tables, but not the ability to comprehend the concept of multiplication. Finally, **emotional memory** is the most powerful type of memory. Experiences that trigger powerful emotions—for example, a class celebration or special event—are much more likely to be remembered. The power of emotional memory also means that students who are thinking about emotionally powerful topics outside the lesson—a problem with a friend or family member, a party after school, a big game last night—are much more likely to attend to the emotionally laden memories than to the lesson at hand, unless the teacher takes special trouble to engage them.

The brain-based education movement also has brought an increased emphasis on the importance of emotion in learning. In addition to the importance of emotional memory, researchers suggest that the emotional climate of the room, particularly the stress level, has an impact on student learning. High levels of stress, which may trigger a fight-or-flight response, are not conducive to optimum learning.

CHECK YOUR UNDERSTANDING

Observe a classroom of your choice. Evaluate how well the teaching methods appeal to the brain's information processing, memory, and ways of constructing meaning. How brain-compatible is the classroom environment? Write a reflective paper that addresses each of these areas.

As you can tell, the ways you plan learning activities will greatly affect how readily students are able to learn and retain new ideas. Opportunities for learning are maximized when learning activities are at the appropriate level and tied to prior experiences with multiple opportunities for active involvement with content.

Practice Activity:

Classroom Observation

Practice Point

With a friend, review the information on learning theory in this section. Examine a lesson in a teacher's edition of a textbook or a sample lesson from one of the many Internet sites containing teaching materials. Analyze the extent to which the lesson optimizes the opportunity for student learning, and list its strengths and weaknesses.

SECTION 3. UNDERSTANDING AND AUTHENTIC LEARNING

Section 3 Objectives

After you have completed this chapter, you will be able to:

1. explain how real problems and authentic projects can promote student engagement in meaningful learning; and
2. plan authentic learning experiences for your students.

It is essential to plan instruction so that students will understand the content. At one level such a statement seems so obvious as to be ridiculous: Of course we want students to understand the content, that's why we are teaching. In fact, students are taught many things they do not really understand, even though they successfully answer test questions on that content. You probably have had this experience yourself. Think of a time you have taken a class in which some of the content never did make sense to you. This may have been a history class in which you learned a series of confusing events or a science class in which you learned a collection of rules or facts. In such circumstances, what did you do? If you are like many students, you memorized the things you needed for the test and forgot them as soon as the class ended. You did not apply the things you learned to real life because you couldn't; you didn't understand what you had "learned."

Spending time in school in this type of learning is wasteful. If students cannot use what they've learned, what is the point of learning it? Contrast this to learning that produces understanding. When an individual understands a concept or skill, he or she can apply it appropriately in a new situation. For example, if I merely memorize the types and functions of simple machines, that information will not help me. However, if I understand that information, I can apply it, perhaps the next time I need to move a heavy piece of furniture. Gardner (1999) describes what he calls an "acid test" for understanding by "posing to students a topic or theme or demonstration that they have never before encountered, and determining what sense they can make of those phenomena" (p. 119). In other words, if students can use what they have learned to make sense of a new situation, they understand it.

Authentic learning allows students to have learning experiences that are grounded in the appropriate context and used in purposeful ways, both powerful assets to learning (Wolfe, 2001). Research on inner-city New York high school students showed that they increased their attendance, learning, and college-admission rates when they were taught with more authentic activities and performance assessments (Darling-Hammond, Ancess & Ort, 2002). The following paragraphs provide several examples of authentic learning within the context of middle and high school classrooms.

In Chicopee, Massachusetts, middle school students studied the problem facing their community since the state had banned the burning of sludge from factories and sewage (Lewis, 1991). During the winter, the sludge froze before it could be hauled to the landfills.

Adolescents like "authentic" schoolwork.

Officials suggested building a brick storage facility to keep the sludge warm, but the $120,000 expense was beyond the city's budget. After study, the students submitted a list of possible alternatives to the chief officer of the sludge plant, including plans for a makeshift solar greenhouse. The city adopted the greenhouse plan at a cost of $500. The student's project provided good opportunities for learning about waste management, city government, and energy conservation, and it saved the community $119,500!

In a different school, seventh-grade students used systematic sampling to plan and conduct phone and door-to-door polls prior to a presidential election. They used the results to predict local election results and, after the election, analyzed the predicted and actual percentages for each candidate.

In some high schools, students have tested the water quality of local streams for a public commission; created communication devices for students with severe impairments; studied whether anaerobic weight training produced aerobic benefits; and written plays to teach younger students about issues such as conservation, child abuse, and drugs. They have lobbied for changes in local laws, created oral histories for the public library, persuaded banks to create art galleries, and conducted population studies of wildlife on school grounds. In each case, students had the opportunity to use the information they gained in schools to solve a problem, investigate an issue, or create something of value to themselves or others. This process, in which teaching is organized around meaningful use of content, is sometimes called **authentic learning** or **authentic achievement**.

Others have defined related constructs. Gardner (1991) distinguished between "rote, ritualistic or conventional performances . . . [that] occur when students simply respond . . . by spewing back the particular facts, concepts, or problem sets they have been taught" and "performances of disciplinary (or genuine) understanding" (p. 9). Performances that demonstrate understanding require students to use information appropriately in a new situation. They may range from physics students using the laws they learned in class to explain a newly encountered game to a first grader to using capital letters and punctuation appropriately in writing a letter to a grandparent or community leader. Perkins (1992) describes "generative knowledge" as a combination of retention, understanding and active use of knowledge "that does not just sit there but functions richly in people's lives to help them understand and deal with the world" (p. 5). In each case, theorists emphasize the importance of knowledge that is related to contexts the students understand and use in meaningful ways.

Newmann (1991, 1996) identified three characteristics of authentic achievement. First, authentic achievement requires the production rather than the reproduction of knowledge. Most traditional learning tasks have asked students merely to reproduce information provided them by the teacher. The teacher gave students the facts; the students gave them back. In authentic achievement, students must go further and do something with the facts, such as create something new, solve a problem, or investigate a question. In this mode of teaching, it is not enough to know something about your community, you must do something to investigate the community or make it a better place.

Second, authentic achievement requires **disciplined inquiry**. In disciplined inquiry, students investigate problems or questions within a particular discipline. Such investigation demands both in-depth knowledge of content and knowledge of how one conducts inquiry within a content area. Students studying the community need to know what kinds of questions professionals ask about communities and how they gather information. Clearly, the sophistication with which students approach this inquiry will vary considerably from sixth to twelfth grade, but at all levels students can be taught to ask questions about content and investigate the answers. In making this decision, the teacher should consider, How do professionals in my discipline gather information, solve problems, and address issues? In many cases, the strategies that allow adults to address authentic tasks can be appropriately taught to students.

The third and fourth characteristics of authentic learning go hand in hand. Authentic learning includes assembling, interpreting, and synthesizing knowledge and results in products that have aesthetic, utilitarian, or personal value. Many traditional school projects have been summaries of information: students read a convenient reference book or encyclopedia, restated the information in their own words, and created some kind of product. In most cases this was the ever-present school "report." In other cases the information might be more creatively communicated through a poster, bulletin board, or display, but it was still basically a reproduction of someone else's ideas. An authentic product contains the student's own thoughts, questions, data, and interpretations in addition to the ideas of others.

Interestingly, the characteristics of authentic learning parallel those identified in a study that asked young adolescents to identify their most memorable and engaging work (Wasserstein, 1995). While some teachers might have guessed that students preferred easy assignments, "Again and again, students equated hard work with success and satisfaction. Moreover, they suggested that challenge is the essence of engagement; when students feel they are doing important work, they are more likely to buy in than not" (Wasserstein, 1995, p. 41). When students were exploring ideas in ways that seemed meaningful and important, they worked hard and felt proud of their efforts. When assignments were perceived as busywork, or unrelated to the real world, students were resentful and uninterested.

What Makes a Problem Real or Authentic?

If we are to engage students in authentic learning, finding and solving problems, and producing information, it is important to first consider, What is a problem? What characteristics define "real" or "authentic" problems or tasks, and how are they distinct from the kinds of problems typically addressed in schools? While Newmann's guidelines provide a beginning, helpful insights can be found in the work of Renzulli (1977), whose Enrichment Triad Model centers on individual and small-group investigations of real problems. While the Triad model was originally developed for education of the gifted and talented (see Chapter 9), many of its components are appropriate for all students, and the strategies for pursuit of real problems can hold the key to authentic learning in many arenas.

First, a real problem has personal interest and value to the student or students who pursue it. Clearly, individual students can be engaged in authentic problems or tasks based on personal interests. The class involved in gathering data for the sludge project utilized the group's shared interest in solving a local problem (particularly one that had stymied local adults) as well as diverse individual interests and skills. The project required students to gather and analyze energy data; communicate with local officials; organize and display ideas in a presentation suitable for a professional audience. At least some part of the project could be interesting to virtually every student.

Second, a real problem does not have a predetermined, correct response. It involves processes for which there cannot be an answer key. As we consider the real problems with which our students have become involved, they seem to fall into three general categories.

1. Some real problems are *research questions.* They involve gathering and analyzing data and drawing conclusions. True research questions entail collecting information from primary sources through observation, surveys, interviews, or document analysis. The students who surveyed food preferences in the school cafeteria, those who interviewed local citizens on life in the community during World War II, and those who observed the effects of various cleaning solutions on bacteria growth on school desks all investigated research questions. Students involved in Ken Cowan's unit on Zimbabwe might become curious as to whether the first settlers in their own geographic area had attitudes towards the native peoples similar to people arriving in Zimbabwe. This interest could lead to a project involving historical research (see Chapter 6); for example, reading the diaries of early settlers and analyzing their beliefs.

2. Other real problems might be categorized as service learning or **activism**. In these activities, students work in the community and/or attempt to improve some aspect of the world around them. Students who organize clothing drives for the homeless, teach peers what to do if they suspect a friend is being abused, set up community hot lines for teens, or lobby for student representation on the school board are pursuing this type of real problem.

3. Finally, real problems in the arts entail the *expression* of some theme, aesthetic, or idea. Adult creators use words, movement, paint, or clay as tools for expression. Students whose art explores the changing light, whose stories reflect their ideas about racism, or whose dance reflects their pursuit of an identity as young adults all address real problems in meaningful ways. Students who create masks to synthesize their understanding of Zimbabwe tackle a similarly authentic problem.

In pursuing real problems, students should use, as much as possible, authentic methodology; that is, they should address the problem as much as possible in the way a professional adult would address it. Newmann's (1991) criterion of "disciplined inquiry" reflects this idea. The students who want to survey cafeteria preferences must learn something about survey design. Those who want to study bacteria on school desks must learn about maintaining cultures and strategies for quantifying bacteria. It will be much easier for students to use authentic historical research techniques in a local history project than one on a distant locale (although electronic networks are making this process more feasible). Even the student with limited access to primary sources can use professional techniques for sharing information in a manner that is appropriate to the discipline. For example, prior to students creating PowerPoint presentations, they need to learn how to use the format to best share what they have learned with others.

Finally, when pursuing real problems, students eventually share information with a real audience. The makeup of a real audience will vary enormously with the age of the students and the sophistication of their problems. The key is that the audience should have a genuine interest in the product, rather than viewing it as a source for a grade or other evaluation. Some real audiences are part of the natural school environment. For example, a group of seniors may write an original play and produce it for the rest of the senior class. Other audiences may be created within schools to provide a vehicle for student efforts: art exhibits, literary magazines, invention conventions, or science fairs (see Schack & Starko, 1998; Starko & Schack, 1992). Many extracurricular activities provide opportunities and/or audiences for addressing real problems. Students who produce a yearbook, argue their case before the student council, or perform the class musical are working for real audiences.

Still other audiences may be part of the local community. In one community, the local chamber of commerce was pleased to display a student-produced brochure on the history of local buildings along with other pamphlets. In another, results of a water pollution study were shared with interested faculty at a local university. In yet another, the radio station often aired student-generated public service announcements. Local access cable TV, historical societies, and other community organizations can provide enthusiastic audiences for appropriate student products.

Certainly, the types of problems pursued, the methodology employed, and the audiences approached will vary enormously from a middle-school student's garden experiment to the high school students' archeological research or investigation of pollution in a local stream. However, at each stage, students may be nudged just one notch closer to professionalism: the seventh grader to consider various question formats in designing a survey, the ninth grader to assess the impact of different types of sampling on survey results, the senior to consider the pros and cons of differing statistical analyses. Each represents a legitimate step toward pursuing real problems.

During instructional planning it would be wise to consider authentic learning activities and projects when designing major objectives and assessments. Whatever the subject, the ultimate goal should be to have students use the content in meaningful ways. Students will learn better when more aspects of real-world problem solving are incorporated into the process. Of course, various types of authentic learning activities can be planned. For example, tenth-grade students studying the Vietnam War could interview local citizens about community events during the war, question veterans about their experiences in the field and upon returning home, study lyrics of popular music of the period, and examine newspaper and magazine coverage of the time. Primary source material would be readily available in most communities. The students would also have many potential opportunities to use their information in meaningful ways, such as creating local histories for the community library or working to provide needed services to veterans.

A unit on Greek mythology would not offer parallel opportunities for activism. However, if a teacher wished to teach techniques of historical research, students might learn to analyze photographs of Greek artworks for evidence of the influence of myth. Their results might be compiled in an "archeologist's report." Alternatively, the teacher might plan to engage students in personally meaningful problem solving by helping students make ties between mythological heroes and heroes today. Students may examine the mythology surrounding contemporary heroes in sports or entertainment and analyze how those heroes influence our lives. Such analyses could result in a variety of literary or artistic products.

Several of the objectives created in the interdisciplinary unit on Zimbabwe involve authentic problems, for example, creating masks or writing contemporary folk tales.

The unit might also serve as a springboard for other real problems. Students may wonder about the impact of expanding modern culture into more traditional cultures today. This could lead to interviews with immigrants from various countries, a study of the history of local Amish communities, or other investigations.

 ## REFLECTING ON THE IDEAS

Think about your own learning experiences in and out of school. When have you been involved in authentic learning? Were most of your experiences in class, in extracurricular activities, or outside of school? In what ways were your experiences powerful for you? What implications does that have for your teaching?

Planning for Authentic Learning

The next section will provide examples for creating authentic learning experiences for students in order to increase the number of connections to their own lives, experiences, and interests.

Gardner (1999) suggested four approaches that appear promising in teaching for understanding. The first recommends that we learn from "suggestive institutions" (p. 126). By examining institutions outside schools in which understanding is fostered, we may gain clues that will enhance our repertoire of teaching strategies. For example, considering how learners function in apprenticeships or how children engage with content in museums may provide models for teaching. The experimentation facilitated in good science museums is very different from the science teaching experienced by many students.

The second avenue is illustrated again by the example of students having a conversation with someone from a different race—direct confrontations with erroneous conceptions. In this strategy, students are given experiences that force them to examine their current concepts. If students believe that metal sinks and wood floats, experimentation with a variety of toy boats can challenge that belief. If students believe all leaders are generals or team captains, that belief may be challenged when they learn how the Daughters of Liberty organized spinning bees that allowed the boycott of English textiles.

The third avenue is a framework for creating activities that demonstrate understanding as instructional goals, or performances of understanding. Chapters 3 and 4 discuss choosing understanding goals and planning for performances of understanding. The fourth avenue suggests that understanding is enhanced as students are provided with learning through multiple intelligences. This is discussed in more detail in Chapter 6.

It can be helpful to think of a series of moments that can occur when we encounter new information in ways that promote understanding. The first moment comes when we say to ourselves, "Oh, wow!" An "oh, wow" moment occurs when we approach new experiences or ideas with curiosity and openness. It allows us to look at things that we do not understand and consequently think, "How interesting," "How curious," or "How puzzling." An experience that encourages students to be curious can serve to motivate them to learn and help them recognize the need for additional understanding. An activity in which students read and discuss historical documents written by different groups of people encourages that type of curiosity and leads to further investigation of conflicting information.

Many adolescents will express a varying level of the "oh, wow" attitude at any given moment, prompt, or encounter. Some will be concerned that showing too much public enthusiasm or interest will cause their peers to think they are "uncool" or a "teacher's pet." As a teacher of middle and high school students, you will need to be mindful that some students will be hesitant to show you their real level of intrigue, but do not make the mistake of thinking they are not curious, interested, or motivated to learn. If we are to facilitate our students' understanding, we must provide them with experiences that prompt curiosity and inquiry.

The second type of moment is one in which new connections and insights occur. It is the moment of, "Aha!" An "aha" moment is one in which the student says (or thinks), "Of course," "How logical," or "Now I see why that happened." You have probably experienced this type of moment, when information that had previously been confusing suddenly made sense. You had enough connections to see a more fully formed logical pattern.

In order for "aha" moments to occur, students must have enough encounters with the information that purposes and patterns emerge. For example, students may have never understood how the teaching of history from a western European cultural perspective could provide them insight into other cultures, their worldviews, and histories, but they may have an "aha" moment when they learn about events from an African's point of view. Simply saying, "The people of Zimbabwe have meaningful rituals that are different than many of those practiced by Americans" is not likely to generate understanding. Students can have a richer context for experiencing their culture by envisioning the people of Zimbabwe, reading literature about their culture, hearing their music, and studying their ways of life. Aha moments can occur when students make sense of how scientific principles are exemplified in the world around them, why historical figures acted the way they did, and why countries with particular geography or history develop. They can make the difference between viewing another culture's traditions as strange and seeing them as logical from another point of view. For example, one group of middle school students thought it was strange that Japanese students ate so much rice, especially for lunch. Why didn't Japanese students eat sandwiches like they did? Once they studied how rice grows and how wheat grows, and compared that information to the geography of the two countries, it all made sense. Rather than viewing the use of this traditional food as peculiar, they saw it as a clever use of the available land.

The final type of moment may not occur often, but it is an important goal for many teaching situations. In this moment a student looks at a new understanding and thinks, "How wonderful!" or "How beautiful!" Every discipline has patterns that are beautiful to those who are immersed in that world. Mathematicians find beauty in elegant equations, anthropologists in the traditions of diverse cultures, biologists in the complex interactions of living things. One of the finest moments of teaching can be helping students find appreciation when they learn things that are beautiful, true, or good.

Projects, whether done in groups or individually, are an imaginative way to build meaning. You might think of a project as the creation of a real-life (authentic) product that represents a synthesis of relevant learning. For example, students in Ken Cowan's unit on Zimbabwe may decide to survey community adults on their knowledge of

African culture or set up a display of the class's sculptures in a local school. Alternatively, they may create a virtual museum on the history of Zimbabwe or create a Hypercard presentation comparing the history of Zimbabwe with other examples of colonialism. In each case, students synthesize a body of information through the creation of some type of product.

To complete projects successfully, students must integrate and apply a variety of skills and understandings. In the examples above, such skills could include survey design, statistics, HyperCard, or museum display techniques. An inventive teacher who favors student-directed learning may encourage students to begin the project, let them discover the need for specific skills and concepts, and then enable them to seek out their own learning materials (already prepared by the teacher). This approach would be similar to the strategy of problem-based learning discussed in Chapter 7. Another teacher might explain the information on survey design directly.

Projects allow students to bring skills, concepts, and generalizations together in a product that is useful to them and is conducted in real-life settings. For example, the survey gives students the opportunity to apply new ideas and gain a deeper understanding of how local attitudes toward Africa may relate to knowledge of African culture. It also demonstrates to the students the real-life utility of data gathering and analysis.

Further Reflecting

In order to plan effectively for the class you are observing, it will be important to learn as much as you can about the students. Learn as much as you can about the general developmental characteristics of the age and grade you are preparing to teach. Through reading and observation, consider how those developmental characteristics will affect the types of lessons that are most effective. Compare your findings with a classmate studying the same grade. Next, consider the characteristics of the specific class for which you are planning. Learn about the major cultural groups represented. Discuss with the teacher any students who have special needs or interests related to your unit topic. If you have the opportunity to correct student work, use it as a chance to analyze student thinking and try to anticipate ways to make your teaching as clear as possible. Think about an authentic project that might serve as the culminating activity or authentic assessment for your unit.

While it certainly will be impossible to learn everything possible about the class, this study will help you remember that unit planning must always focus on students' needs, interests, and characteristics in order to be successful.

CHAPTER SUMMARY

This chapter considered the characteristics of students that influence how they learn, what is known about the process of learning itself, and what it means to understand something one has learned. In making decisions about learning activities, teachers must consider students' intellectual abilities, prior knowledge and life experiences, cultural background, interests, and learning styles. Teachers also must understand that students do not learn by passively receiving information. They construct their own meaning out of what they experience, and this meaning is profoundly influenced by what they already know and have experienced. If students are to understand content, teachers must provide a variety of authentic, complex experiences that allow students to encounter information in many ways and have the opportunity to use it meaningfully.

The examples provided in the last section encourage you to think about alternatives to teaching using the traditional strategies. Field trips, role-play exercises, the use of media and technology, projects, and learning centers are just a few examples to help you, first, think more broadly about how to connect with students, assess their learning readiness, and evaluate their abilities and needs and, second, design activities that respond to them.

Practice Activity

Student Interviews

Select a middle or high school student to interview three times during the term. Conduct your first interview while studying this chapter. Each interview should take no more than 10 to 15 minutes. For each interview, choose something the student has been learning about in school, then try to determine the student's understanding of the topic and how he or she acquired it. Write a case study, including the following information in your study:

Practice Point

Age, grade, gender of student
Topic(s) discussed
Understandings, misconceptions, and interesting ideas you identified
Ways the student used prior knowledge to construct understanding
Teaching strategies that were or were not helpful.

Do not use the student's real name in the case study. Maintaining confidentiality regarding student characteristics and behaviors is an important professional standard you should begin now.

Unit Preparation

Prepare a classroom portrait describing the composition of the class for whom you are preparing your unit. Describe the ages and grade level(s) of the students, the communities from which they come, economic level, ethnicity, and gender. Also describe their learning styles, interests, and other relevant characteristics. Begin thinking about how you will adapt your unit for this particular group of students.

 ## *Portfolio Activity*

In your field placement or other school setting, conduct an assessment of student interests. Prepare a summary for your portfolio. Be prepared to discuss how you will use this information in instruction. Create a "Classroom portrait" describing all relevant characteristics of the students for whom you are planning your unit.

REFERENCES

Armstrong, T. (1994). *Multiple intelligences in the classroom.* Alexandria, VA: Association of Supervision and Curriculum Development.

Banks, J. (1987). *Teaching strategies for ethnic studies,* 6th Ed. Boston: Allyn & Bacon.

Banks, J. (1999). *An introduction to multicultural education.* Boston: Allyn & Bacon.

Borko, H., & Putnam, R. T. (1996). Learning to teach. In D. C. Berliner & R. C. Calfee (Eds.), *Handbook of educational psychology* (pp. 673–708). New York: Macmillan.

Boykin, A. W. (1994). Afrocultural expression and its implication for schooling. In E. R. Hollins, J. E. King, & W. C. Haymen (Eds.) *Teaching diverse populations: Formulating a knowledge base* (pp. 105–127). Albany, NY: State University of New York Press.

Brandt, R. S., & Perkins, D. N. (2000). The evolving science of learning. In R. S. Brandt (Ed.), *Education in a new era: ASCD yearbook 2000.* Alexandria, VA: Association for Supervision and Curriculum Development.

Brooks, J. G., & Brooks, M. G. (1993). *In search of understanding: The case for constructivist classrooms.* Alexandria, VA: Association for Supervision and Curriculum Development.

Brown, J. S., Collins, A., & Duguid, P. (1989). Situated cognition and the culture of learning. *Educational Researcher, 18*(1), 32–42.

Bruer, J. T. (1999). Neural connections: Some you use, some you lose. *Phi Delta Kappan, 81*(1), 4, 264–277.

Butler, K. (1986). *Learning and teaching style in theory and practice.* Columbia, CT: Learner's Dimension.

Butler, K. (1995). *Learning styles: Personal exploration and practical applications.* Columbia, CT: Learner's Dimension.

Butler, K. (1996). *Viewpoints.* Columbia, CT: Learner's Dimension.

Caine, R. N., & Caine, G. (1997). *Educating on the edge of possibility.* Alexandria, VA: Association for Supervision and Curriculum Development.

Checkley, K. (1997). The first seven . . . and the eighth. A conversation with Howard Gardner. *Educational Leadership, 55*(1), 8–13.

Cline, Z. (1998). Buscando su voz en dos culturas—Finding your voice in two cultures. *Phi Delta Kappan, 79,* 699–702.

Cross, W. (1995). The psychology of Nigrescence: Revising the Cross model. In J. G. Ponterotto, J. M. Casas, L.A. Suzuki, & C. M. Alexander (Eds.), *Handbook of multicultural counseling* (pp. 93–122). Thousand Oaks, CA: Sage.

Darling-Hammond, L., Ancess, J., & Ort, S. W. (2002). Reinventing high school: Outcomes of the coalition campus schools project. *American Educational Research Journal, 39*(3), 639–673.

Dewey, J. (1902). *The child and the curriculum.* Chicago: University of Chicago.

Dunn, R. (1996). *How to implement and supervise a learning styles program.* Alexandria, VA: Association for Supervision and Curriculum Development.

Dunn, R. (1997). The goals and track record of multicultural education. *Educational Leadership, 54*(7), 74–77.

Dunn, R., & Dunn, K. (1975). *Educator's self-teaching guide to individualizing instructional programs.* New York: Parker.

Dunn, R., & Griggs, S. A. (1995). *Multicultural curriculum and learning styles.* Westport, CT: Praeger Publications.

Dunn, R., & Others. (1995). A meta-analytic validation of the Dunn and Dunn model of learning styles preferences. *Journal of Educational Research, 88*(6), 353–62.

Ford, D. Y. (1996). *Reversing underachievement among gifted Black students: Promising practices.* New York: Teachers College Press.

Gardner, H. (1983). *Frames of mind: The theory of multiple intelligences.* New York: Basic Books.

Gardner, H. (1991). *The unschooled mind.* New York: Basic Books.

Gardner, H. (1993). *Multiple intelligences: Theory into practice.* New York: Basic Books.

Gardner, H. (1999). *The disciplined mind.* New York: Simon and Schuster.

Gay, G. (1994). *At the essence of learning: Multicultural education.* West Lafayette, IN: Kappa Delta Pi.

Gregorc, A. (1982). *An adult's guide to style.* Maynard, MA: Gabriel.

Guild, P. B., & Garger, S. (1998). *Marching to different drummers,* 2nd Ed. Alexandria, VA: Association for Supervision and Curriculum Development.

Hannafin, M. J., Hannafin, K. M., Land, S. M., & Oliver, K. (1997). Grounded practice and the design of learning environments. *Educational Technology, Research and Design, 45*(3), 101–117.

Hunt, D. E. (1979). Learning and student needs: An introduction to conceptual level. In J. W. Keefe, *Student learning styles: Diagnosing and prescribing programs* (pp. 27–28). Reston, VA: National Association of Secondary School Principals.

Jensen, E. (2000). Brain-based learning: A reality check. *Educational Leadership, 57*(7), 7–80.

Ladson-Billings, G. (1994). *The dreamkeepers: Successful teachers of African American children.* San Francisco: Jossey-Bass.

Ladson-Billings, G. (1995). But that's just good teaching! The case for culturally relevant pedagogy. *Theory Into Practice, 34,* 159–165.

Lewis, B. (1991). *The kid's guide to social action.* Minneapolis: Free Spirit Press.

Lipsitz, J., Mizell, M. H., Jackson, A. W., & Austin, L. M. (1997). Speaking with one voice: A manifesto for middle grades reform. *Phi Delta Kappan, 78,* 533–540.

Manning, M. L. (1994). *Celebrating diversity: Multicultural education in middle level schools.* Columbus, OH: National Middle School Association.

Newmann, F. M. (1991). Linking restructuring to authentic student achievement. *Phi Delta Kappan, 41,* 463.

Newmann, F. M. (1996). Authentic pedagogy and student performance. *American Journal of Education 104*(4), 280–312.

Oakes, J., & Lipton, M. (1999). *Teaching to change the world.* Boston: McGraw-Hill.

Ogbu, J. U. (1983). Minority students and schooling in pluralistic societies. *Comparative Education Review, 27*(2), 168–190.

Pang, V. O. (2001). *Multicultural education: A caring-centered, reflective approach.* New York: McGraw-Hill.

Perkins, D. (1992). *Smart schools.* New York: The Free Press.

Perkins, D. (1999, November). The many faces of constructivism. *Educational Leadership, 57*(3), 6–11.

Philips, D. (1995). The good, the bad, and the ugly: The many faces of constructivism. *Educational Researcher, 24*(7), 5–12.

Piaget, J. (1970). Piaget's theory. In P. H. Mussen (Ed.), *Carmichael's manual of psychology.* New York: Wiley.

Renzulli, J. S. (1977). *The enrichment triad.* Mansfield Center, CT: Creative Learning Press.

Scherer, M. (Ed.). (2000, November). *Educational Leadership, 58*(3). Theme issue.

Shade, B. J. (1997). *Culture, style, and the educational process: Making schools work for racially diverse students.* Springfield, IL: Charles Thomas.

Smith, G. Pritchy. (1998). *Common sense about uncommon knowledge: The knowledge bases for diversity.* New York: American Association of Colleges for Teacher Education.

Sprenger, M. (1999). *Learning and memory: The brain in action.* Alexandria, VA: Association for Supervision and Curriculum Development.

Starko, A. J., & Schack, G. D. (1992). *Looking for data in all the right places.* Mansfield Center, CT: Creative Learning Press.

Sternberg, R. (1985). *Beyond IQ: A triarchic theory of human intelligence.* New York: Cambridge University Press.

Sternberg, R. (1997). What does it mean to be smart? *Educational Leadership, 54*(6), 20–24.

Sternberg, R. J., Grigorenko, E., & Jarvin, L. (2000). Improving reading instruction: The triarchic model. *Educational Leadership, 58*(6), 48–54.

Sternberg, R. J., Torff, B., & Grigorenko, E. (1998). Teaching for successful intelligence raises school achievement. *Phi Delta Kappan, 79,* 667–669.

Stevenson, C. (2002). *Teaching ten to fourteen year olds*, 3rd Ed. Boston, MA: Allyn & Bacon.

Strong, R., Silver, H. F., & Robinson, A. (1995). What do students want? *Educational Leadership, 53* (1), 8–12.

Swisher, F., & Doyle, D. (1992). Adapting instruction to culture. In J. Reyner (Ed.), *Teaching American Indian students* (pp. 81–95). Norman, OK: University of Oklahoma Press.

Tomlinson, C. A. (1999). *The differentiated classroom: Responding to the needs of all learners.* Alexandria, VA: Association for Supervision and Curriculum Development.

Vygotsky, L. S. (1997). *Educational Psychology.* Boca Raton, FL: St. Lucie Press.

Wasserstein, P. (1995). What middle schoolers say about their school work. *Educational Leadership, 53*(1), 41–43.

Wlodowski, R. J., & Ginsberg, M. B. (1995). Framework for culturally responsive teaching. *Educational Leadership, 53*(1), 17–21.

Wolfe, P. (2001). *Brain matters: Translating research into classroom practice.* Alexandria, VA: Association for Curriculum and Supervision.

Young, F. (1993). Instructional design for situated learning. *Educational Technology, Research and Design, 41*(1), 43–58.

CHAPTER **3**

Choosing and Analyzing Classroom Goals

CHAPTER OVERVIEW

One of the most important decisions a teacher makes is *what* to teach. Of all the knowledge, skills, and attitudes that are possible and all the content suggested as appropriate for a particular grade level, some portion must be selected for a given class in a given day, month, or year. The focus of this chapter is how teachers make decisions about what to teach. We address several key questions about selecting classroom goals: Why is there so much debate and disagreement about the goals and achievements of American education? From what sources does a successful teacher derive educational goals? How does the reflective teacher choose goals that are best for the students?

The chapter consists of three sections. Section 1 focuses on three major educational philosophies and their impact on curriculum goals. In it we will examine the ways varying educational philosophies can shape the ways individuals think about the purposes of schools and the content that is most valuable. Section 2 discusses the processes of selecting educational goals, deciding what we hope students will know or be able to do as a result of our instruction. We will examine how key concepts and generalizations can help shape the content in ways that will facilitate student understanding. Finally, Section 3 provides an overview of unit design, illustrating how curriculum goals and content analysis fit into the overall planning process.

SECTION 1. CHOOSING WORTHWHILE EDUCATIONAL GOALS

The process of choosing educational goals can be thought of as the answers to a series of questions:

1. What is my philosophy? What kinds of learning do I believe are most important in schools?
2. What do I want my students to understand and be able to do as a result of my instruction?
3. What content will I teach?
4. What concepts and generalizations will focus and structure the content for understanding?

These questions are not always answered in this order, or even in any order that is clear and sequential. A teacher's educational philosophy is shaped over time and tends to be slow to change. In most cases teachers do not stop to consider their philosophy each time they begin to plan a lesson or unit. However, that philosophy shapes all the decisions the teacher makes in important ways, determining what a teacher believes is valuable in school, what is essential, and what is trivial.

The answers to the four questions often are intertwined. A teacher may identify a series of goals shaped by district guidelines, state standards, and personal beliefs. Once the teacher identifies the specific content to be taught, that may bring to mind additional goals or lead the teacher to decide that a particular goal is not suitable for this content or students. By identifying the key concepts and generalizations that can be used to help students understand the content, teachers can shape the areas to be emphasized. This weaving of goals, content, and core concepts helps teachers make important teaching decisions.

Section 1 Objectives

After you have completed this section, you will be able to:

1. classify examples of educational statements that reflect progressive perspectives, essentialist perspectives, and critical pedagogy and
2. describe how they relate to your personal philosophy.

Opening Activity

Read the following scenario, and try to determine the different curriculum philosophies expressed by the various speakers.

Practice Point

It was a warm evening in early May as the sun filtered into the school board room of the Landstown, Maryland, schools. Landstown is a suburban community of 110,000 persons. Shenandoah, a large state university, is located within its boundaries. Many students who attend the Landstown schools are children of the faculty, staff, and students of that university. Landstown has a number of private and religious schools as well as two public high schools, four middle schools, and ten elementary schools.

The Landstown families are primarily of White and European background, and there are 15% African American and 10% Asian students. A large majority of the public school students come from middle- and upper-income families, although a significant number of families overall (15% to 20%) would be classified as lower income. About 80% of the youths who graduate from one of the two high schools enroll in higher education programs.

The community is divided educationally. Many Landstown residents pressure the schools to concentrate their attention on intellectual development—in part, so high school graduates are prepared to make the transition into higher education. An equal number of residents urge the schools to play a much larger role in enhancing students' personal and social development. In that regard, the Landstown Public Schools participate in a far-reaching inclusion program, in which children with disabilities are included in the regular classroom for most educational activities. Lastly, a small but vocal group of parents and other members of the community push the schools to be more involved in community action and improvement projects.

Marvin Pancett, the school board president, tried to remain calm in the midst of a spirited exchange between two members of the community task force, which was charged with an examination of "The School Curriculum in the 21st Century." The task force chair, Maude Jones, was completing her majority group report on the place of multicultural/global education in the school curriculum.

Practice Point

Jones said, "In Orwell's novel of tyranny, *1984,* the Party in power's banner reads, 'Who controls the past controls the future; who controls the present controls the past.' Clearly, White males, primarily from western European backgrounds, have controlled the past in the United States. The evidence for that conclusion can be found in the middle school and senior high school history and literature books that were required reading for many adults in this room. The cultural contributions of women, people of color, White males from southern and eastern Europe, Jews, and Muslims were largely overlooked or marginalized. It is true that the textbooks in use today in Landstown have improved. However, the task force majority is unhappy with the lack of meaningful multicultural content in the curriculum. We note the increasing numbers of children of color entering the Landstown schools. However, all students, not just students of color, benefit from a multicultural education. Consequently, the task force majority recommends the inclusion of cultural and historical content about Asia, Latin America, and Africa in addition to content about diverse people in America. In fact, we would like to see Landstown become a leader in the development of a multicultural/global curriculum" (Davidman, 1994).

Paul Smith, from the task force minority, was visibly angry as he rose to speak. "The task force minority cannot defend the past. We agree with Ms. Jones' conclusion that the school curriculum misrepresented the history, cultures, and contributions of the groups she mentioned. We agree that a more balanced curriculum is needed. However, we disagree that a multicultural curriculum is the answer. The saga of human history has both its heroes and villains, its uplifting events, ideas, and individuals and those whose direction is otherwise. If Western civilization has much for which to apologize, it also gave birth to democratic thought and practice, the flowering of human reason, artistic creation, and advancements in science, mathematics, and technology that have bettered the lives of all. To replace the study of Western civilization because some groups feel slighted would be a serious mistake, and I will never endorse it."

Carla Martinez, a member of the task force majority, responded. "Mr. Smith and his followers refuse to recognize the diversity of American society. In many communities and schools people of color are a majority of the residents. Soon we shall see African American and Latino/Latina children become the majority group in the public schools. A multicultural perspective to the study of history, the humanities, and the arts will do honor to the heritage and backgrounds of all children."

Evidence has demonstrated that when multicultural education is appropriately implemented a number of positive outcomes occur. First, multicultural teachers can use case studies, events, and personalities from many cultures to illustrate their lessons. Second, they can consider alternatives to traditional knowledge such as that advanced by scholars in the fields of women's and multicultural studies (Banks & Banks, 2002). Third, multicultural education can lead to greater understanding of people from diverse ethnic and racial groups and thus lead to a decline in prejudice and stereotyping (Banks & Banks, 2002).

Practice Point

Finally, consider the terrorist attack on the World Trade Center in New York on September 11, 2001, and the fact that some American people in their rightful anger blamed all Muslims for the actions of a few hate-filled zealots. The terrorists' perverse image of America was the product of an education that recognizes only one right way to believe and act. Multicultural education is an antidote for this kind of intellectual and emotional "blindness."

The board members listened as advocates with different viewpoints rose to speak. Finally, school board president Pancett, distressed because the hour had reached midnight, adjourned the meeting for one week to cool tempers. The next morning Mr. Pancett showed up at the door of the school superintendent, Dr. Ruth Borkman, to discuss the confusing series of events at the school board meeting the previous evening: "Dr. Borkman, what in the world happened last night? I have to admit that the arguments between the two segments of the task force overwhelmed me. Why is the committee so split?"

"Marv, what happened last night brings the wide differences of opinion about what should be taught in the schools to the surface. These differences obviously are present in the task force."

Dr. Borkman then proceeded to explain the educational philosophies that one might expect to find in a public school in the United States and how the philosophies affect the school curriculum and the teachers' instructional approaches.

REFLECTING ON THE IDEAS

The positions taken by members of the curriculum task force reflect the two most common educational philosophies found in American schools today. Consider what appear to be the key beliefs or values held by each side. Have you seen similar differences played out in schools in your area?

Three Views of Educational Philosophy

Progressivism: Social and Personal

As Dr. Borkman explained to school board president Pancett, the majority group members of the curriculum task force were defending a progressive educational philosophy about society in general and education in particular. **Progressivism** developed as the United States was transformed from a rural to an industrialized society. Although the transformation of American society occurred over generations, social scientists and historians label the period 1880–1914 as the major era of change.

As the pace of industrialization quickened, millions of immigrants thronged into the United States. The surge in population with many new Americans living in crowded homes in big-city neighborhoods changed forever the simplicity of the one-room schoolhouse focusing on the three Rs. Such schools were replaced by multiroom and multigrade comprehensive schools that housed hundreds, even thousands, of students. With rapid and massive changes in the size and composition of the schools, together with similar changes in the society at large, advocates of progressivism believed that education beyond the basics was required. "Progressivism was based on the assumption that the quality of human existence could be improved by the application of scientific reasoning to social problems. Consequently, education as a major social institution could play a key role in developing competent citizens, who would be better prepared to deal with the new challenges facing our modern industrial society" (Stanley & Nelson, 1994, pp. 271–272).

Although it is difficult to identify what beliefs and values were shared by all educational progressives, most favored curriculum experimentation and flexibility (e.g., John Dewey), rather than a prescribed program for the transmission of subject matter. Thus a major focus of the progressive curriculum was on learning to think rather than on learning particular subject matter. In addition, progressives were committed to a child-centered educational program in schools that exemplified democratic values and processes. Ironically, progressive teachers found themselves having to choose between supporting the educational and social choices made by an individual child and a desire to support democratic values in the classroom. For example, a large majority of students might decide to pursue a particular unit of study, with a small group refusing to abide by the decision. Ultimately, it was this recurring dilemma that led to a split in the progressive movement.

One group of progressives, let's call them "social progressives," retained the belief that social development is the primary function of modern education. Social progressives see schooling as a process of preparing young people to be successful adults in a democratic society. They view curriculum in terms of the knowledge, skills, and attitudes that assist young people to confront and master the tasks they will face as adults. In the contemporary educational area, social progressives can be seen leading the fight for an increased emphasis on citizenship education; nutrition, health, and family issues; career education; dropout prevention; and emotional, moral, and character development.

Social progressives are often spokespersons for an educational community that values and respects diversity. Inherent in that respect is an emphasis on the nature and contributions of many cultural groups. Social progressives maintain that the result will be a classroom marked by mutual support and harmony. A curriculum that accomplishes this objective must extend its scope to include instruction about the nature and contributions of multiple groups, including Native Americans, African Americans, Latinos, Asians, and Europeans (Association for Supervision and Curriculum Development, 1993).

Although many members of "The School Curriculum in the 21st Century" task force support a social progressive view of the curriculum, a second group of progressives is also represented on the task force: the *personal progressives.* Personal progressives argue that instruction must be tailored to meet the needs and interests of the many kinds of children who enter the public schools. They are opposed to a predetermined curriculum that rigidly organizes what all children are expected to learn. Many progressive teachers in the period 1930–1960 were influenced by the ideas of William Heard Kilpatrick, who espoused the project method. According to this view, the child's experiences should provide the basis for curriculum decisions; these decisions should not be dictated by subject matter fixed in advance. Understandably, Kilpatrick argued that "subject matter was useful only when it could be combined with the child's interests" (Ravitch, 1983, p. 52).

One of the best known contemporary personal progressives, John Holt, was influential through his books *How Children Fail* (1964) and *How Children Learn* (1970). Holt derided the authoritarian climate he perceived in many schools where control and docility were prized and freedom and spontaneity extinguished (1964). He was a leading proponent of the movement that became known as "open education" or "informal education." In such an approach, learning is individualized, teaching is informal, content is based on student expressions of needs or interests, play is valued, and learning takes place in a noisy and joyful setting. Personal progressives view multicultural education as a process of enhancement of individual children, making each a stronger, more capable, and more independent person. Such persons become "self-directed learners" who gradually take more responsibility for their own educational plans and goals (Davidman, 1994).

Essentialism

A second educational philosophy, espoused by the members of the task force minority group, is essentialism. **Essentialism** is a belief that the purpose of schooling is to impart necessary knowledge, skills, and attitudes to enable young people to function as fully developed human beings. Essentialists believe that to achieve maturity, the learner must understand the external world of observable reality and abstract ideas. Some essentialists focus their attention on what has been called the basic skills: reading, writing, and arithmetic. Others have a more extensive list of essentials.

Still others argue that the essentials are contained in the school subjects: literature, English and other languages, history, the social sciences, chemistry, physics, biology, mathematics, and the fine arts. These essentialists argue that disciplinary knowledge has withstood the test of time. Because it has been examined, refined, and revised over the centuries, the knowledge gained from disciplinary study is more valuable than knowledge gained from any other source of educational content.

A clear example of the essentialist position can be found in the book *Cultural Literacy: What Every American Needs to Know* by E. D. Hirsch, Jr. (1987). Hirsch maintained that ". . . no modern society can think of becoming a classless society except on the basis of universal literacy. To be truly literate, a high school graduate must be able to grasp the meaning of written materials in any field or subject provided that those materials are addressed to a general audience" (p. 129). Hirsch argued that the curriculum should impart intensive knowledge, consisting of mental models—commonly labeled as concepts or ideas. However, Hirsch believed that extensive knowledge is also necessary, for example, essential facts, names, places, terms, dates, and events.

According to Hirsch, the concern for relevance and pluralism so prevalent in schools results in a fragmented curriculum (Hirsch, 2001). Consequently, youths learn few topics, such as literary and historical works, in common. Thus he concluded that U.S. youths share little knowledge of the culture that has shaped and enriched the Western world.

Support for Hirsch's position came from the study *American Memory: A Report on the Humanities in the Nation's Public Schools*, (1987) by Lynne Cheney, former chair of the National Endowment for the Humanities, and wife of the current Vice President of the United States. Cheney drew on the data from an NEH study to reveal that two thirds of U.S. 17-year-olds who were tested did not know when the Civil War was fought (even when granting them a 50-year margin of error), could not correctly identify the Reformation and the Magna Carta, and were unable to identify such literary giants as Nathaniel Hawthorne, Jane Austen, Geoffrey Chaucer, and Walt Whitman (Ravitch & Finn, 1987).

Similar findings were reported from the year 2001 administration of the National Assessment of Educational Progress (NAEP). The 2001 test was administered to 29,600 students (mostly public school) and consisted of multiple-choice, short-answer, and essay questions. The history section of the test revealed that only 43% of twelfth graders had a basic understanding of American history, a percentage that was unchanged from the 1994 test. Education historian Diane Ravitch concluded that ". . . our high schools are failing to teach U.S. history well and awaken mature students to the value of history as a study that matters . . ." (Ravitch, 2002). Essentialists would argue that these results indicate a need for increased emphasis on traditional disciplinary content.

Reconstructionism and Critical Pedagogy

The two educational philosophies known as progressivism and essentialism were in conflict within the Landstown schools curriculum task force and are at war in the general society, as reflected by the various reactions to the cultural literacy controversy. However, a third philosophy should not be overlooked. This philosophy, originally identified as **reconstructionism** or, more recently, critical pedagogy, is characterized by a belief that schools should prepare the future adults of society to work for social justice and to demand societal change. Proponents maintain that the present society is seriously flawed by inequities based on class, race, and gender and that schools have a responsibility to respond to those inequities. "It is a view concerned with promoting more democratic, equitable social relations even if that means challenging the existing order of things" (Reynolds & Martusewicz, 1994, p. 226).

Reconstructionism had its roots in the 1930s when social reconstructionists critiqued traditional educational ideas and institutions in relation to surrounding social, political, and economic structures. George Counts, a noted reconstructionist in the 1930s, wrote:

There can be no good individual apart from some conception of the character of a good society; and the good society is not something that is given by nature: it must be fashioned by the hand and brain of man. This process of building a good society is to a very large degree an educational process. (1932, p. 26)

Counts' (1932) book title, *Dare Schools Build a New Social Order?*, reflects the reconstructionists' hope.

Contemporary philosophers with a similar perspective espouse **critical pedagogy**, an approach to teaching that encourages critical analysis of issues such as race, class, and gender and reflects democratic social relationships. Many of those involved in critical pedagogy are political and social activists who believe that schools often unwittingly serve to reproduce inequalities. They often encourage young people to participate in political activity and social action projects in the community.

If an individual committed to critical pedagogy had been active on "The School Curriculum in the 21st Century" task force, what might that advocate have written as a minority report? Think about what that report might sound like before continuing. The remarks would probably be similar to the following:

There must be more to multicultural/global education than learning some things about persons and groups who have different ways of speaking and dressing, different religions or customs, or different previous histories. Multicultural education must also be an agent for societal change and improvement. It must contain a parental and community component that encourages participation in the education of children and extends that participation beyond the classroom to influence the actions and decisions of school committees, boards, and other community agencies. It must be at the center of an activist education that improves the quality of life in communities that have been oppressed by racism and/or the lack of economic opportunity.

 ## REFLECTING ON THE IDEAS

Which of the three educational philosophies do you support? If you were a member of the community task force examining the topic "The School Curriculum in the 21st Century," what would you include in your report on multicultural education? Would your report have a progressive, essentialist, or critical emphasis?

Planning Educational Outcomes

Given the complexity and diversity of potential educational content, and with a philosophical perspective as a backdrop, how does a reflective teacher go about the task of deciding what to teach? At the beginning of this process is the decision of what we want to accomplish—what it is we hope students will learn and understand—the *outcomes* of our teaching. These may be in the form of goals or standards (usually broad, long-

Common Terms for Student Learning Outcomes (Results)		
Term	**Broad, Long-Term**	**Specific, Short-Term**
Goal	X	
Standard	X	
Benchmark		X
Objective		X

Figure 3.1 Common Terms for Student Learning Outcomes
From *Teaching as Decision Making: Successful Practices for the Elementary Teacher* (3rd Ed.) (p. 63), by
A. J. Starko, et al. 2003, Upper Saddle River, NJ: Merrill/Prentice Hall. Copyright 2003 by Pearson Education, Inc.
Reprinted with permission.

range outcomes), benchmarks (usually more specific outcomes), or objectives (usually specific, short-term outcomes; see Figure 3.1). This chapter will guide you in clarifying educational goals, the broad learning outcomes for your students.

Educational goals are statements of educational intent that provide general direction to the teacher in developing instruction. Educational goals or outcomes are often written to describe student learning within large blocks of content, such as a course of study or a unit of study. Although a goal may be written in specific and precise language, most goals are general in form. Thus they must undergo further analysis before they can be useful as guideposts in the design of lessons.

Dozens of models can assist teachers in selecting educational goals. In the 1930s, Ralph Tyler, one of the major figures in curriculum development in the 20th century, developed a systematic framework that has since been popularly referred to as Tyler's Curriculum Rationale (1969). The rationale appears in Figure 3.2.

In Tyler's conception of the process of curriculum design, the teacher begins by examining a range of available materials on the subject matter to be taught. Such materials include textbooks, books written on the topic, curriculum guides, web sites, magazines and newspapers, and information gained through interviews with knowledgeable educators, students, parents, and other resource people in the community. When the examination has been completed, the teacher lists all the possible goals that emerged.

To utilize the Rationale, the teacher might divide the goals into three groups based on their philosophic source: (1) goals that assist the student to master important subject matter, (2) goals that relate to contemporary societal needs, and (3) goals that relate to the students' personal needs and/or interests. Do you recognize in Tyler's three sources of goals the educational philosophies discussed previously in the chapter? Subject matter mastery

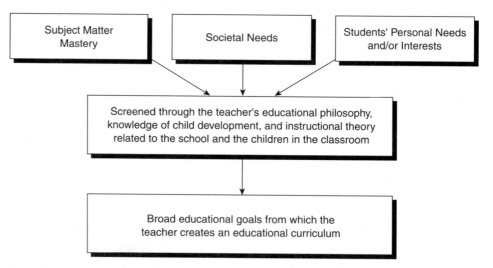

Figure 3.2 Tyler's Curriculum Rationale

From *Basic Principles of Curriculum and Instruction* by Ralph Tyler, published by University of Chicago Press, copyright 1969.

is consistent with an essentialist philosophy. Goals in that area would include competence in communication skills, mathematics, history, and the arts. Societal needs can be confronted from either a critical pedagogy or a progressive perspective. Goals emerging from societal needs could include learning about the environment, health education classes, or gaining skills in decision making that can be used to address a variety of social crises. Attention to student needs or interests is progressive in nature.

 ## REFLECTING ON THE IDEAS

Review the process recommended by Tyler for selecting content goals. Examine the list of goals found in a curriculum guide or teacher's edition of a textbook. Count the number of goals that appear to reflect each major area below. What does your document emphasize?

SECTION 2. ANALYZING CONTENT GOALS

Section 2 Objectives

After you have completed this section, you will be able to:

1. classify examples of affective, psychomotor, and cognitive goals;
2. describe the use of education standards in planning;
3. relate concepts, generalizations, and facts in a content area of your choice;

4. sort examples of concrete and abstract concepts;
5. construct a concept map in a content area of your own choice; and
6. structure a content area into a network of generalizations, concepts, and facts.

Zimbabwe: A World's View from Africa

Joshua Masuko, a graduate student from Zimbabwe at Shenandoah University, is reading for a second time a phone message to call the curriculum director of the Landstown Public Schools, a woman by the name of Millicent Stephens. What could she wish from him, he wonders. Joshua is in his third year of political science graduate work at the university. After a few moments of thought, Joshua decides that the only way to solve the mystery is to make the return call. After reaching Millicent Stephens, Joshua opens the conversation:

JOSHUA: My name is Joshua Masuko and I am responding to your phone inquiry.

MILLICENT STEPHENS: Thank you for returning my call. You are no doubt wondering why I called you. I received your name from Professor Jenkinson of the university political science department who recommended you highly because you are from Zimbabwe and because she thought you might be able to help us with a curriculum development task.

JOSHUA: That is very kind of her.

MILLICENT: Perhaps I should explain my purpose. I am the curriculum director of the Landstown School District. Our schools for youths from ages 11 through 18 have decided to make their course of study in history, the social sciences, the humanities, and the fine arts more multicultural and global in emphasis. At the middle school, a group of eighth-grade teachers have agreed to work together this summer to plan an interdisciplinary unit on Africa. I was hoping that you might agree to be a consultant to the group and advise them when they request help.

JOSHUA: Why don't I meet with the teachers and determine whether I can be helpful to them.

Later that week, Joshua meets with the middle school curriculum development team at Landstown Middle School.

VERONICA SPARLING (A SOCIAL STUDIES TEACHER):   I have just finished reading a biography of Cecil Rhodes [Roberts, 1988], the man many historians credit with establishing the British dominion over southern Africa. I learned he became a multimillionaire from prospecting for diamonds and was the largest stockholder of the DeBeers Mining Company. He was also a prime minister of the European colony that later became South Africa. He bequeathed the Rhodes scholarship, a program that has provided an opportunity for many future American academic, business, and political leaders to study at Oxford University, including two U.S. presidents, John F. Kennedy and William Jefferson Clinton. Given that history, why don't we focus our curriculum development on Rhodes and the settlement of southern Africa? We can use Rhodes as the personal symbol of European colonization in Africa during the period 1850–1900. I can see objectives related to geography, history, sociology, economics, literature, and music.

JIM PAVLOVICH (A LANGUAGE ARTS TEACHER):   That's a great idea. Rhodes called the place he chose for his burial plot "World View," because of its placement at the crest of a hill that overlooked a panoramic vista as far as the eye can see. Why don't we call the unit "Africa: A World's View"? I can see a lot of appropriate literature to include in the unit.

JOSHUA: I like the unit focus very much. There is too little understanding and identification with Africa in your newspapers and television and, I expect, in your schools. In fact, the only mention of Africa that I see is when there is famine, war, or pestilence. The political, social, economic, and educational life in Africa is almost never on view in America. Thus your focus on Africa could be very helpful.

Unfortunately, you have chosen to focus on the past that began when Europeans came to Africa. Cecil Rhodes was a symbol of the European colonialism that took the Africans' land. And I hope you are aware that my country is not Rhodesia, but Zimbabwe. My ancestors lived in a flourishing country long before the Europeans came. For example, our farmers began using iron in A.D. 300. Zimbabwe became an important religious and trading center before A.D. 1450. It was a well-organized country with extensive contacts with other lands and peoples. The British did not arrive until the 19th century. So ignoring our accomplishments before the European arrival, you negate a people's entire cultural history.

In 1964 the northern part of Rhodesia became the African countries of Zambia and Malawi. In 1980 southern Rhodesia became Zimbabwe. With independence, many of the city names created during European rule were changed as well. The capital of Zimbabwe, formerly Salisbury, is Harare. In fact a statue commemorating Rhodes' life was removed from its dominating location in Harare.

LAURA KASSAVAGE (THE FINE ARTS TEACHER IN THE GROUP):   Mr. Masuko, I hope you will agree to assist us. How did Zimbabwe get its name?

JOSHUA: Zimbabwe is a Shona word that refers to "houses of stone." However, the word is probably better derived from *dzimba woye,* literally "venerated houses," and hence usually used for chiefs' houses or graves. The specific reference is to an extensive collection of stone ruins, the most impressive of which is called Great Zimbabwe. These ruins have now become a patriotic symbol and were adopted for use in naming the entire country [Garlake, 1973]. The largest ethnic groups in my country are Shona-speaking Africans, of which I am a member, who make up about 75% of the population, and Ndebele speakers, about 15% of the total. Europeans are less than 2% of the population.

The Great Zimbabwe, a massive set of stone buildings and walls built without mortar, is the most impressive of over 150 remains of stone structures scattered about the territories north of South Africa. At one time the origins were unknown—that Africans built it was considered by Europeans to be impossible. In fact, Cecil Rhodes visited Great Zimbabwe in

1891 and mistakenly pronounced it a Phoenician residence and dated it to the time of Solomon and the Queen of Sheba. It is now identified as a former religious and commercial city built by the powerful Shona kings probably in the 13th and 14th centuries [Randall-MacGiver, 1906].

KEN COWAN (THE FOURTH MEMBER OF THE PLANNING TEAM AND A SOCIAL STUDIES TEACHER): Joshua has given me an idea to combine our knowledge of the European colonialism in Africa in the 1800s with an examination of present and past Zimbabwe. In that way, we can surface the sweet and bitter fruits of European colonization of Africa and in the process teach our students about African history, a history that we all agree is mostly missing from our present course of study. If it's acceptable to everyone, I will develop a preliminary set of goals for a two-week interdisciplinary unit that we will call "Zimbabwe: A World's View from Africa."

JIM PAVLOVICH: Not so fast! I think we also have to recognize the economic and political strife that exists in Zimbabwe today. The government continues to force White-owned farms to turn over their land to poor Blacks. Black squatters claiming the land as their own have occupied hundreds of White-owned farms. Because of mismanagement of the economy, inflation has risen from an annual rate of 32% in 1998 to 59% in 1999 and 60% in 2000. Excessive government deficits and AIDS are steadily weakening the economy; Zimbabwe has the highest rate of AIDS infection in the world.

JOSHUA: I agree that Zimbabwe has more than its share of problems, but I would like to see a unit that does more than describe Africa's problems. As for the issue of land redistribution, about 4,500 White farmers own 40% of Zimbabwe's agricultural land, most of it in prime growing regions, while about 1 million Blacks own 60% of the land, often in drought affected regions. Where they exist together, huge, modern, mechanized estates are next to subsistence farmers living in mud huts. The government argues that Britain should compensate the White farmers since Blacks were forced off their ancestral lands when Rhodesia was a British colony.

KEN COWAN: Let's agree to do both: recognize the contributions of native Zimbabweans and validate their past while looking at the economic and political truths of today. In addition, by taking an interdisciplinary approach we can integrate the history, geography, economics, politics, and current events of Zimbabwe with art, music, and literature and, where appropriate, with science and mathematics.

Everyone, including Joshua Masuko, agrees wholeheartedly. Joshua is enthusiastic. He views the teaching of this unit as an opportunity to dispel the myths and misconceptions about his heritage.

Ken Cowan's Puzzle

Ken Cowan stared out the window of his eighth-grade social studies classroom and recalled the promise he had made to develop a set of goals for the interdisciplinary unit, Zimbabwe: A World's View from Africa. A multicultural global education unit could teach essential subject area knowledge to his students. However, Ken also wanted the unit to connect to the needs of the entire community. Specifically, he was focused on the societal need for greater understanding and appreciation of the racial and cultural diversity in the United States. He viewed with growing concern the media accounts of verbal and physical violence directed at those who are not members of the "right" group. Furthermore, he wanted to use the unit to dispel what he knew was ignorance, misinformation, and stereotypes about Africa and its past. Finally, the unit should include opportunities for students to exercise personal choices. It was important for him to retain these features in the design and implementation of the unit.

Another challenge was to construct the unit from an interdisciplinary perspective incorporating content goals from social studies, mathematics, science, language arts, and the fine arts. Consequently, students could begin to see that useful knowledge was constructed out of threads of knowledge from many subject areas. He wanted to establish connections between geography and history; between social studies, literature, and the fine arts; and ensure that there were mathematics and science activities in the unit. Clearly, a well-done multicultural/global education unit could achieve a number of important subject matter goals.

Ken decided to speak with Jodi Washington, the eighth-grade teacher across the hall. Jodi was on the district social studies committee and could be depended on to have something creative to offer.

KEN: Hi, Jodi! Are you ready for the new school year?

JODI: You bet. You know me, always ready for a new adventure.

KEN: Well, the Zimbabwe unit will be a new adventure for all of us. I thought you might have some ideas to help us make this a strong interdisciplinary unit.

JODI: Interdisciplinary unit planning has certainly helped me. I've found that linking subjects together helps my students and me focus on important ideas. It also has helped me to find the time for some interesting projects for students to do.

KEN: In the Zimbabwe unit social studies and language arts seem to be natural companions.

JODI: I agree. Which areas of language arts will you integrate with social studies?

KEN: Historical fiction would be included and certainly essay writing.

JODI: I would love to help with the planning. By the way, you know I was on the state committee that created the new framework for social studies. We will have to align the goals for the new Zimbabwe unit with the standards and the appropriate middle school benchmarks.

KEN: I'm not sure I understand the big push to incorporate standards.

JODI: Well, the standards movement continues the focus on accountability that has been a theme in education for the past 25 years and has been trumpeted across the country by many, if not all, of the state governors. On January 9, 2002, President George W. Bush signed into law the No Child Left Behind Act of 2001 (CNN.com, 2002). The act continues the process of general federal aid to education begun with the Elementary and Secondary Education Act of 1965. One provision of the 2001 law mandates state testing of students in math and reading in grades 3 through 8 beginning in 2004–2005. In a speech given prior to the signing ceremony, Bush said:

"The fundamental principle of this bill is that every child can learn. We expect every child to learn, and you [the schools] must show us whether or not every child is learning." (CNN. Com, p. 1)

In Michigan, for example, beginning in 2003, students will take the Michigan Educational Assessment Program (MEAP) tests in English/language arts (including reading, writing, and listening) and mathematics in grade 4 and then science and social studies in grade 5. Middle school/junior high students will take the English/language arts test in grade 7 and mathematics, science, and social studies in grade 8. High school students will take all of the tests in grade 11 or 12. The tests are based on standards and benchmarks that define what students are to know and be able to do with the subject matter content within the four major subject areas.

I have some concerns about the top-down nature of the reform; however, I value the framework as one tool for my curriculum development. The standards can help us identify student performance expectations in both content knowledge and thinking processes. As you know, the State of Michigan has gone a step farther than some other states in specifying expectations through the development of more precise statements of outcomes expressed as benchmarks.

Later Ken thought back to his teacher education preparation program and wished that more class time had been spent on the process of standards-based curriculum planning (Carr & Harris, 2001). The state's curriculum framework appeared a bit confusing. He struggled to define the terminology; for example, how to distinguish differences among goals, standards, objectives, and benchmarks. Upon locating his copy of the *Michigan Curriculum Framework* (1996), he first examined the four strands that delineate social studies education (history, civics, economics, geography). These four emphasize content knowledge in specific disciplines (see Figure 3.3).

He noted that the three additional strands—the development of discourse and decision-making skills, inquiry or research skills, and civic involvement in the community—all emphasize the development of thinking processes and communication skills that may be developed in each of the four disciplines. From within each strand, he would have to select standards and then more narrowly defined benchmarks.

He observed that standards are global, long-range outcomes or goals for all students. For example, a sample content standard in the area of geography is stated as follows:

All students will describe and explain the causes, consequences, and geographic context of major global issues and events.

He contrasted this content standard with one found within the inquiry strand that emphasizes thinking processes and communication skills:

Students will engage their peers in constructive conversation about matters of public concern by clarifying issues, considering opposing views, applying democratic values, anticipating consequences, and working towards making decisions.

Figure 3.3 Strands in Social Studies Education
Source: *Michigan Curriculum Framework*, Michigan Department of Education, 1996.

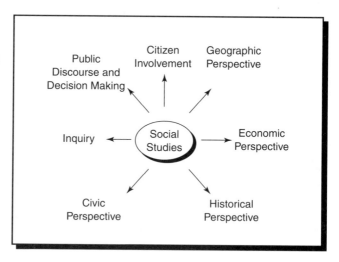

After examining the standards contained within the seven strands, Ken scanned the numerous benchmarks numbered under each standard. Ken observed that the benchmarks seemed more akin to lesson objectives because they were quite narrow in scope. He also observed the developmental progression of the benchmarks. For example, under the geography standard stated above, different benchmarks exist for various age groups:

Middle School: Explain how elements of physical geography, culture, and history of the region may be influencing current events.

High School: Explain the causes and importance of global issues involving cultural stability and change, economic development and international trade, resource use, environmental impact, conflict and cooperation, and explain how they may affect the future.

Ken noted the spiral nature of the benchmarks. As students mature, they are able to grapple with more complex ideas and apply increasingly sophisticated thinking skills. Thankfully, the curriculum director in Ken's district was working with teachers on the use of the curriculum framework as one means of ensuring that content and skills would be taught in a logical developmental sequence from elementary through secondary school.

Ken then looked at the initial planning for the Zimbabwe unit. He knew he would use the unit to fulfill the history and geography curriculum focus on southern Africa (Black, 2000). He thought that the unit would take two weeks of class time, assuming that the students would be engaged in unit activities about an hour each day. Ken then identified benchmarks he wanted students to achieve. For example, one of the middle school geography strand benchmarks for Michigan is "Explain how elements of physical geography, culture, and history of the region may be influencing current events." This unit could be a good place to work toward achievement of that benchmark. Another benchmark that could be appropriate from the inquiry strand is "Pose a social studies question about a culture, world region, or international problem." Since the struggle over land between the wealthy White farmers and the landless Blacks represents a conflict between two points of view, this is another logical benchmark for that unit.

Ken Cowan's Planning

After studying the curriculum standards, Ken Cowan was ready to begin planning the interdisciplinary unit on Zimbabwe. In preparation he has gathered a variety of materials for instruction:

1. state and district standards for social studies and other subjects
2. the district's textbooks, if any
3. a collection of historical fiction from the local library
4. assorted videos on Africa and Zimbabwe
5. websites that provide primary source documents, paintings, timelines, etc.
6. nonfiction books at diverse grade levels on Zimbabwe
7. materials from the historical society and history museum
8. a variety of texts on methods for teaching social studies through an interdisciplinary approach

Along with the collection of resources, he has read some books on Zimbabwe and has constructed a content outline that will guide lesson development. Ken sits at his desk, stares at the materials and content outline, and wonders where to begin. First, he reflects, "I have to know what outcomes are important: What do I want the students to know (content goals) and be able to do (process goals)?" Reflecting upon his recent conversation with Jodi, he recognizes the importance of beginning with the standards. Standards-based reform is an important educational trend both in Ken's district and across the nation (Adler, 2001; Carr & Harris, 2001, Feuer, 1995, Ravitch, 1993). However, there is a difference between genuine standards-driven reform, in which standards are used to focus and improve instruction, and what one author has called its "evil twin," teaching focused on high-stakes testing (Ochoa-Becker, 2001; Thompson, 2001).

Emphasis on a single test is not the only danger in standards-based planning. Ken recognizes that there is a danger in placing too much authority in others while denying one's own abilities as a reflective decision maker (Meier, 2000). The state curriculum framework, while a valuable tool for curriculum development, must not become a rigid and prescriptive set of directives. Ken will continue to examine the standards and select those that appear most relevant and important to the unit. However, he will do this in conjunction with defining for himself those goals he believes should guide unit development. In particular, Ken will be attuned to goals that are essential for the students in his particular community, a decision-making process that is impossible to manage at a state or national level (Falk, 2002).

Ken sought to identify some priorities for himself regarding goals for the unit. First, he reflected on the importance of introducing multiple perspectives in any social studies unit. History is so often taught as a set of facts and truths when, in reality, events of life are marked by controversial interpretations depending upon who is viewing the events. He thought of the many voices that might frame the unit on Zimbabwe. An examination of multiple perspectives goes hand in hand with the inclusion of ethical questions regarding the morality of certain decisions and events in history. Threaded throughout Ken's instruction is his belief that social studies education must further the development of empathic people who consider the moral and ethical sides of any issue

(Brophy & VanSledright, 1997). If some members of the Landstown community were having trouble getting along and understanding the differences in their perspectives, instruction in understanding varying points of view could be particularly crucial.

In addition, he recognized that almost any body of knowledge can be a vehicle for teaching important higher level thinking processes, such as analysis, evaluation, and synthesis. Instruction in important skills such as those related to inquiry—locating materials, taking notes, organizing the content, and presenting it—can also be inserted into any subject matter being taught (Costa & Liebmann, 1997). For Ken, the larger goal of teaching students to independently inquire and solve problems influences the study of any subject.

Another challenge for Ken is to construct a unit from an interdisciplinary perspective. He reflected upon an article he read recently about the benefits of interdisciplinary planning. With so much to teach and never enough hours in the day, it made sense to think about planning ways that two or more subjects could be integrated. Incorporating content standards from language arts seemed like a natural fit (Zarnowski & Gallagher, 1993). For example, reading historical fiction can help students imagine an historical period and become empathically involved in the lives of historical figures. Diverse writing activities such as constructing a newspaper article, creating plays of key events, and constructing diaries from the perspective of different historical figures promotes deep understanding (Lindquist & Selwyn, 2000). Because social studies is by nature an interdisciplinary subject, Ken will also include goals pertaining to civics and economics in addition to history and geography. Drawing upon the theory of multiple intelligences, he will seek ways to develop goals that incorporate analysis of the artwork and music of Zimbabwe as well (Gardner, 1999).

Finally, Ken will develop goals that link the past to the present. One of the greatest challenges social studies teachers must tackle is the seeming lack of relevance between events of the past and students' daily lives. In the Zimbabwe unit Ken will purposefully connect concepts such as colonialism, monarchy, authoritarianism, and democracy so that students can easily relate the content to their lives and current events (Wiske, 1998; Field, Wilhelm, Nickell, Culligan, & Sparks, (2001).

Later Jodi and Ken worked together to create a list of goals for the unit. They shared their individual lists and struggled to come to consensus regarding the most important ones. Their final list incorporated goals derived from language arts, music, art, math, science, and social studies standards.

Ancient Zimbabwe

Students will:

1. determine what life was like in Great Zimbabwe in the 14th century
2. describe daily life in Great Zimbabwe at the time of King Monomatapa who ruled at the beginning of the 16th century (Ransford, 1968)
3. determine the size of structures and enclosures at Great Zimbabwe
4. create an image that is similar in style to the soapstone figures so prominent in Zimbabwean culture
5. develop an educated guess why the culture that created the city of Great Zimbabwe disappeared

Colonial Zimbabwe

Students will:

6. discuss the major events related to the rediscovery of Great Zimbabawe beginning when the Europeans stumbled upon it for the first time in the late 1860s (Blake, 1977).
7. describe the role of Cecil Rhodes in the English colonization of southern Africa.
8. define *colonialism* and *racism.*
9. analyze the role of the Christian missionary in the colonization of Africa by the Europeans.
10. compare and contrast different views of the European colonization of southern Africa in the 1800s.
11. compare colonial stories from an African perspective.
12. perform in a group the singing of a European hymn of the colonial age and an African hymn.

Modern Zimbabwe

Students will:

13. describe the problems facing modern Zimbabwe today such as the spread of HIV, poverty, hunger, landlessness, unplanned urbanization, corruption, lack of democracy, etc.
14. identify characteristics of contemporary Zimbabwean life that can be traced to its African roots and those that can be traced back to European influence.
15. compare and contrast traditional kraal life with life in modern urban Zimbabwe.
16. evaluate the appropriateness of media coverage of Africa that focuses mostly on hunger, disease, poverty, and corruption.
17. evaluate the arguments made by advocates and critics of the Zimbabwean government policy of expropriating White-owned farms without compensation.

Affective Goals

Students will:

18. appreciate the contributions of the people and culture of Zimbabwe.
19. enjoy the musical and literary traditions of southern Africa.
20. value the democratic methods to confront cultural, racial, and economic differences.

As Ken works to prepare his unit, he will use these goals to help shape the specific teaching objectives for his lesson plans. Chapter 4 provides information on writing instructional objectives.

Three Domains of Educational Content

Reflective teacher decision makers are aware of and purposeful about the kinds of learning they are trying to promote. In the previous section we learned that goals could be classified according to philosophical positions: progressivism, essentialism, and reconstructionism. Another way to classify goals is to subdivide them into attitudes (to be like), skills (to be able to do), and knowledge (to know). This book uses a classification scheme that organizes goals into affective, psychomotor, and cognitive groupings or domains. Some goals are clearly classified in one of the three domains. Other goals have characteristics that suggest they reside in more than one domain. That fact will be clearer as we examine various goals.

The **affective domain** involves emotional behavior: feelings, attitudes, preferences, and values. The range of possible behaviors around which affective goals can be written is quite large. For example, an affective goal might be expressed as an appreciation of the differences that exist in the behavior of people in various ethnic and racial groups. A more specific and significant objective would be to expect students to respond to classmates from a different ethnic, racial, or cultural group in ways that are appropriate and supportive. Although a number of Ken's goals have affective elements, goals 18, 19, and 20 are exclusively affective. The concern is for students' appreciation of people and culture of Zimbabwe, the music and literature created by African musicians and writers, and the methods of democratic problem solving.

The **psychomotor domain** consists of learning that is sensory in nature, ranging from involuntary, reflexive movements to complex chains of skillful and purposeful behavior, such as dancing and playing quarterback. Any physical skill that requires repeated practice to perfect is psychomotor. Examples are playing the piano or pronouncing words in an unfamiliar language. In school, sports and the practical and fine arts play a special role in the physical development of learners. In Ken's list of goals, numbers 4 and 12 have psychomotor elements. Goal 12 involves singing African and European hymns and goal 4, the creation of a soap sculpture.

Cognitive domain (intellectual) goals require students to memorize and recall information or to use their intellectual skills to determine meaning and to relate new information to previous learning. Higher level cognitive goals require the learner to disassemble information or to assemble it in new forms, to judge its worth and merit, and to apply it in complex ways to solve everyday problems in life and the workplace.

The other goals in Ken's list are clearly in the cognitive domain. They range from the memorization of information to the creation of original stories and historically accurate portrayals of life in early and contemporary Zimbabwe.

Structure of Subject Matter

In addition to the broad goals, teacher decision makers need to identify the depth and breadth of the particular subject that will be taught. The partial outline in Appendix A shows how the "Zimbabwe: A World's View from Africa" unit might break down the social studies content.

Although the creation of a content outline is a necessary task in the development of a curriculum unit, it is only one task in a long process of decision making. The curriculum developer also must have an understanding of the nature of cognitive knowledge so that the content does not become merely a list of unconnected information. When a content outline is tempered by an understanding of the nature of subject matter, the logical chunks—the groupings and relationships that organize the content—will become apparent.

To understand more deeply the nature of subject matter, consider the work of Jerome Bruner, an internationally acclaimed psychologist. In 1960 Bruner's influential book *The Process of Education* was published. One of these ideas focused educators' attention on the nature of subject matter and the way that subject matter ought to be organized for teaching purposes. Bruner supported the notion that every subject taught in schools has a structure composed of three elements: concepts, generalizations, and facts. He considered all three elements as appropriate for student learning. However, Bruner's central position was that the school "curriculum of a subject should be determined by the most fundamental understanding that can be achieved of the underlying generalizations that give structure to that subject" (p. 31). He argued that instruction should center on the "fundamentals," the generalizations and concepts of the subject, rather than the individual facts. To illustrate his belief, he used the analogy of the fully blooming shade tree (See Figure 3.6): Its trunk and branches represent the subject's organizing generalizations and major concepts, and the leaves represent the multitude of specific facts that describe the nature, history, and scope of the subject and provide examples of its application.

Bruner argued that understanding the structure of subject matter assists learners to make the subject more understandable. It increases retention and transfer of learning, enhances the capability of the learner to relate newly introduced content to previously

Understanding the Structure of the Content Makes Learning Easier.

learned content, and provides a path for learning additional content within the same subject. Philip Phenix, a philosopher and educator, summarized the advantages of teaching through a structured approach by noting that:

> One of the secrets of good teaching is the practice of clearly charting a way through the subject of instruction so that the students know how each topic as it comes along fits into the whole scheme of the course and of the discipline to which it belongs. They understand where they are in relation to what has gone before and to what is to be studied subsequently. The effect of such teaching is a growing appreciation of the inner logic of the subject, resulting at length in a grasp of its spirit and method which will be proof against the erosions of detailed forgetting (1960, p. 307).

Ken Cowan showed an understanding of the underlying structure of subject matter by the way he confronted the task of forming goals for the Zimbabwe unit. Ken recalled his first course in history from a respected professor who emphasized the conceptual structure of a given topic. In her introductory lecture, the professor emphasized that the following fundamental generalizations help to make sense of historical events, issues, and trends.

1. The binding of people through language, religion, tradition, common history, and political boundaries into nationalistic movements has often altered the course of history.
2. Historical events have multiple causes.
3. When two cultures clash, both change. The more powerful culture can be expected to dominate and transform the weaker, while often denying any positive contributions from the weaker culture.
4. Historical events can be interpreted from multiple perspectives.
5. Historical methods involves both an examination of evidence from the past and those who produced that evidence.

Similar generalizations could help Ken's students make sense of the information they learned about Zimbabwe.

Another fundamental generalization is derived from the study of history: regardless of when or where they lived, their race, nationality, or religion, all people possess many characteristics in common. The student who examines unfamiliar cultures with that understanding will be a more accurate, reliable, and productive investigator than one who has not understood this generalization. In the hands of a creative and knowledgeable teacher, this idea can be a connecting thread that is applied as students learn about new peoples and cultures.

It is clear from even this brief discussion that making good decisions about content will take considerable study and content expertise. It is one of the great dilemmas of education that many middle school teachers need to be experts in multiple subjects—a challenging expectation, indeed. Many strategies and resources will help you become more expert in various subjects. Good teachers are avid readers, and you will find many kinds of print resources helpful to you, much like the list of resources Ken collected earlier in this chapter. Other teachers can be helpful, as can content experts in your area. Local museum or historical society personnel might have suggestions regarding the unit. Also, do not forget the vast network of resources available through the World Wide Web and other technological resources.

Concept Learning

After studying his resources, Ken knows he cannot teach everything of importance related to Zimbabwe. Therefore, he has some very important decisions to make regarding what ideas are most important. The outline is a first step in developing a **structured content analysis**. However, before proceeding further, it is necessary to look more deeply into the nature of the three elements of that content: concepts, generalizations, and facts.

Concepts are categories or classes of things that share a set of critical characteristics. Concepts are like lenses or road maps that human beings use to examine the world as identified by the five senses. They permit us to use previous experience and knowledge to place new information in a context, to associate the present with the past, and to recognize new information as a variation of what we have learned previously. We learn many concepts through direct experience, outside of school. However, the learning of concepts, together with the words used to label and describe them, is an essential element in successful school instruction (Erickson, 2002). Many learning psychologists and instructional planners believe that concepts are the essential building blocks in a quality curriculum.

To illustrate how concept learning aids us in understanding what may at first seem like a novel experience, imagine disembarking from a train in a place you have never been before, in a country where you do not speak or understand the language—on the surface a frightening prospect! However, the more you analyze the problem, the lower is your level of fear. Safely stored in your long-term memory are the concepts of hotel, restaurant, and bank. Train stations typically have tourist information centers where it is likely that someone will speak English and provide you with a simplified dictionary that can help you to interpret the unfamiliar language. You know that the bank can exchange your U.S. dollars for the local currency. You can expect to find taxicabs or public transportation. All in all, the concepts you have learned make it possible for you to function in what appears at first to be a totally alien environment.

Concepts have defining characteristics, often called *attributes*. Attributes allow us to distinguish between examples of the concept and nonexamples. Nonexamples are not members of the concept class but are similar enough to confuse the unwary observer. For example, a particular table may look something like a chair, but it is not a chair. A skunk looks like a cat, but it is not a cat. In making the distinction, it is important to distinguish between critical and noncritical concept attributes. Only critical attributes can be used to determine whether a given example fits within the concept class. From the Zimbabwe unit, consider the concept of the traditional family-based life. Everyone has a base in a family, whether we lead a traditional or modern life. However, the critical attribute of a traditional lifestyle is that most or all family members—grandparents, parents, and children—live in close proximity to each other and have always done so. Traditional life is focused on the family, and the informal rules that govern life are laid down by the family. One of these is that the eldest members of the family are the most influential (Kileff & Kileff, 1970).

Concepts can be classified as concrete or abstract. A *concrete concept* is one that exists in the physical world and can be described in terms of its observable attributes. For example, chair is a concrete concept, as are yellow, dog, and girl. The critical attributes that determine whether something is a chair are that (1) it is used to sit on, (2) it rests on usually four legs, (3) it has a back rest, and (4) it is built to seat only one person (*Webster's New Collegiate Dictionary,* 1981). Using these attributes to guide us, we can distinguish among chairs, tables, couches, stools, and so on. We can distinguish between examples and nonexamples.

An *abstract concept* is one that cannot be observed, either because it does not possess physical dimensions or because its physical dimensions are not critical in distinguishing between examples and nonexamples. Consider the concept *citizen.* Although citizens have physical attributes, in that all citizens are human beings and can be observed, you can't tell a citizen from a noncitizen by physical appearance. The physical attributes are not critical in identifying examples. Thus it is an abstract concept.

As complicated as it is, *citizen* is an example of an abstract concept with a clear definition and attributes that together can be used to distinguish examples from nonexamples. Thus a citizen of the United States is either natural born (a child of a U.S. citizen or born on U.S. territory) or completes a process of naturalization. In the Zimbabwe unit, some of the abstract concepts that have clear definitions and attributes are government, resources, culture, president, parliament, and history.

The teaching and learning of abstract concepts whose attributes and/or definitions cannot be used to distinguish all examples from all nonexamples are more difficult. Examples of such concepts in the Zimbabwe unit are inequality, freedom, democracy, and racism. Although these concepts have definitions and attributes, neither can be used to distinguish all examples from all nonexamples. For example, the dictionary definition of political freedom is the "absence of necessity, coercion, or constraint in choice or action" (*Webster's New Collegiate Dictionary,* 1981). Are we free in the United States? Reasonable people would agree that we are. Yet there are restrictions on our freedom. Traffic regulations control how fast we drive. In some communities, smoking is forbidden in public buildings or restricted to designated locations. Individuals must obtain a license to get married, own a dog, or drive a car. In all these cases, our freedom of choice and action is limited. Thus attempting to define the limits of a complex concept such as freedom yields a continuum of examples, ranging from the clearly defined to the ambiguous and debatable. Still, concept learning is critical. We want students to not just memorize definitions of concepts, but to understand and apply them in new situations and to other ideas.

CHECK YOUR UNDERSTANDING

To assess your understanding of different concepts, create two groups of five concepts in a subject area of your choice. You may find it helpful to do this exercise in the area for which you are planning your unit. The first group of concepts should contain concrete concepts; the second group should contain abstract concepts. In your group of abstract concepts, include concepts with clear definitions and/or attributes as well as concepts with unclear definitions and/or attributes. Check your groupings with a colleague.

Concept Mapping

Ken Cowan and the eighth-grade curriculum team were fortunate to have attended a timely in-service workshop on content structures. The in-service leader defined the meaning of a content structure as "the web of facts (words, concepts) and their interrelations in a body of instructional materials" (Shavelson, 1974). He then reviewed the advantages of learning the structure of content as observed by Bruner: (1) it makes the subject more understandable by relating general and specific knowledge, (2) it improves the retention of knowledge by promoting learning concepts and facts as a network of information, and (3) it enhances the capability to relate new knowledge to previously learned content. Finally, he identified "concept mapping" as a helpful curriculum development tool for teaching content structures. *Concept mapping* is a thought process that culminates in a visual display of relevant knowledge and relationships. Each concept, concept attribute, or example is contained in an individual circle. Relationships among concepts, attributes, and examples are shown through connecting lines and arrows and by "linking words" which describe the nature of each relationship (Plotnick, 1997).

The resulting diagram represents a personalized map of the important elements and relationships in a curriculum topic. Typically, a concept map begins with the selection of a focal topic "that is of special interest to the mapper and is the focus of the particular map" (Naidu, 1990). The mapper may choose to begin the map by placing the focal topic at the top, the middle, or the bottom of the map.

Concept mapping has been shown to assist teachers and learners to broaden, deepen, and sharpen their understanding of curriculum topics. It broadens understanding by forcing the consideration of meaningful relationships among concepts. It deepens understanding by identifying concept attributes and examples. It sharpens understanding by providing a visual display of the total set of relationships and elements. The end result may be greater initial learning and retention over time (Bolte 1997, Heinze-Fry & Novak, 1990). It can also assist teachers to plan by helping them identify important relationships among concepts. Figure 3.4 illustrates the relationships among the concepts in persuasive communication.

Ken began his concept map by identifying the focal concepts about Zimbabwe that he wanted to emphasize, namely, its people, history, environment, and culture. Figure 3.5 presents a map using culture as the central concept with its subconcepts of traditional life and modern life.

Generalization Learning

If concepts are the road maps for teaching and learning, then generalizations are the destinations teacher decision makers attempt to reach. A **generalization** is a statement that expresses a generally true relationship between two or more concepts. Understanding a generalization is most likely to lead to an "aha" experience. Whereas a concept is usually expressed in a word or two, a generalization is always expressed as a statement, often as a complete sentence. As opposed to concepts or facts, generalizations allow students to make sense of events in a variety of settings.

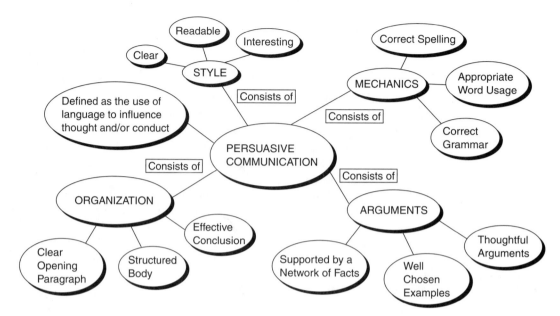

Figure 3.4 Connections among the Concept of Persuasive Communication
From *Teaching as Decision Making: Successful Practices for the Elementary Teacher* (3rd Ed.) (p. 80), by A. J. Starko,
et al. 2003, Upper Saddle River, NJ: Merrill/Prentice Hall. Copyright 2003 by Pearson Education, Inc. Reprinted with
permission.

Examples of generalizations are:

- Metals expand when they are heated.
- The pace of life is slower in small towns than it is in large cities.
- Retired people tend to vote in greater numbers than do voters between the ages of 18 and 21.
- Division is the reverse of multiplication.

A second way to distinguish a generalization from the other elements of subject matter is to contrast it with a fact. Both generalizations and facts have the attribute of being statements. However, facts include specific information about particulars: people, things, places, time, or events. In addition, a fact is typically verified by making a single observation, by conducting a simple experiment, or by consulting a credible reference. Examples of facts are:

- Henry Ford was the creator of the modern assembly line.
- Count Basie played the piano in his orchestra.
- Whales are the largest mammals.
- The U.S. Constitution can be changed through the passage of amendments.
- Gold is more malleable than iron.

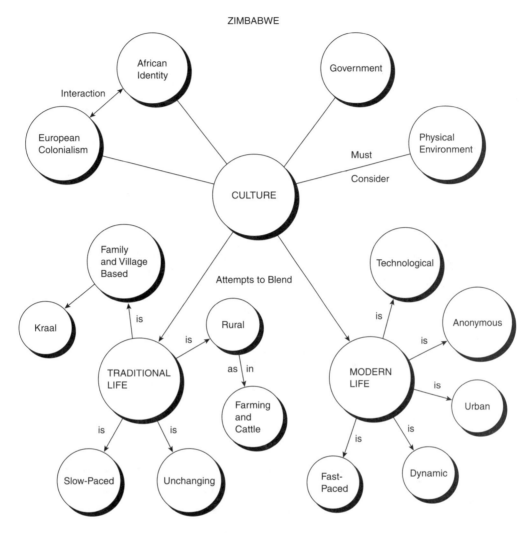

Generalization: Zimbabwe today is the product of the interaction among (1) culture and the physical environment, (2) African identity and European colonialism, and (3) traditional life and modern life.

Figure 3.5 Social Studies Concept Map for Zimbabwe Unit

A generalization cannot be checked through a single observation; the proof requires experimentation or observation through repeated trials over time. In some cases, one must consult and compare many references in order to feel confident that a particular generalization is an accurate description of reality. Table 3.1 displays the differences between facts and generalizations.

TABLE 3.1   *Generalizations and Facts*

Generalization	Fact
Is not absolute (contains some "wiggle")	Is concrete, definite, with no reasonable doubt
Verification requires a good deal of observation/experimentation	Is usually verified by a single observation or reference
Expresses relationship between two or more concepts	Usually refers to one person, event, thing, or place
Applies to many examples	Applies to a single example
Is a hypothesis, explanation, or theory	Evidence that may support a hypothesis, explanation, or theory

From *Teaching as Decision Making: Successful Practices for the Elementary Teacher* (3rd Ed.) (p. 81), by A. J. Starko, et al., 2003, Upper Saddle River, NJ: Merrill/Prentice Hall. Copyright 2003 by Pearson Education, Inc. Reprinted with permission.

After a period of reflection on the goals of the Zimbabwe unit and the outline of the content, Ken Cowan developed the following generalization that would guide the curriculum development process in the Zimbabwe unit:

Zimbabwe today is the product of the interaction between (1) culture and the physical environment, (2) African identity and European colonialism, and (3) traditional life and modern life.

A key question to focus students' inquiry is,

How do developing countries balance modern and traditional influences?

CHECK YOUR UNDERSTANDING

Examine the following examples. Identify those that are generalizations by writing *G* and those that are facts by writing *F* in the space to the left of each example.

_____ 1. In a democracy, the decision-making power is placed in the hands of the majority while at the same time the rights of the minority are protected.

_____ 2. Teaching is both a science and an art.

_____ 3. The color green can be made by combining yellow and blue.

_____ 4. The number of seconds in one month (30 days) is 2,592,000.

_____ 5. As the supply of a product increases, price generally decreases.

_____ 6. If there are x ways of doing one thing and y ways of doing another thing, then there are x plus y ways of doing both.

_____ 7. The term *Karma* is associated with Hinduism.

_____ 8. The earliest alphabet originated in the Middle East.

_____ 9. Paul Bunyan was the subject of tall tales.

_____ 10. Residents of Washington, DC, began voting for president in 1964.

Examples 3, 4, 7, 8, 9, and 10 are facts; examples 1, 2, 5, and 6 are generalizations.

Although generalizations are powerful tools in understanding the past, present, and future, they must not be interpreted mindlessly. In the spirit of scientific investigation, the generalization is valid only if there is no external intervention that changes the relationship between the concepts. For instance, consider the following generalization about past and future educational performance:

> The best single predictor of a young child's educational performance in high school and college is the number of years of schooling (8, 12, 16, 16+) of the child's parents.

That prediction is accurate if nothing intervenes to alter the relationship between the level of education of the child's parents and his or her predicted school performance. However, that is precisely what we expect a good teacher to do—to make it possible for the child to prosper intellectually and emotionally as a consequence of schooling. Good teachers do intervene and alter, for the better, the expected result. Thus a generalization has to be interpreted as a general truth that will prove to be an accurate prediction in a majority of cases. It doesn't guarantee that a particular child will fit the pattern or that intervention from the home or the school or from another significant person in the child's life will not alter the balance in some dramatic way.

Factual Learning

The analysis of the three elements of content concludes with the third element: facts. As indicated in the discussion of generalizations, a **fact** is a statement about particulars (people, things, places, times, or events) and is typically verified by making a single observation, by conducting a simple experiment, or by consulting a credible authority.

To illustrate the importance of facts in learning and living, imagine that you begin reading an article in a news magazine about the stock market. You read the following sentence:

> Wall Street remembers the shantytowns and bread lines of the 1930s caused by the "Great Crash of 1929."

Assume you do not know that the major financial institutions in the United States, as well as the New York Stock Exchange, are located in and around Wall Street in New York City or that a stock market crash in 1929 brought financial ruin. You do not remember that in the Great Depression of the 1930s many unemployed people lost their homes or could not afford to pay rent and buy food. They were forced to live in temporary shacks made of scrap, wood, tin, or cardboard known as shanties. They also stood for hours in long bread lines to receive food donated by the government or by private charities. You do not know that "crash" refers to the stock market collapse that led to the widespread failure of banks, businesses, and farms and then to a worldwide depression. If you had not known any of these facts, what sense could you make of the sentence?

Collectively, the facts that we possess add to our reputation as educated persons. However, for facts to be useful in increasing our understanding and ability to interpret the environment, they must be related to generalizations and concepts. For example, the ability to list the names of the U.S. presidents has little meaning unless the list is organized under concepts such as effectiveness, political party affiliation, and philosophy. Students' ability to recall the scientific names of all mammals would be of little value unless they could identify animals that were mammals and could recognize the critical attributes of a mammal. In the stock market example, you would read with optimum understanding if you were able to place the facts into an existing structural network in your long-term memory. That structure includes knowledge of how the stock market functions, together with generalizations that relate the stock market to the U.S. economy and the banking and monetary system. Finally, it includes the capability to evaluate the likelihood that a stock market collapse today would initiate a catastrophic depression similar to the one that occurred in the 1930s.

Content Analysis

Now that we have analyzed educational content and its three elements—concepts, generalizations, and facts—we can return to Bruner's suggestion to teach content in the form of a fully blooming tree, with the trunk and the major branches representing the generalizations and concepts and the leaves representing the specific facts. Ken Cowan and his eighth-grade planning group could organize their content analysis of the Zimbabwe unit using the fully blooming tree scheme (see Figure 3.6).

Content Analysis in Interdisciplinary Units

Middle and high schools have been organized by traditional subject areas (i.e., English, math, science, social studies, art, and music) through much of the 20th century. This subject-based pattern can be hard to break, but it is changing rapidly. Educational reform proposals have identified a number of advantages to organizing curriculum around interdisciplinary content (Beane, 1997; Jacobs, 1989, 1991; Roberts & Kellough, 1996). First, an interdisciplinary approach models the real world. We do not divide our days and tasks into a time for math, a time for language, and a time for science except in school. In everyday life, disciplines intermingle and relate to one another as individuals use them to solve problems. For example, scientists use language and reporters use math.

Second, interdisciplinary content can help students create multiple ties to important ideas. Students who learn about the concept of balance only in mathematics have fewer opportunities for understanding this concept than students who examine the same concept in art, biology, and political science. Third, interdisciplinary approaches can provide novelty and allow students to look at familiar content with new eyes. For example, students who think they know all there is to know about pioneers, having studied U.S. westward migration in previous years, may come to new understandings if they begin to question what would constitute a pioneer in art, technology, music, or science. Such questions provide opportunities for analysis and critical thinking that would be absent if questions were limited to a single discipline.

Teachers can structure interdisciplinary content in many ways. Examples are:

- using multiple disciplines to investigate a topic
- examining interdisciplinary themes
- addressing complex problems

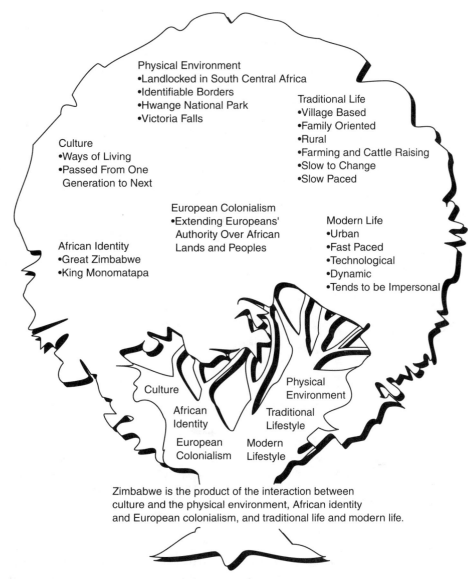

Figure 3.6 The Fully Blooming Tree Example Applied to Zimbabwe

The simplest approach to interdisciplinary content is using multiple disciplines to investigate a single topic or time period. Such investigations may be largely teacher-directed or based on student questions. This is the approach used by Ken and his colleagues in incorporating history, geography, and other disciplines. Students could learn about lifestyles and politics in social studies, about literature or propaganda in language arts, about flags and symbols in art, about the dimensions of the Great Zimbabwe structures in math, and about African dances or games in physical education.

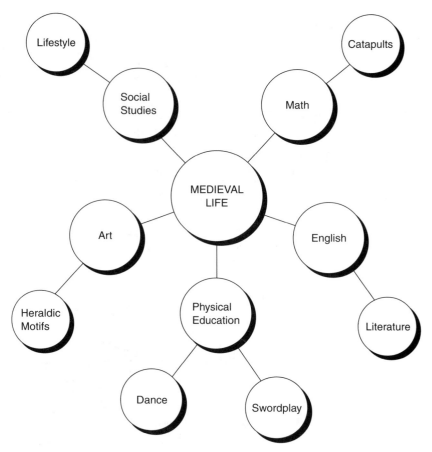

Figure 3.7   A Web for a Topical Unit on Medieval Life
From *Teaching as Decision Making: Successful Practices for the Elementary Teacher* (3rd Ed.) (p. 86), by
A. J. Starko, et al., 2003, Upper Saddle River, NJ: Merrill/Prentice Hall. Copyright 2003 by Pearson Education,
Inc. Reprinted with permission.

A unit based on a time period usually starts as a topic web, with the topic in the center and the content areas at the end of each spoke, as shown in Figure 3.7.

These topics can be used to identify key content, goals, and class activities. Although this web appears similar to a concept map, the key concepts in each topic have
not been identified. In some cases teachers can ask students to raise questions about
the unit. In most cases, such questions will range over a variety of disciplines. Regardless of whether a unit is centered on a single discipline or multiple disciplines, is entirely teacher planned, or is directed by student questions, the teacher will need to
shape the unit to fit current district standards and goals. This ability to tie student interests and questions to key curriculum concepts and generalizations is an important
teaching skill.

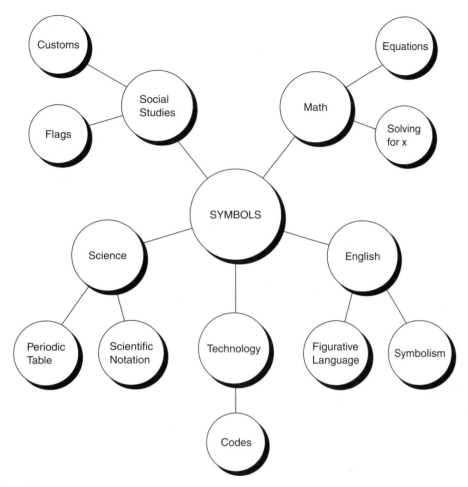

Figure 3.8 A Web for a Thematic Unit on Symbols

A slightly more complicated version of interdisciplinary content involves the use of *interdisciplinary themes.* An interdisciplinary theme is one that is an important idea in a variety of disciplines. Although we could use mathematics to learn about kites, they are not particularly important in the study of mathematics. A true interdisciplinary theme is genuinely meaningful across disciplines. The concept of balance is a good example of an abstract interdisciplinary theme that can easily be related to a variety of disciplines. Other examples of interdisciplinary themes are power, revolution, symbols, interdependence, and cycles. In each case, students increase their understanding by studying the same theme in a variety of disciplines. (See Figure 3.8 for an example of a web for a thematic unit.)

Teachers plan a unit around an interdisciplinary theme in much the same way as one centered on a topic, and they select disciplines for webbing by their relevance to the concept addressed. If Ken Cowan's group wanted to create a thematic unit, they could explore the concept of power: how power operated in Zimbabwe's history, force (power) in science, exponents in math, literature on personal empowerment, and so on.

Another type of interdisciplinary curriculum is structured around real-world problem solving. Virtually all real-world problems are interdisciplinary by their nature. An investigation of life in the pond behind the school may initially appear to be a science problem. However, even the most superficial investigation is likely to require graphing and mathematical problem solving, as well as report writing. If the investigation is extended or the analysis is especially complex, additional disciplines such as computer science, graphic design, or public speaking may be necessary.

It is interesting to witness an interdisciplinary team of teachers in action. Students often become quite enthused by the results.

Final Thoughts on the Structure of Content and Analysis of Learning Process

The following paragraphs focus on two of the most common questions expressed by future teachers, followed by advice that should reduce any anxiety you may have about your ability to analyze content and learning processes.

Question 1

"How do I find out if my students are ready to learn the content I have identified?"

When the content of a particular unit or lesson is analyzed and the concepts, concept examples, generalizations, and facts are identified, half the task of organizing content for instruction is completed. Teacher decision makers must then determine whether the content is a good "fit" with students. This requires an understanding of the developmental needs and capabilities of preadolescents and adolescents at differing chronological and developmental ages. The teachers must be aware that youngsters develop and mature at different rates. A task that is claimed to be appropriate for a 13-year-old may be an accurate barometer of what many 13-year-olds can do; however, the teacher may discover that some students have previously mastered the task and others are not intellectually or developmentally prepared to learn it at the time the teacher wishes to teach it.

For example, many 13-year-olds can interpret the letters to the editor in the local newspaper. They can both comprehend the content and meaning of a letter and identify the writer's emotional state, attachment to the issue, and position. A quick preassessment of a particular classroom of youngsters might reveal that 10% have written such letters before. Another 65% can perform this task with an acceptable level of teacher support. Another 25% may lack the interest or developmental readiness to justify the time the teacher would have to spend encouraging and prompting their efforts. Consequently, the teacher would be wise to postpone the attempt or offer the group other alternatives to persuasive writing. The issue of preassessing students' readiness to learn will be covered in greater detail in Chapter 4.

Question 2

"I can't identify generalizations or key concepts in the subject matter I am expected to teach. The textbooks don't identify them. I feel the way Ken Cowan did before he began his curriculum development task. Can you help me?"

Unfortunately, many textbooks, especially in social studies, provide factual information without any mention of the concepts and generalizations that help to classify and explain the information.

As bleak as the situation appears, some strategies can increase your ability to identify key generalizations and concepts in the subjects you teach. First, the professional journals and national standards of such associations as the International Reading Association (IRA), National Council for the Social Studies (NCSS), National Council of Teachers of English (NCTE), National Council of Teachers of Mathematics (NCTM), National Science Teachers Association (NSTA), and their state affiliates provide articles, papers, and presentations focused on the organization of content for teaching purposes. Some of these associations publish monographs containing lesson and unit plans grounded in fundamental generalizations and concepts.

In addition, some subject areas have specialized curriculum resource and development centers, such as the Joint Council on Economic Education. Further, instructional journals for elementary and secondary teachers publish lesson and unit plans and produce special issues on curriculum. To use magazines and journals productively, consult specialized reference guides to published material organized by topics, titles, and author names.

School district curriculum guides are a second useful source for concept-based lesson plans. Most include sample lesson plans and are oriented toward the teaching of generalizations and concepts. Teachers in other school districts may have prepared the unit or lesson you want to develop, which can then be adapted for your use.

Another source is textbooks and other works on the topic written for adults or for students at a higher or lower grade level than your class. You can then use the organizing framework while increasing or reducing the level of complexity of the reading material and other activities.

A final source is other educators with whom you come into contact. Teachers who are active members of the profession, attend meetings and conferences, and take inservice and graduate courses can especially expect to gain insights into the structure of subject matter.

Question 3

"This whole idea of taking so much time to (1) plan outcomes, (2) analyze facts, concepts, and generalizations, and (3) create a content outline seems like overkill. Do I really need to know all this just to be a teacher?"

Yes! Recall the discussion in Chapter 1 about consumer teachers—who follow others' materials blindly—and reflective decision makers—who design their own curriculum. If you cannot perform these tasks, you will be at the mercy of commercially available teaching materials. With the ability to identify key ideas and structure students' cognitive learning in a logical order, you will have the option of designing your own curriculum when other materials fail. Further, quite often when the textbook-based order of ideas fails to develop the learning you desire, you can use content analysis to rethink the order of the objectives and tasks.

SECTION 3. PLANNING A UNIT OF INSTRUCTION

Section 3 Objective

After you have completed this section, you will understand what you will be able to do when you finish this course: develop your own unit.

This section will help form a vision of what Ken's unit will look like when it is completed. As you read this section you may wish to refer to the sample unit at the end of this text.

Wiggins and McTighe (1998) describe effective curriculum planning as "backward design" (p. 8). Backward design begins at the end, by first identifying the desired results (goals, standards, and performances) and then selecting the learning experiences necessary to get there. Wiggins and McTighe identify three stages in backward design: (1) identify desired results, (2) determine acceptable evidence (assessment) that will help you determine whether you have achieved the desired results, and (3) plan learning experiences and instruction.

An example of backward design is good unit planning. A **unit** is a series of lessons that lead to the accomplishment of a broad goal. You will notice that the chapters in this text follow the stages of backward design as we progress through the unit planning process: identifying objectives, planning assessment strategies, and then considering various types of lessons. Of course there are times when an interesting lesson idea will impact your unit design, but in all cases unit planning should lead toward the achievement of an important goal, not simply provide an opportunity for a favorite activity. The final unit plan usually includes the following components:

- rationale and key questions
- concept map with generalizations and facts
- objectives (aligned with standards) and preassessment activities
- lesson plans with modifications for special needs
- evaluation/assessment procedures (including an authentic culminating activity)
- family and community involvement
- materials and resources

The Appendix includes examples of each of the components for the unit on Zimbabwe.

Rationale and Key Questions

The unit **rationale** is a brief statement that explains the content and purposes of the unit. The rationale is written for the students and for those who will be using the unit. It can focus attention on key unit issues, provide motivation, and justify the importance of the content in terms of subject matter, societal needs, and needs or interests of learners (see Tyler's Curriculum Rationale in Figure 3.2, p. 60).

The **key questions** focus learners' curiosity on the unit, because they have no easy answers and therefore invite exploration.

Concept Map with Generalizations (Aligned with Standards)

As you have learned, the concept map creates a structure showing the main ideas, concepts, generalizations, and facts the students are to learn. Your district and state curriculum frameworks, along with your professional organization's content standards, will prove valuable in making these decisions. A teacher can present information in an orderly way only after a thorough and searching analysis of the content. Since it is not possible to teach everything about a subject, teachers must make decisions about essential ideas—concepts, generalizations, and facts—and then organize those ideas logically. Examples of content outlines and concept maps are provided earlier in this chapter and in the sample unit.

Of course, content can be organized through a single discipline, by multiple disciplines around a single topic, or around an interdisciplinary theme. If your unit is interdisciplinary, or thematically linked to other subjects, your concept map would include multiple disciplines, and the key questions would be interdisciplinary in nature.

Objectives (Aligned with Standards) and Preassessment

After deciding on the most important ideas in the unit, the teacher must decide what students should be able to do in order to demonstrate that they understand the key ideas. These student performances include all cognitive, affective, and psychomotor outcomes relevant to the unit. The state and district standards documents can be helpful in identifying these outcomes. Many standards, however, will be too broad or general, and will need to be broken down into smaller, more specific objectives that lead to the standard. Some states have broken down their standards into grade-level outcomes known as **benchmarks**. (Occasionally these benchmarks are rather vague and need to be broken down further into specific objectives.)

One reason for creating a list of objectives is that they can indicate a logical order for lessons and activities. For example, if students are to conduct research and debate whether Zimbabwe lands should be retained by the European colonists, they first will need to learn many facts about this issue, along with processes for research and debate. When lessons are lacking a logical order, students become confused and learn less.

A second reason for instructional objectives is that they help teachers preassess the learners' readiness for the content (and thinking processes) required by the unit. You have read about the importance of diagnosing learners' prior knowledge, interests, and needs. A list of objectives can help the teacher design a preassessment activity to discover what skills and understandings students bring to the unit. The availability of such information before teaching allows the teacher to fill any gaps or provide extra support for the few students lacking the essential skills required to begin the unit.

Preassessment also helps to determine which students have already learned some of the unit's key concepts or skills. For example, imagine you are teaching an eighth-grade unit on the ecosystems. If some students had a previous teacher who devoted a good deal of time to the subject of the environment, you would want to find out what those students already know and believe about this topic. These students may need more advanced activities—for example, presenting their knowledge to others through a skit or a small play—or they could be encouraged to pursue their learning in another area.

After this process of breaking broader standards (or benchmarks) into objectives, arranging smaller objectives in a logical order, and preassessing students you will be ready to select an objective for your first lesson that is at the correct level of difficulty for most students. You will also know what knowledge, skills, and preconceptions students bring to the learning experiences you will provide in the unit.

Lesson Plans with Adaptations for Special Needs

A *lesson* is a sequence of activities designed to help all students achieve one or more objectives. Once you have an objective for your first lesson, you are ready to design activities that will help students learn. What will these lessons look like? How will you modify some activities so that all students can succeed and be sufficiently challenged? Chapters 4 through 9 discuss various approaches to lessons that systematically lead students to meet the learning objectives. Of course, all learners are not the same, so lessons will need to be adjusted for individual learning needs.

Assessment Procedures

As a teacher, you must find out what meanings, understandings, and beliefs your students are constructing from the activities you design for them. The term **assessment** is used here instead of evaluation or testing in order to convey a continuous process that uses various methods to determine students' achievement of your objectives. Obviously, you should not wait until the end of your teaching to discover if students have learned anything. Chapter 5 stresses the importance of continuous assessment of students' learning. **Continuous assessment** means the teacher assesses how well students are learning throughout the teaching—before, during, and after learning activities (Wiggins, 1998).

One of the best ways to assess student progress during your lessons or units is to talk to students individually (or listen as they work in groups) and hear them explain their thinking. If you begin to use portfolios to document student learning, you will probably include a conference with students that will allow you to gather such information. Teachers can learn a lot by having students write about a product they have created, telling you why they like it and what makes it a "good" product. It is fascinating to read students' analyses of their own reasoning as they approach a problem or a project.

What can be gained by such ongoing inquiry into students' emerging constructions of meaning? The first insight most teachers report is how surprised they are at what they find. Quiet students often evidence profound insights when given time and an attentive ear. Troubled students begin to open up and share their thoughts. Students who take more time to learn often construct meanings in a surprising way (e.g., interpersonal, kinesthetic, spatial, musical). Paper-and-pencil tests given at the end of a unit cannot yield these insights, and they are not very useful in pointing the way toward helping students learn more successfully. Continuous assessment of students' thinking through both written and spoken evidence can be a powerful force in redesigning instruction on the spot.

At the end of your unit, you will conduct a more comprehensive assessment that lets you know which students met which objectives. The final unit evaluation may be a combination of a test (or other individual assessment) and an authentic, culminating project that combines many of the objectives. In the Zimbabwe unit, students might create a play that illustrates how individuals reacted to events during various time periods. They would create the characters, give their backgrounds, and act out a situation that might exist in response to a particular event. The small plays would be presented to the class or to another grade level. They would be graded using a rubric to assess accuracy of life events and other quality standards.

Regardless of the method of assessment, the unit evaluation procedures should provide adequate information about each student's mastery of the most important unit objectives. As a result of this information, the teacher may choose to reteach certain crucial content, especially if later learning is dependent on that content.

Family and Community Involvement

One of the biggest predictors of students' learning is the involvement of their families in their education. This can be done in the lessons, activities, or culminating project. When you plan your unit, you have an opportunity to connect with, communicate with, or bring in both:

a. the students' families (e.g., letter about unit and their role, family volunteer opportunities, interactive homework with guidelines for parents), and
b. the community in which students live (e.g., service-learning project with human service agencies; or consulting with media, government, businesses)

Materials and Resources

What materials and resources do you need in order to teach the unit? Any books, visual aids, films, websites, or other media or materials should be listed at the end of the unit. You should also include a copy of any worksheets, overhead transparencies, computer programs/resources, and other materials you plan to use. Organize your material to help you stay on top of the logistical planning for each lesson. Order a film or special materials well ahead of time. This long-range planning is crucial to smooth-running lessons and makes it easier to share your unit with others.

A bibliography will be useful for those who wish to use your unit. It provides the references for further reading, electronic information (e.g., websites), and other helpful resources on the unit topic.

CHAPTER SUMMARY

The chapter opened at a school meeting in the Landstown, Maryland, school system. During the meeting the approval of a multicultural/global education program became entangled in the continuing debate over the nature and mission of public schools in the United States. We then presented a review of the three major educational philosophies—progressivism, essentialism, and reconstructionism (critical pedagogy)—and a process for generating educational goals using Tyler's Curriculum Rationale. The central challenge of Chapter 3 was introduced when Ken Cowan agreed to lead the eighth-grade team of teachers to design a Zimbabwe unit by creating a set of goals for the unit and analyzing the content to be included in it. He chose to use concept mapping to display the relationships among key concepts.

When you face the challenge of analyzing educational content, you will be aided by your understanding of the distinctions among cognitive, affective, and psychomotor content, especially the breakdown of cognitive content into generalizations, concepts, and facts. The final section of the chapter previewed how content and goals can be used to shape a curriculum unit.

Practice Activity A

Identifying Concepts, Generalizations, and Specific Facts

Write *C* for concept, *G* for generalization, or *SF* for specific fact in the space to the left of each example.

_____ 1. Resources
_____ 2. Mining
_____ 3. European colonization patterns in the 18th and 19th centuries were strikingly different in purpose and results.
_____ 4. The African National Congress was formed by the Reverend John Dube in 1912.
_____ 5. African resistance
_____ 6. If a government attempts to reduce a large deficit by borrowing from citizens and other countries, the value of its currency is likely to decline.
_____ 7. King Monomatapa could put 100,000 soldiers in the field.
_____ 8. Land confiscation
_____ 9. Culture includes ways of living passed down from one generation to the next.
_____ 10. The mines of Zimbabwe produce gold, gems, asbestos, and nickel.

Practice Point

Practice Activity A: Answer Key

1. Concept
2. Concept
3. Generalization
4. Specific fact
5. Concept
6. Generalization

7. Specific fact
8. Concept
9. Tricky one! This reads like a generalization but it's actually a definition of the concept *culture*. If it were a generalization, it would have to relate culture to some other concept. The correct answer is concept.
10. Specific fact

Practice Activity B

Creating a Concept Map for an Interdisciplinary Unit

Practice Point

Imagine you are on an interdisciplinary team planning a unit to be shared with two colleagues. Think of a topic or theme that would apply to at least three content areas. Place the central topic or theme in the middle of a sheet of paper, and create a web that shows how concepts and topics from the various subject areas might be connected.

Unit Preparation

One of the most important parts of your unit preparation is the selection and analysis of content. By now you should have chosen your unit topic, gathered information about it, and talked with the teacher about your class's particular needs. The next step in preparing your unit is choosing the specific content to teach. This will involve several steps. The order in which you take the steps may vary depending on your learning style.

Once you have identified the topic, review relevant state and national standards using the links listed below. Plan an initial set of outcomes (goals) and match them to the relevant standards. Depending on your unit topic or theme, this may include standards from one or more disciplines. Most of your outcomes probably will be cognitive, but you should consider affective goals as well. Some psychomotor goals also may be appropriate.

Next, organize the key content using a concept map. The map will be more helpful if it clearly delineates the relationships among concepts.

Finally, list the key generalization(s) and/or focus question(s) that will form the core of your unit. Limit yourself to one to three generalizations and/or questions around which all other content is organized. You might display these on a tree like that in Figure 3.6. Select facts that will help students understand the concepts and generalizations that frame your unit.

At the end of this process you should have the first draft of your content analysis, including: (1) a concept map and/or content outline and (2) a list of key generalizations, focus questions, and facts to be taught, and (3) the standards you will use to guide the unit. This could be done either through a list of standards and benchmarks or a grid relating unit outcomes to standards.

Do not underestimate the importance of this section of unit planning. For many teachers, this is the most difficult and most crucial part of the planning process. Often those who have trouble planning teaching activities find that the core of their difficulties is in confusion over the key content to be addressed. Take time, share your ideas with colleagues, and get feedback from your instructor. Since this is your first attempt, it is likely that you will need to revise your content analysis at least once before it is ready to use.

Portfolio Activity

Beginning teachers are often asked, especially in interviews, to describe their philosophy of education. You may find that your philosophy flows naturally from the metaphor you developed in Chapter 1. Begin now to write your educational philosophy. Consider what you believe to be the most important purpose(s) of schools and how that will affect your teaching decisions.

Several of the unit development activities above can be adapted as part of a portfolio. A clear concept map can illustrate your ability to emphasize core concepts in your teaching. A tree illustration can serve a similar purpose. Your portfolio can present the outcomes for your unit and how they relate to state and/or national standards. If you plan to apply for teaching positions in more than one state, it would be wise to review information on state standards for each locale.

Search the Web

State and national standards can be found through a variety of websites. To find the state education agencies across the nation, go to www.ccsso.org/seamenu.html. To find national professional organizations in various disciplines, search for "professional associations for educators."

REFERENCES

Adler, Susan (2001, September). The NCSS curriculum standards: A response *Social Education, 65*(5), 315–318.

Association for Supervision and Curriculum Development. (1993, September). *ASCD curriculum update* (p. 2). Alexandria, VA: Author.

Banks, J. A., & McGee Banks, C. A. (2002). *Multicultural education: Issues and perspectives.* New York: John Wiley & Sons.

Beane, J. (1997). *Curriculum integration: Designing the core of democratic education.* New York: Teachers College Press.

Black, M. (2000, October). The geography of connection: Bringing the world to students. *Social Education, 64*(6), 354–358.

Blake, R. (1977). *A History of Rhodesia* (pp. 6–7). New York: Alfred A. Knopf.

Bolte, L. (1997, March 24). *Assessing mathematical knowledge with concept maps and interpretive essays.* Paper presented at the Annual Conference of the American Educational Research Association, Chicago. (ERIC Document Reproduction Service, No. ED 408 160).

Brophy, J., & VanSledright, B. (1997). *Teaching and learning history in elementary schools.* New York: Teachers College Press.

Bruner, J. E. (1960). *The process of education.* Cambridge, MA: Harvard University Press.

Carr, J. F., & Harris, D. E. (2001). Succeeding with standards: Linking curriculum, assessment, and action planning. Alexandria, VA: Association for Supervision and Curriculum Development.

Cheney, L. V. (1987). *American memory: A report on the humanities in the nation's public schools.* Washington, DC: National Endowment for the Humanities.

Costa, A. L., & Liebmann (Eds.). (1997). *Envisioning process as content: Towards a renaissance curriculum.* Thousand Oaks, CA: Corwin Press Incorporated.

Counts, G. S. (1932). *Dare schools build a new social order?* New York: John Day, 7, 9–28.

CNN.com. (2002). *Bush keeps focus on education,* January 9, 2002.

Davidman, L. (1994). *Teaching with a multicultural perspective.* New York: Longman Publishing Group.

Erickson, H. L. (2002). *Concept-based curriculum and instruction: Teaching beyond the facts.* Thousand Oaks, CA: Corwin Press.

Falk, Beverly (2002, April). Standards-based reforms: Problems and possibilities. *Phi Delta Kappan, 83* (8), 612–620.

Feuer, M. J. (1995). *Anticipating goals 2000. Standards, assessment and public policy.* Summary of a workshop. Washington, DC: Educational Resources Information Center. (ERIC Document Reproduction Service, No. ED 389 744).

Field, S. L., Wilhelm, R., Nickell, P., Culligan, J., & Sparks, J. (2001). Teaching middle school social studies: Who is at risk? *Social Education, 65*(4), 225–230.

Gardner, H. (1999). *The disciplined mind.* New York: Simon & Schuster.

Garlake, P. S. (1973). *Great Zimbabwe* (pp. 15–16). New York: Stein and Day.

Heinze-Fry, J. A., & Novak, J. D. (1990). Concept mapping brings long-term movement toward meaningful learning. *Science Education, 74*(4), 461–472.

Hirsch, E. D., Jr. (1987). *Cultural literacy: What every American needs to know.* Boston: Houghton Mifflin.

Hirsch, E. D., Jr. (2001, October). Seeking breath and depth in the curriculum. Educational Leadership, *59*(2).

Holt, J. (1964). *How children fail.* New York: Pitman.

Holt, J. (1970). *How children learn.* New York: Pitman.

Jacobs, H. (1989). *Interdisciplinary curriculum: Design and implementation.* Alexandria, VA: ASCD.

Jacobs, H. (1991, October). Planning for curriculum integration. *Educational Leadership, 49*(2), 27–28.

Kileff, C., & Kileff, P. (Eds.). (1970). *Shona customs. Essays by African writers.* Gwelo, Zimbabwe: Mambo Press.

Lindquist, T., & Selwyn, D. (2000). *Social studies at the center.* Portsmouth, NH: Heinemann.

Meier, D. (Ed.). (2000). *Will Standards save public education?* Boston: Beacon Press.

Michigan Curriculum Framework (1996). Lansing, MI: Michigan Department of Education.

Naidu, S. (1990). *Concept mapping.* Washington, DC: Educational Resources Information Center. (ERIC Document Reproduction Service, No. ED 329 247).

Ochoa-Becker, Anna S. (2001). Critique of the NCSS curriculum standards. *Social Education, 65*(3), 165–168.

Phenix, P. H. (1960, April). The topography of higher liberal learning. *Phi Delta Kappan, 41,* 307.

Plotnick, E. (1997). *Concept mapping: A graphical system for understanding the relationship between concepts.* (ERIC Document Reproduction Service, No. ED 407 938).

Randall-MacGiver, D. (1906). *Medieval Rhodesia.* (pp. 83, 87). London: Macmillan and Co. Limited.

Ransford, O. (1968). *The rulers of Rhodesia.* London: John Murray.

Ravitch, D. (1983). *The troubled crusade: American education 1945–1980.* New York: Basic Books.

Ravitch, D. (1993). Launching a revolution in standards and assessment. *Phi Delta Kappan, 74*(10), 767–772.

Ravitch, D. E., & Finn, C. E., Jr. (1987). *What do our 17-year-olds know?* Washington, DC: National Endowment for the Humanities.

Ravitch, D. "Tests: Most Seniors Lack Basic History Knowledge." CNN.com. Retrieved May 10 2002, from http://fyi.cnn.com/2002/fyi/teachers.ednews/05/10/history.scores.ap/index.html.

Reynolds, W. M., & Martusewicz, R. A. (1994). The practice of freedom: A historical analysis of critical perspective in the social foundations. In R. A. Martusewicz & W. M. Reynolds (Eds.) *Inside out: Contemporary critical perspectives in education,* pp. 223–238. New York: St. Martin's Press.

Roberts, P. L., & Kellough, R. D. (1996). *A guide for developing an interdisciplinary thematic unit.* Upper Saddle River, NJ: Merrill/Prentice Hall.

Roberts, B. (1988). Cecil Rhodes: Flawed colossus (p. 298). New York: W. W. Norton & Company.

Shavelson, A. J. (1974). Methods for examining representations of subject-matter structure in a student's memory. *Journal of Research in Science Teaching, 11*(3), 231–249.

Stanley, W. B., & Nelson, J. L. (1994). The foundations of social education in historical context. In R. A. Martusewicz & W. M. Reynolds (Eds.) *Inside out: Contemporary critical perspectives in education,* pp. 265–284. New York: St. Martin's Press.

Thompson, S. (2001). The authentic standards movement and its evil twin. *Phi Delta Kappan, 82*(5), 358–362.

Tyler, R. (1969). *Basic principles of curriculum and instruction.* Chicago: University of Chicago Press.

Webster's new collegiate dictionary. (1981). Springfield, MA: G. & C. Merriam.

Wiggins, G. (1998). *Educative assessment: Designing assessment to inform and improve practice.* San Francisco, CA: Jossey-Bass.

Wiggins, G., & McTighe, J. (1998). *Understanding by design.* Alexandria, VA: Association for Supervision and Curriculum Development.

Wiske, M. S. (Ed.). (1998). *Teaching for understanding.* San Francisco: Jossey-Bass, Incorporated.

Zarnowski, M., & Gallagher, A. F. (1993). *Children's literature and social studies.* Washington D.C.: National Council for the Social Studies.

Note: For information about present-day Zimbabwe and its geography, economy, political system, and culture, consult the many sites available through searching the World Wide Web. Among them are the following:

www.interknowledge.com
www.teachersoft.com
www.encarta.msn.com

4

Planning Educational Outcomes

CHAPTER OVERVIEW

Once upon a time a Sea Horse gathered up his seven pieces of eight and cantered out to find his fortune. Before he had traveled very far he met an Eel who said, "Psst, Hey bud. Where ya goin'?"

"I'm going out to find my fortune," replied the Sea Horse proudly.

"You're in luck," said the Eel. "For four pieces of eight you can have this speedy flipper, and then you'll be able to get there a lot faster."

"Gee, that's swell," said the Sea Horse, and paid the money and put on the flipper and slithered off at twice the speed.

Soon he came upon a Sponge, who said, "Psst. Hey bud. Where ya goin'?"

"I'm going out to find my fortune," replied the Sea Horse proudly.

"You're in luck," said the Sponge. "For a small fee I will let you have this jet-propelled scooter so that you will be able to travel a lot faster." So the Sea Horse bought the scooter with his remaining money and went zooming through the sea five times as fast.

Soon he came upon a Shark who said, "Psst. Hey bud. Where ya goin'?"

"I'm going out to find my fortune," replied the Sea Horse.

"You're in luck. If you take this short cut," said the Shark, pointing to his open mouth, "you'll save yourself a lot of time."

"Gee, thanks," said the Sea Horse, and zoomed off into the interior of the Shark, and was never heard from again.*

The moral of this fable is that if you're not sure where you're going, you may wind up someplace else, and if you have not clarified what it will look like when you get there, you might never know it when you do arrive!

"The Sea Horse Fable," which first appeared in *Preparing Instructional Objectives* by Robert Mager (1997), provides whimsical support to those who value clearly written instructional objectives. Furthermore, it introduces you to the content of Section 1 of this chapter: the transformation of curriculum goals into clearly stated instructional objectives. Whether you plan to develop your own educational goals or use the standards and benchmarks developed in state or national curriculum frameworks and assessment programs, the process of transforming goals into teachable objectives will enhance your effectiveness.

It is probably obvious that you will be most effective in helping students learn something if you know exactly what it will look like if they have learned it. Clearly stated learning objectives provide another bonus: they help you develop *assessments* that will provide concrete evidence of what students know and can do. You can then use this information before, during, and after lessons to tailor your activities for specific student needs. Without a clear vision of the desired learning, it will be almost impossible to design assessments to determine if that learning is present.

In Chapter 3 you learned how to select and analyze educational goals. In the first section of Chapter 4 you will learn how to write, classify, and evaluate clearly stated objectives for your students' learning. In Section 2 you will learn how to write clearly stated objectives at differing cognitive levels. Then, Chapter 5 will help you learn how to assess student learning.

SECTION 1. WRITING CLEARLY STATED OBJECTIVES

Opening Activity

It's early October and time for family night at the Lincoln Middle School in the Landstown, Maryland, school district. The evening begins with remarks by school officials, who request parent participation on district committees and task forces. The principal closes the general session by reporting on school progress and the opportunities and challenges of the coming year. Finally, the parents disperse to follow their children's class schedule and meet with teachers.

Practice Point

As a result of their children's enthusiasm, many of the parents come expecting to be impressed; only a few anticipate being bored or irritated. Most parents have a "Give the teacher credit, it's a difficult job" attitude. A substantial number of parents seek guidance from teachers concerning the parents' role in reinforcing school goals and tasks.

Imagine yourself as an invisible observer, able to flit from room to room and listen to the teachers introducing their educational plans and programs for the coming year. Specifically, you attend the sessions in two eighth-grade classrooms where the focus of attention is on a new unit titled "Zimbabwe: A World's View from Africa."

The following partial transcript of the sessions in these classrooms is in the form of two case studies. Read the case studies and answer the questions that follow.

Room 214: Mr. Abrams

MR. ABRAMS: A school district curriculum group led by Mr. Cowan of Landstown Middle School developed this unit last year and we are expected to teach it at Lincoln Middle School. So that's what we will be doing in interdisciplinary studies this marking period.

MR. VASQUEZ (PARENT):   Mr. Abrams, what are the goals you hope to achieve as you teach the unit to our children?

MR. ABRAMS: I would have to reexamine the teacher's guide that came with the unit to describe the specific goals, but in general, I expect to teach my social studies students about the history and peoples of Zimbabwe.

MRS. WASHINGTON (PARENT):   That sounds OK to me, but can you tell me a little more about what my daughter will know when she completes this unit?

MR. ABRAMS: I really am not prepared to do that at this time. Remember, some of the responsibility for learning rests with the student and also with the parents. My responsibility is to provide general direction for the students and give them the materials from which they will learn.

MR. LASSIVER (PARENT):   I would like to know what's expected of my child so I can encourage and help him study at home. Under your approach, though, it will be difficult for me to do that.

Practice Point

MR. ABRAMS: Possibly we should discuss that at the parent-teacher conference. Thank you all for coming tonight, and I look forward to meeting with you individually on conference day in November to discuss your children's progress.

Room 212: Mrs. Calzone

MRS. CALZONE: One of the highlights of this year's social studies course of study is the interdisciplinary unit "Zimbabwe: A World's View from Africa," developed last year by a school district curriculum group. I have examined the unit and am prepared to teach it along with some features I have added that make it especially useful for my students.

MR. SARASON (PARENT):   Mrs. Calzone, what are the goals you hope to achieve as you teach the unit to our children?

MRS. CALZONE: That's a good question. This handout includes the goals as well as some recommended activities that you can do at home to assist your youngster in achieving the goals.

MRS. RODRIGUEZ (PARENT):   I'm glad these are written clearly and specify student learning. The goal to "compare and contrast traditional life with life in modern urban Zimbabwe" is of special interest to me. I was born on a farm, and the nearest town of any size was 75 miles away. We live in a suburb next to a big city, and my children have never understood the differences between our lifestyle today compared to when I was their age. I hope you succeed in getting my son, Tony, to recognize the differences.

MRS. CALZONE: Thanks for the expression of support, Mrs. Rodriguez. I am hoping that the adults and the older siblings will be involved in some of the activities in the unit.

You might ask your son or daughter about two instructional objectives. Students will be creating tribal masks that include representations of African culture and history, and they will be writing original stories of life in the capital city of King Monopatama, a powerful king who ruled Zimbabwean Africa at the beginning of the 16th century. I hope you will all show interest in those projects. In fact, we will begin the writing project in two weeks. May I have your participation?

ALL PARENTS IN UNISON: Yes. (enthusiastic applause)

MRS. CALZONE: Thank you all for coming tonight, and I look forward to meeting individually with you on conference day in November to discuss each student's progress.

Consider the interactions that occurred in this scenario. Which teacher do you think was more effective in developing a positive relationship with parents? Why? Think about the relationship between "The Sea Horse Fable" and the two case studies. This chapter will consider what it means to "know where you are going" in planning for instruction and how that will be reflected in your activities as a teacher.

Section 1 Objectives

After you have completed this section, you will be able to:

1. defend or reject the position that teachers who use instructional objectives are more successful in generating student learning than those who do not;
2. explain the advantages and disadvantages of using instructional objectives and make decisions accordingly;
3. analyze the argument for the use of understanding performances;
4. define the A, B, C, and D characteristics of a clearly stated objective; and
5. classify examples of educational statements as clearly stated objectives.

Objectives and Understanding Performances

Few people will argue that one of the most important decisions a teacher makes involves the intended learning of students—the outcomes or results of teaching. Although there has long been a controversy about the value of instructional objectives, those who support them argue that if teachers expect to achieve success, they must be able to define success and then assess students' progress in reaching it.

Although many believe that all learning outcomes can be measured in some useful way, other, more pragmatic proponents are willing to concede that some outcomes are beyond easy measurement by the teacher. However, all advocates agree that *teachers who use clearly stated instructional objectives are likely to be more successful in enhancing the learning of their students than are teachers who do not use them.* Opponents of instructional objectives voice concern that the focus on measurable outcomes may cause educators to emphasize objectives that are easy to measure rather than those that are important, leading to fragmented or shallow instruction.

The authors of this text believe that the argument for and against the use of instructional objectives is a false one. Consider the benefits of planning instruction that includes both the use of higher-level cognitive objectives and the use of meaningful, open-ended, creative activities. When teachers teach for understanding they structure learning to engage students in "understanding performances," authentic tasks that enable students to achieve powerful learning outcomes (Gardner, 1999).

This view of **understanding performances** requires that students continuously apply specific knowledge and skills within a meaningful context—an authentic task, project, performance, or exhibit. That is, students do something that demonstrates their understanding. It is important to clarify that an understanding performance is meaningful only if it has been carefully designed to meet important higher level learning objectives. Some hands-on activities may not address central concepts and generalizations or build important skills. Wiske (1998) makes this point clear when summarizing the characteristics of an understanding performance. An understanding performance:

- relates directly to important learning goals;
- allows students to develop and apply understanding through practice;
- engages students' multiple learning styles and encourages diverse forms of expression;
- promotes reflective engagement in challenging, approachable tasks; and
- requires students to perform in ways that others—peers, parents, or community members—can view and to which they can respond.

What do these criteria look like when enacted within the classroom setting? Imagine a classroom in which cooperative learning groups are engaged in understanding performances. In one area, huddled around a computer, four students use a search engine to find information on a research topic. In another area, students sit in clusters designing maps, using an atlas as a reference. The teacher is meeting with another group to assist them with the organization of their report. Out of the class in the library another group has pulled some books from the shelves and sits at a table reading in pairs.

By posing questions, asking for clarification, and offering suggestions, the teacher guides the groups from the sidelines. Charts, graphs, and reference materials signal a room where students have opportunities to learn according to their needs and interests. In this learning environment teachers view mistakes as opportunities for growth in understanding. The environment is analogous to a laboratory, where students explore, analyze, draw conclusions, and present their ideas in creative and meaningful ways.

In the above scenario, the teacher recognizes the rich possibilities for learning inherent in research activities. The main instructional objectives include teaching students to access multiple resources; to efficiently and effectively gather, organize, and present information; and to analyze and evaluate a body of content in order to draw important conclusions. In this classroom the conflict over the use of instructional objectives has been resolved. Clear instructional objectives guide the open-ended and generative activities and lead to diverse and complex learning outcomes and understanding performances.

In unit planning teachers must consider which aspects of the unit are important enough to merit demonstration in an understanding performance. They must decide which content can be taught for understanding and which can be taught in less depth or not taught at all. Wiggins and McTighe (1998) offer four guidelines for making such decisions. They believe such material should:

- represent a big idea having enduring value beyond the classroom;
- reside at the heart of the discipline (involve "doing the subject");
- require uncoverage (of abstract or often misunderstood ideas); and
- offer potential for engaging students. (p. 23)

Notice how the analysis of key generalizations and concepts and your understanding of authentic learning provide the keys for choosing content to be demonstrated in understanding performances.

As discussed in Chapter 3, an educational *goal or outcome* provides general direction to the teacher in making crucial decisions about instruction. Although both goals and objectives describe student (rather than teacher) behavior, a goal generally covers more content than an objective and thus is phrased more broadly. Goals are related to standards, and instructional objectives are related more closely to benchmarks (although many benchmarks are too broad to be used as objectives). For example, a national, state, or district goal or standard might encompass the content that will be taught in a semester or even a long unit, whereas an instructional objective (and some benchmarks) might cover the content for a week-long unit or for a single day's lesson plan.

An **instructional objective** is defined as a specific statement of what the student will know or be able to do after the unit or lesson ends. Instructional objectives can be developed for all types of content (affective, psychomotor, or cognitive), in all subject areas, and across all grade levels. They can be conceived and written at all levels of subject matter, from facts to concepts to generalizations, and at all levels of learning process, from knowledge to evaluation. When prepared properly, instructional objectives can be used to plan learning activities and develop assessments of student learning.

Recognizing Clearly Stated Instructional Objectives

To help you assess what you know already about clearly stated instructional objectives, read the following examples and be ready to explain which ones are complete instructional objectives.

Students will be able to:

1. recall facts about the people, history, environment, government, resources, and culture of Zimbabwe;
2. compare and contrast different views of the European colonization of southern Africa in the 1800s;
3. listen to the musical and literary traditions of southern Africa;
4. develop a description of life in Great Zimbabwe in the 14th century by writing an original short story that accurately reflects the history and culture of the Shona people who lived there at the time;
5. read some English literature from the 1850–1900 colonial tradition;

6. create an animal figure from soap that is similar in style to the soapstone figures so prominent in Zimbabwean culture;
7. participate in the singing of a European hymn of the colonial age and an African hymn;
8. examine the role of the Christian missionary in the colonization of Africa by the Europeans;
9. describe the meaning expressed in the design of the flag of Zimbabwe;
10. calculate, in a homework assignment, the perimeter enclosed by Great Zimbabwe and modern-day Harare to the nearest foot.

Items 4, 6, and 10 are the most complete instructional objectives. They are classified as such because, using the language of instructional designers, they pass the "behavior test" that distinguishes an educational goal from an instructional objective. That is, both the content to be learned and the expected learning process and level are specifically described. Let's examine item 4 and determine why it is an acceptable instructional objective:

> Students will be able to develop a description of life in Great Zimbabwe in the 14th century by writing an original short story that accurately reflects the history and culture of the Shona people who lived there at the time.

> **Element 1.** *What is to be learned?* The information to be learned is the history and culture of the Shona people who lived in proximity to Great Zimbabwe in the 14th century (clear content description).
> **Element 2.** *What is the learning process?* The learning process is to write a short story (clearly described process using the "by clause").

An instructional objective also must describe specifically how the student is to demonstrate achievement of the objective. In item 4 it is by writing an original short story. In item 6 it is by creating an animal figure from soap. In item 10 it is by calculating the perimeter. These examples illustrate the "by clause" of an instructional objective. Sometimes the by clause adds clarity to the verb that identifies the learning process. In item 4, the learning process is to "develop," and the by clause is "by writing an original short story." Another approach is illustrated in item 6, in which the by clause "create an animal figure from soap" contains the action verb *create*.

CHECK YOUR UNDERSTANDING

Why are items 1 and 3 not complete instructional objectives?

Item 1. Students will be able to recall facts about the people, history, environment, government, resources, and culture of Zimbabwe.
Item 3. Students will be able to listen to the musical and literary traditions of southern Africa.

First, consider item 1:

Element 1. *What is to be learned?* What is to be learned are unidentified facts about the people, history, environment, government, resources, and culture of Zimbabwe (unclear content description, too broad a set of facts to learn).
Element 2. What is the *learning process?* The learning process is to recall. Students could demonstrate that recall through a written exam, in a paper, or in an oral exam (unclear process).

An example of a rewritten item 1 that conforms to the behavior requirement of an instructional objective follows:

When given a list of facts about the people, history, environment, government, resources, and culture of Zimbabwe, students will be able to identify them on an exam, by matching each fact with an identifying statement.

In what other items is the behavior vague and in need of a by clause to clarify exactly how the student will demonstrate proficiency? (They are items 2, 8, and 9. Do you agree?)

The second unacceptable example of an instructional objective is item 3. This item is actually a classroom activity, not an instructional objective (the expected outcome from an activity).

Element 1. *What is to be learned?* The topic (the musical and literary traditions of southern Africa) is somewhat broad. Can these traditions be identified?
Element 2. What is the *learning process?* The learning process is to listen, which is a learning activity, not the result or outcome of the activity. Also, it is unclear whether the process is affective, cognitive, or psychomotor. Thus, an appropriate by clause is needed to accompany the verb (unclear learning process).

An example of a rewritten item 3 that conforms to the behavior requirement of an instructional objective follows:

After listening to examples of Ndebele and Shona musical melodies, both from contemporary sources and from the distant past, students will be able to express an emotional reaction to them.

Look at the list and find the other items that list an activity and not an outcome (items 5 and 7). Be careful of this trap when writing objectives. Many teachers are more comfortable writing the activity the student will engage in rather than the learning that will result from the activity and how it will be demonstrated in an assessment.

Writing Clearly Stated Objectives

A clearly stated instructional objective must contain a behavior statement as well as three other characteristics. A helpful way to remember the four characteristics is to use the A, B, C, and D mnemonic aid, or memory device (See Table 4.1).

TABLE 4.1   *The A, B, C, and D of Clearly Stated Objectives.*

A = *Audience*	*Who?*	*The student will. . .*
B = *Behavior expected at the end (clear, observable)*	*Will do what?*	*Be able to (do x). . .*
C = *Conditions*	*Under what conditions?*	*When given (conditions) or by memory*
D = *Degree*	*How well? [at the end of the lesson(s)]*	*At a _____% performance level (or specify criteria for "proficient" in a rubric)*

Clearly stated instructional objectives contain an *audience (A)* statement that specifies the particular student or students who will be learning. The following examples are acceptable audience statements:

Eighth-grade students will demonstrate the ability to:
Art students will be able to:
Students who complete their other assignments will show they can:
Students in Algebra I will:

Often the audience statement becomes the stem for a set of instructional objectives, as in the following example for a unit:

After completing this unit, eighth-grade students will be able to:

The *behavior (B)* requirement must be a concrete, observable action that illustrates the nature of the learning. Therefore, statements such as "Students will learn to count in Spanish" and "Students will know how to design an experiment" are not observable specific behaviors. The objectives need to specify what it will look like if the students have "learned," or if they "know." Similarly, statements that describe activities designed to produce learning (e.g., "Students will watch a movie") are not clearly stated instructional objectives.

A *conditions (C)* statement is included when special circumstances may affect student performance during assessment. Conditions may be equipment or material to be used by the student, a time requirement, or some other limitations within which the student is expected to perform. If there are no special circumstances, the conditions statement may be omitted from the objective. The following are four examples of conditions statements:

Using the outline map provided
Given a set of data never seen before and class notes
Given a protractor and calculator
As a volunteer

Conditions often describe the materials that may be used by the student when producing the product or performance to be used as evidence of learning, for example, the outline, data, notes, protractor and calculator. The fourth example is used with an affective objective that aims to increase student participation in voluntary social improvement projects.

A *degree (D)* statement describes the criteria (or standards) that will be used by the instructor to determine whether the student has achieved the instructional objective being tested. The degree statement explains how the student product (i.e., written exam, model, painting, essay, research paper) or performance (i.e., speech, demonstration, poster, sprint, debate) will be graded. A degree statement can be expressed in two ways. *Quantitative degree statements* are typically associated with lessons in which the subject matter yields "right" answers rather than "best" answers. Quantitative degree statements usually are associated with the lower-level learning processes of knowledge and application rather than the higher-level processes of synthesis and evaluation. The following five examples are quantitative degree statements:

Achieving 7 out of 10 correct
With 75% accuracy
Listing at least 3 reasons
Using 10 of the unit's vocabulary words
Making 5 of 10 free throws

Qualitative degree statements refer to the teacher's assessment of a complex student behavior. Qualitative degree statements can be difficult to construct. They require teachers to determine the form and substance of the minimally acceptable student product or performance. These criteria, when used to assess a complex task, are often referred to as *rubrics.* Four examples of qualitative degree statements follow:

Essays will be judged on the accuracy of factual statements, relevance to the topic, logic of the argument, and mechanics (sentence structure, spelling, word usage, organization, and coherence).

Radio commercials will be judged on the use of persuasive techniques studied in class, on clarity, and on proper use of language.

Art projects will be graded on whether they show three or more colors and use perspective to present a street scene as described in the assignment.

Travel brochures will be graded according to the following criteria: (1) accurate information on costs, mileage, and other details, (2) use of cultural information studied in class, (3) interest and appeal for the potential customer, (4) correct use of Spanish.

For additional examples of clearly stated objectives, look in Appendix A at the objectives for the interdisciplinary unit "Zimbabwe: A World's View from Africa."

Practice Activity A

Identifying Audience, Behavior, Conditions, and Degree Elements of a Clearly Stated Objective

Write *A* for audience, *B* for behavior, *C* for conditions, and *D* for degree above the words that illustrate those elements in the following clearly stated objectives.

After completing this unit, eighth-grade students will be able to:

1. given the facts about Zimbabwe described in objective 1, create a tribal mask out of materials provided that reflects at least five of the ideas represented by the facts.
2. create a description of life in Great Zimbabwe in the 14th century or in the capital of King Monomatapa's empire at the beginning of the 16th century by writing an original short story (between 1,000 and 2,000 words) that accurately reflects the history and culture of the Shona people who lived there at the time.
3. graph the population density, area, and perimeter enclosed by Great Zimbabwe and modern-day Harare in a homework assignment. Label all work and make your answers accurate to the nearest whole number.

Practice Activity A: Answer Key

After completing this unit, eighth-grade students will be able to:

Conditions

1. given the facts about Zimbabwe described in objective 1,

Behavior

create a tribal mask

Conditions

out of materials provided

Practice Point

Degree

that reflects at least five of the ideas represented by the facts.

Behavior

2. create a description of life in Great Zimbabwe in the 14th century or in the capital of King Monomatapa's empire at the beginning of the 16th century by writing an original short story

Conditions

(between 1,000 and 2,000 words)

Degree

that accurately reflects the history and culture of the Shona people who lived there at the time.

Behavior

3. graph the population density, area, and perimeter enclosed by Great Zimbabwe and modern-day Harare

Conditions

in a homework assignment.

Behavior

Label all work

Degree
and make your answers accurate to the nearest whole number.

Practice Activity B

Writing Clearly Stated Instructional Objectives

Practice Point Write three clearly stated instructional objectives for a lesson or unit of your choice: one psychomotor, one cognitive, and one affective. Each objective should include the behavior requirement and the conditions or degree requirements. Label the behavior, conditions, and degree elements of the objectives.

 REFLECTING ON THE IDEAS

Objectives can give important focus to your teaching, but there may be times when the wisest course is to alter your planned objective or abandon it entirely. When might this occur?

SECTION 2. WRITING AND CLASSIFYING COGNITIVE OBJECTIVES

Section 2 Objectives

After completing this section, you will be able to demonstrate the ability to:

1. identify the six levels of Bloom's taxonomy;
2. correctly label an unfamiliar objective using the taxonomy;
3. use the taxonomy to put objectives into a logical teaching order; and
4. create clearly stated objectives for lessons and units at the knowledge, comprehension, application, analysis, synthesis, and evaluation levels of the cognitive domain.

Teaching for Understanding

As you consider ways to help students understand key content, one of your most important decisions is what students will *do* with the content to demonstrate their understanding. What type of understanding performance will you require? You know that demonstrating understanding requires that students do more than just recall information. Wiggins and McTighe (1998) list six facets of mature understanding. Consider what these facets might look like when demonstrated by young people.

When we truly understand, we:

• can *explain*: provide thorough, supported, and justifiable accounts of phenomena, facts, and data.

How Will You Ask Students to Demonstrate Understanding?

- can *interpret*: tell meaningful stories; offer personal dimension to ideas and events; make it personal or accessible through images, anecdotes, analogies, and models.
- can *apply*: effectively use and adapt what we know in diverse contexts.
- have *perspective*: see and hear points of view through critical eyes and ears; see the big picture.
- can *empathize*: find value in what others might find odd, alien, or implausible; perceive sensitively on the basis of prior direct experience.
- have *self-knowledge*: perceive the personal style, prejudices, projections, and habits of mind that both shape and impede our own understanding; we are aware of what we do not understand and why understanding is so hard. (p. 44)

As you plan for understanding performances, you will want to design activities and assessments that require students to explain, interpret, and apply information; to view ideas from differing perspectives; and to consider their own thought processes.

Bloom's Taxonomy of Educational Objectives

In this section, you will learn to break down a complex intellectual task (e.g., design an experiment using the scientific method) into a list of objectives and place them in order. The most widely used process to order cognitive learning tasks is the taxonomy of educational objectives, first conceived by educational psychologist Benjamin

Bloom and his colleagues in the 1950s. Separate taxonomies occur for each of the three domains of learning objectives: one for cognitive tasks, a second for affective tasks, and a third for psychomotor tasks. This section concentrates on the cognitive domain, first presented in *Taxonomy of Educational Objectives: Handbook I. Cognitive Domain* (1956).

The cognitive domain taxonomy includes six categories of intellectual objectives: knowledge, comprehension, application, analysis, synthesis, and evaluation. These categories are also considered to be hierarchical. The levels range from the lowest cognitive learning tasks (knowledge) to the most complex tasks (evaluation). It is assumed that higher level tasks subsume tasks at a lower level. Thus, an application-level task obligates students to demonstrate knowledge, and an evaluation-level task requires students to perform successfully at the levels below it.

The taxonomy can assist teachers as they create instructional goals and objectives, plan instructional tasks and activities, and design assessment procedures. Over the years, thousands of teachers have derived benefit by using Bloom's taxonomy. For example, as teachers define tasks for each of the six levels, they develop lessons that provide variety and more complex thought for students. Furthermore, the higher level tasks (synthesis and evaluation) can be found only within complex activities with generous amounts of student participation. As teachers attempt to include these tasks, they implement activities that otherwise might be overlooked.

As useful as the taxonomy is, two caveats must be issued. First, the boundaries between some category levels are not sharply defined (e.g., between application and analysis). Second, many complex tasks include a bundle of behaviors. Thus it may be difficult to classify the task into only one of the six levels. Reasonable people can argue over the decision to classify an objective into a particular level. Although these arguments may be interesting, the precise placement of an objective into a particular level is usually not of fundamental importance.

It is fundamental, however, that the instructional tasks planned, implemented, and assessed by the teacher include the higher levels of the taxonomy. Students will then have the opportunity to manipulate information (apply, analyze, synthesize, and evaluate), rather than simply repeat it back to the teacher. When students do something new and meaningful with information, learning is more likely to be enhanced. Each level of the taxonomy is described in the paragraphs that follow.

Knowledge (Memory)

The first level of the taxonomy is knowledge. Tasks at the knowledge level oblige the student to recall, recognize, or reproduce what has been previously learned. Usually, the teacher prompts the recall in the same or similar manner as it was originally learned. Answers are predictable and tend to be either right or wrong. For example, a teacher writes *Shona* and *Ndebele*, the two largest ethnic groups in Zimbabwe, on the chalkboard and then the next day asks the class to recall them from memory and to write them on a sheet of paper. If the teacher had asked for an oral recitation of the names, the task would remain at the knowledge level. Regardless of the nature of the content that must be recalled—

whether generalizations, concepts, or specific facts—if the task is only to recall what was learned from the teacher or from some other source of information, the task remains at the knowledge level.

Examples of knowledge tasks are:

1. Recall the definition of colonialism.
2. State the name of the president of Zimbabwe.
3. List the three most valuable yearly export goods of Zimbabwe in terms of money received.
4. Label the main features of Great Zimbabwe on a map.

Comprehension (Understanding)

The second level of the taxonomy is comprehension. At the comprehension level, students understand material and can express it in their own words or some other form (e.g., drawing). If the teacher asks students to describe in their own words the meaning of colonialism, the task is at the comprehension level. Or, if the teacher asks students to pick out the definition when written by different persons using different words to communicate the same meaning, the task is also one of comprehension.

Other examples of comprehension tasks are:

1. Summarize the major events in the European discovery of Great Zimbabwe beginning with its discovery by Carl Mauch in 1871.
2. Explain the differences between traditional and urban life in Zimbabwe.
3. Describe the meaning expressed in the design of the flag of Zimbabwe.
4. Draw an original map of the main features of Great Zimbabwe.
5. Explain how to translate the area of Great Zimbabwe from meters into yards.

Because both knowledge and comprehension involve only the retrieval of information, they are sometimes referred to as the lower levels of Bloom's taxonomy. That does not mean that lower level tasks are easy or unimportant. Describing the mathematical processes involved in stepwise multiple regression is, after all, a comprehension level task! The information gained at the lower levels often forms the background knowledge needed to successfully complete tasks at the higher levels.

Application

At the application level (and those that follow) students are required to exhibit complex thought. Application and the other higher levels of thought require students to recall and understand content *and* do something with it. If students are to demonstrate that they can manipulate information, the teacher must include some novel element in the task the student is expected to complete. A typical task at the application level is to provide unfamiliar math or science data, an historical incident, quotation, painting, or musical selection and ask the student if it is an example of a concept that has been previously learned. Students might also be asked to make a relatively simple computation to illustrate that they can apply a math concept appropriately.

Some examples of application tasks include the following:

1. Determine the perimeter and area of different shapes.
2. Given a mixed set of items that reflect traditional and urban life in present-day Zimbabwe, students will correctly classify them.
3. Students can generate new examples of the clash between traditional and urban life in the world today.
4. Identify an example of cultural imperialism in a piece of literature not previously studied.

Analysis

At the analysis level, the task given to the student consists of unfamiliar data and/or examples but requires a more complex thought process. Analysis requires the "taking apart" of a complex stimulus. For example, students may examine the information or data provided and make inferences or hypotheses. Analysis demands that students go beyond the information to draw conclusions. For example, students could be given a story of a family's activities, including purchases of goods and services and the family's income and wants. They are told to find the three purchases that are "unwise" buys and three that are "sensible" buys and write a sentence explaining their choices. Another example of an analysis task would be for students to explain why a given household's budget is appropriate or not, given the family's income.

Other examples of analysis tasks are:

1. Given sets of data from three sources, determine the dimensions of various structures and enclosures in Great Zimbabwe.
2. Analyze and explain why a specific characteristic of Zimbabwean life can be traced to its African roots or to European influence.
3. Compare and contrast traditional kraal life with life in modern urban Zimbabwe using information students have discovered.
4. Conduct original research and trace the origins of three musical and literary traditions of southern Africa.

Synthesis

At the synthesis level, students create an original product, exhibit, or performance that involves the selection, organization, and implementation of a number of concepts and principles and requires substantial thought. The key distinction between a synthesis level task and those at a lower level is the necessity that the student produce something that did not previously exist, at least for that student. For example, if students were asked to create an original African tribal mask, they would be engaged in a synthesis task. Original stories, artistic creations, musical compositions, and most projects are also at the synthesis level.

Other examples of synthesis tasks are:

1. Develop an educated guess why the culture that created the city of Great Zimbabwe declined.
2. Develop original stories of life in Great Zimbabwe in the 14th century.
3. Create an original story, poem, or song about the decline and fall of the culture that created Great Zimbabwe.

Evaluation

The highest level of Bloom's taxonomy of the cognitive domain is evaluation. When engaged in an evaluation task, individuals make a judgment about the worth or merit of two or more plausible alternatives, select the preferred alternative, and defend that choice using specified criteria. For example, assume you attend an auction of Renaissance style paintings created by contemporary artists. If you elect to purchase one, the decision combines an affective preference ("This painting appeals to me more.") with a cognitive justification at the evaluation level ("It uses the materials from the artistic period, accurately uses perspective, and is faithful to the dress and man-made structures of the period.").

In an evaluation task, students must defend their decision using a combination of logical argument, evidence, and predetermined criteria. For example, an essay can be judged on one or all of the following standards: organization, coherence, use of language appropriate to the audience, succinctness, and evocative impact.

Other examples of evaluation tasks are:

1. Critique African tribal masks created by classmates according to agreed-upon criteria.
2. Defend or reject the role of the Christian missionary as a positive force in the development of Africa.
3. Evaluate the behavior of King Monomatapa in terms of the standard of conduct of European monarchs who ruled during the same period, such as King Henry VIII of England.
4. In a debate, defend or reject the behavior of European colonization of Africa during the 19th century, with special attention to Cecil Rhodes.

Table 4.2 displays the levels of the cognitive domain, a description of each level, and appropriate learning process action verbs often associated with each level.

Using Bloom's Taxonomy to Break Down Complex Tasks

Although national, state, and district standards are often broken down into grade-level benchmarks, many benchmarks are still too broad to use as objectives. These broader goals then must be broken down into a list of objectives in a logical teaching order. Typically, the objectives are clustered by topic and then placed in order from lower to higher level. This order can be used to guide your lessons. Look back at the Section 2 Objectives. Note how the first objective in the list is lower level and the others build

TABLE 4.2 *Bloom's Taxonomy of the Cognitive Domain.*

Level	Description	Suggested Action Words
6. EVALUATION	Students can use previously learned standard/criteria to determine the worth or merit of a complex product.	defend or reject, develop and critique, judge, state or support a position, justify, argue, decide, appraise,
5. SYNTHESIS	Students can create an original and complex product from a set of simpler components.	create, build, develop an original, compose, write, solve, perform, establish, predict, produce, modify, plan, formulate
4. ANALYSIS	Students can take a complex set of material and break it down into its component parts and/or explain why a complex set of relationships is organized as it is or what caused it to be.	compare and contrast, analyze, break down, explain why, show how, draw a diagram, deduce
3. APPLICATION	Students can apply previously learned material such as concepts, rules, or generalizations to newly taught material.	classify, apply, find, choose, compute, sort, generalize, organize
2. COMPREHENSION	Students can express previously learned material in their own way.	define, put in your own words, describe, summarize, translate, illustrate, restate, demonstrate,
1. KNOWLEDGE	Students can recall, reproduce, or recognize previously learned information as it was taught to them.	reproduce, recognize, recall, list, identify, name, label, underline, place in order

From *Teaching as Decision Making: Successful Practices for the Elementary Teacher* (3rd Ed.) (p. 119), by A. J. Starko, et al., 2003, Upper Saddle River, NJ: Merrill/Prentice Hall. Copyright 2003 by Pearson Education, Inc. Reprinted with permission.

Standard: Establish learning goals that are appropriate for (K–12) students and emphasize critical thinking, creativity, and problem solving (from Eastern Michigan University Teacher Preparation Program Outcomes).

Long-Range Goal:
Future teachers will prepare learning objectives for a two- or three-week unit.

Breakdown of Objectives Leading to Goal:

Clearly Stated Objectives
Students will be able to: explain what A, B, C, and D signify in a clear objective; label the four parts in objectives; and write an objective that contains all parts.

Three Learning Domains
Students will be able to: list the three learning domains (affective, cognitive, and psychomotor); distinguish among affective, cognitive, and psychomotor objectives; and give examples of the three types of objectives.

The Cognitive Domain
Students will be able to: list and explain each of the six levels of cognitive objectives; classify unfamiliar objectives by labeling them; write two objectives of each type; and given a list of objectives related to a certain topic, place them in a logical teaching order.

Uses of Objectives
Students will be able to: explain the uses for objectives in instruction and assessment; and debate the pros and cons of using objectives in the classroom.

Figure 4.1 Illustration of Objectives in a Logical Teaching Order

until the highest level task is last. Bloom's taxonomy is especially helpful for doing this kind of content analysis. Figure 4.1 illustrates how the objectives for teaching future teachers to write objectives would be placed in a chronological teaching order.

Common Questions about Bloom's Taxonomy

Future teachers often ask similar questions. Two of the most common follow with responses.

Question 1

"Just as soon as I think I can classify tasks and objectives at some level of Bloom's taxonomy, I come across one that I can't classify, or a group of us get together and we have three different answers. Even the instructor is unable to persuasively justify why an objective is at the application level or the analysis level. Why does this happen?"

Classifying tasks and objectives is one of the most complex intellectual endeavors in teaching. In order to create a higher level objective for your unit you must access and organize all relevant concepts, generalizations, and facts into a meaningful network. As a new teacher you may not have enough knowledge about the topic to do this structure quickly. Because you are likely to be teaching abstract concepts, it is understandable that you find it difficult to determine whether some element of the content is a generalization or a fact or whether a given instructional objective is at the synthesis or evaluation level. Eventually, however, after teaching a topic and thinking about the ideas within the topic, the conceptual structure begins to emerge and higher level tasks become easier to design and distinguish.

Question 2

"Bloom's taxonomy is too complex. There are too many levels, and it's too difficult to keep the levels straight in my mind. Can't you simplify it further?"

Good question! Here is a simplified, three-level version of the taxonomy for you to consider.

Level A. knowledge/comprehension
Level B. application/analysis/synthesis (higher level)
Level C. evaluation

Level A consists of familiar tasks at the knowledge or comprehension level. At level A, students are asked to remember or recall information—such as names, dates, definitions, items, numbers, labels, statements—exactly as it was taught, summarize it, express it in their own words, or do simple computation. For example, the question, "What happened in the 1970s to the price of gasoline when the supply was drastically reduced?" is at level A.

Level B includes application, analysis, or synthesis tasks. Tasks at level B are triggered by an unfamiliar example, a novel situation, or a set of data that the student must manipulate in some way—classify, reorganize, explain, break down, identify cause and effect, and so on. In contrast to the knowledge level, the assessment situation must contain an unfamiliar element. For instance, "If you were a wheat farmer in the United States and you knew that there would be a severe drought in wheat-growing regions of Canada and Russia in the coming year, would you plan to plant more or less wheat next year? Why or why not?" In synthesis assessment tasks, the students must also create something unique: a story, essay, painting, performance, model, or exhibit.

Level C includes evaluation tasks. For instance, "Write a 500-word essay opposing the rationing of health care in the United States as a way to control health costs" or "Present your arguments to support or oppose the rationing of health care in the form of a five-minute speech to classmates."

For appropriate verbs to use in creating instructional objectives at all levels of the taxonomy, consult Table 4.2.

Practice Activity A

Classifying Tasks into Bloom's Taxonomy

Classify the following objectives using *KC* for knowledge/comprehension, *HL* (higher level) for application/analysis/synthesis, or *E* for evaluation.

Practice Point

____ 1. After practicing calculating the area of squares and rectangles, complete unfamiliar problems using similar shapes.
____ 2. Recall the definition of *colonialism*.
____ 3. Explain why an unfamiliar example of colonialism is similar to European colonialism of the 18th or 19th century. (The example has not been discussed in class.)
____ 4. Provide a definition of *culture* as it is used in a newspaper story.
____ 5. Describe the characteristics of a traditional lifestyle that were presented in class.
____ 6. Defend or reject the thesis "Multicultural education will reduce prejudice and enhance tolerance among adolescents."
____ 7. List one of the sources of information about Zimbabwe taught in class.
____ 8. When given a brief description of a mythical kingdom, explain why it is closer in character to that of the kingdom of Monomatapa or of Henry VIII.
____ 9. Sort a group of unfamiliar statements into a group consisting of historical generalizations.
____ 10. Create an original tribal mask and explain how it accurately reflects the African roots of Zimbabwe.

Practice Activity A: Answer Key

  1. HL (Math objectives are often difficult to classify unless you are able to examine the actual problem. The complexity of the task is the key to whether to classify it at the application or analysis level.)

2. KC (knowledge)
3. HL (analysis)
4. KC (comprehension)
5. KC (knowledge)
6. E (evaluation)
7. KC (knowledge)
8. HL (analysis)
9. HL (application)
10. HL (synthesis)

Practice Activity B

Bloom's Taxonomy

Practice Point

Revise, if necessary, the three clearly stated instructional objectives you wrote in Practice Activity B at the end of Section 1. Make sure one is at the knowledge or comprehension level; a second at the application, analysis or synthesis level; and a third at the evaluation level.

CHAPTER SUMMARY

The first section of Chapter 4 began with the parable "The Sea Horse Fable." Its theme supports the use of instructional objectives as a valuable decision-making tool for teachers. Two arguments favoring the use of instructional objectives are: (1) they assist teachers in focusing student attention on what is expected in the lesson and unit, and (2) they increase the likelihood that activities and assessments will be related to what was actually taught. Two arguments against the use of instructional objectives are: (1) since lower level (memory-type) instructional objectives are easier to construct, some important higher level thinking and affective outcomes may be lost, and (2) some spontaneity may be lost when the classroom is focused too closely on predetermined outcomes.

The middle of this section discussed teaching for understanding through complex authentic performance. The section concluded with guidelines for writing clearly stated instructional objectives.

In Section 2 the focus changed to using Bloom's taxonomy to analyze cognitive learning tasks and write learning objectives at different levels; e.g. knowledge, comprehension, application, analysis, synthesis, and evaluation.

Unit Preparation

Look at the list of goals you prepared in Chapter 3. If necessary, transform them into clearly stated instructional objectives, with well-written behavior statements appropriate for the audience of students who will be expected to achieve them. Analyze whether the objectives will lead students to demonstrate the understandings provided in your state standards and benchmarks. If so, the unit and lesson objectives should include both higher level behaviors and the lower level behaviors required to reach complex learning. Include an authentic culminating objective that will require students to combine and synthesize unit information into an understanding performance.

Again, consider these objectives as a first draft. As you learn more about different types of lesson planning, you are likely to envision alternative ways students may demonstrate their learning. At this stage make sure that your draft objectives are clearly written, focus on key content, and require students to use information in complex ways.

 ## *Portfolio Activity*

Choose one or two of your goals (standards or benchmarks) and prepare a chart that shows how they could be broken down into lesson objectives and placed in a chronological order. Label each with the appropriate level of Bloom's Taxonomy. Be prepared to talk about how your objectives will lead students to higher-level thinking and authentic demonstrations of understanding. You may want to practice this conversation in a mock interview.

REFERENCES

Bloom, B. (Ed.). (1956). *Taxonomy of educational objectives: Handbook I. Cognitive domain.* White Plains, NY: Longman.

Gardner, H. (1999). *The disciplined mind: What all students should understand.* New York: Simon & Schuster.

Mager, R. F. (1997). *Preparing instructional objectives* (3rd ed.). Atlanta, GA: CEP Press, Inc.

Wiggins, G., & McTighe, J. (1998). *Understanding by design.* Alexandria, VA: Association for Supervision and Curriculum Development.

Wiske, M. S. (Ed.). (1998). *Teaching for understanding.* San Francisco: Jossey-Bass, Inc.

Assessing Learning Performances

CHAPTER OVERVIEW

After considering the content to be learned, instructional objectives, and the students to be taught, one important task remains before you can actually plan lessons. You need to design the assessments that will show what students have learned from your lessons. You may ask, "Why plan the assessments before instruction? Don't the tests come after the lessons?" The answer is based on the principle of "backward design"—start with the end in mind (Wiggins & McTighe, 1999). At this point in our planning process, we need to know not only where we are headed (the objectives for student learning), but also how we will assess those objectives. Only then can we design lessons that systematically develop the intended learning.

A well-constructed assessment provides critical information regarding the extent of students' learning and provides feedback regarding the strengths and weaknesses of instruction. Assessment involves:

a. determining what students already know and need to learn (preassessment);
b. using the information to make instructional planning decisions;

c. selecting assessment methods that align with content standards, benchmarks, and instructional objectives;

d. measuring how well students have attained these standards and objectives;

e. providing informative and useful feedback to students and parents; and

f. modifying instruction to better address student learning needs.

SECTION 1. EDUCATIONAL EVALUATION, ASSESSMENT, AND GRADING

Opening Activity

Read the following classroom dialogue between a teacher and a parent at Ken Cowan's school. Then answer the questions that follow.

Practice Point

MRS. CAMPISON (PARENT OF AN EIGHTH-GRADER):   Mrs. Samson, my daughter, Loretta, is in your eighth-grade class this year. I'm afraid that she is very upset about the grade she received from you in math this marking period. She has complained often since she received her report card the day before yesterday.

MRS. SAMSON (EIGHTH-GRADE TEACHER):   Mrs. Campison, I'm sorry about Loretta's reaction to the grade she received. My purpose in teaching is to assist students to be more confident and knowledgeable persons rather than to make them unhappy.

MRS. CAMPISON: Is it true that you are a harder grader than Mr. Carson? Loretta told me that students in your class do more work than her friends in Mr. Carson's classroom.

MRS. SAMSON: I won't compare my requirements to another teacher's requirements, but, it is true that I expect students to do their best work. I have found that if I have high expectations for my students, they will make more learning progress than if I were less demanding.

MRS. CAMPISON: But what about the students who are frightened by your approach to teaching, as Loretta is? What do you do to accommodate these students?

MRS. SAMSON: First, very few students do not benefit from my approach. Consider that we are at the end of the first marking period. Some students need more time to understand that I am serious. Second, I believe that it is the teacher's responsibility to motivate students and to provide the best instruction possible. However, it is also the teacher's responsibility to judge how well the students have learned what has been taught and to assign a grade based on that judgment.

I appreciate the concerns you express about Loretta's schoolwork and hope you will encourage her to respond positively to the challenge to do better in school.

MRS. CAMPISON: Where is the place for effort in your scheme of things? Loretta tells me that she tries as hard as she can but she still fails to satisfy you.

MRS. SAMSON: Effort, if it is strong and persistent, results in improvement. I am absolutely convinced of that.

MRS. CAMPISON: I see that we are not getting anywhere with this discussion. I do intend to speak with Loretta and to offer her additional assistance. I will also encourage her to pay more attention in class and to ask for help from you when she needs it. However, I must say that I find your approach to teaching children unduly threatening and unbending. After all, these children are only 12 and 13 years old. I believe they ought to enjoy their youth and be encouraged to cooperate with each other rather than to compete for your approval and for grades.

MRS. SAMSON: Mrs. Campison, if you and I support each other and motivate Loretta to do her best work in my classroom, I am confident that we can make a significant contribution to her educational development.

What is your reaction to the two persons featured in the dialogue? Do you find yourself more in agreement with the ideas expressed by Mrs. Campison or Mrs. Samson? Why?

Section 1 Objectives

After you have completed this section you will be able to:

1. explain the roles of assessment throughout the instructional cycle;
2. compare and contrast common educational terms such as preassessment (diagnosis), assessment, norm- and criterion-referenced evaluation, formative and summative evaluation, and grading; and
3. list common assessment procedures on a continuum from most controlled to most natural.

Educational Evaluation

Educational evaluation is a systematic process that leads to a judgment about the worth or merit exhibited by a person or persons or by an instructional program. Educational evaluation is considered systematic because it is planned, organized, and completed periodically, and its judgments are subject to revision or redress through established review procedures. Compare this systematic process to the evaluations we make in everyday life. How often do we decide whether something is attractive or unattractive, fair or unfair, good or bad? Normally we are not called upon to defend our evaluative decisions. However, the evaluations that teachers make are fair game for public scrutiny.

Often an educational evaluation entails judgments about both the learner and the instructional program that produced the learning. The conversation between Mrs. Campison and Mrs. Samson involved the evaluation of a student's performance. However, the parent implied that the teacher's instructional approach was a factor affecting the student's performance. Parents have the right to demand that teachers can defend their educational evaluations with appropriate reasoning and evidence using language that a noneducator will understand.

Educational evaluations can be made at any time and for a variety of purposes. Two of these purposes are labeled formative and summative. **Formative evaluation** provides information for improvement while the person or program has the opportunity to improve. Thus, formative evaluation helps a teacher "form" better decisions about student learning and instructional success. Examples of procedures used for formative evaluation of learners are pretests, self-tests, quizzes, drafts of assignments that are reviewed and returned for revision, and practice exercises. Examples of formative evaluation of instruction include exercises to check for understanding and short questionnaires in which students are asked to identify what objectives they have and have not achieved as well as reactions to the classroom activities.

Summative evaluation is used to make educational decisions about persons or programs after instruction terminates. Examples of procedures used for summative evaluation of learners include authentic projects, unit tests, final exams, term papers, student teaching evaluations, report cards, decisions to retain or promote a student, and the like. Examples of summative evaluation of instruction are student evaluations of courses and teachers, formal evaluations of teachers by supervisors, tenure reviews, and other procedures.

The purpose of the evaluation determines whether it is formative or summative. In reality, a given evaluation procedure may serve both purposes. Think for a moment about a unit test that is designed as a summative evaluation of students' performance after the completion of one unit and that also serves a formative purpose to guide students toward improved performance in the next unit.

Educational Assessment

If educational evaluation is a decision about worth or merit, how do we define terms such as assessment and grading? *Assessment* is the process of measuring the quantity and/or quality of a behavior or the indicator of that behavior. It is the foundation information upon which an educational evaluation decision is based. When teachers assess, they determine what students know about some content or their level of skill in performing some task. Teachers might also assess students' motivation to engage in further study of that content.

Assessments can be placed on a continuum between controlled and natural. A highly **controlled assessment** suggests the use of a special testing environment—perhaps having chairs arranged to discourage copying from neighbors, no books or papers on desks, or the requirement that the test be completed within a given time period. In a controlled assessment, the learners are always aware they are being assessed. The most common form of controlled assessment is a standardized or teacher-made paper-and-pencil test, typically administered in the classroom. Teachers can choose other kinds of controlled assessments when appropriate. For example, the observation of a student product or presentation offers a different view of student skill or achievement than does a paper-and-pencil test. Less controlled assessments include written homework assignments, interviews, questionnaires and checklists, observations, and examination of existing records.

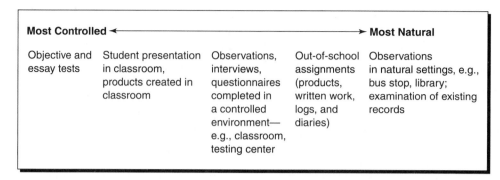

Figure 5.1   Assessment Continuum: Most Controlled to Most Natural
From *Teaching as Decision Making: Successful Practices for the Elementary Teacher* (3rd Ed.) (p. 127), by
A. J. Starko, et al., 2003, Upper Saddle River, NJ: Merrill/Prentice Hall. Copyright 2003 by Pearson Education,
Inc. Reprinted with permission.

Natural assessment procedures are at the far end of the spectrum. Natural assessment requires no artificially constructed testing environment, and the learners are not aware that they are being assessed. For instance, the teacher might observe students while in gym or the library or check the kind and number of library books students choose. A continuum of assessment procedures from most controlled to most natural is shown in Figure 5.1.

The Relationship Between Instruction and Assessment

Consider the following scenario:

A first-year teacher working with Ken Cowan on the Zimbabwe unit has begun assessing her eighth-grade students' first drafts of a formal research report. Using a minimum of three resources, students created two-page reports on the differing perspectives of White farmers and landless Blacks. The teacher is shocked and dismayed by the poor quality of student work. Only 4 of the 25 students have followed the written instructions accurately. Perplexed by the number of students who have submitted papers without important headings, specific comparisons between White farmer and landless Black points of view, and properly labeled timelines, the teacher reflects upon possible reasons for such results.

While some teachers might be inclined to find fault with the students by concluding that they lack research experience or ability, this teacher recognizes that the sheer number of students who failed to meet expectations indicates other causes. An honest assessment of her instruction yields some important insights: the need for clearer expectations and new forms of tiered instruction to promote success. Perhaps a minilesson on comparing and contrasting ideas using a Venn diagram will assist students in their effort to analyze the contrasting perspectives. The teacher considers creating a checklist of report components that students will use as a self-assessment before turning in their final report. Finally, she weighs the potential benefits and drawbacks of presenting students with a model report she could create herself.

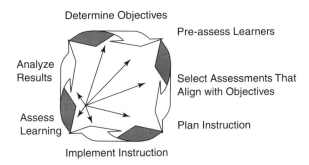

Figure 5.2   The Instructional Cycle
From *Teaching as Decision Making: Successful Practices for the Elementary Teacher* (3rd Ed.) (p. 128), by
A. J. Starko, et al., 2003, Upper Saddle River, NJ: Merrill/Prentice Hall. Copyright 2003 by Pearson Education,
Inc. Reprinted with permission.

This first-year teacher has made an important connection between assessment and instruction. Her students' work provides critical information for the improvement of her own instruction and for future planning. Figure 5.2 shows how selecting instructional objectives, preassessing learners, planning instruction, assessing learning performances, and analyzing results are all part of a continuous cyclical process.

When viewed as an integral part of the instructional cycle, assessment data can be used to generate a wealth of information regarding the quality of our goals and objectives, the effectiveness of our instruction, and of course, the strengths and needs of our students.

Teachers currently use assessment methods at each phase in the instructional cycle (represented by the inner arrows in Figure 5.2). We call this *continuous assessment.* For example, before designing lessons, teachers preassess students to see who may have already learned the objectives or who is lacking prerequisite knowledge. During the lessons themselves teachers informally assess students through the use of observation, assigned work, discussion questions, and one-to-one conferences. At the end of a series of lessons, teachers assess their students' learning of the most important standards and objectives.

Why have teachers begun to embed such formative assessments throughout the instructional cycle? Teachers use the information to clarify and revise their expectations, objectives, and instruction to better address student needs. As a consequence, greater numbers of learners will be successful, and all students will be sufficiently challenged.

One method for continuous assessment is the analysis of student work samples. For example, every week one teacher selects five different students from each period whose work (e.g., class work, homework assignments) will be analyzed in detail. This teacher becomes genuinely curious about why these five students perform as they do, and she attempts to discover the best way to help each one. As she analyzes the work samples, she consults other resources—teachers, books, experts or other professionals—to help her understand the learners' needs more deeply.

Working together with other professionals to interpret and understand student work can be a particularly powerful strategy. In one study of this process (Langer, Colton, & Goff, 2003) teachers changed from seeing student work as merely a grade (or check) in the grade book to analyzing the exact nature of a student's learning and using that information to make instructional decisions. Consequently, their students learned more.

Preassessment

A key idea in this book is that teachers continuously gather information about student learning and use that information to increase student success. One of the more important decisions is where to begin instruction so it isn't too hard or too easy. A powerful tool for making such decisions is preassessment, or diagnosis. For example, if Ken Cowan is about to teach a lesson on the differences between a traditional life in Zimbabwe and a modern life, he should think about two kinds of assessment: *preassessment* and *postassessment*.

When teachers preassess student performance prior to instruction, it is to determine what the student knows or is able to do in relation to the lesson or unit objectives. Teachers also may determine whether students' feelings are positive, neutral, or negative toward the content. They can then use this information to tailor the instruction so it is at the appropriate level of difficulty and interest.

When the teacher assesses student performance after instruction (postassessment), the concern shifts to determine what the students have learned as a result of the lesson and activities. One way for teachers to know if their instruction has had desired results is to compare the students' performance on the preassessment and postassessment of the same objective.

Preassessing students' entry-level competence requires two decisions: what methods to use to gather the information and what content and skills to assess. Preassessment can be accomplished through both *formal* and *informal methods*. An example of a formal method would be a written pretest, similar in style, length, and degree of difficulty to the test that you will administer when the lesson or unit instruction has ended. Formal methods have the disadvantage of feeling like a test—long and possibly scary. One strategy some teachers use is to spread the parts of the pre-test over two or three days, so it does not overwhelm students. Figure 5.3 shows preassessment purposes and methods.

In general, however, you will want to use an informal method, spending as little classroom time as necessary to secure the required information. For example, Ken

---

Preassessment Purposes and Strategies

Area Assessed	Examples of Preassessment Strategies
Interests/feelings	Survey, questionnaire, free-write, rating scales, KWL
General learning skills	Perform (e.g., use equipment, write, do math)
Prior experiences	Free-write, log, daily journal, discussion
Knowledge of content	Pretest, anticipation guide, game, perform task(s), self-assessments (KWL), concept maps

Figure 5.3 Four Categories of Preassessment

From *Teaching as Decision Making: Successful Practices for the Elementary Teacher* (3rd Ed.) (p. 131), by A. J. Starko, et al., 2003, Upper Saddle River, NJ: Merrill/Prentice Hall. Copyright 2003 by Pearson Education, Inc. Reprinted with permission.

Cowan could ask students to list up to three characteristics of a traditional life and three characteristics of a modern life and then choose which life they would prefer to lead. He would collect the papers and analyze each student's level of understanding to determine who may need more or less challenge.

In regard to the content of a preassessment, think of it in two different ways. First, you need to assess the general knowledge and skills you hope students already possess. What *prerequisite* knowledge and skills do students need to approach the objectives in this unit? Do students have the necessary background knowledge to read successfully the written material you have gathered? Can they take notes on lectures and reading? What do they know about library research? Can they do the math required to do the graphing? How well can they cooperate with others during group work? The easiest way to preassess these general skills is to ask students to use them in a simple setting. For example, imagine Mrs. Samson wants to know how well her students can create graphs to represent data they collect about Zimbabwe. She might give them a small set of numbers, explain the task, and see what she gets. It is likely some students will need explicit instruction on this skill while others may not. She may form project groups that include both kinds of students.

Second, preassessment will help you determine each student's prior learning about the content to be taught. The unit concept map and objectives (see Chapters 3 and 4) are very helpful when designing a preassessment of unit content. After completing his concept map Ken Cowan would know that in Zimbabwe a traditional life is typically based on agriculture; and is rural, village-based, family-oriented, and slowly changing; whereas a modern life tends to be urban, technological, impersonal, fast-paced, and dynamic. His preassessment would ask students to list ideas they have about traditional and modern life in Africa or Zimbabwe. Then he would look for the ideas listed above in the students' responses.

This content-specific preassessment may show that some students already have learned what he planned to teach. He will plan independent study or special projects for these students. Such preassessment is extremely useful for teaching decisions. You can use your analysis of the responses to adjust the complexity of the content to be taught, the nature of the activities you will use to initiate study of the unit, and other planned activities and assessments. Further, you will be able to modify (or differentiate) your instruction so individual students are sufficiently challenged and supported.

 ## REFLECTING ON THE IDEAS

If you were Ken Cowan, what would you wish to know about the eighth-grade students' entry level competence before you begin teaching the lesson on the differences between a traditional life in Zimbabwe and a modern life?

You might have considered: Are the students able to read a chapter and gain meaning? Can they take notes from a lecture or movie or field trip? How much do they know about the process of comparing and contrasting?

Grading

How do the terms *assessment* and *evaluation* relate to the issue of *grading?* Ken Cowan has used a preassessment to evaluate how well his students were prepared to study the unit on Zimbabwe. When the results were gathered and examined, he made a judgment (evaluation) about whether the students were ready to study the unit as tentatively planned or if adjustments needed to be made. At the end of the unit, he will postassess the students, evaluate what they have learned, and will assign a *grade* to communicate his judgment to the student, parents, and interested others. Bear in mind that a grade is a label that our society uses to represent value earned. It is a kind of certificate that communicates earned achievement to educators, employers, and the general public. Remember that the value of a grade is only as good as the assessments upon which the grade is based. If they are to be useful to society, grades have to be sufficiently accurate so that they can predict future performance. Thus a student who receives nothing but A's in middle school mathematics should expect to receive similar grades in senior high school.

No doubt you are aware of the intense debate about the relative worth of the grading process. The decision whether to assign grades, the process used to determine the value represented by the grades, and the particular symbols used as grades are political decisions as much as educational decisions. Some educators argue that the symbols traditionally used for grading do not clearly represent the complexities of student achievement and that more specific information would be helpful (Marzano, 2000).

Norm-Referenced and Criterion-Referenced Evaluation

A classroom is sometimes viewed as containing a group of 20 to 35 students who compete against classmates for grades, awards, scholarships, and admission to college. College students may be accustomed to seeing an instructor put a grade distribution curve on the chalkboard showing how many students received an A, B, C, D, or F. Although the concept of normal distribution may remain mysterious, students know that the instructor arranged all the grades in a row and then established cutoff scores between grades—for instance, 92–100 = A, 85–91 = B, and so on.

This view of grading is referred to as **norm-referenced.** The average score and other scores that deviate from that norm become critical determinants of an individual's grade. Scores that fall well above the average get A's and B's; scores that fall well below the average get D's and F's. Scores that cluster around the average get C's.

Norm-referenced evaluation has one major disadvantage. As student performance improves, the average is higher, and the teacher is likely to raise the curve to retain a similar proportion of A's, B's, and C's. Thus, students experience the phenomenon of working harder or doing better without seeing any grade change. A second major disadvantage is that the value of the grade is difficult to interpret from one group to the next. Since the grade is determined by the performance of students in a particular group, a grade in one eighth-grade science classroom taught by teacher A may represent much more or much less educational value than an identical grade in an eighth-grade classroom taught by teacher B. Large testing programs such as the National

Assessment of Educational Progress (NAEP), Scholastic Aptitude Test (SAT), and American College Testing (ACT) can avoid this problem by comparing an individual's score against the average derived from a national sample group.

In contrast, **criterion-referenced grading** considers each individual's performance against predetermined performance standards (or criteria). An evaluation that is criterion-referenced enables the teacher to determine with confidence whether a student's response reaches a predetermined level of accomplishment. Using standards as the definition of success rather than student-to-student comparison makes it theoretically possible for all students to be successful and receive A's. The list of standards (or criteria) that define the desired level of proficiency is referred to as a *rubric* (Wiggins, 1996; 1998).

Some assessment models and types are more appropriate for criterion-referenced grading than are others. One example of a criterion-based teaching/learning model is called **contract learning.** In such a model, the standards for receiving a given grade are described to all students. Each student contracts with the teacher to perform certain tasks at a given quality level in order to receive the agreed-on grade. Objectives and activities are identified, criteria determined, and deadlines established. Contract learning has the advantage of permitting a student to concentrate on certain subject areas or units within a subject and not on others. It also helps prevent the teacher from labeling students, for instance, as A or C students, since students can choose the grade they will seek to achieve.

An example of contract learning is the Brain-Flex program implemented in a secondary school in New South Wales, Australia (Bounds & Harrison, 1997). Each student in the program completes two or three independent projects during a school year. These projects enable them to flex their minds in pursuit of intellectual topics and outcomes of interest to them rather than those selected by the state. The topic must have sufficient breadth and depth to justify the effort that will be devoted to it. That decision is made after the student has written an explanation of the topic and justified its worthiness. Once a suitable topic has been determined, a learning contract is developed with the student's tutor (teacher). The contract includes a rationale of what the student expects to learn, clearly written goals and objectives to be achieved, and standards for assessment of the expected outcomes. Each student is free to use whatever facilities, equipment, and materials are needed to study the topic. Faculty and staff are available to provide counsel and assistance as needed. At the end of the contract, students submit the outcomes of their study and a written summary of what they have learned.

Another example of criterion-referenced grading is known as **mastery learning** (Carroll, 1963; Bloom, 1984). Mastery learning is based on the belief that all students can be successful in achieving all objectives if additional learning time is allowed for those who need it. Mastery learning, if it is to be successful, requires that teachers use clearly stated objectives, employ preassessment and other kinds of formative assessment procedures, and adjust instruction using a variety of strategies and learning activities. Finally, they must be prepared to reteach students when necessary, using alternative methods and materials. Advocates claim that if these assumptions are met and if a sufficient time for learning is provided, all students can master all objectives.

In all these examples criterion-referenced evaluation can be applied to the grading of either tests or authentic performances. Remember it is not the form of the assignment that makes it criterion-referenced; it is how it is scored—by comparing student performance to a set of criteria that defines "mastery."

Tomlinson (2001) suggests that grading needs to accommodate individual differences and variations in instruction. For example, how would a teacher grade a student who is making excellent progress but is working at an instructional level below the other students? Similar puzzles arise for a student who is struggling but working on exceptionally advanced material. In most school settings, these decisions are only partially under the control of the teacher.

SECTION 2. DESIGNING CLASSROOM ASSESSMENTS

Section 2 Objectives

After you have completed this section, you will be able to:

1. explain the importance of validity when evaluating student learning;
2. describe strategies for increasing the validity and reliability of classroom assessments;
3. apply recommended guidelines to construct objective and essay tests;
4. explain how authentic performance assessments can aid evaluation decisions; and
5. design performance tasks to assess student learning.

Classroom assessments used for grading may come from published curriculum materials (e.g., the teacher's guide for a textbook) or may be designed "from scratch" by the teacher. It is rare, though, that a textbook assessment is well matched to state standards, particular students, and what is actually taught. Therefore, most teachers design their own assessments or at least adapt published ones for a better fit. This section introduces key concepts and methods to help you design high-quality assessments. The design and interpretation of assessment information is an extremely complex process. Our presentation is just a beginning; ideally, you will have the opportunity to study this topic in greater depth.

Validity

Validity is the property of being relevant, meaningful, or effective (Merriam-Webster's, 1993). *Educational validity* can be defined as the property of an assessment that makes it an accurate measure of what it purports to measure. Although there are several kinds of validity, only content validity is directly under the teacher's control and responsibility. *Content validity* has often been described through the following teaching prescription:

> Tell them what they will learn, teach them what you told them, and assess what you taught.

However, achieving a high level of content validity is more complex than this simple prescription suggests. Fortunately, your analysis of the content you will teach and the use of clearly stated objectives are the foundations on which valid tests are developed. Two dimensions of content validity are most important. In the first dimension a valid assessment is one that provides an adequate coverage of the content taught in the unit.

In the case of the Zimbabwe unit, adequate assessment of the content includes all the key objectives, including the concepts and generalizations that organize the unit.

If some aspect of the content is missing from the assessment, students can rightfully argue that too much emphasis was placed on some objectives and too little on others. Another common violation of validity occurs when students are assessed on skills or knowledge not taught in class but acquired previously—material learned in earlier courses or through students' personal experiences. For example, consider the injustice that is created when a social studies teacher permits a student to submit a unit project on colonial America that was the result of a summer family excursion through the original 13 colonies. Obviously, one family provided a student with opportunities for cultural enrichment that were far beyond the capacity of other families. To give a substantial grade advantage to the student for this project compounds the effects of economic and class inequity.

The second dimension extends the issue of validity into the learning process. It is necessary not only to "assess what you taught" but also to assess at the same level of learning specified in your objectives. Perhaps you know of instructors who promise lofty aims such as enhancing thinking skills, learning to make informed judgments, and exploring ways to solve problems and then test for the recall of bits and pieces of information. To avoid this error in assessing the Zimbabwe unit, adequate coverage must include (1) questions on the application of concepts such as traditional life and modern society, racism, and colonialism, and (2) tasks that require students to analyze data and to create original products such as a site map and a tribal mask.

Reliability

A second important evaluation concept is reliability. Whereas validity is concerned with accuracy of assessment, **reliability** is concerned with consistency (or stability) from one performance to the next. Educational assessments that have high levels of reliability ensure that if a student were assessed again on the same test, he would achieve an identical or nearly identical score. Thus, if an assessment is both valid and reliable, the teacher can rely on the information as being a reasonable indication of what the student has learned. Validity assures that the assessment measures what you think it measures. Without validity it makes no difference whether the assessment is reliable or consistent. These two concepts can be applied to both written tests and performance assessments.

Enhancing the Reliability and Validity of Teacher-Developed Written Tests

Teachers develop a wide variety of written tests, which can be classified into two types: objective and constructed response. In an *objective test* students are expected to identify or provide the right or best answer. A multiple-choice test is the most common example of an objective test. Other examples include matching, true/false, and fill-in-the-blank. In a *constructed response test* students are expected to build a response requiring the planning, organization, and display of multiple elements. Essay tests and reports are the most common examples of a constructed response test. The following section is designed to help you to plan, design, and grade objective and essay tests.

General Planning Guidelines

1. Are all students expected to complete all items on the test? If so, make sure it is not too long. This is especially important for essay items, since they require additional time for reading, organizing, and editing.

2. Will all students understand the directions for all segments of the test? Are the directions brief and understandable? Is there a potential for students to misinterpret what is expected? If so, consider taking time to discuss the directions for each segment of the test before administering it.

3. Are there a sufficient number of items to adequately sample the content covered by the test? Remember, longer tests are more reliable than shorter tests. However, a series of quizzes that divide the content among a number of periodic assessments can enhance reliability. In addition, frequent assessments even out the variation that affects the reliability (students' health on a given day, the amount of study time, etc.).

4. What other assessments will be used to sample student performance over the same content? Some students perform better on tests where they select the right answer (multiple choice, matching, true/false). Others perform better on essay tests or projects (e.g., creating a product such as a model). A variety of assessment formats (e.g., objective and authentic performances) provides a better assessment of students' learning than a single assessment.

5. The construction and scoring of paper-and-pencil tests affect their reliability. An objective test takes more time to design and construct than an essay test. However, because of their structure, objective tests tend to be more reliable, take less time to score, and provide for a wider sampling of content than essay tests.

Figure 5.4 provides tips for the design of objective test items that will increase test reliability.

CHECK YOUR UNDERSTANDING: OBJECTIVE TEST ITEMS

Write three objective test items that are consistent with the test item tips.

Essay test items, although less time consuming to construct, are much more difficult to score than objective tests. Some tips to aid in the reliability of scores derived from essay tests are shown in Figure 5.5.

CHECK YOUR UNDERSTANDING: ESSAY TEST ITEMS

Write one essay test item that assesses the same content area as one of three objective test items. Ensure that the essay item is consistent with the test item tips.

ALL OBJECTIVE TEST ITEMS
   a. Use language that the student will easily understand.
   b. Avoid testing trivial information.
   c. Avoid using items that depend on value judgments to select the correct answer.
   d. When constructing items, avoid giving clues to the right answer.

MULTIPLE CHOICE
   a. The stem of the item should present an idea, even if incomplete.
   b. All item alternatives should be plausible.
   c. Check carefully to see that the item contains only one correct answer.
   d. Keep choices about the same length.
   e. If you wish to have students find the "wrong answer," express the stem as a positive and include the word "EXCEPT" at the conclusion of the stem.
   f. Don't make the longest answer the correct answer in every case.
   g. Refrain from using "All of the Above" as an alternative.
   h. The use of "None of the Above" is acceptable as an alternative. If you use it, be sure it is occasionally the correct answer.
   i. Vary the stem of items to reduce student fatigue. Include incomplete statements, questions, analogies.
   j. Words to be repeated in each alternative should instead appear in the stem.
   k. The stem should be grammatically correct with each alternative.
   l. Avoid unneeded information that adds to the item's length without adding essential information.
   m. Numerical alternatives should be placed in a logical pattern, e.g., ascending order.

TRUE/FALSE
   a. Express a single thought in the statement.
   b. Avoid the use of a negative statement.
   c. Avoid the use of an absolute statement.

MATCHING
   a. Organize lists around a central idea so that all individual elements are similar in content and form.
   b. Don't have the same number of elements in both lists to be matched; don't indicate that elements may be used more than once.
   c. Don't use long lists of elements; students will take so long to read and organize them they will have too little time to answer the items.

Figure 5.4 Tips to Improve the Reliability of an Objective Test
From *Test Construction* by Dorothy Wood. Columbus, OH: Charles Merrill and Co. Copyright 1961, pp. 103–107.

Performance Assessment

Performance assessment tasks are currently recognized as a powerful form of evaluation (Feuer & Fulton, 1993; Spalding, 2000; Worthen, 1993). When knowledge and understanding are demonstrated through performance in a real context, students clearly perceive the value and relevance of learning. They are engaged in experiences that are valued and useful in the adult world. And, the teacher has the opportunity to see the knowledge and skills in use.

Consider the following performance assessment task from the Zimbabwe unit:

Students are to prepare two radio reports that evaluate the arguments made by advocates and critics of the Zimbabwean government policy of expropriating

WRITING ESSAY TEST ITEMS
    a. A group of short answer essay items are preferable to one or two items that require an extensive response.
    b. Use an essay test item to tap higher level learning (synthesis, evaluation).
    c. Include a sufficient number of items to cover the content to be tested.
    d. Specify the scope and detail expected in the answer, e.g., one paragraph, 500 words, include five reasons, etc.
    e. Require all students to answer all items.
    f. Write a sufficiently detailed set of instructions so students will know what is expected of them.
    g. Inform students before they begin the essay test how much each item will be worth in determining the final score on the test.
    h. Remember, the novice essay test writer usually demands too much writing from students within the available time.

SCORING ESSAY TESTS
    a. Prepare a model correct answer before grading any responses.
    b. Grade papers as anonymously as possible.
    c. Score all responses on a single question before going on to the next question.
    d. If possible, score all papers in a single sitting.
    e. Take a break between questions to reduce fatigue.
    f. If you wish to grade for mechanics as well as substance, it is a good idea to award two grades.

Figure 5.5 Tips to Improve the Reliability of an Essay Test
From *Test Construction* by Dorothy Wood. Columbus, OH: Charles Merrill and Co. Copyright 1961, pp. 21–22

White-owned farms without compensation. The radio report should be timed to be no longer than three minutes. Be prepared to deliver the radio report to your classmates.

In this example, students learn important research and reporting skills as they examine primary and secondary source documents. They analyze and evaluate evidence and draw conclusions. This ability to articulate and support an argument with evidence is a skill students will utilize throughout their lives. Students are more motivated when they are assessed through performances such as this news broadcast assignment (other examples include playlets, musical performances, and debates) and products (exhibits, research reports, models, charts, diaries and logs, other writing assignments, experiments, and art projects) created for real purposes and audiences. Finally, an emphasis on depth versus breadth of content coverage increases students' knowledge retention and understanding (see, for example, Associated Press, 1998).

Designing Performance Assessments

The creation of performance assessments is challenging and time consuming; however, the rewards in student learning are well worth the effort. Performance assessments can be used as both formative evaluation (during the unit) and as summative evaluation at

A Student Presents His Authentic Project.

the conclusion of a unit. In order to construct a performance assessment teachers need to (1) select goals and objectives, (2) design a performance task, and (3) determine assessment criteria (see Figure 5.6).

The following narrative describes the decision-making processes of one teacher as she follows this three-step process.

Step 1: Selecting Goals and Objectives

Jodi Washington wishes to design an assessment task based on the following goal for the Zimbabwe unit.

> **Goal:** Students will describe the problems facing modern Zimbabwe today, such as the spread of HIV, poverty, hunger, landlessness, unplanned urbanization, corruption, lack of democracy, etc.

Jodi aligns her goal with the following state social studies standards/benchmarks:

> Public Discourse and Decision Making Standard: All students will engage their peers in constructive conversation about matters of public concern by clarifying issues, considering opposing views, applying democratic values, anticipating consequences, and working towards making decisions.

Figure 5.6 Steps in Designing Performance Assessments
From *Teaching as Decision Making: Successful Practices for the Elementary Teacher* (3rd Ed.)
(p. 140), by A. J. Starko, et al., 2003, Upper Saddle River, NJ: Merrill/Prentice Hall. Copyright 2003 by
Pearson Education, Inc. Reprinted with permission.

Middle School Benchmark: Engage each other in conversations that attempt to clarify and resolve national and international policy issues.

Geography Standard: All students will describe and explain the causes, consequences, and geographic context of major global issues and events.

Middle School Benchmark: Explain how elements of physical geography, culture, and history of the region may be influencing current events.

History Standard: All students will reconstruct the past by comparing interpretations written by others from a variety of perspectives and creating narratives from evidence.

Middle School Benchmark: Analyze interpretations of major events selected from African, Asian, Canadian, European, and Latin American history to reveal the perspectives of the authors.

Economic Standard: All students will describe how government decisions on taxation, spending, public goods, and regulation impact what is produced, how it is produced, and who receives the benefits of production.

Middle School Benchmark: Use case studies to assess the role of government in the economy.

Step 2: Developing the Performance Task

After defining her goals, Jodi brainstorms the elements of a task that will incorporate the goal and be faithful to the standards and benchmarks. She wants her students to empathetically enter the lives of the Zimbabwean people. She wants to link the past with the present and wants differing points of view to be represented. She wants to ensure that accurate, contemporary data are collected and disseminated.

Jodi expects her students to explore the many electronic sources of information about Zimbabwe available on the Internet. Of special interest is the use of WebQuests, "inquiry-oriented activities in which most or all of the information used by learners is drawn from the Internet" (Milson & Downey, 2001). (For examples of such sites, see Internet websites about Zimbabwe listed at the conclusion of Chapter 3.) Perhaps she can motivate students to use the data from Zimbabwe to reflect on American issues and problems and on their own lives.

After brainstorming, Jodi Washington refines the task and creates directions for the students. Her formulated task follows:

> In two weeks we will produce a *Challenges Facing Zimbabwe* newsletter that will focus on seven issues that the country faces in 2003. The seven challenges are:
>
> 1. hunger
> 2. HIV/AIDS
> 3. unplanned urbanization
> 4. environment deterioration
> 5. racial and ethnic disputes
> 6. political need for reform
> 7. economic underdevelopment
>
> The class will be divided into seven groups of four students each. We will draw straws to select the challenge each group is to research and then write an article about the challenge, including its present circumstances, causes, and potential solutions. Then we'll culminate with the group's consensus about whether the challenge will be successfully met. Your grade will be based on the attached rubrics for both individual and group projects.

Step 3: Creating Assessment Criteria and Scoring Guides

First, Jodi outlines the major elements that encompass the task. Then she begins to outline the criteria she will use for grading.

- Each group will meet with her prior to the start of research to identify the specific responsibilities of each group member.
- Each student will research and take notes, and will participate in constructing the article.
- Each student will have to examine a minimum of five sources and submit a series of index cards that contain his or her notes. (She develops a rubric for this element of the project.)
- She lists the characteristics of a good newspaper article, such as accuracy, clarity, comprehensiveness, mechanical correctness, human interest, and originality.
- She constructs a rubric related to the investigation and construction of information by distinguishing the difference between partially proficient, proficient, and advanced performance (see Figure 5.7).

In addition to grading each group's project, Jodi will need to assess each student's individual learning. She may do this by requiring specific documentation of each student's contribution to the project (e.g., the research notes) and by asking each student to write his or her own summary of how the geography, culture, history and government impacts Zimbabwe today. She would use a rubric to grade these summaries.

Partially Proficient	Proficient	Advanced
• constructs an inadequate information-gathering strategy • does not use electronic technology • gathers irrelevant or insufficient data • uses only one way of organizing information • makes inaccurate statements based on information	• constructs an information strategy using secondary and primary sources and electronic means to complete a task • uses multiple ways of organizing the information • draws valid inferences from the information	• constructs an information-gathering strategy using a variety of sources, including little-known information resources to complete a task • uses multiple ways of organizing information • draws valid generalizations from the information

Figure 5.7 Gathering and Organizing Information Rubric
From Michigan Curriculum Framework. (1996). Lansing, MI: Michigan Department of Education, Section V Assessment, 13. Used with permission.

Developing rubrics, and sharing them with students, can be particularly helpful in promoting self-assessment and goal setting for students (Luft, 1997; Pate, 1993).

Self-Assessment, Goal Setting, and Student Ownership of the Learning Process

A fundamental way to help students understand teacher expectations and criteria for successful achievement is to involve them in the creation of scoring guides and rubrics. Sample exemplary products from previous years can be helpful in allowing students to identify characteristics of successful examples. Include adolescents in performance assessment through peer evaluation and personal goal setting, which promotes greater individual autonomy and responsibility for learning (Marzano, Pickering, and Pollock, 2001). Self-assessment enables students to internalize criteria for exemplary performance that they can then apply to new situations. Simple reflection forms, such as the one in Figure 5.8, enable students to analyze their performance and establish goals for future performance.

Self-assessment guides can facilitate student discussion about their work during peer, teacher/student, and student-led parent conferences. These self-assessment activities foster the development of vocabulary and communication skills that enable students to assume greater ownership for their learning.

Portfolios and Exhibitions

One approach to performance assessment emphasizes the collection and display of student work in a **portfolio.** A portfolio should include various kinds of products and exhibits. In some cases, students are encouraged to maintain a portfolio of revisions of a significant assignment, such as a research report, story, or art project. Students can attach to these exhibits their own assessment of the development of their competence on

Reflection and Goal-Setting Form

Name: _____   Date: _____

Project: _____

1. I think the strengths of my project are. . .

    _____

    _____

2. My favorite part of the project was. . .

    _____

    _____

3. Some things I understand now that I did not know before are. . .

    _____

    _____

4. One thing I would do differently next time is. . .

    _____

    _____

5. A learning goal I have as a result of this project is. . .

    _____

    _____

Figure 5.8 Reflection Form

From *Teaching as Decision Making: Successful Practices for the Elementary Teacher* (3rd Ed.) (p. 145), by A. J. Starko, et al., 2003, Upper Saddle River, NJ: Merrill/Prentice Hall. Copyright 2003 by Pearson Education, Inc. Reprinted with permission.

these projects. Thus, the students demonstrate a continuing commitment to the task and awareness of their progress.

For example, for the Zimbabwe unit, students could include some or all of the following assignments of their work in their assessment portfolio.

1. a brief account of a fictional person living at the time of King Monomatapa
2. an original poem or song lyric appropriate to Zimbabwe
3. a Zimbabwean tribal mask
4. a drawing or painting of Victoria Falls

5. a set of definitions of key terms from the Zimbabwe unit
6. a letter to the editor of a Harare newspaper expressing a point of view about one of the challenges facing contemporary Zimbabwe
7. a segment of the report they created for the newsletter, *Challenges Facing Zimbabwe.*

Each of the assignments contained in the portfolio could be evaluated (by the teacher, peers, and/or the student) and become important elements in determining the summative grade for the unit.

An exhibition is another form of performance assessment. An ***exhibition*** is designed to be a broad, preferably interdisciplinary, culminating experience that requires the application of knowledge within a stated set of conditions (Sizer, 1992; 1994). Typically an exhibition entails some type of presentation to an audience outside the class.

Imagine an exhibition, complete with producers and consumers, on creating and running a market economy in a middle school. The centerpiece of the economy is the creation and operation of a bank. Businesses are planned and created to produce and sell a variety of goods and services within the school and the community. Students assume the duties and responsibilities of entrepreneurs, salespeople, advertisers, illustrators, bankers, and other related positions. Banks lend money to entrepreneurs; consumers invest in new and existing businesses, save, and borrow money from the bank. Parents and community people add their expertise as guest speakers and consultants. At an end-of-year school fair, all participants and sectors of the economy can exhibit their products and services and explain their roles and contributions to the economy.

Returning once more to the "Zimbabwe: A World's View from Africa" unit, the portfolio requirement could be organized as an exhibition. Students from other classes, faculty, school board members, parents, and community guests could be invited to view exhibitions of student work from the unit. African tribal masks, site maps, and scenes from short stories created by groups of students could be featured in displays and performances in the auditorium.

Final Thoughts about Assessment

A variety of educators view high-quality assessment as a potential driving force for school improvement (Rothman, 1997; Simmons & Resnick, 1993; Smith, 1997). Stiggins (2000) advocates the use of diverse forms of assessment. He claims the classroom has a place for both teacher-made tests and performance assessment. Stiggins identifies four primary forms of assessment that offer different assessment capabilities:

- selected response
- essay
- performance assessment
- personal communication

Selected response assessments include short-answer, multiple-choice, true/false, and matching exercises. These are particularly useful if the teacher seeks to assess broad areas of knowledge mastery; however, selected response assessments cannot directly assess skill application and mastery in an authentic context.

Essays are defined as exercises that call for extended written answers. They provide an excellent opportunity for the examination of student reasoning processes. Similar to selected response tests, essays often do not directly assess skill development and application in context.

Performance assessments are used to accurately assess problem-solving ability, skill development, and mastery as observed in a performance. This can show student proficiency in applying knowledge through a project or product development. However, performance assessments are not effective tools for assessing student mastery of a broad area of content.

Finally, personal communication includes assessment strategies such as conferencing, oral examinations, interviews, debates, question posing during instruction, and group discussion. These strategies allow the teacher to assess student thinking processes and evaluate the depth of knowledge mastery. They are less effective as tools for assessing knowledge of a large body of content.

Each of these four assessment methods can be an effective tool when matched thoughtfully with a specific set of objectives. Consequently, a primary challenge for the teacher concerns the alignment of objectives with assessment methods.

 ## REFLECTING ON THE IDEAS

Examine the following instructional objectives, and describe an appropriate assessment method or methods:

1. Objective: When given a list of facts about the people, history, environment, government, resources, and culture of Zimbabwe, match each fact with a statement that identifies it. Assessment:

2. Objective: Create a description of life in Great Zimbabwe in the 14th century or in the capital of King Monomatapa's empire at the beginning of the 16th century that accurately reflects the history and culture of the Shona people who lived there at the time. Assessment:

CHAPTER SUMMARY

The chapter began with a confrontation between a teacher and a parent over a student's academic performance. The confrontation brought to the surface the complex and difficult issues involved in assessing and judging academic learning. Often, assessment problems occur because the evaluator has made a validity error, either (1) assessing what was not taught or failing to assess adequately what was taught, or (2) assessing at a different level of learning from what the student had practiced. Diverse assessment methods including selected response, essays, personal communication, and performance assessments must be carefully chosen to align with instructional objectives. Of the four types, performance assessment has unique qualities that facilitate student application of knowledge and skills within a realistic context. When students participate in the development of assessment criteria and reflect on their own progress through self-assessment and goal setting activities, they develop assessment skills and increased responsibility for their own learning.

Regardless of the particular mix of assessment methods chosen by the teacher, a high-quality assessment program includes the following characteristics:

- A clear and succinct statement of policy describes the purpose of the assessment program, indicating the role of assessment in measuring student performance, diagnosing learning needs, and identifying elements of instruction and assessment that should be modified.
- Learning goals and objectives are coordinated with assessment practices into a functioning system.
- Where available and appropriate, the assessment practices are aligned with local, state, and national content standards and benchmarks.
- A test grid (or blueprint) that displays a breakdown of content and learning levels has been constructed and is available for scrutiny. It reveals the assessment weights of different lessons, topics, and/or units and types of assessment formats such as multiple choice and essay.
- Issues of fairness, equity, and respect for diversity are openly addressed, and policies ensuring their presence in the assessment practices are publicly available.
- A wide variety of assessment practices are used, with special attention to those practices that facilitate student inquiry and conversation and those that require students to analyze, synthesize, and evaluate data in novel contexts.
- When a particular assessment task requires higher-order learning and/or requires students to engage in substantive conversation, either orally or in writing, or requires the production of a performance or product, a thoughtful, valid, and reliable scoring guide is developed and shared with students prior to the initiation of the task.
- Scoring guides (rubrics) distinguish among performance levels; e.g., highly proficient, proficient, not yet proficient.
- Reports of student performance and progress on assessments are disseminated according to a timely and predictable schedule.

Practice Activity A

Reviewing Your Educational Evaluation Philosophy

Practice Point

At the beginning of this chapter, you read about a confrontation between a teacher, Mrs. Samson, and a parent, Mrs. Campison, involving the grade Mrs. Campison's daughter received in math. Given what you have learned in this chapter, how would you have responded to the parent's concerns if you were Mrs. Samson?

Practice Activity B

Multiple-Choice Test Items

The following objective test items are flawed. Using the guidelines for "Enhancing the Validity and Reliability of Teacher-Developed Written Tests" presented earlier in this chapter, identify one or more errors illustrated by each item.

1. What is 20% of 50?
   a. 20
   b. 25
   c. 40
   d. 10

2. Zimbabwe is located in
   a. Africa
   b. The Northern Hemisphere
   c. Asia
   d. The Southern Hemisphere

3. Imperialism is defined as the extension of rule or authority of one nation or empire over a foreign country or countries. Although imperialism has been practiced for thousands of years, after 1500 A.D. the imperial nations came largely from which continent?
   a. South America
   b. Europe
   c. Africa
   d. Asia

Practice Point

4. All of the following statements about Great Zimbabwe are true EXCEPT:
   a. It was constructed in the pre-Christian era by the ancient Phoenicians, Greeks, or Hebrews.
   b. Its stone structures were built without using mortar.
   c. It was the center of a great inland empire.
   d. The people living there traded with other countries.

5. Choose the best answer to complete the statement, A walrus:
   a. is a fish.
   b. lives in water.
   c. is a mammal.
   d. breathes through gills.

6. Before the year 1500 A.D., the spoken or written words of which of the following were not believed by most Europeans?
   a. results of scientific experiments
   b. papal pronouncements
   c. scripture
   d. the works of Aristotle

7. All of the following are necessary factors for industrialization EXCEPT the:
   a. type of government
   b. adequate labor supply
   c. technical improvement
   d. adequate supply of capital

8. The best way to improve the future for the people of modern Zimbabwe is through:
   a. investments in education
   b. family planning
   c. economic development
   d. investments in health care

9. Cecil Rhodes was a/an
   a. European imperialist
   b. utopian socialist during the 19th century
   c. industrialist who competed for the contract to build the Suez Canal
   d. character in a Walt Disney movie

10. Which of the following statements is true?
    a. Motivation lessens as we move closer to a goal.
    b. The higher the degree of anxiety, the greater the learning.
    c. As feedback is reduced, effective learning is vitiated.
    d. Young children (0–5 years) are motivated more by extrinsic factors than older children.

Practice Activity B: Answer Key

1. Alternatives should be arranged in a logical sequence, such as ascending order.
2. Two answers are right. To prevent this particular error, use only similar alternatives, such as all continents.
3. The stem includes some unneeded information.
4. The longest answer is the correct one.
5. The stem does not express an idea; two answers are right.
6. Express the statement as a positive and conclude with *EXCEPT*. Eliminate the unneeded expression "the spoken or written words."
7. The last word in the stem gives a grammatical clue to the answer.
8. Without reference to an authority or a standard, best answer is impossible to determine.
9. Alternative *d* is implausible.
10. The use of *vitiated* makes the item a test of vocabulary rather than of psychological knowledge; the longest answer is correct.

Practice Point

Practice Activity C

Designing a Performance Assessment

Practice Point

Imagine you are teaching a unit. You have analyzed the content and identified the key generalizations, concepts, and facts. Write the instructional objectives for your unit, and order the cognitive ones in a logical sequence. Be sure to include affective and psychomotor objectives as appropriate. Design a culminating exhibition in the form of a project or performance task that would assess the students' learning in your unit. Finally, create a scoring guide (rubric) that includes key categories for assessment and the criteria that apply to each category.

Unit Preparation

Prepare an assessment plan for your unit. Start with a grid (or blueprint), listing your outcomes and how each one will be assessed. Outline your assessment materials, including at least one sample of a traditional test and a performance assessment with rubric. In most cases your performance assessment will parallel the culminating objective you created in the last chapter. It also may tap other outcomes. You should continue to develop and refine assessment materials as you develop your lessons.

Portfolio Activity

The assessment plan and materials created for your unit are good items to include in any portfolio. Be prepared to discuss why you made the assessment decisions you did and how your choices reflect valid and reliable assessments.

Select a sample of a student's work and remove any identifying information. Analyze the work sample and write a brief description of what you learned from the work and how it affected (or would affect) your teaching decisions. Be prepared to talk about using student work to plan instruction.

REFERENCES

Associated Press. (1998, April 23). Top teacher has students act out history. *Detroit Free Press.*

Bloom, B. S. (1984). The search for methods for group instruction as effective as one-to-one tutoring. *Educational Leadership, 41*(8), 4–18.

Bounds, C., & Harrison, L. (1997). In New South Wales: The Brain-Flex project. *Educational Leadership, 55*(1), 69–70.

Carroll, J. (1963). A model of school learning. *Teachers College Record, 64,* 723–733.

Feuer, M. J., & Fulton, K. (1993). The many faces of performance assessment. *Phi Delta Kappan, 74*(6), 478.

Langer, G., Colton, A., & Goff, L. (2003). *Collaborative analysis of student work: Improving teaching and learning.* Alexandria, VA: Association for Supervision and Curriculum Development.

Luft, J. (1997, February). Design your own rubric. *Science Scope, 20*(5), 25–27.

Marzano, R. (2000). *Transforming classroom grading.* Alexandria, VA: Association for Supervision and Curriculum Development.

Marzano, R., Pickering, D., & Pollack, J. (2001). *Classroom instruction that works.* Alexandria, VA: Association for Supervision and Curriculum Development.

Merriam-Webster's collegiate dictionary (10th ed.). (1993). Springfield, MA: Merriam-Webster, Incorporated.

Milson, A., & Downey, P. (2001, April). WebQuest: Using Internet resources for cooperative inquiry. *Social Education, 65*(3), 144–146.

Pate, E. P. (1993, November). Rubrics for authentic assessment. *Middle School Journal, 25* (2), 25–27.

Rothman, R. (1997). Measuring up: Standards, assessment, and school reform. San Francisco: Jossey-Bass.

Simmons, W., & Resnick, L. (1993). Assessment as the catalyst of school reform. *Educational Leadership, 50*(5), 14.

Sizer, T. (1992). *Horace's school: Redesigning the American high school.* Boston: Houghton-Mifflin.

Sizer, T. (1994). Better high schools: What would create them? *New England Journal of Public Policy, 10*(1), 29–35.

Smith, J. (1997, December). Alternative assessment and successful school reform. *Equity and Excellence in Education, 30*(2), 61–70.

Spalding, E. (2000, June). Performance assessment and the new standards project. *Phi Delta Kappan, 81*(10), 758–760.

Stiggins, R. J. (2000). *Student-involved classroom assessment.* Upper Saddle River, NJ: Prentice Hall, Incorporated.

Tomlinson, C. A. (2001). Grading for success. *Educational Leadership, 58*(6), 12–15.

Wiggins, G. (1996, January). Designing authentic assessments. *Educational Leadership, 153*(5), 18–25.

Wiggins, G. (1998). *Educative assessment: Designing assessment to inform and improve practice.* San Francisco, CA: Jossey-Bass.

Wiggins, G. & McTighe, J. (1999). *Understanding by design handbook.* Alexandria, VA: Association for Supervision and Curriculum Development.

Worthen, B. (1993). Critical issues that will determine the future of alternative assessment. *Phi Delta Kappan, 74*(6), 444–454.

Implementation: Hands-on Teaching

6

Reflective Lesson Design

CHAPTER OVERVIEW

Teachers frequently ask themselves, What experiences can I design that will allow students to develop the skills, understandings, and attitudes specified in my district's curriculum guide? The next chapters provide frameworks for planning lessons and activities. *Activities* are the elements of well-designed, well-organized *lessons* that help students attain specific learning objectives (outcomes). These lessons should not be isolated events. When organized into *units,* they lead systematically to the accomplishment of long-range goals (standards/benchmarks) that reflect useful skills and ideas for daily living.

The choice of lesson types and activities is based on the students' needs, the content and outcomes, the teacher's philosophy and style, and the context. A reflective teacher decision maker attempts to weave together a variety of types of activities when designing lessons and units.

In this chapter we introduce general principles for designing and analyzing a variety of teaching approaches. Then we provide a structure for lesson planning and two basic approaches to teaching: direct and inductive. The chapter closes with a discussion of formal and informal modes of instruction in secondary classrooms and differentiated instruction, instruction that flexes to meet many students' needs simultaneously.

SECTION 1. PRINCIPLES FOR DESIGNING LEARNING EXPERIENCES

Section 1 Objectives

At the end of this section, you will be able to:

1. describe elements of constructivist teaching, and
2. explain six principles for designing learning experiences and use them to analyze lessons.

Constructivist Learning Theory: Schooling for Democracy

Constructivism is one of the theories that strengthens the strategies for teaching and learning in this book. Recall that constructivism is the result of a synthesis of the work of Piaget, Vygotsky, Bruner and others. It implies that learning is an active process—individuals construct the schema that constitute their understanding, as opposed to passively absorbing information. The theory suggests that in-depth learning of concepts and ideas occurs only when a person has the opportunity to actively construct knowledge through experience, inquiry, and exploration. Most constructivist theorists also emphasize the important role that dialogue and cooperative learning play in the development of understanding (Perkins, 1999). General principles of instruction and learning derived from constructivist theory appear below. Consider how they mesh with what you know about the ways human beings learn.

1. Learning is not the result of development; learning *is* development. It requires invention and self-organization on the part of the learner. Thus, teachers need to allow learners to raise their own questions, generate their own hypotheses and models of possibilities, and test them for viability.

2. Disequilibrium facilitates learning. It occurs when individuals perceive something that does not fit easily into their existing cognitive structure. Remember from a previous chapter the child encountering a skunk. Initially the child labeled the skunk "cat." When the child recognized that events surrounding this animal were inconsistent with previous experiences with cats (producing disequilibrium), new learning was possible. Errors, such as the mislabeling of this animal, need to be perceived as a result of the learners' conceptions and, therefore, not minimized or avoided. Challenging, open-ended investigations allow learners to explore and generate possibilities, both affirming and contradictory. Contradictions, in particular, need to be explored and discussed as opportunities for learning.

3. Reflective abstraction is the driving force of learning. Human beings seek to make meaning, to organize and generalize across experiences in a representational form. That is, we label patterns in our experiences, usually through language. When a teacher allows reflection time through journal writing, discussion, or representation in other symbolic forms, this action may facilitate reflective abstraction.

4. Dialogue within a community generates further thinking. Human beings learn through interactions with others. For this type of learning to take place, a teacher needs to see the classroom as a community engaged in activity, reflection, and

what does an A, B, C, D look like?

conversation. The learners are responsible for defending, proving, justifying, and communicating their ideas to the classroom community.

5. Learning proceeds toward the development of structures. As learners struggle to make meaning, progressive structural shifts in perspective are constructed—in a sense, "big ideas." These big ideas are learner-constructed, central organizing principles that can be generalized across experiences and that often require the undoing of earlier conceptions. This process continues throughout development (Fosnot, 1996).

The role of the constructivist teacher emerges from an examination of these principles. The teacher must first seek to understand students' conceptions and then extend, refocus, or direct their thinking while preserving students' ownership of the learning process. Perhaps the greatest challenge for the teacher involves the preparation of learning experiences that include appropriate forms of **scaffolded instruction.** Just as scaffolding can be used to support and facilitate the construction of a building, scaffolded instruction helps students bridge the gap between current understanding and new meanings. It refers to the use of graphic organizers, graduated instruction, verbal hints and guiding questions, and some forms of direct instruction that guide the students while they maintain independence and move forward. Brooks and Brooks (1999a) describe the challenge that is implicit in constructivist teaching.

> As educators, we develop classroom practices and negotiate the curriculum to enhance the likelihood of student learning. But controlling what students learn is virtually impossible. The search for meaning takes a different route for each student. Even when educators structure classroom lessons and curriculums to ensure that all students learn the same concepts at the same time, each student still constructs his or her own unique meaning through his or her own cognitive processes. In other words, as educators we have great control over what we teach, but far less control over what students learn. (p. 21)

Still, principles emerge to define effective constructivist teaching. Brooks and Brooks (1999b) outline five overarching principles evident in constructivist classrooms. Consider how each principle ties to what you know about student learning and development.

- Teachers seek and value their students' points of view.
- Classroom activities challenge students' suppositions.
- Teachers pose problems of emerging relevance.
- Teachers build lessons around primary concepts and "big" ideas.
- Teachers assess student learning in the context of daily teaching.

These principles can be used to shape instruction in a variety of lesson types, enhancing their effectiveness in facilitating student learning.

Effective student learning is not the only rationale for constructivist teaching approaches. As in the title of their engaging book about exemplary instructional practices, Daniels and Bizar (1998) declare, "Methods matter." When a teacher plans a lesson, he or she chooses both a method of instruction and a process that sends implied messages about who holds information and how learning takes place. The means and ends cannot be separated, for they are related; each lesson teaches content, but it also teaches about learning. For example, imagine a classroom where teacher-directed learning predominates. If students spend the large majority of their time listening, they may learn that the only way to gain information is to listen to others. In such a classroom, students are likely to associate learning with passivity and obedience. They may have little opportunity to realize the power that comes through personal discovery or to envision themselves as individuals who can take initiative in the world. Of course, it would be foolish to suggest that teacher-directed learning is unacceptable. However, when used to the exclusion of other approaches, it can teach unintended lessons.

In order to wisely select instructional practices, it is helpful to look beyond the immediate classroom context to the skills and abilities students will need for participation in our society. Passivity and obedience, for example, are more appropriate citizen behaviors in an authoritarian society. In a democracy, skills such as locating, analyzing, and evaluating information; collaborative problem solving; and reasoned public decision making are of critical importance (Beyer, 1996; Glickman, 1998).

Advocates of democratic classroom practices speak of the value of providing students with the opportunity for choices and increased ownership over the learning process. As students progress through school, this ownership is particularly important—after all, in a few short years high school students will make critical decisions controlling their postsecondary school lives. Substantive conversation among students in which they challenge each other's thinking through debating multiple perspectives also fosters democratic sensibilities. As you consider the principles and teaching methods in the next chapters, think about how the teaching practices you select will affect both your students' understanding of content and their preparation to be citizens in a democracy.

Six Principles for Instruction

This section synthesizes much of what you have learned about students and authentic learning into a small number of learning principles.

You may recall that Ken Cowan was conducting a textbook-based lesson and his students were inattentive. He was frantically trying to determine how to change the lesson to engage and interest students. In addition to reviewing what he knows about his students' characteristics and best ways of learning, he could use the following principles: *cultural context, congruent continuous assessment, conceptual focus, higher level thinking, active processing,* and *variety* (see Figure 6.1). Teachers can use these principles to plan lessons and to understand how and why lessons were successful or less successful.

1. Cultural Context Principle:

Make sure classroom events and activities draw on the strengths of a variety of cultures and both males and females.

The discussion of this principle is divided into two sections: (1) race, class, and gender issues, and (2) social and political contexts. Treating people of various races, classes, and genders with equity differs somewhat from having an awareness of the political and social realities of the society in which our schools exist. Both are important for reflective teacher decision making.

1. Cultural Context Principle: Make sure classroom events and activities draw on the strengths of a variety of cultures and both males and females.
2. Congruent Continuous Assessment: (a) Match your objectives, activities, and assessment; and (b) discover what your students understand about a topic, plan activities to build on or reconstruct that knowledge, and assess them continuously.
3. Conceptual Focus Principle: Make sure the activities are focused on developing a few key concepts and generalizations—the structure of the information—rather than on memorizing a series of facts.
4. Higher Level Thinking Principle: Aim learning activities toward an authentic project or display that requires higher level thinking.
5. Active Processing Principle: Help students make new ideas more meaningful through direct experience and active involvement with the ideas in meaningful contexts.
6. Variety Principle: Appeal to the different styles, needs, and preferences of students.

Figure 6.1   Six Principles for Designing Learning Experiences

Race, Class, and Gender Equity

Recall the discussion of students' cultural backgrounds in Chapter 2. Every activity you undertake, every example you use, and all the written or visual materials you provide can influence students' appreciation for diversity. These activities also can impact students' self-esteem. If students see examples of people like themselves in the stories they hear, the history they learn, and the images they see, they are more likely to make ties to their own experiences. If the stories, history, and images are affirming, students develop more positive images of themselves. If, in addition, they hear positive anecdotes, learn important history, and see beautiful images of people very different from themselves, they learn to value diversity.

To understand issues of diversity, one must do more than merely teach about Crispus Atticus while studying the American Revolution or discussing Women's History during March. It involves an awareness of how the examples and images used in every aspect of the curriculum may inadvertently reinforce stereotypes. Are boys and girls portrayed in equal numbers? Do the examples using girls all entail cooking? Are cooperative groups organized so that roles rotate among boys and girls and majority and minority students? How do the stories we read or the accomplishments we praise reflect the ethnic diversity of the world around us?

Activities designed to teach about important contributors to our society should include males and females representing various cultural groups. They should not reinforce stereotypes, such as teaching about important Native Americans only as warriors and important African Americans only as entertainment or sport figures. Although subtle, these aspects of teaching can exert a powerful influence over your students' attitudes toward themselves and others. For example, think about scientists with whom students may become familiar in the traditional curriculum. In most cases, the group is not very diverse. However, if the teacher shares additional information about the contributions of women scientists and people of different races, students can better envision their potential in those roles (see, for example, information on women of NASA at NASA's website).

In every classroom, examples, materials, and treatment of students need to reflect a bottom-line respect for all classes, races, genders, and religious beliefs. This takes commitment and time. You may need greater cultural awareness yourself so you can communicate an appreciation of all cultures. Many teachers have been conditioned by society to hold certain prejudices. In this case it is better to acknowledge the fact and avoid inadvertently sending demeaning messages to students.

Teachers also need to learn about the cultures represented in the community. This may require visiting gathering places, attending community functions, and becoming active in the community in other ways. Join an organization or group that has many people from different cultural and economic backgrounds. Become well acquainted with someone who has had experiences very different from you in this society. Soon you can begin to see how each social group has its own strengths and challenges. Finally, once you are equipped with a better understanding of yourself and cultural diversity, examine the available teaching materials for obvious or hidden biases.

Cultural competence is the essence of respecting students and their backgrounds, which can provide a powerful model of democracy and fairness for students. In Lisa Delpit's (1995) view, this respect should not extend so far that the teacher fails to teach the student Standard English and other keys to success in the dominant culture. For example, a teacher can celebrate and highlight the expressiveness of Ebonics while at the same time teaching children the conventions of English as used in the workplace. When a teacher helps students understand and appreciate the cultural conventions appropriate to a given time and place, a valuable lesson is learned.

Social and Political Context

The second aspect of the cultural context principle refers to the power relationships among groups and their influence on your decisions as a teacher. Figure 6.2 shows concentric circles expanding outwards from the classroom—school, community, district, state, nation, and planet. Each of these social and political entities is important to consider in decision making. Sometimes you will find yourself selecting activities based on school factors, such as your school's collaboratively developed "school improvement" goals. For example, a planning team might set a goal to improve students' informational reading scores. All teachers would emphasize reading for information, especially in social studies, math, and science activities. The school improvement team might also plan to improve students' sense of identity with the school community. In response, a teacher might plan more activities that allow students to work in groups or might set up a weekly game that many of the lower achieving students could play successfully, raising their status among other children (Cohen, 1994). A service learning activity could be helpful, for example, in which students work together to create something new for the school: a nature trail, a school store, or a literary magazine.

Other factors that may influence the choice of activities include the size of the school, the grade levels served, and the physical school facility. Some schools are designed for open-space learning, reflecting a progressive orientation. In such schools,

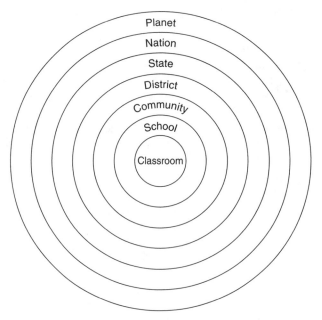

Figure 6.2 Influences on Teacher Decision Making
From *Teaching as Decision Making: Successful Practices for the Elementary Teacher* (3rd Ed.) (p. 157), by
A. J. Starko, et al., 2003, Upper Saddle River, NJ: Merrill/Prentice Hall. Copyright 2003 by Pearson Education,
Inc. Reprinted with permission.

classes can be easily combined for joint activities, which offers greater flexibility for
team teaching and sharing of resources.

School district policies and politics also influence what occurs in your classroom.
Most teachers work for a school system that is governed by a school board, a group of
elected citizens or appointed officials. Members of the board reflect the attitudes, values, and philosophy of the community that the schools serve. Thus board members exercise an important influence on school programs, policies, regulations, and
curriculum. Although school board members rarely spend large amounts of time examining the actual teaching activities used, they do have a vested interest in what happens in classrooms. As representatives of the community, they want to be sure that
students are learning appropriate skills and attitudes.

Imagine yourself teaching in an ethnically diverse community that has experienced
conflict between the Latino and Anglo cultures. Perhaps the school board has expressed
concern over this issue and has made conflict resolution a goal for the year. Therefore,
you would strive to select classroom activities that would enable students to deal with
conflict and learn how to resolve it. For instance, when deciding how to teach about representative government, you might have teams of students work together to solve a
problem. You would teach, model, and give feedback on the social skills needed for students to work together constructively. This type of activity would better meet the dis-

trict goal than a lecture that offers little opportunity for interaction or conflict resolution. To apply the principle further, you might decide how attention to differing cultures would apply to this goal.

State and national policies also influence what happens in the classroom. A few of the larger factors that need to be considered by teachers on a daily basis include state curriculum frameworks, testing programs, statewide school improvement initiatives, and funding formulas.

In the cultural context principle, classrooms do not exist in a vacuum. Teachers form an important socializing function in this society. The attitudes they develop and model will influence the actions of future generations toward the opposite sex, various races, and other cultural and economic groups. Chapter 10 contains more information about working with diverse students.

2. Congruent Continuous Assessment:

(a) Match your objectives, activities, and assessment; and (b) discover what your students understand about a topic, plan activities to build on or reconstruct that knowledge, and assess them continuously.

Congruence (Alignment)

Congruence refers to the crucial match—or alignment—among standards, lesson objectives, activities, and assessment procedures. See Figure 6.3 for a visual illustration of this concept. The following example may help clarify this concept.

One high school chemistry teacher started every class with a story about football. As the students continued to ask questions, he would continue talking—until the bell rang—about his experiences as a football star. No congruence existed between his chemistry objectives and his football stories. Even worse, he used tests from the teacher's manual, even though he had spent only a fraction of class time presenting content covered by the test. His teaching method was clearly an infraction of the congruence principle.

Simply put, when you select activities, make sure they lead to your objectives. Be certain that tests and projects assess the skills and ideas you have developed through learning activities (Stiggins, 1994; Wiggins, 1999). For instance, if you want students to be able to solve word problems of a certain type, they will need adequate demonstration and practice activities on solving those word problems. When you assess your students'

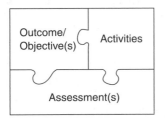

Figure 6.3 Congruence in Planning
From *Teaching as Decision Making: Successful Practices for the Elementary Teacher* (3rd Ed.) (p. 158), by A. J. Starko, et al., 2003, Upper Saddle River, NJ: Merrill/Prentice Hall. Copyright 2003 by Pearson Education, Inc. Reprinted with permission.

learning, your test should include new word problems of the same type. You may be reminded of the idea of content validity (see Chapter 5) as you read about congruence.

An important aspect of congruence is to match the activities with the level and type of learning stated in the objective(s). If you want students to be able to recite geometry formulas, one set of activities may be appropriate (drill with flash cards, use of manipulative materials to illustrate formulas, or group oral games). If your objective is that students be able to solve real-life problems using geometry, your activities need to include small-group problem solving, demonstration of thinking strategies (e.g., by explaining your thinking as you solve a problem on the board), or an inquiry task in which students discover how to calculate the volume of air in the gymnasium. Thus, lower level and higher level objectives may require different types of activities.

Your choice of activities will depend on whether the objective is affective, psychomotor, or cognitive. Affective outcomes usually take a longer time to develop and are often best taught through direct experience; for example, role-playing or group work. Imagine that as an objective, you want students to be able to disagree in a courteous way. You might discuss and demonstrate specific words and actions you desire and negative words and actions you want to discourage. You could have two students act out both types of behavior, and then discuss the reactions with the class. Next, you could observe students during classroom group work and give feedback on their treatment of their classmates. This affective objective may require several weeks or months for students to achieve.

A second important aspect of congruence is to match the assessment or evaluation with the objective(s) (Wiggins & McTighe, 1999). Congruence can be a bit tricky with higher level objectives. For example, to compare and contrast the characteristics of a mammal and a reptile, you could discuss in class the similarities and differences between a cat and a snake. On the test, however, if you included a question about a cat and a snake, you would be testing only memory of a prior lesson. To see whether students can engage in higher level thinking, test them with new situations. In this case, students would be asked to compare a mammal and a reptile not previously discussed in class, perhaps a dog and a lizard, or they could create an imaginary mammal or reptile with the correct characteristics. This task would require students to apply their understanding to a situation not previously encountered.

In addition, make sure that, if you are teaching to a higher level objective, class activities provide opportunities to practice functioning at those higher levels of learning. Too often, teachers teach information and skills at the lower cognitive levels and then expect students to be able to apply the knowledge at higher levels on an assessment, without ever having been asked to do so before.

One way to provide congruent activities is to tell students repeatedly the instructional objective(s) and remind them periodically of how they will be assessed. This reminds you and the students of where the lessons are heading and how the classroom activities relate to the objectives. As an example, one excellent teacher kept showing his students the final project on water quality from the previous year's class. This kept the current students motivated and focused on the outcome while they were learning the content and skills required for the project.

CHECK YOUR UNDERSTANDING

Mrs. Zarett is teaching limericks, and her objective is for students to be able to write a limerick. She presents examples and describes the characteristics of a limerick. For practice, students describe the characteristics and identify them in examples. Then, to evaluate their learning, Mrs. Zarett asks students to write a limerick. Determine whether the principle of congruence has been followed by comparing the objective with the activities and evaluation.

Answer: The assessment was at the higher level (synthesis), while the activities took the students only to the lower levels of comprehension (understanding). This mismatch is a lack of congruence. Mrs. Zarett should have provided modeling and practice on writing limericks before asking the students to do so.

You may ask, What is the purpose of "and assess them continuously" in this principle? You will need to know how well the students are doing in achieving desired learning objectives, whether it is before you begin to teach, during your teaching, or after. You can examine students' work, ask them to "think aloud," have students self-assess, and observe their work in groups—all valuable sources of informal "assessment" information. Without such assessments, students' developing understandings (or misunderstandings) will be a mystery and you will lose a crucial source of information for teacher decision making (Stiggins, 2000).

Continuous Assessment

Often teachers begin a lesson with a preassessment activity that shows the prior knowledge, experiences, or feelings students have about the topic in the lessons to come. For example, one teacher wanted students to conduct inquiries into local water quality. To find out about their prior experience with the topic, she had them write down everything that came to mind about how water is made safe for cooking or swimming. The teacher read the responses, which helped her find a few students with a deep interest in the subject and others who had never played in a stream or considered the cleanliness of water. She then could ask the students with more background knowledge to share their experiences and build a knowledge base for the others.

The teacher also wanted to know if students had enough math knowledge to construct pie charts that would illustrate the findings of their investigations. To preassess this skill, she gave them a set of data and had them construct a pie chart. From their results she was able to see who needed explicit teaching on this skill before reaching that part of the project.

Preassessing students' knowledge and attitudes about a topic or skill allows you to determine what existing knowledge might be useful in helping students understand the new ideas. Linking new information to prior knowledge is an important key to learning. Recall the discussion of constructivism in Chapter 2. If you had never studied Piaget, that idea would have been difficult to grasp; but because you had prior knowledge of Piaget's ideas about assimilation and accommodation, it was probably easier to understand.

Teachers have to present information in a way that is easily understood by students. One very effective way to do this is to "hook" the new idea to something the students already know. For example, when teaching about fractions and decimals, use a pizza cut into ten slices. Let the students see that fractions and decimals are not mysterious. In fact, they will realize that they have been dealing with fractions at the dinner table for years!

Many teachers assume children have no knowledge of something because it has not been formally taught to them, such as the topic of historical accuracy. Although students may not have had any lessons in school on how history is written, they have been around history, stories, and the news media their entire lives. They also have learned the concept of history from family discussions and activities. It would make sense for the teacher to preassess students to learn what conceptions about history, stories, and the news students bring to the classroom. The teacher can build on helpful ideas (e.g., "History is a record of events") and reconstruct misconceptions ("There is only one interpretation of an event—the true one") through hands-on, mindful experiences with various accounts of the same event told from different perspectives.

The idea of *misconceptions* is an important aspect of constructivist teaching. Recall our discussion on misconceptions in Chapter 2. For example, most students (and many adults!) believe that plants gain their nutrition solely from plant food, just like humans do. In their minds an early search for meaning has constructed an explanation that seemed very reasonable. This entrenched belief, though, interferes with student learning about photosynthesis. Such early constructions of meaning (misconceptions) are very powerful and must be identified and challenged in order to change them. Teachers need to learn about such prior conceptions and then design experiences that eliminate students' misconceptions. In the photosynthesis example, students could be asked to find out what would happen if plants received plenty of plant food, but no light. They would be pressed to explain the results using their old ideas. Such discrepant events are very powerful in helping students reconstruct misconceptions. For a teacher to lecture on new information without acknowledging how students have created meaning is not likely to produce the kind of learning that stays with students.

3. Conceptual Focus Principle:

Make sure the activities are focused on developing a few key concepts and generalizations— the structure of the information—rather than on memorizing a series of facts.

This principle relates to the discussion of concepts and generalizations in Chapter 3. Concepts allow us to classify ideas and objects we have never seen before and allow us to transfer our learning. Consider a unit on Colonial America. Many units devote a large percentage of the time to memorizing key people, dates, and events. If these are merely treated as isolated facts, little transferable learning occurs.

On the other hand, the unit could be organized around the concept of "symbols" instead of around isolated facts. Students could discuss what symbols are and how they are chosen. They might discover that many symbols of past and present life were selected because they represent the colonial era or played an important part in colonial history. Further, students might wonder if other symbols are chosen in similar ways.

They might learn that every group—nation, state, or ethnic—has specific symbols of its own culture. This is a powerful idea that will transfer to many settings and will aid students in understanding the world around them.

It is important for you to clarify for yourself the main ideas before beginning to teach a topic. As there simply is not enough time to teach thoroughly everything in a given textbook or unit, you must sift out what is crucial. One suggestion is to talk to the curriculum coordinator in your district about the district outcomes (standards or benchmarks). Then you can select the ideas and skills that relate most directly to the district grade-level and long-term goals. Other teachers are also a valuable source of information on curriculum. Try to become as knowledgeable as possible about the topics of importance at your grade level and subject areas. As you develop your own deeper understanding of the content, it is easier to choose the most powerful ideas.

Once you have identified the key concepts and generalizations (as discussed in Chapter 3), you will want to design instruction so the conceptual structure of the content is clear to students. Since the brain naturally wants to organize information into meaningful networks, or schemata, the teacher can capitalize on this inclination by helping students see the patterns and structure in new information (Wolfe, 2001).

Many teachers use an overhead projector, computer display, chalkboard, or poster to show the organization of information as they explain it. When you decide how to display the material, you may find that your learning style does not match your learners' styles. You may prefer lists and outlines, but some of your students may need to see the information displayed spatially or in pictures. A variety of visual tools—from brainstorming maps to sorting trees—can help students visualize the structure of the information. See Hyerle (1996) for a good assortment of examples. Nonlinguistic representations (e.g., drawings, models, or diagrams), as used by the teacher and as created by students, are powerful tools for enhancing memory (Marzano, Pickering, & Pollock, 2001). The outline of the Zimbabwe unit found in Appendix A shows one way to organize that information. Figure 3.5 presents it as abstract and spatial. Visual aids such as concept maps, graphic organizers, and webbing also help show the "big picture" and the interconnections among ideas.

Students can have trouble making sense of information when it is unclear how one piece relates to another. They may like to see the big picture first and then fit the details in later. Others cannot understand the big picture until they have understood all the details. You will have both types of learners in your classes. Therefore, show the structure before, during, and after instruction so that all learning preferences are met. In any case, be sure to focus students' attention on the structure and organization often during presentation of information. Statements such as these help students focus on the relevant information: "This next point relates to the one we just discussed in this way. . ." or "We've been talking about mammals. Now look up here and see how our next topic, reptiles, relates to . . ."

Not all information lends itself to easy organization. For example, when there are many disparate facts to be memorized (e.g., the times tables), it may be hard to find any meaningful way of categorizing them. In such cases, you may wish to use a **mnemonic device,** a memory aid. You have probably used such devices at one time or another, especially when cramming for a test. HOMES is a mnemonic device used to remember the names of the Great Lakes: Huron, Ontario, Michigan, Erie, and Superior. Other mnemonic devices include a story or sentence using the first word or letter of items in a list (e.g., "Every Good Boy Does Fine" for the lines on the treble clef) or an image for each item on the list.

 ## REFLECTING ON THE IDEAS

Imagine you are creating a checklist, to use as you create lesson plans, that will include important ideas in the first three principles for designing learning experiences. What questions would you list?

4. Higher Level Thinking Principle:

Aim learning activities toward an authentic project or display that requires higher level thinking.

When designing learning activities, it is important to foresee a culminating experience that will allow students to create something original with their knowledge. Developing a product for a real audience that illustrates their learning is the essence of authentic learning.

Such activities allow students to develop the kind of higher level thinking that will be required of citizens in the 21st century. It includes the processes of problem solving and decision making in real or simulated situations. In short, higher level thinking requires students to use information rather than merely recall it. Students may be asked to compare one concept or generalization with another; to use a skill in a new situation; to analyze the causes, effects, motivations, or other aspects of an event; to make judgments; to apply logic; or to combine information and prior experience in new and creative ways.

This type of learning is in marked contrast to rote learning or memorization of facts that are not used in a meaningful way. Lower level learning—recalling and understanding basic facts, concepts, or generalizations—is still important, but it is only one step in a larger process. Sound higher level thinking is built on a solid foundation of understanding. A teacher first needs to find out students' understanding of an area and then must provide the guidance and encouragement they need to build toward higher level tasks.

In selecting learning activities, note that some have greater potential for enhancing higher level thinking than others. Tasks that are especially good for this purpose are role-playing, simulations, and assignments that require students to relate a number of generalizations to one another in a debate or other creative display. Authentic student projects that include performances and problem solving are also excellent vehicles for developing thinking skills.

5. Active Processing Principle:

Help students make new ideas more meaningful through direct experience and active involvement with the ideas in meaningful contexts.

Information is more easily stored and recalled when it is embedded in a rich network of meaning created through direct experience with the ideas, concepts, and generalizations to be learned. The idea of active processing is fairly simple: If teachers can engage students' minds in thinking about, using, applying, and reflecting upon new ideas or skills, the learning will be deeper and more permanent. When giving an explanation, a teacher can pause after each one or two main ideas and ask students to answer a question, write a brief summary, or discuss one of the ideas with their partner. These activities require students to work with the ideas in their short-term memories so the new ideas can become integrated into the structures of meaning in long-term memory.

For example, one objective in the Zimbabwe unit was for students to be able to contrast an African folktale with a Joseph Conrad novel. Rather than just lecture or assign a worksheet on the topic, the teacher could have students form literary criticism groups. In the groups, roles would be assigned requiring each student to analyze a particular aspect of the story and the novel. These people would combine their information to prepare an analytical criticism for presentation to the class. Such direct experience and active involvement promote a significantly deeper understanding of the topic than a teacher-centered lecture with follow-up worksheets.

We have discussed the "active processing" part of this principle. What is meant by "direct experience . . . in meaningful contexts"? Imagine Ken Cowan determining different ways to teach his students about the lifestyles in ancient Zimbabwe. He considers the following ideas: using a worksheet, demonstrating some of the customs, showing a movie or video, taking a virtual tour via a museum website, having students analyze period artwork, creating a classroom simulation including the meeting of cultural groups, and role-playing a talk-show interview with students as expert historians. Analyze which activities seem to be the most meaningful in terms of actual real-life applicability. The last two occur in a meaningful context where students can directly experience the ideas being learned. The other activities can teach important information, but to exclude the more authentic ones would greatly curtail meaningful learning.

The cone of experience (Dale, 1969) in Figure 6.4 is a useful way to portray this continuum. From the bottom to the top are concrete, more meaningful contexts for

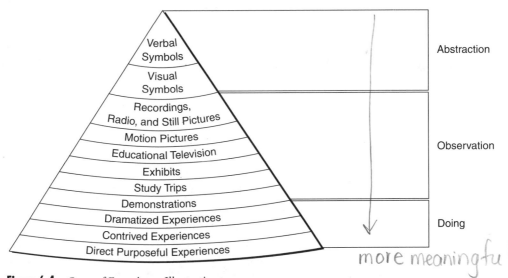

Figure 6.4 Cone of Experience Illustration
From *Audio-Visual Methods in Teaching, Third Edition*, by E. Dale, © 1969. Reprinted with permission of Wadsworth, an imprint of the Wadsworth Group, a division of Thomson Learning.

learning to abstract, less meaningful contexts. As you consider each level, recall what you know about Piaget's theory of cognitive development: your students are moving slowly from concrete to more abstract thinking (formal operations). Also recall what you learned about multiple intelligences theory and learning styles.

Doing

Direct purposeful experiences involve students in activities in the world outside the classroom and outside school. Examples include participating in community cleanup projects, establishing a working banking system in the school, managing and staffing a school store, and assuming the duties of tutor in a kindergarten class. Kavolik (1994) referred to this level as "being there."

Contrived experiences approximate real-life situations. They are edited versions of reality. For example, chemistry students may be introduced to certain chemical reactions by simulating the results on a computer. In this case the simulated situation is preferred over the real-life one because of safety concerns. In other cases simulation may be used because of a need for simplification, for example, using a model of the solar system—physical or virtual—to illustrate the orbits and rotation of the plants.

Dramatized experiences include role-playing and dramatic re-creations of actual or fictional events, perhaps of scenes from history or literature. Kavolik (1994) referred to these activities as "immersion or simulation."

Observation

Demonstrations, study trips, virtual trips via the web, exhibits, educational television, motion pictures, recordings, radio, and *still pictures* all represent gradations from more concrete to more abstract learning activities. Remember, when the experience is more hands-on, the learning is better (Kavolik, 1994; Wolfe, 2001).

Abstraction

The layer *visual symbols* includes activities where students work with maps, games, and other kinds of diagrams. The top layer, *verbal symbols,* refers to activities such as writing, speaking, and reading, in which students work with symbols (e.g., words and numbers) that do not look like the objects they represent. That is, the symbols, in and of themselves, do not provide any visual clue to assist in meaning and thus are abstract concepts.

The cone of experience teaches us that teachers should think about whether they are providing enough "learning by doing" activities. In most classrooms, too many abstract reading, writing, and listening activities and too few direct-experience activities are available. Many students are not developmentally ready to learn from the more abstract activities without significant preparation, and they may need more time with concrete experiences.

One goal of schooling is to allow students to function at the higher, more abstract levels. Middle school students need a large proportion of concrete activities, and high school students need to be gradually weaned away from a predominance of concrete experiences. Even among older students, however, some concepts are best introduced through concrete, real-life activities.

CHECK YOUR UNDERSTANDING

Assume you are teaching students about bird migration. Label the following activities according to the type of learning: *D* for *doing*, *O* for *observation*, or *A* for *abstraction*.

_____ 1. Teacher lecturing from a textbook on migration
_____ 2. Field trip to a bird sanctuary, including an interview with a sanctuary guide
_____ 3. Reading and then completing a workbook exercise on the topic
_____ 4. Seeing a filmstrip about bird migration
_____ 5. Groups of students role-playing movements of birds on a map

Did you label items 2 and 5 as doing, 4 as observation, and 1 and 3 as abstraction?

6. Variety Principle:

Appeal to the different styles, needs, and preferences of students.

Students do not all learn in the same way, and teachers need to acknowledge this in planning and teaching. Students must attend to information in order to learn it, but most adolescents and preadolescents have trouble attending to one topic for any length of time. In light of these facts, teachers can plan a variety of activities that will appeal to learners' multiple learning styles, preferences, and intelligences. In addition to enhancing learning, such variety also holds students' attention throughout the lesson (Wolfe, 2001).

In preparing his lesson on Zimbabwe, Ken Cowan might start the day with students brainstorming in small groups all the "things" they believe about ancient civilizations and how Africans fit into those events. Then Ken might focus student attention on the outcome of the lesson—their projects showing different aspects of life in Zimbabwe using multimedia presentations. He might have students research Zimbabwe's location on current and older maps. The students could structure the information by grouping different eras of history and corresponding geographic maps. Finally, students could work in groups to draw maps of Zimbabwe and create rap or other songs that illustrate and describe the changes in the area over time.

With this lesson structure, Ken would use visual, auditory, and kinesthetic learning modes. He also would appeal to musical intelligence. The organization of his activities may have appealed to sequential learners, while those who prefer a more random style would probably feel comfortable with the brainstorming. By having students work in groups and alone, Ken would have allowed for different learning preferences. Because the lesson included a variety of activities that appealed to different learning styles and needs, more students would be likely to achieve success. The guideline to follow is, Have a good deal of variety in your lessons, not only to maintain students' attention but also to "hook into" students' particular styles.

One aspect of this principle deserves greater attention. **Modeling,** which is a variation on appealing to the visual learner, means to show, demonstrate, or illustrate something as you explain it. Most educators suggest that explanations, stories, or other verbal lessons be illustrated visually. Teachers can use several techniques. One teacher put on a costume each Friday to illustrate a different idea the class had been studying. In a unit on westward expansion, for instance, she dressed up as a pioneer one Friday and as an explorer on another. You can also simply draw pictures on the board to illustrate how sod huts were built, or fill a tank with water to show how different weights and densities of materials float and sink. Students can role-play the numbers in a problem to illustrate the process to balance an equation. Red chalk could be used to highlight adjectives in a story on the board.

In modeling it is also important to provide an example of an assignment or project so students can see the specific qualities being sought in the product. Some experts (e.g., Stiggins, 1994) call this a target paper. Be sure to save (or download from the web) examples of the type of work you hope to receive from students. Write notes on these examples to show why they are strong or weak. Modeling can help you reach the variety of learners in your class.

You can add variety to your lessons in many ways. Talk to other teachers, read teacher magazines, and be creative. Try new approaches and remember that *humor, novelty,* and *emotion* are excellent ways of providing variety. Dare to be a little outrageous occasionally—it is rewarding when you finally see a hard-to-reach student "tune in."

 ## REFLECTING ON THE IDEAS

Complete the list of questions you began in the last activity by writing prompts or thought questions for the remaining three principles. As you prepare lesson and unit plans, refer to your list of questions to see if you are using the planning principles to guide you.

Practice Activity A

Remembering the Learning Principles

Practice Point

First, review the six principles of learning and make notes for yourself. Then, create a mnemonic device or memory aid that will help you remember the six principles. Practice saying them from memory until you think they are in your long-term memory. Write or draw your mnemonic device on a card, and keep it with you when you plan lessons and assignments.

Practice Activity B

Applying the Learning Principles

Use the six principles of learning to analyze the actions taken in the scenario that follows. In the right-hand margin, write the name of the principle that is illustrated by the activity described in the scenario. Be ready to explain why this principle aids learning. You also can use the principles to analyze real-life classroom observations and your own teaching.

> Mr. Jones is working with a group of eleventh graders on a local government unit. He hopes that, as one objective of his lessons, students will be able to create a news report based on interviews with two public officials (mayor, city clerk, comptroller, or city council member).
>
> First, Mr. Jones focuses students on the lesson by asking them to make a list of what they know about the impact of local government in their everyday lives. After a short discussion of the importance of government, he then describes the objectives and presents the project to the students. Next, he shows a diagram of the structure of local government and a list of city workers. To convey information about each job, he has small groups of students research the responsibilities of each official, and then he assigns these "experts" to new teams so they can teach each other about the jobs. He appoints a coach for each team and has them quiz the other team members on descriptions of workers' roles. Then the students play a game in which teams answer questions about the local government officials. Next, students complete a brief worksheet so he can see how much they have learned.
>
> To move to the higher level of applying the information, Mr. Jones has each student write down two questions to ask one of the officials. Together the class chooses two officials to invite to their class for group interviews. Interview techniques are studied, and students practice in pairs. They also are given an outline for recording their findings, and they analyze examples of interviews in the news. After the interviews are conducted, students work in small groups to prepare reports for the school paper.

Practice Point

Your responses may have included some of the following observations:

- Mr. Jones has selected an authentic activity as his outcome. This represents the Active Processing Principle and its "meaningful context" aspect. Students will be active as they research their jobs and teach their peers. The interview with a real community official is also meaningful and rich.
- The Cultural Context Principle is illustrated as the lesson represents an awareness of the surrounding social and political realities.
- The Conceptual Focus Principle is evident in the diagram of the structure of local government.
- The Congruent Continuous Assessment Principle is seen in the alignment among the objective, activities, and assessment. Making a list about local government and the quiz are both examples of continuous assessment.
- The Higher-Level Thinking Principle is involved in designing the questions, analyzing the responses, and writing the news reports.
- Finally, the Variety Principle is apparent when students write, read, listen, create, work alone and together, and engage in more concrete and abstract tasks.

SECTION 2. TEACHING APPROACHES AND LESSON PLANNING

Section 2 Objectives

After you have completed this section, you will be able to:

1. describe two categories of instructional approaches;
2. describe a format for lesson planning;
3. explain the difference between formal and informal instruction; and
4. describe differentiated instruction and why it is important.

Assume that you are about to plan a lesson to fit into Ken Cowan's Zimbabwe unit. You must select learning activities to lead students from where they are to where you expect them to be, as stated in your outcomes. Remember that there is no single activity or lesson type that will work with all objectives, classroom environments, and students. Teaching involves planning, day-by-day experimentation, and responsive adjustments as you discover what works best for you and your students. Consequently, an effective teacher must employ a wide repertoire of skills, methods, and learning activities in the classroom. This section will provide a simple yet powerful lesson format with the flexibility and creativity you need to provide rich learning experiences for your students.

Plan lessons carefully, keeping your students, goals, and objectives clearly in mind. Use what you can glean from research, teaching principles, experience, and intuition, while also considering classroom conditions and surrounding context. After you teach the lesson, take a few minutes to reflect on it, noting what went well and what did not. Use the learning principles in these chapters and other resources to try to determine why students did or did not achieve the objective. Note changes that might improve the lesson; share your thoughts with colleagues and ask for their suggestions. Use your notes to redesign the lesson and test it with a different class, then revise it again as needed. This approach will help keep your teaching fresh and provide the most positive learning results (Garrison, 1997).

Approaches to Teaching

This chapter will preview several approaches to teaching. If you like to see the big picture first, proceed. If you are a more concrete learner, you may wish to come back to this section after reading about the various approaches in the next two chapters.

 ## REFLECTING ON THE IDEAS

To further understand the first two types of lessons, examine the following two teaching episodes involving a seventh-grade classroom.

Example 1

TEACHER: Class, I have written the definition of *honesty* on the board. It is freedom from fraud and deception. Raise your hand if you know what *fraud* is. (Wait) Janet?

JANET: Miss Morrison, I think it means cheating to get something you want from someone else.

TEACHER: Good! Now, everyone, think: What does *deception* mean? (Wait) Larry?

LARRY: It means using tricks or not telling the truth.

TEACHER: That's right. Now that we have looked at the definition and agreed that honesty requires that you tell the truth and don't cheat or use trickery to get what you want, I would like you to examine these three newspaper stories that I have gathered. Be ready to tell me if the person identified in each story is being honest. Later, we'll apply this idea in your courtroom plays.

Example 2

TEACHER: Class, we are going to examine a very important aspect of people. Instead of telling you what it is, I would like you all to examine three newspaper stories that I have gathered and use your thinking skills to find what the stories have in common. Also, be ready to tell me what the person identified in each story is like. (Students look at the stories provided.)

TEACHER: Cross your arms when you have an idea of what the three stories have in common. (Wait) Larry?

LARRY: The people in each story tell the truth even though they could make more money or be thought of as more important if they lied. In one story, a company wanted to pay a thousand dollars for a poem written by this man's great-grandfather so they could use it on a greeting card. They thought it had been written by the man. He told the company the truth even though the company could then use the poem without paying anything for it. In the second story, this woman returned a purse with over five thousand dollars in it. In the third story, a woman told her daughter that the daughter had been adopted, although the mother could have kept it a secret. They were all honest!

TEACHER: Excellent, Larry! Now, everyone jot on your paper your ideas about what it means to be honest. (Wait) Mary?

MARY: It means to tell the truth, even when the truth hurts!

TEACHER: That's an excellent answer, Mary. That is one of the lessons to be learned from the story you have been reading this week. Now let's look at three different news articles and see if the people involved in them are being honest.

What are the key differences you notice between the two episodes? Which lesson do you think is better? Why? How might you label each?

The first lesson is a **direct lesson.** When the lesson begins, the teacher tells students the concept or generalization to be learned and leads them through most of the activities. The second episode is **inductive** because students discover the concept through finding patterns.

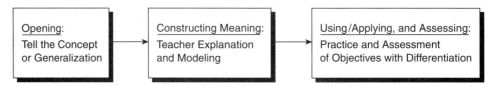

Figure 6.5 A Direct (Deductive) Lesson
From *Teaching as Decision Making: Successful Practices for the Elementary Teacher* (3rd Ed.) (p. 170), by
A. J. Starko, et al., 2003, Upper Saddle River, NJ: Merrill/Prentice Hall. Copyright 2003 by Pearson Education,
Inc. Reprinted with permission.

A direct lesson is also referred to as *deductive.* Direct lessons are deductive because
the teacher typically states the instructional objective(s), presents the material to be
learned with examples and nonexamples, provides practice, and assesses students'
learning. For instance, assume that the English teacher on Ken Cowan's team wants to
teach students about the concept "figurative language" before having them write their
stories about Great Zimbabwe in the 14th century. If she decided to use a direct approach, she would tell them the objective, present the definition and characteristics of
figurative language, show students examples and nonexamples, engage them in practice
exercises, give them feedback and more practice, and then assess them. These activities
would be modified (differentiated) for specific student needs. Figure 6.5 illustrates the
structure of the direct (deductive) lesson.

In contrast to a direct lesson, an **inductive lesson** begins with exploratory activities
and leads students to discover a concept or generalization. For the preceding topic,
Ken's colleague might begin by giving students several passages with and without figurative language. She would ask them to select the passages that give them the most vivid
image of the idea being presented. Next, she would ask them to identify the phrases that
made the passages so interesting and try to figure out their common characteristics.
Only then would she label these phrases as examples of figurative language, define the
term, and describe its essential attributes. As with the deductive lesson, the final step
would be to provide practice exercises and then to assess students' accomplishment of
the objective. Again, activities would be adapted for specific student needs. You may
have noted that inductive lessons require the students to do more of the thinking, at
least in the beginning of the lesson—an added bonus of inductive lessons. Figure 6.6 illustrates the structure of an inductive lesson.

These approaches can serve as a starter kit for your first year of teaching, although
they are not the only approaches to teaching. Weil, Calhoun, and Joyce (1999) provide
an excellent presentation of several other models of teaching. Many approaches can be
explored, especially in the area of student-directed learning (Darling, 1994; Johnson,
1999; Maushak, Wigans, & Bender, 1999).

The two lesson categories are not necessarily kept separate in daily teaching; they
are often combined in a particular lesson or unit. For example, a lesson might have an
inductive introduction and a direct section that builds understanding, or vice versa. As
you observe and practice teaching, you will be able to make decisions about the various
types of lesson categories and to mix and match them yourself.

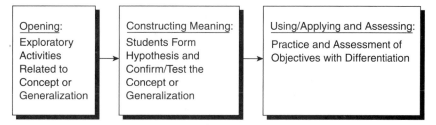

Figure 6.6 An Inductive Lesson

From *Teaching as Decision Making: Successful Practices for the Elementary Teacher* (3rd Ed.) (p. 171), by A. J. Starko, et al., 2003, Upper Saddle River, NJ: Merrill/Prentice Hall. Copyright 2003 by Pearson Education, Inc. Reprinted with permission.

CHECK YOUR UNDERSTANDING

Without reviewing the text on the two lesson categories, explain their definitions and differences to a classmate. See if you agree on the critical attributes of each lesson type.

A Lesson-Planning Framework

A basic framework is necessary to structure lessons. When discussing lesson planning, however, it is helpful to note the distinction between a lesson plan and a lesson design. A **lesson plan** describes the activities for one day of instruction. A complete **lesson design** includes all the activities needed to help students achieve mastery of one or more objectives. It will include your plans for differentiation and some assessments of how students are progressing. A lesson design may span one or more days.

When planning for a week of teaching, it is most helpful to think of a lesson design rather than a lesson plan. A lesson is rarely a one-day event to be performed and then to be left, with no further work on that topic. Even if you think you have taught something well on a particular day, you should definitely plan to revisit the same topic or skill on another day. One-time lessons have little lasting power.

A series of lessons may not necessarily all be in the same content area; they may form the puzzle pieces of an interdisciplinary unit, like the Zimbabwe unit Ken Cowan's team has planned. In any case, the lessons will build upon one another and culminate in an authentic activity that illustrates much of what students have learned. Figure 6.7 shows how activities are combined to form lessons and units. The lessons are all congruent with the central themes and objectives of the unit. They are modified (differentiated) as needed. The learning is then demonstrated through the authentic culminating project(s) and other assessments.

A simple but powerful frame for lesson design can accommodate most approaches to teaching. It organizes lessons into five phases: *opening, constructing meaning, using* and *applying, assessing learning,* and *differentiation.* Each of these is summarized in Figure 6.8 and discussed later.

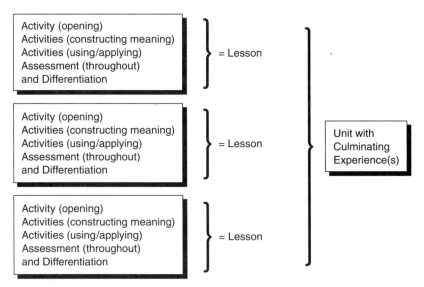

Figure 6.7   Activities, Lessons, and Units

From *Teaching as Decision Making: Successful Practices for the Elementary Teacher* (3rd Ed.) (p. 172), by
A. J. Starko, et al., 2003, Upper Saddle River, NJ: Merrill/Prentice Hall. Copyright 2003 by Pearson Education,
Inc. Reprinted with permission.

Opening

The beginning of any lesson should serve to *focus students' interest and attention* on
the topic, for example by showing a puzzling event; having students discuss their personal experiences; asking a provocative question; or sharing a story, popular song, or
poem.

The opening is also a time to access students' *prior knowledge* or skills that may be
relevant to the lesson. For example, if students will need to use the concept of equality
for the poem they will write, the opening should require them to recall what they know
about equality. Note that having students review prior concepts (rather than you reviewing them) also gives you valuable preassessment information about who may need
reteaching in that area. Another reason to have students access prior experiences, feelings, or knowledge relates to how students construct meaning through experience. Recall how new information is retained when it is seen as connected to information in
one's mind. Teachers can create this readiness for learning new concepts by activating
students' prior knowledge.

The opening can help students understand the *objectives* of the lesson and how they
will be *assessed* on the knowledge or skills. Finally motivate students by telling them the
purpose of the lesson—why it is important, how it will be used in their personal or work
lives, and how they will apply the knowledge in their authentic culminating projects.

OPENING: Readiness, preassessment, activate prior knowledge and experience, focus attention, invite inquiry/puzzlement, clarify culminating authentic projects/assessments, state objectives and purpose.
CONSTRUCTING MEANING: Students receive, gather, interpret, share, and digest: information, data, problems, ideas, events.
USING/APPLYING: Students apply new learning in problems, experiments, group or individual projects, productions, or exhibitions.
ASSESSING LEARNING: Teacher continuously gathers information from student responses and products to provide feedback and design next steps.
DIFFERENTIATION: Before or during the lesson, the teacher adapts activities for diverse student needs.

Figure 6.8 Lesson-Planning Framework: Five General Phases
From *Teaching as Decision Making: Successful Practices for the Elementary Teacher* (3rd Ed.) (p. 173), by A. J. Starko, et al., 2003, Upper Saddle River, NJ: Merrill/Prentice Hall. Copyright 2003 by Pearson Education, Inc. Reprinted with permission.

Constructing Meaning

In the next section of the lesson, students' minds construct new meanings and understandings by interacting with stories, ideas, objects, materials, and other learners. The authentic learning activities described in Chapter 2 would fit into this category. Many less complex activities that help prepare students for higher level thinking also would fit this category. Teachers can provide inductive or cooperative group activities to help students construct meaning. Finally, the teacher can use more direct approaches, including teacher lecture, demonstration, or storytelling. This phase may require more than one day.

Using and Applying

In this section of a lesson, students actively use the new understandings in a variety of settings. The concepts of problem solving, application activities, writing a story or poem, and classroom practice fit into this category. Even though a new understanding has been gained, it will become more solid and meaningful when used multiple times in meaningful settings. This phase, too, may require more than one day and may include activities in and out of school. Some evidence exists that out-of-school practice (homework) is most effective in increasing achievement for high school students, only about half as effective for middle level students, and much less effective for younger children (Cooper, 2001a, 2001b).

Assessing Learning

In addition to continuous assessment during the lesson, the teacher will provide later, more formal assessments of the learning resulting from one or more lessons. The assessments can include projects and/or tests.

Differentiating (Adapting)

During planning the teacher already may have made some accommodations for those students with special learning needs (e.g., for limited English or special education students).

At any time during the lesson, however, formal or informal assessment information may indicate the need to adapt or differentiate specific activities for other students. This may involve reteaching those who are confused, simplifying assignments, or it can include extension (enrichment) for those students who need more challenge.

Differentiation

Although Chapter 10 discusses *differentiation* in greater detail, it is important to consider this idea in the context of lesson planning. Recall the complex dynamics of individuals and learning discussed in Chapter 2. Any class—or even small group—of students includes multiple, diverse individuals. Those individuals vary in many ways based on their prior experiences, culture, patterns of intelligences, learning styles, and so forth.

Given this reality, the idea that a teacher can plan one lesson for a class and expect all students to learn similar things is not realistic. In fact, whatever the subject, some activities will match particular students and some will not. A teacher who is committed to all students learning must recognize that sometimes only multiple differentiated lessons can accomplish that goal.

Differentiated instruction is instruction that flexes to meet the needs of multiple learners simultaneously. It recognizes that in any given classroom there will be some times when students work together, in small groups, and individually. Some individuals or small groups may work on the same or similar tasks; at other times their tasks will be completely different.

It is possible to consider differentiation both across lessons and within lessons. Differentiation across lessons requires that key concepts and skills be taught in multiple ways, targeted at different needs. In many ways it parallels the Variety Principle, and its implementation may look very similar. However, when teachers differentiate across lessons, they use varied methods and materials in an effort to match specific student needs and characteristics.

For example, a teacher who has observed several students who learn best through kinesthetic (using the whole body) experiences might include activities in which students learn the electron bonds in chemical changes by portraying parts of the molecules coming together. This would be a good general strategy for all students, but particularly effective if the teacher made sure the kinesthetic learners had key roles in the demonstration. A literature teacher could differentiate across lessons by including a variety of literature that portrays families and communities similar to those of particular students as well as those that are very different. In this way more students have the opportunity to tie to prior knowledge and contribute unique information to class discussions.

The variety in students' needs also requires that teachers be able to differentiate within lessons. Differentiated instruction has at least three overarching organizational patterns. First, at some times particular lessons or activities are not appropriate for some students and require *alternate activities*. This is most likely to be true when students have very strong skills, interests, or a great deal of prior knowledge. If, after preassessment, a teacher determines that one or more students are highly skilled in basic computation, it would not be a good use of those students' time to review and practice computation exercises. If students already know how to punctuate the ends of sentences, read a map key, or distinguish a noun from a verb, they may be assigned alternate activities rather than spend large amounts of time on skills they have already mastered. There also may be occasions when a skill that is being taught is so far beyond the prior knowledge of a student or group of students that it would present an unreasonable level of frustration. In this case, too, that student or students may be assigned alternative activities at the appropriate level of difficulty. This strategy requires that both teacher and students be able to manage multiple activities occurring simultaneously in the same room.

Another general strategy that can be used for differentiation is *multiple levels of activities or assignments* within the same lesson or series of lessons. For example, to teach the genre of historical fiction, all students could read historical fiction, but they would not necessarily all read the same book. Students could choose from among a collection of historical fiction, or they could be divided into groups and assigned texts of varying levels of difficulty. Class discussions could compare the accuracy, plot development, and use of language across texts. This approach allows for a variety of reading levels to be accommodated and provides multiple examples for a richer development of the concepts.

Finally, curriculum can be differentiated through the *levels of supports or extensions* offered individual students. Students who are struggling may be quietly offered a guide for notetaking or allowed to do alternate problems on a math assignment in order to accommodate a slower pace of work. Students who complete assignments quickly and easily may be offered the opportunity to study topics of interest or work on a challenging project with a mentor from a class of older students. Whatever the strategy chosen, differentiated instruction requires that planning be done for the individuals who require it within the class.

To plan for multiple levels or types of instruction simultaneously is a daunting task, particularly for beginning teachers. It will not be possible to plan differentiated instruction for every moment of the day. Nevertheless, it is important to understand from the beginning of a teaching career that effective teaching requires acknowledgment and accommodation of differences among individuals. Though beginning adjustments may be somewhat limited, they will provide important connections to students and important inroads into expert teaching.

Formal and Informal Instruction

We close this chapter by considering the different types of learning activities that are important in the ebb and flow of teaching. For example, teachers who participate in extracurricular activities have valuable opportunities to develop rapport with students. The many interactions that take place throughout the school day form the totality of student learning, not just the parts of the day that are outlined in formal lesson plans.

The formal designs for different types of lessons are helpful in planning, particularly as a beginning teacher. In fact, such designs are often like the training wheels on a bicycle, good for getting a sense of how things work best until you are ready to ride more flexibly on your own. A number of formal lesson designs and strategies are presented in Chapters 7, 8, and 9, which you can use to plan the instruction throughout the school day, although many teaching opportunities are less formal.

For example, many concepts can be built simply by the way you arrange your room and the things in it. Remember from Chapter 2 that we develop understanding through interactions with our environment. As individuals notice patterns in those interactions, concepts emerge. For example, classrooms in which the calendar includes birthdays of notable men and women from multiple cultures provide important data for developing the concepts of "famous," "important," or "scientist." Sometimes these ideas are taught directly, but often students learn them inductively through many experiences over time.

Of course, the classroom environment also can teach important lessons about how disciplines are organized and used, how materials are cared for, and what it means to be thoughtful and educated. The arrangement of the furniture, decorations on the walls, and routine interactions of the day all combine to teach students concepts beyond the evident content; for example, "leader," "team," and "adult." It is important that we ensure the unspoken lessons in our classrooms teach what we want.

Daily interactions with young people bring countless opportunities for teachable moments, both big and small. A brief conversation on the nature of friendship with a student whose best friend is moving away, a class discussion on drugs spurred by a flippant remark, or a morning spent in preparing cards in response to a tragedy in a student's family all develop concepts that are essential for students' growth. An accomplished teacher can skillfully integrate the immediacy of such moments into carefully laid plans.

Informal Learning Can Occur Just by What a Teacher Chooses to Put on the Shelves and Walls.

Practice Activity A

Planning in Detail

You may have asked yourself, "Why should I spend a lot of time writing lesson plans when the teachers I observe seem to do so little planning? Their lesson plans fit into a tiny box!!" Attempt to answer that question.

Answer: You are a new teacher, whereas teachers with years of experience rely on memory and prior years' lesson plans guide them. A novice needs to do much more detailed planning (e.g., logistics, questions, group size, and directions) than does an expert. You will not always need to plan at this level of detail, but it is a good idea to plan extra carefully when you teach something for the first time, try a new strategy, or have an evaluation visit by a supervisor.

Practice Activity B

Differentiated Instruction

Examine a lesson plan, either from a teacher's edition of a textbook or from your own collection of materials. What information is provided there that could help you plan for differentiated instruction? Is the lesson designed to suit all students? Compare notes with a classmate. Think about how you might adapt the lesson for specific students you are observing in a school.

Practice Activity C

Reflection Journal

Observe a teacher or teach a short lesson yourself. Then fill in the following journal using the ideas from this chapter to help explain what you saw. (Use extra paper if you need more space.)

Reflection Journal

Objective(s) for student learning:

What was done (attach lesson plan or describe activities):

How it worked in terms of student learning:

Describe in detail one successful aspect of the lesson:

Why did this part go well? What do you know about teaching and learning that might explain why? What conditions were operating that might explain why?

Describe in detail one less successful aspect of the lesson:

Why did this part not go well? What do you know about teaching and learning that might explain why? What conditions were operating that might explain why?

How would you change the lesson if you could teach it again? (Redesign notes.)

What you learned from this experience:

CHAPTER SUMMARY

This chapter has provided information on principles for planning, approaches to teaching, and lesson planning. It has discussed formal and informal teaching opportunities and the importance of differentiation.

Teaching is a sophisticated process of decision making in which many factors are considered. Avoid a haphazard method of planning. Select activities that match the instructional objectives and relate to students' learning needs. A purposeful, analytical, caring approach to teaching will guide the best decisions possible for the students, content, and conditions at the time.

Plan activities to meet your objectives while taking into consideration the context, content, students, learning theories and principles, assessments, and teaching techniques. Then, design a lesson or action plan for the teaching period.

When you finish a lesson, spend a few moments reflecting on what went well and what did not go well. Examine the evidence you have of students' progress toward your learning objectives. Try to figure out why students did, or did not succeed. Review your decisions, considering the context, students, content/objectives, learning theories, and techniques. Also consider the six learning principles to see if any of these ideas can help explain why things went as they did. Then decide how to pursue or develop the successful parts of the lesson, emphasizing the factors or principles that made them work. Plan an alternative approach that might make the less successful parts of the lesson work better. The Reflection Journals at the end of this chapter and Chapter 7 can guide the reflective analysis of your experiences. Finally, test the modification with students, analyze the students' learning, and repeat the process until you have a sequence of activities that help students reach your objectives. Be prepared, however, to modify further when students, goals, or content change. Teaching is an ever-renewing process.

UNIT PREPARATION

This chapter provides general background information that will help you prepare the lessons for your unit. At this point you should have studied the needs of the students you are to teach, prepared your content analysis and concept map, written lesson goals and objectives, and outlined your assessment plan. As you continue in unit planning, you may find that the goals you have set are too lofty or could be higher. You may identify a better culminating activity than the one you first planned. Unit planning is an iterative process; each new stage may affect previous stages, and it often is necessary to review and revise each piece.

At this stage in the planning process you should create a broad time line for your unit, outlining which objectives you plan to emphasize each day. Think about the order that will best help students understand the structure of your content and build toward your culminating activity. Planning the time line before doing specific lesson planning can help you focus on the content to be addressed each day and may give you information on whether the goals you have set are realistic for the time available. Of course, as you actually teach the unit, your time line will almost certainly have to flex to account for student progress and reactions.

Portfolio Activity

The Reflection Journal in the Practice Activity above can make a good portfolio activity. Choose a lesson in which you are able to discuss students' learning and what you learned from the experience. Many beginning teachers focus their attention solely on whether students are behaving and enjoying themselves. Of course it is important that your classroom atmosphere be conducive to learning and, hopefully, happy. Yet, the most important question for your reflection is, What were students learning and why? Your reflections focused in that direction can be very powerful.

As another possible portfolio activity, plan for parent involvement. Carefully consider ways to involve parents and other community members in your class, which is an important part of the Cultural Context Principle. The web links cited below may help you compile a set of strategies that will enhance both your teaching and your communication with students' families.

REFERENCES

Beyer, L. E. (1996). Creating democratic classrooms: The struggle to integrate theory and practice. New York: Teachers College Press.

Brooks, J. G., & Brooks, M. G. (1999a). *In search of understanding: The case for constructivist classrooms.* Alexandria, VA: Association for Supervision and Curriculum Development.

Brooks, M. G., & Brooks, J. G. (1999b). The courage to be constructivist. *Educational Leadership, 57(3)*, 18–24.

Cohen, E. B. (1994). Complex instruction: Higher-order thinking in heterogeneous classroom. In S. Sharon, *Handbook of cooperative learning methods.* Westport, CT: Greenwood Press.

Cooper, H. (2001a). *The battle over homework: Common ground for administrators, teachers, and parents.* Newbury Park, CA: Corwin Press.

Cooper, H. (2001b). Homework for all—in moderation. *Educational Leadership, 58(7)*, 34–38.

Dale, E. (1969). *Audiovisual methods in teaching.* New York: Holt, Rinehart and Winston.

Daniels, H., & Bizar, M. (1998). *Methods matter.* Portland, ME: Stenhouse Publishers.

Darling, J. (1994, Fall). Summerhill from Neill to the nineties. *Educational Forum, 58(3)*, 244–251.

Delpit, L. (1995). *Other people's children: Cultural conflict in the classroom.* New York: New Press, Norton & Co.

Fosnot, C. T. (Ed.). (1996). *Constructivism: Theory, perspectives, and practice.* New York: Teachers College Press.

Garrison, J. S. (1997). *Dewey and Eros: Wisdom and desire in the art of teaching.* Monograph Accession No. BEDI970031555, *Education Abstracts* (Internet).

Glickman, C. D. (1998). *Revolutionizing America's schools.* San Francisco: Jossey-Bass.

Hyerle, D. (1996). *Visual tools for constructing knowledge.* Alexandria, VA: Association for Supervision and Curriculum Development.

Johnson, G. M. (1999). Inclusive education: Fundamental instructional strategies and considerations. *Preventing School Failure, 43*(2), 72–78.

Kovalik, S. (1994). Brain compatible learning. *Video Journal of Education, 3*(6).

Marzano, R. J., Pickering, D. J., & Pollock, J. E. (2001*). Classroom instruction that works: Research-based strategies for increasing student achievement.* Alexandria, VA: Association for Supervision and Curriculum Development.

Maushak, N., Wigans, L. M., & Bender, C. (1999). Technology, teaching, and learning in Iowa high schools. In proceedings of selected research and development papers presented at the National Convention of the Association for Educational Communication and Technology [AECT] (21st, Houston, TX, February 10–14), ED436183.

Perkins, D. (1999, November). The many faces of constructivism. *Educational Leadership, 57*(3), 6–11.

Stiggins, R. J. (1994). *Student-centered classroom assessment.* New York: Merrill.

Stiggins, R. J. (2000). *Student-involved classroom assessment (3rd Ed.).* Upper Saddle River, NJ: Prentice Hall.

Weil, M., Calhoun, E., & Joyce, D. (1999). *Models of teaching (6th Ed.).* Boston: Allyn & Bacon.

Wiggins, G. (1999). *Assessing student performance: Exploring the purpose and limits of testing.* San Francisco: Jossey-Bass.

Wiggins, G. McTighe, J. (1999). *Understanding by design handbook.* Alexandria, VA: Association for Supervision and Curriculum Development.

Wolfe, P. (2001). *Brain matters: Translating research into classroom practice.* Alexandria, VA: Association for Supervision and Curriculum Development (ASCD).

Models for Teaching: Direct

CHAPTER OVERVIEW

Secondary teachers plan a lot of lessons. Every day provides many opportunities to teach. In order to address the variety of intelligences, learning styles, interests, and background of your students—and to keep teaching fresh and interesting—it will be important to have a wide repertoire of teaching strategies. The next three chapters will help you build this repertoire. This chapter examines approaches to teaching that can be categorized as *direct instruction*. The next chapter features *inductive* approaches. Both chapters describe how direct and inductive teaching can be used in both formal lesson plans and informal teaching moments. Chapter 9 will describe structures and strategies that can be used with both types of teaching.

Opening Activity

Think about two things you have learned recently, one in secondary school and one outside a formal educational institution. As an adult, you might remember learning about Bloom's Taxonomy, or laws of planetary motion, and how to read an e-mail attachment, bake bread, install a muffler, or develop photographs. Perhaps you learned what plants grow best on the west side of the house or how to calm an anxious student.

* * *

You may have learned some things when someone explained them to you, either in person or through the written word. Perhaps a professor explained the planets or a friend taught you the finer points of working with yeast. You may have learned to install a muffler from a clear how-to book, complete with photographs. You likely learned other things through multiple experiences that led you to draw conclusions, such as several years of gardening that helped you learn what kinds of plants thrive in your soil. You have been involved in both direct and inductive learning throughout your lifetime. This chapter will help you build on those experiences to structure effective direct lessons. Chapter 8 will present similar information regarding inductive teaching.

CHAPTER OBJECTIVES

After you have completed this section, you will be able to:

1. describe formal and informal instances of direct teaching;
2. debate the advantages and disadvantages of direct lessons;
3. evaluate appropriate and inappropriate uses of direct teaching; and
4. design a direct (deductive) lesson consistent with the principles of such lessons, teach it, and reflect on it.

Direct Teaching: Formal and Informal

Direct, or deductive teaching, is exemplified by the word *direct*. Direct teaching may be provided in person or in some mediated form; for example, through an instructional video or videoconference. In direct teaching, one person gives another information needed to learn. It is to the point, straightforward, and clear.

Direct teaching may be formal or informal. Successful informal direct teaching usually includes giving information, demonstrating, and providing practice. Think of a person learning to hit a baseball, play the guitar, or use a sewing machine. In each case the teacher is likely to explain what is needed, demonstrate how to do it, and allow the youth to practice. It is understood that practice is important and worthwhile because it will lead to success in doing something now.

Formal direct teaching in school will have similar characteristics. Beginning teachers might think direct teaching is equivalent to long, boring lectures and is to be avoided. Like all good teaching, however, direct instruction should engage students in constructing their own knowledge by sharing information and actively engaging them through questioning or practice activities.

Direct teaching is used in school in both formal and informal ways. Informal direct teaching is likely to be used in brief teachable moments when a student needs instruction in a skill you had not planned to teach or when a student asks a question about content outside your plans. A student might come in after a storm asking how hail is formed. In those moments it is helpful to remember the basic components of effective direct instruction: sharing information, demonstrating (modeling), and giving students the opportunity to practice and receive feedback.

Direct Lesson Design

Formal direct teaching is often organized in a format called (naturally enough) a *direct lesson.* The direct lesson design presented here is based on research on teaching effectiveness conducted in traditionally structured classrooms during the 1970s and 1980s (Hunter, 1976; Rosenshine, 1987; Wang, Haertel, & Walberg, 1993). Researchers prepared teachers to use the methods of more successful teachers and determined that direct teaching tended to produce higher student learning scores on standardized tests in reading and math. This method, however, did not produce more creative thinking or better attitudes toward learning. Direct teaching, then, is not necessarily the best way to teach everything, but it does have its advantages and is the best decision under certain circumstances.

For example, the method for constructing a papier-mâché mask from Zimbabwe would need to be taught directly. It would be very difficult and time consuming for students to discover this process (inductively) on their own. The opening of the lesson could invite students to figure out ways they could make a mask, but the lesson would not spend more than a few minutes on this part before going on to direct teaching.

Direct teaching provides valuable guidelines for strengthening the effectiveness of your lectures (Marzano, et al. 2001). The following seven elements in a direct lesson design are labeled to indicate how each fits into the general phases of most lessons described in Chapter 6. Remember that for many objectives, not every element can be included in a single period of instruction.

1. Set (opening)
2. Objective(s) and purpose (opening)
3. Information and modeling (constructing meaning)
4. Checking for understanding (constructing meaning)
5. Guided practice (using/applying)
6. Formative assessment (assessing learning)
7. Reteaching, extension, and/or independent practice (differentiation)

alike a lesson plan

When planning and teaching your first direct lessons, use all the elements in the order presented. However, with more experience, you will become more comfortable using the sequence flexibly. You may then question if each one is necessary and make a conscious decision whether to include it or not. Eventually you may develop your own order, integrate other steps, and blend the direct design with elements of other types of lessons.

Remember that you are a reflective decision maker; therefore, any one approach to teaching is not a recipe to be followed exactly (Hunter, 1976; Putnam & Borko, 2000).

Think of it as a road map that suggests alternative pathways—some direct and quick, others less direct but possibly more picturesque.

1. **Set**

- Provides focus (active involvement of learner)
- Transfers relevant prior knowledge
- Provides an advance organizer for key ideas
- Preassesses appropriate skills as necessary (diagnosis)

The set activity begins or introduces a lesson or can be used after any break in a lesson (or when continuing a lesson from a previous day) to focus students' attention. A set activity is not merely saying to students, "OK, now we're going to work on math" or "Please turn to page 26." The sensory memory is the gatekeeper for what we remember (Wolfe, 2001). If students are not stimulated to attend actively to the information a teacher presents, they will probably forget it immediately. Further if the set activity does not tie to students' prior knowledge, they are unlikely to understand the new information.

Set activities are usually short, lasting no more than three to five minutes for older students and much less time for younger ones. A film or a field trip would typically not be considered a set activity, because such an activity might take several hours and would support a variety of topics. Pick a set that is interesting, but not so engrossing that it distracts students from the activities after it. As Madeline Hunter used to say in her workshops, "Don't bring in an elephant to teach the color gray." The main purpose is to focus the students actively on the content, transfer existing knowledge to the new topic, and when necessary, assess students' prior relevant skills and understandings.

The set has four key aspects. First, a set activity provides a focus for the learners' minds by requiring *active involvement* with the content. Active involvement means more than passive listening. To be actively involved, the student imagines, writes, pictures, says, or reads, always with some question in mind. For example, one teacher introduced a lesson on creative writing by asking students to discuss in pairs a new ending to a story they had just finished reading. Then, after a short period of time, the teacher asked students to share what they were thinking.

A second aspect of the set is **prior knowledge**. The set activity should enable students to relate the new information to something they have learned before. In the previous example, the set activity motivated students to relate the new topic (creative writing) to a familiar story. Think about how this example relates to discussions in Chapters 2 and 5. Students construct information in long-term memory in networks of meaning (schema). New information is more meaningful and more memorable when it is hooked in with relevant information in the brain.

The beginning of the lesson is an excellent time to provide an **advanced organizer,** a structure to help students organize the information in their minds (Ausubel, 1968; Weil, Calhoun, & Joyce, 1999). For example, when introducing a direct lesson on the history of Zimbabwe, it would be helpful to let students get the big picture first. This might be done by showing a time line with the highlights of each century, a short written passage, or a discussion. These ideas would then provide "ideational anchors" for the information to follow (Weil, Calhoun & Joyce, 1999). This is consistent with the Conceptual Focus Principle discussed in Chapter 6.

A third aspect of the set activity is *preassessment,* or diagnosis. This step may not be necessary when a teacher has just finished a prior lesson or activity that gave good information about students' levels of performance. For example, consider a math class that just completed a lesson on single-variable problems. The next lesson, on two-variable problems, might not require extensive diagnosis, because the teacher already knows how well prepared the students are to move on.

In many cases, however, inadequate information may be available to make necessary instructional decisions about students' current understandings or skills. When student teachers conduct practice lessons in real classrooms, one of the most frequent comments is, "I made a false assumption about what the students already knew. I wish I had done a preassessment."

This diagnosis will help find students who need extra help and others who are already beyond the upcoming lesson. Some students will need reteaching of key prerequisite skills. For example, if students are going to conduct surveys of their neighbors' buying habits, make sure they have the necessary math skills to summarize their data. Starting the lesson with a quick exercise (not a lecture) that requires students to graphically portray a set of data may provide useful information about who needs a review of this key skill.

Preassessment also can help target those students who already know some of what you are about to teach. For example, in an earth science class, the teacher probably would want to diagnose students' knowledge before a unit on rocks and minerals. He or she could pass around three rocks and have students write about what they observe and know about them. Even if some students have already studied the topic, their understanding of the information could vary widely. In this way the lesson could be tailored for those who have more or less experience with rocks and minerals. Gathering such information is especially important at the beginning of the year to understand each student's background knowledge and general skills.

2. Objective(s) and Purpose
- Communicates to the students the learning goal(s)
- Motivates students (by explaining the purpose, how the lesson relates to real life)

When students know both the *objective*(s) and the *purpose* of the lesson, it provides further focus for them as well as motivation. In direct lessons, tell students what they should be able to do by the end of the lesson (the *objective*), how you will assess them, and what level of performance or culminating authentic activity will be expected. Students also want to know the *purpose*—why it is important to study the topic and how it will be useful to them or others in real life.

Clearly stated objectives are crucial to help keep your lesson on track and to motivate students. Tell the students the objective in their language, not in the formal way listed at the top of your lesson plan. So instead of making a statement like, "The students will be able to define 'point of view,'" you would say, "By the end of the week, when I ask you to define point of view, I would like you to be able to explain what it means and give two examples from books we have read."

To tell the students, "Today we're going to work on point of view" is not an example of conveying the objective, because you have not stated any expected behavior. The students do not know how they will be assessed, nor do they know the learning they will be expected to demonstrate as a result of the teaching activities.

When students know the *purpose,* it further motivates them. It lets them see the usefulness of the new knowledge, skill, or attitude. In the lesson example above, you would provide the objective and then say, "It's important for us to understand 'point of view,' because later we will be writing stories in which you will use at least two different points of view and we will be publishing those stories for our English Book Fair next month."

When explaining to students the objective and purpose of the lesson, it is important to clarify how the lesson relates to the overall objectives and purpose as expressed in the unit rationale. The principle to follow is to relate "this" to "that." Thus when giving the objective and purpose for the lesson about point of view, emphasize that understanding "why the Revolutionary War was revolutionary" (a key question) requires taking multiple points of view.

CHECK YOUR UNDERSTANDING

Look back at some objectives you have written. Pick one that you believe is suitable for direct instruction. Write two ideas for set activities that will (1) focus your learners actively and (2) encourage them to transfer their existing knowledge of your topic. Also indicate how you'll find out what they do and don't know already (preassessment). Then indicate how you will tell students the objective and purpose of the lesson.

Share your ideas with a classmate to see if you understand each component similarly.

Lesson objective
Set (focus, transfer, preassessment)
Objective told to students
Purpose told to students

3. **Information and Modeling (with Checks for Understanding Throughout)**
   - Explains and demonstrates information
   - Uses variety to appeal to various learning styles
   - Provides a visual conceptual structure for information
   - Uses verbal labels to point out key elements of examples and demonstrations (modeling)
   - Involves learners actively after each chunk of information

In this phase, provide the relevant *information* about the topic at hand. Teachers can provide information through a variety of sources, such as lectures, experts (in person or on the Internet), readings, movies, filmstrips, multimedia presentations, or the Internet. As you present information, *model,* or show, it. Periodically *check for understanding*—meaning stop to allow students to summarize or use the material just presented. The information in Chapter 2 on learning and memory provides some guidelines to keep in mind during the presentation of information.

First, consider students' individual learning needs. Because of the varied backgrounds and experiences of students, it is important to appeal to as many learning preferences as possible. This will require, in particular, applying the learning principle of Variety (see Chapter 6). Give students the opportunity to encounter the material in a number of ways; for example, through reading, listening, viewing, and touching (Wolfe, 2001).

Modeling occurs while you are presenting information. Remember to show the information, not just tell it to them. Posters, overhead transparencies, multimedia materials, pictures, objects to pass around and explore, demonstrations, charts, graphic organizers, chalkboard illustrations—all of these aids help make the verbal information visual and tactile, thus appealing to the learning needs of your students. Think about the difference between a description of a desert environment without visuals and one that is accompanied by a video, or imagine visiting a website that illustrates a trip across desert terrain. Even the best verbal description is likely to be more effective when supported by a model. Of course, it is essential to model each skill we teach, whether it is using a microscope or storing paints safely.

Verbal labeling is the technique of pointing out in words an idea or element students are to notice while the teacher is modeling. Verbal labeling of the essential aspects of a visual aid or demonstration is important when explaining how to do a project or a particular procedure. For example, when teachers give directions for an assignment, they should show an excellent example of that assignment and explain why each part is exemplary (Stiggins, 2000; Wiggins, 1996). The verbal labeling is necessary because students may look at the model and not understand which elements are the most important. For instance, a student might look at a poster and assume it's good because of its size, rather than because it conveys the essential information and the colors are vivid. Similarly, as a procedure or skill is demonstrated, it is essential to label what is happening so students recognize important steps.

Next, consider the principle of Conceptual Focus and the fact that the memory searches to structure information into meaningful networks. To present information in an organized way, first divide the information into logical chunks in your mind. Outline it or diagram it so that the concepts, the generalizations, and the links between the elements of information become clear. (Remember the concept map you created in Chapter 3.) Then create a poster, an overhead transparency, or other visual aids that make this organization obvious to students (Wolfe, 2001). Figure 3.6 (p. 81) shows the organization of the information in the Zimbabwe unit. When presenting the information, refer to the concept map or graphic organizer often to let students know how the current pieces of information are related to those that they've already covered and those they will study soon. Have students actively process each chunk after it has been presented. After each main point in your minilecture, stop and have students work with what they have learned. For example, a minilecture on the water cycle would be more effective if supported by a diagram and if the teacher stops at each stage of the cycle to actively involve students' minds with the content. Ask students to summarize, act out the water's path, or add to their own diagrams at each stage.

CHECK YOUR UNDERSTANDING

Take the objective you used for the set activity designed earlier and outline a few essential ideas. Plan two or three specific ways you could present the information so your students will remember it. How will you appeal to different learning styles? How can you help students see the conceptual organization of the information? Share your ideas with others.

Objective
Content outline (key concepts)
Ways to make information meaningful (use ideas from Chapters 2 and 6)

4. Checking for Understanding (Active Processing).

- Is done periodically during information giving to focus attention
- Allows students to actively process information (e.g., write, talk, vote)
- Provides information about student understanding of information presented

Although it is listed as a separate phase of the lesson, checking for understanding is interspersed with the information and modeling phase as shown in Figure 7.1. One researcher (Rowe, 1974) suggested the "10-2 rule," which refers to about two minutes of active student involvement for approximately every ten minutes of information presented. According to this idea, in a unit on rocks, the teacher might explain the characteristics of sedimentary rocks and show examples (with verbal labeling of essential qualities) for about ten minutes. He or she would not go on to explain the second type of rock (igneous rocks) until students were given a short activity in which they could summarize or apply the information already presented; for instance, classifying examples and nonexamples of sedimentary rocks. Next, the teacher would explain and model the characteristics of igneous rocks and again check for understanding.

Checking for understanding has three purposes. The first is to enable students' minds to digest the information in small chunks, so that each phase is meaningful to them before the next piece is presented. Most students probably have had the unpleas-

Figure 7.1 Checking for Understanding During Information and Modeling
From *Teaching as Decision Making: Successful Practices for the Elementary Teacher* (3rd Ed.) (p. 193), by A. J. Starko, et al., 2003, Upper Saddle River, NJ: Merrill/Prentice Hall. Copyright 2003 by Pearson Education, Inc. Reprinted with permission.

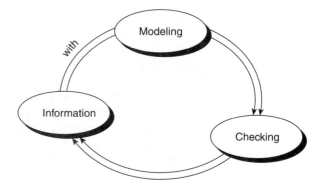

ant experience of sitting in an hour-long lecture with no opportunity to process, digest, or otherwise interact with the material presented. When students are given large amounts of complex information without any time to actively process it, they retain little of it. Therefore, when showing a long movie or video, preview it to determine where to stop so students can actively process the information. In this way, they will solidify their understanding of the material.

Recall that short-term memory has a limited capacity. If students receive too many pieces of information at once, they overload and begin to forget. Their attention usually wanders and they are no longer learning—or at least not the content planned for them to learn. Younger students tend to wander sooner.

The second reason to check for understanding is to allow students to actively process information in logical chunks, thus making it more easily remembered. The word *active* is important here. Recall the principle of Active Processing from Chapter 6; it is more meaningful than passive learning. Discussing the ideas or answering a few true/false questions about the information presented keeps that information in the memory system longer and increases the likelihood of transfer to long-term memory (Wolfe, 2001).

In reviewing research on effective classroom strategies, Marzano, Pickering, and Pollock (2001) note that making and testing hypotheses can help students process information. Although hypothesis testing is often associated with inductive teaching, it is effective to have students generate and test hypotheses based on principles they have been taught. This idea could fit well into several sections of a direct lesson, including checking for understanding. Students could be asked to imagine "What would happen if . . ." and later test their hypotheses. When students explain their hypotheses, the teacher gains important information on students' thinking, and students gain practice in logical thinking.

A third purpose of checking for understanding is to find out how well students have absorbed the material. This relates to the principle of Continuous Assessment (see Chapter 6). Without information on students' understanding of the material presented, a teacher would have a difficult time deciding what to do next: go on to a new idea or stay with the current one. You may think of this process as *formative assessment*—not for grading but for formulating decisions about where to go next with students (Black & Wiliam, 1998).

Often teachers find that their students have misunderstood something they said. Perhaps the teacher just didn't explain it clearly enough or said something that was confusing. When teachers check for students' understanding, they can find out what was misunderstood. They may choose to reexplain and model the original information in a new and clearer way.

What activities are useful in checking for understanding? Table 7.1 lists some active participation strategies. They might include techniques such as having students write a one-minute summary, giving true/false questions on which students vote, or having students think of questions for others to answer. The least helpful way to check for understanding in most situations is to ask, "Are there any questions?" Many students (especially the shy or less successful ones) do not want to call attention to their lack of understanding. Thus the fact that no one has any questions may reveal little about students' actual grasp of the material.

TABLE 7.1   *Suggestions for Increasing Student Participation (to be used during Set, Checking, Guided Practice, or Review)*

Small-Group Activities

1. *Discuss with a partner*
   Examples:
   - In your own words, explain to your partner how the pistons in a car engine work.
   - Share with your partner the guidelines to keep in mind when writing an expository paragraph.
   - Discuss with your partner the meanings of these 10 terms from our anatomy unit.
2. *Discuss in small groups*
   Keep the group size to three, four, or five so that each student can participate. Appoint a recorder to summarize the findings of the discussion.
3. *Write questions*
   Examples:
   - Write one question about what we have just been studying. Try it out on a person near you. If that person can't answer the question, pass it to me. At the end of the period, I'll answer all questions that have been turned in.
   - Write two questions based on the topic "Planning Nutritional Meals." We'll use them tomorrow for a review of the unit.
4. *Brainstorm*
   Brainstorming can be done as a group or with a partner. Define the topic or problem. For example, the topic may be "questions students think will be covered on an exam."
   Examples:
   - On your scratch paper, jot down as many terms as you can think of that are related to the topic we began studying yesterday. In 5 minutes we'll discuss these terms.
   - Repeat the same process as in the previous example, but share the ideas with a partner.
5. *Debate*
   Discussion of both sides of a question involves more students when done in small groups. In teaching debate techniques, first explain the structure and guidelines. Then, with the help of a student, demonstrate a debate for the group.
6. *Peer group teaching*
   Using students as tutors can be an effective learning device for both the tutor and tutored.
7. *Role-playing*
   Simulating an event brings new perspectives to any lesson. Role-playing involves more students when done in small groups (rather than by one group in front of class), and it reduces the risk factor.

Whole-Group Activities

8. *Oral reading*
   Oral reading can be done in two ways.
   a. One student can read while the rest of the class follows with markers, their eyes, or their fingers.
   b. The entire class can read aloud together. For special dramatic effects, the boys and girls can alternate reading, etc.
9. *Whisper answer in teacher's ear*
   The teacher can select random students to whisper the answer to him or her.
10. *Provide wait time for covert rehearsal of responses* (Tobin, 1980)
    Waiting at least 3 seconds for an answer is a critical element in effective questioning of an entire class. Ask the students who have arrived at an idea to do something overt, such as put their right hand on the table, fold their arms, etc. Promote even greater participation by telling the class how many have given the signal. For

example, say, "Well, already 12 people have signaled that they know the answer." Wait until a sufficient response number is obtained. Then call on one randomly selected student to answer the question.
Examples:
- Which were the three Axis countries during World War II? (Pause.) I can tell you're thinking. I see five hands, six, eight, lots more. Let's see, I think I'll call on Ted. (He responds.) How many agree?
- I want you to think about whether this blueprint would be practical for a house in an area that has a climate like southern California's. I'll call upon someone in about 1 minute.

11. *Unison response*
A teacher signal will indicate when the class should respond. For example, the slow raising of the teacher's hand means preparation. The abrupt lowering signals the point for the class response.
Examples:
- I'll point to a word and say a definition. If the definition I give is correct, please reply all together, "Yes." If it's incorrect, all say, "No."
- I'll read some statements about the digestive process. If the statement is true, everyone responds together, "True," etc.
- We'll check the answers to this worksheet together. I'll say the number of the question, then all of you respond with the answer on your paper. If the response is clear, we won't need to discuss that question. If it's garbled, we'll stop to clarify. (This will work only with short, one-right-answer responses.)

12. *Consecutive response*
Each student is responsible for recalling the previous student's response.

13. *Polling by raised hands*
Casting votes or canvassing for information—the data can be recorded on a chart visible to the entire class. Or, when a student responds, teacher can ask those who agree to raise their hands.

14. *Pointing*
Using an individual pictorial representation (map, diagram, picture), the students can point to the correct answer.

15. *Cross/uncross arms*
Examples:
- I'll read a series of statements about different kinds of angles. If you agree with the statement, cross your arms; if you don't agree, don't cross your arms.
- If you agree with Toby's opinion, cross your arms.

16. *Flash answers in groups*
Flash cards made by students can be used in a variety of ways: true-false cards (color-coded for ease of reading), chemical elements, vocabulary review, and color-coded classifying.
Examples:
- We've talked about the three branches of our federal government. (Students are divided into groups, and each group has three cards, each one stating a different governmental branch.) I'll read a government duty (such as making laws). As a group, decide which branch of government would be responsible for that duty, and then hold up the correct card.
- There are three animal classifications listed on the board, and they are color-coded. Each group has three pieces of paper, each a different color. I'll read the name of an animal, and as a group you decide which category that animal belongs to. Then hold up the appropriate piece of paper.

17. *Flashers*
A short answer can be written either on a laminated notebook with a water-soluble pen or on an individual chalkboard.

continued

TABLE 7.1 *continued*

18. *Thumb signals (done at chest level in a personal, low-key manner)*
    Examples:
    • I'll read several statements about how to make a collar for a blouse. If the statement is true, put your thumb up. If it is false, put your thumb down. If you're not sure, put your thumb to the side.
    • If you agree with Jim's explanation of a zone defense, put your thumb up, etc.
19. *Finger signals (done at chest level in a personal, low-key manner)*
    Examples:
    • The three kinds of rock formations are listed on the board by number. I'll say a characteristic of a certain rock formation; you put up the appropriate number of fingers for the one that is being described.
    • The five main characters from the novel are listed on the board by number. If the statement I read refers to the first one, put up one finger. If it refers to the second one, put up two fingers, etc.
    • I'll play several chords on the piano. If it's a major chord, put up one finger; if it's a minor chord, put up two fingers.
20. *Flash cards*
    Examples:
    • You've made flash cards for your new Spanish vocabulary. Study them alone for 5 minutes. Then we'll do some spot checking.
    • You've made flash cards for this week's vocabulary words. Practice then with a partner for 10 minutes. Then we'll have our quiz.
21. *Cross/uncross arms or legs, look up or down, thumbs up or down, pencils up or down*
    The opposite positions can indicate positive/negative, higher/lower, or any two-part test of opposites.

Adapted from Napa County, CA, Essential Elements of Effective Instruction Training Materials.

CHECK YOUR UNDERSTANDING

Try this exercise to check your own understanding of this section. Write *T* if the statement is true and *F* if it is false.

_____ 1. An informational lecture is the opening activity of a direct lesson.
_____ 2. The best way to model is to state the information.
_____ 3. Understanding is checked after all the information is presented.
_____ 4. A movie is one way to provide information.
_____ 5. It is impossible to check for understanding during a film or video.

The only true statement is item 4. Why are the others false?

5. Guided Practice
   • Allows students to improve learning through practice
   • Provides activities that match the objective(s) (congruence)
   • Allows teacher to monitor learning and adjust accordingly

Guided practice gives students an opportunity to practice with the skills or information until they are confident and have achieved the objective. Recall the importance of rehearsal and meaningfulness for the transfer of information into long-term memory (Wolfe, 2001). Marzano, Pickering, and Pollock (2001) drew two key generalizations from the research on practice: (1) mastering a skill takes a fair amount of focused practice and (2) during practice students should adapt and shape what they have learned. The practice sections of direct lesson design are planned to accomplish both aims.

It is critical that the teacher guide the practice by constantly monitoring to check student progress. If students are in a large-group practice activity responding to teacher questions with hand signals, the teacher can see how they are doing and correct any misunderstandings. If the students do a few problems or exercises from a book or worksheet, the teacher can circulate among students without spending too much time with any one student. In this way, errors can be caught early before they become ingrained by repeated practice. If the teacher finds many students are making the same kinds of errors, the teacher can adjust the lesson by reteaching the whole group or a subgroup in a different manner.

Guided practice may be written or oral and may include the same participation activities referred to in Table 7.1. Long worksheets or book assignments may not provide the best guided practice, because students may actually be practicing errors or may become confused for a long time while the teacher is trying to get around to everybody. Therefore if worksheets or book assignments are used, students should work on a few of the problems or questions before the teacher brings the whole class together to check their success on those few items. If students comprehend the activity, then they may proceed on their own, with light supervision from the teacher.

The guided practice activities should follow the principle of Congruence by being relevant to the lesson objective. Most practice activities should lead directly to the accomplishment of the objective. For example, if the teacher wants students to be able to interpret the Declaration of Independence and tie it to their lives, and they read multiple reports on the development of the document, the activity and the objective are closely matched. If they understand the origins of the document, it will be helpful in understanding (and later interpreting) the text. If, however, the teacher asks students to copy the first parts of the Declaration from the book, this provides little match between the rote copying activity and the higher level objective of interpreting and applying such a complex document.

What is the difference between a check for understanding exercise and guided practice? Although monitoring student progress is a key aspect in both phases of the lesson, they differ in purpose and in scope. The goal of guided practice is mastery of the skill; the goal of checking for understanding is merely to find out if students understood what was just presented.

Both concepts also differ in the scope or the amount of information. Guided practice encompasses all the information presented in the lesson, whereas checking focuses only on the small chunk just presented.

6. Formative Assessment
- Gathers information about individual achievement of the objective
- Helps teacher decide how to proceed with each student

It is essential to find out who has and has not met the objective by conducting a brief formative assessment. This activity may be a quick miniquiz or a short project that students do on their own, such as completing two or three math problems or writing a short poem. If students cannot perform the skill adequately at this point, they are likely to experience failure when going on to independent work. The assessment may show, however, that some students are bored by more practice and need to proceed to extension or independent work. Teachers can differentiate the instruction here to meet the needs of each student by deciding who needs reteaching and who can proceed to extension activities or more practice.

Some teachers ask if guided practice is enough to ensure that students have met the objective. Remember, students' correct performance on a guided practice activity does not necessarily mean they can perform well on their own. During the practice, they may have received help from the teacher or from their peers. At this point, the teacher will not know which students are capable of succeeding independently and, therefore, may need a special assessment activity to indicate how well each student can perform without assistance.

Sometimes it is possible to gather enough information about achievement during guided practice so that a separate assessment activity is not required. If this phase is skipped and many students are unsuccessful during independent work, you may conclude that you did not obtain adequate information about who was ready to proceed and who was not.

It is a reality of teaching that not all students learn at the same rate. Thus, some students may be ready to go on to extension activities or independent work while others will need reteaching or more teacher-assisted practice. At this point in the lesson, use your assessment information to decide who falls into which group and to differentiate the instruction.

7. Adaptation/Differentiation

Reteaching (for those still struggling) or Extension (for those who need more challenge) or Independent Practice (for those who need more practice)
- Attends to individual needs by reteaching, or
- Extends learning, or
- Provides further practice to develop fluency/automaticity

At this point, teachers know which students have or have not achieved the learning stated in the objective and can differentiate their instruction accordingly. *Reteaching* may be necessary for some students because the activities provided so far did not help them learn what you hoped for. Look for evidence of misunderstanding in these students' guided practice and assessment activities, or orally check with them. In any case, once the problem is found, reteach.

Reteaching may include further direct instruction or some other approach. It is not, however, just covering the content in the same way a second time. Chances are that the first teaching approach did not work. Therefore, try appealing to a different learning style or type of intelligence, or try a different type of guided practice activity. For example, if you presented the information on air pressure using illustrations from a science text, then during reteaching you might use an experiment or demonstration or have the students make up a song about air pressure.

Often you will find that several students have not succeeded on the lesson and need reteaching. If so, it may be wise to pull those pupils aside while the other students are working independently. The teacher also could assign students to mixed-ability cooperative learning teams, in which the misunderstanding must be clarified before the group proceeds. Another idea is to use peer teaching (Ernst, 1995; Powell, 1997) to help the student master the objective. Individual help before or after school also may be useful. More ideas for modifying instruction for special student needs may be found in Chapter 9.

Experience has shown that it is well worth the time and effort to reteach. Not all students succeed on the first try, and they should have a second chance. Furthermore, research on mastery learning (Bloom, 1984) indicates that, with continuous assessment of student learning and reteaching where needed, students who would normally be near the average of the class can rise to achievement levels typical of the top 10%.

While some students will need reteaching, others will need *extension*. For the students who have already achieved the objective, more work of the type done in guided practice would seem boring and repetitive. For example, after students have shown that they can distinguish a noun from a verb in sentences, having them repeat that activity during independent practice would seem senseless. To extend their learning, they might look at magazine articles and find nouns and verbs or look for nouns in poetry or on TV.

In extension activities, students who are ready for more challenge work with the same skills, but in a different setting with more complex examples or at a slightly higher level of learning. For example, activities that ask students to identify similarities and differences among key concepts and to portray those differences through a variety of means (such as graphically, through metaphors, through classifying) are particularly effective at enhancing student understanding of content (Marzano, Pickering, and Pollock, 2001).

Independent practice is designed to increase students' fluency and ability to perform with ease the activity stated in the objective. For example, although some students may be able to slowly do algebra problems correctly, they may need more practice before they can do them quickly and without much effort. Independent practice takes place with little or no teacher guidance; it may be performed in or out of class. Homework is one example of independent practice.

The extension and independent practice activities do not have to be closely guided by the teacher, but students should receive immediate feedback on their work. Since many students have difficulty working independently, they will also need feedback on how well they work on their own. Thus, teacher monitoring (or at least visual scanning) is a good idea, especially if you are reteaching a small group at the same time. Chapter 9 contains more ideas on structuring independent work.

CHECK YOUR UNDERSTANDING

With another student, trade off explaining and giving examples of the following terms: guided practice, assessment, reteaching, extension, and independent practice. Each of you should write definitions of two or three of the terms, then exchange your work with your partner's. Try not to look at your notes. Be sure to explain the terms in your own words. Check the accuracy of your understanding by looking back over the previous section.

When to Use Direct Lessons

The direct lesson is not recommended for every type of content. For example, you might initiate a teaching sequence for some concepts with an inductive lesson and use direct lessons for follow-up and practice. Direct lessons tend to be less effective with (1) abstract, "fuzzy" concepts, such as majority, equity, justice, discrimination, freedom, ethics, and beauty; (2) holistic content that does not lend itself easily to sequencing of skills, such as reading comprehension and the writing process; and (3) content that includes a high degree of judgment and/or that has a substantial affective flavor, such as politics, artistic expression, or debates (Cawelti, 1995).

Content that has a high degree of structure lends itself well to direct teaching. Examples of such content are writing an introductory sentence, concepts with clear rules, many math and science operations, problem-solving steps, study skills, rules for debating, how to find resources for research, classroom rules and procedures, and some foreign language instruction. In fact, disadvantaged high school students in New York City improved writing, reading, and were more prone to attend college when directly taught the "tricks" of succeeding in college-level learning (Darling-Hammond, Ancess, and Ort, 2002).

Some people think direct lessons can be used only with lower level cognitive skills (memorization and comprehension). However, researchers (Beyer, 1995, 1997; Brown, 1978; Rosenshine, 1992) have shown success in using direct teaching to enhance students' higher level cognitive skills (e.g., learning strategies, concept learning, comparison, contrast, and analysis). These researchers argue that too often students are given a higher level task without explicit direct teaching on how to attack that task (Williams & Colomb, 1993).

Many students have not learned such skills on their own and need modeling, explanation, and guided practice before they can operate at the higher levels of thinking. For example, students who are taught procedures designed to enhance creative thinking, such as brainstorming, SCAMPER, or Creative Problem Solving, are more likely to be successful in tasks that require creative thinking (see Starko, 2000). Teaching the skills or procedures themselves might be considered lower level, but they can then be applied to many more complex activities. Thus direct teaching may be used to support both lower and higher level cognitive objectives as well as with psychomotor and some affective objectives.

Storytelling and Curriculum

Storytelling can be a vehicle for direct teaching in a variety of curriculum areas. Stories told well almost always hold our attention. They include vivid descriptions, interesting characters, and conflicts to be resolved.

History told as story can be as interesting as any television drama. To be a successful teller of history, one must have a sense of the big and the small, an overall sense of the structure of the story being told, and an alertness to the details that make it interesting. In much of Western culture, stories have a beginning, a middle, and an end. Some conflict or challenge forms the backbone of the story, and the resolution of the challenge—even temporarily—provides a natural ending. For example, Washington's crossing the Delaware to attack the Hessians at Trenton is a dramatic story. In textbooks, however, it is often reduced to colorless recounting of facts.

Once you have established the story outline, find the details of sight and sound that can bring the story to life for students. In this case, help them picture the comfortable well-trained Hessian forces and the untrained, cold, and discouraged Colonial soldiers. Sometimes you might have access to quotes of people present at key moments. Imagine, for example, the soldier who wrote these words.

Christmas, 6 p.m. It is fearfully cold and raw and a snow-storm [is] setting in. The wind is northeast and beats in the faces of the men. It will be a terrible night for the soldiers who have no shoes, Some of them have tied old rags around their feet, others are barefoot, but I have not heard a man complain. They are ready to suffer any hardship and die rather than give up their liberty. I have just copied the order for marching. . . .

December 26, 3 a.m. I never have seen Washington so determined as he is now. He stands on the bank of the river, wrapped in his cloak, superintending the landing of his troops. He is calm and collected, but very determined. The storm is changing to sleet, and cuts like a knife. . . . We are ready to mount our horses (Peacock, 1998, pp. 25, 28).

Notice how the details of the wind beating, the snow turning to sleet, and the image of Washington wrapped in his cloak against the wind as the barefoot soldiers land their boats bring this story to life. If you share details of history that make its humanity real, students will learn and remember. They will be able to make ties, not just to their textbook, but to all their memories of cold, rain, determination, and courage. Good stories also can come from less dramatic moments, brought to life through the sights, sounds, and smells that made them come alive.

To be a good storyteller takes practice, but it is worth the effort. Take the opportunity to hear professional storytellers, either in person or through television. Sometimes reading historical fiction or biographies can help you envision a time and place well enough to make it real for students. Visiting museums and restored historical sites can help bring a time and place to life for both the teacher and students.

When you use storytelling in teaching, give students the chance to retell the story in some way. In some cases students can literally retell the story in their own words. In others they can transform it into another form—illustrate it, write a song about it, dance it, or create a model. In any case, storytelling lessons should fit the phases of a lesson described in Chapter 6. For example, any good story needs an interesting *opening* to catch the listeners' attention. This could be a puzzling question, a dramatic description, or any other story technique that signals to the listener that something interesting is coming. A good story *builds meaning* by tying events to concrete images students can experience—sights, sounds, smells, and feelings that are vivid enough to become real. Students *apply understanding* through activities that follow the story, transforming it into some new form or using information in a new way. Finally, you will constantly *assess students' learning*, and *adapt* or *differentiate* your instruction based on students' progress.

CHECK YOUR UNDERSTANDING

Think about a unit you plan to teach. Consider how storytelling might be used in the unit. Identify material that may be shared in story form, or devise a story that contains principles you want to teach. Try telling the story to a friend or colleague. Ask for feedback on the parts that were the most vivid or interesting.

Examples of Direct Lessons

These lessons can be used as a model when designing your own lessons. Note that the teacher has placed the curriculum standard or benchmark and the lesson objective at the top of the lesson. To consider differentiation for these lessons, teachers may use a pre-assessment to see if some students already have this skill. If so, those students might skip directly to the extension activity. More direct lessons may be found in the Appendix.

A Direct Lesson on Latitude and Longitude

Benchmark

Locate and describe major geographic features of Africa.

Objective

(The objective is for teacher use and should be placed in brackets at the top of the lesson.)

 Given latitudinal and longitudinal readings, students will be able to find a city on a map.

Set

(The lesson begins with this activity.)

 The teacher holds up a flat Mercator projection map and says, "How are this map and a football field alike? How are they different? Everyone jot down a few ideas and be ready to tell me." The teacher walks around and reads what students write, waits a few seconds, and then calls on four randomly selected students and comments on their

A Direct Lesson on Latitude and Longitude

ideas. She says, "We studied earlier about the difference between a globe and a flat map. Now we'll learn just a few more details about flat maps."

Objective

(This is a learning outcome told to students in *their* words.)

"By the end of this lesson, you will be able to use these lines on a map to find cities on the map."

Purpose

(The purpose explains why students are learning this and how they will use it in the future.)

"We'll use this skill later when we role-play the pioneers' trips in our Westward Expansion unit."

Information and Modeling

(First chunk of information)

The teacher explains and labels latitude and longitude lines, the Equator, the Prime Meridian, and the numbering system used for degrees of latitude and longitude. The teacher points to these lines on a large wall map and uses a memory aid (mnemonic device): "La*ti*tude is *at* the equator; *long*itude is a *long* up and down line."

Checking for Understanding

The teacher asks students a series of questions based on information that has been presented. Examples include: "What are these lines called?" "What is the Prime Meridian?" (The teacher asks the question, waits while all students prepare an answer, and selects students randomly to respond.)

Information and Modeling

(Second chunk of information)

With a globe, the teacher explains and illustrates how latitude and longitude lines intersect and how to determine north and south latitude and east and west longitude.

Checking for Understanding

The teacher asks a few oral true/false questions, to which all students respond (after wait time) with an overt signal (e.g., thumbs up or down). Depending on responses, the teacher decides to reinforce some concepts or proceed.

Information and Modeling

(Third chunk of information)

The teacher writes three latitudinal/longitudinal readings on the chalkboard and illustrates how to use this information to determine which city is at each of the specific locations. The teacher thinks aloud to illustrate the thinking process, metacognition. (Metacognition is discussed in the next chapter on inductive lessons.)

Guided Practice

(The teacher plans three activities that appeal to multiple intelligences and styles. If not all are needed, the extra ones can be used later for reteaching or review.)

1. The teacher passes out cards containing three latitudinal/longitudinal readings and gives students two minutes to work in pairs to find the cities on the globe.

Then the teacher has a few students of varied achievement levels come to the globe to identify each city and asks the other students if they agree.

2. The teacher distributes a copy of a flat Mercator projection map to each student. The teacher has large cards with a latitudinal/longitudinal reading listed on each card and holds up one at a time. Students individually determine the correct city for each reading and jot down the name of the city on a piece of scratch paper. After students determine the answer for each card, they compare their findings with their neighbor. Then the teacher points to each correct city on the wall map and names the city. Students who agree raise their hands.

3. Students create a song or short play about how they find a city. Volunteers perform for the class. (If students are successful after the two practice activities, this activity may be used for reteaching or later review.)

Formative Assessment

(Assessment makes sure every student has achieved the objective.)

The teacher writes two final latitudinal/longitudinal readings on the chalkboard. Each student uses the map to determine the cities at each location and writes down the name of each. The teacher does not provide help at this point.

Adaptations/Differentiation

At this point the teacher checks each student's progress and decides who needs reteaching, extension, and/or independent practice.

Reteaching

(Reteaching is for students who need more teaching and practice.)

Those students who do not complete the assessment correctly are given help in small group with a globe, while the others do independent practice or extension.

Extension

(Extension is for students who need more challenge.)

Students create fictional maps with cities and latitudinal/longitudinal coordinates.

Independent Practice

(This is for students who need more practice. It can be done without teacher guidance, perhaps as homework.)

The teacher provides a worksheet that lists ten latitudinal/longitudinal readings. Students use their maps to determine which city is being described and write the name of the city on the worksheet next to its description.

On the following day, the second step in working with latitude and longitude will be introduced: determining the latitude and longitude of specific cities.

A Direct Lesson for Art Class: Putting Away Supplies

(Classroom Management Lesson)

Objective

(This objective is for teacher use.)

Students will be able to return project materials and supplies to the correct location with minimal confusion.

Set

(The lesson begins with this activity.)

While students are working, the teacher has put the rack of scissors in the wrong place. Teacher role-plays being unable to find the scissors. "What am I going to do? I need scissors and I can't find them. Someone must have put them in the wrong place." She then spots the scissors and returns them to their correct location.

Objective

(This is a learning outcome told to students in *their* words.)

"That was really a problem. I thought I wasn't going to be able to cut out the things for this bulletin board because I couldn't find the scissors. Today we are going to learn how to put away some of our most important supplies so everyone can find them when they need them."

Purpose

(The purpose explains why students are learning this and how they will use it in the future.)

"This is important because when we work together to create projects, we'll be using many materials. If the supplies are in the right place, we'll always be able to find them."

Information and Modeling

The teacher explains the labeling system for the shelves, showing where each item is to be stored.

Checking for Understanding

The teacher asks students a few questions (using wait time). Examples include, "Where would these markers go?" and "If I found this colored paper on the floor, what should I do with it?" She asks students to put the supplies where they belong.

Information and Modeling

The teacher explains and demonstrates procedures for returning unused paper and paper scraps to the shelves.

Checking for Understanding

The teacher holds up pieces of paper, and students signal one finger if they should go in the paper pile, two fingers if they should go in the scrap pile, and thumbs down if they should go in the recycling pile.

Guided Practice

The teacher places an object to be returned on each table. Students are to decide where the object goes and point to the correct location. At the teacher's signal, the materials person for each table returns the object. If the students are successful, the teacher indicates students are now ready to work on a collage.

Formative Assessment

(Assessment makes sure every student has achieved the objective.)

Assessment will take place after the next activity. The teacher asks students to complete a simple project. At the end of the activity she signals for cleanup (as previously taught) and observes students, making note of those who appear to have difficulty putting materials back correctly.

Adaptations/Differentiation

Reteaching

(This skill will be practiced throughout the school year, especially when the process begins to break down. As new materials are added to the classroom, additional instruction may be required.)

Students with limited motor abilities or other impairments that would make cleanup difficult, may be assigned a rotating "Pickup Buddy" to assist with the tasks.

Extension

Students with exceptional organizational or language skills may be asked to devise a system for storing new supplies or to create labels for additional classroom items.

CHAPTER SUMMARY

This chapter has discussed formal and informal teaching and two approaches to formal direct teaching. Direct lesson design is an efficient way to help students learn well-structured content; it may be less effective with loosely structured, abstract, or affective content. Direct teaching incorporates many aspects of effective instruction: congruence among objectives, activities, and evaluation; organization of concepts for long-term learning; rehearsal and practice; appeal to a variety of learning styles; active student involvement; and continuous assessment of learning. Although you will not use direct teaching every minute of every day, it is a valuable structure for the design of some lessons.

Practice Activity A

Designing and Teaching a Direct Lesson

Create a direct lesson to meet one of the cognitive objectives you have written. Use the first example lesson as a guide. Be sure to write the related standard and the formal objective at the top of the page. Just for practice, include each element of the lesson design as if it were a recipe. Describe each activity you would do with students. You do not have to write every word you would say, except when telling students the objective and purpose. Be sure to plan carefully how to ask each question so *all* students have a chance to form an answer before you begin calling on them.

If possible, teach the lesson in a classroom, and have the teacher or observer complete the Feedback Form (Figure 7.2).

Practice Point

Date: _____

Time Started: _____

Name of student teacher: _____   Time Ended: _____

Name of observer: _____

FEEDBACK FORM
FOR DIRECT LESSON

1. SET

_____ Elicited active involvement
_____ Diagnosed (pre-assessed) learners
_____ Referred to previous learning

2. OBJECTIVE(S)

_____ Told students the *behavior* expected at the end
of the lesson (and how they would be assessed)

3. PURPOSE

_____ Told students *why* it is important to learn
(authentic project/real use)

4. INFORMATION AND MODELING

_____ Communicated the structure/organization of
information
_____ Showed it through modeling

5. CHECKING FOR UNDERSTANDING

_____ Used questioning strategies that got *all* involved

6. GUIDED PRACTICE

_____ Helped students to use the information
_____ Gave enough practice to lead to success
_____ Practice exercises matched the objective(s)

7. FORMATIVE ASSESSMENT

_____ Checked each student's mastery of objective

Look for examples of *principles of learning:*

1. CULTURAL CONTEXT

2. CONGRUENT CONTINUOUS ASSESSMENT

3. CONCEPTUAL FOCUS

4. HIGHER LEVEL THINKING

5. ACTIVE PROCESSING

6. VARIETY

COMMENTS:

Figure 7.2   Feedback Form for Direct Lesson

Practice Activity B

Reflection Journal

Complete this Reflection Journal, based on your experience in Practice Activity A.

Name_____   Date_____

Reflection Journal

Direction: Use these questions to help you understand and learn from your teaching experiences. Please write out the answers on a separate sheet of paper and submit the journal to your professor. These reflections can be very helpful in the development of your professional thinking and decision making.

*************** **Please include your lesson plan to help your instructor understand what you did in your lesson.**

Practice Point

1. What "big idea" (concept, principle, or generalization) were you trying to get across?

2. What was (were) the learning objective(s) for you lesson?

3. What evidence can you provide that the students learned (or began to learn) what you wanted them to? How well did *each* student do?

4. If you were the teacher, what would you do with the students tomorrow?

5. What specific activity went as well as (or better than) you had hoped? What did you do to cause this success?

6. What was not as successful in this lesson? Why was it less successful?

7. If you were to teach this lesson again, what would you plan to do differently, and why?

8. Every action (or lack of action) taken by the teacher in relation to students, subject matter, or events promotes specific social values. What particular values were promoted in your teaching today? How, specifically, were these values promoted? (Critical Reflection)

Unit Preparation

Examine the unit time line you prepared for your two-to-three week unit. Consider each objective to determine whether you believe it would be most effectively taught through direct or inductive strategies. You may need to read the next chapter before finalizing the decisions. Begin preparing direct lessons that meet the criteria listed above. Begin with a lesson that teaches a specific skill, a set of procedures, or well-organized facts. Submit at least one lesson for feedback before proceeding.

Depending on your instructor's requirements, you may create a few detailed lesson plans and only brief outlines of the remaining lessons, or you may prepare detailed lesson plans for the entire unit. Your lessons will probably evolve as you continue to learn about teaching strategies. As you plan, remember to keep in mind all the things you have learned about the students in your class and adapt your activities to meet their needs.

 ### *Portfolio Activity*

Include your strongest direct lessons in your portfolio. Select ones that illustrate your ability to design activities that actively engage students' multiple intelligences, use visual displays of information, assess students, and adapt lessons for different student needs.

 ### *Search the Web*

Many websites exist on which teachers share their lessons. The quality of those lessons varies widely. Examine some of the lessons at Ask Eric Lesson Plans (http://ericir.syr.edu). Notice how many activities are primarily inductive and how many are direct. Select a lesson you consider particularly outstanding to share in class. Use the principles you have learned to explain why the lesson is a good one.

REFERENCES

Ausubel, D. (1968). *Educational psychology: A cognitive view.* New York: Holt, Rinehart, & Winston.

Beyer, B. K. (1995). *Critical thinking.* Bloomington, IN: Phi Delta Kappa.

Beyer, B. K. (1997). *Improving student thinking: A comprehensive approach.* Boston: Allyn & Bacon.

Black, P., & Wiliam, D. (1998, October). Inside the black box: Raising standards through classroom assessment. *Phi Delta Kappan, 80*(2), 139–144.

Bloom, B. (1984, May). The search for group instruction as effective as one-to-one tutoring. *Educational Leadership, 41*(8) 4–17.

Brown, A. L. (1978). Knowing when, where, and how to remember: A problem of metacognition. In R. Glaser (Ed.), *Advances in instructional psychology* (pp. 77–157). Hillsdale, NJ: Erlbaum.

Cawelti, G. (Ed.) (1995). *Handbook of research on improving student achievement.* Alexandria, VA: Association for Supervision and Curriculum Development.

Darling-Hammond, L., Ancess, J., & Ort, S. W. (2002). Reinventing high school: Outcomes of the Coalition Campus Schools Project. *American Educational Research Journal, 39*(3), 639–673.

Ernst, M. P. (1995). *The effect of peer teaching on middle school learners' skill performance, cognitive performance and comfort level.* Thesis, University of Wyoming. Accession No. 32651139, ERIC (Internet).

Hunter, M. (1976). *Rx: Improved instruction.* El Segundo, CA: T.I.P. Publications.

Marzano, R. J., Pickering, D. J., & Pollock, J. E. (2001). *Classroom instruction that works: Research-based strategies for increasing student achievement.* Alexandria, VA: Association for Supervision and Curriculum Development.

Peacock, L. (1998). *Crossing the Delaware: A history in many voices.* New York: Simon & Schuster.

Powell, M. A. (1997). *Peer tutoring and mentoring services for disadvantaged secondary school students.* Sacramento, CA: California Research Bureau, California State Library.

Putnam, R., & Borko, H. (2000). What do new views of knowledge and thinking have to say about research on teacher learning? *Educational Leadership, 29*(1), 4–15.

Rosenshine, B. (1987). Explicit teaching. In D. C. Berliner & B. V. Rosenshine (Eds.), *Talks to teachers* (pp. 75–92). New York: Random House.

Rosenshine, B. (1992, April). The use of scaffolds for teaching higher-level cognitive strategies. *Educational Leadership, 49,* 26–33.

Rowe, M. B. (1974). Wait time, review, and instructional variables. *Journal of Research in Science Teaching,* 11, 81–84.

Starko, A. (2000). *Creativity in the Classroom: Schools of curious delight* (2nd Ed.). Mahwah, NJ: Lawrence Erlbaum.

Stiggins, R. J. (2000). *Student-involved classroom assessment* (3rd Ed.) Upper Saddle River, NJ: Merrill Prentice Hall.

Wang, M., Haertel, E., & Walberg, H. (1993). What helps students learn? *Educational Leadership, 51*(4), 74–79.

Weil, M., Calhoun, E., & Joyce, B. (1999). *Models of teaching.* Boston: Allyn & Bacon.

Wiggins, G. (1996, Spring). Anchoring assessment with exemplars: Why students and teachers need models. *Gifted Student Quarterly, 40*(2), 66–69.

Williams, J. M., & Colomb, G. G. (1993, October). The case for explicit teaching: Why what you don't know won't help you. *Research in the Teaching of English, 27*(3), 252–64.

Wolfe, P. (2001). *Brain Matters: Translating Research into Classroom Practice.* Alexandria, VA: Association for Supervision and Curriculum Development.

Models for Teaching: Inductive

CHAPTER OVERVIEW

In Chapter 7 we described ways in which to use direct instruction, where the teacher provides information directly to the students. Many times, however, powerful learning occurs not when a teacher tells students something directly, but when they discover something themselves through their own experiences. This chapter will explore strategies for teaching that follow this pattern of experience and discovery. These strategies are characterized as inductive teaching.

Opening Activity

Think of a time outside of school or other formal class settings when you learned something that was really interesting. It may have happened during a trip to a local science museum, a walk on the beach, or any other time when exciting learning occurred without the specific guidance of a teacher. Share your experiences with one or two classmates. Discuss what, if anything, your experiences have in common.

CHAPTER OBJECTIVES

When you have completed this chapter you will be able to:

1. describe key components of inductive teaching; and
2. design, teach, and reflect upon inductive experiences, including those designed to build concepts, inquiry lessons, authentic research, problem-based learning, role-play, and simulation.

Inductive Teaching: Formal and Informal

When an argument or process of logic is said to be inductive, it proceeds from the specific to the general. That is, individuals draw general conclusions based on particular examples. If you notice that your four red-haired friends also have fair skin and draw the conclusion that red-haired people are fair-skinned, that is inductive reasoning. If you read five fables and conclude that they have characteristics in common, that is also inductive. Detectives (particularly the TV variety) use inductive reasoning when they draw conclusions about what happened at the crime scene from isolated bits of evidence. Similarly, **inductive teaching,** as presented in Chapter 6, occurs when the teacher provides data or experiences from which students can draw conclusions to uncover concepts or generalizations.

Much of the learning that occurs in daily life is inductive. We learn most concepts through experience with examples rather than through direct teaching. Perhaps you can remember the first time you noticed the similarities between the pattern of the veins on a leaf and the branches of a tree, and started looking around for other things that branched. Perhaps you recall more recent discoveries: suddenly seeing connections between Greek mythology and a contemporary movie or noticing words in a politician's questionnaire designed to bias the results. Each of these is an important insight, yet none were covered by teachers in a direct learning experience.

One of the teacher's roles is to structure school experiences to allow students to discover important ideas. Individuals construct meaning best when they interact with new information in real contexts and use it in meaningful ways. Like direct teaching, inductive teaching in school occurs in both formal and informal ways. Much informal inductive teaching occurs through the physical environment of the classroom and the routine of the school day. Minute by minute we are providing students with valuable experiences that build concepts such as fairness, honesty and participation in governance.

It is important to note that informal teaching is not necessarily unplanned. It is true that school days are full of teachable moments, some of which cannot be anticipated, but it is also true that good teachers plan their classrooms and their days to increase the likelihood of teachable moments. A bulletin board of "Amazing Events," a poster of careers using mathematics, a stuffed chair next to a few interesting books, or a space for displaying collections all offer the opportunity for informal conversation and learning. Classroom weather stations, collections of artifacts borrowed from a local museum, a collection of books displayed on a table, online bookmarks for independent browsing, or a portion of the school yard "adopted" for careful observation throughout the year all provide experiences that form the basis of new concepts. Careful thought about the teaching environments we provide and the cues we give students for interacting with those environments are important parts of planning. Sometimes these environments are structured in centers, as described in Chapter 9.

Field trips are a complex example of structuring the learning environment to provide experiences on which concepts can be based. Restored villages that allow students to simulate life in the past, museums with interactive exhibits, or visits to a theater with a backstage tour provide learning beyond the direct instruction that usually takes place. For example, students touring the wings of a theater probably will hear the guide point out the ropes used for flying scenery, the counterweights, the area for set construction, and controls for the many lights. While there, students also are experiencing a host of sights and sounds that build new concepts and new connections about the illusion of scenery, the use of pulleys, and the roles of individuals behind the scene. These connections may prove valuable far beyond the immediate moment. In those settings it is important to focus on the key ideas we hope to teach without losing our appreciation of the additional learning that takes place in a rich environment.

Thoughtful use of technology can enrich a classroom environment without leaving the physical classroom. Consider the informal lessons learned by electronically following an expedition across the desert, or exchanging data with a class from another state or country. In addition to the core content of the project, students will learn many other concepts and lessons through their exposure to new environments, new people, and new ideas. More specific ideas for technology-infused curriculum can also be found in Chapter 9.

 ## REFLECTING ON THE IDEAS

Observe a middle or high school classroom. Think about the concepts that are being built through the classroom environment. Does the environment support the curriculum? Try to identify things the teacher says or does that maximizes student learning through that environment.

Think about your own classroom. You might want to begin a list of things you would like to include in your classroom to support inductive learning.

Formal Inductive Teaching

If students are to develop a clear understanding of the concepts and generalizations we are trying to teach, they will have to experience the ideas and interact with them in ways that make sense in their lives. Formal inductive teaching focuses on structuring such interaction so that it happens as a carefully planned aspect of instruction.

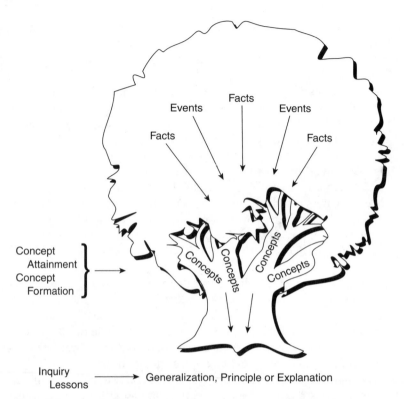

Figure 8.1   The Relationship of Bruner's Structure of Knowledge to Inductive Lessons
From *Teaching as Decision Making: Successful Practices for the Elementary Teacher* (3rd Ed.) (p. 213), by A.J.
Starko, et al., 2003, Upper Saddle River, NJ: Merrill/Prentice Hall. Copyright 2003 by Pearson Education, Inc.
Reprinted with permission.

In direct lessons a teacher is likely to present an idea or skill and then cite specific examples of how it may be applied. In inductive lessons the students are given
the examples or information, and they figure out the concept or generalization that
ties the examples together. *It is only an inductive lesson if the students engage in inductive thinking* (Weil, Calhoun, & Joyce, 1999). As a teacher, it is often tempting to
present the examples and/or and then point out to students the conclusions they
should draw, which shortcuts the process. While students often benefit from cues
that direct them to new understanding, powerful learning can result from the opportunity to discover independently. The resulting "Aha" moment is not likely to be
forgotten.

The tree image of Bruner's structure of knowledge (Figure 8.1) illustrates how
facts, concepts, and generalizations relate to one another and shows how several types
of inductive lessons relate to that structure-of-knowledge tree. Inquiry lessons tend to
result in the discovery of a generalization, principle, or explanation (theory or rule).
Concept attainment and concept formation lessons result in deep understandings of

concepts and key ideas. The three basic types of inductive lessons are: (1) experiences designed to build concepts, (2) inquiry experiences requiring the interpretation and application of data to arrive at an explanation or principle, and (3) authentic research.

Experiences Designed to Build Concepts

This section presents two types of concept-based lessons. The **concept formation lesson** allows students to classify data or information into categories and label the key organizing features as concepts. The **concept attainment lesson** allows students to look at examples and nonexamples of a particular concept, find common characteristics, and then determine the name of the concept.

Concept Formation Lessons

Taba's (1967; see also Weil, Calhoun & Joyce, 1999) concept formation lessons have three basic components. First, students are asked to *list,* or enumerate, data regarding a particular question or problem. For example, students might be asked to list all the uses of water they can name. Next, students are asked to *group* items with similar characteristics. For example, they may be asked, "How might we categorize types of water usage?" This process may be assisted through questions such as: "You have said that drinking water and cooking with water can be grouped under 'human consumption.' Are there other uses that could fit that category?" or "You have listed many ways that human beings use water. Are there other ways that other living things use it?" The final step of a concept formation lesson is *labeling* the concepts. In these lessons, the teacher may be hoping to develop the concepts of individual, environmental, agricultural, and industrial uses of water. These could be important concepts in understanding the effects of water resources in the development of Zimbabwe.

In planning a concept formation lesson, two major factors must be considered. The first key is planning a question or problem that will allow students to generate a list of data rich enough to include the concept you wish to develop. Imagine, for example, that a teacher wanted to plan a concept development lesson around the concepts renewable resources and nonrenewable resources. If the first question were, "How are your homes heated?" it is possible that all the items listed might be nonrenewable resources. In that case, it would be impossible to develop the desired concepts without asking additional questions. Alternatively, the teacher could pose the question, "Imagine that you could design your own house. What are all the possible ways you could provide power to your home? You will want to make sure that your house is both comfortable and economical to live in." With that introduction, it is more likely that at least some students will mention solar power, windmills, and the like.

The second key to a successful concept development lesson is recognizing when students need additional questions to assist them in focusing on the categories. It is always wise to try to predict in advance what types of categories may be initially formed and how to guide students to the desired concepts. Sometimes very general questions may be helpful. For example, you may ask students to form the smallest number of categories they can in which all items are still alike in some way. Other times you may need to be more specific: "If we relied on wood for heat, perhaps we could plan a wood lot near the home so we would never run out of fuel. With our other sources, could we plan for additional fuel?" Concept formation lessons or activities may stand alone or be part of a sequence of activities designed to help students achieve the objective.

Concept Attainment Lessons

A related type of lesson also can help students develop new concepts. Whereas a concept formation lesson requires students to determine criteria and develop categories, concept attainment lessons require them to identify the attributes that differentiate unlabeled categories already formed by someone else. This is done through the analysis of examples and nonexamples of the concept to be attained (Bruner, Goodnow, & Austin, 1977; Weil, Calhoun & Joyce, 1999). The examples and nonexamples are called *exemplars*.

A concept attainment lesson begins with the teacher presenting exemplars and categorizing them as *yes* (an example of the concept to be developed) or *no* (a nonexample). By comparing yes and no exemplars, students begin to silently form ideas about the critical attributes of the concept. After a number of exemplars have been presented, students are asked to describe the common characteristics or attributes of the yes examples presented thus far. As additional examples are presented, students may be asked to categorize them as *yes* or *no* and determine whether the criteria originally developed continue to hold. Criteria may then be refined and concept labels developed. After the teacher assigns a concept label, students are asked to produce examples of their own. Finally, students describe their thinking and how their ideas changed as they moved through the activity (metacognition).

Imagine, for example, that Ken Cowan wanted his students to be able to use inductive thinking to discover the meaning of traditional lifestyle (Objective No. 1) so they could explain the critical aspects of this life (Objective No. 2). Note that the lesson develops two objectives/outcomes: the inductive thinking skill and the content understanding. The lesson might proceed as follows.

1. The teacher introduces the activity by presenting the following exemplars, one at a time, and asks students to find common characterstics of the positive examples. They should use the negative examples to clarify what the concept is *not*.

slow paced (yes)	skyscrapers (no)
extended family (yes)	cattle raising (yes)
impersonal (no)	computers (no)
village (yes)	quickly changing (no)
factories (no)	

2. Students form ideas about what the yes examples have in common and write a definition using critical attributes. For example, one guess might be "life in the old days," with the critical attribute that all the items happened long ago. Students do not initially share ideas.

3. The teacher gives additional unlabeled exemplars for the students to label as *yes* or *no*. For example, "today" (yes) or "high fashion" (no). Teacher asks students to share their definitions.

4. The teacher names the concept and restates the definition in terms of the critical attributes. Students are then asked to generate more exemplars. For example, the teacher might listen to students' ideas and then say, "Yes, the critical attributes of the 'yes' examples are that they are rural, family-based, and low technology. Now, jot down one or two more examples that could be part of a traditional lifestyle." Students are called on to read their examples, which might be "gardens" or "respect for elders."

5. Students describe (in writing or discussion) their thoughts on how they formed their definitions and labels and how they tested them when new exemplars were given. Students might say that they put into one category two exemplars that had a similar quality and then looked at another *yes* item to see if it fit into that category. Then they would contrast those three examples with a *no* item. When a new exemplar was given, they would again test it against the *yes* and *no* examples to see if it fit. (This metacognition helps develop their thinking skills.)

6. Application, practice, assessment, and adaptations (e.g., reteaching or extension) would follow this activity.

Follow three major steps to develop a concept attainment lesson. First, carefully define your concept. Decide on its key attributes. Think about which attributes are critical (essential for this concept) and noncritical (common but not essential). For example, if the concept is plant cell, critical attributes are that plant cells have a cell wall. A noncritical attribute is that many plant cells have chloroplasts. Chloroplasts would not be considered a critical attribute because nongreen plants (mushrooms, for example) do not have chloroplasts. It is important to select your examples to clarify as many of the critical attributes of the concept as possible.

Next, select your exemplars. Exemplars may be provided in the form of words, phrases, pictures, or even concrete items (e.g., works of art or music). Select examples and nonexamples that highlight critical attributes. When selecting the exemplars for a lesson on plant cells, you would want to choose illustrations in which the components of the plant cells are clear. A photograph in which the cell wall cannot be distinguished would not be a helpful exemplar, because it would not clarify a critical attribute.

Finally, consider the order in which you will present the examples and nonexamples. In most cases, give broadly differing examples first, and present finer and finer distinctions as the concept is developed. In ordering your illustrations of plant cells, you might want to start with green plants as examples and animal cells as nonexamples. Later examples might include nongreen plants.

In determining the order of the exemplars, consider the purpose of the inductive activity. If the intent is to provide students with information from which they can build a new concept, it is most appropriate to start with clear examples and save those that demand careful analysis for later in the lesson.

Occasionally, activities resembling concept attainment lessons are used to review or reintroduce already learned concepts. In this case, teachers sometimes use "trickier" examples first and allow clues to become more and more obvious until students "guess" the concept. This can be a highly motivating and appropriate activity; but it is not a concept attainment lesson, because students are attempting to identify a concept they have already internalized. See Figure 8.2 to compare key features of various types of inductive lessons.

 ## REFLECTING ON THE IDEAS

Do the concept attainment activity that follows, completing steps 1–5 of the preceding lesson verbally with a partner.

   The number on a football jersey (no)
   The second place-winner in a race (yes)
   The serial number on a radio (no)
   The seventh person in a graduating class (yes)
   A telephone number (no)
   The number-one song on the charts (yes)

What did you attain from this exercise that you would have missed if you had been taught the concept of ordinal data using direct teaching?

Inquiry Lessons: Interpreting and Applying Data

Experiences that involve interpreting and applying information or data are frequently called inquiry lessons. **Inquiry lessons** require students to inquire, examine information, make hypotheses, gather data, and draw conclusions. They get students actively involved in discovering a generalization, principle or theory that explains a puzzling event or set of data. Inquiry lessons are particularly valuable because they involve students in many of the processes of authentic investigation used by adults in a variety of fields. They also capitalize on students' natural curiosity and desire to find solutions to puzzling or problematic situations (Caine & Caine, 1997).

Suchman's Inquiry

One variety of inquiry lesson was developed by Suchman (1962; Weil, Calhoun & Joyce, 1999). In this model, the teacher begins the activity by explaining the inquiry process and the ground rules. During the questioning period the teacher gives students no response except "yes" or "no". The teacher presents a puzzling event, something that conflicts with our typical notions of reality. Students ask questions to get more information and see under what conditions different results would occur. Through their questions, students begin to isolate relevant variables and to form hunches about causal relationships (hypotheses). Through questions or experiments that test their hypotheses, they formulate an explanation for the puzzling event. Finally, the teacher helps students verify the explanation and leads students to analyze their own thinking processes (metacognition).

Lesson Type	Use	Key Attributes/Student Activities
Concept formation	Development concepts	1. List data 2. Categorize data 3. Label concepts
Concept attainment	Develop concepts	1. Examine examples and nonexamples of concept 2. Identify new exemplars as examples or nonexamples 3. Generate rules/criteria for concepts 4. Develop or receive concept labels
Suchman's inquiry	Form generalizations	1. View a puzzling event 2. Ask "yes" and "no" questions to explain the event and/or identify important variables 3. Test hypotheses by asking questions or manipulating variables 4. Draw conclusions
Other inquiry	Form generalizations	1. Examine data set 2. Make hypotheses regarding data 3. Test hypotheses on additional data 4. Draw conclusions
Authentic research	Produce new knowledge	1. Learn about a topic 2. Pose questions that can be investigated through descriptive, historical, or experimental research 3. Choose the appropriate research design and sources of data 4. Gather data 5. Examine data 6. Draw conclusions

Note: Final step in each approach is metacognition

Figure 8.2 Inductive Approaches

From *Teaching as Decision Making: Successful Practices for the Elementary Teacher* (3rd Ed.) (p. 127), by A.J. Starko, et al., 2003, Upper Saddle River, NJ: Merrill/Prentice Hall. Copyright 2003 by Pearson Education, Inc. Reprinted with permission.

A concrete example will show how this model of inquiry works. The objectives for this activity are to develop students' ability to:

1. see patterns in the evidence and form a hypothesis to explain why an event occurs, and
2. describe how air pressure, direction, and speed interact to create lift.

Note that the first objective relates to the inductive thinking skill, and the second one relates to content understanding to be discovered.

1. The teacher presents a discrepant event (after clarifying ground rules). He or she blows softly across the top of an 8 1/2 by 11 inch sheet of paper, the paper rises, and the teacher tells the students to determine why.

2. Students ask questions to gather more information and to isolate relevant variables. The students ask if temperature is important; the response is *no*. They ask if the paper is of a special kind; the response is *no*. They ask if air pressure has anything to do with the paper rising; the response is *yes*. Questions continue.

3. Students test causal relationships. In this case, they ask if the nature of the air on top causes the paper to rise (yes). They ask if the fast movement of the air is important (yes). Then they test the rule with other material; for example, thin plastic or paper airplanes.

4. Students form a generalization: If the air on the top moves faster than the air on the bottom of a surface, the object rises. This is because fast-moving air exerts less air pressure. Later lessons can tie this experience to other important effects of air pressure, for example airplane wings and flight.

5. The teacher leads students in a discussion of their thinking processes. What were the important variables? How did they put the causes and effects together?

6. Application, practice, assessment, and adaptations/differentiation would follow this activity.

Other Inquiry Lessons

Other inquiry lessons involve students in drawing conclusions, not about a particular puzzling event, but about a set of data. For example, in one lesson students made and investigated hypotheses about the relationship between advertising strategies and product type by examining a collection of advertisements cut from magazines. Students examined the *data set* (magazine ads), made *hypotheses* about *variables* (product and strategy), and tested their *conclusions* (looking at additional print or TV ads). The key attributes of inquiry lessons are examining data or events, making hypotheses, and drawing conclusions. This cycle may be repeated as many times as it seems productive.

For example, you might want to create an inquiry lesson to help students develop a generalization regarding the relationship between scarcity and cost. You might divide students into small groups and provide them with a set of data regarding an imaginary product. For example, the data might be presented in a chart showing the number of floogles available in various years and their cost. Students may be challenged to investigate the data and make hypotheses about the cost of floogles. Hypotheses may be tested by examining additional data on floogles in more recent years. You could ask students to extend their investigation of the hypothesis by looking at data for other items. If the cost of floogles rises when floogles become scarce does that pattern hold for other commodities? Data may be examined for real items that have changed dramatically in availability, for example DVD players. Like other inductive experiences, this lesson would include drawing conclusions about the relationship of scarcity and price, and discussion of the thinking processes students used to reach the conclusions. This inquiry lesson could end with the floogles after one or two class periods or extend to include many areas over a week of investigation.

Many fascinating inquiry projects can be conducted when classrooms share data from different parts of the country or the world through a web-based teacher exchange. Imagine sharing information on the acidity of rain, the numbers of various types of insects, or weather conditions with students in different geographical locations. Students can make and test a variety of hypotheses—while also having the opportunity to learn about another location in a meaningful way.

As schools face increasing pressures regarding test scores and accountability, some teachers are concerned about the amount of time necessary to complete an inquiry project as compared to the time necessary to "just tell students what they need to know." Jorgenson and Vanosdall (2002), for example, fear that forces pushing students and teachers away from inquiry could mean "the death of science" (p. 601). It is true that inquiry activities can be time consuming; that is why it is important to choose carefully the content for inquiry (and other inductive) activities. Yet the in-depth knowledge and thought processes gained through inquiry activities can, in the end, lead to more in-depth understanding and long-term gain than activities that may initially appear more efficient (Wolfe, 2001).

REFLECTING ON THE IDEAS

Two teachers are discussing a student, John, in the teachers' lounge. John attends class regularly, turns in all his homework, seems to be succeeding in practice activities, but is failing most of the quizzes. This is a puzzling set of circumstances! With a partner, develop four hypotheses that might explain the apparent contradiction. For each hypothesis, give a strategy for finding out if it is true.

Present your hypotheses and strategies to another team. Discuss your thinking as you move through the process. Assume that the correct explanation of John's performance is test anxiety. What did you get out of the exercise that you would have missed if you had been told directly about John's test anxiety?

Authentic Research with Students

Traditional inquiry lessons and most research conducted in schools are planned by teachers. Teachers develop the questions, structure the activities, and know in advance the conclusions students should draw. Many valuable activities take this format. However, few researchers in the real world would undertake inquiry projects for which the end result is predetermined. If students are to experience authentic learning, at least some of their inquiries should result in genuine research.

Whereas inquiry activities entail drawing conclusions from data selected and controlled by teachers, authentic research analyzes data as it is found in the world around us. Such activities appeal to the way the human brain naturally learns by engaging students with meaningful, complex experiences (Caine & Caine, 1997; Wolfe, 2001). Because this type of research entails drawing conclusions from specific bits of data, it can be considered an inductive experience. For more information on conducting research with your students, see Schack and Starko (1998) or Starko (2000).

Defining Authentic Research

What is authentic research? Although there are a variety of activities that might be appropriately labeled *research*, most research efforts share certain basic characteristics.

Students Can Do Research

Random House Webster's Dictionary (1993) defines research as "diligent and systematic inquiry into a subject in order to discover facts or revise theories" (p. 565). The essence of research is the production or discovery of new information; it is not merely finding resources and summarizing information. Researchers address questions and problems for which they do not have ready solutions, and through their efforts they add to the body of knowledge. This role as a *producer of information* is key to this type of research and to authentic learning. Thus, in **authentic research** students collect and analyze data to draw new conclusions.

If teachers are to help students function as true researchers, it is necessary to tackle problems for which the teachers do not have ready answers. Teachers and students cannot conduct research to determine the items in the USDA Food Guide Pyramid, but they could investigate food preferences of ninth graders in their school. Although the class cannot research the name of the first U.S. president, they might research the history of their school building. In authentic research, the teacher must give up holding the final solution and take on the role of fellow investigator, never quite sure what the data will bring. The key to this changed role of the teacher is to assist students in posing genuine research questions, questions to which there are no predetermined answers and for which data are available.

A full discussion of research techniques appropriate for middle and high school students is beyond the scope of this book (see Schack & Starko, 1998). It is, however, appropriate to consider basic types of research questions that might be investigated by students. Consider how each type might be used to enhance the basic curriculum or to encourage students to investigate areas of interest.

Types of Research

Three types of research can be particularly appropriate for students: *descriptive, historical,* and *experimental* (Schack & Starko, 1998). A knowledge of the various types of research is helpful in deciding the kinds of questions that might be asked. If, for example, students are interested in recycling or recycling is to be studied as part of the regular curriculum, one way to develop possible research questions is to think about how the topic of recycling might be explored through each of the major research types. What kind of descriptive research might be conducted about recycling? How might recycling be studied from a historical perspective? Could the students design an experiment dealing with recycling?

Descriptive Research. **Descriptive research** is research that describes. It can be thought of as research that answers the question, How are things now? Its main purpose is to portray a current situation as systematically and accurately as possible. Public opinion surveys, descriptive observations, consumer research, and analyses of current test data are all types of descriptive research. If a school reports average reading test scores for a building or grade, if *Consumer Reports* describes the repair records of various types of CD players, or if *Parade* lists the ten top-selling snack foods in the country, they are reporting the results of descriptive research. Students who survey the community regarding recycling practices, conduct election polls, plan taste tests to determine the preferred brand of pizza, or observe the types of insects found on school grounds are conducting descriptive research.

Descriptive research is probably the easiest type of research for students. Such studies often can be conducted in a relatively short period of time. Observation, surveys, and interviews lend themselves to this type of research. For example, in a unit on wellness, you might include a simple survey to determine how many students exercise regularly or an observational study on food choices in the cafeteria. If you plan a unit on the political process, the class might survey adults to find out how many voted in years with and without a presidential election, or interview senior students regarding voting when they turn 18. Students curious about why they had never heard about the early civilization in Zimbabwe might examine the district's elementary school textbooks to find the number and types of references to Africa.

Some data collection activities are brief, conducted in a single class period. Others might be more elaborate and span a period of weeks, for example, a study collecting data on the percentage of sugar in students' favorite cereals. In one class a similar study culminated in letters to cereal companies suggesting that sugar content of some favorites be reduced to allow students to add sugar to taste. Think of the number of skills and content areas encompassed in that study: nutrition, percentages, graphing, letter writing and composition, and consumer activism. The data collection and analysis necessary in these types of surveys are essential parts of the math curriculum in many schools. Students can learn to plan survey questions to minimize bias and to identify bias in political or commercial surveys. This understanding can be essential in making good sense of advertising that claims, "The research says. . . ."

Historical Research. Descriptive research answers the question, How are things now? Similarly, **historical research** answers the question, How did things used to be? Its purpose is to reconstruct the past as accurately and objectively as possible. You probably do not see historical research reported in popular publications as often as you do descriptive research, but it still surrounds us. A newspaper interview with a former mayor about his or her term, a book on pioneer women based on their diaries, or even a magazine article on "Fifty Years of Swimsuits" are reporting historical research. Students who interview their parents about the parents' school experiences, investigate the past occupants of stores on Main Street, or learn about the American Revolution by examining diaries, etchings, or the lyrics of popular music of the period are also doing historical research.

Much historical research is interesting and appropriate for adolescents. One of the key differences between historical research and typical library research is the reliance of historical research on *primary sources*. In a typical research report on clothing of the Civil War period, a student would go to an encyclopedia, reference book, or other *secondary source;* take notes; and summarize the information read. A student doing historical research on the same topic would look for primary sources of information. This might include looking at paintings of the period, reproductions of catalogues, museum displays, or old magazines. The student would look for similarities and variations and draw conclusions from the data.

Many types of resources can be used in historical research. Some may be available in local libraries or museums or through interlibrary loan. In many cases, reproductions of paintings, books, magazines, or catalogues are available and are more durable than the originals. Most libraries have archives of older material on microfiche or other media. Every year students have access to a growing number of primary sources through the Internet and other forms of electronic communication.

Although locating materials for historical research may seem daunting, historical research provides benefits to students that are unavailable by any other means. Aside from the obvious benefits of library and critical thinking skills, this type of research makes history come alive. Students who have been touched by the words and sounds and images of real people from long ago, who have considered those people's lives and points of view, and have drawn conclusions from those lives, form links with history that are not forged in other ways. This power to touch the reality of history makes historical research a vital tool to consider, especially for intermediate teachers who are charged with teaching state and local history. You may find many local resources in your library, and you may also find it worthwhile to visit flea markets and used book stores to find sources that tie in with major units in your curriculum.

For example, a teacher who commonly teaches the history of the state may canvass library sales or flea markets for reproductions of early maps, old postcards depicting the key events, or histories of Michigan families. Such materials could allow students to investigate questions as diverse as: How have the customs of our state changed since 1800? Who were the most common immigrants in our state in 1870?

A teacher of American history may want to acquire a few old *Life* magazines or recordings of period music (such as "Goodbye Mama, I'm Off to Yokohama") to add to a unit on World War II. Such additions might result in a class investigation into point of view in news coverage, or an individual study comparing music written about World War II with that written about the Vietnam War. Students are able to experience the thrill of touching the world of the past through investigating as historians.

Simulated artifacts can be used in place of the real ones. Many books include drawings, paintings, and etchings from the time period being studied. Students can analyze them, as historians do, for information about events, clothing, and architecture. The famous Paul Revere etching of the Boston massacre provides an outstanding opportunity to discuss bias in primary sources as well as the use of propaganda during the Revolution. *Cobblestone* magazine (American history for ages 9–14) regularly includes segments from primary sources, as does *Footsteps,* a similar magazine for African American history.

Museum shops often contain rich resources for real and simulated historical research. An author of this text returned from a trip to a local museum with a small lamp that could have been used in the revolutionary period and a reproduction of the first cookbook printed in the United States (Simmons, 1958). Both artifacts could be analyzed in the same ways the originals might have been, thus enhancing understanding of the lifestyle in the Revolutionary period.

Experimental Research. Perhaps the most typical image that enters your mind when you hear the word *research* is that of the bubbling tubes and strange concoctions of a scientist in the midst of an experiment. Of course, true experimental research is an important type of research design—with or without the test tubes! This type of research investigates cause-and-effect relationships by exposing experimental groups to some type of treatment. It answers the question, What would happen if . . . ?

Experimental research, unlike descriptive or historical research, manipulates variables. That is, the individual conducting the experiment must be able to change at least one aspect of the situation being studied in order to determine the effects of those changes. For example, a researcher investigating the effects of a particular drug must be able to give the drug to some patients and not to others in order to determine its effectiveness. This manipulation of variables is called the *treatment.* All experimental research involves a treatment (though it is usually not a drug). Researchers do not merely describe a situation; they change it.

Examples of true experimental research are many medical studies—some studies comparing the effectiveness of teaching techniques and research comparing the effects of various insecticides. Many science fair winners are students who have conducted experimental research. For example, one student compared the growth of beans under normal classroom conditions with that of beans grown on a rotating "Ferris wheel," on which centrifugal force would interfere with the force of gravity. The student provided a treatment—a change in gravitational forces—and studied the results.

Experimental research can sometimes be complex and difficult. However, even very young students can conduct simple experiments with sufficient guidance. One humorous example happened in a first-grade classroom. In the midst of a typical discussion of the needs of plants, Alex raised his hand. "Do you think," he asked thoughtfully, "that if we put milk on the plants instead of water, they would grow better?"

His teacher replied, "I don't know. Why do you think that might happen?"

"Well, milk makes us grow stronger than water. Maybe it would work for plants, too." Alex had made a hypothesis!

"How could we find out?" the teacher asked.

"Well, we could pour milk on our bean plants and see if they grow."

"But how will we know if the milk made any difference? Maybe they would have grown just the same anyway."

(Long pause.) "We could put water on some and milk on some and see which grow more. That would be fair."

Alex had seen the necessity for the other key component of experimental research, the *control group*. To assess the effects of any treatment, it is necessary to have an equivalent group that does not receive the treatment in order to compare results. Alex did pour milk on some bean plants and water on others and carefully observed their growth.

After about 2 weeks, he drew two conclusions:

1. The plants that were given milk grew to just about the same height as those that were given water.
2. Milk, when left in the sun for two weeks, is not pleasant to have in the classroom.

The experiment ended when neither the researcher nor his teacher could tolerate the smell another day! Despite its untimely end, Alex's research was a true experiment. A treatment (milk) was applied to an experimental group, which was compared to a randomly selected control group. Students had the opportunity to make hypotheses, gather data, and draw conclusions like any investigator.

CHECK YOUR UNDERSTANDING

Identify the following as examples of descriptive *(D)*, historical *(H)*, or experimental *(E)* research.

_____ 1. A report of repair records of new cars in a given model year
_____ 2. Taste tests comparing popular cola drinks with generic brands
_____ 3. Interviews with all living former superintendents of a particular school district
_____ 4. Using different brands of fertilizer in different areas of the garden and comparing results
_____ 5. Examining paintings from the 1860s to learn about clothing of the era
_____ 6. Counting number and type of birds that come to feeders painted different colors

Answers: D, D, H, E, H, E

Problem-Based Learning

Another approach that demands inductive thinking is **problem-based learning,** which is structured around a complex problem (Glasgow, 1997). In some ways, problem-based learning stands the traditional learning sequence "on its head." In traditional classrooms (or at least in those traditional classrooms engaged in projects), first, students are taught the content and skills associated with a particular body of knowledge.

Then they are assigned a project that requires them to use their newly acquired knowledge in complex ways. Such projects are a tried-and-true method of teaching and are the backbone of many classrooms. Suppose, however, that you were to assign the project at the beginning of the unit, before students had the knowledge or skills necessary to succeed. Problem-based learning proceeds in much the same way.

As you might guess from the name, problem-based learning starts with a problem. It has its roots in medical schools where, instead of presenting medical students with lists of symptoms to memorize, some educators began presenting students with hypothetical patients whose complaints must be investigated. In most cases, in or out of medical school, the problem is contrived. It simulates a real-world problem, but is selected or created by the teacher. The problem is chosen because it requires students to use content and processes the teacher wants to address. Content and skills are acquired by students and taught by the teacher as students become aware that they are necessary.

As students explore various aspects of the problem, teachers prompt the types of inquiry they hope students will pursue. Examples are: What is going on here? What do we know? What do we need to know in order to understand the situation? As students become more proficient at questioning, teachers are able to fade into the background as fellow problem solvers.

For example, one problem-based unit created for middle level students has students facing a large truck overturned in a creek, blocking traffic and spilling liquid (Center for Gifted Education, 1993). As students ask questions about the situation, it becomes clear that the liquid, hydrochloric acid, poses a danger to the ecological systems of the creek. Over the course of several weeks, students investigate the likely course of the acid and experiment with strategies for neutralizing acids and bases. Core content includes the concepts of systems, acids and bases, and methods of scientific investigation.

Older students have investigated simulated outbreaks of Legionnaires' disease, taken on the role of German gallery directors forced by the Nazi government to rid their collections of degenerate art, or acted as marriage counselors in a family relations class (Dooley, 1996; Savoie & Hughes, 1994; Stepien & Gallagher, 1993; Stepien, Senn, & Stepien, 2001). Problem-based activities can extend for weeks, an entire school year, or only a few days.

The success of a problem-based unit is determined by two things: (1) the structure of the problem and (2) the skill of the teacher in guiding students. A good topic for a problem-based unit can be described as a well-structured, ill-structured problem. The problem is ill structured in that it is "fuzzy," containing multiple avenues for investigation and no clear answer. It is well structured in that the situation presented to students has been designed carefully to require the content and skills planned by the teacher. If, for example, you wanted to plan a problem-based activity that would include students experimenting with simple machines, you would have to make sure that the situation presented requires simple machines for solution.

The teacher in a problem-based activity can shift between traditional and nontraditional roles. During much of the activity, the teacher is encouraging students to be independent investigators through questioning and modeling. At other times, when students have determined that specific content is necessary, teachers may shift to a more traditional role and provide needed information. For example, in the acid spill problem described earlier, once students realize they need more information on acids, the teacher provides several lab activities in which students can learn the required information. Problem-based learning can be powerful. It parallels quite closely what people in business and other professions do every day and students love it.

Metacognition and Planning Inductive Experiences

The various inductive activities provide ample opportunities for higher level thinking. Regardless of whether students are engaging in authentic research, problem-based learning, or any other type of inductive activity, the basic processes of categorization, analysis, hypothesis testing, and drawing conclusions from data remain the same. Each experience also provides opportunities for **metacognition,** thinking about one's own thinking processes. Metacognition can be a valuable asset for students' understanding of content and skills of effective learning (Costa & Liebman, 1997; Tishman, Perkins, & Jay, 1995).

Imagine that while reading a chapter in this book, you turn a page and suddenly realize that you do not understand a word of what you have read. You are thinking about your own understanding, engaging in metacognition. As a result of this insight, you decide to reread the page. Many students are unsuccessful at learning tasks because they lack awareness of their own thinking or because their preferred strategy is ineffective. To make matters worse, they often lack the tools to examine their own thinking and to generate a more successful strategy.

One part of metacognition is an awareness of one's own commitment, attention, and attitude toward a task. A second aspect is the exertion of metacognitive control over the learning process: knowing what information is important, which strategies to use, and how to apply a selected strategy. For example, when solving a math word problem, a student might need to select the relevant information and decide whether a chart would be helpful in analyzing the data.

The third aspect of metacognition occurs when the student monitors how well the planned strategies are working and checks progress made toward the goal. In the math problem, the student checks to see whether the chart does, in fact, help solve the problem or whether another strategy might be more helpful (Marzano et al., 1988).

What does all this have to do with inductive approaches? Teachers select inductive strategies because they want to develop their students' thinking and problem-solving skills. Notice that the last step of many of the lessons described is metacognition. In any inductive experience, students can share how they approached the task, what strategies they used, and how they monitored their performance during the task. Such discussions are especially useful for students who lack adequate planning and self-monitoring strategies; they benefit from their peers' modeling of metacognition (Caine & Caine, 1997; Huffman, 1997).

Although each type of inductive experience discussed has unique attributes, they usually include five basic stages:

1. *exploring data*
2. *finding patterns or making hypotheses*
3. *examining additional data to test hypotheses*
4. *using conclusions to form concepts or generalizations*
5. *metacognition*

Lesson Objectives 1. Inductive Thinking/Metacognition Skills
2. Content Understanding, Application, etc.

1. *Exploratory activity:*
   Examine data or view a puzzling event.
2. *Find patterns and/or make hypotheses:*
   Attempt to make sense of the data by creating categories, looking for patterns or making hypotheses.
3. *Test hypotheses:*
   Examine additional data to test hypotheses and see if patterns or categories still make sense.
4. *Form concepts or generalizations:*
   Students draw conclusions from data.
5. *Metacognition:*
   Examine the thought processes used to find patterns and draw conclusions.
6. *Apply understanding in a new situation:*
   Guided or independent practice activities use concepts or generalizations.

Note: Stages 2 and 3 may be repeated as often as necessary.

Figure 8.3   Steps to Inductive Approaches
From *Teaching as Decision Making: Successful Practices for the Elementary Teacher* (3rd Ed.) (p. 228), by A.J. Starko, et al., 2003, Upper Saddle River, NJ: Merrill/Prentice Hall. Copyright 2003 by Pearson Education, Inc. Reprinted with permission.

The middle stages, finding and testing patterns or hypotheses, may be repeated as many times as necessary. The five basic steps are frequently followed by a step 6, application activities, practice, and/or formative assessment. The list in Figure 8.3 may be helpful in planning inductive lessons.

Role-play

Another activity falls somewhere between a structured inquiry lesson and the informal experiences that provide the basis for so much concept development: role-play and simulation activities. In these activities situations are planned in which students can interact with important concepts, much as we might plan a classroom environment. However, in these activities the environment is structured so that students can simulate interaction with places, materials, and situations that would be impossible in the actual classroom. Role-play and simulations can provide opportunities for students to build new understanding and to demonstrate understanding developed in other activities.

Role-plays can be effective tools for enhancing understanding of content and developing social understandings (Weil, Calhoun, & Joyce, 1999). In **role-playing** activities, students take on a role—that is, pretend they are a particular person or thing—to solve a problem or act out a situation. Role-playing may be done in small groups simultaneously or by one group in front of the whole class. For example, students might form pairs to act out effective listening with a partner by reflecting back what was heard. Unlike a skit or play, role-plays are not scripted; the words to be spoken are not planned in advance. Students improvise the words and actions they believe to be most appropriate to the problem situation. A role-play is usually a brief activity, completed in one class session.

Role-playing is an excellent way to assist students in developing varied points of view by considering issues from more than one perspective. Such understandings are particularly valuable in social studies and language arts, in which exploring the reasons for individuals' actions is essential. Students may role-play Cecil Rhodes' first encounters with indigenous peoples, Eleanor Roosevelt explaining her activities after her husband's death, or a literary character devising a new ending to a story.

Role-playing can also be a valuable tool in developing students' social and life skills. It may be used in a planned sequence of dilemmas devised by the teacher as well as for dealing with particular classroom issues. Students may role-play alternate solutions to conflicts, methods for dealing with peer pressure, interview or telephone skills, or appropriate responses to students with disabilities. Taylor (1998) uses the term "process drama" to describe extensive use of role-play type activities in drama and social studies. He found such activities particularly important in challenging participants' perspectives and experiencing multiple points of view. Similarly, Manley and O'Neill (1997) describe the use of process drama as an effective strategy for investigating African American history, art, and literature. The opportunity to explore and experience multiple points of view is of particular value when exploring cultural differences.

The four main steps in planning a role-play are:

1. Select the general problem area to be addressed. In choosing a topic, consider your students' needs, interests, and backgrounds. In addition to selecting a problem area that is relevant and interesting, it is important to select a topic on which students have sufficient prior knowledge to take on roles understandably (or provide such background before attempting the role-play). If you are role-playing in content areas, background knowledge can make the difference between an amusing skit and a powerful learning experience.

2. Define the specific situation to be portrayed. A good role-play puts the characters in a specific situation that requires action. For example, if the general topic is dealing with peer pressure, set up a situation in which a student walking home is invited by another student to a party at which the student knows drugs will be used. Content-related role-play activities must also be clearly defined. If the topic is westward expansion, a situation might be created in which a parent discusses the move west with a son or daughter who does not want to leave home, friends, and possessions behind. Choose the specific characters to be portrayed, the situation, and the action that must be taken. For example, the son or daughter moving west must make a decision about which one possession he or she will bring. It would probably be helpful to provide information to the students about the available possessions during that era.

3. Plan a role for the audience. Students not playing particular roles must have an active part in the role-play experience. For example, they may be listening for particularly effective arguments, deciding which of several solutions they think is best, or deciding what they might do in a particular character's place.

4. Decide how you will introduce the role-play. Some role-play situations might be introduced by a story, others by a discussion of the issue or by small-group sharing.

When actually conducting the role-play experience, follow these steps:

1. Provide the introductory activities (readiness, objective, purpose, directions).
2. Explain clearly and explicitly the situation to be enacted.
3. Select students for each role and assign the observation task to the audience.
4. Provide students with necessary time to prepare for their roles and to clarify responsibilities.
5. Give the audience their observation task to perform during the role play.
6. Conduct the role-play one or more times. If you repeat a scenario, you can give more students the opportunity to participate and obtain varied points of view. You may also have students perform the role-play in small groups all at one time or in paired groups with one performing for the other.
7. Debrief the experience in a class discussion. For some role-plays you may wish to discuss each version as it occurs; for others you may prefer to withhold discussion until after several versions have been portrayed. In either case, be sure to allow ample time for students to respond to the role-play experiences. Much can be gained from role-playing activities: helping students understand why individuals made particular choices, what those individuals were thinking and feeling, and what alternative choices might have been made.

REFLECTING ON THE IDEAS

Nancy teaches theater classes. In her warm-up activities she sometimes has students portray animals, inanimate objects, or imaginary situations such as standing inside a shrinking box or walking across hot sand. How are these activities similar to or different from role-playing as it has been described here? Discuss your ideas with a partner. Consider both the activities themselves and the purposes of the activities.

Simulations: Human and Electronic

In role-play activities, the goal is to allow students to understand people, perspectives, and events by taking on the roles of particular individuals in specific situations. They generally encompass short, tightly defined problem-solving situations. **Simulations,** on the other hand, are designed to allow all students to experience a simplified version of reality over a more extended period of time. Role-play usually involves a small number of students at a time and is generally completed within a class period. Simulations are likely to involve many students over a period of days, weeks, or even months. For example, a role-play activity regarding local government might involve a student portraying a citizen discussing an issue of concern with a member of the town council. If several pairs of students portrayed the same situation, the activity might take approximately 45 minutes. In contrast, a simulation on local government would probably involve the entire class. Each student might have a role as a citizen or member of the government. Citizens might organize into special interest groups to lobby officials; public hearings might be held and testimony given by interested parties; and bills might be introduced, pass through committees, and be addressed by the council. Such activities might easily last several weeks.

In good simulations a variety of roles demand differing strengths and interests. Students address complex situations from points of view that vary with the needs and interests of their roles. The results of a simulation must not be predetermined. Events should take place as a natural consequence of student actions. For example, one common form of simulation is a courtroom reenactment. These may range from realistic contemporary situations to trials of historical or literary figures. The guilt or innocence of the character should be assessed by the jury based on evidence presented. If one attorney does a better job arguing and preparing than the other, he or she is likely to win the case. Teachers may provide information on procedures or other necessary input, but they should not direct students' actions. Students should act as they believe their role demands. To do this will quite often require time for students to research their roles so they can be as accurate as possible in their portrayal of the character and situation.

Naturally, the depth and complexity of a simulation that is appropriate for a group of students will vary with the age of the students and their familiarity with simulations and role-play. Middle or high school students may set up businesses, a banking system, or a simulated stock market. Some classes (or even whole schools) have created mini-societies, complete with currency, daily expenses, and employment for all students. In such minisocieties, students may spend a portion of each day earning the classroom currency necessary to rent their desks, pay their portion of the lighting bill, and cover other expenses. Some may earn their living as part of the government and others by operating banks, businesses, or publishing companies. Minisocieties may operate for a few weeks or for most of the school year.

Other common simulations for older students include model United Nations activities and simulated marriages, in which students learn to hunt for housing, plan a budget, and other activities. It is also possible to simulate historical events. Students might take on roles of individuals organizing a party traveling westward or spend a day (or longer) simulating life in medieval times.

Some interesting and challenging simulations are available commercially. For example, a commercial archaeology simulation (Lipetsky, 1982) asks teams of students to create imaginary societies and appropriate artifacts. The artifacts are exchanged (or actually buried) and other students try to learn as much as possible about the civilizations from the remaining artifacts. The resulting difficulties can bring new appreciation for both the field of archaeology and the tentative nature of research. Bear in mind that not all materials labeled *simulation* actually involve students in important aspects of real life, such as those that involve students with dragons or talking space creatures and probably have other goals.

A variety of excellent simulations are available for computers. Although computer simulations are less likely to involve an entire class simultaneously, they allow students to experience the results of decisions that would be impossible or dangerous in real life. Computer simulations can allow students to impact their environment, travel to dangerous places, and conduct elaborate experiments that could not be managed in a school.

Some computer simulations allow students to interact with participants in other states or countries taking on a variety of roles. For example, The Global Schoolhouse houses many simulations connecting schools across the globe in a variety of roles. One of their simulations allows students from various schools to interact with real world adventurers as they re-enact history. (See www.globalschoolnet.org for more information).

The guidelines for assessing computer simulations are similar to those for other simulation materials. The simulation should present a version of reality that is simplified for students' use, but as complex and authentic as is appropriate for the grade level. Results should be determined by students' participation and should be a natural consequence of students' actions and real-world forces, not primarily of luck or chance. For an in-depth discussion of computer-generated simulations, see Dowling (1997).

Four key questions may prove helpful in order to create a simulation activity for your class (Jones, 1985). (See also Adkins, 1996, for steps in designing environmental simulations.) The questions may be considered in any order, but all need to be answered before the simulation can begin.

1. *What is the problem?* In this question consider the general topic, area, or problem to be addressed. Imagine, for example, that you have decided to develop a simulation around the idea of waste disposal, particularly landfill.

2. *Who are the participants?* Participants in a landfill simulation might include homeowners and businesses that use the landfill, city officials, scientists studying groundwater, the owner of a waste disposal company that transports material to the landfill, and others.

3. *What do they have to do?* In this question determine the goal of the simulation. It is usually helpful to set up a situation in which some sort of problem needs to be addressed in a particular format. In the landfill simulation, you might set up a situation in which the local landfill will be too full within the next 18 months. The town council must hold a hearing to obtain community input then prepare a long-range plan for waste disposal.

4. *With what do they have to do the simulation?* This concerns the physical materials that will be available for participants. You may consider creating "role cards" for some roles, for example: "You are B. G. Hauler, owner of Waste, Inc. You have a contract with the city to haul waste to the current landfill. It represents 85% of your company's business." You may also consider providing documents such as a regional map showing alternative landfill sites or procedures for conducting hearings. Materials for a simulation may be simple or elaborate, depending on your needs, desires, and creativity. You may want to start with a fairly simple simulation and add complexity (and materials) over several years.

CHAPTER SUMMARY

In inductive teaching approaches, the teacher's role shifts from that taken in direct instruction. In direct teaching the teacher is responsible for the explicit presentation of content, through lecture, reading, storytelling, or the use of media. In inductive approaches the teacher provides the data and experiences from which students can draw conclusions. The success of inductive approaches is increased by selecting data and structuring experiences so that students are likely to discover important ideas. Whenever students need practice in inductive thinking, select an inductive approach. When you feel students need structured experiences with particular concepts in order to construct meaning (when telling is not enough), an inductive approach may be appropriate. In order to encourage metacognition and higher level thinking, inductive approaches are good choices as well. Inductive lessons may take more time than direct lessons, but they have the advantage of meeting at least two objectives at the same time: they teach the content *and* a higher level inductive thinking strategy useful in everyday life.

Practice Activity A:

Designing a Role-Play

Practice Point

Select a belief, attitude, or value that you listed at the beginning of this section as one you wanted to enhance in your students. With a partner, design a role-play activity that may help students grow toward that value.

Practice Activity B:

Designing a Simulation

Imagine that you want to plan a simulation that would help students understand the functioning of state government or some other topic suitable to your subject area. Work with a small group to decide:

Practice Point

1. Who might be participants in such a simulation?
2. What situation could form the framework for the simulation? What would the participants try to do?
3. What materials would you need to prepare or gather for the simulation to function effectively?
4. How would you debrief (conduct a discussion) so students gain meaning from the activity?

Practice Activity C:

Designing a Concept Attainment Lesson

Practice Point

Develop a concept attainment lesson for the concept of figurative language or another concept taken from one of your college courses. Try to choose a concept that is not completely familiar to most adults. Teach the lesson to several friends or classmates. Pay particular attention to how the order of your examplars affects their experience. Reflect on how their learning might have been different if you had taught the same content as a direct lesson.

Practice Activity D:

Designing an Inquiry Lesson

Practice Point

Think of a generalization, principle, theory, or rule that is important in a unit you might teach. Consider whether the generalization can best be demonstrated through a puzzling event or a set of data. Plan an inquiry lesson to teach the generalization, and teach it to a small group.

Practice Activity E:

Authentic Research

Practice Point

Imagine that you are teaching a ninth-grade class. Like most ninth graders, your students are very interested in rock music. You have decided to take advantage of this high level of interest to teach research skills. List as many projects as you can in which your students might conduct authentic research that relates in some way to rock music. Try to include descriptive, historical, and experimental research.

Practice Activity F:

Problem-Based Learning

Practice Point

Design a problem-based project for your unit. Carry out the investigation yourself before assigning it to students. Share what you designed with classmates. How did you feel doing the research? How might these feelings affect students carrying out similar projects?

Practice Activity G:

Observing an Inductive Lesson

Observe an inductive lesson taught by a classmate (or teacher). Use the Observation Guide that follows to analyze the elements of the lesson and the use of the six learning principles. After the lesson, discuss what you recorded with the "teacher."

Observation Guide

Take notes on a separate sheet.

Practice Point

1. Students were engaged in an exploratory activity
2. Students found patterns and/or made hypotheses
3. Students tested hypotheses
4. Students drew conclusions: concepts or explanations (generalizations)
5. Students discussed their thinking (metacognition)
6. Students applied the concept or explanation in a new situation (practice and/or formative assessment with adaptations)

Note: Steps 2 and 3 may be repeated as often as necessary.

Learning principles

The following learning principles are used in this lesson:

Practice Point

- Cultural context
- Congruent Continuous Assessment
- Conceptual focus
- Higher level thinking
- Active processing
- Variety

Unit Preparation

Review your unit outline and plan inductive lessons for the appropriate objectives. Submit at least one lesson for feedback to make sure you are using the lesson structure correctly. Consider these lessons to be in draft form until you read the next two chapters; they are likely to give you ideas for revising your lessons to make them more effective for the range of students in your class.

Portfolio Activity

Prepare several examples of inductive lessons. Be sure to include a variety of lesson types and to review your lessons with the six principles in mind. Be prepared to explain why each lesson is particularly suited to the content you are teaching.

You may wish to create a diagram of the classroom you would like to prepare. Consider the concepts that could be developed through your classroom plan, and label the diagram accordingly.

Search the Web

Many of the Ask Eric Website links you visited in Chapter 7 also contain inductive lessons or sources that could be used to structure inductive lessons. Think, for example, how some of the historical materials under the topic Discipline-Specific Resources could be used to create lessons incorporating historical research. You also will find many materials under the topic Libraries, Museums, and Archives that can be used to create inductive lessons.

REFERENCES

Adkins, C. (1996, April). Ten steps to better simulations. *Science Scope, 19,* 28–29.

Bruner, J., Goodnow, J., & Austin, G. (1977). *A study of thinking.* New York: Wiley.

Caine, R. N., & Caine, G. C. (1997). *Education on the edge of possibility.* Alexandria, VA: Association for Supervision and Curriculum Development.

Center for Gifted Education (1996). *Acid, acid everywhere.* Williamsburg, VA: College of William and Mary School of Education.

Costa, A. & Liebman, R. (1997). Supporting the spirit of learning: When process is content. Thousand Oaks, CA: Corwin Press.

Dooley, C. (1996). Problem-centered learning experiences: Exploring past, present, and future perspectives. *Roeper Review, 19,* 192–195.

Dowling, C. (1997). Simulations: New worlds for learning? *Journal of Educational Multimedia and Hypermedia, 6,* 3–4, 321–327.

Glasgow, N. A. (1997). *New curriculum for new times: A guide to student centered problem-based learning.* Thousand Oaks, CA: Corwin Press.

Huffman, D. (1997, August). Effect of explicit problem solving instruction on high school students' problem-solving performance and conceptual understanding of physics. *Journal of Research in Science Teaching, 34,* 551–570.

Jones, K. (1985). *Designing your own simulations.* New York: Methuen.

Jorgenson, O., & Vanosdall, R. (2002). The death of science? What we risk in our rush toward standardized testing and the three r's. *Phi Delta Kappan, 83*(8), 601–605.

Lipetsky, J. (1982). *Dig 2.* Lakeside, CA: Interact Publications.

Manley, A., & O'Neill, C. (1997). *Dreamseekers: Creative approaches to the African American heritage.* Portsmouth, NH: Heinemann.

Marzano, R. J., Brandt, R. S., Hughes, C. S., Jones, B. F., Presseisen, B. Z., Rankin, S. C., & Suhor, C. (1988). *Dimensions of thinking.* Alexandria, VA: Association for Supervision and Curriculum Development.

Random House Webster's Dictionary. (1993). New York: Random House.

Savoie, J. M., & Hughes, A. S. (1994). Problem-based learning as classroom solution. *Educational Leadership, 52*(3), 54–57.

Schack, G. D., & Starko, A. J. (1998). *Research comes alive: Guidebook for conducting original research with middle and high school students.* Mansfield Center, CT: Creative Learning Press.

Simmons, A. (1958). *The first American cookbook: A facsimile of "American Cookery" 1776.* New York: Dover Publications.

Starko, A. J. (2000). *Creativity in the classroom: Schools of curious delight.* 2nd Ed. Mahwah, NJ: Lawrence Erlbaum.

Stepien, W., & Gallagher, S. (1993). Problem-based learning: As authentic as it gets. *Educational Leadership, 50*(7), 25–28.

Stepien, W. J., Senn, P. R., & Stepien, W. C. (2001). The internet and problem-based learning: Developing solutions through the web. Tucson, AZ: Zephyr Press.

Suchman, J. R. (1962). *The elementary school training program in scientific inquiry.* Report to the U.S. Office of Education. Urbana: University of Illinois.

Taba, H. (1967). *Teachers' handbook for elementary school social studies.* Reading, MA: Addison-Wesley.

Taylor, R. (1998). *Redcoats and patriots: Reflective practice in drama and social studies.* Portsmouth, NH: Heinemann.

Tishman, S., Perkins, D. & Jay, E. (1995). *The thinking classroom.* Needham, MA: Allyn & Bacon.

Weil, M., Calhoun, E., & Joyce, D. (1999). *Models of teaching* (6th Ed.). Boston: Allyn & Bacon.

Wolfe, P. (2001). *Brain matters: Translating research into classroom practice.* Alexandria, VA: Association for Supervision and Curriculum Development (ASCD).

9

Facilitating Structures and Strategies

CHAPTER OVERVIEW

Now that we have presented two main approaches to teaching, let us turn to the variety of activities that can be embedded in lessons. First, consider the meaning of *student activity*. Phil Schlechty, a prominent school reformer, has coined the term *knowledge work* to describe student activity in the classroom. "Knowledge work is nothing more or less than using ideas, concepts, problem-solving skills, analytic skills, and applying facts to achieve some end. . . What teachers are trying to do is engage students in working on knowledge, rather than having students passively absorb knowledge." (Sparks, 1998, p. 25)

This chapter discusses how to engage students in "knowledge work" so that they actively construct learning.

Opening Activity

If students' learning and retention require that they interact with, rehearse, and critically examine information, how will you provide the opportunity for this to happen? Think of some strategies or learning structures that will engage students in meaningful ways with the ideas you want them to learn.

You probably thought about some of the most interesting things you did in middle or high school; or perhaps you recalled some creative teaching strategies used by teachers you have observed. One of us recalled a school weather station that "broadcast" reports during announcements each morning. It is the teacher's job to give the students opportunities to work with content in ways that will help them learn.

The purpose of this chapter is to introduce several structures and strategies that actively engage students in "knowledge work." These include:

- questioning and discussion
- group learning activities (e.g., cooperative learning)
- academic service learning
- technology
- centers, contracts, and skills for independent learning

The end of the chapter includes a discussion on how to plan for the use of classroom time.

SECTION 1. QUESTIONING AND DISCUSSION

Section 1 Objective

After you have completed this section, you will have the ability to describe effective strategies for questioning and discussion and apply them in lessons.

This section deals with two important teaching techniques: questioning and discussion. Questioning and discussion can take place in many types of educational experiences. For example, direct lessons may use questions to check for understanding. Inductive lessons use questions to help students form categories, to challenge them to make a hypothesis, or to prompt generalizations among their thoughts and experiences. Excellent questioning and discussion skills are particularly essential in inductive lessons (Caine & Caine, 1997). Discussions can be used to practice, develop, and challenge ideas introduced in any type of lesson. Many units are organized around key questions.

Questioning

Questioning, one of the most powerful interaction tools available to teachers, can focus student attention, help students to interact with content, encourage students to express values or opinions, and facilitate classroom management. In summarizing some of the key research regarding questioning and cuing, Marzano, Pickering and Pollock (2001) made four generalizations.

1. Cues and questions should focus on what is important, as opposed to what is unusual. Teachers tend to structure questions around what they believe students will find interesting or unusual, rather than around key ideas. The irony is, the more students understand about a topic, the more interested they tend to be. Thus, questions that increase understanding will increase interest, but not necessarily vice versa.

2. Higher level questions produce deeper learning than lower level questions. Unfortunately, teachers tend to ask lower level questions.

3. If a teacher waits briefly before accepting responses from students, the depth of student responses increases. You will read more about wait time in a few pages.

4. Questions are effective learning tools even when asked before a learning experience. In this case questions focus students' attention rather than check their understanding.

This section provides techniques for phrasing questions effectively and strategies to promote interaction with all your students: planning questions, pacing and phrasing questions, distributing questions, and responding to student answers. Figure 9.1 illustrates these aspects of questioning.

Planning Teacher Questions

A carefully planned sequence of questions can lend clarity and structure to a lesson, leading students from one main idea to the next. Although it is important to maintain flexibility to respond to students' ideas, needs, interests, and opinions, it is equally important to begin questioning with a clear plan. Questions that are prepared in advance are more likely to focus on lesson objectives and provide for both higher level and lower level thinking than questions produced on the spot.

A key consideration in planning questions is *why* you are asking the question(s) in the first place. The type of question you would use to check students' comprehension of previously presented material is likely to be different from questions designed to have students evaluate content or defend opinions. Some of the *purposes* for questions are to:

Figure 9.1   Teacher and Student Questioning and Discussions
From *Teaching as Decision Making: Successful Practices for the Elementary Teacher* (3rd Ed.) (p. 240), by A. J. Starko, et al., 2003, Upper Saddle River, NJ: Merrill/Prentice Hall. Copyright 2003 by Pearson Education, Inc. Reprinted with permission.

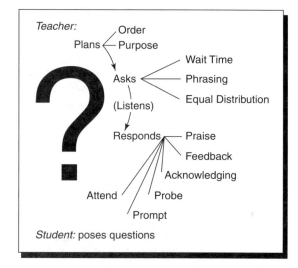

- check students' understanding (formative assessment);
- tie information to students' prior knowledge or experiences;
- have students process information by looking for inferences, implications, and related items;
- allow students to practice supporting ideas and opinions with evidence;
- lead students to discover a new concept, principle, or generalization;
- learn about students' interests, ideas, or concerns;
- focus students' attention on important ideas; and
- model the importance of forming and seeking answers to questions.

It is also important to consider the *order* in which you will ask questions, and there is more than one correct way to sequence questions. Sometimes you may wish to begin with an open-ended (divergent) focusing question and narrow the topic down through questions that involve descriptions and comparisons for answers. At other times you may prefer to proceed from lower level to higher level questioning. Select the sequence of questions that corresponds best to your lesson objectives.

Plan ahead of time how you will ask the questions so you don't fall into the trap of having the same few students answering every question. Will you use wait time by asking the whole group the question, telling all students to think of an answer, and randomly selecting students to respond? Will you raise a question, and then ask students to tell the answer to a partner? Will you pose a question to be discussed in small groups before calling for a response? If you note these ideas in your plans, you will be more likely to provide variety and equity in questioning techniques. Review Table 7.1, page 186 for a wealth of questioning strategies that promote maximum student participation.

Pacing and Phrasing Questions

How will you pace and phrase your questions? One of the most important concepts in pacing questions is wait time. Wait time is the period between the time a teacher asks a question and the time he or she asks another question, questions another student, or answers the question (Atwood & Wilen, 1991). Rowe (1974) discovered that the average wait time for each teacher was shorter than 1 second. No wonder students sometimes have trouble finding time to think! In studies in which wait time was increased to 3 seconds or longer, numerous changes were observed (Tobin, 1980; Tobin & Campie, 1982):

- The length of responses increased.
- The number of voluntary responses increased.
- Complexity of responses increased.
- Student questions increased.
- Student confidence increased.
- Student failure to respond decreased.

There is no perfect amount of wait time. In quickly paced recall questions, short amounts of wait time are appropriate. In divergent questioning, or questions requiring higher level thinking or evaluation, longer wait time allows students sufficient time to formulate answers, consider more than one perspective, or reflect on other students' responses. In general, however, it may be best to pace questions more slowly than feels natural at first, allowing "think time" before asking for responses.

At the beginning of the year, you will probably need to carefully structure your wait time. If both you and your students are accustomed to a rapid-fire pace of questioning or calling only on volunteers, it will take practice to change those habits. Some teachers use a formal think time in which a hand signal communicates that no responses will be accepted until everyone has a chance to think. Other teachers simply discuss the idea of wait time with their students and do not call on anyone until an appropriate time has passed. The key is to communicate to students that you will wait until they *all* have an opportunity to think and that you expect *every* student to think carefully and be prepared to respond.

The *phrasing* of questions also can have an impact on students' thinking processes. In general it is best not to start a question with a student's name, such as, "Gina, why did Lafayette agree to help the colonists?" All the other students know immediately that they are not being questioned and can ignore both the question and the answer. In this case, more students would have thought about Lafayette's motivation if the question had been phrased as follows: "Everyone think about why Lafayette agreed to help the colonists and be ready to tell me if I call on you." (Wait time) "Gina?" (Wait time) It is also advisable to avoid the "Who can tell me" manner of asking questions. Such phrasing invites students to call out the answer, thus depriving the others of valuable mental rehearsal of the material.

Distributing Questions Equitably

Even when teachers call for responses after a question, students do not always have an equal chance for classroom interaction. Research has noted numerous inequalities, for example, many teachers call on high-achieving students much more frequently than low-achieving students, males more than females, White students more than minority students, students at the front more than students at the back, or even students on one side of the classroom more than the other.

Any time an unequal pattern of questioning develops, some students have greater opportunity to meaningfully process the material and transfer the information to long-term memory than others. It also sends nonverbal messages to students about which youths in the classroom are considered more capable or important. Research conducted in classrooms indicates that more equitable questioning patterns lead to greater interaction by all students, more willingness to respond, and increased questioning by students (Good & Brophy, 1999).

How can you distribute questions and teacher attention equitably to your students? Some teachers use props to ensure that all students have an equal chance of being asked a question. Popsicle sticks or index cards with student names on them can be pulled at random. Other teachers keep track of whom they call on by making a mark on their seating chart each time they call on or speak to a student. Every day or two they check to see who is getting called on and who needs to be called on more. In this way they can monitor their own distribution of attention and questions. Finally, you can ask a friend or peer to observe a lesson you teach and note the students with whom you interact. Such observations can provide valuable information for improving questioning patterns.

Responding to Student Answers

Once a student has responded to a question, you will need to decide whether to praise, acknowledge, redirect, probe, prompt, correct, or ask a new question. Major factors in making this decision are saving the dignity of the student and knowing how a student will react to different types of public responses by the teacher.

Although *praise* can be important in creating a positive classroom atmosphere and building self-esteem, it must be used carefully (Brophy, 1998). Praise that is vague, routine, or repetitive quickly becomes meaningless. A response of "good" after every student answer is almost like no response at all. Praise that is global ("You are always such a good student.") does not help students identify the characteristics of their work that led to their success. It is better to give specific feedback about the performance, not the student ("You made excellent use of figurative language in your description of the forest.").

Global, vague praise also has the potential to create or increase emotional problems. Individuals who are led to believe that they are always expected to be good students may become fearful of challenging tasks or open-ended situations. Teachers must also be alert for students who are embarrassed by being praised publicly. For many students, a private comment is more welcome than public praise given during class (Good & Brophy, 1999).

Finally, praise can be seen as a terminal response, ending discussion or thought. If you ask a higher level or divergent question and give elaborate praise to the first answer, other students are less likely to respond, assuming the "right" answer has already been given. Some research has indicated that giving rewards too early may have a detrimental effect on problem solving or higher level thinking (Costa & Liebman, 1997). Other research suggests that the use of *evaluative praise* ("Good work") can be damaging to motivation and creativity in higher level tasks. Students may be left with the impression that something is good or bad simply because the teacher says so (Good & Brophy, 1999).

Informational feedback is less problematic, because it tells students which characteristics of their efforts were particularly effective (for example, "You really had a lot of evidence to back up your ideas."). Each teacher needs to be sensitive to the effects of praise in the classroom. In many cases, praise is most appropriate for unmotivated or reluctant learners, lower grade students, lower level cognitive tasks, or practice of previously learned material. In other cases, silence or *acknowledgment* of responses ("I understand." or "That's one possibility.") may be more appropriate and lead to continued student efforts. You may also wish to accept the response nonverbally (perhaps through a nod) or *redirect* the question to another student ("What do *you* think, Ben?").

When student responses are unclear or incomplete, it is important to probe in order to further clarify the response or to get more information. A general probe such as "Please explain further." or "Tell me more about your thinking on that." may be appropriate. In other cases it is best to be more specific. If, for example, a teacher asks the class "How did Washington's troops feel at Valley Forge?" and a student responds, "Happy," the teacher should probe, "Why were they happy?" If the student replies, "Well, they were cold and hungry, but they knew they were fighting for an important cause, and I think that would have made them happy," the teacher would plan a much different response than if the student had said, "They were camping out and camping is fun."

When probing, be aware of responses to ethnic, achievement, and gender groups in the classroom. Probing must be equitable; teachers who seek responses from as many students as possible send the message that all students are considered capable and are expected to participate.

If a student answer is inaccurate or incomplete (or if the student gives no answer), you may wish to **prompt**, or cue, the student toward a more successful response. It is important to help students understand which parts of an answer were correct and which were incorrect, while providing information that may lead to a completely correct response. The process of prompting students requires care and sensitivity, so that students have every opportunity for success without embarrassment. For example, assume a teacher asks, "What are the characteristics of commedia dell'arte?" and Cheryl, a student, replies, "They hit each other." The teacher might respond, "We did talk about the use of the slap stick as one of the conventions of commedia dell'arte, but it is probably not the most important characteristic of that form. What can you tell me about the characters in these plays? You might think about Pantalone or Harlequin." This type of prompting may lead Cheryl to a more complete response.

Good teachers should not only question students, but listen effectively to what students say. Teachers can improve their listening through attending behavior and through active and reflective listening. **Attending behavior** refers to a variety of verbal and nonverbal responses that signal to students, "I am listening to you. I believe that the things you have to say are valuable." Verbal signals can include silence, which is a chance for the teacher to reflect and the speaker to continue; brief verbal acknowledgments, such as "I see." or "Yes."; or brief summaries of the speaker's statements. Nonverbal signals include eye contact, an empathetic facial expression (for example, nodding or smiling), relaxed body posture (signaling "I have time to listen to you"), and comfortable physical proximity (distance).

Attending behaviors are often viewed as common courtesy. Unfortunately, without conscious attention, they may be lost in the flurry of classroom activity, in which the critical moment of silence or careful eye contact may seem difficult to maintain. However, with care and practice, you will be able to signal to your students that no matter how busy you are, you value the things they are saying.

You can also signal students that you are paying attention to them by active and reflective listening. **Active listening** entails identifying both the intellectual and emotional attitude of the speaker. If Jared says, "This is a dumb book," he is conveying an emotional as well as an intellectual message. Carefully observe nonverbal cues and consider all you know about Jared to discern his message. Jared might be saying, "I am upset because I don't understand this book," or "I am offended by the stereotypes presented here," or "I read this three years ago and I am bored."

After actively listening to a student, you may reflect, or restate, the message you thought you received, which is called **reflective listening** and can involve paraphrasing the statements ("You don't like the book.") or expressing both the statement and the inferred emotion ("You seem upset about reading this book."). Reflective listening is a powerful tool that must be used with care. It is particularly valuable when emotions are high and misunderstandings easy or in situations in which clear understanding is critical. Try to be sensitive to the amount of reflecting that is sufficient to elicit clarity without becoming monotonous or parrot-like.

CHECK YOUR UNDERSTANDING

How might you use reflective listening to respond to the following students' comments?

JANE (LOOKING AT THE FLOOR):   I hate going to lunch.
MIGUEL (SMILING BROADLY):   I'm going to be on the citywide quiz bowl team!

Encouraging Students' Questions

The teacher should not be the only person asking questions in the classroom. Eisner (2002), in describing "the kind of schools we need," said that such schools "would be staffed by teachers who are as interested in the questions the students ask after a unit of study as they are in the answers students give" (p. 579). Students' questions are important in at least two ways. First, it is important that students feel free to ask questions when they do not understand a lesson or assignment. If students sense that such clarifying questions are unacceptable, they are likely to languish in confusion or move forward practicing content incorrectly. Neither experience is likely to lead to effective learning.

Second, students should feel free to ask questions that go beyond the content being taught. The essence of this type of question is not, "I do not understand," but "I wonder." Wondering is an important key to learning and creativity. Productive people wonder all the time—about the things they see, the things they hear, the things that trouble them, and the things that bring them joy. Unfortunately, students seldom experience this type of questioning in school. A typical school question generally has one correct answer, and it can be found in the back of the book. The real world is not like that. Teaching students to question and to wonder is to provide them with a skill for lifelong learning.

Consider the following five strategies for encouraging student questions:

1. *Teach students to appreciate genuine questions, ones that have no easy answer.* Help them understand that you will ask two kinds of questions: (1) "checking for understanding" questions, to which you already know the answers and (2) genuine questions. You ask checking questions because you need to see if students are learning important content. Sometimes they, too, may want to ask clarifying questions to make sure they understand something you are teaching. Make sure students know you will be pleased to respond to such questions. Help students understand the difference between these activities and your real questions—questions that show your curiosity because you don't have an answer.

2. *Model questioning behaviors.* Share your puzzlement and curiosity with your students. Sometimes this may be as simple as a casual comment, "Isn't it interesting how some fashion trends return and some don't? I wonder what determines which fashions recycle and which don't? Will I ever get to wear my [insert your favorite fossil fashion here] again?" Other times your questions will be more serious: "I have always wondered what makes people follow different leaders. Did people follow Hitler for some of the same reasons they followed Gandhi, or were there totally different factors at work? What do you think?"

3. *Teach students to ask questions.* You may want to do a lesson on what constitutes a question, why people ask questions, and why questions are important. Consider lessons focusing on questions one could ask about a given event, experiment, story, or idea. Rosenshine, Meister, and Chapman (1996) found that teaching students the cognitive strategy of generating questions resulted in significant gains in reading comprehension.

4. *Respond to student questions with respect.* One student came stomping home from school, disgusted with her teacher's use of the K-W-L reading strategy. (K-W-L discussed in Chapter 1 is a technique in which students are asked what they Know about a topic, what they Want to know, and later what they have Learned.) Her complaint was, "I don't know why they bother with the *W* anyway. She asks us what we want to learn and then we just do what the teacher wants to do anyway!" Although it is impossible to investigate every question posed by an enthusiastic group of students, they should have confidence that at least some of their questions will be addressed and others will be met with enthusiasm and suggestions for follow-through. One teacher even created a bulletin board on which to hang interesting questions. Not all the questions were investigated, but they all were acknowledged as valuable.

5. *Teach students the investigative skills of the disciplines.* That is, teach them how to ask good questions within various subjects. History teachers should help students understand what kinds of questions historians ask and how they investigate them. Science teachers should teach students how scientists develop questions and design experiments to test them. (This is a far cry from the follow-the-book procedures of many science activities.) Such activities can be a natural outgrowth of existing labs. For example, as part of a lab in which students observe the effects of light and incline on earthworm behavior, students could be invited to consider what other variables they might wonder about and how to investigate them. Language arts teachers can discuss how authors decide what to write and the kinds of issues they try to address. In each case, students are exposed to the mental processes of wondering within the context of a particular discipline.

Conducting Discussions

What is the difference between asking questions and having a discussion? Think about the differences before you read further.

Some of the possible points you may have thought of are (1) the relative extent of participation by students and by the teacher, (2) the focus of communication, and (3) the classroom atmosphere. In questioning, the teacher is almost always the focus of attention. Communication travels from teacher to student, back to teacher, and is redirected to another student, forming a pattern like a many-legged spider with the teacher at the center.

In a discussion, the patterns of communication are much more diverse. The initial stimulus may come from the teacher. Additional comments may travel from student to student, with students adding questions or comments as desired. Figure 9.2 illustrates the difference between questioning and discussion. Whereas questioning is sometimes directed at quizzing students, discussion is an open-ended exchange of ideas designed to share information and possibly to reach consensus, rather than to seek the so-called right answer (Gall & Gall, 1990).

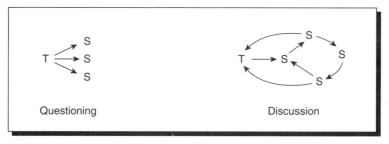

Figure 9.2 Interaction Patterns in Questioning and Discussion
From *Teaching as Decision Making: Successful Practices for the Elementary Teacher* (3rd Ed.) (p. 246), by A. J. Starko, et al., 2003, Upper Saddle River, NJ: Merrill/Prentice Hall. Copyright 2003 by Pearson Education, Inc. Reprinted with permission.

A good classroom discussion is a valuable learning experience, full of opportunities for higher level thinking and ties to student interests and experiences. Like many worthwhile goals, it is a challenge that requires planning, patience, and practice. Many students spend years in school without participating in a real discussion. Their inexperience can sometimes turn discussions into questioning sessions in which all attention is focused on the teacher, with students attempting to discern exactly what the teacher wants. Because they find it difficult to imagine that the teacher wants them to express opinions (to say nothing of asking questions of their own), they expend enormous energy trying to find the right answer.

An open-ended topic is key to a successful class discussion. There is little point in discussing the year the American Revolution started or the sequence of events in *Johnny Tremain*. Facts, sequences, or issues on which there is already consensus do not make good discussion topics. Concepts that are fuzzy, issues generating a genuine difference of opinion, or opportunities to tie personal experiences to content provide more chance for successful expression.

If you want students to raise questions during class discussions, you may wish to structure activities to practice such behaviors. Students can be asked to write questions about stories they have read, current issues, historical dilemmas, or almost any other content. Some teachers even explain the levels of Bloom's taxonomy (see Chapter 4) to their students, to enable them to write higher level questions for class discussions. Try to reinforce students' questioning behaviors, letting them know you are glad that they are seeking information, clarification, or opinions.

In many classes it is useful to plan numerous experiences with paired or small-group minidiscussions before attempting to share ideas with an entire class. Students may be asked to describe to a partner their favorite character in a story or to discuss in a group of five the items they would choose to best represent American culture. A pair of students might debate the pros and cons of proposed legislation, with a third student noting major arguments. Such activities accustom students to talking to one another without depending on the teacher to direct the conversation. They also provide needed variety, even in classes already adept at whole-group discussion.

During a discussion, the teacher (or other discussion leader) may serve several roles:

1. Provide the initial stimulus for discussion.

2. Provide additional information, clarification, or correction of misinformation as needed.

3. Paraphrase, summarize, or compare student positions to add clarity.

4. Maintain the focus of the discussion. This role demands good judgment and a gentle hand. Although class discussions must not stray far from the topic at hand, occasional diversions can provide significant information about students' needs, wants, and values. In general, discussion leaders should try to keep discussion on the topic of concern.

5. Respond to student comments with acceptance, rather than praise or criticism. Remember that either praise or criticism can be viewed as a terminal response, cutting off further discussion. If one student's response is effusively praised, other students are apt to think that it was the right answer and may hesitate to comment further. Of course, if students' comments are met with personal criticism or harassment, neither they nor others are likely to continue. Students will benefit from instruction on expressing disagreement without fear of being insulted.

6. Draw the discussion to a close through summarizing and/or seeking compromise or consensus. As you conduct classroom discussions, be aware of the patterns of student interactions. You may want to ask an observer to keep track of student contributions during class day. You can encourage contributions from all students by using small groups and by teaching skills of discussion and cooperation.

It is not sufficient planning to write in your lesson plan, "Conduct class discussion." The reflective teacher makes many key decisions to engage students successfully in question-and-answer and discussion activities. The selection of questions, how they are phrased, the teacher's reactions to student answers, and equity in response opportunities are just a few of the considerations when planning lessons. Discussions must be carefully planned to evoke students' engagement, curiosity, and energy. The best teachers take care to plan their questions and discussion prompts before the lesson begins. They also plan structures (e.g., wait time) to make sure every student has an opportunity to participate. Finally, think deeply about how to respond to students in ways that maintain students' dignity and interest.

Practice Activity A

Planning Teacher Questions

Practice Point

Reread the section of text dealing with questioning and discussion. Develop two questions that could be used to check students' understanding of the section. Next, plan two questions that would be appropriate for a discussion of some controversial issue raised in the section. Take turns asking your questions in a small group, and don't forget to use wait time.

SECTION 2. GROUP LEARNING ACTIVITIES

Section 2 Objective

After you have completed this section, you will have the ability to design various types of group learning activities and critique their strengths and weaknesses.

Adolescents naturally socialize. Years ago "socializing" was considered a problem in schools, often a cause for disciplinary action. Now we know that a silent classroom is not necessarily a good one. Remember from Chapter 2 that social learning theory suggests that students need to interact with adults and with peers in order to develop new concepts. Glasser (1990, 1997) identified "affiliation" as one of the five basic needs of young people. "Collaboration" and "absence of threat" are two of the eight key factors present in a classroom that are compatible with how the brain learns (Caine & Caine, 1997; Wolfe, 2001).

Group learning fulfills students' need for affiliation while teaching explicitly how to work productively and courteously in a group. In addition, the research base supports the effectiveness of this method for promoting both cognitive and affective learning (Johnson & Johnson, 1999; Manzano et al, 2001; Slavin, 1995). Almost any set of recommendations for school and instructional improvement includes greater use of small cooperative learning groups.

Making Student Grouping Decisions

One of the most important decisions a teacher makes in planning learning experiences is how to form instructional groups. The most reasonable question about grouping does not seem to be, "Should we group or shouldn't we group?" Rather, it seems to be, "What grouping arrangements best meet the needs of these students for this particular activity?" Although the effectiveness of rigid, long-term groupings based on ability can be questioned, flexibility within—or between—class groupings based on particular academic needs is associated with increased achievement (Slavin, 1994).

Most students should probably spend part of the school day working in larger, heterogeneous groups. They should also spend some time on individual tasks, projects, and interests and some time in small groups. The small groups may be heterogeneous or homogeneous or skills-based or interest-based, depending on the needs of the students and the demands of the task. Most experts agree, however, that students should be included in multiple groupings so they do not become labeled or stereotyped as a result of always being in the same group (Cohen, 1994, 1998).

At times, you may want students to work in groups based on the need for a particular skill. This type of grouping is particularly appropriate for basic skills instruction or instruction in areas that have been previously introduced but not mastered by all students (e.g., for reteaching). More targeted groupings can provide an appropriate level of challenge for every student. Few things will kill motivation more quickly than repeated practice in a long-mastered skill or instruction on a task that is impossibly beyond a student's current skill level. Remember, however, that research indicates negative effects when low-ability students are grouped homogeneously for longer periods of time (Lou et al., 1996).

In addition to specific skills needs, some complex tasks are best suited to more homogeneous groups. Particularly challenging problem-solving activities or projects may be appropriate for students with demonstrated abilities in a particular area, but may be unsuitable for a whole-class task. At times, groups of students with more limited skills can benefit from tackling a research task that presents a challenge to them but would be less challenging to others. Managing the task this way can provide chances for problem solving and persistence that might not occur in a more heterogeneous group. Chapter 10 contains more information on differentiated instruction that may assist you in generating ideas for both homogeneous and heterogeneous groups.

At other times, groups may be based on students' expressed interests. Sharan and Sharan's (1992) group investigation model has students generate questions they would like to explore about a particular topic. Then students divide into groups according to the questions they would most like to investigate For example, a class studying the Renaissance may be divided into groups examining Renaissance art, music and dance, weaponry and warfare, or other areas of interest. Some students may be interested in learning about culture and events in Asia or Africa during the time of the Renaissance in western Europe. Similarly, a math class might divide into groups to investigate the use of mathematics in different types of careers in science, the performing arts, business, emergency services, or fashion/design areas. The groups may be heterogeneous in skill level, but homogeneous in interests. The next section discusses a particular way of teaching with heterogeneous groups that can develop the ability to work harmoniously and productively with others.

Cooperative Group Learning

Cooperative group learning is a mixed group that "sinks or swims" together because each person is responsible for the others' learning. When discussing cooperative learning (Johnson & Johnson, 1999), it is important to contrast it with individualized learning and competitive learning.

In **individualized learning**, students work individually to accomplish an objective. Students are not compared with one another; they work to achieve a preset standard. Individual structures are useful when students are well motivated and need little guidance.

Competitive learning, often present in today's schools, judges student performance against the average performance of all students. Recall the characteristics of norm-referenced evaluation presented in Chapter 5. If some students succeed, others must be less successful because of the limited number of A grades available. Tests in competitive classrooms are graded on the curve, so the idea is to do better than someone else. The effect of too much competition on students may be selfishness, low self-esteem, and poor communication skills.

Cooperative classrooms, on another hand, are characterized by an attitude of interdependence. Students work to help their team members achieve the objectives. Each student is held individually accountable and receives an individual score. Teams with a score greater than the minimum level set by the teacher may receive special recognition or a reward. Students in such classrooms learn to value giving and receiving help. They also learn to work together toward a common goal—a skill that is essential for both effective workplaces and democratic communities.

REFLECTING ON THE IDEAS

Discuss with friends their experiences in school. Do they remember examples of individualized, competitive, or cooperative learning? What was your experience with each type of structure? How did you feel? How did your friends feel? Come to class prepared to discuss your own and your friends' experiences.

The main reason to use cooperative learning, in addition to its obvious social benefits, is that it can assist student learning. The research on cooperative learning is impressive. Students at many levels who received some cooperative activities (approximately 60% of class time, with the balance spent in individual and competitive learning) had higher achievement, better retention, higher level reasoning skills, greater empathy for those who are different, and higher self-esteem than students who had little or no cooperative learning (Johnson & Johnson, 1999; Walberg, 1999).

Cooperative learning does not work by simply putting students into groups and assigning a task. The four critical components of cooperative lessons are face-to-face interaction, positive interdependence, individual accountability, and cooperative skills learning.

Face-to-Face Interaction: Grouping Decisions

As you learned in Chapter 2, many students learn best when involved in purposeful interaction about authentic tasks. Cooperative learning is an excellent way to structure such interaction. Group size is an important factor. As groups become larger, it is harder to get every student actively involved; thus groups of two, three, or four seem to be most productive. Students must learn to work closely together; face-to-face interaction is essential to group learning.

Most long-term cooperative groups are mixed in ability or in social makeup. For example, a group of three students may contain one high achiever, one low achiever, and one middle level achiever. If social integration is a goal, the groups may be composed of popular and less popular students. Ethnic and home background may be the basis for creating heterogeneous groups. Language proficiency and gender could also be taken into account in setting up mixed groups.

When students who don't typically interact with one another are in a face-to-face, interdependent situation, many social barriers are broken down and students learn to value those who are different from themselves. This social integration can be particularly important in secondary grades where the need to fit into a peer group is a primary motivating force. One teacher forms long-term groups by having students privately list the names of three students they would like to have in their group. In this way students get to have some input into the group structure. The teacher uses this information to mix students who appeared on few lists with those who are particularly outgoing and caring with others. In such groups the isolated student begins to feel included and valued.

For informal, short-term groups you might assign students randomly by counting off, by the color of clothes, or by giving playing cards to students as they enter the room.

Such random groupings make sense at the beginning of the year when little is known about each student and for quick on-the-spot activities (e.g., checking for understanding with a neighbor).

Positive Interdependence

When groups work together, all too often only one of the students does all the work, and therefore, the other students may learn little. One way to avoid this pitfall is to deliberately structure the task so all students must depend on one another to succeed. Such positive interdependence causes the group to sink or swim together.

How is a sense of positive interdependence achieved? First, it can be achieved by **limiting materials;** such as giving only one copy of a worksheet or one pencil to the group. Second, it can be achieved by jigsawing the material into sections and assigning an expert on each piece of the puzzle to teach the other group members. Third, it can be achieved by assigning roles, such as a checker, an encourager, and a recorder. Fourth, it can be achieved by offering group rewards; for example, if all members succeed, each member receives a privilege or points. **Reward interdependence** appears to be one of the most powerful aspects of group learning (Slavin, 1995).

In such interdependent structures, all students must do their part in helping the others learn the material or accomplish the task. If one person does not learn, the whole group has failed. Thus students learn how to help each other. One of the simplest ways to use reward interdependence is to have a group of three coach each other for a quiz or test. Then, after assigning individual grades, give special recognition, privileges, or rewards to the groups in which every member reached the minimum performance level specified.

The assigning of specific roles to students is another way to introduce interdependence. The students will need to receive very clear directions on their particular role. Many teachers do this by using laminated role description cards. Table 9.1 displays several roles.

Occasionally you may find a student who either wants to dominate the group or refuses to get involved. These students will require coaching and support in the social

TABLE 9.1 *Cooperative Group Role Descriptions*

Reader	Reads the material aloud to group; makes sure all are listening
Writer/recorder	Fills in forms; writes as group dictates
Materials manager	Gathers materials, supplies, information
Timer	Keeps track of time; keeps group on task
Checker	Checks to be sure all agree on group's answer or information selected for a project Makes sure each member can explain the answer or information selected and say why
Summarizer	Periodically stops to summarize what has happened so far, or to clarify information gathered
Coach/organizer	Makes sure each member has a chance to participate equally; checks that each member agrees on directions; mediates disagreements
Encourager	Gives praise and encouragement to group members
Presenter	Presents the group's product to class or other audience

From *Teaching as Decision Making: Successful Practices for the Elementary Teacher* (3rd Ed.) (p. 252), by A. J. Starko, et al., 2003, Upper Saddle River, NJ: Merrill/Prentice Hall. Copyright 2003 by Pearson Education, Inc. Reprinted with permission.

skills required for group work. They also can be assisted by thoughtful assignment of roles. For example, the role of recorder might suit a shy student or one who needs to learn to listen carefully. The encourager role is appropriate for students who are tentative and need a positive, low-key role, and for those who tend to use put-downs. Being a summarizer is good for those who tend to isolate and for those who need practice in putting thoughts into words. The timekeeper role is good for those who need an important or easy role, or for those who tend to wander (mentally or physically) away from the task. As a caution, do not always give students the same role; they need to learn to stretch into other areas and responsibilities.

Individual Accountability

Have you ever worked on a group project and felt resentful because one or two people did all the work, but everyone got the same grade? This should not happen in well-structured cooperative groups because every group member is held individually responsible for his or her own learning. It is always crucial for the teacher to continually assess each student's understandings and growing competence. This is especially true in cooperative groups, where one person's understanding can too easily be assumed to represent everyone's level of understanding.

Individual accountability is similar to Formative Assessment as discussed in Chapters 4 and 7. It may be accomplished by giving students a quiz, with grades recorded in the teacher's book as usual. Or the teacher may rotate among the groups with a clipboard, making random spot checks by asking students questions about material they are supposed to have learned. When students are completing a worksheet together, you may ask all the students to sign their name on the sheet, to indicate that all members agree with the answers and that every student can explain why each answer is correct. Another way to encourage individual accountability within the group is to assign the role of checker to a student who is responsible for gauging each person's understanding by asking questions, requesting summaries, and quizzing the other group members. A deeper discussion of the role of assessment in cooperative learning may be found in Johnson and Johnson (1999).

 ## REFLECTING ON THE IDEAS

With a partner, explain how cooperative learning differs from more traditional group work. Be sure to include the three essential attributes of cooperative learning discussed so far.

Cooperative Social Skills Learning

Students don't always walk into the classroom knowing how to help other students or how to work in a group to complete a task. Yet such skills are crucial at home, in the workplace, and in myriad social situations. One of the key skills listed in the Secretary's Commission on Achieving Necessary Skills (SCANS) report (1993) is teamwork and collaborative problem solving. It is, therefore, important to teach students how to build and maintain trust, to communicate, to lead, and to manage conflict or controversy. Imagine how successful our relationships would be if we all had such skills!

Cooperative skills must be preassessed before they can be taught. It is instructive to put students in cooperative groups to complete a simple task. For example, ask them to solve a puzzle and to make sure every person can independently explain how to find the solution. Then, walk around with a clipboard, taking notes on which social skills are present or lacking. You may find that many students do not know how to share, do not know how to give each other positive feedback and encouragement, or interrupt each other. If you find some important social skills lacking, teach them in your cooperative lessons—one at a time.

Most experts agree that it is sufficient to focus on only one or two social skills per lesson. You may see improvement only after several weeks of work on one area. For example, you might spend an entire grading period emphasizing the skills of giving encouraging comments to others, listening without interrupting, and using the other person's name. Refer to Figure 9.3 for a list of common social skills. Remember, students will need long-term practice and reinforcement before a social skill will become automatic, so do not try to do too much too fast.

You may use a variety of strategies to teach social skills: direct explanation and modeling; discovery or inductive activities; or role-playing. Of course, the work in cooperative groups provides practice of the skills. This is where monitoring, feedback, and self-assessment are crucial.

Use the following ideas for teaching cooperative skills:

1. *Explain and Model.* Help students understand the specific social skill. If you tell students to "cooperate," that is too vague and will result in little success. Many young people cannot comprehend an abstract idea, like respect, until they see and hear it in action. You can ask specific questions about the behaviors included in the social skill to make it concrete and easier to understand. For example, you may lead students in a discussion, asking "What does giving encouragement look like?" (e.g., leaning forward, smiling) and "What does it sound like?" (e.g., "Good job!" "That's a good idea"). You may write these behaviors on the board on a T-chart, as shown in Figure 9.3. You may also wish to have students demonstrate what the skill looks like through role-playing.

2. *Give the Purpose.* Make sure students know the usefulness of a particular skill. For example, show students how learning to give encouragement will make it easier for them to get along with their siblings and friends. Let students know how they will be rewarded (personally and externally) by using the skill.

3. *Practice.* Help students practice the skill while they work in groups. At first, you may create a special nonacademic activity that promotes application of the skill; for example, having students talk in pairs about a hobby while making a conscious effort to encourage the other student to talk and share. Observe the groups and record examples of encouraging behaviors. To encourage practice you may assign roles ("Today Joe is the encourager.") or you may assign a group observer ("Lola, today you put a check mark next to each person's name when he or she encourages another

Social Skills	T-Chart on Encouraging Others	
	Looks like 👁	Sounds like 👂
• Staying with the group • Using quiet voice s • Taking turns • Not using put-downs • Asking for help • Summarizing aloud • Criticizing ideas, not people • Using first names • Contributing ideas • Praising • Encouraging others • Saying "please" and "thank you" • Paraphrasing	• Smiling • Leaning forward • Eye contact	• "Good job" • "That's a good idea" • "Yes!"

Figure 9.3 Common Social Skills and T-Chart

From *Teaching as Decision Making: Successful Practices for the Elementary Teacher* (3rd Ed.) (p. 254), by A. J. Starko, et al., 2003, Upper Saddle River, NJ: Merrill/Prentice Hall: Copyright 2003 by Pearson Education, Inc. Reprinted with permission.

student."). Eventually, this skill will become more automatic for students as they work together on academic tasks.

4. *Process or Debrief.* Allocate class time for students to discuss their use of the social skill. This discussion may be done within the small group ("Lola, show your observation results to the group and have members discuss how well they encouraged each other today."). Or you can ask each member to rate themselves (1–5) on their own use of the social skill and to set a professional goal. Finally, give specific feedback to individuals or groups by reading aloud the encouraging statements you recorded as you observed the groups. These feedback and debriefing sessions will take approximately 10 minutes a day at first. Later, you may need to spend only a few minutes per week to discuss how the desired social skills are progressing.

Developing cooperative groups takes time, persistence, and effort. Keep in mind the main cooperative skills on which the students need to focus. Then, every time you do an activity, remind students to think about the one or two social skills that need polishing. Review the T-chart if necessary. At the end of every activity, make sure the groups assess their progress on the cooperative skills and discuss how they can improve. Keep groups together long enough to learn how to be productive; switching affords little opportunity to resolve conflicts and build trust.

It is important to consider the topic of developing trust. Think of a group you are in and how long it took you to become comfortable. Trust does not develop overnight, but teachers can help to develop it. The first weeks of the academic year are a particularly important time for building a sense of community in the classroom (see

Chapter 11). When students don't feel comfortable on a team, they often are less productive. Early on, invest some time in group trust-building activities, which will pay off in the long run.

Other Models of Cooperative Learning

In **Teams-Games-Tournaments** (TGT) (Slavin, 1995), heterogeneous teams of four to five members coach one another as they prepare for team competitions. The teams practice with the content questions for part of each period over a few days. At the tournament on Friday, students from each team are assigned to different three-person tables with other students of similar achievement levels. The questions are usually taken from a current chapter, study guide, or other resource. All tables play at once. The first contestant picks a number card and tries to answer the corresponding question on a handout. Points are earned by successfully answering a question or correcting another's answer. Each person at the table scores points for his or her own team. Play continues by picking another number card and answering the corresponding question, until all number cards have been drawn. Points are then totaled to determine each team's score. Rewards and recognition are provided often in the form of a newsletter announcing the team scores. Before the next tournament, the teacher may change the composition of the tournament tables to ensure even competition. The students practice in heterogeneous groups, but compete only against those of similar achievement levels, with questions geared to that level.

In **Student Teams–Achievement Divisions** (STAD) (Slavin, 1994), a similar process is used to prepare for the tournament, but teams compete against one another by taking an individual quiz. Quiz scores are converted into team points by computing each member's improvement over the last quiz score and summing them or by awarding points based on the team's improvement over past group averages.

In **Jigsaw** (Aronson, Blaney, Stephan, Sikes, & Snapp, 1978; Clarke, 1994; Draper, 1997), each "home" group member is given a topic or set of materials to teach to the other team members. Students then meet with others who have the same topic (expert groups). This is a good time for the teacher to exert some quality control by providing clarification of key points or misunderstandings with each expert group. Next, students return to their home group to teach their part to the others. A quiz or other form of individual accountability results in a group score and a reward or recognition for the winning team.

Jigsaw is a complex structure that can work well with many secondary school students. For example, imagine a jigsaw review activity with different groups teaching others about the parts of speech or a science activity in which different groups became expert on one living thing in an ecosystem. Only when all the information is shared can students envision the entire habitat topic.

In summarizing research on cooperative learning strategies, Marzano, Pickering, and Pollock (2001) recommend the following:

- Organize groups based on ability levels sparingly.
- Keep cooperative groups small in size, no more than 3–4 students.
- Apply cooperative learning consistently and systematically, but do not overuse it.

Examples of Cooperative Learning

Example 1

Writing Business Letters

The following example illustrates a cooperative learning lesson on letter writing. The teacher has finished several lessons on correct formats for business letters and now wants students to apply these ideas. Notice how two objectives are specified (one content and one social skill objective). All four decisions about grouping, interdependence, individual accountability, and cooperative/social skills must be clear in the teacher's mind before the lesson can be planned.

Content Standards

Integrate listening, viewing, speaking, reading, and writing skills for multiple purposes in varied contexts.

Objectives

- Students will be able to recognize and correct errors in letters. (content—cognitive objective)
- Students will disagree courteously during the task. (social skill—affective objective)

Decisions Made before Lesson Begins

GROUP SIZE

3 (mixed according to proficiency in writing)

COOPERATIVE SKILLS

Disagreeing courteously taught directly at beginning, monitored by teacher during task, and self-assessed and discussed by students at end.

MATERIALS

3 letters with formatting and grammar errors per group; 1 pencil per group; 1 piece of paper per group

TASK

One person in the group will show his or her letter to the rest of the group. He or she will explain to the group what is incorrect. Then he or she will illustrate how to correct the letter. Group members check accuracy. Roles are then rotated.

POSITIVE INTERDEPENDENCE

Provided by limited materials, group rewards (points given for correct answers during spot check), and job roles that are rotated after each student's turn:

Writer: holds letter, explains the error, and corrects it
Checker: checks writer's correctness
Encourager: gets all group members involved

ASSESSMENT OF LEARNING (INDIVIDUAL ACCOUNTABILITY)

Spot checks by teacher while recording on a chart the level of each student's ability to correct the errors.

Lesson Procedures

OPENING

Set and Teaching Social Skill: First, the teacher asks students to jot down two things they could say or do to "disagree courteously with someone." The teacher uses their ideas to fill in T-chart and reminds them that he or she will be rotating among the groups looking for this skill.

Cognitive Objective and Purpose: The teacher explains the other objective (correcting letters) and clarifies the purpose; later they will be using the skills when they write business letters to gather information about jobs in their areas. Reminds students to use examples and rules in their textbook as references when necessary.

CONSTRUCTING MEANING AND USING/APPLYING

The teacher forms the groups, assigns and explains roles, and gives directions for the task. The teacher explains the group rewards and how students will be held individually responsible for their learning (spot checks). Students perform the task as teacher walks around and takes notes on "disagreeing" behavior. When the task is completed, students share correct answers with another group.

ASSESSMENT OF COGNITIVE LEARNING (INDIVIDUAL ACCOUNTABILITY)

Toward the end of the group time, the teacher goes to each group and picks two students to justify the corrections made in the group's letters.

SOCIAL SKILL PROCESSING

Next, using a self-assessment form, groups rate themselves from 1 (low) to 5 (high) on their ability to disagree courteously and then discuss needed improvements in their groups. Finally, the teacher reads examples he or she heard of students disagreeing courteously and gives positive feedback.

ADAPTATIONS/DIFFERENTIATION

The teacher provides reteaching and/or extension the next day (based on quality of letters).

 REFLECTING ON THE IDEAS

In the lesson above heterogeneous groups are used to teach about letter writing. What are the benefits of this structure? What are the potential difficulties?

Example 2

A Cooperative Learning Lesson on Journey to Jo'burg

In this lesson students read a novel about the journey of a young Black South African girl and her brother from their small village to a large city in search of their mother. The novel illustrates how the adolescent girl begins to have a different perspective about her life during apartheid. This lesson includes all four elements of cooperative learning, and it illustrates how to differentiate the activities by offering choices for students needing more or less challenge.

Objectives

- Students will be able to describe how oppression and apartheid affected Black South Africans' lives. (cognitive)
- Students will be able to contrast how life for many Black South Africans during apartheid is different than the students' own lives. (cognitive)
- Students will use active listening when working in groups. (affective social skill)

Decisions Made before Lesson Begins

GROUP SIZE

5 (racially diverse; 1 strong reader, 2 average readers, and 2 struggling readers)

COOPERATIVE (SOCIAL) SKILL

Active listening (or paraphrasing) (taught at beginning of lesson, monitored with teacher feedback during group work; assessed and discussed by the group at the end)

MATERIALS

- Novel *Journey to Jo'burg,* by Beverley Naidoo
- Overhead projector with vocabulary words
- Individual role sheets with clear instructions

TASK

Once a week after students have read a section of the novel, each student will complete an individual role sheet (different role for each group member). In the group they share the information they have collected. Afterwards a class discussion will explore the groups' findings.

POSITIVE INTERDEPENDENCE

Provided by limiting materials (only one copy of each completed role sheet), jigsaw (each student has one piece of the entire task), and roles (rotated each week)

Connector: finds connections between novel and outside world;
Discussion Director: creates open-ended questions and directs the discussion
Analyzer: finds situations, feelings, or locations that are different from the experiences of characters in the book

Vocabulary Definer: finds new, puzzling, or important words; looks them up in a dictionary; and creates a sentence with each one
Illustrator: draws 2 pictures related to the reading

ASSESSMENT OF LEARNING (INDIVIDUAL ACCOUNTABILITY)

Each student makes a project (e.g., diorama, poem, letter, or journal entry) to show understanding of the key objectives related to the novel. Each project will be assessed using a common rubric that reflects the understandings stated in the lesson objectives.

Lesson Procedures

OPENING

Set: Before beginning to read the book, put several vocabulary words on overhead. In assigned groups, students make predictions about the book, based on the words given. These are discussed as a large group. Daily when the book is discussed, students review their predictions to see how well they match the actual story.

Cognitive Objectives and Purpose: The teacher tells students about the final project. They will each use narratives and graphic data to (a) explain and show how oppression and the apartheid affected Black South Africans' lives and (b) contrast life for many Black South Africans during the apartheid with the students' own lives. The teacher explains how important it is to recognize that each person has value regardless of their race; that each student needs to value the input of fellow classmates no matter how much they differ from one another.

Social Skill (Teaching, Objective, and Purpose) The teacher asks students to discuss with their neighbor what it feels like when an adult or friend just does not listen to you. A few randomly selected students share their feelings. Then the teacher explains the importance of listening actively (paraphrasing what a person has said) and demonstrates it. Students practice in pairs by discussing what they did the night before. The teacher explains that they and the teacher will be using active listening during their group work. At the end of the group work, students will discuss how well they listened to each other.

CONSTRUCTING MEANING AND USING/APPLYING

The teacher explains the task, assigns the roles, and clarifies each role and the importance of each person doing his or her part. (The roles have been modeled and practiced on prior days.) As the groups are discussing the novel, the teacher walks around, checking to see that each role sheet is completed, observing students' use of the social skill, and answering questions. After 20 minutes, the teacher leads a discussion of the themes and examples of how the students' lives here are different or the same as the main character's life during apartheid.

ASSESSMENT OF COGNITIVE LEARNING (INDIVIDUAL ACCOUNTABILITY)

At the end of each session, the groups discuss and write down what they felt were the most important parts of the novel and why they thought this. Then the teacher leads a group discussion on this topic. (At the end of the entire novel, each student does the individual project described above and presents it to the group.)

SOCIAL SKILL PROCESSING

Students individually complete a Group Reflection form including the following items:

- I listened actively to each of my group members and tried reflecting back to them what they said.
- I encouraged the views of the person speaking (rating from 1—true to 2—false).
- My group could have listened more effectively by . . .
- We made sure everyone understood the material (yes or no).
- Everyone felt comfortable about sharing his/her thoughts. (yes or no)
- One thing we did well was . . . .

The teacher leads a class discussion about what students liked and disliked about the activity and if they changed their mind about something because of something said by a group member.

ADAPTATIONS/DIFFERENTIATION

- Cultural Diversity: Groups are formed so students from different cultures are together.
- Struggling Students: Readers of different levels are grouped together; struggling readers can begin reading the novel at home or after school with parental or mentor assistance.
- Advanced and Gifted Students: Will have more complex roles and assignment choices; e.g., creating ideas for final projects.
- Learning disabled students will have specific segments broken down with specific direction as teacher monitors the groups (e.g., stand up if you need to while you read).

Cautions, Differentiation, and Cooperative Groups

Much of the literature on cooperative learning stresses the importance of heterogeneous groups. Students in heterogeneous groups can learn to help one another, get along with those who are different from themselves, and understand the value of diversity. Unfortunately, improperly used heterogeneous groups also can cause a host of problems (Cohen, 1994, 1998). Less able students can rely on more able students to carry out the tasks for them. More able students can become resentful or bored at having to repeatedly explain to team members information that they themselves easily mastered.

Either of these two difficulties could occur in the letter writing lesson cited above, particularly if skill levels are highly diverse. If, for example, one of the group members is unable to read the letters—or one member has been writing business letters in an after-school job for years—finding errors in a letter may not be an appropriate group task.

This difficulty might have been minimized through differentiation. If, for example, students who were already extremely adept at letter writing were engaged in alternative activities, they may be more appropriately challenged. The groups would still be heterogeneous, but only within the range of students needing practice on that skill. Students who have difficulty reading could work with an assigned buddy or a particularly sensitive and helpful group member. Alternatively, students could be given varied assignments within the group—perhaps letters of varying difficulty with more or less complex errors. The second cooperative lesson (on the novel) provides examples of varied assignments in the roles. Chapter 10 provides additional information on differentiating cooperative groups.

When using cooperative learning, look carefully at the tasks and make sure that the interdependence assumed in the group goals is real. Sometimes group tasks produce group efforts that are more illusion than substance. Cohen (1998, 1994) suggested guidelines for cooperative learning tasks that avoid these pitfalls. The key is that cooperative learning tasks, particularly those for heterogeneous groups, should be tasks for which having group participation is a genuine asset for everyone in the group. This emphasis reflects the way groups function in business and society. Automobile manufacturers do not typically use groups to fill out reports or gather facts; those tasks are more efficiently done individually. Groups are important on design teams, in think tanks, and in many other problem-solving situations. A good group task is one that benefits from many strengths, abilities, and points of view. Cohen's guidelines may be grouped in the following clusters:

1. Cooperative learning tasks should have more than one answer and/or more than one path toward a solution. No student or students should be able to come to the task with the solution in hand. For example, imagine that instead of gathering facts about Sitting Bull as a cooperative learning exercise, the class had the opportunity to learn the basic facts surrounding Sitting Bull and the events at Little Big Horn from a movie or class discussion. Then, cooperative groups might be charged with designing a suitable monument for the battle site of Little Big Horn, which would have no simple solution. Each student's opinion could be valuable in helping the group decide on a focus and perspective for their monument.

2. Cooperative learning tasks should be intrinsically motivating and should offer challenge to all students. Students should work together to create a worthwhile product, not simply to earn team points. Intrinsically motivating tasks, like the monument assignment, involve making choices about interesting topics at a level of challenge suitable for students' knowledge and skills.

3. Group tasks should allow students to make different kinds of contributions. They should demand a variety of abilities and skills. Jan may be able to read and analyze reference materials easily. Jose may be able to see issues from more than one point of view. Sally may be able to draw and Cherilyn to organize materials and keep the group on task. Each contribution is needed and valuable. Inequality can be combated powerfully by pointing out the real contributions of group members considered "low status" by their peers. (Cohen, 1998).

4. Cooperative learning tasks should involve multiple media and multisensory experiences in addition to traditional text. Complex experiences are good education under any circumstances. In a heterogeneous group, they increase the probability that each student will have the opportunity to receive information and express ideas in the form that best matches his or her learning style.

Practice Activity B

Jigsaw Activity

In your class, count off so that you have teams (home groups) of four members. Spend five minutes getting to know each person (learn and use first names). Now join with another group of four, and each person pick a partner from the second group so that there are four pairs. The first pair will become experts on face-to-face interaction; the second pair, on positive interdependence; the third pair, on individual accountability; and the fourth pair, cooperative skills.

With your partner for 10 minutes, prepare to explain your assigned area of expertise to the others in your original team. Provide specific examples in your explanation, and create a visual aid to help you convey the information.

Now return to your original team (home group) and have each person explain and model his or her area of expertise. The others should discuss the ideas and create their own examples. For added interest, have the person whose birthday is the earliest in the year be the checker to make sure each person can explain the section before moving on to the next point. You have 20 minutes to make sure all members of your group can explain all four aspects of cooperative learning and give examples. You will be quizzed orally at the end of this time. Remember to use first names as you work.

Practice Activity C

Teaching a Cooperative Learning Activity

Use the following form to design a cooperative lesson that you will teach in a classroom. Be sure to include the four aspects of cooperative learning in your plan. Share your written plans with your professor and the teachers and use the feedback to fine-tune it. As you teach the lesson, ask the teacher to observe the lesson and complete the following form. After the lesson, use the Reflection Journal questions at the end of Chapter 7 to analyze your students' learning and your own performance.

Decisions to Make When Planning for Cooperative Learning

Related standards or benchmarks:

Content (cognitive) objective(s)

Cooperative/social skill (affective) objective

Group size and composition (trust activity needed?)

Social skill teaching, modeling, and group processing (e.g., self-assessment)

Positive interdependence (plan more than one type: limiting materials, jigsaw, roles, group reward)

Roles for group members

Assessment of cognitive learning (Individual accountability)

Adaptations/Differentiation

Materials

Procedures

Opening (set, objectives, purpose)

Directions for task

Teaching/reviewing social skills (may be part of opening)

Teacher monitoring social skills/helping during the task

Formative assessment (individual accountability) of cognitive learning

Social skill processing

- individual, group, and/or whole class?
- form for self-assessment?

Adaptations/Differentiation

Practice Point

SECTION 3. ACADEMIC SERVICE LEARNING

Section 3 Objective

After you have completed this section, you will have the ability to design academic service-learning activities related to a unit of study.

Throughout this text we have emphasized the importance of authentic learning—learning that engages students in meaningful tasks. One structure that engages students in such activities is academic service learning. As an introduction to academic service learning, it may be helpful to examine a successful curriculum project that incorporated the use of this methodology. As you read, think about the characteristics of this project that would lead it to be classified as academic service learning.

Imagine a cross-age tutoring program in which culturally and linguistically diverse students who are labeled at-risk mentor younger students in reading. In order to develop their mentoring ability, the tenth graders videotape the mentoring sessions and analyze their strengths and weaknesses through written observations. Through discussion, they work together to find ways to increase their repertoire of teaching strategies and increase their effectiveness. In addition, they develop a mentoring handbook for parents that describes key reading strategies for helping young children learn to read. Throughout this project the tenth graders gradually become confident as readers themselves. Their characterization of themselves as poor readers begins to change as they take on the role of "expert."

All of the critical attributes of an academic service learning project are present in this mentoring project. The following definition of academic service learning highlights these key attributes:

Academic service learning is a teaching methodology that utilizes community service to help students gain a deeper understanding of specific course objectives, acquire new knowledge, and engage in civic activities. (Jacoby, 1996; Stacey, Rice, Hurst, & Langer, 1997)

Academic service learning encourages students to provide a *service*. Unlike service projects that are conducted by clubs, church groups, or civic organizations, it is *academic* in that it is structured to teach key concepts and skills specified in curriculum standards and goals. However, that is not all. From this definition, we can infer that providing real-world experiences alone will not lead to optimum learning unless teachers provide structured opportunities for student **reflection**—thinking about and interpreting experiences to improve practice or learning. For learning to be meaningful, students must have ample opportunities for metacognition and reflection on their experiences. For example, metacognitive reflection activities in the context of the mentoring program might take the form of journal prompts such as, "What presented the most challenge as you mentored the student?" and "What mentoring strategy seemed most effective and why?" Other valuable activities are partner dialogue, whole-class discussion, and the progress reports that require both description and analysis.

You may have parallel experiences as you engage in field activities as part of your teacher preparation program. If you have the opportunity to teach in a classroom using the lessons you have designed (your academic content), this is academic service learning at an adult level. You are able to learn and reflect about teaching while serving students and schools. Those experiences will result in much more powerful learning if you discuss your experiences and thought processes with an expert professional, record them in a reflection journal, and/or share them with peers.

One of the most important aspects of academic service learning is a developing sense of community. In a community all of us have opportunities to both serve and be served. Each individual is an important contributor to the whole. Academic service learning experiences will be most successful when students enter a community ready to share responsibility with and respect those they serve rather than to "fix" things (Jacoby, 1996). In the tutoring example, the tenth-grade students will be more effective and caring mentors if they respect the challenges faced by the younger students and appreciate the difficulty of learning to read. They will gain more from the experience if they recognize how much they can learn from the younger children. To ensure such mutual appreciation, teachers can describe, model, and practice positive communication skills such as active listening, probing for clarification or more information, and encouraging others.

For academic service learning to be successful, it is important that everyone involved understand the goals and organization of the activities. Teachers should communicate important outcomes to all stakeholders in the project—community members, students, and parents. These outcomes are often quite diverse. They include cognitive, affective, ethical, civic, and career-related outcomes. Think for a moment about the diverse outcomes that could be attained through the project described on page 256. Certainly there were cognitive outcomes, as students' reading skills improved, but there were important affective, civic, and ethical outcomes as well. The older students developed confidence, learned to respect the struggles inherent in learning, and experienced the ethics of care and service. Perhaps some of them even began thinking about teaching as a career.

Academic service learning projects are most often designed to engage students in problem solving around authentic societal problems. The following activities could be used for academic service learning.

- creation and implementation of strategies to welcome and support newly arrived immigrant children in the school community
- development of oral histories for individuals living in nursing homes or past local government officials
- instruction of younger students to become critical television viewers
- creation of promotional materials on important local history sites
- creation and implementation of solutions to environmental problems in the community, such as a neglected park
- data gathering on local environmental issues
- surveys or statistical analyses carried out for a local nonprofit agency
- creation of a nature trail to teach about local plant life
- generation of strategies to solve a problem provided by a local business or nonprofit agency

Projects such as these help students recognize the relevancy of their education and realize their own role in improving the quality of life in their communities. As an instructional methodology, academic service learning promises to promote young people's activism and academic achievement through service.

 ## REFLECTING ON THE IDEAS

With a partner, brainstorm ideas for service in your community that could be suitable for middle or high school students. Choose one or two and think about how you could teach important academic outcomes through that service. You might make a chart listing the service learning opportunity on one side and the standards or outcomes to be taught on the other. Consider including this chart in your portfolio as a demonstration of your understanding of academic service learning.

SECTION 4. INFUSING TECHNOLOGY IN INSTRUCTION

Section 4 Objective

After you have completed this section you will have the ability to create activities that use technology to enhance the depth and quality of learning.

One of the challenges and adventures of teaching in the 21st century is finding ways to use emerging technologies to improve teaching. The use of technology has been heralded as the key to educational reform and a necessity for holding the attention and interest of the "net generation" (Dede, 1998; Tapscott, 1999). Schools have been given the responsibility to develop the technological skills essential for success in our rapidly changing environment while also attending to students' developmental needs (see cau-

1. Identify capabilities and limitations of contemporary and emerging technology resources and assess the potential of these systems and services to address personal, lifelong learning, and workplace needs.
2. Make informed choices among technology systems, resources, and services.
3. Analyze advantages and disadvantages of widespread use and reliance on technology in the workplace and in society as a whole.
4. Demonstrate and advocate legal and ethical behaviors among peers, family, and community regarding the use of technology and information.
5. Use technology tools and resources for managing and communicating personal/professional information (e.g., finances, schedules, addresses, purchases, correspondence).
6. Evaluate technology-based options, including distance and distributed education, for lifelong learning.
7. Routinely and efficiently use on-line information resources to meet needs for collaboration, research, publications, communications, and productivity.
8. Select and apply technology tools for research, information analysis, problem solving, and decision making in content learning.
9. Investigate and apply expert systems, intelligent agents, and simulations in real-world situations.
10. Collaborate with peers, experts, and others to contribute to a content-related knowledge base by using technology to compile, synthesize, produce, and disseminate information, models, and other creative works.

Figure 9.4 Technology Standards Students Must Meet Prior to Completion of Grade 12

tions in Healy, 1998; Tell, 2000). To this end the International Society for Technology in Education (ISTE) has developed National Educational Standards (NETS) for students, outlining the technical literacy skills appropriate for each level. The NETS standards for students' secondary schools are included in Figure 9.4. The complete standards are available at the ISTE website.

It is certainly true that technology has enormous potential for challenging traditional ways of teaching and learning. Since no teacher can possibly equal the volume of knowledge available electronically, emerging technologies can shift the roles of teacher and learner alike (Medina, Pigg, Desler & Gorospe, 2001). Just like any other strategy or tool, however, it can be used wisely or unwisely, effectively or ineffectively. While it is beyond the scope of this text to fully review either the issues surrounding emerging technology or provide comprehensive guidelines for its use, this section will briefly discuss some ways technology can effectively be infused in our instruction—providing both improved instruction and opportunities for students to address NETS standards.

A basic premise is key to understanding the effective use of technology: Technology is not a type of lesson, nor is it a teaching approach. Technology provides us with an assortment of tools that can be used in a variety of lessons. They will work more or less well depending on the context. For example, various types of presentation software (e.g., PowerPoint) can be used in the "information and modeling" portion of a direct lesson. The electronic presentation can provide clear cues to the organization of the content and allow links to interesting graphics, video clips, and other features.

This illustration leads to another, perhaps obvious but important premise: Use technology when it allows you to do something new or something you already do more effectively. Reflective teachers do not use technology simply because it is new. It can be exciting for a reflective teacher to find ways to enhance teaching using technology.

Technology Helps Learning.

Technology and Direct Teaching

In direct instruction, technology can be used at several stages of a lesson. In an opening (set), a video clip from a multimedia encyclopedia or other data source (CD, DVD, Web) can catch students' attention. The same types of sources, with or without presentation software, can provide illustrations to clarify or enliven lectures. A projection system that allows you to create and display a spreadsheet can be helpful for teaching data analysis, particularly when a graph can be created and presented with a few clicks of the mouse. Personal digital assistants (PDA) can provide hand-held data collection and analysis systems that can move from classroom to outdoor activities and back again.

In many cases technology can provide appropriate practice or application activities. These may range from drill-and-practice software packages to complex activities that require students to use technology to show their expertise. Students only a few years ago were often limited to writing reports, painting murals, and creating an occasional diorama. Today's students, with appropriate instruction and technical support, can create multimedia presentations, digital videos, and websites. Such projects, if carefully constructed, require complex thinking and problem solving in addition to knowledge of the content being presented.

Technology and Inductive Teaching

One of the most powerful ways to use technology is for inductive teaching, both formal and informal. As students develop concepts through interaction with posters, plants, art, and animals in a classroom, they also can develop concepts as they use the Internet to follow scientists exploring under the ocean, communicate with classes in other parts of the country, or problem-solve with an electronic mentor. Each of these opportunities provides experiences with other people and places on which concepts and principles will be built for years to come.

Using the Internet and other technologies can vastly expand the opportunities for data collection and analysis in inductive teaching. For example, instead of conducting a study of weather data and patterns at school, the Kids as Global Scientists project (www.onesky.umich.edu) allows students to study and compare weather data from across the country. On a smaller scale, many students have graphed the numbers of various colors of M&M's® candies in a bag for a classic inductive activity on probability. Teaching students to use a spreadsheet to collect and organize data adds both a new level of sophistication to the activity and a new, useful skill. This is a good example of using technology to do an activity in a better way.

The Global Schoolhouse (www.globalschoolhouse.org) is a good source for collaborative data sharing activities. It can also be a fine source for other collaborative activities. For example one activity offered the opportunity to send messages of hope to those affected by the September 11, 2001, tragedy. Another activity, Friendship through Education, was designed to link students in the United States with those in Muslim countries, with the hope of gaining greater understanding.

More and Better Tools

Many effective uses of technology allow students to do their work more easily or powerfully. Using word processors to facilitate student writing greatly eases the editing and revising processes. This is of particular assistance to students whose penmanship presents challenges. Material taken from the World Wide Web—particularly lessons on critical reading and analysis—can be timely and effective. Computer graphics programs can help students illustrate their ideas.

The research opportunities presented by the Internet—while demanding careful consumerism and media savvy—vastly expand the materials available in the school library. In particular, students have access to primary source materials that are unlikely to be available any other way. For example, students might study three accounts of the Boston Massacre, analyzing the point of view expressed in each one. By bookmarking the relevant sites, teachers can help students make the most efficient use of research time.

Finally, the global communications made available through the Internet provide new and powerful opportunities for real-world problem solving. Through electronic communication, students can gather and analyze data, share concerns across state and national boundaries, and work with others on areas of common concerns. This type of activity, when tied to a teaching unit, provides opportunities for authentic learning beyond those available to any single classroom.

Virtual Architecture

Judi Harris (2002) described a wide variety of activities that can be used to infuse technology into instruction in meaningful and often powerful ways. She uses the term "virtual architecture" to describe structures that define various types of "telecomputing activities." The structures are divided into two broad categories: those focused primarily on collaborating with distant colleagues and those focused on research using resources located elsewhere. Numerous examples of such activities can be found at the website associated with the book: http://virtual-architecture.wm.edu. The following text is a brief description of her structures for the first category of activities, "telecollaboration and telepresence" (p. 17).

- *Keypals.* Students pair off with students in another location to communicate electronically, often on topics of mutual interest.
- *Global Classrooms.* Two or more classrooms in different locations study a common topic during the same time period. Students might read a common novel or study the same topic.
- *Electronic Appearances.* Students have the opportunity to communicate with a subject matter expert, usually on a one-time basis. For example, they might conference with a NASA scientist or favorite author.
- *Telementoring.* Sometimes subject experts are available for longer term relationships as mentors for individual or class projects.
- *Question-and-Answer Activities.* A variety of "ask the expert" sites allow students to pose questions to individuals in many areas of expertise.
- *Impersonations.* Impersonation projects are activities in which individuals communicate with each other in character. For example, a project at Monticello allows students to "communicate" with Thomas Jefferson.
- *Information Exchanges.* Information exchanges from around the world can provide data for inductive analysis, ranging from slang words from around the world to indigenous insect species.
- *Database Creation.* Some information exchanges also entail organizing information into databases that can be exchanged and studied. The exchanges include information on bird sightings and a collection of children's artwork illustrating animals around the world that start with different letters of the alphabet.
- *Electronic Publishing.* Many classes and schools have created websites to share information and student work. Larger scale publishing opportunities include student journals and art galleries created via the Web.
- *Telefieldtrips.* Students can visit locations around the world via the Web. They can visit specific sites or follow adults researching historical sites or specific environments in a type of virtual expedition. Some expeditions provide students with daily updates and the opportunity to pose questions to the travelers. For example, Conyers and Rauscher (2000/2001) describe the ways students shared in a trip across Antarctica, learning about everything from weather to the effects of temperature on various lubricants.
- *Pooled Data Analysis.* Like database creation activities, these projects involve students in collecting and analyzing data. In this case, both the data collection and the

analysis are collaborative activities, including a variation of the M&M®'s probability activity mentioned earlier.

• *Information Searches.* In these game-like activities, students are provided with clues and must use reference materials to answer questions. For example, one game asked students to research an interesting landmark and design clues to its identity. Clues were posted weekly in a competition to identify the most landmarks.

• *Peer Feedback Activities.* These activities encourage students to give helpful suggestions regarding peers' efforts, often as a type of long-distance editing.

• *Parallel Problem Solving.* Students in multiple locations work to solve a similar problem then compare experiences and data. One of the most popular of these activities involves creating crates to protect dropping eggs.

• *Sequential Creations.* Students join with distant classrooms to compose sections to a poem, song, or other work.

• *Telepresent Problem Solving.* Students come together in virtual conferences, often to discuss topics of global importance.

• *Simulations.* Like "in person" simulations, Internet simulations provide students the chance to experience slices of life ranging from Western expedition to the Mideast peace negotiations.

• *Social Action Projects.* The Internet can serve as a vehicle for global humanitarian efforts, many focusing on environmental issues.

Some projects illustrate how technology can change the nature of schooling in fundamental ways. For example, Pearlman (2002) described technology-intensive high schools that include required courses in math, English, etc., with technology integration and personalized learning plans, internships for seniors in local businesses, and environments that seem more like a technology-rich workplace than a traditional school. Students work on short- and long-term projects and organize the products in digital portfolios. In this case, technology facilitates individualization (differentiation) of learning, not through tutorials or computer-assisted instruction, but by providing tools that assist students in developing and attaining their own learning goals. Some believe that this contextual learning—learning that is embedded in projects and structured toward individual goals—will be necessary as schools prepare students for a 21st-century economy (Thornburg, 2002).

Access and the Technology Gap

It is important to consider ways to structure technology-infused curriculum activities to provide access to all students. A gender divide exists in the ways boys and girls use technology, and the divide continues into adulthood (American Association of University Women Educational Foundation, 1998; Weinman & Haag, 1999). In a similar fashion, use of technology varies enormously along cultural lines. As you use the Diversity Principle to reflect on gender and cultural issues throughout teaching, pay special attention to activities involving technology. For example, make sure that boys and girls of all cultures have opportunities to experience technical competence. If you have a limited number of computers in the classroom, require all students to do some of the activities.

Otherwise students who may be interested but are less assertive (or a bit unsure of their technical expertise) may not be willing to compete with other students for time on the machines.

Many students do not have ready access to computers outside school. It is important to be sure that students who come from technology-rich homes do not have unfair advantages in class assignments over those who must complete their work in school or in the community library. Understand the delicate balance between accepting and appreciating students' outside efforts and discouraging students for whom such activities are an unreasonable expectation. As we work to infuse technology in our curriculum, it will be important to help all our students become involved in meaningful ways.

SECTION 5. CENTERS, CONTRACTS, AND SKILLS OF INDEPENDENT LEARNING

Section 5 Objectives

After you have completed this section you will have the ability to plan, implement, and assess the effects of various types of centers and contracts, and describe key activities to prepare students for independent learning.

Students' pursuit of independent learning activities allows flexibility in planning large- and small-group lessons—with or without technology. Such activities can provide opportunities for students to practice skills appropriate for individual needs (e.g. reteaching) but not for the whole group. They can also allow students the opportunity to investigate questions of interest or to design creative projects that are unique to their individual concerns, styles, or needs (e.g., extension). If students are to have opportunities for individualized practice or investigative activities, all students in the class must be taught the skills of independent working. These skills are not just for the most able, the most creative, or the most motivated. If you are to concentrate your attention on helping a group or individual, at some point each student must be able to work without your direct guidance.

Treffinger and Young (2002) describe five goals of independence and self-direction. Students should be able to:

- function effectively in their total environment (classroom, school, home, and community) as they relate and work with peers, teachers, parents, and other adults;
- make effective, appropriate choices and decisions based on their knowledge of their own needs and interests;
- assume responsibility for their actions by completing their own work at a satisfactory level of achievement and in an acceptable time frame;
- identify and define the problem, identify a possible solution, determine a course of action for implementing the solution, and deal effectively with change; and
- evaluate their own work and be able to answer for themselves the question, "How well can I do what I want to do?" (pp. 26–27)

Treffinger's goals are most likely to be achieved if teachers teach students explicitly how to work independently. Two of the most common vehicles for implementing independent learning activities are *centers* and *contracts*. Each of these strategies has many possible variations. This section describes general definitions, uses, and patterns. Adapt the general framework provided to the needs, interests, and abilities of your students.

Centers

While various authors define their terms differently, we will make a distinction between two kinds of centers: learning centers and interest-development centers. Physically, the two types of centers look much the same. They entail a designated area of the classroom for independent work on a particular topic or discipline. Centers may be constructed in study carrels, on tabletops, on a pair of desks in the corner, or with virtually any structure that can store materials. Learning centers and interest-development centers differ in intent. A **learning center** is designed to introduce and/or reinforce a specific part of the regular curriculum. An **interest-development center** is designed to spur curiosity and interest in areas outside the regular curriculum. While centers have traditionally been used most extensively in elementary grades, they also can provide important experiences in independence for middle and high school students.

Because a learning center is designed to reinforce the core curriculum, all or most students will probably be required to complete work there. However, the nature of a center makes it easy to provide choice within the requirements and to vary the difficulty of assignments for individual students. Students may be required to complete two activities of their choice, or one "red" (easier) and one "blue" activity. You may also vary center assignments according to students' strengths and needs.

Organizing Centers

The first decision to make in constructing a center is, of course, the topic. Some centers are focused on particular skills; for example, reading maps or solving word problems. Some may be focused on specific materials, such as lab equipment or interactive software. Still others center on areas of content, such as electricity, local government, or Impressionism. You may choose to create a center for a topic that needs extra reinforcement, one for which you want to provide differentiated assignments for varied student needs, or one for which the limited quantity of materials makes it impossible for a large group of students to work at one time. For example, a history teacher may decide to devote one corner of the room to a center on local historical research. While the material is important for all students, the limited number of resources available might make it difficult for an entire class of students to be working with them at one time.

Once the topic has been determined, the next step is to gather available materials. If, for example, the topic were local history, you could start by gathering books, magazines, old postcards, family histories and any other available materials. You might find computer software on doing historical research. Next, you could brainstorm a list of possible activities that could be pursued independently by individuals or small groups. Typically, activities would focus on, or branch off from, key concepts and generalizations planned for the unit. Activities should include opportunities for data gathering, problem solving, individual research, and creative expression, in addition to more traditional vocabulary practice and fact-gathering exercises. Such an activity allows for higher-level thinking and authentic learning that may vary from student to student.

For example, a unit on state history might be planned around four general content clusters: mapping the settlements, changes in population, economic growth, and changes in lifestyle, all dealing with the period 1910–1950. The list of possible activities could include a scavenger hunt of relevant vocabulary and a worksheet from the text explaining how to create local histories. A computer station also could provide information on techniques of historical research. Perhaps the library has an interactive video program that allows students to investigate changes in 20th-century advertising. In addition, you might decide students could read copies of census reports and graph trends, examine photos of their city during different decades; plan an interview with someone who lived in their town during 1940 or 1950; read excerpts from a local teacher's diary and examine old maps, yearbooks, and memorabilia to draw conclusions about changes occurring during the target years.

Each of these activities has the potential to be carried out independently and reinforces one of the content emphases for this unit. You would need to decide which activities might be done during class time with teacher supervision, which will be required center activities, and which will be electives. It will also be important to decide if and how assignments will be varied to meet students' needs. You will also need to make decisions about the physical format of the center, when the center will be used, and how/if you will correct or monitor activities done at the center.

In most ways, the construction and use of interest-development centers parallel those of learning centers. They, too, start with a topic, although it is generally not part of the regular curriculum. It may be selected because of student interest, as an extension of a unit, or as an offshoot of some local or national event. Next, activities are listed that will spur student interest. The activities are not intended to reinforce content, so they are likely to be more broad and less tied to specific generalizations.

Such centers are particularly appropriate for the types of exploratory studies that are important for middle grade students. For example, if you were to plan an interest-development center on photography, you could include activities on constructing pinhole cameras; taking and developing pictures; studying the lives and art of great photographers, the development of photography, historical research based on photographs, the use of photography in motion research, stop-action photography, and the development of moving pictures. The goal is to have as many students as possible find some question, idea, or activity that looks interesting enough to investigate, rather than to have everyone in the class understand basic processes of photography. Interest-development centers reinforce content and the values of choice and independence.

The ability to select and pursue individual goals needs to be supported in classrooms. It could be a challenge in secondary schools to find time for students to work at centers and other independent learning activities, because students are with the teacher for only a limited time each day. Some teachers have solved this problem by rotating center activities among students. Some teachers excuse a small number of students each day from required class activities so they may complete center activities. For example, an English teacher who plans five days of discussion of a novel may schedule one fifth of the students per day to work at a center on a related topic.

Centers also can be used as enrichment for students who have completed required work or have already mastered concepts. One eighth-grade math teacher pretests his students at the beginning of each unit and divides the class into three groups depending on the differentiated instruction needed. At any given moment, one group is working on skills instruction with the teacher, one group is at a center on problem solving, and one group is at the computer. Because the class periods are too short for him to meet with each group each day, the teacher meets with two groups per day on a rotating basis. He feels that he accomplishes more in targeted small-group instruction two out of three days than he does meeting every day as a whole group. Plus, the students have the added bonus of individualized computer and center activities.

Experiment with some center activities. You will probably want to start by offering a few center activities to one class and then build from there.

 ## REFLECTING ON THE IDEAS

Which type of center would you be more likely to use in your classroom—a learning center or an interest-development center? Why? Compare your reasons with at least one other person.

Using Multiple Centers

Some teachers use centers as a key organizational feature in their planning. In most of these classes multiple centers are operating throughout the school year, often organized around a curriculum theme. Because these classrooms include multiple centers, each center is usually simpler than those described above, often containing only one or two key activities. These change at regular intervals; usually at least some change every week. It is easier to organize multiple centers in schools that have longer periods of time with the same group of students; for example, those with interdisciplinary planning or block scheduling.

One effective way to organize multiple centers is around subject areas, such as a math center, a language arts center, an art center, or a science center. Activities may be focused around a particular topic or work of literature. Imagine a class reading *Johnny Tremain*. The language arts center could contain writing prompts related to characters in the novel or exercises in analyzing and writing historical fiction. The art center could provide opportunities to illustrate the book or learn more about Colonial silversmiths. The history center could provide opportunities to analyze documents from the time period and learn more about the Sons of Liberty. The teacher may or may not decide to link science and math activities to the novel as well. In this case the centers are related by a topic and used to teach and reinforce a variety of concepts and skills.

It is also possible to take the same approach to an abstract interdisciplinary theme. For example, imagine the same classroom organized around the theme "interdependence." This theme could provide an organizing framework for a semester or a whole year. The literature center could still discuss *Johnny Tremain,* but one of the activities would include an analysis of the interdependence of the characters. The history center would examine the American Revolution, noting in particular the relationship between England and the colonies across time. This more abstract theme could extend to science or math centers that would include an examination of the interdependence among organisms in a habitat or in mathematical relationships.

Another approach to organizing multiple centers is to create centers around multiple intelligences rather than subject areas. Imagine the *Johnny Tremain* centers focused around the following intelligences.

Linguistic	Read and write about the novel.
Logical-Mathematical	Solve problems about distances traveled by Colonial soldiers or identify important decisions Johnny had to make, and chart the pros and cons of each option.
Visual-Spatial	Create a diorama or computer illustration that best represents the key dilemma of the novel.
Bodily-Kinesthetic	With two friends create a tableau that best represents the relationships among three characters in the novel.
Musical	Create or choose music that expresses the idea of "revolution."
Interpersonal	Discuss how Johnny might have felt when he realized his hand would not be the same as before the accident.
Intrapersonal	Write or draw about something for which you would be willing to fight.
Naturalist	Learn about how the environment in New England has changed since Colonial times. How has that affected plant and animal life?

As you can see, organizing centers around multiple intelligences often leads to some ideas that are very similar and some that are quite different from those organized around traditional subject areas.

 ## REFLECTING ON THE IDEAS

Imagine you are creating multiple centers to support a thematic unit on "uses of power." Decide whether you would prefer to organize your centers around subjects or intelligences. Jot down some ideas for center activities and share them with a colleague.

Teachers who use centers as a major part of the curriculum typically have blocks of time set aside for center use. Some teachers divide students into groups and assign them to rotate among centers in a block of time. Other teachers require students to complete specific activities at each center but allow them to choose the order in which they complete the work. Many variations exist on both approaches. It can be helpful to visit a variety of classrooms that use centers in different ways in order to envision the flexibility available with this structure.

Contracts

Learning **contracts** allow a student and teacher to agree upon a series of tasks to be completed in a given time frame. For example, a few students might work independently through a body of required content and/or carry out an individual project when part of the class is involved in other activities.

At the secondary level, contracts are most commonly used to accommodate (differentiate instruction) for individual students' needs. They can be used to provide careful structure for students who have difficulty learning or to supply extra challenge for students with a high level of ability, interest, or background in a particular area. The appropriate complexity and duration of contracts vary enormously with the students' maturity and experience with independent work. While most teachers would immediately agree that the first independent contracts completed by younger students should entail no more than one or two work periods, the same is true for many older students who have never before worked outside of whole-group, teacher-directed lessons. Like other aspects of independent learning, facility with contracts must be developed gradually, starting with simple short-term forms and working up to complex tasks.

Most contracts entail specific assignments drawn from the regular curriculum and optional activities that may be drawn from the curriculum or planned around student interests. Regular curriculum assignments may be specific pages to be completed and/or concepts that must be mastered in preparation for some type of assessment. When dealing with basic skills, the use of preassessment will help you tailor the context to individual students' needs.

Optional activities can be planned by the teacher and/or student. The older the student and the more experienced in independent learning, the more input he or she should have in planning the contract. Open-ended activities based on student interests and those emphasizing individual investigations, problem solving, and creative ideas should be an important part of this section of the contract (see Figure 10.1, p. 283 in Chapter 10 for an example).

Contract activities may be pursued during any independent work time: while other students are involved in skills instruction or projects, when other assignments have been completed, or at any other time designated by the teacher as appropriate for independent work. You may want to begin with a small group of students who have demonstrated independent working skills. As the year progresses, the opportunity to work on independent contracts can be expanded or rotated to other students.

Teaching Skills of Independence

The first key to making the transition to independent work is to realize that you need to teach students how to work independently. It is not sufficient to tell them to be independent; you must *teach* them how to do it.

Do not assume that because your students have been through several years of school, they already have mastered skills of independent learning and are ready to learn on their own. Many students may have had little or no experience with independent tasks. In fact, students who have experienced many years of teacher-directed instruction may have particular difficulty making the transition to a more autonomous learning style. They will not have acquired necessary skills of planning, time management, and organization, and they may view the teacher as their primary source of information and direction. They may have little confidence in their own efforts and little desire to take responsibility for their own learning. We are all aware of students who, while they performed successfully in high school, were unable to manage their time and tasks independently in higher education or the workplace. It is essential that these important skills be taught, not left to chance.

In most cases you may start this process by planning a series of lessons on "independent work time." These lessons should be planned and executed with as much (and possibly more) care, planning, and practice as any other part of your curriculum. Major topics should include:

- importance of independent work
- long-term versus short-term goals and planning for time use
- expectations about noise, conversation, and so forth
- what to do if you are stuck or don't understand a task
- how to signal the teacher for assistance or a conference
- choice activities and what to do when tasks are completed
- rules about materials

No set procedures exist that are better than all others. Likewise, no single best strategy exists for students to follow if they are stuck or don't understand a task. The key is that there must *be* a strategy. Strategies could include asking tablemates, posting a sign or signal so the teacher knows there is a problem, or going on to alternative activities. Students should know (and practice) which procedures are to be followed and in what order.

Once procedures are established and taught to students, students may begin to work on their own without teacher direction. The goal is to move students from seatwork, during which they may be quiet but all activities are chosen, directed, and monitored by the teacher, to a period of time in which many activities are planned, organized, and implemented by students.

Don't try to introduce any new content the first time you have independent work time. The important lesson is independence. Give the students an assignment (preferably one with enough challenge that some students may practice getting assistance) and two or three choice activities. During the work time, do not try to give other instruction. You may wish to circulate and give feedback on their independent work skills, but do not assist with content except through the procedures established for independent work time. After the independent work time, discuss the results with the class. Identify areas of difficulty and devise strategies to reduce them. Students should be aware of independence as a goal and monitor their progress toward that end.

The next stage in establishing independent work time involves students working independently while you work with individuals or small groups. This is a good opportunity to pull together groups needing work on a particular skill or to work with individuals needing help with projects. Be sure that you are seated so that you can easily see the class while working with small groups. Students need to know that you are aware of all activities in the room. Try not to interrupt the group to answer individual questions, but refer students to the established procedures for independent work. You may wish to circulate and answer questions between your work with instructional groups.

Remember that independent work skills are complex and will be built over time. Early in the year, most choice activities should be fairly simple, building in complexity as the year progresses. You may wish to progress from activities not directly tied to academic content (such as brainteasers or logic puzzles) to activities reinforcing class content, to activities that explore new content such as interest-development centers or independent projects. Gradually increase students' responsibilities from short- to long-term planning and time management. Initially, long-term projects may be broken into subsections with due dates that you determine for your students. Later, scheduling may be planned together as a group and by individuals.

REFLECTING ON THE IDEAS

Imagine you are planning a lesson on "What is an independent worker?" How would you teach independence to your students? What characteristics or behaviors would you emphasize? How would you help them practice these skills? Be ready to share your ideas in class.

SECTION 6. PULLING IT ALL TOGETHER

Section 6 Objective

After you have completed this section you will have the ability to make decisions about the use of instructional time.

One of the most challenging—and interesting—parts of planning is figuring out how everything fits together. In many secondary schools teachers typically plan for single subjects to be taught in specific blocks of time. In middle schools teachers may be planning in teams for multiple subjects to be taught throughout the entire school day. It is tempting to spend each day at a frantic pace, attempting to cram as much as possible into each individual minute. Often you will find your teaching most effective if you devote more time to fewer topics in depth and to developing relationships with students that help them learn (see, for example, Wood, 2002).

Teaching requires many levels of planning in order to use instructional time wisely. At the broadest level, teachers often create a global plan for the school year, either for single subjects or interdisciplinary themes, identifying large blocks of time for particular areas of content. This type of planning can be particularly helpful for beginning teachers who are concerned about teaching required content in a timely way.

For example, a science teacher might block out the content by months, using the district curriculum guide, state standards, and knowledge of the local environment. If students are to study animal habitats in the Midwest, that study might logically take place in fall or in the spring, when outdoor activities can be most easily planned. A unit on weather could take place any month.

When planning in interdisciplinary teams you need to identify in advance times that may be challenging for particular subjects. For example, if, as part of your language arts curriculum, you plan to put on a play during January, it is likely that the large amount of rehearsal time may cut into time for other team members' subjects. You will need to work together to identify how to incorporate content from the other subject areas into the play. Or, you may plan for other times during the year when time for language arts may be expanded into other areas (for example, writing the text for science projects).

Of course, it is also possible to divide the year into time periods according to interdisciplinary themes or even to have a single theme for the year divided into subcategories. For example, a team might choose to divide the year into quarters with a main theme for each: exploration, interdependence, power, and heroes. Not all subjects will fit each theme, but the themes can be used to organize much of the curriculum. Science energy concepts could fit into the "power" theme along with the balance of power in the Constitution and literature exploring uses of power. Kovalik (1994) suggests creating a year-long theme that will integrate one or more subjects across time.

This type of planning is complex—primarily as the demands increase to incorporate specific content standards in particular years—and will not be mastered your first year. Many teachers find that using a year-long theme helps them make connections among units and provides a helpful context for students.

Like most beginning teachers, you will probably find that many things take more or less time than you planned. Having a year-long outline will help you gauge whether you and your students are moving toward your long-range outcomes in a timely manner. It can be very helpful to talk to more experienced teachers as you make your first attempts to plan for an academic year.

Similar processes will help you plan for shorter periods. When you plan your units, plan the number of days you expect to spend on each key idea and outcome. Of course, these plans may be subject to change according to your students' needs. Finally, it will be important to plan the timing and order of subjects and activities through the class period or school day. Some guidelines will be helpful.

First, establish routines that give shape to the time you spend with students, whether it is 50 minutes or longer. Some teams start each day with a class meeting; some teachers begin with homework issues or a challenge-of-the-day activity. Class might end with a read-aloud or class headline (interesting accomplishment or event). A predictable routine makes it easier to plan and provides security to students with a high need for structure. While these time allocations should never be rigid, they can be helpful in outlining the period.

Second, As you think about your time with students, plan for whole-group, small-group, and individual activities. It is important to have enough variety, support, and challenge so that each student—regardless of learning style, prior knowledge, or skill level—has appropriate activities every day. Since students differ in so many ways, this will not be easy. It will require careful planning and differentiation of some activities.

Here are two examples of planning for two hours in a block schedule centered on language arts. Notice how the team has allowed for some whole-class activities and some activities that are differentiated according to students' needs. Each day begins with whole-class activities during the Morning Meeting (Kriete, 1999) and then varies according to student needs.

Teacher 1
Monday

8:30–9:00	Morning Meeting
9:00–9:20	Preassessment of skills
9:20–10:00	Whole-group experiences with novel
10:00–10:30	Journals; individual reading; teacher works with students with particular skill needs—some who need additional assistance, some who need to plan for additional challenge

Tuesday

8:30–9:00	Morning Meeting
9:00–9:30	Whole-group experiences with novel
9:30–10:00	Begin small-group assignments on genre: students read one of three novels based on interest and/or skill level
10:00–10:30	Skills lesson for students identified through preassessment; other students work on genre assignment, contracts, or individual reading

Wednesday

8:30–9:00	Morning Meeting
9:00–9:40	Trios of students work on genre assignments with those reading the same book, using graphic organizer to identify characteristics of characters
9:40–10:00	Whole-class discussion comparing novels
10:00–10:30	Journals, as on Monday

Teacher 2
Monday

8:30–9:00	Morning Meeting
9:00–9:40	Introduce theme for the week
9:40–10:00	Preassessment of language arts skills
10:00–10:30	Students rotate to two theme centers (these may focus on language arts or include multiple subject areas)

Tuesday

8:30–9:00	Morning Meeting
9:00–9:30	Skills instruction for students identified in preassessment; any students not needing skills instruction work at centers with choice activities
9:30–10:00	Students from skills group work on practice activity; teacher introduces other group to contracts
10:00–10:30	Student from skills group work in centers with choice activities; contract students work on contract assignments

Wednesday

8:30–9:00	Morning Meeting
9:00–9:45	Students rotate through required activities at two more centers
9:45–10:15	Students who need additional skills (on the basis of Tuesday's practice activity) work with teacher; contract students work on contracts; other students choose either to begin contracts or use choice activities at centers
10:15–10:30	Students with contracts check in with teacher; other students practice or do choice activities

Notice the amount of variety that was planned in a short period of time. Students had the opportunity for whole-group, small-group, and individual activities. Both teachers provided extra support and practice to students who needed additional skills instruction or more challenge, without resorting to traditional inflexible groups.

In a similar fashion, activities within a single class period should vary and, when possible, provide opportunities for differentiation. Within a 50-minute class period you might have five minutes of "housekeeping," five minutes of active student involvement in review activities, 15 minutes of whole group minilecture or inductive activity, 20 minutes of small-group or individual activities, and five minutes of closing and assignments. Opportunities for differentiation would be most likely to occur in small group or practice activities.

CHAPTER SUMMARY

As a beginning teacher, you will need a variety of strategies for planning large and small tasks. From the moment-to-moment planning of questions and responses to broader planning for days or months, each decision affects the ways students learn and the relationships in your classroom. Use strategies to help students learn independently and activities to help them learn together. Plan activities that open your classroom to the world. Mastery of this complex set of strategies is part of the process of becoming a professional educator. As you progress from field experiences to student teaching to the beginning years of your teaching career, you will find that returning to the information in this chapter will help you incorporate these ideas in increasingly sophisticated ways. Support from other teachers, professional reading, and professional development also will be important as you continue the journey into professionalism.

Practice Activity D

Interviewing Teachers

Do one or both of the following:

- Interview a teacher about the processes he or she uses for long-range planning. If possible, obtain a copy of the long-range plan for one or more subject areas. Compare your findings with a colleague. Think about the processes you think will work best for you.
- Interview a teacher about the structure he or she uses to organize the school day. Make a template or diagram to describe the day's routines. Compare your findings with colleagues.

Unit Preparation

During this time you should be refining your lesson and assessment plans. Using what you have learned in this chapter, consider how you can add variety, challenge, differentiation, and interest to your plans. Your instructor may have specific strategies or assignments to add to your basic unit. For example, you may want to create an independent learning activity that could be placed in a center to supplement your unit, or compile a list of resources that could facilitate independent work.

 ## *Portfolio Activities*

Create a plan for your school day, outlining the routines you believe will be important. Be prepared to discuss your choices and how you believe they will support student learning.

Create and use a learning center. Include one or two photographs of your center in use, along with descriptions of the activities.

 ## *Search the Web*

Continue to search the Web for new lesson ideas and materials. One of the richest resources is provided by the federal government of the United States; FREE (Federal Resources for Educational Excellence) is a source of thousands of materials that can be used by teachers.

http://www.ed.gov/free

Education World provides lesson plan databases in all subject areas and monthly updates regarding new sites on particular topics.

http://www.education-world.com

REFERENCES

American Association of University Women (AAUW) Educational Foundation. (1998). *Gender gaps: Where schools still fail our children.* Washington, D.C.: Author.

Aronson, E., Blaney N., Stephan, C., Sikes, J., & Snapp, M. (1978). *The jigsaw classroom.* Beverly Hills, CA.: Sage.

Atwood, V. A. & Wilen, W. W. (1992). Wait time and effective social studies instruction: what can research in science education tell us? *Social Education, 55*(3), 179–181.

Brophy, J. (1998). *Motivating students to learn.* Boston: McGraw-Hill.

Caine, R. N., & Caine, G. C. (1997). *Education on the edge of possibility.* Alexandria, VA: Association for Supervision and Curriculum Development.

Clarke, J. (1994). Pieces of the puzzle: The jigsaw method. In S. Sharan, *Handbook of cooperative learning methods.* Westport, CT: Greenwood Press.

Cohen, E. B. (1994). Complex instruction: Higher order thinking in heterogeneous classrooms. In S. Sharan, *Handbook of cooperative learning methods.* Westport, CT: Greenwood Press.

Cohen, E. G. (1998). Making cooperative learning equitable. *Educational Leadership, 56*(1), 18–21.

Costa, A., & Liebman, R. (1997). *Supporting the spirit of learning: When process is content.* Thousand Oaks, CA: Corwin Press.

Conyers, J. G., & Rauscher, W. C. (December 2000/January 2001). An Antarctic adventure. *Educational Leadership, 58*(4), 69–72.

Dede, C. (Ed.). (1998) *ASCD Yearbook 1998: Learning with technology.* Alexandria, VA: Association for Supervision and Curriculum Development.

Draper, R. J. (1997, September/October). Jigsaw: Because reading your math book shouldn't be a puzzle. *The Clearing House, 71,* 33–36.

Eisner, E. W. (2002). The kind of schools we need. *Phi Delta Kappan, 83*(8), 576–583.

Gall, J., & Gall, M. (1990). Outcomes of the discussion method. In W. Wilen (Ed.), *Teaching and learning through discussion: The theory and practice of the discussion method.* Springfield, IL: Chas. J. Thomas.

Glasser, W. (1990). *The quality school: Managing students without coercion.* New York: Harper Row.

Glasser, W. (1997, April). A new look at school failure and school success. *Phi Delta Kappan, 78*(8), 597–603.

Good, T., & Brophy, J. (1999). *Looking in classrooms* (8th Ed.). Needham, MA: Allyn & Bacon.

Harris, J. (2002). *Virtual architecture* (2nd Ed.) Eugene, OR: International Society for Technology in Education.

Healy, J. M. (1998). *Failure to connect: How computers affect our children's minds—for better or worse.* New York: Simon Schuster.

Jocoby, B. (Ed.). (1996). *Service-learning in higher education.* San Francisco: Jossey-Bass.

Johnson, D., & Johnson, R. (1999). *Learning together and alone: Cooperative, competitive and individualistic learning.* Boston: Allyn & Bacon.

Kovalik, S. (1994). Brain-compatible learning. *Video Journal of Education, 3*(6).

Kriete, R. (1999). *The morning meeting book.* Greenfield, MA: Northeast Foundation for Children.

Lou, Y., Abrami, P., Spence, J. C., Paulson, C., Chambers, B., & d'Appollorio, S. (1996). Within-class grouping: A meta-analysis. *Review of Educational Research, 66*(4), 423–458.

Marzano, R. J., Pickering, D. J. & Pollock, J.E. (2001). Classroom instruction that works. Alexandria, VA: Association for Supervision and Curriculum Development.

Medina, K., Pigg, M., Desler, G., & Gorospe, G. (2001). Teaching generation.com. *Phi Delta Kappan, 82*(8) 616–619.

Pearlman, B. (2002). Reinventing the high school experience. *Educational Leadership, 59*(7), 72–75.

Rosenshine, B. V., Meister, C., & Chapman, S. (1996, Summer). Teaching students to generate questions: A review of intervention studies. *Review of Educational Research, 66,* 181–221.

Rowe, M. (1974). Pausing phenomena: Influence on quality of instruction. *Journal of Psycholinguistic Research, 3,* 203–224.

Secretary's Commission on Achieving Necessary Skills. (1993). Teaching the SCANS competencies. Washington, D.C.: United States Department of Labor.

Sharan, Y., & Sharan, S. (1992). *Expanding cooperative learning through group investigations.* New York: Teachers College Press.

Slavin, R. E. (1994). Student teams—Achievement divisions. In S. Sharan, *Handbook of cooperative learning methods.* Westport, CT: Greenwood Press.

Slavin, R. E. (1995). *Cooperative learning: Theory, research and practice* (2nd Ed.). Boston: Allyn & Bacon.

Sparks, D. (1998) The Educator, examined: An Interview with Phillip Schlechty. *Journal of Staff Development, 19*(3).

Stacey, K., Rice, D., Hurst, K., & Langer, C. (1997). *Academic service-learning K–12 training manual.* Ypsilanti, MI: Eastern Michigan University.

Tapscott, D. (1999). Educating the net generation. *Educational Leadership, 56*(5), 6–11.

Tell, C. (2000, October). The I-generation—from toddlers to teenages: A conversation with Jane. M. Healy. *Educational Leadership, 58*(2), 8–15.

Thornburg, D. (2002). *The new basics: Education and the future of work in the telematic age.* Alexandria, VA: Association for Supervision and Curriculum Development.

Tobin, K. (1980). The effect of an extended teacher wait time on science achievement. *Journal of Research in Science Teaching, 17,* 469–475.

Tobin, K., & Campie, W. (1982). Relationships between classroom process variables and middle school science achievement. *Journal of Educational Psychology, 74,* 441–454.

Treffinger, D. J., & Young, G. C. (March, 2002). Fostering independence and self-direction. *Parenting for High Potential.* United States Department of Labor, 26–29.

Walberg, H. J. (1999). Productive teaching. In H. J. Waxman & H. C. Walberg (Eds.), *New directions for teaching practice and research* (75–104). Berkeley, CA: McCutcheon Publishing Corporation.

Weinman, J., & Haag, P. (1999, February). Gender equity in cyberspace. *Educational Leadership, 56*(5), 44–49.

Wolfe, P. (2001). *Brain Matters.* Alexandria, VA: Association for Supervision and Curriculum Development.

Wood, C. (2002). Changing the pace of school: Slowing down the day to improve the quality of learning. *Phi Delta Kappan, 83*(7), 545–550.

Diversity and Differentiation

CHAPTER OVERVIEW

Throughout this text we have discussed the importance of recognizing students' individual differences and using various approaches to instruction for students with a variety of learning styles, interests, and abilities. This chapter takes another look at strategies that will be useful as you work to differentiate the curriculum for a variety of learners. We offer information and techniques to help you make decisions regarding the particular needs of students with educational disabilities, gifted and talented students, culturally diverse and bilingual students, and students in urban schools. Each of the chapter sections focuses on the characteristics and needs of students discussed, describes teaching strategies appropriate for such students, and explains how these strategies may sometimes be useful for all students.

Opening Activity

Hannah Lewis, a first-year teacher, sits at her desk at the end of a long October day. So far, she has found her eleventh-grade English classes to be extremely hectic but rewarding. Hannah has enjoyed the diversity in her large urban school. Her carefully prepared management system has proved valuable in creating a classroom atmosphere that is warm but businesslike. Although much of the material so far has been review, Hannah is pleased that most of her students are completing their assignments successfully. Best of all, Hannah feels as if she is beginning to really know her students—their likes, dislikes, strengths, weaknesses, and interests. Today, however, that knowledge is starting to cause her some concern.

The students are all so different. It is easiest to worry about John. Although he is the oldest child in his class, his reading is slow and laborious, and he has not mastered basic writing skills. So far he has not caused any trouble, but last year's teacher said he used to argue with her and would not participate in class.

Diedra, on the other hand, has caused some problems already. Her ready wit sends the class into fits of laughter, often at the teacher's expense. She is a leader in class and out, devising creative sets for drama club productions and elaborate pranks at the expense of rival schools and local faculty. Her work is erratic. While her creative writing is outstanding, her grammar and spelling are average at best, and she frequently hands in late or incomplete assignments. Hannah often wonders if Diedra is really listening to her.

Rosa is another story. Raised in a Spanish-speaking home, Rosa spent her first two years in school in bilingual program. While she speaks English fairly well, her grammar is weak and her reading is not much better than John's. Rosa never volunteers in class, and Hannah is seldom sure whether she understands the lesson.

Tony is the star of the class. Whenever a lesson is lagging or a point seems unclear, Hannah can count on Tony to come up with the correct answer. His assignments are always complete and accurate. If a topic is mentioned in class, Tony frequently finds a newspaper article or book from home that can serve as an additional resource. Hannah has heard other teachers reminiscing about how much they enjoyed Tony in previous years. Hannah enjoys him, too, but she continues to have nagging doubts about the work he is doing in class. Is Tony really learning anything?

As she thinks about John, Diedra, Rosa, and Tony and her carefully prepared unit on mythic heroes and heroines, Hannah wonders how she can ever teach the subject in a way that will reach all her students.

Practice Point

Think for a moment about John, Diedra, Rosa, and Tony. What characteristics of each student may have an impact on his or her learning in Hannah's class?

Hannah is facing a common dilemma. Although teachers learn important principles of planning and instruction, those principles are always put into practice on a particular day, in a particular lesson, and with a particular group of students. The artistry in teaching consists of knowing how to take into account the context of the lesson—that is, which principles and strategies are most important to emphasize in each set of circumstances.

This chapter will help you differentiate your planning and instruction for learners like John, Diedra, Rosa, and Tony. As you read, remember that none of the special needs addressed are mutually exclusive. A student may be gifted and bilingual; another may come from a cultural background that affects school performance. Many other combinations exist as well. It is important to consider each student first as an individual. Only then is it helpful to think about the special needs often found in particular groups of young people.

SECTION 1. DIFFERENTIATED INSTRUCTION

Section 1 Objective

When you have completed this section, you will have the ability to explain several strategies for differentiating instruction to meet students' needs.

As we discussed in Chapter 6, differentiated instruction flexes to meet the varying needs of students within a class. If you intend for all students to learn, you must plan instruction that can accommodate many types of learners with widely varied backgrounds. Now that you know more about different types of lessons and instructional strategies, you can better reflect on how differentiation can (and must) occur. This section describes principles and characteristics of differentiated instruction.

Tomlinson (1999) outlines eight guidelines for differentiated classrooms. Think about how each of these principles already guides your planning.

1. The teacher focuses on the essentials. Teachers in differentiated classrooms focus instruction around core concepts, principles, and skills of a discipline. (See Tomlinson, 2000, for a discussion of standards-based instruction and differentiation.)

2. The teacher attends to student differences. Teachers in differentiated classrooms are aware of individual differences and of their responsibility to all the students in their classrooms.

3. Assessment and instruction are inseparable. In these classrooms assessment is ongoing and diagnostic. Instructional decisions are based on assessment, not on what is found on the next page of a teacher's guide.

4. The teacher modifies content, process, and products. Modifying *content* may mean skipping practice of already mastered skills, or additional practice activities on content some students should have learned in previous years. It also can mean variation by interest or prior knowledge. Modifying *process* may require that some students work with the teacher in a small group while others work independently on similar material. It could mean that some students receive a homework assignment to read about key terms before they are introduced in class, or others are given resource materials that are too complex for most of the class to analyze. Modifying *products* could entail choice among different products or variations on a product assigned to different students. For example, if all students are writing historical fiction, some students may be challenged to write a new ending for an already familiar story, some to recount a major event in story form, and still others to write in first person—a task requiring greater abstraction and flexible thinking. All three are higher level tasks at varying levels of difficulty.

5. All students participate in respectful work. A differentiated classroom is not a room in which some students learn important content or engage in challenging higher level thinking and others do not. All of the children work toward essential goals. Teachers in these classrooms understand that you cannot show respect for student differences by ignoring them. Respectful teaching entails acknowledging the readiness level of each student, expecting each student to grow, offering escalating challenges as students develop understanding, and providing all students with equally interesting, important, and engaging work. The writing example above represents an

effort to provide all students with interesting, creative work while still allowing differing levels of challenge.

6. The teacher and students collaborate in learning, The teacher in a differentiated classroom is the leader, with students as the important participants in the community. Students help the teacher identify appropriate goals, monitor progress, analyze successes and failures, and learn from experience. As they do this, they become active participants in their own learning.

7. The teacher balances group and individual norms. Differentiated instruction requires attention to group goals (often outlined as state standards and benchmarks) and individual goals. If a student enters a grade without having mastered a key part of earlier curriculum, the teacher will need to balance targeted activities designed to teach earlier skills with supported appropriate instruction in grade-level content. Both sets of goals are essential. In a parallel fashion, students who enter a grade well above the expected skill level will need both group and individual goals to learn.

8. The teacher and students work together flexibly. As described in earlier chapters, good teaching entails great variety in strategy, group structure, and amount of choice. Differentiated instruction requires a large and varied repertoire of teaching strategies and the flexibility to use them in diverse combinations as they meet students' needs.

Many of the strategies already discussed can be used to facilitate differentiation. Differentiated classrooms do not make these modifications all day long, but only when they make sense. Tomlinson (1999) recommends:

> Modify a curricular element only when (1) you see a student need and (2) you are convinced that modification increases the likelihood that the learner will understand important ideas and use important skills more thoroughly as a result. (p. 11)

Contracts also can facilitate differentiation. They can be used for individual assignments or as a class activity with two or three possible contracts, each with challenging options appropriate to a particular level. Figure 10.1 shows the beginning of two possible contracts that might be used in a unit on insects.

Agendas, another similar structure, also provides students with an individualized list of tasks to be completed in a specified amount of time. Generally, students determine the order in which they work on the tasks, often while the teacher circulates, providing coaching and monitoring. Agendas can work well in conjunction with centers. Figure 10.2 is an example of a personal agenda.

Tiered activities can ensure that students all work on key skills or essential ideas while they address varied learning needs. For example, a student who struggles with reading or abstract thinking still needs to be able to understand the dilemmas of a character in a particular story. A student who reads several years above grade level still needs to learn from the character's choices. If both students are given identical assignments, at least one is likely to be frustrated and experience limited learning.

A tiered activity could be used to provide multiple avenues to the same key learning, with varied levels of difficulty. Students could discuss the plot and the influences on the character in a whole-class discussion or in heterogeneous groups with guide

Contract 1

Insect Study

Name _____

1. Draw a diagram of an insect, illustrating all the major body parts.
2. Choose one insect and create a flip book illustrating its life cycle. Attach a written description of the life cycle to the flip book. Explain how this insect's life cycle is like or unlike that of other insects.
3. Using your science notebook, observe at least five insects in your environment. Sketch or describe each insect. Note when and where you observed it, what the insect was doing, and what you observed about the insect's environment.

Contract 2

Name _____

Science Choose an insect that interests you. Draw a diagram of your insect, labeling all important body parts.	**Science** Investigate your insect's environment. Write a description of the environment and how your insect is suited for the environment(s) in which it lives.	**Science/Technology** Use a search engine to locate three sites that describe your insect. Using the rating form, rate the sites for information, ease of use, and potential bias.
Music Create a work of music inspired by your insect. You may use the collection of percussion instruments or other instruments of choice.	**Language Arts** Write your autobiography as if you were your chosen insect. Create at least three illustrations for your story.	**Math** Calculate how much space would be needed to hold 10,000 of your insect. If you want, calculate the space for 1 million insects.

Figure 10.1 Sample Contract Segments
From *Teaching as Decision Making: Successful Practices for the Elementary Teacher* (3rd Ed.) (p. 291), by A.J. Starko, et al., 2003, Upper Saddle River, NJ: Merrill/Prentice Hall. Copyright 2003 by Pearson Education, Inc. Reprinted with permission.

questions. Some students (including the first student) might create a collage illustrating the influences they felt were most important in the character's choices. Others might write a dialogue in which one character explains the choice to another. Still other students (perhaps including the more advanced student) could write about an original character who responded to similar influences in a different way.

Schniedewind and Davidson (2000) describe several strategies for *differentiating within cooperative learning*. One strategy entails varying the complexity of tasks within heterogeneous groups. For example, in a jigsaw activity students can each become expert on key pieces of information, but they do not have to work from resources of equal

Personal Agenda for _____

Starting Date _____

Completion Goal _____

Teacher and Student Initials	Task	Special Instructions
	Complete first-person descriptions of Boston Massacre.	Be sure that at least one of your descriptions is from someone not involved in the combat.
	Read your historical novel.	Keep track of new vocabulary in your reading log. Make notes of areas in which you identify historical consistency or inaccuracies.
	Complete problem-solving activities 26–30.	Try to find at least three ways to solve problem 28.
	Write a rough draft of your plan for your demonstration project using simple machines. After the draft has been reviewed, complete the plan according to the directions.	Do not begin your final draft of your project until the rough draft has been reviewed. Remember that the final report must be word processed.

Figure 10.2   Personal Agenda

From *Teaching as Decision Making: Successful Practices for the Elementary Teacher* (3rd Ed.) (p. 292), by A.J. Starko, et al., 2003, Upper Saddle River, NJ: Merrill/Prentice Hall. Copyright 2003 by Pearson Education, Inc. Reprinted with permission.

length or complexity. Cooperative groups also can enhance individualized work. For example, students can help partners study individualized spelling lists or help each other stick to time lines on long-term projects.

Many students can benefit from carefully planned peer tutoring activities. Keep in mind, however, that pairing students from the two extremes of your class—those who learn most easily and quickly with those who have the most learning difficulties—may not be the best strategy. Students learn best from a model they perceive is similar to themselves. If the perceived differences are too great, modeling may be less effective. In any peer tutoring structure it is important to also make sure that tutoring represents only a limited portion of the school day, particularly if the tutor is already highly skilled in the content being taught. For the majority of their day, tutors, too, should be learning content that is new to them.

We have found that a matter-of-fact *acknowledgement of differences* among students—in the context of a classroom in which it is clear that all are valued—merely recognizes what students already know. Different students are good at different things. Discussing and appreciating those differences, rather than acting as if difference is something to hide, can be the basis of an accepting community that genuinely celebrates differing accomplishments.

In their article, Schniedewind and Davidson (2000) respond to an important question about differentiated instruction.

> Do students feel awkward or resentful about such differentiated assignments? We have found that students know one another's capabilities quite well although they don't necessarily talk about them. One teacher explained to her students that differentiated assignments help her fulfill her job of challenging each student. We've found that students feel more comfortable when teachers acknowledge and engage them in discussion about the tension-producing subject of academic difference. Afterward, students can focus on learning with less anxiety. (p. 25)

Whatever the strategy, the key to successful planning for your classes is to remember this: *Classes never learn anything; only individual students learn, one at a time.* As you look at your lesson plans and think about the challenge of meeting so many students' needs, you probably are feeling a little overwhelmed. Sometimes good teaching can feel like a daunting task to even the most experienced professionals. Few teachers with typical sized classes can differentiate for every student or for every lesson. It is important to begin to prioritize your lessons to determine when differentiation is most important.

First, consider the *content*. Content that focuses on basic skills or is primarily a review from previous years is most likely to be strengthened through differentiation for able learners. Content that requires numerous prerequisite skills or complex abstract thinking may pose enough of a challenge that some students will need extra levels of support. Next, consider the *students* themselves, particularly those with the most extreme individual needs. If you have students whose current levels of achievement are a year or more above or below grade level, work with those students' most clear-cut needs in order to provide a place to start.

Finally, in planning for a day or a week, consider each student's experience over that period of time. A reasonable rule of thumb is that all students—even those whose needs are significantly different from the norm—should spend at least part of every day engaging in activities that specifically target their needs. The following sections discuss the students with particularly diverse needs for whom differentiation will be most crucial.

SECTION 2. STUDENTS WITH EDUCATIONAL DISABILITIES

Section 2 Objectives

After you have completed this section, you will have the ability to:

1. describe characteristics of students with educational disabilities;

2. describe special instructional needs of students with educational disabilities and design instructional strategies for them;
3. plan lessons in your curriculum area that are adapted to meet the needs of students with educational disabilities; and
4. explain how activities that are appropriate for students with educational disabilities may be used in lessons for an entire class.

For much of the history of American education, students with physical, emotional, and mental disabilities were taught in special educational environments by instructors trained to teach such children. In the case of a severe disability, the student was taught in a location other than a regular school. If the disability was modest, the student's classroom was typically in a public school, usually in an area set apart from the school's traffic patterns. In either case, young people with disabilities were isolated from the regular public education system and thus from teachers and students in regular classes. However, the second half of the 20th century saw dramatic changes in the education of such students. Almost every public school classroom now includes one or more students with educational disabilities. Although special education teachers are trained in these disabilities, all teachers must become familiar with the major types of disabilities and strategies for accommodating them in the regular classroom.

What Are Educational Disabilities?

A **disability** is a condition that results in a reduced competency to perform some task or behavior, whether the condition is physical, emotional, or intellectual. A disability that impedes regular educational activities is called an *educational disability*. Everyone suffers from some degree of disability, in the sense that we all have traits that keep us from performing some tasks at optimum levels. Many people have poor eyesight or poor color discrimination, are awkward at sports, or are shy with strangers. However, these disabilities are mild enough so that we can easily reduce their effects or correct them. It may be useful to think of disabilities as existing within a continuum of competency. For example, consider a continuum of visual acuity, from individuals with excellent eyesight (perhaps those who can read the numbers on the jerseys from the top row of a football stadium!) to those who have no sense of sight. We would begin to classify persons as disabled who are somewhere in the lower 25% of that continuum. Reduced competency can be categorized as *mild, moderate, severe,* or *profound.* The major classifications of educational disabilities include the following:

1. *Mental disabilities.* Students with mental disabilities function below the norm in all areas of learning. In the set activity at the beginning of this chapter, John may have a mild mental disability. Many students with mild mental disabilities need extra assistance with both traditional school curriculum and basic social and communication skills. In its moderate and severe form, intellectual disability is accompanied by difficulty in adapting to regular classroom expectations and routines, and difficulty in getting along with the teacher and other students. Students with such disabilities will need instruction and special support in daily living skills.

2. *Physical or other health impairments.* Students with physical or other health disabilities may have reduced capability to perform psychomotor tasks involving small- and large-muscle movement, such as manipulating writing instruments and books or moving around the classroom. Often the disability results in a reduction in the students' stamina, alertness, and vitality, although many students with physical disabilities have no mental disability. Common causes of physical impairment are disease and accidents.

3. *Sensory impairments.* Students with sensory disabilities have reduced visual or auditory competency. Some teachers have performed a great service for students and their parents by identifying a mild sensory disability that could be reduced with the use of glasses or hearing enhancements. In more severe cases, the young person has limited or no vision or hearing, and teaching must be adapted to reduce the effects of the disability on learning. Many forms of adaptive technology can assist students who have sensory disabilities in learning and communicating what they have learned.

4. *Speech impairments.* Students with speech disabilities have reduced competency in speech communication. A common source of speech disability is a hearing loss that reduces the student's ability to reproduce speech patterns.

5. *Emotional impairments.* Students with emotional disabilities display repeated inappropriate behavior to the extent that it affects their academic growth, social maturity, and relationships with adults and peers. It is important to distinguish a person who acts out from time to time from the person with emotional disabilities whose inappropriate behaviors are frequent and distinctive. Some individuals with emotional disabilities are identified because they are verbally or physically aggressive and prone to repeated outbursts that upset classroom routines. However, students with emotional disabilities may also be fearful, passive, or withdrawn.

6. *Learning disabilities.* Students with learning disabilities demonstrate a reduced competency to perform some behaviors, while performing as well as or better than peers on other tasks. Unfortunately, because of the limited nature of the disability and an individual's efforts to compensate for areas of weakness, learning disabilities may not be identified until many years of schooling have passed. Conversely, some young people are wrongly identified as having learning disabilities when the true cause of disability may be a physical, mental, or emotional impairment. In fact, of all the disability areas, learning disabilities are the most controversial. Because of the imprecise nature of diagnosis, major disagreements exist about the nature of a learning disability and the criteria to be used to classify a student as having a learning disability.

More than 40 definitions of learning disabilities have been proposed, but none has been universally accepted (Heward, 2000). Sternberg and Grigorenko (2001) argue that learning disabilities represent an interaction between the individual and the society; we consider individuals as having learning disabilities if they have difficulty with a skill valued by our culture. They suggest, for example, that an individual we identify as having a disability in mathematics might be considered perfectly able in a hunter-gatherer society; but some other individuals might be identified as "hunting disabled" if they could not track effectively.

Varying types of learning disabilities may impair a student's ability to read, attend to stimuli, understand figurative language, or accurately assess spatial relationships. Some kinds of impairments are much more commonly occurring than others. Ninety-one percent of the children and youth receiving special education services are reported in four disability categories: learning disabilities (51.1%), speech and language impairments (20.1%), mental impairments (11.4%), and emotional disturbances (8.6%). The vast majority of these individuals (85%) have mild disabilities. Children with disabilities in special education represent approximately 10% of the entire school-age population (Heward, 2000). These statistics make it clear that virtually every teacher will encounter students with disabilities in general education classes.

All of the listed disabilities may occur in a range from mild, to moderate, to severe, to profound. At some level of disability a person loses the capacity to function in society without external assistance. The degree to which individuals are assisted determines the degree of handicap they experience. A **handicap** is the disadvantage one suffers from the effects of a disability. The extent to which an individual is handicapped is a result of both the severity of the disability and the degree of assistance offered by society. For example, a person with physical disabilities who uses a wheelchair will be handicapped by facilities that are inaccessible, but not in areas designed to accommodate wheelchair access. A student with a learning disability who is unable to read a science test is handicapped if required to take a written exam. Although it is impossible to prevent all handicaps caused by disabilities, teachers have a responsibility to minimize the handicapping effects of disabilities in their classrooms. In the case of a reading disability, the teacher could allow the students to take the science test orally. The student would still have a learning disability, but would not be handicapped in taking the science exam.

Educational Disabilities in School

It is helpful to understand the relationship between a disability and a handicap in order to interpret the motivation for the events of the late 1960s and 1970s that culminated in the passage of the Individuals with Disabilities Education Act (IDEA). Originally known as the Education for All Handicapped Children Act (EAHCA) or Public Law 94-142, this legislation has been amended four times. The 1990 amendments renamed the law, often referred to by its acronym, IDEA.

The purpose of IDEA is to:

> . . . assure that all children with disabilities have available to them . . . a free appropriate public education which emphasizes special education and related service designed to meet their unique need, to assure that the rights of children with disabilities and their parents or guardians are protected, to assist states and localities to provide for the education of all children with disabilities, and to assess and assure the effectiveness of efforts to educate children with disabilities. (IDEA, 20 U. S. C., 1400 [c]).

The law has six major principles, as follows:

1. Schools must educate all children. Regardless of the nature or the severity of the disability, no child with disabilities can be excluded public education.

2. Schools must use nonbiased and multifactored methods of assessing disabilities. Tests must be administered in the child's native language, and placement cannot be made on the basis of a single score. This principle is intended to protect students from inaccurate assessments affected by cultural bias or single observations.

3. Education for students with disabilities must be provided at public expense, including an Individualized Education Plan (IEP) designed to meet the child's unique needs.

4. Students must be educated in the least restrictive environment (LRE) appropriate to their needs. Students with disabilities cannot be segregated into special classes or schools unless the nature of their disabilities is such that they cannot receive appropriate education in a general education setting with supports. To ensure that students have access to the least restrictive environment possible, schools must provide a continuum of services.

5. Schools must provide due process to protect the rights of students with disabilities and their parents. Parental consent must be obtained for evaluations and placement decisions. When the school and the parents disagree, specific requirements must be adhered to for due process.

6. Parents (and where appropriate, students) should have the opportunity to collaborate with schools in the design and implementation of specialized services (Heward, 2000).

In a 1987 review of the impact of the Education for All Handicapped Children Act, Singer and Butler concluded that the EHA had been a singular success. They stated that 20 years earlier, most Americans

> . . . would have flatly denied the feasibility of instituting in every school system in the country, a program of individualized education, however imperfect, for 11 percent of the nation's children. Yet, this was done within a few years of EHA's implementation. Regular education teachers, special education teachers, school administrators and others at the local level have demonstrated a remarkable degree of dedication to the law's goals and an equally remarkable willingness to subsidize the program with their own efforts. (p. 151)

In fairness, it must be noted that this success was not accomplished without significant problems. Then and now, the sheer size of the change and the number of disability areas created administrative, logistical, clerical, and instructional burdens for the schools. Each disability area has its unique characteristics and challenges. Many students with physical and sensory disabilities need special equipment, materials, and support personnel. Some students who are classified as disabled qualify for government support because they are also economically disadvantaged; others do not. Some disabilities are hard to identify, particularly in students with multiple disabilities or students for whom English is not the primary language. Despite such difficulties, however, IDEA has successfully mandated enormous changes in the education of students with disabilities.

To provide all students with the least restrictive environment possible, a continuum of services has evolved.

1. *Full-time regular classroom.* In this option, students with disabilities spend the entire school day in a regular classroom, which is called mainstreaming or, more

recently, inclusion. The teacher in a classroom with one or more students with disabilities may receive support and consultative services from a special education specialist. In some cases, the specialist may also provide supplementary services or instruction to students within the regular classroom. In other cases, the student may be accompanied by a part- or full-time assistant appropriate to the student's disability. Full-time placement in a regular classroom is an increasingly popular option for many students with a wide range of disabilities.

2. *Regular classroom for a majority of the school program.* In this case, the student has the outside support of a resource teacher trained in special education and other professional personnel who specialize in the particular disability involved. The student is with his regular student peers for most of the day but may spend several hours each week in a resource setting.

3. *Self-contained classroom for a majority of the school program.* In this option, the student is taught in a special education classroom and mainstreamed into the regular classroom for varying amounts of time and for appropriate content activities. Such students may join a regular classroom for a limited amount of time each morning or afternoon or for special subjects such as music or physical education.

4. *Self-contained classroom for the instructional program but within the regular school building.* Placement in the regular building permits the students with disabilities to participate in individually prescribed experiences and extracurricular activities.

5. *Separate school.* When special schools are located on the same campus as other school buildings, the proximity can permit students with disabilities to participate in appropriate parts of the extracurricular program. Students with severe disabilities may need more protective services than the public schools can provide and may require full-time residential programs.

It is likely that you will have one or more students with disabilities in your classroom for all or part of the school day. Each of these students will require an **individualized education plan (IEP),** an educational plan outlining goals and strategies. An IEP must include the following for each student:

(A) a statement of the child's present levels of educational performance,
(B) a statement of annual goals, including short-term instructional objectives,
(C) a statement of the specific educational services to be provided and the extent to which the child will be able to participate in regular educational programs,
(D) the projected date for initiation and anticipated duration of such services, and appropriate objective criteria and evaluation procedures and schedules for determining, on at least an annual basis, whether instructional objectives are being met. (IDEA, 20 U.S.C., 1400 [c])

In addition to describing the nature of the IEP, the law stipulates that the plan must be cooperatively developed by the student's teacher and the student's parent(s) or guardian and approved by the designated school administrator or special education supervisor. Although the federal law does not do so, some states require that IEPs be prepared not just for students with disabilities but for students identified as gifted as well.

If a student in your classroom requires an IEP, a specialist should work with you to plan the individualized program and to clarify your role in carrying out the plan.

Note that the IEP has a similar structure to a unit plan or lesson design. Each is a system beginning with goals that are analyzed and phrased as clearly stated objectives. Activities are designed to help students meet the objectives, and evaluation (assessment) procedures are used to determine if the objectives have been met. If additional instruction is needed, it is provided. Throughout instruction, there is consideration for students' learning styles, prior knowledge, and experience.

The major differences between an IEP and a unit plan or lesson design are that the IEP is a learning prescription for an individual student and that parents are more directly involved in its preparation and execution. The IEP rests on criterion-referenced evaluation rather than norm-referenced evaluation principles; that is, evaluation is based on a student's achieving a predetermined performance standard rather than on a comparison with the performance of other students. Because of the attractive characteristics of the IEP process, its individual perspective on achievement, the way in which it involves parents, and its systematic structure, some educators have proposed that all students be taught through individualized education plans.

REFLECTING ON THE IDEAS

Assume that an influential group of citizens recommended that all students be taught through the IEP process. What would be the advantages and disadvantages of that recommendation? Is it a worthy goal? Is it workable and practical? Briefly explain your views, and discuss the recommendation with others.

Inclusion

The passage of IDEA has meant that many students with disabilities spend all or part of the day in regular classrooms, which is often referred to as **inclusion.** There is no clear consensus on the definition of inclusion (Kauffman & Hallahan, 1994/5). Some individuals use the term only to refer to full-time placement of students with disabilities in general education classrooms. Others would include more limited time in regular classrooms within the definition. Some advocates for individuals with disabilities believe that the best way to ensure equitable treatment for students with disabilities is to place all students in regular classrooms all the time, which is known as *full inclusion.*

Inclusion involves the integration of students with severe disabilities into regular classrooms. Generally the educational programs for students with severe impairments center on the development of functional life skills—eating, communication, and hygiene. Although such students often spend the majority of their time in special education, they are sometimes able to join regular classrooms for appropriate activities (Raynes, Snell, & Sailor, 1992; Rogers, 1993). In an inclusion classroom the test is whether the severely disabled student benefits from participation in the regular classroom work and not whether the student is able to maintain a work performance level similar to that of other students (Goodlad & Lovitt, 1993).

Where inclusion is common practice, the student does not follow assistance personnel and services; rather, the personnel and services follow the child. These personnel may include resource teachers who work with students individually or in small groups, paraprofessionals who assist with physical care and other needs, translators for students with physical impairments, readers for those with visual impairments, and many others. In an inclusion program, a cooperative relationship and a shared sense of responsibility develop between the student's regular classroom teacher and these special education personnel. If inclusion is to be successful, all members of the educational community must work together to meet the needs of students with disabilities.

A school that successfully implements inclusive education has been characterized as a place where the following occur on a regular daily basis.

1. *Heterogeneous grouping.* Students are organized in classrooms in which the proportion of students with disabilities approximates the natural proportion in the population. In a secondary classroom this might include one student with severe disabilities, several with mild disabilities, and many students without identified disabilities.

2. *A sense of belonging to a group.* The students with disabilities are considered part of the group rather than special guests. They are welcomed into a classroom community.

3. *Shared activities with individualized outcomes.* Students may share learning activities without necessarily sharing the same goals within the activity. This could include differentiated objectives within a curriculum or social objectives for some students being pursued at the same time as content goals.

4. *Use of environments frequented by persons without disabilities.* Educational experiences take place in environments in which most individuals do not have disabilities, such as general education classrooms.

5. *A balanced educational experience.* Inclusive education seeks a balance between academic and social goals. Neither is given absolute priority. (Giangreco, Cloninger, Dennis & Edelman (1994).

An inclusive school would not be characterized by a particular set of practices as much as by the commitment of its staff to continually develop its capacity to accommodate the full range of individual differences among its learners. Simply placing students with disabilities in general education does not constitute inclusion and will not guarantee that children with disabilities will learn and behave appropriately or that they will be accepted by other students. It is important that teachers, often with the help of special education specialists, educate nondisabled students about their classmates. Properly implemented, inclusive classrooms have demonstrated successes from preschool to high school and for mild to severe impairments (Esposito & Reed, 1986; Guralnick, 1981; Hanline & Murray, 1984; Johnson, Rynders, Johnson, Schmidt, & Haider, 1979).

Despite these successes, full inclusion has its critics (see, for example, the variety of positions in the January 1995 issue of *Educational Leadership*). The levels of support provided, type and severity of disabilities, and number of inclusion students in a particular classroom all contribute to the success or failure of the effort. Snell and Janney (2000) describe some of the lessons they learned in creating successful inclusion experiences. Teachers who were successful in implementing inclusion modified their typical role to share responsibility for the focus (included) students with a special education professional. Typically, classroom teachers maintained primary responsibility for the class and the focus child when he or she was being treated like nonfocus classmates. Special education professionals took the lead when the focus child was being treated differently. Classroom teachers modified classroom routines and arrangements to accommodate physical needs of focus students and modified instructional activities in order to allow focus students to participate. This might entail modifying activities to allow academic participation (for example, a reduced or differentiated list of spelling words) or simply social participation (for example holding a book while other students are reading). Special education teachers taught individualized objectives separately but within the classroom. Relationships with other students were most successful when teachers treated focus students as much like other students as possible, encouraging age-appropriate behavior and social interactions with other children.

Farlow (1996) described strategies for successful inclusion at the secondary level. They include supports for inclusion students and curriculum adaptations to maximize their success. Farlow's suggestions are summarized as follows.

Supports for Students

1. Allow peers to facilitate learning. Reading buddies, study pals, and other types of assistants can help students function in general education settings.

2. Structure class activities to make peer support available. If cooperative learning and peer tutoring are part of the classroom routine, inclusion becomes part of a natural climate of helpfulness. It is important, however, to be sensitive to the amount of time nondisabled students spend as peer tutors, particularly if the material being studied is something they mastered long ago. Peer tutoring can be a powerful learning experience, but it is also important to make sure all students spend most of the school day learning material that is appropriate to their own level.

3. Prime students to be successful. Being introduced to ideas or materials before they are presented to the class can add to students' success. Communication with parents, reading guides, and early assignments can help students gain important prior knowledge before a new topic is introduced to the class as a whole.

4. Give students valued roles. Students with disabilities often have strengths that can allow them to play important roles in school organizations, teams, and classrooms. To the degree they successfully manage roles that are valued in the school community, students become an accepted asset of the group. For example, a student who may not be able to play on a varsity sports team may serve a valuable role in organizing and storing equipment, encouraging the team, and being its most enthusiastic supporter.

5. Use existing expertise. Learn from teachers who are successful with inclusion students. One graduate student did a research project in which she interviewed teachers in her district who were particularly successful with inclusion students. Her conversations with those teachers enriched her own teaching practice, and it provided an interesting graduate project!

Adaptations of Curriculum

1. Use independent prompts. If students need cues to classroom routines or other skills, written or audiotaped directions can provide assistance without disrupting others. For example, direction cards taped to a desktop can remind students of classroom routines or steps in an assignment.

2. Vary the amount of work required. Some students with disabilities work much more slowly than other students. In such cases, a reduced assignment can provide needed practice without placing an unreasonable burden on the student. Some students are much more successful if an assignment is literally cut into smaller sections; for example, strips of problems one at a time rather than a whole page of problems.

3. Adjust delivery of information. A variety of means of presenting information—computers, pictures, media, storytelling, oral reading—can assist students for whom reading is a challenge.

4. Allow students to express information in varied ways. Students who may not be able to express content in writing may be able to explain it, draw it, or choose from among several possibilities.

5. Present alternative activities. At times a class activity may be inappropriate for a particular student. A reasonable solution is to provide an alternative activity. In a classroom in which many students frequently do differing kinds of assignments, such flexibility will seem natural.

Strategies for Teaching Students with Disabilities

Some general recommendations can be made for teachers regardless of the nature of the students' disabilities. Several of the ideas are also recommended for optimum learning for all students.

• Learn as much as you can about the needs of students in your class. Consult with the special education professional in your building or district to gain additional insights into students' learning styles and strengths as well as strategies to accommodate the disabilities. For example, a student with a mild mental disability is more likely to be successful if presented with small chunks of information and given considerable reinforcement. A student with a mild hearing disability will benefit from sitting near the speaker, with an unobstructed view for lip reading. A more severely disabled student may need an interpreter. You can also use your knowledge of students' interests and strengths to plan individual or class activities particularly suited to their needs.

• Avoid calling special attention to the student's disability. Although a matter-of-fact acceptance of a disability is appropriate—you certainly cannot ignore the fact that Paul cannot see the board or Susan cannot read—it is important to relate to students as individuals, not as members of a group of people with disabilities. It is no more appropriate to make generalizations about groups of people with disabilities than it would be to base broad generalizations on race or gender.

• Do not make assumptions based on disabilities. Do not assume that people with disabilities are unhappy. Similarly, do not assume that individuals with disabilities are disabled in all areas or are less mature than those without disabilities. It is inappropriate to treat a mentally disabled 15-year-old whose intellectual level is that of a 10-year-old in the way you would treat a typical 10-year-old. Likewise, it is inappropriate to treat a preadolescent who is blind or has a physical disability like a small child (Biklen & Bogdan, 1977).

• Establish a classroom environment in which it is a common practice for students of different backgrounds and capabilities to learn from each other. Use cooperative learning activities to integrate students of different backgrounds and abilities so they can teach each other. Use a clear management system. Do not accept inappropriate behavior from students with disabilities that you would not accept from students without disabilities. You may choose a less serious consequence, but do not communicate the message to the rest of the class that you will ignore unacceptable behavior. Such inconsistencies may lead to misbehavior or resentment by other students.

• Be enthusiastic and give positive reinforcement in response to the performance of students with disabilities. However, as for all students, do not give praise that is repetitious, insincere, or overly broad, as it is not helpful and can be damaging.

• Be sure to have a systematic framework to organize your classroom activities. Some students with emotional, intellectual, or learning disabilities need a carefully established structure in order to work most effectively. Clearly defined objectives, with activities and assessment procedures that logically follow from these objectives, communicate a sense of security and predictability to all students.

• Consider using a criterion-referenced evaluation approach in judging the performance of students with disabilities. Students with disabilities are more apt to be successful if your goal is to move them to greater competence rather than to rank them in comparison with others.

• Consider using the IEP format for all your students. Begin with a small portion of your requirements and assess how it works. You could meet with each student to develop a plan for an individual project. Help each student develop a project goal and transform it into objectives, activities, and a product that can be evaluated to determine if the objectives have been met.

• Become an advocate for students with disabilities. Lobby for alternative learning materials; for example, interesting literature and books that parallel the text for regular students but are at a different reading level. Lobby for facilities and materials that can reduce the handicaps of students with visual or hearing disabilities. See education for students with disabilities as their right as members of society rather than as a privilege granted to them.

• Finally, continue to learn about educational disabilities. As our understanding of learning processes and brain functions increases, so does our understanding of educational disabilities. There differences can have important implications for teachers. For example, a teacher who understands Attention Deficit Hyperactivity Disorder (ADHD) as a learning disorder will be more effective than one who believes it to be behavioral disorder (Tannock & Martinussen, 2001).

It is impossible in this brief space to provide a comprehensive description of teaching methods for students with disabilities. However, a brief list is given below of additional strategies that may prove useful for students with varied types of disabilities. While strategies are suggested for a particular type of disability, many strategies are appropriate for multiple student needs. By working as a team with a special education professional, you will be able to devise strategies most suited to the students in your class.

Students with *mental* disabilities often find it easier to learn skills and procedures in small incremental steps. They will need more detailed and elaborate directions than other students. Carefully analyzing the task at hand can allow you to provide appropriate directions and prompts. For example, a student with a mental disability initially may need a set of reminder pictures inside his or her locker to remember the materials to be carried to class each day. In a similar fashion, it may be necessary to provide a detailed checklist for a student learning to write a complete sentence or to add fractions.

Students with mental disabilities benefit by active involvement in lessons, with the opportunity for frequent responses. Response cards or other signal devices can be helpful. Other types of active involvement can include choral reading, computer-aided instruction, and activities that call for physical responses, such as clapping or moving in specific ways. Students with mental disabilities benefit from feedback when it is immediate, positive, frequent, and differential ("You did five more than yesterday."). This type of feedback is not difficult in a small group but can be challenging when working with a whole class. When students are participating in large-group activities, it can be helpful to create "secret signals" to let the student know you notice and appreciate his or her appropriate responses and behavior. For example, walking by and briefly touching the student's desk or giving a subtle thumbs-up signal or other agreed-upon gesture can provide needed reinforcement. As the student matures, time without reinforcement can increase.

Students with *learning disabilities* benefit from explicit descriptions of what is expected. It also can be helpful to be clear about objectives and provide support materials and examples. For example, you can provide graphic organizers and diagrams for students with learning disabilities. Many students benefit from templates to guide their notetaking or help them follow a minilecture. Mnemonic devices can help some students recall content more readily. Also, you may provide very explicit teaching of study, organizational, and problem-solving strategies. For example, students may need clear step-by-step directions about how to record homework assignments, address a word problem, or structure a story.

Many other types of support strategies can be effective, depending on the nature of the disability. Special education teachers will assist you with specific strategies targeted to students' disabilities. Some students with learning disabilities benefit from guides to help them follow along a line of text or transparent overlays that cut the glare on their papers. Some students will need adjusted deadlines or adjusted assignments to accommodate a slower pace of work. If a disruption in routine is expected, for example a school assembly, many students with learning disabilities will benefit from advanced preparation and rehearsal of the new activity. Sudden changes in structure can be distressing.

Similarly, students with *emotional disabilities* benefit from predictable routines and preparation for anticipated changes. For many such students, learning self-management skills is as important as content learning. For example a check list on which the student assesses his or her success in keeping class rules can develop self-monitoring skills. Students with emotional disabilities also need many opportunities to see positive models of peer interactions. Morning meetings, class counsels, cooperative learning activities, and peer mediation programs can all be helpful sources of peer modeling. Perhaps most importantly, students with emotional disabilities need teachers who can accept them without accepting inappropriate behavior and who can develop empathetic relationships. This is not easy; it demands patience, maturity, and self-control. With the assistance of an empathetic teacher and a skilled specialist, many students with emotional disabilities can learn the skills and behaviors necessary to succeed in school and in life.

Learning Together

The integration of students with disabilities into regular school classrooms has been a consistent element of local, state, and federal education policy since the 1970s. It has a number of advantages: the opportunity for cooperative learning; the reduction of isolation experienced by students with disabilities; strengthened democratic values; reduction in stereotypes, prejudice, misconceptions, and outright superstition concerning individuals with disabilities; and the promise it holds for the continuation of such values into the adult world.

Drawbacks of inclusive education can include the costs of educating students with disabilities in multiple environments and instructional demands on the regular classroom teacher. Most educators believe that integrating a student with disabilities into a regular classroom requires additional effort and commitment on their part. Nevertheless, these same educators are working toward an adaptive education system in which all young people can achieve their maximum potential.

SECTION 3. GIFTED AND TALENTED STUDENTS

Section 3 Objectives

After you have completed this section, you should be able to:

1. describe characteristics of gifted and talented students;
2. describe special instructional needs of such students;
3. list instructional strategies that are appropriate for gifted and talented students;
4. plan lessons in your curriculum area that are adapted for gifted and talented students; and
5. explain how activities that are appropriate for gifted and talented students may be used in lessons for an entire class.

What Are "Gifted" Students?

No consensus exists on what constitutes a "gifted" student. Traditionally, giftedness has been identified by a high score on an IQ test, a measurement closely associated with school success. A student who scored in the top 1%, 2%, or 5% of the population (depending on the district) was likely to be highly adept at school learning and was considered to be gifted. One of the problems with equating giftedness with high IQ is that IQ is not a particularly good predictor of adult giftedness. If all students are given an IQ test, it will not necessarily identify the next Einstein or Marie Curie or Phillis Wheatley. Moreover, the information that is being learned from studies in human intelligence makes the limitations of IQ tests increasingly clear.

As you learned in Chapter 2, contemporary theories of intelligence are multifaceted. Whether you consider Sternberg's (1985) triarchic theory, Gardner's multiple intelligences theory (Gardner, 1983; see also Checkley, 1997), or other emerging theories, it is clear that no single number can represent the complexity of any individual's intellectual ability. Individuals may demonstrate outstanding capabilities in many dimensions. For example, according to Gardner's theory, a student with exceptional linguistic intelligence will probably have different abilities and needs than one who is exceptional in logical-mathematical, spatial, or interpersonal intelligences. Whatever model of intelligence is considered, there is no doubt that students' prior knowledge, cultural background, and previous school experiences have a significant impact on test scores. Although IQ scores may reasonably predict the ease with which students may succeed in traditional schooling, they cannot assess an individual's total intellectual or academic potential—or identify giftedness (see Colangelo & Davis, 1997, for a more complete discussion of conceptions of giftedness).

In 1993 the U.S. Department of Education proposed a definition that limited the use of the word **gifted** to adults and focused on developing talent in children. It defined young people with outstanding talent as those who

> . . . show the potential for performing at remarkably high levels of
> accomplishment when compared with others of their age, experience, or
> environment . . . in intellectual, creative, and/or artistic areas . . . leadership
> capacity . . . or specific academic fields. (p. 26)

The definition further notes that such young people "require services or activities not ordinarily provided by the schools" and that outstanding talents are present in "all cultural groups, across all economic strata, and in all areas of human endeavor" (p. 26). This definition marks an important shift from an emphasis on giftedness as a trait—either you have it or you don't—to a characteristic that is developed over time and affected by experience. The emphasis in the definition on talented students' needs for specialized services has provided support for programs for the gifted and talented.

Another definition was proposed by Renzulli (1978), which might best be understood through the following exercise. Take a moment and think of five people, living or dead, whom you would consider to be gifted. What do the people you named have in common? It is likely that you thought of individuals who developed an important idea, were responsible for a major invention, made a scientific discovery, or created a work of art, literature, or music. One way to describe these individuals is to call them creative producers, producers of information and art rather than simply consumers. (Does this bring to mind the discussion of authentic learning?) Now think about the ways in which we have traditionally labeled students as gifted. Is the rationale the same? In most cases, students have been labeled as gifted because they are skillful consumers of information. They take the input teachers give them and "return" it on tests, without necessarily doing very much to change or improve it.

Renzulli believes that we have attached the gifted label to two different types of ability, so he devised two new categories. Schoolhouse giftedness is the ability to consume, analyze, and reproduce information, whereas **creative productivity** is the ability to generate new information. Both schoolhouse giftedness and creative productivity are important. Einstein certainly could not have devised the theory of relativity if he had not

Figure 10.3 The Three-Ring Conception of Giftedness
From *The enrichment triad,* by J.S. Renzulli, 1977, Mansfield Center, CT: Creative Learning Press. Reprinted with permission.

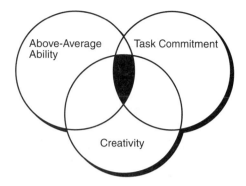

consumed his physics! However, schools have traditionally paid much more attention to the consumption than to the production of information. Renzulli's Three-Ring Conception of Giftedness (see Figure 10.3) was designed specifically to reflect research on creative producers, in the hopes that, if we identified the ways in which giftedness "works" in adults, we might be able to identify or encourage it in young people.

Important ties exist between Renzulli's concept of creative productivity and authentic learning. Schoolhouse giftedness emphasizes that the reproduction and analysis of information must be only part of what students achieve in schools. It may be useful to consider the definition of giftedness that Renzulli believes can help explain high-level creative productivity in adults.

The Three-Ring Conception of Giftedness consists of three interlocking circles: above-average ability, creativity, and task commitment. Adult creative producers are of above-average intelligence, but not necessarily from the top 1% or even the top 5% of the population. They also work creatively and with great commitment to the tasks they choose. Of course, their ability, task commitment, and creativity must be in the same area. If an individual has above-average ability in math, creativity in cooking, and task commitment to an improved golf swing, it is not likely that gifted behavior will result. One of the functions of schools can be to help students identify areas of ability and interest and work to develop creativity and task commitment in those areas. It is unrealistic to expect even the brightest students to come to school with their abilities, creativity, and commitment already fully developed; that is part of the teacher's responsibility.

CHECK YOUR UNDERSTANDING

List three different ways in which giftedness may be defined. Think of someone you know who might be considered gifted according to each definition.

What are the Characteristics of Gifted Students?

There is no simple answer to the question, What are the characteristics of gifted students? Some students may be very good at one or more school subjects. Others may be creative, always ready with a new idea. Some will have a wide variety of interests;

others will pursue one specialized area. Special interests or abilities do not always show up in obvious ways, or even in ways that make the teacher's job easier. Diedra, at the beginning of the chapter, showed creativity in her writing and extracurricular activities, but also in the humor directed against her teacher. Picasso was frequently reprimanded in school because he refused to do anything but paint. He was demonstrating creativity and task commitment, but not in the ways his teachers may have expected.

CHECK YOUR UNDERSTANDING

The following characteristics are often associated with gifted students:

- large knowledge base
- good memory
- unusually varied and/or intense interests
- highly developed verbal skills
- ability to process information rapidly and accurately
- flexibility in thinking, with ability to see many points of view
- persistence
- awareness of relationships among diverse ideas
- ability to generate original ideas
- enjoyment of abstract ideas
- intense opinions or emotions
- sensitivity to feelings of self or others
- concern for global issues: war, hunger, and so forth
- sense of humor

Choose three characteristics and describe how they might be manifested in schools in positive (1) or negative (2) ways. For example, a student with a fine sense of humor may add zest to the class or disrupt lessons with inappropriate comments.

Under what circumstances do you think the negative behaviors would be most likely to take place? Although there are many possible causes for negative behavior, bright students who are not intellectually challenged by class work sometimes find alternative forms of challenge through disruptive activities. In fact, one study found that highly gifted boys (defined in this study as those with IQ scores over 140) demonstrated levels of behavior problems more similar to students with learning disabilities than to those defined as more moderately gifted (IQ scores 124–139) (Shaywitz, et. al., 2001).

Characteristics of giftedness also may be hidden. Think back to the beginning of the chapter. It is easy to see evidence of intelligence in a successful student like Tony, but what about Rosa? Teachers should look for signs of special interests or abilities in students whose other needs may prevent teachers from noticing students' giftedness. Sometimes cultural differences may obscure teachers' understanding of students' abilities. If they think that all bright students ask many questions, they may be less open to noticing the abilities of a Native American student whose tribal customs promote silent watching and listening as signs of respect.

Non-white students and students in troubled urban settings are less likely to be identified as gifted, both because of teacher expectations and the ways in which gifts may be manifested. This is particularly problematic for those who have a "dichotomized view of race and achievement" (Rowley & Moore, 2002). This dynamic was brought to public attention by Fordham (1988, Fordham & Ogbu, 1986) when she described urban African American students' dilemma when school achievement was perceived as "acting white." Students who believe that behaving in ways that schools consider successful is disloyal to their friends, families, and culture are likely to display their gifts and talents outside those venues. A similar dynamic can play out in other cultural groups who do not identify with the school culture. Particular attention must be paid to diverse ways in which extraordinary abilities may be displayed and to provide appropriate supports (see, for example, Hebert, 2001; Cross, 2002).

Various types of disabilities also may lead teachers to miss signs of advanced ability. It may be more difficult to recognize advanced reasoning in children whose hearing disability has delayed the development of language or whose learning disabilities affect their reading. Some students may—consciously or unconsciously—hide their gifts, either because they fear social isolation or because their experience has taught them that good work is rewarded with more work. If most math students are assigned 20 problems and above-average math students are assigned 30, many bright students "beat the system" by performing like average students.

The assumption that gifted students will make it on their own is a fallacy, especially if "making it" means living up to their potential. Like all learners, bright students need instruction appropriate to their individual capabilities. Some districts provide special programs for bright students. Students identified as gifted and talented spend part or all of the day in classes designed to provide challenging experiences. Sometimes these classes focus on specific sections of content and are designed for students with strengths in particular areas. For example, an advanced creative writing class may be offered for especially able or interested writers. Other schools offer advanced independent study options or seminars that allow students to investigate a variety of interests or strengths. In still other cases, resource people assist teachers in planning for gifted students in their classrooms. In some areas the appropriateness of specialized instruction for gifted students has been questioned regarding elitism and the distribution of resources (see, for example, Sapon-Shevin, 1994). However, even in districts with special programs, most gifted students spend the majority of their time in regular classrooms, under the direction of a classroom teacher.

What Do I Do with Gifted Students?

Giftedness is a complex concept, and identifying it is not simple. Therefore, the question remains, What can teachers do with bright students in their classrooms, regardless of whether they have been officially labeled as *gifted?* One course of action is to consider two basic questions: (1) Which parts of the regular curriculum has the student already mastered (or could the student master quickly with little assistance)? and (2) What alternative activities will allow the student to learn and be challenged at an appropriate level?

A basic assumption underlies these questions that is simple but profoundly important: Every teacher is obligated to make sure that each student in the classroom has the

opportunity to learn. The teacher's first obligation is not to the body of content designated seventh grade English or Biology I or even the state standards—it is to the students.
It is a challenge to meet that assumption with students who have special needs. In the case
of particularly able learners, it means finding things for students to learn even if they arrive in September already knowing large amounts of designated curriculum. If, for example, a seventh-grade student enters the classroom having worked her way through an
advanced algebra book during the summer, she is not likely to improve in mathematics if
the only experiences provided are the same as those provided to most seventh-graders.
Students who spend eighth grade reading *Mein Kampf* or *Macbeth* need challenges beyond the typical ninth-grade language arts program (see, for example, Callahan, 2001).

Students who enter one or two years "ahead" have less extreme needs, but the principle is still the same. Teachers faced with such students may not breathe a sigh of relief
and assume they need not worry about students who can already meet the grade-level
goals. Rather, it is their responsibility to set new goals for the students to reach. The importance of preassessing mastery of curriculum goals is not limited to the top few students in a grade or class. In one study, fourth-grade students were tested on the content
of their math text before they had used it for the school year. Sixty percent of the students in one suburban group could score over 80%! Similar results were obtained with
students in fourth- and tenth-grade science and tenth-grade social studies (Educational
Products Information Exchange, 1979). Preassessing students' regular curriculum is
important for all students, and it is particularly vital for able learners, who often enter
a grade having already mastered a substantial portion of the content to be taught.

Regular Curriculum

One strategy for dealing with the regular curriculum is called curriculum compacting
(Reis, Burns & Renzulli, 1992; Reis & Purcell, 1998; Renzulli & Smith, 1979). In its simplest form, **curriculum compacting** involves diagnosing which of the skills in a particular unit of study some of your students have already mastered. Throughout this text
we have emphasized the importance of preassessing students' prior knowledge before
beginning instruction. In curriculum compacting, this assessment is particularly focused on identifying areas of the curriculum that may be unnecessary or repetitious for
some students. For example, before beginning a math chapter, you might give a pretest
covering the main skills in the unit. Some teachers use unit tests for this purpose; others use excerpts from textbooks or devise their own tests. If you discover that any of
your students have already mastered these skills, it would not be appropriate for them
to spend a lot of time practicing or reviewing the same material.

In 1888, J. M. Greenwood wrote, "When once a child has learned that four and two
are six, a thousand repetitions will give him no new information and it is a waste of time
to keep him employed in that manner" (p. 13). Instead of repeating previously learned
content, students could test out of some material and be provided with alternative activities. In the unit on Zimbabwe, Ken Cowan may discover that two or three students
have already mastered the map skills he plans to incorporate in the unit. If so, he can allow those students to pursue other activities during the time he plans to focus on map
work. This form of compacting works best when the material to be taught consists of

specific skills or procedures, such as computation strategies, reading maps or charts, grammar, spelling, or procedures for various technical processes (i.e., PowerPoint), etc.

In other cases, especially when the instruction deals with concepts rather than skills, gifted students may not have mastered the materials yet but can do so more quickly than other students. For these students you might consider contracts (see Chapter 9) or other forms of independent study. Recall that a *contract* generally identifies activities that must be completed to help a student master the regular content as well as related enrichment activities. The contract also specifies how new knowledge and skills will be evaluated.

However, the use of independent contracts or other independent work does not release you from your responsibility as a teacher. Although many bright students can master material with much less direct instruction than average students, you must still identify areas in which instruction is needed. Sometimes such instruction may be provided on an individual basis, perhaps while other students work on a practice activity, or a student may receive instruction with a large or small group of students who need to learn the same skill. Periodic individual conferences can be helpful in assessing students' progress, identifying areas of difficulty, and planning further activities. A sample contract can be found in Figure 10.1.

Alternative Activities

If students' curriculum has been compacted, they will complete the regular assignments in less time than average students. It is necessary to decide how to best use the additional time, choosing between acceleration and enrichment. **Acceleration** is the pursuit of the regular curriculum at a faster pace (for example, proceeding to the eighth-grade math book while in seventh grade). Acceleration can encompass advancement in a single subject (such as going on to the next math book), grade skipping, or early entrance to college. Since acceleration affects students' studies years after it occurs, many districts have guidelines for its use. It is important to know the policies in your district regarding acceleration.

Enrichment, the incorporation of activities outside the regular curriculum, can be divided into three general categories. One type of enrichment can be developed by *adapting assignments* or techniques in the regular curriculum to provide additional challenge. Many gifted students thrive on inquiry, induction, role-playing, simulation, and other activities that encourage higher level thinking while teaching content. The higher levels of Bloom's Taxonomy can be helpful in generating ideas for assignments. Of course, teachers must take into account the students' abilities and their prior knowledge of the content to be taught. For example, in the unit on the Zimbabwe, Ken may consider substituting additional higher level assignments for those designed to teach basic facts for students with a great deal of prior knowledge or exceptional independent learning skills. Such students, rather than constructing a time line of basic events, may be challenged to investigate events occurring at the same time in other areas of the world or to compare events in Zimbabwe with the impact of colonists in America on the indigenous people.

A second category of enrichment is *interdisciplinary teaching.* Of course, interdisciplinary teaching can be an appropriate organizational strategy for all students. However, it is particularly suited to students whose excellent abstract reasoning abilities allow them to make ties among ideas in various disciplines. *Interdisciplinary thematic instruction* planned

Alternative Activities Can Meet the Needs of Students Who Have Mastered the Regular Curriculum.

for gifted students is usually organized around abstract themes, such as patterns or revolution. For example, students studying the American Revolution might also examine the idea of revolution in other disciplines. How might scientists like Barbara McClintock be considered revolutionaries? What would constitute a revolution in art? In sports? How are revolutions in other disciplines similar to or different from the American Revolution?

The third type of enrichment often recommended for bright students is an *independent investigation,* which culminates in some type of product. The types of projects pursued should encompass the same categories as the "real problems" described in Chapters 2 and 8: investigation of research questions, involvement in activism, or communication of some aesthetic. The skills of independent learning discussed in Chapter 9 can be particularly valuable as individuals or small groups investigate topics of interest. Many times parent volunteers or other community mentors can give valuable assistance to students interested in particular topics.

These activities may or may not parallel the general curriculum. A group of Ken's students may wonder whether the attitudes of 19th century missionaries toward African people were in any way different from those of other colonists. They could investigate their question by reading diaries or autobiographies from the period. Another student might want to study the use of Central African motifs in contemporary American art. The student might study slides, art books or local galleries in search of evidence. In other schools, students have analyzed the water quality of local ponds for the Cooperative Extension Service, created taped interviews of past mayors for the library, conducted "metric fairs" for younger students, and founded school literary journals.

In some schools, enrichment specialists can help locate resources or mentors for such projects. Individual investigations can be challenging, but they are much easier within classes where differentiated instruction is the norm. Even small beginnings can be important; for exceptionally able students, the opportunity to be challenged in an area of strength and interest part of the time is better than no opportunity at all.

Whole-class activities that function as real-world projects also can offer natural opportunities for differentiation. For example, Lesko (2001/2002) describes a series of activities in which high school students worked as activists regarding school safety and students' rights. In other cases, students collaborated with nonprofit and government agencies to work toward preventing teen pregnancy, smoking, and other youth-oriented problems. In such activities (and other complex authentic and/or service learning options) students can play a variety of roles. For example, particularly able or interested students can delve into an aspect of the project to such depth that it becomes functionally an independent investigation.

The Enrichment Triad

Renzulli (1977) referred to independent investigations as "Type III enrichment," individuals or small groups pursuing real problems. Two other types of enrichment can help lead students to Type III projects. The three types of enrichment form the Enrichment Triad Model (see Figure 10.4).

Type I enrichment consists of general exploratory activities designed to help students identify their interests and to encourage them to further investigate these interests. It

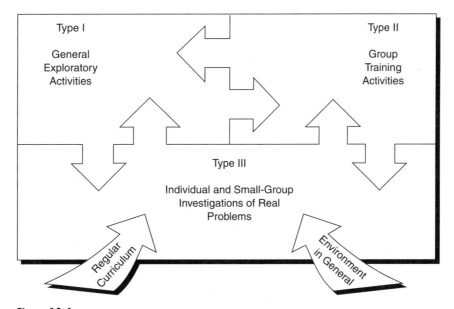

Figure 10.4   The Enrichment Triad Model
From *The schoolwide enrichment model* (2nd Ed.), by J.S. Renzulli, 1997, Mansfield Center, CT: Creative Learning Press. Reprinted with permission.

includes activities, materials, and resources (e.g., guest speakers, displays, movies, books, and interest-development centers) that extend education beyond the regular curriculum. Any time you set up an interesting display, show a movie expanding the curriculum, or have a guest speaker in your classroom, you are providing a Type I activity. It is best to present the broadest range of topics during the year. The key to providing a meaningful Type I activity is the debriefing questions that follow it. Because a Type I activity is intended to help students identify their interests, the questions should not simply assess whether students have understood the material; they should raise additional questions, pose problems, and find out which students are interested in pursuing the topic. For example, after an environmentalist has discussed acid rain, you could ask students whether they think there is acid rain in their area, what questions they still have about acid rain and how they could find answers, or if they would like to learn how to test for acid rain. The most important purposes of Type I enrichment are to expose students to as many varied topics as possible and to encourage them to identify areas of interest and learn more about them.

Type II enrichment is composed of group training activities that can provide students with the tools they need to become independent investigators. Skills of independent learning can be taught as described in Chapter 9. Other activities might include the development of advanced skills in research, data gathering, problem solving, or interviewing. The gifted-education specialist in your district can provide ideas, techniques, and materials. If your district does not have such a specialist, consult the professional literature or your state Department of Education for suggestions.

Type III enrichment depends on Type I and Type II enrichment. Activities in both Type I and Type II enrichment can help you identify those students with the interest and motivation to pursue a Type III individual investigation. Some leaders in the field of education of the gifted and talented are recommending that many students be provided with the skills and opportunities necessary to develop diverse abilities (Feldhusen, 1992; Renzulli, 1993). They envision a shift from concern about identifying students who can be labeled as gifted to a focus on developing talents in all students. This text's emphasis on authentic learning and real-world problem solving reflects a similar view. However, it is clear that students with exceptional abilities still will need additional challenge and support in pursuing enrichment opportunities that may not be suited to the needs of all students.

You may, at times, wish to provide students with a choice of assignments and encourage able students to select challenging tasks. Of course, not all bright students have the same interests and strengths. If you expect students to put forth efforts that are beyond those expected of other young people, the tasks must challenge and interest them. Make sure that gifted students do not spend too much time working in isolation. If students are able to bypass or condense significant amounts of the regular curriculum, it may be helpful to identify a group of intellectual peers with whom they can work for part of the school day. Sometimes advanced classes or independent study seminars provide this opportunity. Students also may form a cluster group in a heterogeneous class, a group of same-grade students from different classes who come together for instruction or independent work, or a group of mixed-grade students working on a particular project. Such arrangements may demand creative scheduling, but they can be invaluable in helping students meet important intellectual and social needs.

A curriculum model that attempts to integrate all the major strategies of curriculum differentiation is the Parallel Curriculum Model (PCM) (Purcell, Burns, & Leppien, 2002). PCM is a complex model that examines opportunities to differentiate instruction through ten different curriculum components. This can be accomplished through examining the core curriculum (analyzing content), making more interdisciplinary connections, working toward professional methodologies, and seeking ties to individuals' needs and growth.

It should be clear by now that students with gifts and talents are a diverse group with needs that vary enormously both by the students' individual characteristics and cultures and by the nature and strengths of their abilities. No one strategy is best for all students identified as gifted any more than one strategy would be suitable for all students with disabilities. Throughout students' school experiences a continuum of services should be available to meet diverse and changing needs. These should include the types of classroom strategies described above as well as more specialized programs that may include magnet, charter or specialized schools, advanced placement opportunities, specialized enrichment programs, and dual-enrollment opportunities at local colleges or those available through Internet access (see Renzulli & Reis, 1997).

 ## REFLECTING ON THE IDEAS

Choose a unit topic you might teach. Briefly list three enrichment activities that might be suitable for a student who has already mastered much of the unit content.

Did your activities require higher level thinking, interdisciplinary ties, and/or independent investigation and problem solving?

Affective Needs of Gifted Students

Like all young people, highly able students have affective as well as cognitive needs. Like all students, they need to have friends, feel part of the group, and enjoy social interaction. While characteristics may vary with degree of exceptionality (Shaywitz and others, 2001), most exceptionally bright students are well liked and socially adept. Some characteristics of bright students, however, can impact their emotional needs.

One of the factors that most affects bright students is the differences in their levels of physical, intellectual, and emotional maturity. Bright secondary-level students can display levels of cognitive and affective development even more disparate than the usual roller coasters of adolescence. These can be magnified by the sensitivity and intense emotions that characterize many highly able learners. Students may be extremely depressed over social issues or dateless Saturdays. They may frustrate teachers who cannot understand how anyone who can manage college-level calculus cannot tell the difference between appropriate and inappropriate jokes in class. Adolescents with the intellectual reasoning of adults generally have the unpredictable moods and inconsistent judgment of their agemates. It is important that the adults around them recognize that advanced intellect does not necessarily correlate with advanced maturity or social development. In addition, the adults must allow bright adolescents the latitude to sometimes "act their age" even when such actions seem inconsistent with students' other abilities.

These disparities can become particularly troublesome when intellectual pursuits conflict with traditional social or gender roles. The achievement of many bright young women plummets in adolescence when fears of social stigma may overpower individual interests or aspirations. While the achievement of young men does not display a similar decline, adolescent males with talents and interest in literature or the arts can face the same social trials as young women working in math and science. For those students, opportunities to meet and work with similarly interested peers are essential to the development of their talents.

Diverse needs make it important that gifted students have many types of peers. As mentioned above, it is important that they have interaction with others working on the same instructional level. A ninth-grade girl who does math at the twelfth-grade level may need bright female math peers, an adult friend with whom to discuss politics, and ninth-grade friends on the soccer team or yearbook staff.

Finally, teachers of bright young people must be wary of the dangers of perfectionism. Some children go through years of school without ever encountering challenging work. Naturally enough, they come to expect that everything they do in school will be easy and that they should be able to complete their tasks without struggle. Sometimes students develop an image of themselves that demands that everything they do be done perfectly—they see anything less as failure. Some evidence suggests this type of perfection is a particular risk for middle school girls and may increase through the middle school years (Siegle & Schule, 2000). Perfectionism can be disabling and potentially dangerous to healthy emotional development. If students' needs are correctly diagnosed and challenging work is provided beginning in early grades, some perfectionism can be avoided. If you encounter students who have difficulty taking risks or attempting challenging tasks for fear of making an error, it will be important to start with small challenges and increase gradually, while modeling your own willingness to try, fail, and try again.

Serving Many Students

Strategies recommended for gifted students are important for other students as well. Many students will benefit from preassessment and curriculum compacting, especially at the beginning of the year. Interdisciplinary teaching, Type I exploratory activities, instruction in Type II skills, and involvement in real-world problem solving can be appropriate for a wide range of students. One of the most important trends in the field of education of the gifted and talented is the adoption of many of the strategies used with gifted students into general education (Feldhusen, 1996; Renzulli, 1993). In fact, the accelerated school model uses strategies typically employed with gifted students (including accelerated math) to accelerate and enrich the whole-school curriculum for urban, at-risk students (Brandt, 1992; Goldberg, 2001, Hopfenber, Levin & Chase, 1993). This trend brings many benefits for a wide range of students. Renzulli and Reis (1997) described a Schoolwide Enrichment Model in which enrichment activities are used to structure a range of activities for all students.

However, one potential danger is apparent. If many of the strategies recommended for bright students are used for all students, some teachers may be led to believe that gifted students' needs are automatically being met within the regular curriculum and thus need no further concern. This is not true. In a 1993 report, *National Excellence: A Case for Developing America's Talent,* the U.S. Department of Education called the lack of achievement in our most able learners a "quiet crisis" in education.

> In a broad range of intellectual and artistic endeavor, America's most talented students often fail to reach their full potential . . . . Despite sporadic attention over the years to the needs of bright students, most of them continue to spend time in school working well below their capabilities. The belief espoused in school reform that children from all economic and cultural backgrounds must reach their full potential has not been extended to America's most talented students. They are underchallenged and therefore underachieve. (p. 5)

An enormous range of students may be considered gifted. Students who are functioning slightly above grade level may need only slight adaptations in curriculum. However, some students in virtually every school are functioning (or are capable of functioning) substantially beyond grade-level expectations. Sometimes such students are easy to spot, such as the first-grader who enters school reading near-adult books. Other students may appear to be only slightly advanced, either because they have learned to hide their abilities in order to avoid sticking out or because no one has asked them to attempt anything more difficult. A few years ago, the authors became aware of a sixth-grade student who was particularly able in math. Neither the student nor his parents felt he was being challenged by the math curriculum. The teacher had planned a flexible program that allowed students to progress through the sixth-grade curriculum at different paces, so she felt the student's needs were being met. Finally, the parents had the student take part in a "talent search" program in which 12-year-old students take the SAT test along with high school juniors. The student scored over 700 on the math portion of the SAT, well ahead of most high school students. Only then did the teacher realize that small adaptations of curriculum would not be sufficient to meet this particular student's needs.

The challenge, then, is to help *all* children learn. Much of what is good for bright students can be used with most students in the classroom. However, educators still must be open to recognizing special needs and advanced abilities that demand more challenge than even the best general curriculum can offer. Providing needed adaptations can help all students find school to be a place of learning, challenge, and opportunity.

SECTION 4. TEACHING CULTURALLY DIVERSE AND BILINGUAL STUDENTS

Section 4 Objectives

After you have completed this section, you should be able to:

1. list instructional strategies that are appropriate for culturally diverse students, with special attention to non-white and bilingual students;

2. plan lessons in your curriculum area that are adapted to meet the needs of each group; and

3. explain how activities that are appropriate for culturally diverse and bilingual students may be used in lessons for all students.

Home and family backgrounds are important in determining the experiences, attitudes, interests, and beliefs that pupils bring to school. In totality, students come to school with a diversity of languages, cultures, and experiences that affect their school performance. Just as you should know as much as possible about your students' learning styles and prior academic experiences, you need to take into account their language and cultural diversity.

Teaching for Equity

In Chapter 2 the definition and characteristics of *culture* were introduced and discussed. The differences between the Anglo-Western European macroculture and the several microcultures that coexist with it in the United States were identified.

Because of their skin color, early immigrants from Europe often were willing and able to assimilate into American culture without having to give up their unique cultural attributes. They could identify with the Anglo-Western European culture and adopted the concept of the "American Melting Pot." However, some people were forced to come to this country, expected to assimilate, and prevented from practicing their own culture, beliefs, traditions, and language. Historically, because of enforced segregation, many have been underserved by our schools. Despite the abolition of most formerly legal forms of discrimination, the continued shadow of racism remains (Quality Education for Minorities, Project 1990).

In recent years, **cultural pluralism**—where ethnic groups retain their cultural heritage, traditions, and values while adopting aspects of another culture—emerged as an alternative to the "melting pot" in America. Unfortunately, this concept of cultural pluralism has not been completely accepted in our society. Judgments about students' abilities, potential, or even interests are sometimes made through the cultural lens of the Anglo-Western culture. For example, John at the beginning of the chapter had trouble learning basic skills and often argued in some classes. When majority children have such difficulties, the school is most likely to contend that there is a problem with the instruction or a mismatch between the curriculum and the child's level of development (Hale-Benson, 1986). If John is a non-white student, however, he is 2.3 times more likely to be labeled as educable mentally disabled than a White child ("Status of Black Children," 1989). Certainly there are educable mentally disabled students of all races, and such children need special educational support, but it is crucial that the evaluation of students' abilities be based on their performance on appropriate tasks, not on racial or cultural stereotypes.

Three main conditions support cultural pluralism in the schools (Banks, 1999; Banks & Banks, 2001):

1. positive teacher expectations
2. learning environment that encourages positive intergroup contact
3. pluralistic (multicultural) curriculum

Other helpful approaches for diverse groups of students are to raise self-esteem and use culturally relevant teaching.

Positive Teacher Expectations

Students tend to perform at the level expected of them by the teacher. Research has indicated that in classes where teachers held higher expectations for all students, higher general student performance resulted.

Too many African American, Native American, or Latino students are considered slow and difficult to teach. These expectations of inferiority are often passed on to the students, who, by their behavior, turn the expectations into self-fulfilling prophecies. In other words, students tend to behave as teachers expect them to behave. If a teacher labels a student as a low achiever, he or she expects and demands less from that student. If the teacher perceives a student to be a high achiever, he or she expects and demands more from that student. This view of a student's expected performance is communicated to the student by verbal and nonverbal behaviors. Good & Brophy (1999) cited many ways in which teachers behaved toward students they perceive as *low achievers.* The teachers studied:

- provided general, often insincere praise;
- provided them with less feedback;
- demanded less effort from them;
- interrupted them more often;
- seated them farther away from the teacher;
- paid less attention to them;
- called on them less often;
- waited less time for them to respond to questions;
- criticized them more often; and
- smiled at them less.

Students who were perceived as *high achievers,* on the other hand:

- were given more opportunities for responses;
- were asked higher level questions;
- received more praise and detailed feedback;
- were given prompts or probes if they seemed to be having difficulty;
- were allowed more time to respond to questions; and
- were provided supportive communications (i.e., active listening, physical closeness, courtesy, acceptance of feeling, compliments).

Positive Learning Environment

Four basic conditions are necessary in order for social contact between groups to lessen prejudice and lead to friendly attitudes and behaviors (Bennett, 1986):

1. Contact should be sufficiently intimate to produce reciprocal knowledge and understanding between groups.

2. Members of various groups must share equal status.
3. The contact situation should lead people to do things together. It should require intergroup cooperation to achieve a common goal.
4. There should be institutional support—an authority and/or social climate that encourages intergroup contact.

One research study found that successful teachers in culturally diverse situations were flexible, creative, well organized, enthusiastic, warm, firm, and consistent risk takers. They had high expectations, a high energy level, and a commitment to the teaching of all children. They had a repertoire of many teaching strategies, and they were able to find a compatible mode that would engage students in learning (Shade, 1990). Teachers who have studied learning style differences, particularly cross-cultural differences, will have an advantage in developing such a repertoire (see, for example, Shade, 1997).

To teach students from culturally diverse backgrounds also requires a restructuring of teaching attitudes, approaches, and strategies. It requires becoming a facilitator and director of the learning process, rather than an information giver. The classroom should become more group-oriented and cooperative. Students should become more involved in their learning, and the telling of facts must be replaced with demonstrations and modeling (Hollins, 1994). While all young people, regardless of their race, benefit from the general teaching strategies outlined in this text, some teaching and learning activities are particularly important in culturally diverse classrooms.

Effective teachers in culturally diverse situations:

- have a clear sense of their own ethnic and cultural identities;
- look at cultural differences among students as cultural assets (Boykin, 1994);
- communicate high expectations for the success of all students and a belief that all students can succeed;
- are personally committed to achieving equity for all students and believe they are capable of making a difference in their students' learning;
- develop a bond with their students and cease seeing their students as "the other";
- provide an academically challenging curriculum that includes attention to the development of higher level cognitive skills;
- add meaning to instruction in an interactive and collaborative environment;
- include contributions and perspectives of the various ethnocultural groups that compose our society by using a multicultural curriculum;
- use an affective curriculum (Harmon, 2000);
- encourage community members and parents or family members to become involved in students' education and give them a significant voice in making important school decisions related to school programs (i.e., resources and staffing); and
- use culturally congruent teaching methods. (Cole, 1995)

Multicultural Curriculum

As described in Chapter 2, the American culture is a macroculture composed of many microcultures, making it a multicultural and pluralistic society. According to Banks (1999), ". . . education within a pluralistic society should affirm and help students understand their home and community cultures" (p. 4). A multicultural curriculum is designed to promote and value the diversity of all cultures in our country, while helping students to see the commonalties among all groups. In a positive multicultural environment:

- teachers expect all students to achieve, regardless of race, sex, class, or ethnicity;
- the learning environment encourages positive contact between all students;
- instructional materials are reviewed for bias;
- the curriculum includes the historical experiences of all cultures;
- efforts are made to develop an understanding and appreciation of and respect for all cultures;
- goals and strategies reflect cultural learning styles of all students;
- time is spent dispelling misconceptions, stereotypes, and prejudices; and
- bulletin boards and classroom exhibits display people of many backgrounds.

Students in a multicultural classroom learn to appreciate the capabilities of others as well as their own strengths. Multicultural education involves providing the best education for students that preserves their own cultural heritage, prepares them for meaningful relationships with other people, and enables them to lead productive lives in the present society without sacrificing their own cultural perspective (Hollins, 1994).

Goals for multicultural education should provide for:

1. the development of historical perspectives and cultural consciousness;
2. the development of intercultural competence;
3. the reduction of racism, ethnic prejudice, and discrimination; and
4. the development of social action skills (Bennett, 1986).

Historical perspectives involve knowledge of the world views, heritage, and contributions of diverse cultures, including one's own culture. In a music class a teacher might include music from many different cultures, rather than just focusing on classical music from Europe. Intercultural competence is the ability to interpret intentional communication (language, signs, gestures), some unconscious cues (body language), and customs in diverse cultures. Simulation activities could be used with adolescents to experience how a lack of communication and knowledge of other cultures affects interactions with each other.

One way to reduce prejudice and discrimination is to teach students strategies for detecting bias in the media. Such activities can help students clarify their own values and help them clear up misconceptions and erroneous beliefs about the superiority of some races. Social action skills include self-expression, decision making, making choices, goal setting, and problem resolution. Student's feelings of personal and political effectiveness can be developed through these activities, community activism, or classroom projects.

Activities That Enhance Self-Esteem

Because culturally diverse students and students from lower socioeconomic status often feel less valued, it is important to find ways to increase their self-esteem. The following activities build students' self-esteem through positive relationships among teachers and students.

- Check your perception of students. Ask yourself if you really expect the students to achieve. A study from the University of Chicago found that the major factor in student performance was not parent demography or per-pupil expenditure, but teacher expectations (Kunjufu, 1984). Don't use students' home environment or social status as an excuse for poor achievement.
- Encourage students to take a more challenging educational path. This will convey the message that you have confidence in their abilities. Provide role models with others from the same cultural background. Inform students about opportunities in many fields. Involve community organizations and local businesses and industries. Recruit school graduates to assist in this area.
- Watch the language you use: Teachers also can be guilty of discrimination in vocabulary. Grant (Hale-Benson, 1986, p. 179) found that social scientists used harsher terms when describing African Americans and more neutral terms when describing Whites. For instance, African Americans were seen as belonging to the "drug culture" while Whites had a "chemical dependency problem." African Americans had "illegitimate children"; Whites chose "single motherhood."
- Learn about your students' cultures. Understand their traditions to help you see how students view and interpret their world (see, for example, Banks & Banks, 2001; Spring, 1995).
- Let students know that effort is valued. Attribution theory indicates that students' beliefs about the reasons for success and failure can greatly influence their perception of the task and their achievement of a successful outcome. When students believe that they are successful because they have put effort into a task, they experience a greater feeling of pride and are more likely to work hard on tasks in the future than if they feel their success was caused by luck.
- Strive to maintain a positive classroom climate. Clear explanations, positive reinforcement, and activities that encourage interaction among students all can contribute to classroom tone.
- Acknowledge students' value and promise. Find opportunities to tell students how much you value them and their efforts. Let them know how bright and promising you find them (Collins, 1992).
- Provide opportunities for students to discuss their concerns regarding prejudice, discrimination, and other kinds of social injustices. Bibliotherapy, or the use of carefully selected literature containing characters and challenges similar to those of the students, is a highly effective technique.
- Look to the community and the family for role models and mentors for students. Posters of famous and exceptional individuals contribute to students' appreciation of diversity, but real-life role models that are accessible to students have the greatest impact.

Culturally Relevant Teaching and Other Instructional Strategies

Culturally relevant teaching refers to methods of teaching that empower students to grow intellectually, socially, and emotionally by using cultural referents in teaching knowledge and skills (Harmon, 2000; Pang, 2001). The following strategies can help to make the classroom more stimulating and students more flexible learners.

• Take cultural characteristics into consideration when beginning instruction and selecting instructional strategies. Students in some cultures prefer oral/aural communication and are field-dependent, expressive, flexible, and humanistic. Preassessment of your students early in the year will give you insights into these variations in learning preferences.

• Check students' prior knowledge. Some students miss the point of a lesson because they don't have the background knowledge that could put the text and ideas presented in meaningful context.

• Provide field trips and other background-enriching activities. If students have not had the experiences necessary for learning a particular subject, plan appropriate activities to provide the requisite background knowledge.

• Relate content to students' lives. Know about their interests and background to help you provide valuable links. Use examples, similes, metaphors, and stories from students' cultures to provide bridges for understanding.

• Provide kinesthetic activities (writing, physical games, role-playing); visual images (photographs, charts); auditory experiences (records, music); and interactive (group discussion) and haptic strategies (drawing, painting, sculpturing) (Shade, 1990).

• Engage students in meaningful real-world tasks. When students see that learning has a purpose (e.g., solving a real problem or doing an authentic project), they are more likely to stay engaged.

• Use cooperative learning strategies. Many students who do not achieve individually do well with group activities (see Chapter 9).

• Be flexible in grouping students. Heterogeneous grouping can be effective. Research shows that using interracial work teams is one of the most powerful ways to improve performance (Bennett, 1986). If you do group students homogeneously for some activities, don't always put the same students together.

• Teach students test-taking skills. Practice test-taking environments. Familiarize students with the routines of tests, use practice drills, teach relaxation skills for reducing stress, and discuss time management.

• Assess students through multiple measures. Allow students to be evaluated through personal interviews, oral tests, and practical assignments.

• Beware of cultural differences in communication styles. One of the hallmarks of culture is patterns of communication. Understanding that many cultural groups have communication styles that are more interactive than western European cultures will make a difference in the way a teacher interprets student comments during a lecture. Understand differences in narrative style in order to understand students' communication more readily and to provide more effective cues for communication strategies that will be effective with differing audiences (Gay, 2002).

• Remove bias from materials used in teaching. Materials that are biased ignore the existence and often demean the personal characteristics of some students. They can distort conditions and largely ignore the students' perspective. If biased or racist language passes unchallenged, students are harmed by the demeaning depiction of the group (Southern Poverty Law Center, 2001).

Pang (2001) focuses on culturally relevant teaching that is structured by an ethic of caring. Her work is powerful regardless of school setting, but is particularly important in diverse urban settings. She suggests five approaches for restructuring curriculum to incorporate both cultural diversity and a focus on caring relationships.

1. Include themes or threads in your curriculum that focus on language, culture, power, and compassion.
2. Present diverse perspectives on the issue, theme, event, or concept.
3. Employ an issues-centered orientation.
4. Restructure existing units by using a culture/caring/justice filter.
5. Teach by example. (p. 204)

As Pang observes, the fifth approach is one of the most powerful. When teachers treat students with respect, fairness, and open mindedness, students are likely to respond in kind. If teachers demonstrate interest in diverse ideas and cultures, it is much more likely students will do so as well.

 ## REFLECTING ON THE IDEAS

Observe a teacher interacting with students in a variety of circumstances, such as in class, in the hallways, or in the cafeteria. Observe the interactions that you believe convey high or low expectations for students. Observe actions you believe demonstrate an ethic of caring.

Teaching Bilingual Students

Some culturally diverse students whose family traditions and customs are quite different from those associated with the majority culture also may be impacted by limited proficiency in English—the language spoken by the macroculture and, therefore, the medium of communication in the nation's public schools. Bilingual students will benefit from good teaching and planning as well as from many of the activities suggested for culturally diverse students. In addition, the following ideas may be helpful:

• Review students' files extensively. Make sure you are clear on the history of the students' educational experiences. A student who was successful in algebra in her native country needs different strategies in math from one who is unable to learn algebra because of language difficulties, even if neither can express knowledge of algebra in English.
• Make and maintain contact with parents. Realize that some parents may be reluctant to contact the schools because of their limited English proficiency. Others may view American schools as a threat to their native culture or to their authority as parents. Convey both your respect for the students' native culture and your academic goals.
• Learn as much as you can about the cultures of the students in your class. Make contact with parents, local cultural associations, bilingual education specialists, academic specialists in various cultures, and others with knowledge of the countries.

- Be especially attuned to patterns of communication, taboos, and structures of authority.
- Consider a buddy system or cross-grade tutoring. A buddy within the class might be assigned to help a bilingual student communicate and learn the logistics of school. An older, successful bilingual student can provide tutoring and serve as a powerful role model.
- Be cautious about cooperative learning in the beginning, particularly structures in which groups compete with one another. Cooperative learning assumes an ability to communicate and function within an educational system that may not be reasonable for a non-English-speaking student. Avoid putting students in situations they are unable to handle; the results are likely to be a sense of personal inadequacy and a feeling of disappointing their groups.
- Present as much material visually as possible. Videos, pictures, graphics, and demonstrations can assist students with language development. Graphic organizers can be particularly helpful in visually depicting the relationships among concepts.
- Whenever possible, share information and positive role models from diverse cultures, with emphasis on those cultures represented in your room. Parent presentations, studies of the contributions of varied groups, and the selection of music, celebrations, and games from non-Western lands send a message that all cultures are important.
- Be patient. Adapting to a new language and culture is a long and difficult task, even for a young person. Time, energy, and genuine affection will be necessary for students to integrate that task into the already complex demands of school.

REFLECTING ON THE IDEAS

Imagine that the principal comes to your room and informs you that in one week a Polish student will be joining your class. The student speaks limited English and will receive one hour per day of specialized language instruction. How will you prepare for the student's arrival? What strategies might you use once the student has arrived? Write down your ideas, then discuss them with one or more colleagues.

SECTION 5. TEACHING IN URBAN SCHOOLS AND OTHER SETTINGS

Section 5 Objectives

After you have completed this section, you should be able to:

1. discuss the major factors influencing the success of some teachers in urban schools;
2. compare and contrast the influencing factors for successful urban teachers with those for successful rural and suburban teachers;

3. compare and contrast the views of successful urban, rural, and suburban teachers concerning such important factors as learner needs and characteristics, society, home, community, culture, and the availability of funding and resources;
4. relate the PREMIER model of successful urban teaching with instructional principles presented elsewhere in the text; and
5. describe the potential benefits of parental involvement and integrated service schools on student achievement.

Teaching in Urban and Other Settings

Although schools cannot accomplish everything, Edmonds (1979) argued, "We can, whenever and wherever we choose, successfully teach all children whose schooling is of interest to us. We already know more than we need to do that" (p. 24). If this belief is to be proven true, it will have to be demonstrated in urban schools. It is in such schools that the racial, cultural, and social contradictions between the teachers and students often create barriers that significantly endanger learning.

Consider that the teaching force in the United States is predominantly White; almost 90% of those currently teaching trace their family histories back to Europe (Pasch, Krakow, Johnson, Slocum, & Stapleton, 1990). Most were fortunate enough to be nurtured as children in emotionally and financially secure families. They were successful students and graduated from small-town or suburban schools and then achieved a college degree. Their background and experiences were overwhelmingly influenced by the dominant Anglo-European culture.

Differences in resources between urban and suburban districts, especially given the needs of many urban populations, can cause striking levels of inequality (Kozol, 1992).

Teachers employed in the foreseeable future can expect to be employed in urban schools. They are likely to be teaching non-White children, from African American and Latino cultures, but also children from families who recently emigrated from one of the many Asian countries. It is a good bet that the urban school districts in which these teachers work will be large, underfunded, and bureaucratic. The buildings are likely to be old and possibly deteriorating. There may be little money available for necessary supplies and equipment. Too many students in each urban classroom will come from families facing unemployment, financial problems, and health emergencies. Often families will be headed by a single parent who must face these problems with inadequate support.

Given the importance of the need, it is vital to identify those factors that allow some teachers and students to succeed, even in potentially difficult environments. In a recent study of high-achieving culturally diverse inner-city students and their teachers, students identified characteristics of effective teachers (Harmon, 2000). Exemplary teachers:

* were culturally competent;
* viewed cultural differences as cultural assets, not deficits;
* held high expectations for all students;
* used a multicultural curriculum incorporating higher level thinking skills and creative problem solving;

- used an affective curriculum including conflict management skills;
- used culturally relevant teaching methods;
- used differentiation;
- used role models and mentors;
- provided a disciplined environment through an authoritative and democratic management style; and
- involved the family and the community;

One of the key concepts in the above study is **cultural competence.** Culturally competent teachers possess self-awareness and self-understanding, cultural awareness and understanding, social responsiveness and responsibility, and use appropriate techniques for teaching all students. The process of becoming culturally competent begins with the opportunity to learn about one's own cultural heritage and the influence of that culture on teaching.

Cultural awareness and understanding involves learning how cultural differences and conflicts influence teaching and learning. Teachers who work to develop racial harmony in their classroom by demanding respect for individual differences are demonstrating social responsiveness and responsibility. Armed with this knowledge and understanding, culturally competent teachers are able to use instructional methods that enable all of their students to learn.

 ## REFLECTING ON THE IDEAS

Consider your own cultural heritage. Think about the values that are most important to you, the standards you consider for exemplary behavior and achievement, and the ideas you consider most interesting. How will those ideas and values affect your interactions with students whose cultural norms are different from yours?

One of the authors has been active in a consortium of three urban teacher education projects engaged in a two-year research project to identify the factors that influence successful urban teachers (Pasch et al., 1992). After analyzing data from 90 urban teachers in three large cities, the researchers developed a model for teaching success in urban schools represented by the mnemonic *PREMIER*. These elements and others are supported by Haberman's (1995) research on "star" teachers of children in poverty. Note, too, the similarity to the Harmon study above. Successful urban teachers do the following:

1. *Teach Purposefully.* They set high, yet achievable expectations, identify the purpose(s) for learning in each new unit and lesson, establish and communicate clearly stated objectives, and teach the relationships between previous learning and upcoming learning tasks.

2. *Respect Diversity.* This principle encompasses the importance teachers attach to knowing the characteristics of students, the environment in which the students live, and its probable effects on the students. Finally, teachers add to their success

when they accept and care for young people from backgrounds and lifestyles different from their own.

3. *Use Experience-Based Methods and Activities.* The importance of a curriculum that has relevance to the life of the urban student captures the essence of experience-based learning. The curriculum should identify the contributions of culturally diverse people to American and world civilization and culture and challenge students to interpret, analyze, compare, and evaluate these contributions. This principle also subsumes the benefits derived from role-playing, simulations, and activities that permit young people to observe, touch, and manipulate objects in contrast to activities that rely exclusively on verbal symbols.

4. *Manage the Urban Classroom Effectively.* The focus of this principle is on physical, emotional, and relational environments and their impact on student behavior. Chapters 11 and 12 discuss the research- and experience-based principles and practices that enable any teacher to be successful as a classroom manager.

5. *Individualize Instruction.* Each student is an individual and has the right to be treated as such. Alternating direct lesson designs with those based on active, discussion-based activities helps meet the needs of a variety of students. Inductive lessons that require students to investigate and discover concepts and principles also should be used.

6. *Communicate Proficiently.* This principle suggests that purposeful teaching is not complete until ideas, relationships, and expectations are communicated before, during, and after instruction. Teachers in the study often referred to the importance of responding appropriately to students' answers, questions, and comments.

7. *Reflect in Thought.* This principle develops the importance of self-evaluation and metacognition while teaching, with special attention to reflection after instruction. Successful teachers also communicate to students what they are teaching, share alternative ways to structure a lesson or activity, and thus assist students to become more aware of their own thought patterns (see also Cole, 1995).

It also is important to look at models of urban success that involve whole schools. One important example is Meier's (1995) description of the Central Park East (CPE) schools in East Harlem. While some of the variables that promoted CPE's success are beyond the control of an individual teacher (such as school or class size), some principles can be effective in other environments—and reflect those emphasized in this text. CPE schools build a democratic community; promote strong, respectful relationships with parents and community; foster inquiring intellectual habits; integrate the curriculum and teach fewer topics in depth; and connect learning to the real world.

 ## REFLECTING ON THE IDEAS

Leaving the principle "Manage the Urban Classroom Effectively" aside, consider how the other PREMIER principles relate to concepts taught in other chapters. What ideas have you learned so far that you think will be most important in teaching in an urban environment?

Parental Involvement

In the 1990s, growing attention was paid to the importance of cooperative home-school efforts to improve educational outcomes. Research studies over a 30-year period have demonstrated the positive results on school performance from school/home partnerships (Henderson & Berla, 1995). After examining over 85 studies, Henderson and Berla concluded that when parents are involved with a school, their children perform better in that school. In wealthy communities where family income and educational achievement are high, parents have traditionally been active in school activities. As the pace of life increases and parents work to juggle careers and families, maintaining those levels of involvement is difficult. In urban and rural communities extra effort is needed to bring parents and school administrators and teachers closer together. Strong parent/school relationships can even enhance relationships between parents and children (Galinsky, 2001).

The evidence has been so persuasive that it encouraged the National PTA to develop and disseminate the booklet *National Standards for Parent/Family Involvement Programs* (National PTA, 1997). Parent involvement has been identified as one of the eight national education goals:

> Every school will promote partnerships that will increase parental involvement and participation in promoting the social, emotional, and academic growth of children. (National PTA, 1997, p.4)

The PTA describes six types of home/school involvement based on the framework established by Joyce Epstein (Epstein, 1995, Sullivan, 1997). The standards include (1) frequent and predictable two-way communication between home and school, (2) enhancing parenting skills and capabilities, (3) assisting and enhancing student learning, (4) encouraging parents to engage in volunteering activities in the school, (5) participating in school decision making and advocacy, and (6) enabling parents and schools to create additional partnerships for collaborating with the community. Of course, these standards are applicable in urban and nonurban communities.

One important area for parent/community interaction is after-school programs. As more and more parents spend their days in the workforce, high-quality after-school activities are extremely important. For example, collaborations between schools and community organizations can provide opportunities for secondary students to provide service and learn important skills in a safe after-school environment (McLaughlin, 2001).

Practice Activity A

Home and Family Involvement

Practice Point

Working with colleagues in class, divide into six groups, one focusing on each of the types of home/school involvement. Brainstorm things you will be able to do as a beginning teacher to support each type of involvement.

Integrated Services Schools

In his last book, *Basic Schools: A Community for Learning*, Boyer (1995) argued for an integrated approach to schooling, one that serves the "whole child." In addition to a solid academic program and a partnership between home and school, an integrated services school provides "basic health and counseling services for students, referrals for families, and a new calendar and clock, with after-school and summer enrichment programs for learning and creative play" (Boyer, 1995, p. 153). The move toward integration of school and community services can take a variety of forms. In some areas, schools establish more formal links with health and social service agencies than in traditional schools. In those agencies educational personnel have systematic communication with a variety of agencies, allowing for quick and convenient referrals and consultation. In other schools, sometimes called full-service schools, the school itself becomes the hub for services. Health, government, and social service agencies establish a presence within the school itself (Dryfoos, 1994; Williams-Boyd, 1996). In these cases teachers do not have to refer a student or parent to a health clinic, counselor, or social service agency somewhere in the city; they can simply walk them to another part of the building. In urban settings (or in impoverished rural settings) in which many students have complex sets of needs, such supports can be particularly valuable.

Boyer gives credit to James P. Comer, a Yale University child psychologist, for his early and continuing efforts to create schools that provide a range of professional services to children (Boyer, 1995, p. 168). Today hundreds of "Comer Schools" exist across the nation, predominantly in low-income school districts. These schools utilize the Comer School Development Program to integrate pupil services with parental collaboration in order to foster child development as a necessary foundation for educational progress and academic achievement (Finn-Stevenson & Stern, 1997; Goldberg, 1997; Haynes, 1996; Squires & Kranyik, 1996). When a Comer School Development Program is fully functioning, every student in the school is supported by a significant adult presence at home, at school, and in the community.

As we consider the directions schools must take during the 21st century, it seems likely that they will take on services not traditionally considered part of the school mission. Think about the impact on your effectiveness—and on your students' lives—if basic health, safety, and economic concerns could be addressed efficiently and effectively as discussed above.

CHAPTER SUMMARY

The extraordinary range of student strengths, needs, interests, experiences, values, difficulties, learning styles, and a host of other variables makes it impossible for a one-size-fits-all approach to be very successful in any classroom. On the other hand, the realities of classroom life dictate that you will have few opportunities to plan individually for each one of your students. This poses a dilemma that has puzzled teachers for generations: How do I balance the seemingly limitless variety of students' needs with the basic limits of time, space, and human energy?

Fortunately, a host of options is available between inflexible planning and infinite variety. If teachers assume that the right way to teach is when all students do the same things in the same way, any variation in that pattern is likely to be deemed an unreasonable expectation. On the other hand, if teachers assume that having students engage in a variety of activities is the normal process of teaching, fewer adaptations will need to be made, because the regular classroom routines will already accommodate a variety of students' needs. If you plan differentiation and variety as part of your normal course of teaching, you will have fewer worries about adapting to the needs of individual students. A more flexible curriculum will need to be adapted less.

Practice Activity B

Adapting Mythic Heroes and Heroines

Practice Point

Think back to the four students described at the beginning of this chapter and to Hannah's planned unit on mythic heroes and heroines. What advice might you give Hannah for activities or strategies that would enhance the unit for her students? List at least two suggestions for each student. Compare your list with a friend's list. Discuss the characteristics that helped you diagnose each student's instructional needs.

Unit Preparation

As you have planned your teaching unit, you should have kept in mind the needs, interests, and circumstances of the students for whom you are planning. Now that you have some basic plans in place, it is important to examine those plans in order to determine points where you need to differentiate instruction. Here are some questions to get you started. Where necessary, note the kinds of adaptations or alternative plans that will be necessary to meet all your students' needs.

1. When planning class activities what skills are you assuming students already have? These might be skills associated with the content you are teaching or general skills, such as taking notes, reading charts, or using a calculator. How will you determine who is lacking these prerequisite skills? What supports will you plan for these students?

2. Which students in your class may not have had experiences common to other students, or are likely to have trouble learning through the types of lessons you are planning because of a disability? How will you adapt your instruction?

3. Which students in your class learn exceptionally rapidly or have a great deal of background knowledge about your topic? How will you make sure they have the opportunity to learn information that is actually new to them?

4. Which parts in your unit could be omitted for some students? Which parts in the unit might allow multiple options for differing styles, backgrounds, or levels of challenge?

Portfolio Activity

Your plan for differentiating your teaching unit can make a good portfolio activity. It is enormously challenging to learn to differentiate instruction for various groups of students simultaneously. Be prepared to talk to interviewers about how you hope to accomplish this. You will not become expert at differentiation during your first year, but you can begin the important habit of thinking of students as individuals first.

 Search the Web

You may refer to many websites on special education to find links related to both disabilities and gifted education. Also, websites geared toward parents and community often include links related to parent involvement and community-school partnerships.

REFERENCES

Banks, J. A. (1999). *Introduction to multicultural education.* Boston: Allyn & Bacon.

Banks, J. A., & Banks, C. A. M. (Eds.). (2001). *Handbook of research on multicultural education.* San Francisco, CA: Jossey-Bass.

Bennett, C. I. (1986). *Comprehensive multicultural education: Theory and practice.* Newton, MA: Allyn and Bacon.

Biklen, D., & Bogdan, R. (1977). Handicappism in America. In B. Blatt, D. Biklen, & R. Bogdon (Eds.). *An alternative textbook in special education* (pp. 205–215). New York: Love Publishing.

Boyer, E. (1995). *Basic schools: A community for learning.* Princeton, NJ: Carnegie Foundation for the Advancement of Teaching.

Boykin, A. W. (1994). Harvesting talent and culture: African American Children and educational reform. In R. Rossi (Ed.), *Schools and students at risk.* New York: Teachers College Press.

Brandt, R. (1992). On building learning communities: A conversation with Hank Levin. *Educational Leadership, 50*(1), 19–23.

Callahan, C. (2001). Beyond the gifted stereotype. *Educational Leadership, 59*(3), 42–46.

Checkley, K. (1997). The first seven . . . and the eighth. A conversation with Howard Gardner. *Educational Leadership, 55*(1), 8–13.

Colangelo, N., & Davis, G. A. (1997). *Handbook of gifted education* (2nd ed.). Boston: Allyn & Bacon.

Cole, R. W. (Ed.). (1995). *Educating everybody's children: Diverse teaching strategies for diverse children.* Alexandria, VA: Association for Supervision and Curriculum Development.

Collins, M. (1992). *Ordinary children, extraordinary teachers.* Charlottesville, VA: Hampton Publishing Co.

Cross, T. (Ed.) (2002). Underrepresentation among ethnically diverse students in gifted education. Special Edition, *Roeper Review, 24*(2).

Dryfoos, J. (1994). *Full-service schools.* San Francisco Jossey-Bass.

Edmonds, R. (1979). Effective schools for the urban poor. *Educational Leadership, 37, 15–24.*

Educational Products Information Exchange (EPIE). (1979). *Grant progress report NIE-G-790083.* Mimeographed. Stony Brook, NY: Author.

Epstein, J. (1995). School family, community partnerships: Caring for the children we share. *Phi Delta Kappan, 77*(9), May, 1995, 701–712.

Esposito, B. G., & Reed, T. M. (1986). The effects of contact with handicapped persons on young children's attitudes. *Exceptional Children, 54, 224–229.*

Farlow, L. (1996). A quartet of success stories: How to make inclusion work. *Educational Leadership, 53*(5), 51–55.

Feldhusen, J. F. (1992, August). *Talent Identification and Development in Education (TIDE).* Paper presented at the Second Asian Conference on Giftedness, Taipei, Republic of China.

Feldhusen, J. F. (1996). How to identify and develop special talents. *Educational Leadership, 53*(5), 66–69.

Finn-Stevenson, M., & Stern, B. (1997). Integrating early-childhood and family-support services with a school improvement process: The Comer-Zigler initiative. *Elementary School Journal, 98*(1) September, 1997, 51–66.

Fordham. S. (1988). Racelessness as a factor in African American students' school success: Pragmatic strategy or Pyrrhic victory? *Harvard Educational Review, 58*(1), 54–84.

Fordham, S., & Ogbu, J. U. (1986). African American students' school success: Coping with the "burden of acting white." *The Urban Review, 18*(3), 176–206.

Galinsky, E. (2001). What children want from parents—and how schools can help. *Educational Leadership, 58*(7), 24–28.

Gardner, H. (1983). *Frames of mind.* New York: Basic Books.

Gay, G. (2002). Preparing for culturally responsive teaching. *Journal of Teacher Education, 53*(2), 106–116.

Giangreco, M. F., Cloninger, C. J., Dennis, R. E., & Edelman, S. W. (1994). Problem-solving methods to facilitate inclusive education. In J. S. Thousand, R. A Villa, & A. I Nevin (Eds.), *Creativity and collaborative learning: A practical guide to empowering students and teachers.* Baltimore: Brookes.

Goldberg, M. (1997). Maintaining a focus on child development. An interview with Dr. James P. Comer. *Phi Delta Kappan, 78*(7), March, 1997, 557–59.

Goldberg, M. (2001). An interview with Henry Levin: A concern with disadvantaged students. *Phi Delta Kappan, 82*(8), 632–634.

Good, T. & Brophy, J. (1999). *Looking in Classrooms.* Needham, MA: Allyn & Bacon.

Goodlad, J., & Lovitt, T. (Eds.). (1993). *Integrating general and special education.* New York: Macmillan.

Greenwood, J. M. (1888). *Principles of education practically applied.* New York: D. Appleton.

Guralnick, M. J. (1981). The social behavior of preschool children at different developmental levels: Effects of group composition. *Journal of Experimental Child Psychology, 31, 115–130.*

Haberman, M. (1995). *Star teachers of children in poverty.* W. Lafayette, IN: Kappa Delta Pi.

Hale-Benson, J. (1986). *Black Children: Their roots, culture, and learning styles.* Baltimore: Johns Hopkins University Press.

Hanline, M. F., & Murray, C. (1984). Integrating severely handicapped children into regular public schools. *Phi Delta Kappan, 66,* 273–276.

Harmon, D. (2000). They won't teach me: The voices of African American inner city students. *Roeper Review.*

Haynes, N. (1996). Creating safe and caring school communities: Comer School Development Program schools. *Journal of Negro Education, 65*(3), Summer, 1996, 308–314.

Hebert, T. P. (2001). If I had a new notebook I know things would change: Bright underachieving young men in urban classrooms. *Gifted Child Quarterly, 45*(3), 174–194.

Henderson, A. T., & Berla, N. (1995). *A new generation of evidence: The family is critical to student achievement.* Washington, DC: Center for Law and Education.

Heward, W. L. (2000). *Exceptional children: An introduction to special education.* Upper Saddle River, NJ: Prentice Hall.

Hollins, E., (Ed). (1994). *Teaching diverse population: Formulating a knowledge base.* Albany, NY: State University of New York Press.

Hopfenber, W. S., Levin, H. M., Chase, C. (1933). *The accelerated school resource guide.* San Francisco: Jossey-Bass.

IDEA: Individuals with Disabilities Act of 1997. U. S. Public Law 105-17. 105th Congress, 4 June 1997.

Johnson, R., Rynders, J. R., Johnson, D. W., Schmidt, B., Haider, S. (1979). Interaction between handicapped and nonhandicapped teenagers as a function of situational goal structuring: Implications for mainstreaming. *American Educational Research Journal, 16,* 161–167.

Kauffman, J. M., & Hallahan, D. K. (1994/5). *The illusion of full inclusion: A comprehensive critique of a current special education bandwagon.* Austin, TX: PRO-ED.

Kozol, J. (1992). *Savage inequalities.* New York: Harper.

Kunjufu, J. (1984). *Developing positive self-images and discipline in Black children.* Chicago: African-American Images.

Lesko, W. (2001/2002). Student activism for the next generation. *Educational Leadership, 59*(4), 42–44.

Marland, S. P. (1972). *Education of the gifted and talented: Report to the Congress of the United States by the United States commissioner of education and background papers.* Submitted to the United States Office of Education. Washington, DC: Government Printing Office.

McLaughlin, M. W. (2001). Community counts. *Educational Leadership, 58*(7), 14–18.

Meier, D. (1995). *The power of their ideas: Lessons for America from a small school in Harlem.* Boston Beacon Press.

National Education Association. (1978). *Education for all handicapped children.* Washington, DC.

National PTA. (1997). *National Standards for Parent/Family Involvement Programs.* Chicago, IL: National PTA: Author.

Pang, V. O. (2001). *Multicultural education: A caring-centered, reflective approach.* New York: McGraw-Hill.

Pasch, M., Krakow, M. C., Johnson, C., Slocum, H., & Stapleton, E. (1990). The disappearing minority educator: No illusion, a practical solution. *Urban Education, 25,* 207–218.

Pasch, S., Pasch, M., Johnson, R., Ilmers, S., Snyder, J., Stapleton, E., Hamilton, A., & Mooradian, P. (1992). Reflection of urban education: A tale of three cities. In *Diversity, the 1992 Research Yearbook.* (pp. 9–30) Reston, VA: Association of Teacher Educators.

Purcell, J. H., Burns, D. E., & Leppien, J. H. (2002). The parallel curriculum model (PCM): The whole story. *Gifted Children Commique, 14,* 3. Insert: Teaching for high potential 1–4.

Quality Education for Minorities Project. (1990). *Education that works: An action plan for the education of minorities.* Cambridge, MA: Massachusetts Institute of Technology.

Raynes, M., Snell, M., & Sailor, W. (1992). A fresh look at categorical programs for children with special needs. *Phi Delta Kappan, 73*(4), 327.

Reis, S. M., Burns, D. E., & Renzulli, J. S. (1992). *Curriculum compacting: The complete guide for modifying curriculum for high ability students.* Mansfield Center, CT: Creative Learning Press.

Reis, S. M., & Purcell, J. H. (1998). An analysis of content elimination and strategies used by elementary classroom teachers in the curriculum compacting process. *Journal for the Education of the Gifted, 16*(2), 147–170.

Renzulli, J. S. (1977). *The enrichment triad.* Mansfield Center, CT: Creative Learning Press.

Renzulli, J. S. (1978). What makes giftedness? Reexamining a definition. *Phi Delta Kappan, 60,* 180–184.

Renzulli, J. S. (1993). *Schools are places for talent development: Applying "gifted education" know-how to total school improvement.* Storrs, CT: National Research Center for Gifted and Talented.

Renzulli, J. S., & Reis, S. M. (1997). The schoolwide enrichment model (2nd Ed.). Mansfield Center, CT: Creative Learning Press.

Renzulli, J. S., & Smith, L. H. (1979). *A guidebook for developing individualized educational programs for gifted and talented students.* Mansfield Center, CT: Creative Learning Press.

Rogers, J. (1993). *The inclusion revolution. Research bulletin no. 11.* Bloomington, IN: Phi Delta Kappa Center for Evaluation, Development and Research.

Rowley, S. J. & Moore, J. A. (2002). When who I am impacts how I'm represented: Addressing minority student issues indifferent contexts. Racial identity in context for the gifted African American student. Roper Review, *24*(2), 63-67.

Sapon-Shevin, M. (1994). *Playing favorites: Gifted education and the disruption of community.* Albany, NY: State University of New York Press.

Schniedewind, N., & Davidson, E. (2000). Differentiating cooperative learning. *Educational Leadership, 58*(1), 24–29.

Shade, B. J. (1990). *Engaging the battle for African American minds.* Washington, DC: National Alliance of Black School Educators.

Shade, B. J. (Ed.). (1997). *Culture, style, and the educative process: Making schools work for racially diverse students.* (2nd Ed.). Springfield, IL: Charles C. Thomas.

Shaywitz, S. E., Holahan, J. M., Freudenheim, D. A., Fletcher, J. M., Makeuch, R. W., & Shaywitz, B. A. (2001). Heterogeneity within the gifted: Higher IQ boys exhibit behaviors resembling boys with learning disabilities. *Gifted Child Quarterly, 45*(1), 16–23.

Siegle, D., & Schule, P. A. (2000). Perfectionism differences in gifted middle school students. *Roeper Review, 23*(1), 39–44.

Singer, J. D., & Butler, J. A. (1987). The Education for All Handicapped Children Act: Schools as agents of social reform. *Harvard Educational Review, 57*(2), 125–152.

Snell, M. E., & Janney, R. E. (2000). Some things we've learned about inclusion. In W. L. Heward, *Exceptional children: An introduction to special education,* pp. 236–237. Upper Saddle River, NJ: Prentice Hall.

Southern Poverty Law Center (2001). *Responding to hate in school.* Available at http://www.splcenter.org/teachingtolerance/ttindex.html.

Spring, J. (1995). *The intersection of cultures: Multicultural education in the United States.* New York: McGraw-Hill.

Squires, D., & Kranyik, R. (1996). The Comer program: Changing school culture. *Educational Leadership, 53*(4), 29–32.

Status of Black Children. (1989). [Special issue]. *Black Child Advocate, 15*(4).

Sternberg, R. (1985). *Beyond IQ: A triarchic theory of human intelligence.* New York: Cambridge University Press.

Sternberg, R. J., & Grigorenko, E. L. (2001). Learning disabilities, schooling, and society. *Phi Delta Kappan, 83*(4), 335–338.

Sullivan, P. (1997). The PTA's national standards. *Educational Leadership, 55*(80), 43–44.

Tannock, R., & Martinussen, R. (2001). Reconceptualizing ADHD. *Educational Leadership, 59*(3), 20–25.

Tomlinson, C. A. (1999). The differentiated classroom: Responding to the needs of all learners. Alexandria, VA: Association for Supervision and Curriculum Development.

Tomlinson, C. A. (2000). Reconcilable differences: Standards-based teaching and differentiation. *Educational Leadership, 58*(1), 6–11.

U. S. Department of Education. (1993). *National excellence: A case for developing America's talent.* Washington, DC: Author.

Williams-Boyd, P. (1996). A case study of a full-service school: A transformational dialectic of empowerment, collaboration and communitarianism. Unpublished doctoral dissertation, Lawrence, KS: University of Kansas.

Creating a Positive Learning Environment

Classroom Management: Traditions, Programs, and Goals

CHAPTER OVERVIEW

An understanding of effective classroom management is basic to professional practice and should be a significant part of a teacher's decision making. Sound classroom management principles can provide answers to a new teacher's numerous questions. How does a teacher establish an environment that enhances learning? What are the forces that affect a teacher's responses to student behaviors? What management programs or strategies have proven to be most effective?

This chapter describes and analyzes the beliefs, guidelines, and practices of two approaches to classroom management: behavior management and humanistic/developmental. In addition, it offers insights and practical suggestions gleaned from researchers who observed successful classroom managers in action, and it considers how a variety of management strategies can be considered part of a developmental continuum. Reflective teachers will make decisions by selecting the approaches that best fit their philosophy, meet student needs, and complement school expectations.

Chapter 12 will describe one approach, the Rational Approach to Practical School Discipline, which blends features of the management approaches described in this chapter. Here, again, the teacher decision maker will have to select appropriate strategies that meet the individual problem, set the tone for positive interactions, and structure the environment to match the teacher's style.

Opening Activity

You are a new member of the Landstown School staff. During a prep period in mid-September, you overhear Ken Cowan discussing a discipline problem with two teachers. Examine the responses made by Sandy and Marilyn to the problem Ken is having with Kevann, one of his students.

Practice Point

KEN   Kevann disrupts my class every five minutes. It's so frustrating. He is such a nice, respectful young man, but I have to tell him to stop talking, visiting, or wandering aimlessly in my class. I plead with him to stop. He stops for a few minutes, and then he is back disrupting again. I'm at my wit's end. I need to observe a bit more, maybe talk to last year's teacher.

SANDY   Ken, have you taught students your classroom rules and consequences for misbehavior? I spend the first two weeks of class creating an environment in which the students learn that they will receive rewards for positive behavior and punishment for negative behavior.

MARILYN   My approach is very different. I want students to develop self-discipline, to take responsibility for their own behavior, and to realize that when they misbehave, they disappoint me and diminish what we can do together that day. I use group meetings and individual conferences to gain insights about my students' needs, resources, and feelings. I find that these practices make it possible for the students to participate actively in managing the classroom.

Using the information provided, describe the approach to classroom discipline management reflected by each teacher.

Sandy and Marilyn represent differing traditions of classroom management. These traditions often are defined by psychological principles. The behaviorist tradition in psychology holds that human behavior is shaped through experiences with reward and punishment. This is the perspective held by Sandy. Humanist psychology holds that healthy human development is a natural process of growth that will unfold in positive directions unless blocked. Humanist approaches are more likely to lead to management strategies like those described by Marilyn. The degree to which you implement strategies based on these traditions is likely to be based on your own beliefs and values, school requirements, and your students' experiences and developmental levels.

In nearly every yearly opinion survey between 1973 and 2002, the national Gallup Poll reported that parents, students, and teachers regarded discipline among the most serious problems facing the public schools (Rose & Gallup, 2002). The public has remained consistent in its perception that (1) students in the public schools of the United States lack discipline and (2) improved discipline is the answer for many of the schools.

Unfortunately, as the case study about Kevann reveals, there are serious differences of opinion about what methods and practices are most effective in addressing discipline and management problems in schools.

The achievement of a disciplined and well-managed classroom is not as simple as most packaged, widely marketed discipline programs would suggest. On the other hand, it is not as awesome a challenge as many people believe. Rather, the reality lies somewhere between the two extremes.

The decisions you make in setting up your room and interacting with students are critical. With increasing numbers of young people coming to school from families in which both parents are working, from households headed by a single parent, or from troubled homes and communities, you must be able to enhance students' personal and social development if you wish to be successful in teaching academic content.

SECTION 1. TWO TRADITIONS OF CLASSROOM MANAGEMENT

Section 1 Objective

After you have completed the activities in this section you will be able to classify examples of the behavior management and humanistic/developmental traditions of classroom management.

Tradition 1: Behavior Management

The behavior management tradition is based on the behaviorist learning theory of B.F. Skinner. Skinner believed that future human behavior is determined by the consequences that followed past behavior. Behaviorist learning theory was derived from scientific experimentation, including numerous types of animal studies. It was Skinner who developed language that could communicate the nature of behavior theory to people within the field of education (but outside the field of psychology) and thus became its primary spokesperson. According to behaviorist learning theory, students are more likely to repeat behaviors that have led to positive consequences and less likely to repeat behaviors that have led to negative consequences. Consequently, the teacher's responsibility is to assure that positive actions yield positive results.

Many behavior management programs, although based on behaviorist theory, incorporate practices derived from other psychological theories. For example, a behavior management program may include a component that dignifies the importance of students' feelings and values, a practice derived from humanistic psychology.

What are the common elements of behavior management programs? Among the best known are contingency management, contracting, the use of praise, noncontingent reinforcement, and rules/reward—ignore/punish. Since these approaches use rewards and punishments, keep in mind that the consequences of the student behavior should be as *logical* as possible (Albert, 2002; Dreikurs, Grunwald, & Pepper, 1982; Fay & Funk, 1995). That is, the reward or punishment should reflect as closely as possible what would logically follow in real life. So, if students are quiet during a video, their reward is a small amount of free time. The free time is a logical consequence because no time was lost during the video by pausing to quiet students down. Logical consequences avoid the sense of coercion often present when an illogical consequence (e.g., doing extra homework problems because of misbehavior) is seen as a random "power play." As you read about each element, consider how behaviorist theory might be applied with such logical rewards or punishments.

Contingency Management

Contingency management, sometimes referred to as an *incentive system,* is a widely practiced element in behavior management. Contingency management requires that the teacher provide reward and punishment in the classroom based on specified criteria. Rewards are *contingent* upon behavior. Students who are ready for the next activity may be praised; students who complete their math in a specified amount of time may earn five minutes extra free time.

The basic theme of contingency management is that the worth of a reward you receive in school should be based on the worth of your actions. Contingency management often involves the use of tangible rewards to reinforce appropriate behavior. For example, tokens of different values are given and then exchanged for such rewards as books, magazines, free time, or preferred classroom activities. Instead of tokens, play money may be used to redeem desired products from a student store. In some cases, individual adults and the business community contribute products and services to support the token exchange.

Contracting

Contracting is a formalized contingency management process that involves an agreement with an individual student specifying the work to be accomplished by the student, the period for which the contract will remain in force, and the reward (reinforcement) to be given to the student after successful completion of the contract. The teacher and the student sign the contract; in some cases the student's parents do so as well. The legal overtones of the process are intended to convey a sense of importance and responsibility to the student. Teachers can help students assess and monitor their own behavior by asking them to periodically reflect on their compliance with the contract. Similar, less formalized arrangements can be made using charts. For example, a student agrees that he or she will receive a "star" for each day's assignments completed without disruption and that a specific reward will follow a whole week of stars.

The Use of Praise

"Catch 'em being good," or the use of praise as reinforcement, is a specific form of contingency management. Praise provides an immediate reward that reinforces a desirable behavior. For example, after a teacher gives an assignment, he or she may say, "Take out your social studies book and do so without talking to your neighbor. Thank you, Maxine, for being so prompt in getting out your book. You, too, Tanya and Ivan." These students are recognized because they responded promptly and appropriately. The teacher's recognition both reinforces the desired behavior, as exhibited by Maxine, Tanya, and Ivan, and signals the others that desired behavior will be recognized.

Many educators suggest that this method is most effective at the elementary school level. Certainly it occurs most frequently at that level. It can be applied at other grade levels, even at the college level. As students get older, they may prefer praise given privately over publicly.

Noncontingent Reinforcement

Noncontingent reinforcement is reinforcement that takes place without reference to any particular behavior on the part of the student. At first, this practice would seem contrary to a behaviorist approach. Rather than a systematic structure or process, it uses only the teacher's smile, the granting of privileges or special activities, or the giving of tokens to deserving students. Students are given positive reinforcement (reward) without a specific contingency behavior (although not when they are actively misbehaving). When positive noncontingent reinforcement is implemented, students generally behave better, even in settings other than the ones in which they received reinforcement. For example, giving a big smile in the hallway could result in improved student attitude and behavior during independent math seatwork. The smile had no specific reference to student behavior, nor was it based on merit. It was just a humane thing to do.

Rules/Reward—Ignore/Punish (RRIP)

Some behavior management programs tell students that if they obey the rules, they receive a reward; if they ignore the rules, they receive a punishment. Referred to as rule/reward—ignore/punish (RRIP), this approach uses freedom from unpleasant consequences as a form of control. In the RRIP system, logical consequences for misbehavior are given the same status as are rewards for good behavior, and rules are established to set the limits of behavior. In many cases, students participate in the development of the rules. The teacher then acts as the enforcer of the rules. Students who are compliant are rewarded, and those who are not are punished. Rewards and punishments are administered as quickly as possible after the behavior that prompted them.

Different philosophies are apparent in two groups of RRIP advocates. One group maintains that certain disruptions—soft talking, unobtrusive movements, whispered profanity, and the like—should be ignored. This is based on the belief that such minor disturbances do not disrupt classroom activity and that the attention given to misbehavior for some students can be rewarding. The second group cautions that at some point the teacher will have to confront the behaviors that are ignored, because they will increase either in frequency or in intensity. This group charges that ignoring some misbehavior sets up a continuing negative pattern that will be more difficult for the teacher to break the longer it remains in force.

CHECK YOUR UNDERSTANDING

Examine the following case study. Then review and critique the contract agreement between Mr. Griffiths and Sam. Develop your own contract to deal with Sam's behavior. Share it in a group of three to five persons, and reach a consensus about what the contract should contain.

CASE: Sam, a tenth-grader, has been absent from school three times within the last month. Each time this happens Sam seems distracted in class and he picks on another student before the day ends. Mr. Griffiths is frustrated by Sam's behavior. He decides to design a behavior management contract for Sam. After analyzing Sam's behavior pattern, he focuses the contract on Sam's habit of picking on his classmates. He discusses the proposed program with Sam and they agree on the following contract:

> Contract: On Monday, Sam will sign an agreement that he will avoid using any negative words or actions with his classmates on Monday and Tuesday. At the conclusion of the period on Tuesday, if Mr. Griffiths has observed no negative incidents, Sam will be given time (5 to 10 minutes) after the work is done to choose one of his preferred learning activities.

You may have been concerned in your critique that Mr. Griffiths chose to focus on Sam's habit of picking on classmates rather than on his distractedness. Focusing on one behavior per contract (and one contract at a time) makes monitoring easier for the teacher and enhances the student's likelihood of success. Mr. Griffiths chose to emphasize safety and the reduction in interpersonal conflict as his first priority—thus the contract to eliminate Sam's picking on other students. When Sam has mastered that behavior, the teacher then may create a contract to address Sam's attention in class.

Assertive Discipline: An Example of a Behavior Management Program

Assertive discipline (Canter, 1989, 1996; Canter & Shank, 1992) is based on the rules/reward–ignore/punish approach. Canter recommends that teachers create a discipline plan for their classroom with the participation of the parents and the school principal. This system includes the following:

1. List of rules and series of lessons. This will teach students the difference between acceptable and unacceptable school and classroom behaviors. The rules and lessons should help students understand which behaviors will result in punishment and which behaviors will reap rewards.

2. List of discipline consequences for misbehavior. The short list should be organized from least serious to most serious. For example, the least serious consequence could be a warning, such as writing of the misbehaving student's name on the blackboard. The most serious consequence could involve a conference among the teacher, the principal, and the student's parents.

3. List of rewards for acceptable behavior. The list should include those behaviors that contribute to classroom learning success. For example, students could exchange tokens for material rewards (less logical), or they could receive verbal praise, written notes of appreciation, or independent reading time (more logical).

4. Timely and frequent communication with parents. Communication should include the classroom rules and consequences. Contacts also are made with parents of misbehaving students.

The important thing to remember is that students must be *taught* how to behave, as described later in this chapter and in Chapter 12. Also, the consequences should be *logical*—that is, logically related to the misbehavior. The consequence of writing "I will not talk to my neighbor in class" 100 times has no logical relationship to the lost learning time due to students talking in class. A more logical consequence would be for the student to lose some socializing time. The following is an example of an assertive discipline system:

Rules

1. Listen while others are talking.
2. Walk quietly in the classroom and halls.
3. Bring materials to class every day.
4. Respect others' property and bodies.

Consequences

Discipline

1st infraction = warning
(name on board or card)
2nd infraction = check by name
(miss 30 seconds of passing time)
3rd infraction = second check (detention)
4th infraction = third check (call home)
5th infraction = fourth check (see principal)

Rewards

Points accumulated until 50 =
class party
Positive note to parents
Free games
Special movie
Computer time
Lunch with teacher
Free time

Letter To Parents

Dear _____ ,

I will be (student's name)'s teacher this year. I look forward to working with your student in my class. [Explain goals of the class, both cognitive and affective, and any special projects that will involve parents.]

To maintain a positive classroom, we have established the attached rules and consequences. If your student must remain after school, I will give you one day's notice.

I appreciate your support in helping me uphold this system. Please feel free to call or visit me to discuss anything of concern to you.

Sincerely,

(Sign your name)

Criticisms of the Behavior Management Approach

In recent years, much criticisms has been made of the behaviorist approaches to classroom discipline. Alfie Kohn (1994, 1996) has raised serious concerns about the coercive nature of behavior management strategies. He claims that students become merely compliant and do not learn about the crucial aspects of human cooperation. Other research calls into question the result of external rewards on students' creativity, critical thinking, and motivation (see for example, Amabile, 1996; Amabile, DeJong, & Lepper, 1976; Collins & Amabile, 1999; Deci, 1976; Deci 1971; Lepper & Greene, 1975). According to this body of research, when rewards are given for activities that could be intrinsically rewarding, motivation for those activities can actually decrease. Some teachers wonder. "If students' behavior is 'managed,' at what point to students learn to control themselves without external rewards or consequences?"

Similarly, Glickman (1988) maintains that the emphasis on obeying rules precludes the development of a democratic atmosphere in the classroom. Thus, valuable opportunities to develop character and care are lost. In 1996, even Lee Canter (the developer of assertive discipline) stressed the importance of (1) establishing rapport with students before moving on to discussions of rules and (2) involving students in the development of the rules and consequences. His critics (for example, Kohn, 1996) would argue that the teacher-centered focus of assertive discipline would make it an ineffective means for developing a classroom community, even with established rapport.

Tradition 2: Humanistic/Developmental

Although the humanistic tradition has a long history, its application in classrooms became popular in the 1960s and 1970s. Recent years have seen a resurgence of this approach in programs such as Love and Logic (Fay & Funk, 1995), and Discipline with Dignity (Curwin & Mendler, 1999). Humanistic practices can be traced to the work of clinical psychologists, school counselors, and mental health professionals studying emotional development. The goal of this approach is to establish a classroom atmosphere in which students' healthy emotional growth and development are supported. Humanists hope to create and maintain a classroom environment that emphasizes clear, effective communication, shared responsibility, conflict resolution, and the development of students' self-control and need fulfillment. Indeed, in this approach the teacher may act more as a guide in the classroom rather than as a figure of authority.

The remainder of this section describes two programs that emerged from the humanistic tradition. The first program, cooperation through communication (Ginott, 1972), emphasizes the importance of communication in the classroom. The second humanistic program, reality therapy (Glasser, 2000), stresses the role of individual conferences and group meetings in establishing a positive environment for learning. These two programs are discussed in detail along with Glasser's (1998a, 1998b) work on quality schools and choice theory. As you read, think about how each approach exemplifies a humanistic approach.

Haim Ginott: Cooperation through Communication

Ginott suggests that good behavior is inextricably tied to a good self-concept. The latter is, to a significant extent, built on the messages that adults generally and teachers specifically convey to students. It is logical, then, that his model for enhancing students' development—and, in turn, improving their behavior—is based on improving communication. This teacher student communication model focuses on reducing chaos through *congruent communication*, which Ginott describes as honest messages that are in harmony with students' and others' needs (Ginott, 1972). In pursuit of this harmony, Ginott proposes that teachers must (1) express sane messages, (2) deal with feelings, (3) eliminate stereotypes and labels, (4) use praise carefully, (5) build cooperation, and (6) communicate anger. These six principles are the essential building blocks of Ginott's conception of a humanizing, orderly environment.

Express Sane Messages. According to Ginott, the best teachers send sane messages, in which feelings are appropriate to the situation and the individuals. He observes that adults are too often predisposed to preach, condemn, force, accuse, threaten, and humiliate, resulting in the dehumanization of young people.

One of the essential principles designed to break this pattern is to separate the student's behavior from the teacher's conception of the student. The student should hear very clearly that "your behavior is unacceptable and will not be tolerated, but there will always be a guaranteed safe place for you in my heart." For example, Leesha, a ninth-grade student, was not writing the assigned essay and was walking about the room without permission. The teacher said, "You have 10 minutes to finish the essay. Let me see how much you have done." This is a sane message because the emphasis is on the student's off-task behavior. An accusing (less sane) message from the teacher is communicated when she says to Leesha, "Why do you keep walking about? You are always inconsiderate of the others in the room."

Deal with Feelings. One of the most challenging tasks teachers face is to confront feelings about self and others. Ginott counsels that teachers must help students to sort out their feelings. He suggests that teachers actively listen to students' feelings and ideas. For example, students may exaggerate the facts about some situation to impress or to gain attention. Suppose Lauri says to the teacher, "I got all the math problems wrong. I know I am dumb." The teacher may try to prove that Lauri is not dumb. Such an attempt to argue the logic or dispute the facts may be laudable, but Ginott feels a better decision would be to address Lauri's feelings of inadequacy by saying, "That has really made you upset. Well, we all feel that way sometimes. Let's see where you made the mistakes. Understanding that should help you feel better." Thus, the teacher accepts the student's right to feel bad about her math performance and has confidence in Lauri's ability to improve.

Eliminate Stereotypes and Labels. According to Ginott, teachers have often used irresponsible labels to describe students. Labeling creates stereotypes for others to apply to the student in future years. It also fosters a negative self-image in the student. Labeling, Ginott suggests, is especially dangerous when the teacher, from a position of authority, draws conclusions about a student's academic and social future. Some students have had a teacher call them by a nickname related to a misbehavior or less desirable trait or action. Decades later they can still struggle with the memories of that label and the need to overcome it.

When students are negatively labeled, their imagination, aspirations, and possibilities for personal growth are disabled to the degree that they accept the label. Any conclusion about a student's social or academic standing may become a self-fulfilling prophecy that stifles the student's potential. To avoid negative labeling, it is best to communicate to the class that you care about your students' future possibilities. Identify their goals and aspirations, and use that knowledge to prompt behaviors that will motivate them to work toward their goals. For example, if a student expresses an interest in an educational career, a teacher might say, "So you want to be a teacher. If I can help in any way, let me know." This does not mean that you confirm the student's choice. It only means that you are ready and willing to communicate with the student about the goal.

Use Praise Carefully. Ginott Stresses four cautions when using praise, First, avoid giving judgmental praise. Statements such as "Leesha, you are a good student" or "Maria, you are the best student in the class" may make students dependent on others for self-validation, or they can alienate students. Praise should be focused on a particular performance: "Leesha, I particularly enjoyed the way you used your own experience to show how we can welcome new students in the class," or "Maria, this is the fourth time in a row that you have gotten 100 percent on your math test. That kind of work will help you achieve your goal to become a math teacher."

Second, when using praise, be cautious about the tendency to associate correctness with personal worth. If the teacher—consciously or unconsciously—connects the two traits, some students may feel their success allows them to exercise more liberties than are reasonably allowed. Conversely, students whose work is less successful may conclude that they are not worthy.

Third, avoid praising minimally acceptable behavior, such as sitting down or working quietly. Instead, the teacher should praise the results of that behavior, as in "I appreciate your working so quietly and hard. We really accomplished a lot today." Praise should be expressed when students behave appropriately in an unusual circumstance: "I'm so glad that you solved the problem of who would clean up our lab equipment."

Fourth, refrain from overusing praise, especially when it is not warranted by student behavior. It is tempting to believe that if praise rewards behavior, then more and more praise will lead to even better behavior. Unfortunately, students will quickly perceive that the praise is insincere and it will lose its positive reinforcement value.

Praise can be worthy and effective if used carefully to avoid potential pitfalls. Chapter 12 provides more guidelines on the use of praise.

Build Cooperation. Ginott encourages teachers to build an atmosphere of cooperation in the classroom. He suggests that this is done most effectively when students feel a sense of independence and a sense of personal responsibility for the environment. Conversely, when students are dependent on external authority, their desire to exercise self-control is diminished.

He recommends several ways to enhance cooperation through the development of student independence. First, give students alternative ways to solve classroom problems. For example, in the event that room cleanup after art projects has been unacceptable, the teacher can offer the students a choice of (1) selecting a cleanup committee that quits 10 minutes early and cleans up for everyone or (2) having the entire class end art activities 5 minutes earlier and begin to clean up.

Second, Ginott reinforces the notion that it is more productive to invite cooperation than to legislate it. He encourages teachers to give students opportunities to make decisions about ways to increase cooperation in the classroom. For example, he suggests that when students are off task, the teacher should reemphasize positive expectation, as in, "Remember, it's now 10:00 and the period ends at 10:20. You should be working on your projects so we can present them to the other English class tomorrow." Such a message reminds the students that they have a personal responsibility for what they do during the next 20 minutes.

Communicate Anger. All human beings—no matter what their profession—get angry in both their personal and work lives, and teachers are no different. In contrast to some other working people, however, teachers are in physical proximity to those they serve (students) for five to seven hours a day, day after day. It is, therefore, not uncommon for a teacher's irritation and anger to be fueled by fatigue, student rudeness, classroom emergencies, or disputes with students, parents, or other teachers and administrators. Because the teacher is expected to be warm, gentle, and sympathetic, the public may be surprised when a teacher reveals anger. Yet, Ginott points out that showing anger in front of a class is one of the few times the teacher has the students' full attention.

He advises the use of the *I-message* when showing anger. An I-message contains both a description of the behavior that prompted the anger and an expression of how the behavior makes the teacher feel—angry, frustrated, disappointed. The following are examples of effective I-messages:

- "I'm disappointed by the put-downs you used during group work, because it shows that we are still treating one another poorly."
- "Tony, when you use those words in class, I feel very sad."
- "Sarah, when you interrupt me while I am giving instruction, I get really frustrated because I lose everyone's attention."

Ginott contrasts an I-message with an accusatory *you-message*, which is much less effective. In a you-message the focus is on the student, not the behavior. For instance, "Stop that fighting. You are making me angry," or "Tony, you must stop saying those nasty words in my class," or "Sarah, you are being rude when you interrupt me!"

 ## REFLECTING ON THE IDEAS

Assume that you are an advocate of Ginott's principles of classroom management. Analyze the following case study:

> Mrs. Weaver explained to her twelfth-grade class that she had to speak to a parent outside the classroom. "I will be just outside the door for five minutes," she informed them. "When I return, everyone working on their assignments and behaving will receive five minutes extra free time. Remember, you have an assignment that should take you ten minutes or more. Stay on task." She

returned in four minutes to find most of the class out of their seats, some chatting and some engaged in a scuffle. She realized that if someone had been hurt, she would have been liable for damages. She clenched her right fist and pounded it into the palm of her hand. Her eyes narrowed in anger, and she stood ramrod-straight as students began scurrying back to their seats. In a hissing voice forced through clenched teeth, she slowly and deliberately spoke to them:

"I am not going to let myself get mad. I am not going to blame your behavior on your parents and your upbringing. I am not going to let the behavior of some of you ruin the day for me and for the few good students who remained in their seats and continued to do their work. Instead, I am going to calmly ask that you *all* take your seats, and we will continue with class. I trusted you and you responded by being disrespectful of my directions."

How well did this teacher follow Ginott's principles of cooperation through communication? What would you have said if you had been the teacher? Discuss your responses with a classmate.

If you and your classmates decided that Mrs. Weaver was angry but did not express that anger well, you were correct. If you concluded that she was labeling students by mentioning their upbringing, you were correct again. Finally, her reference to the few "good" students violated Ginott's principle that correctness (behavior) should be separated from goodness (a person's worth).

If Ginott had observed the scene, he might have suggested that Mrs. Weaver express appreciation for those students who settled down quickly when she entered the room. She would have then told the class that she was angry and disappointed about their behavior while she was gone and explained that her feelings were caused by the fact the many of the students had not honored her trust. She would then ask the class how they should have behaved. Finally, she should express a willingness to give them a second opportunity soon to show that they can exercise positive classroom responsibility.

William Glasser: Reality and Therapy and Quality Schools

William Glasser, a noted psychiatrist, developed his educational program after years of working with troubled youngsters. The basic premise of reality therapy (1969, 2000) is that a student's past is over and cannot be altered. Regardless of that happy or sad past, students make choices when they select good or bad behavior.

Glasser rejects the idea that students' environment determines whether they will behave well or badly. He is impatient with teachers who find sociological and economic causes to explain or excuse the inappropriate behavior of students. Even though he may concede that these factors influence behavior, he maintains that teachers should not accept them as justifications for inappropriate behavior.

Glasser places the responsibility for deciding to misbehave squarely on the shoulders of students. He believes that since humans are rational beings, they should make choices that are conducive to their present and future well-being. The fact that students become disruptive indicates that they are not making good choices. The teacher's responsibility is to assist students to make better choices.

In reality therapy, teachers must help students see the value of desired behaviors in the classroom. Teachers also can provide opportunities for students to explore alternative approaches to problem solving. To perform these responsibilities, Glasser recommends two activities: *class meetings* and *individual conferences*. His more recent work (1998a, 1998b) extends these ideas into creating a quality school environment where students are most likely to meet their basic needs. This includes strong relationships, sound management strategies, and instruction that supports success for all students.

Class Meetings. Class meetings, according to Glasser, must be held on a frequent and regular basis. Glasser encourages, as part of the routine curriculum, three types of classroom meetings. In the *social conduct and problem management meeting*, the group discusses issues related to school and classroom conduct and ways to improve them. In the *student progress meeting*, the focus is on students' educational progress and ways to enhance it. The *open-ended discussion* allows students to make decisions about issues that are important to them.

In class meetings the emphasis is on the analysis and evaluation of solutions for one or more problems affecting the class. The teacher facilitates the discussion while permitting students to set the direction and momentum. Glasser recommends that participants be seated in a circle and that the discussion be limited to 30 to 45 minutes. Before closing, the teacher or a designated student should summarize the findings and recommendations.

Individual Conferences. Despite the success of class meetings, individual conferences with students about their behavior and school performance may be necessary. While it can be difficult to find time for an individual conference during a school day, it is best to keep the conference private without other students looking on—perhaps before or after class, during lunch, or before or after school. Glasser emphasizes that the teacher must demonstrate caring to the student during an individual conference. Caring reinforces self-worth, and self-worth produces a belief that the student can be successful. This one-on-one time usually yields positive results in rapport and clarity.

Glasser recommends that an individual conference consist of the following eight steps:

Step 1. Be sure that individual conferences stress students' responsibility for their own behavior.
　　　TEACHER : Newton, why are we meeting?
　　　STUDENT : I dunno.
　　　TEACHER : Newton, why are we meeting?
　　　STUDENT : Because you want to talk to me.
　　　TEACHER : Why are we meeting for me to talk to you?
　　　STUDENT : I guess because I would not stay seated.
　　　TEACHER : Right!
Step 2. Have students identify the rule that has been broken and explain why the rule is important to individual and class success.

TEACHER : Which rule did you break by moving around in class without permission?

STUDENT : No off-task movement.

TEACHER : And why do we have the rule?

STUDENT : Because we would lose too much class time if everyone were moving around the room and disturbing others.

Step 3. Regardless of students' background or status, accept no justification that will excuse inappropriate behavior.

TEACHER : OK, Newton. Let's figure out a solution to this problem of your movement.

STUDENT : But I was only up a couple of times.

Teacher: The rule was broken, no matter how many times, Newton.

Step 4. Be sure students acknowledge explicitly or implicitly that their action was inappropriate.

TEACHER : So what causes you to move without permission?

STUDENT : I know I shouldn't get out of my seat, but I can't sit for so long without moving.

TEACHER : I understand, but we must work out a plan that keeps you on task.

Step 5. Suggest two or three acceptable alternatives for students to select from if the urge to break a classroom rule should become irresistible.

TEACHER : Of the three alternatives I suggested, which one do you think is best for you?

STUDENT : Number two. I'll let you know with a signal before I move.

TEACHER : OK, Newton, when you get the urge again, that is what I expect you to do. Do you need me to remind you when you come to class the first few times?

STUDENT : It will help.

TEACHER : Then I will.

Step 6. Communicate and affirm logical, reasonable consequences. Firmly and consistently administer the consequences if students choose an unacceptable alternative.

TEACHER : As you know, if you choose not to inform me before you need to move, you will be isolated from the class for fifteen minutes. Neither of us wants that, right?

STUDENT : Right.

Step 7. To be effective, persist—never give up. This may mean repeating the process again with some students, being consistent and patient, and communicating a positive expectation that they can learn to behave.

TEACHER : Let's see how this works out. We will talk again at the end of the week to see how well you've done.

STUDENT : All right.

TEACHER : If you want to talk with me about it before the end of the week, just let me know.

STUDENT : OK.

Step 8. Evaluate progress at the end of the trial period. Never give up on your students; you are their hope for a positive future.

CHECK YOUR UNDERSTANDING

Now that you have examined the eight steps as advocated by Glasser, summarize each in a word or two. Try to do this exercise without reviewing the steps.

Glasser's Quality Schools and Choice Theory

Glasser (1998b) has extended his examination of classroom behavior to emphasize the individual control that students have over their own actions, which he refers to as choice theory. In these writings he decries the "boss management" approach to governing students and believes that such coercive measures have alienated students and lowered motivation to learn. Glasser's books (1992, 1998a) describe how schools and classrooms can use a "lead management" approach that will result in true motivation. Fortunately, he advocates many of the ideas already presented in this text; for example, authentic projects, differentiation, and cooperative learning.

Glasser states that students must have some real control over their destiny through participating in decisions about the classroom and school. In this way they learn about their own power and the responsibility that comes with such freedom. Teachers must understand that students come to their classes with five basic needs:

1. Survival
2. Love
3. Power
4. Fun
5. Freedom

Glasser states that students' actions are aimed at fulfilling these five needs. If the teacher can remember that the student's behavior is merely an attempt to satisfy one of these needs, then the approach taken will be more sensitive and responsive. As one middle school teacher said, "It is important to remember that when a kid is giving you trouble, it is not really your problem. It is the student's problem, and it's simply your job to help the kids resolve their problems. By keeping yourself on the kid's side as you think through a classroom problem, you can avoid about 90% of the pitfalls that most teachers fall into in terms of discipline" (Ayers, 1998).

The satisfaction of these needs is one of the most important factors for a reflective teacher to consider when making classroom decisions. It will affect the strategies you use (direct, cooperative, or inductive learning), how you set up your rules and procedures (amount of choice and student participation), and how you interact with students. As a lead manager, you can search for and find ways to meet many of the students' needs while still engaging them in valued learning.

Practice Activity A

Examining Tony's Pattern of Misbehavior

In the first year of your first teaching job at Landstown School, you are drawn into a lunch-hour conversation between two veteran teachers who are exchanging impressions about Tony.

> MR. GRIFFITHS: Tony is helpless. He sits and stares. He does nothing. He is just plain lazy. I told him on Tuesday that if he did not change, I was going to get him out of my class.
>
> MR. HENRY: He is not the only one. Most of the kids around here learn nothing at home that is helpful in school. They are insolent and lazy. I asked one of them if he was planning to spend his whole life sitting around watching television and he responded, "I don't care."
>
> MR. HENRY turns to you and says: You don't look very happy with my hypothesis. What would you recommend we do about Tony?

Write a response to Mr. Henry's question. Include at least four principles/practices found within either the behavior management or the humanistic classroom management traditions. Also, try to help the teachers develop more appropriate conclusions about the students' home situations.

If you began your response by showing respect for the feelings of the two teachers (e.g., "You sound frustrated"), you have understood what Ginott means about dealing with feelings. Dealing with feelings is necessary with colleagues as well as with students. If you counseled that good people can occasionally behave unacceptably, you will have encouraged the teachers to send sane messages instead of messages of condemnation. You may then suggest that they analyze Tony's unacceptable behavior and evaluate his motivation in relation to the tasks assigned to him. By prompting the teachers to consider the needs of their students (e.g., "What do you think they really want?"), you may help them gain some empathy and understanding of the students' needs. You could ask the teachers about the students' cultures; for example, many Native American and Latino populations value collaboration. If they come to the conclusion that Tony seems more engaged when talking to other students, you may suggest that they try structured group work. These four principles—deal with feelings, send sane messages, eliminate stereotypes and labels, and consider student needs—should be communicated to the two veteran teachers.

SECTION 2. BUILDING THE CLASSROOM COMMUNITY

Section 2 Objectives

After you have completed the activities in this section, you will have the ability to describe the components necessary for developing a classroom learning community.

One of the first steps in building a productive classroom is to stop for a moment and consider your goal. Remember from Chapter 3 that it is necessary to identify instructional goals in order to meet them. Similarly, in order to meet them you must first determine your classroom management goals. Few teachers today aim for the atmosphere that may have characterized some schools 100 years ago: complete silence broken only by the scratching of writing implements. Stop for a moment now and think about the type of atmosphere you would like to have in your ideal classroom.

Like many teachers, you may envision a classroom full of happily engaged students working together on tasks and contributing without conflict. This is a vision of a learning community—one of the most important goals you can have for adolescents. If students learn to work together and value one another, they are likely to carry those habits and beliefs into their adult lives. Two key questions must be answered: What makes a group a community? Which type of management system will best get us there?

Sapon-Shevin (1999) described five characteristics of a community.

1. *Security.* In a community it is safe to be yourself, take risks, ask for support, and occasionally fail. In a safe classroom students are free to share concerns without fear of mockery and are free to share successes trusting they will be met with enthusiasm and support. In one seventh-grade class a boy had struggled all semester with solving math word problems. One day while working individually with his teacher, something "clicked" and he found a strategy that worked for him. He shouted out loudly, "All right!" In that community, success was shared and his outburst was not punished. A safe environment also is one in which racist or otherwise demeaning comments are not accepted and evidence of prejudice is addressed, not ignored (Southern Poverty Law Center, 2001).

2. *Open Communication.* In a community questions are accepted and differences are embraced. A student who uses a walker or speaks a different language is treated matter-of-factly. "Jason uses a walker because his legs aren't strong enough for him to walk without it." "Kim is just learning English because he recently arrived from Taiwan." "We'll need to listen carefully to Jessica because it is hard for her to pronounce some words. Perhaps she can spell them for us."

3. *Mutual Liking.* Students in a community genuinely enjoy each other's company. Multiple opportunities to share positive experiences and express appreciation support the development of many friendships.

4. *Shared Goals and Objectives.* In a community people work together toward common goals. This can be as simple as completing the cleanup in time to listen to an extra chapter from a favorite book or as complex as joint planning of a class trip.

5. *Connectedness and Trust.* The feeling of connectedness entails sharing good and bad, excitement, sadness, and fear. It means explaining how hard it is to return to class after the death of a loved one, trusting that the absence has been noticed.

According to Sapon-Shevin (1999, p. 17), "Community is important not just as a place where we feel connected and supported, but as a solid base from which we move out into the world. Being a member of a community can help us to understand that together we are better, together we are stronger." Seven factors can contribute to classroom community. They are displayed in Figure 11.1 and discussed next.

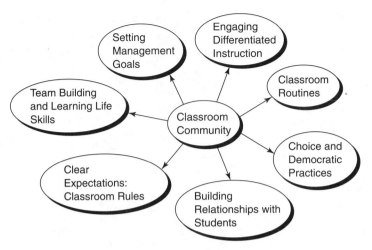

Figure 11.1   Building a Classroom Community.
From *Teaching as Decision Making: Successful Practices for the Elementary Teacher* (3rd Ed.) (p. 354), by A. J. Starko, et al., 2003, Upper Saddle River, NJ: Merrill/Prentice Hall. Copyright 2003 by Pearson Education, Inc. Reprinted with permission.

Setting Management Goals

As a teacher, you will need to have clear management goals and an understanding of your own management philosophy. An important goal is to have students work together as a community, which blends aspects from both humanistic and behavior management approaches.

One way to view the process of community building is helping students grow along a developmental pathway from external control to self-management. Think about a toddler walking near the street. A responsible adult will want to make sure that the toddler does not walk into the path of cars. Most toddlers are not ready for a complicated explanation of the dangers of motor vehicles. If the student walks near the street, he or she is likely to be stopped by an adult shouting loudly, "No! Do not run in the street!" This command is consistent with a behavior management approach, but as students grow older, we know it will not always be possible to watch their every movement. Nor do we want them always stuck on one side of the street fearing the traffic. So as time passes, students are taught how to look both ways and make good judgments about crossing. At first these habits may be undertaken out of fear or obedience, but hopefully young people eventually will realize that careful maneuvering in public places makes life safer and more pleasant for everyone.

Similarly, our goal in classroom management is to help students become more self-directed. As students move from early to later adolescence, they should become more adept at self-monitoring and making good judgments about their own behavior. Students' point on that pathway will be dependent on their past experiences at home, in the community, and school. Just as we must adjust our teaching to address students' prior knowledge, so our management choices must reflect students' needs at a given moment. Students' culture and prior experience will shape their concepts of what constitutes authority, how directions are given, and what behaviors do and do not elicit respect. A deep understanding of our students can guide our selection of management styles.

Students Can Learn Responsibility Through Classroom Routines.

For example, in many urban environments the cultural expectation of authority is that it is direct, sets high standards, and conveys seriousness of purpose. Delpit (1995) quotes a young Black man describing a former teacher.

> We had fun in her class, but she was mean. I can remember she used to say, "Tell me what's in the story, Wayne." She pushed, she used to get on me and push me to know. She made us learn. . . . There was this tall guy and he tried to take her on, but she was in charge of that class and she didn't let anyone run her. I still have this book we used in her class. (p. 37)

Delpit clarifies that this young man was proud of the teacher's "meanness." Her straightforward, no-nonsense leadership style commanded his respect. Someone else viewing the same behavior might have characterized it as negative or authoritarian, but for that young man at that moment it was appropriate. Similarly, Delpit describes the indirect style of giving directions, "Isn't it time to put that away now?" or "Would you like to take out your math books?" as characteristic of upper middle-class parenting styles. Students who are accustomed to such directives—which sound like questions but are, in reality, commands—are much more likely to obey them. Students from working class families are much more likely to respond to a clear directive, "Please take out your math books now."

If we want our students to be successful in their education, and in life, it is essential to move students toward self-management by building on their current understanding. Students who understand only direct commands can be explicitly taught about indirect language. Students who are accustomed to external control can be taught self-regulation, but it will take time. Even in circumstances where external rewards are important—for example, a reward system for a special-needs student who has trouble attending for more than a few moments—the goal is to wean students from external control and move toward self-monitoring and self-control. Clear goals and a management philosophy help us understand that control is not the end product of effective classroom management. Good classroom management has two goals: the creation of an effective learning environment and teaching the self-management skills of successful adults.

Clear Expectations: Classroom Rules

A **classroom rule** is a statement that informs students which behaviors are acceptable and which are unacceptable in the classroom. Rules are few in number (usually three to seven, for easy recall) and are designed to clarify expectation in the classroom. One group of authors describes rules as intended to instill "habits of goodness" (Horsch, Chen, & Nelson, 2000, p. 224) that promote and sustain community. Just as we feel safer approaching an intersection with a traffic signal (because it is easier to predict the behavior of oncoming traffic), effective rules can make a classroom a more predictable and pleasant place. Although students may participate in establishing class rules, it is the teacher who has the ultimate responsibility for determining the rules. When students participate in the process, they are more likely to take ownership of and cooperate with the rules. The following guidelines are helpful for establishing classroom rules.

- Effective rules are clearly stated and phrased with positive expectations.
- Students should have input and discuss reasons for the rules.
- Rules should be linked to logical consequences.
- Rules need to be explained, practiced, and enforced.
- Rules and consequences should be communicated to parents.

While virtually every writer in the area of classroom management agrees that rules should be clear, authors differ in how they define "clear." Some writers suggest that all rules result in observable behaviors much like a behavioral objective. This results in rules such as "Remain seated during lessons." However, teaching students to interpret rules that are written a bit more broadly can be an effective life skill. The following are examples of effective rules for secondary-age students.

1. Be polite and helpful.
2. Focus on today's tasks.
3. Protect all property.
4. Use words to solve problems.

Of course, students will need assistance in defining what polite and helpful look like, what it means to be focused on tasks, and how to solve problems with words. Conversations regarding the meaning of such rules are especially important at the beginning of the school year but may be initiated any time the rules are being forgotten.

REFLECTING ON THE IDEAS

Write five rules for your classroom. Make them understandable, reasonable, and enforceable. Share them with classmates and invite suggestions for improvement.

Classroom Routines

Next, it is important to consider classroom organization and the use of classroom routines—the many small things that either go smoothly or are a source of confusion and wasted time. For example, teachers are constantly passing out and collecting papers. If students have been taught exactly how it is done and have done it many times before, the task can be accomplished quickly with virtually no disruption. If, however, each time papers are distributed everyone has to stop and consider how the papers will go and who will manage the effort, large amounts of time can be wasted.

Such routines are accomplished automatically, with little lost time because they are *taught and practiced* as the beginning of the year. For example, at the end of the first day, eleventh-grade students would be told the procedure for entering class: "When you enter class, pick up your work from your folder, go to your seat, check the board for bell work, and begin your work." The teacher would provide a demonstration, and ask the students to remember to do this tomorrow. The next day, the teacher would have the procedure written on the board, with the bell work. Students would be reminded or praised, depending on how well they followed the routine. The next section of this chapter provides more information about how to "teach" students to function as a productive community.

In contrast to the small number of classroom rules described next, a teacher may have a large number of routines, including how to form classroom groups, pass out material, begin class, use the restroom, and so on. Some routines will be established by the teacher and should be taught immediately. For example, fire drill procedures should be taught on the first day. Other routines and procedures can be developed cooperatively with students.

Choices, Democratic Practices, and Conflict Resolution

If you are teaching in the United States, most of your students soon will be adults who participate as citizens in a democratic society and political system. They will need to understand core democratic principles and be able to participate productively in making choices and conflict resolution.

In a classroom based on democratic practice, students have opportunities for making reasoned choices, sharing in decision making, and engaging in problem solving. Choices can range from helping to plan the games for a class party to deciding which of several topics to investigate in a social studies unit. Reasoned choice is more than just providing options. It entails helping students think through the possible options, consider the reasons for making a particular choice, and later evaluating the selection. For example, a class making decisions about games for a class party might list criteria to be used in selecting games: Can everyone play at once? Will it make a mess? Do we have the equipment we need? Is it fun? Some teachers teach Creative Problem Solving (CPS) as a strategy for decision making and planning (Isaksen, Dorval & Treffinger, 2000; Treffinger, 1995; Treffinger, Isaksen, & Dorval, 2000).

One area in which shared problem solving can be particularly effective is conflict management. Many programs teach students how to deal with peer conflicts productively (see, for example, Levin, 1994; Prutzman, Butrger, Bodenhamer, & Stern, 1988). A typical strategy includes four steps.

1. calming down
2. explanation of the problem
3. discussion and resolution
4. some kind of acknowledgement of closure (handshake, etc.)

First, students use I-statements to deliver emotion-laden messages using the formula "When you_____, I feel_____, because_____, so what I would like is _____" (p. 1). Students may hold conflict resolution meetings (at first with the teacher present) to solve problems. For example, John might ask for a meeting (after calming down) and present the I-statement, " When you ignore me in the group I feel left out, so what I would like is to be included on the team." Next, David summarizes what he heard John say: "You want to be included more." The meeting would continue until a resolution is achieved, perhaps with David agreeing to ask John his opinion occasionally.

Engaging, Differentiated Instruction

The next factor in establishing an effective classroom community is engaging, differentiated instruction that allows every student to feel successful. Nothing is more motivating than success. Therefore, one of the most effective managements tools of all is good teaching. If the instruction is differentiated so that students are working on tasks that are not too hard, not too easy, but "just right," they are less likely to encounter the frustration that so often can lead to misbehavior. It is certainly true that even the best teachers will encounter management challenges, but sufficiently challenging activities that lead to success can greatly reduce student misbehavior.

All of the information in Chapters 1–10 will help you develop activities and assessments that contribute to the development of your classroom community. Differentiation is a vital part of a classroom community, not just because it makes it possible for many students to be appropriately challenged simultaneously, but because of the messages it conveys about individual differences. Good differentiated instruction by its very nature conveys respect for differences. It says that different students have different needs and that is OK. Everyone has interesting and important work to do. This attitude is fundamental to a classroom in which diverse students work together cooperatively.

Building Relationships with Students and Families

In the first chapter we talked about the necessity of building relationships with students in order to teach effectively. Using the model of the bridge, we said that even if the bridge links the students and the content, it would be of no use unless the student trusts the teacher enough to cross the bridge. Similarly, the most carefully planned management system will be ineffective without positive personal relationships with students. Glasser (2000) put it succinctly, "Successful teaching is based on strong relationships"(p. 1).

Many of the practices described in this section help foster positive relationships—treating students with respect, giving them choices, and planning instruction that acknowledges their individuality. It is also necessary to take the time to make sure each student realizes that you value him or her as an individual by asking about the student's dog, concert, athletic performance, or some other personal interest. One popular high school teacher selects five or six students per class to connect with in this fashion. By the end of the week, each student has received his or her personal attention. It is challenging to get to know each student individually, but it is worth it.

One of the most powerful tools in building relationships with students is to get to know their families. Frequent communication with the home—particularly about positive things—can provide important opportunities for sharing. Some teachers make a special effort to call home whenever a student does something particularly well. Others set up a system in which they contact one family per night, just to touch base and see how things are going. A brief phone conversation can help build relationships with both the student and important family members.

Team Building and Learning Life Skills

The final component necessary for building a classroom community is teambuilding, where teachers plan activities specifically designed to promote a cooperative, inclusive classroom atmosphere. They also will teach values, attitudes, and skills that promote community and real-world success. These might include initiative, perseverance, organization, patience, curiosity, and caring (Kovalik, 2000). Sapon-Shevin (1999) describes strategies that help students know each other well, set mutual goals, be honest with one another, and work together. These include the use of literature, songs, and class activities. Choosing a class name can build group identity. Activities designed to help students practice effective listening or helping strategies also build classroom community.

The Responsive Classroom Model (Horsch, Chen, & Nelson, 1999; Wood, 1999) brings these components together in an effort to establish classroom communities. The model is built around seven beliefs.

1. The social curriculum is as important as the academic curriculum.
2. How students learn is as important as what students learn. Students need both student-directed and teacher-directed experiences as well as opportunities for choice and discovery.
3. The greatest cognitive growth occurs through social interaction.
4. Students need a set of social skills in order to be successful academically and socially. These skills form the acronym *CARES*: cooperation, assertion, responsibility, empathy, and self-control.
5. It is important to know the students we teach and the content we teach.
6. It is just as important to know the parents of the students we teach as knowing the students.
7. Teachers and administrators must model the social and academic skills that they wish to teach their students. (Wood, 1999)

Many of the elements of the Responsive Classroom model probably sound familiar to you, since they echo basic principles of this text: active learning, understanding students, and the importance of relationships in teaching. Basic elements used in implementing the model include classroom meetings, rules with logical consequences, classroom organization designed to maximize students' independence, academic choice, assessment and reporting to parents, and guided discovery. Guided discovery is an inductive model that uses open-ended questions to help students think about ways to use materials and implement procedures that will work best for everyone. If you are interested in more details on this model, you may want to review the website listed at the end of this chapter.

SECTION 3. USEFUL INSIGHTS FROM RESEARCH

Section 3 Objectives

After you have completed the activities in this section, you will be able to

1. explain contemporary research principles related to
   a.   establishing classroom rules and routines,
   b.   behaviors of effective classroom managers,
   c.   preventing classroom disruption, and
   d.   saving instructional time;
2. develop classroom rules and routines that are consistent with sound principles of classroom management; and
3. develop and refine your own philosophy of classroom management.

Whatever management philosophy or system you espouse, it is helpful to examine research regarding well-managed classrooms. One of the most important findings is related to "**proactive classroom management.**" In the most productive classrooms studied, teachers spent considerable time during the first weeks of school to "teach" students the systems and rules of the classroom; this was a proactive (preventive) rather than a reactive strategy. More detail on proactive classroom management is provided at the beginning of Chapter 12. The following other strategies have emerged from classroom research regarding management practices.

Research on Classroom Routines

Some teachers are more effective classroom managers than others, in part because of their development and use of effective classroom routines. The following recommendations have been gathered from a number of research reports. They are presented in two groups—a general list and a list specific to the beginning of the school year. As you read them, think about how each contributes to some of the classrooms you have experienced.

General Guidelines

1. Greet students on entry to your classroom—meet them at the door, give a pat on the shoulder, shake hands, and/or smile. Use your educational philosophy to guide you in developing a greeting style, and be consistent and regular in using it.

2. Begin your class promptly with a mental exercise (e.g., "bell work" or "starter activity"). This exercise may be a review of a homework assignment, a response to something on the chalkboard, or a discussion by pairs of some issue. During this time, you may take attendance, deal with an individual student, or monitor the students. Be prepared to actively engage students' minds each day as soon as they enter your classroom.

3. Take time to communicate your objective(s) and purpose(s) for each lesson. Attentive, focused students are less likely to be disruptive. Active involvement of students and a variety of activities during lessons also help to maintain students' attention.

4. Rely on established rules and routines during lessons. Among these are signals for attention, responding to teacher questions, appropriate behavior while someone is speaking, rules for movement in the room, guidelines for working in pairs or small groups, and so on. The more complex the behaviors, the more time you will need to teach and reinforce them. For example, working at multiple centers or in cooperative groups are complex behaviors. In most classes you will need to build toward those activities over time, introducing one skill at a time.

5. Give directions *once*. Begin preparing students in the first week to listen carefully. They will learn to listen after two or three days of practice.

6. Clarify student behavior at independent work stations, computers, or centers. Include issues related to availability and scheduling, use of resources, and potential problems.

7. Make sure students know which legitimate activities they may pursue when their work has been completed. For example, reading appropriate materials or writing in a journal may be long-term assignments.

8. Establish a routine for ending class. Students should understand the routines for closing, cleanup, storage of supplies and equipment, and dismissal.

9. Develop routines for interruptions. Students should be taught what to do if they or the teacher are interrupted. Most students are willing to help develop a list of appropriate activities or behaviors. Let them discuss ideas for staying on task during interruptions. Crossword puzzles, brainteasers, and word searches may be developed for such purposes.

10. Teach students routines for emergencies. Schools should work with law enforcement agencies to establish routines for major safety emergencies. Be sure to learn these procedures and review them regularly. Fire, hurricane, and tornado warnings are not the only emergencies. Be prepared to handle other emergencies, such as possession of weapons, fights, or someone in danger. Help students know what is expected of them during those times. It is important to be mindful of the different needs in various types of emergencies. For example, in a fire emergency the goal is to evacuate the building as quickly as possible. However, if an intruder enters the building with a gun, many law enforcement agencies would prefer that classes remain in locked rooms until the entire situation can be secured. Exiting prematurely could add danger. Consult with your building and district officials to determine what is recommended for your school.

During the *first week or two of classes* the knowledge students gain from your proactive orientation activities may be more important than the academic content you teach. The first impression students have of you will determine, to a great extent, the way they respond to you throughout the year. Recall our discussion earlier about the importance of establishing a set for each lesson. The classroom management set you create during the first week of class is even more critical to your success as a teacher. To make this management set a supportive one, extend your proactive orientation activities across a full week or two.

Guidelines for Beginning the School Year

You will make several important decisions prior to starting the school year. General planning ahead for management, setting a tone, being aware of your first impressions, and establishing order are some of the areas about which you will make decisions. One popular source of ideas for beginning the school year is *The First Days of School* by Wong and Wong (2001). Their recommendations include the following.

A. Planning
   1. Establish clear management objectives about what you want to happen the first day and thereafter. Pay particular attention to the first 15 minutes of class. Anticipate possible external interruptions and determine, ahead of time, responses that will leave in your students' minds the impression that their teacher is businesslike and nice.
B. Setting the Tone
   1. Make sure that your meeting and greeting of students leaves them with a warm and expectant feeling.
   2. Introduce humor into your orientation activities and remarks.
   3. Be authentic. Do not play Dr. Jekyll and Mr. Hyde with the sensitivities of students. Introduce them on the first day of class to the teacher you plan to be for the entire year. Contrary to common belief, there is no need to refrain from smiling until December. Be firm and friendly from the beginning (Johns, Macnaughton, & Karabinus, 1989, p. 6).
   4. Expose students to a repertoire of reinforcers the first week. Joke, smile, touch, praise, encourage, compliment, use names, incorporate student ideas, and make positive references to the school and the community.
C. Developing Awareness of Students
   1. While you try to make a positive impression on students, be equally conscious that you do not develop a negative impression of any students during this first week. Remember that some students will attempt to impress you, others will be fearful, and still others may have had some external experience that will negatively affect their behavior.
   2. Develop an awareness of individual students during this first week. You may pre-assess key knowledge and skills you hope they already possess and attempt to fill in any significant gaps. Try to establish a climate that meets their physical and psychological safety and security needs.

D. Establishing an Orderly Environment
   1. Make sure that on the first day you discuss seating arrangements and classroom routines. If you have planned start-up activities for each day, describe and demonstrate them. It is very beneficial to have students practice all procedures and to provide feedback throughout the first weeks of school.
   2. Introduce the rules during the first three days of class. Students may participate in creating the rules in your room. Be certain they understand the purpose of these rules, by allowing discussions and clarification where necessary. It is your responsibility to enforce rules and to see to it that they are focused on learning tasks. Teach the rules each day during the first week at both the knowledge and the higher cognitive levels of learning.
   3. Establish a sense of order by keeping your class together in a large group for the first few days. Allow students to develop a sense of community and to know that you are securely in charge before you break into small-group activities. When you do, teach and discuss the rules and routines for small-group work. Give plenty of feedback, both positive and corrective as necessary.
   4. Implement initial activities that require a high level of student participation. Such activities should be simple, interesting, and pleasant and should guarantee that all students will achieve a high degree of success.
   5. Prepare smooth transitions from one activity to the next. This is a time when a classroom routine can be especially helpful. Teaching a classroom procedure by explaining, demonstrating, and rehearsing it greatly reduces transition time. For example, you may teach students how to get quiet when you raise your hand and say, "Give me five." You would practice this and time students each day until the response is quick and automatic.
   6. Plan activities to soak up "dead time" at the beginning and end of class and during transition periods. These activities, often referred to as "sponges," add instructional time and reduce the opportunities for disruption. They should be easy, pleasurable, and related to valued learning. Brainteasers, writing in journals, board work, and puzzles are some commonly used sponge activities.

All these guidelines should be acted on during the first weeks of school. Begin in the first hours, and continue through the following weeks. Reinforce your rules, routines, and expectations throughout the remainder of the year.

Preventing Classroom Disruptions

In the late 1960s and early 1970s Jacob Kounin (1970) received a grant from the National Institute of Mental Health to undertake several studies of teachers' skills in preventing discipline problems. Based on his study of elementary, high school, and college classrooms, he introduced valuable concepts and terms into the discipline literature. Among the most useful four are *overlapping*, *group alerting*, *with-it-ness*, and *smoothness and momentum*. A fifth concept, *low-profile interventions*, was contributed by Fred Jones' research (1988).

Overlapping

Overlapping is the teacher's ability to attend to more than one event or activity at the same time. Assume the teacher is working with an individual or a small group and a disruption occurs elsewhere in the classroom. The teacher who is able to handle both events without becoming sidetracked is effectively overlapping. For example, an earth science teacher discussing mountain formations with one group becomes aware of loud chattering and off-task behaviors among the group working on rock formations. The teacher poses a question to the group with whom he or she is working and leaves them to find an answer while he or she gets the rock formation group back on task. Two minutes later the teacher can return to the mountain group to discuss the question posed before leaving them.

 REFLECTING ON THE IDEAS

Observe a skilled classroom teacher. Note the number of times the teacher attends to multiple needs simultaneously. Begin now to practice attending to multiple areas of the classroom simultaneously. It can be helpful to observe a classroom in pairs. Afterwards, discuss what you saw. Consider whether there were areas of the classroom of which you were less aware.

Group Alerting

Group alerting is the technique of keeping students' attention when they have yet to be called on to respond. A helpful group alerting strategy is to use wait time—to ask the question, pause, remind all students to prepare a response, and only then select a student to respond. Thus you ensure that all students will consider the question since they may be selected. Beware of first naming the student to whom a question will be asked or having a predictable pattern of questioning (alphabetical or by row and seat). This allows students to mentally check out of class discussions.

With-it-ness

With-it-ness is the extent to which the teacher demonstrates an awareness of student behavior in all situations and in all sectors of the classroom. Students believe that teachers who possess with-it-ness have eyes in the back of their heads. With-it-ness can be measured by the number of times the teacher identifies disruptive behavior as compared with the actual number of times it occurs.

Smoothness and Momentum

Smoothness and momentum measure how easily the teacher moves from one activity to the next without interrupting the instructional flow and student attention. *Overdwelling* is one threat to smoothness and momentum and occurs when the teacher badgers or nags the students about an issue, especially one that is irrelevant to the lesson at hand. It is essential for the teacher to maintain movement, activity, and attention toward a specific goal.

Low-Profile Interventions

Fred Jones (1988) observed hundreds of classrooms and concluded that about 50% of the available instructional time in the classroom was lost because of disruptive behavior. He developed the following low-profile strategies (among others) to reduce student disruption.

Jones advocates the use of eye contact, facial expressions, gestures, and a take-control appearance to communicate the message that the classroom is a place for work. These *low-control* or *low-profile methods* have been identified by other researchers as highly effective in preventing disruptions and loss of instructional time. For example, the teacher's *physical proximity* is an effective technique in classroom management. Thus it is recommended that teachers move frequently throughout the classroom.

Jones also examined the way time was allocated in helping students. He reported that teachers believed that they were spending an average of one to two minutes with each student who needed help when, in actuality, they spent an average of four minutes with each student. Consequently, Jones counseled teachers to be more conscious of the way they distributed time to individuals and the group and to be more equitable in that distribution.

One technique for achieving Jones' goal is called *praise, prompt, and leave* (Jones, 1988). First, the teacher approaches the student needing help and praises what the student has done independently: "Oh, good! You've got the first problem correct." Then the teacher prompts the student to make another try by giving a hint or a suggestion: "Number 2 is just like the one on page 16. Try it and I'll be back to check in a minute." The leave step is obvious; the teacher leaves as the student makes another independent attempt. The student has not been reinforced for helplessness by several minutes of undivided teacher attention, but has been reinforced for independent work and will receive a second praise, prompt, and leave when the teacher returns in a few moments.

CHAPTER SUMMARY

Since the 1970s classroom discipline has been identified as one of the most serious problems facing the public schools. Classroom management can be a formidable challenge for teachers during their beginning years in the profession. The first section of this chapter focused on the behavior management and humanistic discipline philosophies. Strategies of each were presented to provide guidance in using them in the classroom. The classroom community must have rules and routines in order to run smoothly. Insights about classroom management from the work of contemporary researchers can help the teacher begin the school year effectively and prevent disruptions.

If this array of approaches to classroom management seems confusing right now, understand the words of teacher Lynn Ayers (1998). In the first chapter we identified relationships among teachers and students as the heart of the instructional process. Likewise, those relationships are key to developing a productive classroom community.

> My motivation has always been very clear to my students: I want to help them learn. If the kids know I am motivated by a concern for them, they will help me teach a camel to swim, if necessary. The key (with controlling behavior) is that the kids have to know the teacher really cares about them and is implementing a behavior system, no matter how dumb or how well researched it might be, in order to provide a classroom atmosphere that will be in the best interest of the kids themselves. As long as the kids know that, I think any system can work.

Chapter 12 will present a rational approach to classroom management.

Practice Activity B

Classroom Observation

Observe a middle or high school classroom and make note of the use of as many classroom management strategies as possible. See if you can label any of them using the theories, guidelines, and research presented in this chapter.

Unit Preparation

By now you should have completed the first draft of your unit plan and be ready for revisions. Try to read through your lessons as if you had never seen them before; imagine that all the content is new to you. Think about the questions you would ask, where ideas might be confusing, and where you could make connections. One of the important skills for planning is the ability to view the world from another perspective—that of a student who does not already know the material you are teaching.

Consider whether ideas build logically and think about whether you have provided students with ample opportunities to work with key concepts. Pay particular attention to your culminating activity/assessment, and be sure you have used a variety of lesson types to appeal to varied learning styles. Check that your directions and criteria are clear and that you have provided students with the experiences they will need to succeed. You may want to have a colleague review your materials and give you feedback. As a final note, the formatting necessary to put your unit into final form will take longer than you think, so be sure to allow yourself plenty of time before the due date for final preparations.

Portfolio Activity

Create your own discipline philosophy, one that best reflects your personality and beliefs. Consider the traditions from which classroom management philosophies emerge, your own experiences as a student, and your goals as a teacher. Be conscious of the extent to which these traditions influence your philosophy about student behavior.

Write your philosophy carefully, understanding that you will one day be called upon to explain it to parents and administrators. Be concise and clear, keeping the philosophy to a paragraph or two. You may wish to discuss your philosophy with a peer or a group. This philosophy statement should be included in your professional portfolio.

Search the Web

You may want to read more about specific approaches to classroom management. You can find information on Love and Logic at loveandlogic.com and the Responsive Classroom approach at www.responsiveclassroom.org. You can also get details on Susan Kovalik's Likeskills in the ITI Overview found at www.kovalik.com.

REFERENCES

Albert, L. (2002). *Cooperative discipline resources.* Circles Pines, MN: American Guidance Service.

Amabile, T. M. (1996). *Creativity in context: Update to the social psychology of creativity.* Boulder, CO: Westview.

Amabile, T.M., DeJong, W., & Lepper, M. (1976). Effects of external imposed deadlines on subsequent intrinsic motivation. *Journal of Personality and Social Psychology, 34,* 92–98.

Ayers, L. (1998), Personal Communication.

Canter, L. (1989). Assertive discipline: More than names on the board and marbles in a jar. *Phi Delta Kappan, 17*(2), 37–40.

Canter, L., & Shank, M. (1992). *Assertive discipline: Secondary workbook.* Seal Beach, CA: Canter & Associates.

Collins, M.A. & Amabile, T. M. (1999). Motivation and creativity. In R. J. Sternberg (Ed.), *Handbook of creativity* (pp. 297–312). New York: Cambridge University Press.

Curwin, R. & Mendler, A. (1999). *Discipline with dignity.* Alexandria, VA: Association for Supervision and Curriculum Development.

Deci, E. (1971). Effects of externally mediated rewards on intrinsic motivation. *Journal of Personality and Social Psychology, 28,* 105–115.

Delpit, L. (1995). *Other People's Students.* New York: The New Press.

Dreikurs, R., Grunwald, B., & Pepper, F. (1982). *Maintaining sanity in the classroom.* New York: Harper & Row.

Fay, J. & Funk, D. (1995). *Teaching with love and logic.* Golden, CO: Love and Logic Press.

Ginott, H. G. (1972). *Teacher and Student: A book for parents and teachers.* New York: Macmillan.

Glasser, W. (1969). *Schools without failure.* New York: Harper & Row.

Glasser, W. (1992). *Quality schools.* New York: Harper Collins.

Glasser, W. (1998a). *Quality school teacher.* New York: Harper Collins.

Glasser, W. (1998b). *Control theory in action.* NewYork: Harper Collins.

Glasser, W. (2000). *Reality therapy in action.* New York: Harper Collins.

Glickman, C. (1998). *Revolutionizing America's schools.* San Francisco: Jossey-Bass.

Horsch, P., Chen, I., & Nelson, D. (2000). Rules and rituals: Tools for creating a respectful, caring, learning community. *Phi Delta Kappan, 8*(3), 223–227.

Isaksen, S.G., Dorval, K.B., & Treffinger, D.J. (2000). *Creative approaches to problem solving* (2nd Ed.). Dubuque, IA: Kendall/Hunt.

Johns, F. A., MacNaughton, R., & Karabinus, N. G. (1989). *School discipline guidebook.* Boston: Allyn and Bacon.

Jones, F. (1988). *Positive classroom discipline.* Santa Cruz, CA: Fred Jones and Associates.

Kohn, A. (December 1994). The Risks of Rewards. *Eric Digest*, EDO-PS-94-14.

Kohn, A. (1996). *Beyond discipline: From compliance to cooperation.* Alexandria, VA: Association for Supervision and Curriculum Development.

Kounin, J. (1970). *Discipline and group management in the classroom.* New York: Holt, Rinehart, & Winston.

Kovalik, S. (2000). ITI Overview[on-line]. Available: http: www. Kovalik.com

Lepper, M., & Greene, D. (1975). Turning play into work: Effects of adult surveillance and extrinsic rewards on students' intrinsic motivation. *Journal of Personality and Social Psychology, 31,* 479–486.

Levin, D. E. (1994). *Teaching young students in violent times: Building a peaceable classroom.* Cambridge, MA: Educators for Social Responsibility.

Prutzman, P., Burger, M.L., Bodenhamer, G., & Stern, L. (1988). *The friendly classroom for a small planet: Student' creative response to conflict program.* Wayne, NJ: Avery Publishing.

Rose, R. C., & Gallup, A. M. (2002). The 34th annual Phi Delta Kappa/Gallup Poll of the public's attitudes toward the public schools. *Phi Delta Kappan, 82*(1), 41–57.

Sapon-Shevin, M. (1999). *Because we can change the world.* Boston: Allyn & Bacon.

Southern Poverty Law Center. (2001). *Responding to hate at school.* www.splcenter.org/teachingtolerance/tt-index.html. Retrieved April, 2003.

Treffinger, D. J. (1995). Creative problem solving: Overview and educational implications. *Educational Psychology Review, 7,* 301–312.

Treffinger, D.J., Isaksen, S. G., & Dorval, K.B. (2000). *Creative problem solving: An introduction* (3rd Ed.). Waco, TX: Prufrock Press.

Wood, C. (1999). *Time to teach, time to learn: Changing the pace of school.* Greenfield, MA: Northeast Foundation for Children.

Wong, H., & Wong, R. (2001). *The first days of school.* Sunnyvale, CA: Harry K. Wong Publications.

A Rational Approach to Classroom Management

OVERVIEW

Chapter 11 examined two traditions from which classroom management philosophies emerge: behavior management and humanistic/developmental. The two approaches can be viewed as stages on a continuum from external control to self-management. You were asked to create a discipline philosophy that reflects your personality, beliefs, and values. This emerging philosophy—probably a blend of elements taken from more than one tradition—will be a powerful influence on your teaching decisions.

This chapter describes the Rational Approach to Practical School Discipline (RAPSD), which was developed by one of the authors (Gardner, 1989). Section 1 focuses on what the teacher can do to prevent disruption. Section 2 emphasizes responses to disruptive students. Finally, Section 3 provides a menu of techniques that can be used by the successful rational manager.

Opening Activity

Based on your knowledge from reading Chapter 11, evaluate Mrs. Henry's responses in the following incident:

> Leesha is a student in Mrs. Henry's ninth-grade room. In mid-November Mrs. Henry was 10 minutes into a lesson on reading graphs when Leesha began playing with Tanya's hair. Mrs. Henry said, "Leesha! Pay attention to the explanation being given, dear." Leesha turned her face to the teacher but continued to play with Tanya's hair. Mrs. Henry continued, "I'm waiting." At this point, Leesha let go of Tanya's hair, Mrs. Henry resumed her explanation, and Leesha began playing with Gerald's jacket. While looking at the teacher in what seemed like a very attentive manner, Leesha continued to play with Gerald's jacket. After about 6 minutes she initiated a tug of war with Cori over a pencil. Mrs. Henry then told Leesha, "Watch it."

How would a behaviorist evaluate Mrs. Henry's handling of Leesha's behavior? How would a humanist evaluate Mrs. Henry's responses?

What philosophy would you use in handling this behavior? Why would you take that approach?

Rational Philosophy of Classroom Discipline: An Overview

The rational philosophy is eclectic in that management decisions are guided by sound behavioral and humanistic psychology. The rational manager takes from the behavior management tradition an emphasis on consequences following positive or negative behavior. The rational manager also believes that the teacher's needs must be met, but not at the expense of the student. External reinforcers are used to emphasize that the student has a choice to behave well and avoid punishment or to behave inappropriately and be punished.

Similarly, the rational philosophy includes some elements from the humanistic tradition. Constructive expression of students' wants and desires is supported, responsibility is highlighted, anxiety is reduced, and shared authority and a warm environment are advocated. Although in this system teachers are responsible for selecting and enforcing rules and consequences, they are encouraged to involve students in the management of the classroom.

In the rational philosophy the emphasis is on the classroom as a society in which teacher and students learn to work together to develop a more cooperative and just community (Hoover & Kindsvatter, 1997). The laws that govern how teachers manage must be considered and taken seriously. Teachers must make informed decisions about student behavior. Responsibility to the community is of great importance in the rationalist approach to management. The rational classroom manager educates students to be accountable for the standards of behavior in the classroom. This attitude, when held by both teacher and students, works effectively to create a disciplined environment.

Because of the sense of mutual respect built on a belief that all students have equal rights and responsibilities, the rational philosophy can be more responsive to students' cultural, ethnic, and social backgrounds (Hernandez, 1995). At the same time, the teacher must be true to the essential management structure that ensures each student a safe, orderly, and cordial classroom environment.

Rational Approach to Practical School Discipline: Its Structure

The **Rational Approach to Practical School Discipline** (RAPSD) program, an eclectic blend of behavior management and humanistic ideas, was developed by Trevor Gardner (1989) at Eastern Michigan University. It exemplifies the rational philosophical approach and has two essential elements:

1. It is proactive. This means:
   a. both the teacher's and students' needs are considered before classroom rules and consequences are established;
   b. the physical organization of the classroom is planned to maximize learning and minimize disruption; and
   c. understandable, reasonable, enforceable rules, classroom routines, and desirable social behaviors are specifically taught through a discipline curriculum.
2. It includes a system for responding to classroom misbehavior. This system:
   a. uses Dreikurs' classification system of misbehavior to evaluate the causes of misbehavior,
   b. establishes an information system to record student misbehavior,
   c. uses quality circles to confront disruptive behaviors and disruptive students,
   d. gives students some decision-making power in the class,
   e. implements the positive moments strategy with pattern-disruptive students, and
   f. develops a set of procedures in preparation for classroom emergencies.

SECTION 1. PROACTIVE STRATEGIES TO PREVENT CLASSROOM DISRUPTIONS

Section 1 Objectives

After you have completed this section, you will be able to:

1. describe the rational approach to classroom management;
2. discuss and defend student behavior management decisions based on a rational integration of philosophy, attitudes, behavior types, and classroom management techniques; and
3. design a plan for the physical arrangement of your classroom to optimize your classroom goals and objectives.

The rational manager believes that the management of classroom discipline is divided into two equally important stages. Unfortunately, many teachers spend too much of their creative thinking on the second phase—being reactive to disruptive student behavior. What will I do if Joanna speaks out in class without permission? How will I respond if Paula threatens my authority in front of the entire class? Should I send Mike to the principal's office if he misbehaves again tomorrow? All of these questions are important. However, teachers would gain greater benefits if they were more proactive—understanding teacher and student needs, organizing the classroom to promote learning and prevent disruption, and establishing a discipline curriculum to teach classroom rules, routines, and consequences before disruption occurs.

Teacher and Student Needs

Keith knocked his pencil on the back of the chair in front of him. It was the fourth time Mrs. Ronberg had to tell him to stop in the last 35 minutes. When he was not hitting the pencil, he was pulling someone's hair, throwing spitballs, flying airplanes, or talking without stopping until she reprimanded him for his behavior. Even when he stopped after she spoke to him, he was back at it within 5 minutes. "How does one deal with those irritating behaviors?" Mrs. Ronberg asks.

Keith's behaviors express a need. As a teacher, you should spend a significant part of your planning time assessing and predicting student needs as a way to prevent disruptive behaviors and maintain effective management. If you view student misbehavior as the result of a misplaced attempt to fulfill a need, you are more likely to be effective in channeling or changing the behavior. There are many theories of need and its relation to human motivation. Perhaps the best known is the hierarchical arrangement of needs as developed by Abraham H. Maslow (1954). Maslow conceived of five levels of need at the bottom:

Level 5, Self-fulfillment Needs: Attainment of your full potential, being all that you can be
Level 4, Self-Esteem Needs: Reputation, recognition as a valuable and important person, being your own person
Level 3, Love/Belonging Needs: Acceptance by others, friendship, love
Level 2, Safety/Security Needs: Protection from physical and psychological threats and attacks
Level 1, Physical Needs: The most basic and obvious needs: oxygen, water, food, sleep, sex

It requires little imagination to create a scenario in which a student's misbehavior could be the result of unfulfilled needs at level 1 (hunger), level 3 (peer pressure), level 4 (drive to achieve academic recognition), and so on. Note the close correlation with the needs highlighted by Glasser in chapter 11: survival, love, power, fun, and freedom.

The teacher's needs are also important to consider in classroom management. The emphasis on the teacher's needs by Canter and Canter (1976) was a significant addition to the literature on classroom management (see Chapter 11). When asked by the Canters what teachers want from students, teachers responded with need statements, such as "I don't want hassles from the boys who are troublemakers" (level 2) and "I want them to be good citizens and have positive attitudes" (level 4).

Consideration of the teacher's needs must be balanced by a concern for the needs of students. Failure to balance these two legitimate needs may result in teacher behaviors that encourage rather than prevent disruptive student behaviors. Gartrell

(1987) emphasized this very point in his critical review of Canter's *assertive discipline program*. Gartrell believes that students are controlled but do not learn *self-control* if the teacher follows the principles espoused by Canter. The students' sense of responsibility may be neglected in an effort to satisfy the teacher's need to control student actions.

Glasser's (1998, 2000) approach appears to strike the appropriate balance. Although teachers are not responsible for fulfilling every need of their students, a major part of their job is creating learning experiences that do fulfill some important student needs while at the same time producing the desired learning. In such environments, students have some decision-making power, so they begin to learn self-control and self-regulation.

Classroom Arrangement

The classroom arrangement can either facilitate or hamper various types of class activities. For example, desks in immovable rows make cooperative learning more difficult. The physical arrangement of the classroom also has a significant impact on the way teachers manage and the way students behave. Student desks, the teacher's desk, computers and multimedia equipment, bookshelves, cabinets, learning centers, and other materials and tools must be arranged to maximize instructional results and effective management.

From a management perspective, the primary guidelines for good room arrangements are visibility, proximity, accessibility, and safety (Emmer & Evertson 2002). Although there is no one right way to arrange classroom furniture, equipment, and materials, these guidelines provide a foundation on which an effective design can be constructed:

1. Students should be easily visible from all areas of the room. (visibility)
2. The teacher must be able, without difficulty, to move close to each student during instruction. (proximity)
3. Frequently used instructional materials and supplies should be kept within easy access. (accessibility)
4. Students should be able to see and hear instructional presentations, demonstrations, and displays. (accessibility/visibility)
5. High-traffic areas—for example, around pencil sharpeners—should be free from congestion. (accessibility)
6. Arrangement of furniture, centers, and equipment should be designed to facilitate safety in case of emergency situations—fire, accidents, fights, and so on. (safety)

The traditional seating arrangement of five rows of six seats, shown as A in Figure 12.1, has at least two disadvantages. First, it affords too little opportunity for eye contact (visibility). An observation of more than 500 teachers documented that in the traditional pattern most of the teacher's attention is directed to the students inside the boxed area. Students outside the boxed area tend to be ignored and are likely to become

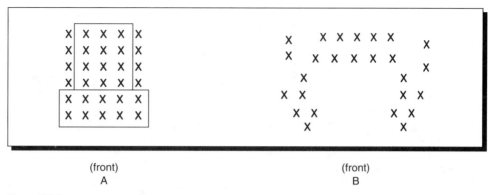

Figure 12.1 Alternative Student Seating Patterns
From *Teaching as Decision Making: Successful Practices for the Elementary Teacher* (3rd Ed.) (p. 375), by A.J. Starko, et al., 2003, Upper Saddle River, NJ: Merrill/Prentice Hall. Copyright 2003 by Pearson Education, Inc. Reprinted with permission.

disruptive. Teachers may compensate for this fact by circulating often among students during instruction. However, during whole-class direct teaching (especially when teaching at the board, overhead, or computer) it is difficult, if not impossible, to be mobile. A second disadvantage is that it is difficult to get close to students (proximity) when you have to pick your way through rows of desks and chairs. Of course, the arrangement has instructional disadvantages as well, as it provides little flexibility for varied instructional spaces.

Because of the disadvantages of the traditional pattern, you will wish to consider alternatives. Some teachers of older students recommend a semicircular or horseshoe pattern, such as B in Figure 12.1. They find that they can maintain eye contact and move quickly and easily among students. Other teachers recommend a rectangle with one end open for teacher access, or some recommend groups of four or five students at desks or table clusters. In planning seating arrangements, consider areas for class meetings, centers, storage, and passageways for students to move from one area to another. In a room with multiple instructional areas you may find it helpful to watch the ways students use your room and adjust the arrangement to suit the flow of student traffic. Check any classroom arrangement you select for visibility, proximity, accessibility, and safety.

CHECK YOUR UNDERSTANDING

Keith is your busy eighth-grader. He is constantly moving in your class and always ready to start a conversation or examine the activities of other students. Although his behavior is not seriously disruptive, it is annoying. He is especially active when he believes that you cannot see him. How can you use your room arrangement to help solve this problem?

The location of the students' desks is a key concern in planning a room arrangement. The teacher's desk should be strategically placed to facilitate the teacher's management style and philosophy. In order to offer any instruction while seated at the teacher's desk, it should be placed so that students can gain easy access and the teacher has visible control over the entire class. If you plan to be up and about most of the time, place your desk in an area where you will spend much of your time and be close to routinely used materials. When contemplating a room arrangement for support furniture, equipment, and materials, consider where to place the following:

1. learning resources—charts, maps, books, models, artifacts, and so forth
2. bookcases
3. overhead projector
4. other audiovisual equipment
5. teacher supplies
6. classroom materials (paper, textbooks, etc.)
7. computer(s)

When planning the location of instructional tools and materials, make sure each decision is consistent with the guidelines of visibility, proximity, accessibility, and safety. After that, consider the aesthetics of the placement.

Remember that the room arrangement is likely to affect student responses. Some teachers suggest that cluttered rooms may lead students to value disorder and to submit messy work.

Teaching a Discipline Curriculum

Several studies have shown that a teacher's failure to adequately explain, teach, and enforce management rules and routines often leads to nonproductive student behaviors such as confusion, incomplete assignments, disruption, frustration, and lower academic achievement (Emmer & Evertson, 2002). You may wish to review the processes for developing classroom rules and routines, together with the illustrative examples presented in Chapter 11.

The most important rules and routines should enhance a young person's skills as a participant in small and large social groups. Johnson and Johnson (1995) argued that the development of social skills leads directly to the building of personal relationships (see also Kelly, 1982). They asserted that the fostering of such skills is critical for students, since they are learning how to get along with others. The degree to which students accept themselves is a significant predictor of the likely strength of their relationships with others. As Matson and Ollendick (1988) stated: "A person's ability to get along with others and to engage in prosocial behaviors determines popularity among peers and with teachers, parents and other significant adults" (p. 1).

A curriculum for teaching acceptable social behavior should consist of two units: (1) the teaching of classroom rules of conduct and routines, with an appreciation of the reasons for rules, limits, and consequences, and (2) the development of social skills that lead to supportive social relationships among students and thus to a more productive classroom atmosphere.

Teaching Classroom Rules of Conduct

In teaching rules in a classroom following the RAPSD philosophy, follow the seven basic steps presented below. These steps also can be used to teach classroom routines such as passing and collecting materials, classroom start-up activities, and end-of-class routines.

1. Have three to five rules that cover the essential behavior management needs of your class. (The students may participate in developing the rules, but it is your responsibility as the teacher to decide what are the rules.)
2. Present and explain the rules and consequences to your students on the first days of school.
3. Be sure that your students understand these rules and consequences so that they can explain them in their own words by the second day.
4. By the third day, provide simulated situations that allow your students to practice appropriate behaviors. Give ample positive and corrective feedback.
5. Continue this practice and feedback until the behaviors and routines are well established. This may take one to three weeks.
6. Post the rules in a very visible place.
7. Periodically review and practice the rules to reemphasize their importance and value in the environment.

For example, if you want to teach your students to sit quietly during independent work, begin by explaining and modeling the desired behavior. Then check students' understanding of the rule by giving examples and asking them to label appropriate behavior (sitting, feet on floor, eyes on work) and inappropriate behavior (standing, crowding around the teacher's desk, talking to a neighbor). Or, you could use the same processes to teach students to ask two friends for help with directions before approaching the teacher. Have your students practice during an independent activity while you carefully monitor and give positive or corrective feedback, perhaps applying rewards or negative consequences later in the week. Before each independent activity, ask the students to state appropriate and inappropriate behaviors. Continue to monitor behavior and give feedback and consequences. By the end of a week or two, students will have learned how to behave during independent work, and less monitoring will be necessary.

Teaching Social Skills

While one unit of the discipline curriculum focuses on social rules, the second unit emphasizes social skills that help students enhance and strengthen their self-concepts and thus their standing in social groups (Lee, Pulvino, & Perrone, 1998). For example, students should be taught how to avoid being the perennial victim of the class aggressor.

To illustrate, consider the following incident:

SARAH: John, you're big, fat, and ugly. (the aggressor)
JOHN: I'm not! (potential victim)
SARAH: Yes, you are! You're as big as a truck.

JOHN: I'm going to tell the teacher. You're calling me names.

SARAH: (gets a parting shot) You're a crybaby, too.

John runs to the teacher and reports Sarah's behavior. Too often the teacher will respond by moving immediately to discipline Sarah. A scenario like this is played out in some classrooms every day. In a rational classroom, however, the pattern is broken, not just by making it clear that bullying will not be accepted, but also by coaching students to be assertive, poised, and confident in responding to bullies and their verbal taunts. For example, John can learn two simple sentences to use in response to Sarah on subsequent occasions:

SARAH: John, you're big, fat, and ugly. (the aggressor)

JOHN: When you say that, it hurts my feelings. (potential victim)

After that response, most aggressors feel embarrassed and slink away. However, a few will be so hurtful that they may go on to say:

SARAH: That was the whole idea. You *are* big, fat, and ugly.

JOHN: Then you succeeded in hurting me.

SARAH: What?

JOHN: I am hurt. You're successful.

Most aggressors will apologize and never repeat the performance. Strategies that help students deal with difficult social situations facilitate individual development and promote a more positive classroom environment.

The teacher's responsibility is to help students learn assertive responses that build confidence and the willpower to confront a bully. Your knowledge about individual students will guide you in shaping the counsel you give to the student who is being victimized. In all cases inform the victim that a helping adult will not always be ready and available; stress that self-help is the best solution. The goal is for every student to feel responsible for the social environment in the classroom. One technique for achieving cooperation is to teach students how to discourage their peers from undesirable behaviors through conflict management. Other social skills might include being supportive, sharing feelings, listening actively, and participating constructively in a group.

Students do not usually learn these skills on their own. They will need explicit training through a social skills curriculum. This curriculum may be designed specifically for young students with social behavior deficits or for all students. The skills should be taught at the beginning of the year and reinforced periodically throughout the year. Role-playing, simulations, cooperative learning, classroom meetings, direct lessons, and inductive lessons are all appropriate for teaching these crucial social skills.

Practice Activity A

Designing Your Own Classroom

Practice Point

As a new teacher in your school, you have been assigned an eleventh-grade class with 23 students in a room 25 by 30 feet. Design two room arrangements and organize the furniture and space as you would in the week preceding your first day of school. One design should reflect a room with the basics—desks, chairs, bulletin boards, and so on. The second design should include everything you ever wanted in your classroom. Compare and contrast your designs with others in your class.

Practice Activity B
Teaching a Social Rule or Skill

Practice Point

Select a rule or social skill appropriate for a class you might teach. Design a lesson to introduce and model the desired behavior. Make sure that students practice it and receive feedback. Indicate how and when you will follow up to continue teaching the rule or skill.

Practice Activity C
Evaluating Classroom Arrangements

Practice Point

Visit two teachers' classrooms and evaluate the layout of the rooms on the basis of the four guidelines of successful room arrangement. If it is useful and the teachers are willing, discuss your conclusions with them. Write a brief report to share with your class for discussion. Be prepared to learn from the teachers; if their rooms are not consistent with the guidelines, there may be extenuating circumstances.

SECTION 2. RESPONDING TO DISRUPTION AND THE PATTERN-DISRUPTIVE STUDENT
Dreikurs' Classification System of Misbehavior
Section 2 Objectives

After you have completed this section, you will be able to:

1. analyze examples of student and teacher behaviors and using Rudolf Dreikurs' misbehavior classification system;
2. select proactive elements and techniques that are consistent with your classroom philosophy and teaching style; and
3. select management elements and techniques that deal effectively with pattern disruption and disrupters.

In spite of your best efforts to prevent disruptive behavior by developing effective classroom rules, routines, and lessons, students will misbehave. Students who misbehave repeatedly and often are sometimes referred to as pattern disrupters. Before deciding how to respond to a pattern of disruption, you need to analyze why all students misbehave. One of the best known theories of student misbehavior is that of Rudolf Dreikurs (Dreikurs, Grunwald, & Pepper, 1982). Dreikurs characterized students' misbehavior according to the goal being sought: attention seeking, power seeking, revenge seeking, or sympathy seeking. The student may or may not be conscious of the reason for the misbehavior. However, it is clear that the goals reflect mistaken efforts to fulfill Maslow's level 3 (love/belonging) needs or level 4 (self-esteem) needs. An excellent resource for more information on Dreikurs' system is *Cooperative Discipline Resources* (Albert, 1996/2002).

Attention Seeking

As social beings, students share a need to belong and to be accepted by others. Students who lack social skills or who have developed patterns of antisocial behavior still seek to be accepted by their peers. Such students may rise frequently to sharpen a pencil, poke other students, or engage in a myriad of distracting activities. They may ask repeated questions or may blurt out answers during oral exercises—both legitimate answers and silly ones. Recognition from the class and the teacher reinforces the belief that the attention seeker is an acknowledged member of the group, albeit one who is recognized for the wrong reasons.

A student engaging in these behaviors legitimately needs attention. However, the teacher should decide the time and the circumstances for giving that attention. Gather enough information to determine the frequency of the inappropriate behavior. When you judge that it occurs often enough to be considered a pattern disruption, decide how and when you will give attention. For example, students who like to talk may be given the opportunity to present information to the class, read a story, or take part in a lesson demonstration. Allowing students to gain attention within the structure of class activities can lessen the need to be disruptive.

Power Seeking

Power seeking is a more desperate attempt on the part of the student to be recognized as an important member of the group. The student can see the teacher's authority as a barrier to the goal of achieving power in the classroom. When Joan calls the teacher a name in front of the class, she hopes that her friends will admire her for her courage. Joan wants other students to conclude that she is free to do whatever she wishes in the classroom.

To confront students seeking power, you must know that you are the legitimate authority in the classroom. There is no need to enter a contest that pits you against a student, since it is impossible to "win" a power struggle with a child. Simply engaging in the conflict implies that your authority is in question and that your goal is to prevail. Neither of these is supportive of a classroom atmosphere focused on either learning or community.

Prepare a series of alternatives to an open war of words. Consider ways to use humor to reduce the level of conflict, invite dialogue, give the student an escape route, or postpone immediate action. In any power confrontation, keep cool. When a student attempts to argue after a reprimand by saying, "I wasn't doing anything. You're always picking on me," don't argue the point. Merely repeat your request ("Please get to work") each time the student attempts to argue. This repetition of your expectation, sometimes referred to as the broken record technique, does not allow the student to pull you into a power struggle. Some authorities suggest taking deep breaths and saying to yourself, "I'm in charge here" before saying anything to a power seeker. Your calmness and dignity let the class know that the problem is being handled with care and respect. Most students do not relish a fight with a teacher. When given an opportunity to avoid one, they will gladly take it.

Unlike other disrupters, most students seeking power seem to be able to do the classwork. You can use this advantage to find ways to give them legitimate status and prominence. The classroom offers many status-enhancing opportunities—for instance, to be discussion leaders, run errands, interview important adults, direct role-playing activities, distribute classroom papers and materials, monitor other students during field trips, and so forth. Students who are granted such opportunities will usually work to preserve the teacher's authority. Although power seekers are typically better than average academically, sometimes less able students exhibit power-seeking characteristics. They, too, can benefit from most of the same leadership opportunities.

Revenge Seeking

A struggle for power with the teacher may result in the student's losing face in the eyes of peers. Or struggle for recognition or other events outside the classroom can result in anger toward adults or authorities in general. In response, the student may turn to ridicule, taunts, and physical attacks in an attempt to hurt and humiliate the teacher. For example, a student many taunt you with the charge that "You can't even spell right" or ask, "Who sold you that ugly tie?" Respond with humor ("Gee, you're right; my dad has bad taste!") and a willingness to work on the problem. Students seeking revenge expect you to get flustered and defensive. Shock them by not indulging this expectation!

Treat this type of student behavior thoughtfully. Instead of giving vent to your first reaction, demonstrate instead that you understand and care: "John, that comment is not like you. Is there anything I can do to help?" Such a response is more likely to prevent further attacks and to help you understand and help the student. It is better to step outside the traditional role of teacher and let the revenge-seeking student see you as a humane person. Most belligerence in a student requires greater understanding from the teacher. Find out what things interest the student and initiate a conversation. Take every opportunity to build a relationship with the student; positive attention reduces the urge for revenge.

Sympathy Seeking

Barbara spends most of her class time daydreaming. It makes no difference whether the activity is direct instruction or group work. Ivan's most common statements are, "I can't do it," "It's too hard," "I don't understand," or "Will you show me how?" Kezia is satisfied with a D in spelling. She boasts, "My daddy is a worse speller, but we have a house, two cars, and a boat."

Sympathy-seeking students will indulge in one or all of the behaviors illustrated in these examples. They have given up hope that the teacher or their parents will help them. They have given up on themselves, too. They know that you, the teacher, cannot force them to do anything. Yet they depend on you. When students whine or complain, there is a tendency to leave them alone. However, you must recognize their behavior as a display of passive resistance, defiance, and personal defeat. Students engaged in sympathy-seeking behavior should be told in clear and precise terms what is expected of them. They must experience success at the initial levels of performance; nothing is more powerful in changing their lowered self-concepts than success in reaching expectations.

In Chapter 11 you were introduced to a strategy called praise, prompt, and leave (Jones, 1988). The first step is to praise something the student has done independently: "Good, Mary. You've gotten the problem copied." Asking, "What's the trouble?" only reinforces the student's sense of inadequacy. The next step is to prompt the student's attempt to solve the problem by giving a hint or providing direction: "OK, now look on page 68. It helps you with this part." Finally, the teacher leaves, saying, "Try that on your own, and I'll be back to check in five minutes." By praising, prompting, and leaving, the teacher does not rescue Mary and thus does not reinforce her helplessness. Rather, Mary is praised for her efforts and nudged to try to solve it on her own—a lesson in self-sufficiency.

Table 12.1 displays Dreikurs' four classes of misbehavior, the beliefs that support each misbehavior, an example of a student behavior associated with each type, a typical teacher response, and a constructive action guide. To analyze misbehaviors, you must (1) describe the pattern of student misbehavior, (2) classify the behavior into one of the four types, (3) examine your own feelings, and (4) select your response.

CHECK YOUR UNDERSTANDING

Reread the set activity in Chapter 11, in which three teachers—Ken, Sandy, and Marilyn—discussed the misbehavior pattern exhibited by Kevann. Based on your knowledge of Dreikurs' classification system of misbehaviors, answer the following questions:

1. What was the pattern of misbehaviors exhibited by Kevann?
2. Into which type of misbehavior does the pattern best fit?
3. How did the teacher's pattern of responses support your conclusion?
4. Suggest some constructive actions that Ken might have implemented.

If you concluded that Kevann was seeking attention, you are correct. First, look at his misbehavior pattern. He initiates a behavior, stops when the teacher commands him to do so, but repeats the behavior or a similar behavior minutes later. Next the teacher's response indicates annoyance: "I'm at my wit's end," "...disrupting," "...so frustrating." Kevann's behavior has annoyed him beyond composure. The behaviors of both the student and the teacher suggest that the student is seeking attention. Kevann appears to believe that he belongs to the class only when he draws everyone's attention to himself. He is not conscious that his peers are annoyed at his repeated disruptions. He thinks that no one will remember he is there unless he takes some unusual steps to remind them.

As you decide on constructive actions to change his behavior, be certain, first, to document and analyze the pattern of attention-seeking behavior the student exhibits.

TABLE 12.1 *Four Classes of Misbehavior*

Student Behavior Pattern	Student Belief	Teacher Responses	Behavior Type	Constructive Action Guide
Student stops the behavior on teacher command. But soon starts same behavior or another behavior of the same type. Teacher must observe . pattern	Feels that acting out will draw attention of peers or teacher. "I belong only when people are noticing me."	Teacher feels annoyed and frustrated. Wants to coax, guide, and react to student's behavior.	Attention seeking	1. Resist temptation to coax, guide, or overtly react. 2. Code behaviors to ascertain basic pattern. 3. Formalize process to give attention on your own terms. 4. Reinforce possible behaviors. 5. Give noncontingent reinforcement.
Student continues the behavior that the teacher says should stop. May increase intensity of behavior. Seems to ignore teacher although is well aware of command intent.	"I am important and a part of a group only when I control, or when I am proving how strong I can be by standing up to authority."	Teacher feels angry, challenged, provoked, and needs to show who is in charge. Thinks, "I'll show who is boss in this class."	Power seeking	1. Withdraw from the conflict interaction. 2. Provide students with some control. 3. Teach students how to work for and use power constructively. 4. Use students in meaningful ways in the lesson.
Student seeks to hurt teacher or other students physically or verbally. Calls unkind names, tries to ridicule, shows malice, and so on.	"I am worthwhile only when I let others feel fearful of me. I do not expect anyone to like me, so I will not be kind to anyone."	Teacher feels hurt and defensive. Desires to retaliate for self or on behalf of others.	Revenge seeking	1. Do not visibly show hurt. 2. Demonstrate that you care. 3. Be warm and trusting.
Student does not attempt to do work. Always asks for help. Often complains of lack of understanding, although teacher knows student can do the work.	"People will accept me only when they are convinced that I am helpless and unable to do things on my own. My position in the group is enhanced when somebody gets a chance to help me."	Teacher feels despair, discouragement, and helplessness. Will say, "I do not know what else to do with (student)."	Sympathy seeking (display of inadequacy)	1. Make sure the assignment is at the correct level of difficulty for the student. 2. Do not pity, sympathize with, or criticize. 3. Encourage all positive efforts. 4. Do not be mean, but be firm about your expectations.

From *Teaching as Decision Making: Successful Practices for the Elementary Teacher* (3rd Ed.) (p.383), by A.J. Starko, et al., 2003, Upper Saddle River, NJ: Merrill/Prentice Hall. Copyright 2003 by Pearson Education, Inc. Reprinted with permission.

Second, do not include coaxing in your actions, which only reinforces attention seeking. Third, choose an action that ensures Kevann receives some legitimate attention. For example, as indicated in Table 12.1, you may use noncontingent reinforcement. As you will recall from Chapter 11, noncontingent reinforcement is physical or nonverbal attention or other rewards given even though the student has not done anything in particular to earn it. It may be a pat on the back, a smile, or a piece of candy. Positive reinforcement is equally important—an action taken immediately after the student has behaved appropriately. Catch the attention seeker being good whenever possible. In this case, you would give Kevann legitimate attention when he is not deliberately seeking it. (Positive reinforcement and "catch 'em being good" are discussed in Chapter 11.)

Do not assume that your days in the classroom will be taken up analyzing student misbehavior patterns. For the most part, you will worry only about the few students who exhibit frequent and recurring nonproductive behaviors. Distinguish between incidental disruption and patterns of disruption before you select instructional and behavior change strategies. After several class meetings it is usually possible to predict which students exhibit these behaviors. Although there is no magic formula or precise recipe for managing discipline effectively, the approaches presented here can make a significant difference when they are consistently applied.

Establishing an Information System

An accurate information system is a key component of a rational discipline system, after you have determined which student behavior is pattern disruptive. The purpose of such a system is to record the nature and incidence of disruptive behavior so that the teacher can make appropriate responses. The system permits the teacher to plot patterns of disruption on a behavior log and include information such as student's name, description of behavior, place, date and time, and teacher responses. Table 12.2 shows an example of a teacher's behavior log.

With the availability of menu-driven computer spreadsheets, the record keeping, analysis, and retrieval of information can be greatly facilitated. The information in the behavior log helps the teacher detect patterns of student behavior. The identification of these patterns is essential for the teacher to (1) respond appropriately to a pattern-disruptive student and (2) communicate the pattern to the student, parents, and administrators. In any case, the RAPSD teacher acts in a consistent manner in administering consequences, because decisions are based on informed judgment. The teacher makes decisions based on observable patterns of student behaviors.

When a student has demonstrated a pattern of disruption, the RAPSD teacher may decide to place the student in a positive moments program for a defined period of time. In this strategy, the teacher blends ideas and practices from the humanistic and the behavior management traditions. Together with an emphasis on individual student differences and an understanding of the social context, the combination of approaches produces the rational tradition of classroom discipline.

TABLE 12.2 *A Teacher's Behavior Log*

Student's Name	Student's Behavior	Location	Date and Time	Teacher Response
John Doe	1. Moves out of seat and wanders around room while seatwork is in progress	In math class	5/4 9:30 a.m.	Warns John that if the unacceptable behavior continues, he will be consequenced
	2. Calls two students names of which they disapprove	Math period in class	5/10 9:10 a.m.	Points to logical consequences in rules-teaching week and administers consequences—miss 10 minutes of free time
	3. Gets up four times within 30 minutes to sharpen his pencil	In class right after math class	5/20 10:15 a.m.	Administers logical consequences—stay in seat during choice time
	4. Calls Sarah a "rag doll who has no brains"	In class during math	5/30 9:35 a.m.	Administers logical consequences—detention and calls home
	5. Calls the principal a "bag of wind with no direction"	In the hallway between classes	5/30 10:30 a.m.	Administers logical consequences—conference with teacher

From *Teaching as Decision Making: Successful Practices for the Elementary Teacher* (3rd Ed.) (p.385), by A. J. Starko, et al., 2003, Upper Saddle River, NJ: Merrill/Prentice Hall. Copyright 2003 by Pearson Education, Inc. Reprinted with permission.

Use of Positive Moments

The time the teacher devotes to students, individually or in small groups, is related to their motivation for academic excellence and constructive social behaviors. A positive moments strategy is built on an appreciation of the importance of teacher time spent with two groups—pattern disrupters and cooperatives. Pattern disrupters refers to students who indulge in social behaviors that are inappropriate in the school environment. Cooperatives refers to students whose behaviors are desirable and thus promoted in schools.

The **positive moments** approach is translated into a set of techniques that teachers use in the classroom to encourage acceptable behaviors. As you review the techniques, consider how the teacher/student interaction affects both the pattern disrupters and the cooperatives. As a result of the interaction, will the pattern disrupter feel that the teacher "knows me, listens to me, helps me, and protects me"?

The techniques are organized into logical groupings related to equity, feedback, rule enforcement, and courtesy and caring. As you read about these techniques, you may wish to develop measuring skills and tools to evaluate yourself on each of them.

Equity

Equity entails fair time, proximity, distribution of questions, and rephrasing and cuing.

Apportioning Fair Time. Fair time is the equitable apportionment of positive time to all students. Positive time includes comments of agreement or encouragement and expressions of praise and appreciation, Negative time includes critical comments, commands to stop in disrupting the class, requests for justification, or discussion of tasks that do not result in productive learning. Repeated classroom observations have documented that teachers spend more positive time with cooperatives and more negative time with pattern disrupters. Even when more total time is spent with the disrupters, the major portion of the time is negative.

To alter this relationship, teachers should spend at least 15 seconds of positive time each hour with each disruptive student. Use those 15 seconds to comment on something good about the student: Note behavior changes, attendance improvement, pleasant smile, family, favorite sport, favorite subject, and favorite pastime. Though short, fifteen seconds can work miracles in changing student attitudes toward knowledge and constructive social behavior. In about three weeks, the teacher is likely to observe an increase in fair time, as more positive time is added to the equation and there is less need for negative time with the student.

Teacher Proximity.   The results of many studies indicate that, in a typical classroom, there are differential attention patterns. In each case, students nearest the teacher receive more attention than do students in the rear of the classroom or the farthest from the teacher. Students who work at tables get more positive attention if they are in the group of cooperatives. Teachers should consciously spend more time in the proximity of disruptive students. Thus you will want to review your class seating chart to see where pattern disrupters are seated and adjust seating patterns to focus more positive time on these students.

Distributing Classroom Questions.   As you learned in Chapter 4, Bloom developed a taxonomy of cognitive behavior that included six categories, from knowledge through evaluation. The taxonomy may be used to classify classroom questions into two categories: (1) questions that ask only for the recall of information (knowledge and comprehension) and (2) questions that ask students to use the information (application through evaluation).

Just as some teachers distribute questions inequitably among cultural groups (see Chapter 9), questions asked of pattern disrupters can show systematic bias that denies them the opportunity to extend their minds to the thinking level. Teachers have many reasons why they ask the kinds of questions they do of different students, but when students become aware that discrimination exists, they will resent it. To prevent this inequity, teachers should:

· ask for opinions from all students;
· ask questions that requires students to identify relationships among concepts and generalizations and to organize information;
· use inquiry lessons that have no right answers, to help all students think through puzzling phenomena; and
· create a system that uses wait time after a question and ensures a random order of student selection to eliminate systematic bias and increase classroom attention.

The teacher's goal is to distribute low-level and high-level and convergent and divergent questions equally between pattern disrupters and cooperatives as well as between boys and girls, high achievers and low achievers, and among students from all cultural groups. The reasoning is that all students will then have less time to be disruptive.

Rephrasing and Cuing. When a teacher rephrases a question to make it more understandable to a student or cues a student to assist in the search for an appropriate response, the results are usually positive. Teachers have reported that rephrasing and cuing are made available to a greater degree to cooperatives than to pattern disrupters. Teachers typically do less probing for the correct answer when questioning pattern disrupters. Whether teachers fear embarrassing their students or believe that they may have failed to teach the material thoroughly, the result is that those who need help the most receive help the least.

Feedback

Giving Feedback. Feedback can be positive or negative, constructive or destructive. Positive feedback may not always be constructive. In the example "Right, Keith, you are always correct," the positive feedback creates an unrealistic pressure on Keith and puts him above other students, who by implication are not always correct. Conversely, negative feedback may not always be destructive, as in "Lara, it is better for all of us if you wait your turn." In this example, the negative feedback is a signal of disapproval; however, the feedback contains constructive advice.

Each student, including the pattern disrupter, should expect and get as much positive validation and correction as other students. In an ideal classroom environment, the teacher promptly affirms and corrects the behavior of each and every student.

Sensitivity to the Ripple Effect. A response to one student is a response to all students. Kounin (1970), in observations of K–12 and college classrooms, discovered that teacher responses to a single student were perceived by all students as if the teacher were talking to them. When the response was negative, it had a more extended and deeper ripple effect than a positive response. Pattern-disruptive students are particularly sensitive to the way teachers speak to others. They consistently compare the teacher's response to others with the way the teacher speaks to them, and they feel resentment when they see themselves as victims of the differences in the two treatments.

Giving Praise. The teacher must find a reason to praise each student, each day. When praise is given judiciously, one clearly recognizable praise statement for each student each day is sufficient. The total amounts to about 7 1/2 minutes out of each day for a class of 30 (15 seconds of praise for each student). Brophy (1981) has shown that not enough praise is given to the pattern disrupter who responds with a right or helpful answer. Teachers should be sure that every student receives positive recognition. Bear in mind that students get too much unwarranted praise and too little genuine recognition when they deserve it (Sadker & Sadker, 1985). Consider delaying your praise until you can give it genuinely. Other ideas for effective praise come from Brophy (1981, 1998):

- Praise should express appreciation for achievement, effort, and determination.
- Praise should specify the particulars of the accomplishment.
- Praise should highlight students' effort and ability (not luck).
- Praise should use prior work or performance as the context for describing the present accomplishment.
- Praise must excite. Use variety and spontaneity. Give it energy!

- Praise must be specific to the event, not general to the person.
- Private praise may be as effective as—and for some students, more effective than—public praise.

CHECK YOUR UNDERSTANDING

Describe some examples of positive moments equity and feedback techniques that you have seen used in any classroom.

Rule Enforcement

The teacher should enforce the rules by applying various techniques.

Being Consistent. The teacher's consistent behavior in enforcing the classroom rules conveys a message of fairness. Regardless of whether the disruption is a minor or major one, the teacher must respond to it in a consistent manner. Keep in mind these guidelines:

- Similar disruptions call for similar consequences.
- Teachers must use care to enforce all rules for every student.
- Establishing too many rules will reduce consistency.

Observing. A teacher must be observant. Recall the concept of with-it-ness, created by Kounin (1970) and discussed in Chapter 11. Pattern disrupters who perceive that the teacher is observing them at all times are likely to engage in appropriate behavior. Teacher must remain alert to classroom behavior, rhythms, and relationships. A behavior that the teacher may find irritating but that does not affect the learning environment should not be made into an overt issue. Instead, teaching energy is best concentrated on pattern disruptions and clearly unacceptable behaviors in an effort to change them. Teachers should:

- continually scan the room visually, even when working with an individual student;
- observe and respond to patterns of behavior, both negative and positive; and
- demonstrate that they also observe and appreciate effort and appropriate actions.

Using Desists Appropriately. A desist is a verbal or nonverbal command that identifies the behavior causing the disruption and commands the disrupter to stop. Since there are no ideal classrooms, desists will be needed. It is crucial that they be used accurately and equitably. They should signal or verbally indicate what behavior is required at the moment without calling too much attention to the individual student and without stopping the flow of instruction. If there is no response, then the next step in the discipline agreement or code of conduct should be taken.

Courtesy and Caring

Modeling Courtesy. Visitors from other countries, and many U.S. citizens as well, have accused our nation of lacking civility. Considering the public treatment of the aged, the weak, and the poor, it is not surprising that our schools mirror the lack of hospitality and civility. Teachers should look for ways that they can enhance respect in such relationships as parent/child, teacher/student, and student/student. Teachers must model that respect, especially when conversing with a disruptive student, and remember these principles:

- Use courteous words, particularly when dealing with a disruption.
- Show sincerity and an absence of anger in nonverbal expressions (posture and facial expressions).
- Use complimentary verbal and nonverbal expressions. On occasion, because of cultural differences, some nonverbal behaviors may be confusing to some students. However, the true intent will come through if there is congruence with the spoken words.

Exploring Personal Interests. Students have to be convinced that you are interested in them as individuals. The process you use to help pattern disrupters talk about their lives outside the classroom will be invaluable in promoting their cooperation in school. Students feel respected and worthwhile when teachers listen to them and respond to what they say. The personal nature of sharing gives students a sense of importance and belonging, and it permits you to respond as a human being rather than in your role as teacher. Make it a point to:

- find our what you can about students' hobbies and mention them in class at appropriate times;
- ask students to share their experiences;
- give writing assignments that require the integration of personal experiences; and
- show interest in the revelations from pattern disrupters.

Listening. Students who listen learn. Teachers who listen also learn. The art of listening may be one of the teacher's most important assets. Listening is essential for justice, appropriate response, gaining time, and thinking in the classroom. As students talk, the teacher should be sensitive both to what they are saying and to what their words indicate about their feelings and needs.

For example, if Joseph is yelling and speaking abusively to another student, it can be best to let him finish. Extract the essentials from what he said, and respond to those essentials in a constructive manner. If your response is disapproval, take time to make him aware that your disapproval is of his behavior and not of him as a person. It is important that you listen to what is said and demonstrate an understanding that the student is hurting. Remember the following:

- Listen for feelings, needs, and for facts.
- Recognized all on-task contributions.
- If you must interrupt a student who is speaking, acknowledge the interruption.

Touching. Babies in a crib move toward a corner, a doll, a blanket—any object with which they can feel contact. The desire to be physically close to another human being is instinctive in students and in adults. As a teacher, look for the appropriate opportunity to touch a student.

Touch can be a useful management technique in the classroom. A light, friendly touch can dissuade a student from engaging in disruptive behavior. The teacher must be careful, however, when touching a student to make it a brief encounter, to ensure that the student will not see the gesture as a threat. Touching a student's hand or tapping the student on the shoulder or upper arm may be sufficient to gain attention. In case of a violent incident, the firm touch should have immediate and commanding effect.

Some school districts expressly forbid the touching of students. The teacher should know district policies on such matters and adhere to them. For some students, touching may help focus their attention; for others, it may be a bewildering or frightening experience. Therefore, it is essential that both the nature of the situation and the student's likely response guide the teacher's decision.

Be aware that the pattern disrupter is less likely to be touched by adults, in school and at home. You should not touch a student in the midst of an argument or if the student is angry at you. If the student's anger or disruption is directed at someone or something else, approach from the front and try to accompany the touch with eye contact or words that inform the student that it is the teacher who will be touching.

Following are two examples of how touch may be effectively used as a classroom management technique:

1. Ms. Sand has assigned an exercise, but David is reading a motorcycle magazine. She calmly approaches his desk, touches his hand briefly, and then, while facing him, places her hands on his desk and points to the exercise that has been set. She looks him in the eyes for the count of three and leaves.

2. Cindi and Mike are talking excitedly as Mr. Francis gives a dictation. As he continues to dictate, he moves to the desk closest to Mike's and grasps his shoulder gently but firmly. As Mike looks at Mr. Francis, the teacher makes eye contact with Cindi and points to their books. He leaves as quietly as he came. His touching was timed to coincide with the end of a sentence. They will begin to write on the next sentence.

Remember:

- Teachers should touch, but always use it with care.
- A touch may be a pat on the shoulder or a gentle nudge.

Accepting Feelings. One of the most mysterious areas of human behavior is feelings and dealing with them. Goodlad's research reported in *A Place Called School* suggests that many classroom tasks are accomplished in a bland environment "with little emotion, from interpersonal warmth to hostility" (1983, p. 230). To help overcome the sense of emotional sterility, teachers should be alert to ways of generating feelings in students. Teachers who are able to do this mobilize positive feelings among students and possess the skill to control negative feelings. Experience has shown that students, especially pattern disrupters, learn more in classrooms in which teachers are apt to accept, encourage, and validate student feelings.

Implementing Positive Moments: A Summary

The following list summarizes key suggestions involved in the implementation of a positive moments approach in your classroom.

Preparation

1. Select two students with disruptive behavior patterns.
2. Establish a baseline frequency (how many times the misbehavior occurred) for two weeks before implementing your positive moments approach with the two students.

Implementation

1. Every classroom hour, include 15 seconds of positive time with each student.
2. Touch each student three times each week.
3. Administer consequences when one of the students breaks a rule.
4. Praise each student at least once a week.
5. Give feedback about inappropriate behavior. Clearly articulate that the behavior is unacceptable and why. Reinforce acceptable behavior.
6. Stand close to the students in a friendly way at least twice each week.
7. Use quality circle meetings to explore alternatives to disruptive behavior (see the discussion that follows).
8. Place the two students in a visible location at all times.
9. Plan and implement a strategy that will encourage the students to tell you something about themselves.
10. At the end of each week inform the two students that you have been pleased with their improved behavior. Mention three or four specific good things they have done.
11. Call or write to the parents of the two students and tell them something good about each student.
12. Give each student a responsible task each day for the first week and one each week thereafter.

If the First Approach Fails

1. If you do not observe a 30% reduction in disruption in three weeks, establish a contract with the student and shake hands on it.
2. Ask the student, "What rules have you been breaking?" "What have you been doing that breaks these rules?"
3. Ask, "What are your plans for stopping what you have been doing?" (Work toward a goal. Help the student be realistic.)
4. Ask, "How do you plan to reach the goal?" (Work to develop a plan.)
5. Ask, "How long will it take before I see a change?" (Work toward a specific and realistic time period; a shorter time interval is better.)
6. Ask, "How can I help you achieve the goal?" (You may even suggest a way to help.)

7. At the end of the agreed upon period, assess, praise, and/or guide to another contract, reducing or lengthening the time period as necessary. (The goal is one week of nondisruptive behaviors. Be realistic, as this may not happen until the third or fourth week.)

Organizing and Conducting Quality Circle Meetings

A common activity in RAPSD classrooms is the use of meetings called quality circles. Based on Glasser's classroom meetings (See Chapter 11), **quality circles** are used to reinforce personal and group responsibilities, to process the causes of and the alternatives to misbehavior, to recommend changes in past behavior, and to discuss community issues that affect school life. In a quality circle the group helps the disruptive student to acknowledge the behavior and plan ways of reducing the severity and incidence of the behavior.

Public disclosure is excluded during a quality circle. That is, the student whose behavior is being discussed is not publicly identified with the disruption. Rather, the students discuss what they would do if faced with the situation that led to the disruptive behavior. The disruptive student listens to the discussion of the problem, without being referred to in person, and privately or publicly decides what changes will be made. In this approach, the problem, not the person, is the focus.

The seating arrangement should be a closed circle, with the teacher seated as a group member. Although misbehavior should always be discussed in the third person, the issues and concerns can be discussed either in the first person or the third person, depending on individual choice. No names should be used except when giving positive reinforcement. The teacher's role is to be a facilitator. Students should be allowed freedom to initiate issues that they believe are affecting class behavior and performance. In closing a quality circle session, everyone is encouraged to summarize what occurred, but no one is required to speak.

When a case of disruptive behavior is being discussed, the teacher will usually close by asking, "What should be done if circumstances create a similar situation that causes another disruption?" This strategy embedded in a quality circle is called decision therapy. The focus of decision therapy is to have pattern disrupters make decisions about what they will do in the future. The rationale is that each time a pattern disrupter hears or states a positive, constructive action, it reinforces the chances that an appropriate behavior will be selected on future occasions.

Responding to Emergencies

The RAPSD model also recommends that the teacher develop a set of predetermined procedures in the event of a classroom emergency. For example, what will you do if two students begin a fight in the classroom or in the hallway? If a student brings in a toy gun or knife, what action will you take? If a student uses expletives or physical, psychological, or racial slurs to describe you or another student, what will be your response? What will the administration do in any of these emergency cases? Since emergencies are handled in different ways in different schools, you must be prepared for them. Consider four factors when developing an emergency procedure:

1. Personal behavior
   - Be firm and consistent.
   - Develop discipline by putting a series of correct social habits together progressively.
   - Focus your actions on improving your relationship with the disruptive student(s).
2. Incentives
   - Use an incentive system as a first step to prevent emergencies, but incentives should be soon phased out. Students should be taught to find value in a disciplined environment rather than to behave to earn token rewards.
3. Standards
   - Teach students the socially acceptable behavior in your classroom.
   - Be sure that students know what behaviors are unacceptable in your classroom.
   - Do not permit students to avoid responsibility for and the consequences of their actions.
4. Analysis
   - The rational approach emphasizes low- rather than high-control management.
   - Keep Dreikurs' four types of misbehavior in mind as you analyze what the disruptive student did to create the emergency.

What specifically should you do if a fight breaks out in your classroom or nearby on school property? Even when you are at your best, a fight places you in a tense, irrational, and potentially dangerous situation. Expect to make mistakes in judging who started the fight and what proportion of the responsibility each combatant should be assigned. Be cautious in judging. Avoid, if you can, the role of fight arbitrator. Do two things when encountering a student fight.

The first thing to do when encountering a fight is to decide whether it is an individual or a group fight. Individual fights involve only two combatants. Other students may be encouraging the fight, but each of the two combatants represents a social, racial, ethnic, or other subgroup in the class merely by chance. When you investigate, the noncombatants are willing to assign blame to each of the combatants. In the case of an individual fight, stop the fight and then send the two fighters to different corners of the room or to different locations in the school. In some cases, you may need to have the other students leave the room for their own safety. Your school will have procedures for handling fights. Most recommend that a teacher not try to break up a fight alone, and getting help is usually a good idea.

When you have a conference with the two students involved in the fight, try to reconstruct the incident as accurately as possible. You may have each combatant write what happened. Bring the students together and inform them that the only story you wish to hear is the correct sequence of events. Let them tell their version to each other without interruptions. After the facts have surfaced, expose and explore feelings (Lee, Pulvino, & Perrone, 1998). In most cases, the students will agree on what occurred, thus avoiding the necessity for you to be the judge. Avoid identifying a winner and a loser. Even if there is an admission of guilt, let the guilty party leave feeling as if he or she were a winner because you recognized the honest and cooperative behavior.

A group fight can be inferred if (1) three or more students are involved, (2) social, racial, religious, ethnic, or other identifying group epithets are heard, (3) there have been rumors about conflicts between groups, (4) there has been a previous history of group divisiveness, and (5) the atmosphere becomes silent as soon as you attempt to investigate what caused the fight. In the case of a group fight, first make sure students not involved in the fight are safe and anyone needing medical attention receives it. Then, divide the class into the respective groups, and let each group list all the things the other group has done to cause harm. Let each group review the other's lists and correct inaccurate perceptions. Facilitate an open dialogue to restore a community atmosphere and positive attitudes. Have students discuss what should happen if the situation becomes ripe for a repeat fight.

The second and most important thing to do when encountering a fight is to teach students that a fight is the responsibility of both parties. The only excuse for fighting is for the protection of life and limb. A student who is attacked should feel safe in reporting the incident to the teacher and expecting that something appropriate will be done about it.

Practice Activity D

Analyzing Misbehavior Patterns

To assess your understanding and analysis of the characteristics of Dreikurs' misbehavior classification system, read the following cases and:

1. determine the category of misbehavior present in each case,
2. write a response consistent with the recommendations for effective actions on a separate sheet to be shared with colleagues,
3. critique your responses with a peer or with a group, and
4. be aware of the need to recommend practical actions.

Practice Point

Case 1

Miss Gardner feels that Maxine is the most passive and whining student she has ever had in class. Maxine's mottoes are, "I can't do it," "I don't know how," and "Please show me." In the fifth week of the school year Miss Gardner walks into the staff room with her hands in the air and in exasperation announces, "I give up." After a moment she addresses a fellow teacher, "Molly, you had Maxine in class last year. How did she do?" Molly replies, "I suspect the same as she does for you. We did not seem to do well together. I wish you good luck."

Assume that Maxine is in your class. Analyze her behavior and plan a course of action.

Case 2

While Ms. Pettigrew is at the back of the classroom preparing supplies for a science activity, Brian climbs up on his desk. As he jumps from one desk to the other, she says to him, "Brian, you are not supposed to be on the desk." The rest of the conversation goes like this:

BRIAN: I know.

MS. PETTIGREW: Well, come down, now.

BRIAN: I don't want to.

MS. PETTIGREW: But you know it's against the rules for you to damage the desks' surface.

BRIAN: I'm just showing them something.

MS. PETTIGREW: Get down, I said.

BRIAN: I'll get down pretty soon.

MS. PETTIGREW: Listen, young man. . . .

The dialogue continues for two to three minutes while the rest of the class looks on.

If you classified the misbehaviors in Case 1 as sympathy seeking, you were correct. The student's helplessness and the teacher's surrendering behaviors are evidence of a sympathy-seeking child.

Case 2 illustrates a power-seeking incident, because the student continues his inappropriate behavior as he argues with the teacher.

Practice Activity E

Planning for an Emergency

Create a plan of action to use if you find three students fighting in the hall. Use the ideas presented in this section.

SECTION 3. ADDITIONAL MANAGEMENT TECHNIQUES

Section 3 Objectives

After you have completed this section, you will be able to:

1. recognize and incorporate nonverbal management techniques to further develop your ability to manage and discourage classroom disruptions;
2. respond to classroom disruptions with greater confidence;
3. incorporate verbal cues as a management technique;
4. recognize differences among cultures when planning for and implementing a management style; and
5. demonstrate confidence in analyzing and determining responses to classroom discipline situations by providing a rational base for your choices.

The techniques that follow are used by effective managers to maintain order in the classroom. The rational management approach recommends and uses all of them.

Consider which ones are most consistent with your discipline philosophy and give you the most confidence as a classroom manager.

Nonverbal Classroom Management Techniques

The teacher continuously communicates in every classroom through verbal and nonverbal messages. These messages—conscious or unconscious, purposeful or inadvertent—prevent, help, control, or encourage discipline problems. The following represents a sample of the nonverbal management techniques organized within each of the major sources of nonverbal messages.

Attire

Significant data exists from the business world, observers of fashions, and social science literature to substantiate the effect of dress on people's behavior. Thus it is not surprising that the way teachers dress affects the responses of their students and helps set the tone for classroom control. As a teacher, your dress communicates your attitude toward order, neatness, and appropriateness of behavior for different settings. It conveys a message about your feelings toward societal standards. The community in which you teach has determined acceptable dress standards for teachers. Do not be enslaved by these standards, but do respect them. Your attire should be professionally appropriate for each occasion: gym, science class, picnic, and so on. If your choice of dress is of the stiff-collar-and-tie fashion, the hidden message may be one of an exacting and uptight individual—a headmaster or headmistress with little room for understanding. Sloppy clothes, on the other hand, may indicate sloppy attitudes toward students, academics, or order in general.

Dress as the professional person you are. Be conscious of the image you want to project. Of course, a professional image in a first grade classroom can be very different from one in a bank or office building. A sweater with a teddy bear motif or alphabet socks may not be appropriate for many business meetings, but they could convey positive and appropriate messages to students. Clothing goals of the rational manager should be modesty, professionalism and appropriateness.

Eye Contact

Eye contact may be the most potent nonverbal management technique available to the teacher. Teachers who develop the skill of periodically surveying their room usually control marginal problems by that means alone. An eye survey may be slow and deliberate with no specific student as a target, or it may be swift and certain in order to jog memories that the teacher is still there and in charge.

Eye contact with an individual says something different from eye contact with a group. The situation and severity of the behavioral problem will dictate the method of eye contact that you use. Look at the individual or visually roam around the group so it is obvious who is the target. Communicate expressions of approval and disapproval with brief flashes of eye contact. A look must always be purposeful, certain, and

Good Communication Is Essential for Effective Classroom Management.

timed—not so quick that the student loses the impact, and not so slow that the student believes you are deliberately trying to cause embarrassment. Practice using your eyes as a discipline technique.

Facial Expressions

Intentional or unintentional facial expressions make a difference in the way students respond to the teacher's management. Teachers should use facial expressions appropriately in an effort to prevent discipline problems or to maintain an air befitting the classroom situation. Facial expressions can indicate concern or anger in order to give students the opportunity to change their behavior before the teacher must resort to verbal cues (spoken anger, for instance). Anger may be demonstrated by slanting the brows inward and downward, close to the eyes, with the lips firm. The knitted brow can express concern rather than anger. The stern look—taut cheek, downturned corners of the mouth—can mean there is no room for tolerance. Be careful not to use mocking smirks—students are quick to note these—unless they are intended in good humor and the students clearly understand that. Smiles can be a powerful means for showing approval and can be much more personal than verbal cues, particularly in some cultures. It can be both a help and a time-saver to use nonverbal rather than verbal cues and to make requests with a smile.

Movement

A teacher must be at ease in the physical setting of the classroom. Teachers should move in a manner that is purposeful, deliberate, and self-confident (Zirpoli & Melloy, 1997). Too often, teachers' movements are unrehearsed, haphazard, or thoughtless. Such movements can have disruptive effects on the classroom environment. For example, when the teacher gets involved with students or materials right after giving directions, many students will continue to visit.

Control of movement as a form of nonverbal communication is an important aspect of the disciplinary encounter. Fast attack-like motions in response to minor offenses can result in much more severe behavior if a student becomes defensive. A teacher has to quickly appraise the problem and decide on its potential to erupt into something more serious. This decision will dictate the urgency with which the teacher moves and the subtlety or the obtrusiveness of the movements.

Most classroom situations are not emergencies. Thus, do not overreact to the particular circumstances or students. Finally, do not turn away from the class for a long period of time, as this may indicate lack of communication and invite talking or other behavior that is irrelevant to the lesson.

Hands

The appropriate use of your hands is a highly effective management technique. Hand messages can be as precise as verbal messages. Hands can point out a particular student, draw attention, signal silence, and so on. For example, after Mr. Roshaw established eye contact with the three girls in the back row, his hand pointed at Cindy and his index finger signaled a "no" to cue her to stop stuffing paper down Todd's shirt. The gesture communicated to Cindy the teacher's disapproval of a potentially disruptive behavior without interrupting the class. Cindy quickly stopped, to avoid drawing negative attention to herself.

Finally, do not be tempted to use hands to maintain control in a threatening fashion, as the hands may elicit a physical reaction.

Posture

The teacher's posture affects classroom management as much as—sometimes more than—the posture of students. Standing tall (straight posture) during the execution of a discipline procedure may suggest command or superiority. On the other hand, slouched shoulders may indicate defeat and hopelessness and lead to challenge by some students or to fear by those who feel that the teacher is not in control.

The examples that follow illustrate some effects that posture may have on management success:

- Leaning over students to supervise their work or social behavior is more threatening than stooping.
- Moderately slow, deliberate steps, with upright frame and a businesslike facial expression indicate that the teacher is in command.

If your authority is challenged by a student exhibiting a defiant posture, do not back down. After you have given a reasonable direction, move close enough so that you are about two long steps away. Look directly at the student, and repeat your command slowly. Maintain a comfortable stance, wait, and maintain eye contact. If and when the student breaks eye contact, acknowledge the response and return to the lesson. If a student does not break eye contact, calmly ask to speak with the student in private after class and resume teaching.

 ## REFLECTING ON THE IDEAS

Assess yourself on each of the six nonverbal techniques. Which one(s) do you need to improve?

	OK	Needs Work	Not Sure
Attire			
Eye contact			
Facial expression			
Movement			
Use hands			
Posture			

Verbal Cues in Management Techniques

As nonverbal techniques may be called the silent treatment, verbal cues may be thought of as the audible treatment. Verbal cues may consist of complete sentences, phrases, exclamations, grunts, or laughter. The sensitivity of the teacher toward the student and toward the situation will dictate what verbal response is selected. Verbal cues stand as good a chance of being misinterpreted as nonverbal cues. Quite unconsciously, a teacher may use a word that is loaded—culturally, sexually, or racially. Care in the choice of verbal cues is especially crucial at the beginning of the term, because the students and the teacher do not know each other.

When properly used, verbal expressions can open doors of communication. What a teacher says, how it is said, when it is said, and to whom it is said are all significant elements in a verbal management technique.

Voice

The teacher's ability to manipulate the voice is an essential skill in controlling a classroom. Through tone and volume, voice communicates meaning during an interaction, particularly in a stressful disciplinary situation. The tone and volume of the voice can create, increase, or lessen stress.

Teachers must enunciate clearly. When commands are given, they should be brief and specific. "John, please be quiet." Sharp, short phrases may be sufficient for reprimands or for attracting students' attention. You may calmly say to students who are talking: "Trevor, Marge." The voice should reflect calm and assurance. Pause long enough for them to regain composure, and then proceed with the lesson. Speak distinctly, in a pleasant, friendly voice. Students will listen more attentively and be more likely to ask questions spontaneously if the sound effects are pleasant and harmonious. Tape-recording a few lessons and listening to the tapes can reveal poor speech habits, such as lack of tone variation or too many "uhs."

The teacher who yells is likely to find that students will yell back. If the teacher yells, "John! Be quiet!" the student is likely to shout back, "I'm not talking!" or "OK!" or "I'm not making any noise!" or "What for?" In such a situation no matter what is said, the result may be anger, a threat, defensiveness, or a contest for power. The teacher's tone often sets the atmosphere for the student's response.

Feelings such as disapproval, annoyance, and anger should be carefully expressed with appropriate voice tone and volume. Know your students. Some are very sensitive, whereas others do not appear to be bothered. Some students are just beginning to experiment with the expression of their own feelings. Others have had disapproval expressed to them in a destructive manner all their lives. Teachers must learn to recognize these feelings in students' voices and modulate their own voices accordingly.

Content and Control

The content of verbal communication can become the essence of a teacher's management technique. The message should not be focused on personal approval but on task accomplishment. Instead of saying, "I don't like it when you keep rapping on the desk," the teacher might say, "We will never learn how to do equations if the noise continues" or "It is more difficult for us to understand equations with the continuous rapping." A statement like the first example can be used, but it depends on the relationship of teacher and students for its effect. The latter two examples are task-oriented, and students respond more appropriately to such messages.

Verbal commands such as "Hey, stop that!" have minimal effect in controlling a situation. To maximize the effect of a command, the teacher should be sure that it helps the student involved and the other students who are aware of the situation. Give a clear message: "Mike, stop playing with that car, and start writing your essay." When teachers increase the clarity of verbal desist messages, students are less likely to become disruptive.

Coercive threats are bad management techniques. For example, some teachers often say things such as, "If you do that again, I'll deal with you" or "If you don't stop, you will see what happens." The use of threats will not lessen the chance that the disruption will be repeated. In fact, it may encourage such behavior. The credible use of a threat should more appropriately be called a warning. For example, you might say: "John, this is the third time you have shouted without reason in this class. When you choose to do that again, you will miss your free time." Leave it right there. Do not wait for a response, but continue the academic task at hand.

The teacher's message should be delivered with firmness. You are more likely to achieve control if you use a businesslike tone of voice, walk closer to the disrupter, or continue to look at him or her as you go on with the lesson. These actions, when judiciously undertaken, convey to the students the professional quality of your teaching. To quickly lose control of the class, say, "I wish you people would pay attention." Instead, your message should have power. "You have to learn how to identify the sources on these websites so you are not fooled by someone with a particular bias, so let's stick to it." Such a statement demonstrates power accompanied by respect and expectations. Power is in the implication that the teacher has information to give. Respect and high expectations enhance power by establishing a relationship between effort and the achievement of a worthwhile goal.

Responding to Student Blockers

"I Didn't Do It." Students commonly use this response. Many teachers unwisely try to use logic to prove to students that they did do what they were accused of doing. That is precisely what the students want the teacher to do. Teachers should resist the temptation to justify a reasonable action each time one is taken. For example, if you are sure that James behaved inappropriately but he denies it, simply administer the logical consequence you normally use. Do not provide an opportunity for the student to lie. Close the dialogue after the first denial with "James, I know you did it. I saw you do it, and you know that such behavior is unacceptable."

"I Didn't Know." In the rational classroom management program, it is unlikely that a student will say, "I didn't know." The teacher would have spent the first weeks of school teaching which behaviors are acceptable and which are not. Therefore, students will have had opportunities to explore both the behavior examples given in class and unfamiliar examples that may emerge later. However, as much as a teacher prepares, a few students generally end up saying, "I didn't know." Your response is to affirm the rule that was broken, in the context in which it was taught. Be calm and professional in the process. You may respond by saying, "Let me remind you of when and how we covered this incident." Administer the consequence that had been agreed upon earlier. In most cases, the student is prepared to accept it. Finish with, "Now that you know, I'm sure we will not have to deal with this again from you," and return to your academic instruction.

"I Wasn't the Only One." Another comment students will make is, "I wasn't the only one doing it. Why are you picking on me?" The teacher should firmly but quietly reply, "Vonda, I'm sorry. You are the only one I saw, so right now I can deal only with you." Administer the logical consequence. Be very careful that you are not being unfair to the student. Some students develop a reputation for being disruptive, and it becomes easy for others (students and teacher) to see them as the disrupter in any situation. Be sure that social and cultural stereotypes are not predisposing you to "pick on" certain students unconsciously. For example, if you believe that students from a particular minority group are usually more disruptive than other students, you may, without being aware of doing so, pick on such students disproportionately. However, if you have examined your motive, your judgment, and your decision, and you are confident that you are being fair and equitable, go ahead and do what you have to do without fear.

"You're a Racist." Students may say, "You're the man," "You are for the man," "You've forgotten your roots," "You yell at us but not at them," and a host of other statements that may be summed up as: "You're a racist" or "You're selling out." Statements like these

are used by both the dominant and the minority student cultures in an effort to make the teacher feel guilty. Teachers of all races often find themselves defending their actions to prove that they are not what they are made out to be (Hernandez, 1995). Some teachers unwisely try to explain how much they have worked for or supported desegregation efforts. You must remember three points in responding to such accusations:

1. The students know you, and if you are racist, nothing you can say at this point will disprove that belief. If you are not racist, they know that and are merely trying to anger you.
2. The students' main objective is for you to feel guilty and begin to defend yourself.
3. When you begin to put up a defense, you are responding to students' manipulation.

Instead of offering an explanation, say, "You know that what you did was unacceptable. The consequences are. . . ." Repeat the statement as many times as you deem necessary as you administer the consequence. Sometimes it is hard to leave it at that; however, it is the most constructive decision you can make at that point. There are some considerations you may want to contemplate as you make decisions that may be affected by the culture of the student.

Cultural Continuity and Discontinuity

As teachers consider students' behavior, it can be useful for them to reflect on the students' culture of origin before making a decision (Hernandez, 1995). This reflection may be by race, but it should not be assumed that a student's race is enough to predict his or her culture. All students enter the school with a culture that is different from the school culture.

For many White students the cultural difference is minimal. They enter a system that looks and behaves like a business, much like life is at home. This cultural continuity quickly provides for them an environment that is less forbidding than it would be for a minority child. Most teachers are White, even in school districts where the population is overwhelmingly minority. The formality and language is reflective of the White population more than it is of any other group. Therefore, White students have far less cultural dissonance than do other students.

In contrast, where the difference is minimal for most White students, it is great for many other students. **Cultural discontinuity** is the difference between the culture of the school and the home according to Ogbu (1992). It is the process through which education as a cultural transmission agent impinges on the normal culture of the student's home and imposes an institutional culture on the child.

Some students accept this imposition as a normal part of education, and others rebel against it. Effective teachers will consider this fact in any analysis of student behavior and design ways to reduce the potential problems inherent in cultural discontinuity. Planning the first week of school is particularly important because that is when the student begins to feel a sense of identity or isolation. During the first week the student must be made to feel that as much is expected of him or her as of all other students in the class. This expectation must be directed to academics as well as social behavior.

Equally true, you must pay attention to the idiosyncratic behaviors that are common in groups. Make a note of such behaviors without typing them as "good" or "bad."

If students do not look you in the eye, avoid the temptation of thinking that they are lying or shy. A student who responds to you with, "Yes, I would prefer not to have you call my parents," is not necessarily attempting to confuse you. Students may only be responding as those in their cultures have been trained to respond, or expressing concern for parents' language skills. You will need to understand the cultures of your students in order to make effective decisions.

Some cultures are more animated than others, but it would be disastrous to decide that because someone is from any one ethnic group they are very passionate. You must get to know your students and respect them for their differences without tolerating unacceptable behaviors. Acceptable behavior does not mean that they behave as you do; rather, it may best be measured in the context of how it prevents or aids learning. The teaching process is a complex web of decisions. Experience progressively reduces the complexity for reflective teachers.

Despite the cultural discontinuity that some students experience in the school setting, you can reduce the negative impact in the way you manage your room. Validate the importance of each member of your class. Find an opportunity to reinforce the value of each culture, either in lectures, discussions, or as model examples. Effective managers are careful to create a family-type atmosphere in their class where students have an opportunity to question without fear and to disagree freely but appropriately.

REFLECTING ON THE IDEAS

In Section 3 nine additional techniques were presented that have been used by rational managers to assist them in responding to disruptive students. Which three or four techniques were the most meaningful to you? Why? Be prepared to share your list with classmates.

CHAPTER SUMMARY

Maintaining an environment conducive to learning is a primary responsibility of the classroom teacher. The rational leader-manager formulates policies to communicate reasonable expectations, disciplinary practices, and consequences—both positive and negative—that create a constructive environment in the classroom. Integrating essential elements from the behavior management and humanistic philosophies into the Rational Approach to Practical School Discipline (RAPSD) results in a proactive position that will earn the respect of students, parents, and administrators. Adopting this approach is the first constructive step of the rational manager.

The second step taken by the rational manger is to build a predictable, comfortable, and secure learning environment in the classroom. To create that environment, teach collective responsibility for managing the classroom, helping peers stay on task, sharing, safety, and respect within the first weeks of school. Furthermore, your prudent integration of rules, routine procedures, and management techniques will promote positive individual and group behaviors. Your efforts to be consistent, to respect the civil rights of students, and to prevent rather than punish will be well received.

However, in spite of your best efforts as an effective discipline manager, conflicts and other disruptive behaviors will occur in your classroom. Your knowledge of the causes of misbehavior, combined with your use of quality circles and positive moments strategies, will enable you to be as rational in response to discipline situations as you are in creating a proactive classroom environment in which many discipline situations fail to develop.

Your understanding of the cultural discontinuity that students experience in the classroom and school community will aid the quality of the decisions you make in responding to student needs and managing social behaviors.

Your decisions about management will create or destroy a safe and productive climate in the classroom. Make those decisions with your best heart and your best skills. Be aware that you will make some mistakes in the process of establishing your management style. Do not despair in such cases, but take Glasser's advice given in Chapter 11: "Never give up."

Practice Activity F

Revising Your Classroom Discipline Philosophy

Practice Point

Examine the discipline philosophy you wrote at the conclusion of Chapter 11. What characteristics of the rational approach to classroom management might you use in revising your philosophy? Think specifically of the proactive elements—teacher and student needs, physical organization of the classroom, use of a discipline curriculum—and the elements in a system to respond to discipline situations (Dreikurs' classification system of misbehavior, an information system, quality circles, positive moments, and procedures for responding to classroom emergencies).

Unit Preparation

By this time you should be fine-tuning your unit. Be sure that you have a complete reference list and a list of necessary materials. See that any handouts or required visual aids have been completed so that the unit is clear to the reader. Check to make sure that after any revisions you still have continuity from your goals and objectives to your lesson plans and your assessment. Use the six principles from Chapter 6 to examine your unit. Trade units with a classmate, and give each other helpful suggestions. Proofread your unit carefully for grammar, spelling, and technical errors. Parents, administrators, and the public expect teachers to have exceptional communication skills. It is essential that you be able to express yourself clearly in grammatically correct Standard English.

If you have the opportunity to teach your unit, it is important to analyze your students' learning. Compare the knowledge your students demonstrated in the preassessment with the knowledge demonstrated at the end of the unit. This will take careful analysis if you have used complex assessment, since some of the knowledge demonstrated will be embedded within larger activities. Compare the achievement of subgroups within your classroom. Do you see equivalent gains for boys and girls or for students of different cultures? How do the gains of high-achieving and low-achieving students differ? After your analysis, consider how the information you gained would affect your next teaching decisions.

Portfolio Activities

If necessary, adapt your management philosophy from Chapter 11. You also may want to create or revise a map of your ideal classroom to take into account management and instructional goals. Talk to experienced teachers, observe a variety of classrooms, and examine a number of texts on management strategies. Practice with friends and colleagues until you can easily discuss the types of management strategies you will use and your rationale for discussing them.

If you had the opportunity to teach your unit, your analysis of student work can make a powerful portfolio activity. Be prepared to discuss how your teaching affected your students' learning and how you can use that information to inform your teaching.

Search the Web

Many general web sites targeted at teachers have sections on classroom management; for example, Education World (http://educationworld.com) and the American Federation of Teachers site (www.aft.org). Use any search engine to see what other links you can find.

REFERENCES

Albert, L. (1996). *Cooperative discipline.* Circle Pines, MN: American Guidance.

Albert, L. (2002). *Cooperative discipline resources.* Circle Pines, MN: American Guidance Service.

Brophy, J. E. (1981). Teacher praise: A functional analysis. *Review of Educational Research, 51,* 5–12.

Brophy, J. E. (1998). *Motivating students to learn.* Boston: McGraw-Hill.

Canter, L., & Canter, M. (1976). *Assertive discipline: A take-charge approach to today's education.* Seal Beach, CA: Canter & Associates.

Dreikurs, R., Grunwald, B., & Pepper, F. (1982). *Maintaining sanity in the classroom.* New York: Harper & Row.

Emmer, E. T., & Evertson, C. M. (2002). *Classroom management for secondary teachers.* Needham Heights, MA: Allyn & Bacon.

Gardner, T. (1989). *Rational approach to school-wide discipline.* Ann Arbor, MI: Pedagogic Press.

Gartrell, D. (1987, January). Assertive discipline: Unhealthy for students and other living things. *Young Students Journal, 42*(2) 10–11.

Glasser, W. G. (1998). *The quality school teacher.* New York: Harper Collins.

Glasser, W. (2000). *Every student can succeed.* San Diego, CA: Black Forest Press.

Goodlad, J. I. (1983). *A place called school.* New York: McGraw-Hill.

Hernandez, H. (1995). *Teaching multicultural classrooms.* Upper Saddle River, NJ: Merrill/Prentice Hall.

Hoover, R. L., & Kindsvatter, R. (1997). *Democratic discipline: Foundation and practice.* Upper Saddle River, NJ: Merrill/Prentice Hall.

Johnson, D. W., & Johnson, R. J. (1995) *Teaching students to be peacemakers* (3rd Ed.). Edina, MN: Interaction Book Company.

Jones, F. (1988). *Positive classroom discipline.* Santa Cruz, CA: Fred Jones and Associates.

Kelly, J. A. (1982). *Social skills training: A practical guide for interventions.* New York: Springer.

Kounin, J. (1970). *Discipline and group management in the classroom.* New York: Holt, Rinehart and Winston.

Lee, J. L., Pulvino, C. J., & Perrone, P. A. (1998). *A guide for managing conflicts in schools.* Upper Saddle River, NJ: Merrill/Prentice Hall.

Maslow, A. H. (1954). *Motivation and personality.* New York: Harper & Row.

Matson, J. L., & Ollendick, T. H. (1988). *Enhancing students' social skills.* Elmsford, NY: Pergamon Press.

Ogbu, J. U. (1992, November). Understanding cultural diversity and learning. *Educational Researcher, 21*(8) 5–15.

Sadker, D., & Sadker, M. (1985). Is the O.K. classroom O.K.? *Phi Delta Kappan, 66*(5), 358–361.

Zirpoli, T. J., & Melloy, K. J. (1997). *Behavior management: Application for teachers and parents.* Upper Saddle River, NJ: Merrill/Prentice Hall.

Afterword

This text has discussed a variety of decisions you will make as a reflective teacher. You will select and analyze instructional goals and objectives, and develop activities based on your knowledge of student needs and child development, the subject matter, pedagogy and learning principles, the political and social context, and your educational philosophy. As you begin your first years of teaching, we hope you will choose to continue your growth as a professional.

GROWING IN YOUR PROFESSIONAL DECISION MAKING

You have the opportunity to begin the process of continuous learning now as you observe teachers in your prestudent teaching or student teaching experiences. Try to enter each situation reflectively. The examples you see in those classrooms will have an enormous impact on the way you teach a class of your own. Watching experienced teachers

can give you a chance to learn the practical ins and outs of teaching. It can help you understand how the instructional techniques and principles in this book can be applied with a variety of students in a variety of situations.

On the other hand, no teacher is perfect, and no two individuals' educational philosophies and values are identical. Don't be afraid to question, to consider alternatives, or even to say to yourself, "This is something I'll do differently in my own class." You may find, in the end, that your view changes and you decide to adopt a technique you had earlier rejected. Likewise, you may decide that just because something works for one teacher does not mean it is the best way for you.

As a teacher, you will want to find ways to examine your own decision making and the effects of your actions on students. A helpful way to improve your teaching may be to keep a journal of your teaching experiences, or you may prefer to discuss your experiences with a trusted colleague. If you do ask another teacher to discuss your teaching with you, choose someone who is competent, positive, and willing to be helpful and who can maintain confidentiality about students.

Peer coaching can be of immense help when you are trying to learn more about teaching. Peer coaching in its simplest form occurs when you visit another teacher's classroom or that teacher visits yours. You may ask the colleague to look for something specific, such as whether you are giving all students attention and response opportunities, or you may just want the teacher to help you examine your entire lesson from a different perspective.

Another way to gather information on your teaching is to make an audiotape or videotape of your lesson or of a particular group of students. The observation forms in Chapter 7 can be useful for analyzing what you see and hear on the tape.

Many teachers have found student questionnaires to be a valuable source of insights. Teachers ask students their impressions of certain activities and classroom events, but student names are not required to be recorded. One simple form is made by having students draw a vertical line down the center of a paper and then listing on the left all the "Pluses" they feel exist in your classroom and teaching and listing on the right all the "Wishes" they feel could make the classroom and teaching better. This provides fascinating reading!

Finally, you may wish to conduct your own study of student learning where you select two or three target students who represent fairly typical teaching challenges. Once a week or so, take examples of these students' work (or behavior) and analyze (preferably with another teacher) the reasons for the students' performance. Then brainstorm ways to improve each student's progress, select some strategies, and test them during the next week or so. Next, collect more work samples, analyze them, select new strategies that might help the student, and test them. Repeat the cycle until you believe you have found a way to help each of your target students. In this way you can build case strategies that work with different kinds of student challenges.

You will find many opportunities for professional growth through workshops offered during student teaching and your first years of teaching. Take advantage of these opportunities for learning new ideas and gaining new perspectives. In such settings you can sit back and reflect on your own practice. You will receive support for change and experimentation, and you will have the comfort of hearing that other teachers struggle with the same issues that puzzle you! As each year of teaching goes by, you will feel more confident, more comfortable with what you are doing, and clearer about your goals and student learning.

Your role as a professional decision maker will continue throughout your career. If you are to learn and grow as an educator, it is important that you gain information that will contribute to your effectiveness in the classroom. Because knowledge about teaching and learning is increasing rapidly, teachers must make an effort to stay current on trends in educational research. Review the research carefully and look for ways to put the new principles and ideas to use in your classroom. The information in this textbook is just a beginning.

Subscribe to professional publications, join educational organizations, and continue to study through graduate and in-service education. As you do so, view the information you learn critically. See how new ideas fit in with tried-and-true principles. Don't be afraid to experiment, to retain ideas you find effective and appropriate, and to reject others. Very few educational trends need to be swallowed in their entirety. Your professional judgment will allow you to choose what is best for your students and what fits your personal philosophy and values.

As you enter your fourth or fifth year of teaching, you may find that you have the inclination to face a larger challenge—pursuing an advanced certificate from the National Board for Professional Teaching Standards (NBPTS). Preparing for National Board certification entails honing and demonstrating your reflective decision-making skills. The process involves the preparation of a portfolio that documents your best teaching and collaborative efforts and your analysis of what made those efforts effective. You would also go through a series of assessment tasks at a centralized location. If you attain this certificate, you will find that the process has greatly enhanced your own sense of professionalism and respect.

THE MOST IMPORTANT DECISION

As you approach the beginning of a career that is focused on the hope of the future, let us consider a few of the ways teaching makes a difference to you and to others.

Teaching will make a difference for you. Good teaching will never be boring. As you have learned, a reflective teacher is surrounded by information, challenges, and puzzles about which to reflect. It is true that some teachers choose to teach the same content the same way year after year, which certainly can become boring. However, teachers who are attuned to the individual differences among students, to new ideas about pedagogy, and interesting ideas from the world around them will find that each day brings fresh challenges.

Sound teaching will bring chances to learn interesting things. Teaching gives you the opportunity to learn more about the content you teach, and it provides the chance to see the content with new eyes. Teaching helps you remember that seeing a butterfly or eating something that has been supplied from across the ocean—or even adding two fractions—can be a strange and wonderful thing. It can inspire you to continue to learn, whether it be about Internet adventures that can link your classroom to far corners of the Earth or local history that can make your neighborhood come to life. Each new bit of information can be doubly interesting as you consider how it will affect the students who share your days.

Most importantly, *teaching makes a difference to the students and to the future.* We teach because we believe our efforts matter. The best curriculum helps young people understand the things we find to be good, true, and ethical. In the sciences we help students see how exciting the natural world can be, balancing new understanding with a sense of wonder. In social studies we help them see the equal wonder of human beings. We teach the ways human beings make decisions based on many factors. As we understand these factors—a moment in history, the forces of geography or economy, the values of a culture—we teach that humans' actions make sense.

Literature and the arts uncover human lives and emotions and begin to explore what is beautiful, what is ethical, what is true. Math is important not just for calculation but for building appreciation of all that is ordered and seeing patterns in myriad aspects of life. Understanding the workings of the world and the people and other living things that populate it can be a source of interest and delight for students and teachers, now and for years into the future. It also prepares students to be contributors to that knowledge, with hope that they can solve the many dilemmas that have puzzled society for decades.

In schools we also teach important values. Although the idea of teaching values can be controversial, the fact of the matter is that every teacher and every classroom teaches values. We teach values through our choice of content, teaching strategies, and interactions with students. As teachers, we play a vital role in helping students understand the world they live in; the heritage they share; and the values, attitudes, and actions we consider important.

In the United States one of our most important roles is to prepare students to function in our democratic society. This involves more than learning American history or the structures of government, although those are important. Preparing students to work in a democracy means helping them to consider issues carefully, make decisions, work together, think about others, and believe that their efforts make a difference. The experiences they have in classroom communities form the patterns by which they understand larger communities and the decisions they make about their roles in them. If our curriculum brings diverse groups of young people together to live and work on a daily basis, it teaches the following lessons about democratic living. People matter. Kindness matters. Prejudice is wrong. Problem solving works. Hard work pays off. Differences are often interesting and good. We can disagree and still work together. We can make a difference in the world. It takes a whole class to make a community.

In the end, what is it like to be a teacher? Teaching, and the young people it brings into your world, will change who you are and how you live your life, in ways from the silly to the profound. For many people it means closets full of egg cartons, feathers, rock samples, and scraps of plastic—just because you never know when you might need some. For others it means being the only adult on the block to wear pumpkin earrings or shoelaces in school colors or never being able to pass a bookstore or sale at an office supply store without looking for something for "your" kids.

Teaching will make you laugh. Whether you are surrounded by the silliness of youngsters or teenagers or the more sophisticated humor of older students, you will have days when humor abounds. It will bring you moments of joy—to watch a student perform an unexpected kindness or observe students find new courage in difficult situations. There will be days when all your planning pays off and students who could not understand before now do understand, and you know you have made a difference. On those days you'll think, "Yes, I am a teacher!"

Teaching also will bring harder days. You will have days when you drag yourself out of bed ill, because it is easier than planning for a substitute. Because you are human, there will be days when your patience runs thin. There will be lessons that fail, fire drills that interrupt you, and paperwork that will drive you crazy. There will be days when teaching breaks your heart, when your students face situations you cannot change. There will be times when your best efforts to help students fail. Yet you still choose to keep trying.

Teaching means being in close touch with the everyday dramas of young lives. It is remembering what it is like to have a best friend—or not have one—to discover the excitement between the covers of a book or to bang the desk in frustration because your pencil won't create the drawing your mind envisions. It is about being there to celebrate a successful recital or a perfect math paper. It is also about being sad together when pets or people die, about being stable when families change, and about being a predictable source of learning and care.

It is a tall order. Teaching is about careful planning, but it is also about unplanned moments and unscripted lessons. When we are with our students, we teach them what it means to be an adult, to be a professional, to be a caring human being.

This book was written to help you become the best teacher possible: an empowered reflective educator capable of making thoughtful and appropriate instructional decisions. No single path exists and no prescription can be given for this goal, but the information, tools, and guidelines provided here will help you begin. The art and science of teaching demands the best of learning, intellect, and decision making, and it requires insight, sensitivity, persistence, humor, patience, stamina, and joy in the process of learning. While the goal may seem daunting, no profession has greater potential to communicate, make change, or touch individual lives. May you similarly touch the lives of your students, as John Steinbeck (1957) wrote of a teacher who touched his life.

Like Captured Fireflies

In her classroom our speculations ranged the world.
She aroused us to book waving discussions.
Every morning we came to her carrying new truths, new facts, new ideas
Cupped and sheltered in our hands like captured fireflies.
When she went away a sadness came over us,
But the light did not go out.
She left her signature upon us
The literature of the teacher who writes on children's minds.
I've had many teachers who taught us soon forgotten things,
But only a few like her who created in me a new thing, a new attitude, a new hunger.
I suppose that to a large extent I am the unsigned manuscript of that teacher.
What deathless power lies in the hands of such a person. *

Many professional organizations can support you in your ongoing efforts to be the best possible reflective teacher. One of the most comprehensive lists available is found at the website of the American Association of Colleges of Teacher Education. Log on to www.aacte.org and follow the link under Other Resources. In addition, read more about the National Board for Professional Teaching Standards at www.nbpts.org.

Appendix

Example Unit:

Zimbabwe: A World's View From Africa

Below we provide an example of a short unit similar to the one you will design for your methods class. Read it carefully and be ready to ask questions in class about the structure of this unit.

Rationale and Key Questions

In this unit we will learn about an African country named Zimbabwe, a mysterious ancient city whose ruins we will explore, and the modern life lived by many people who call Zimbabwe home. Zimbabwe today is the product of the interaction between (1) culture and the physical environment, (2) African identity and European colonialism, and (3) traditional life and modern life. This unit connects concepts such as colonialism, monarchy, authoritarianism, and democracy so that students can easily relate the content to their lives.

Ancient Walls in Zimbabwe

The unit will include opportunities for students to exercise personal choices, develop group work skills, and have individual independence. To connect the unit with their own lives, students will write an original short story about the Shona people (14th century) or King Monomatapa's empire (16th century).

The unit stresses important higher level thinking processes such as analysis, evaluation, and synthesis. The larger goal of teaching students to independently inquire and solve problems also is addressed in this unit; for example, locating materials, taking notes, organizing the content, and presenting it.

The unit focuses on the societal need for greater understanding and appreciation of the racial and cultural diversity in the U.S. Concern is growing over the media accounts of verbal and physical violence toward those who are not members of the "right" group. The unit is designed to dispel the ignorance, misinformation, and stereotypes about Zimbabwe and its past.

The unit is interdisciplinary through the integration of language arts. For example, reading historical fiction will help students imagine the historical period and become empathically involved in the lives of historical figures. Diverse writing activities, such as constructing a newspaper article, creating short stories, and constructing diaries from the perspective of different historical figures, will promote deeper understanding.

A key question to focus students' inquiry is, How do developing countries balance modern and traditional influences?

In addition, they may ask, what would it be like to live in a different time, sometime in the 14th to 16th centuries when kings ruled grand cities?

Concept Map with Generalization(s)
Content Outline. Zimbabwe: A World's View from Africa

    I. Zimbabwe: Its Physical Environment, People, and History
       A. Borders
          1. Landlocked in southern Africa

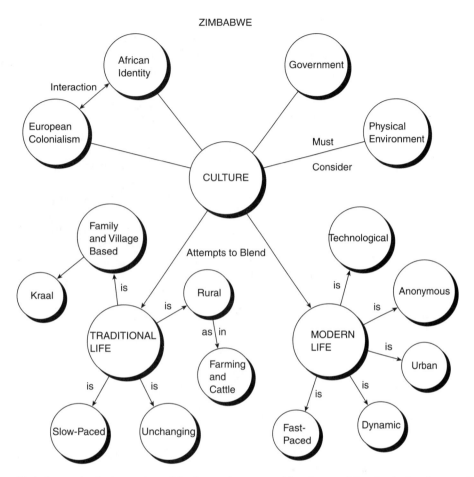

Figure A.1 Zimbabwe Culture Concept Map

2. Physically identifiable borders
   a. Bordered on the north by the substantial flow of the Zambesi River
   b. Bordered on the south by the slowly moving Limpopo River
   c. Bordered on the west by the dry sands of the Kalahari Desert
   d. Bordered on the east by the mountains that separate it from Mozambique and the Indian Ocean

B. Other Interesting Features
   1. The middle and high plateau (veld), which cuts through the center of the country from east to west, is temperate in climate and contains spectacular scenery.

      2. The middle and high plateau provides the setting for most of the urban centers including the two principal cities: Harare (Salisbury), the capital; and Bulawayo, the second most principal town.

      3. The two most often visited tourist attractions are Victoria Falls and the Hwange National Park.

  C. People

      1. The population is over 10 million.

      2. Ninety-six percent are Black.

      3. The largest ethnic group is Shona (Mashona).

      4. The second largest ethnic group is Ndebele (Matabele).

      5. Less than 3% are White.

      6. One percent are Asian and people of mixed races.

  D. History

      1. Zimbabwe ruins point to a well-organized country during the 14th through 16th centuries with a considerable empire.

      2. In the 19th century a branch of the Zulu, the Ndebele, was forced into Zimbabwe from South Africa.

      3. Discovery of gold in southern Africa and ambitions of Cecil Rhodes to see England dominant in the region accelerated settlement by Europeans in the late 19th century.

      4. In 1896 the Matabele and Mashona tribes were conquered by the European settlers. The country was named Rhodesia and divided into Black and White areas.

      5. The struggle for independence resulted in a seven-year civil war followed by a transitional government in 1979.

      6. On April 17, 1980, Zimbabwe became an independent country under Black majority rule.

II. Zimbabwe's Cultural Lifestyles: A Blend of Traditional and Modern Life

  A. Traditional Life

      1. Family and village based (kraal)

      2. Rural, primarily farming and cattle raising

      3. Slow paced, slowly changing

      4. Religion, education, arts

  B. Modern Life

      1. Urban

      2. Fast Paced

      3. Dynamic

      4. Technological

      5. Impersonal

III. Zimbabwe's Government: A Combination of British and American Patterns

  A. Parliament makes laws.

  B. President Robert Mugabe has multiple roles.

      1. Chief executive

      2. Political leader

      3. Head of state

      4. Military leader
      5. Manager
      6. Chief law enforcer
      7. Appoints vice-president and cabinet
  IV. Economy
   V. Current Events
 VI. Problems and promise

Unit Objectives/Outcomes (Aligned with Standards)

Social Studies Content Standards (Michigan Curriculum Framework)

History Standard: All students will reconstruct the past by comparing interpretations written by others from a variety of perspectives and creating narratives from evidence.

> Middle School Benchmark: Analyze interpretations of major events selected from African, Asian, Canadian, European, and Latin American history to reveal the perspectives of the authors.

Economics Standard: All students will describe how government decisions on taxation, spending, public goods, and regulation impact what is produced, how it is produced, and who receives the benefits of production.

> Middle School Benchmark: Use case studies to assess the role of government in the economy.

Geography Standard: All students will describe and explain the causes, consequences, and geographic context of major global issues and events.

> Middle School Benchmark: Explain how elements of physical geography, culture, and history of the region may be influencing current events.

> Public Discourse and Decision Making Standard: Students will engage their peers in constructive conversation about matters of public concern by clarifying issues, considering opposing views, applying democratic values, anticipating consequences, and working towards making decisions.

> Middle School Benchmark: Pose a social studies question about a culture, world region, or international problem.

Unit Objectives: Zimbabwe: A World's View from Africa

When this unit is completed, eighth-grade students will be able to do the following tasks.

Ancient Life

1. When given a list of facts about the people, history, environment, government, resources, and culture of ancient Zimbabwe, identify them on an exam and match each fact with a statement that identifies it. (Social Studies)
2. After reading the African folktale, *Mufaro's Beautiful Daughters*, work in cooperative groups to identify five differences between the narrative and the novel *Outpost of Progress*, by Joseph Conrad. Identify reasons for the differences, and be ready to explain and justify them in a class discussion. (English)
3. Write an original short story or folktale (1,000–2,000 words) that includes a description of life at Great Zimbabwe in the 14th century or in the capital of King Monomatapa's empire at the beginning of the 16th century that accurately reflects the history and culture of the Shona people who lived there at the time. (These will be published for the class to share with other classes.) (Social Studies and English)
4. Graph the population density, area of, and perimeter enclosed by the Great Zimbabwe and modern day Harare in a homework assignment. Label all work and round answers to the nearest whole number. Present work to a classmate. (Math/Technology)
5. Create a scale drawing of Great Zimbabwe and a comparative area of their home town in the form of an archeological site map. Include a legend and description of ten artifacts that are representative of the cultures that lived there. These will be displayed in the school hallways. (Social Studies/Math)
6. Given the facts about Zimbabwe, create a tribal mask from materials provided that reflects at least five of the ideas represented by the facts. (Art)
7. After listening to examples of Ndebele and Shona musical melodies, both from contemporary sources and those from the distant past, show an interest by seeking out more music. (Affective: Music)

Modern Life

(This is a continuation of the unit: The lessons are not included in the Appendix.)

8. Discuss the major events related to the rediscovery of Great Zimbabwe, beginning when the Europeans stumbled upon it for the first time in the late 1860s (Blake, 1977).
9. Define *colonialism* and *racism*.
10. Describe the role of Cecil Rhodes in the English colonization of southern Africa.
11. Analyze the role of the Christian missionary in the colonization of Africa by the Europeans.
12. Compare and contrast different views of the European colonization of southern Africa in the 1800s.
13. Develop an educated guess why the culture that created the city of Great Zimbabwe disappeared.
14. Identify characteristics of contemporary Zimbabwean life that can be traced to African roots and those that can be traced back to European influence.
15. Describe the problems facing modern Zimbabwe today, such as the spread of HIV, poverty, hunger, landlessness, unplanned urbanization, corruption, and lack of democracy.
16. After finding an article in a magazine or newspaper that discusses some event involving racism, write a brief report to be shared with one or more classmates.

The paper must compare and contrast the racism involved in European Imperialism in Africa with present-day examples. The report should be three or more double-spaced typed pages. (Social Studies)

17. Assume you are a critic of the mass media. Prepare a brief (three-page) report that evaluates the appropriateness of media coverage of Africa focusing mostly on hunger, disease, poverty, and corruption.

18. Prepare two radio reports that evaluate the arguments made by advocates and critics of the Zimbabwean government policy of expropriating White-owned farms without compensation.

19. In a brief (no more than 1,000 words) newspaper article that focuses on two Zimbabwean families (one who lives in a remote, rural village and one in Harare), compare and contrast traditional kraal life with life in modern urban Zimbabwe.

20. Value the democratic methods to confront cultural, racial, and economic differences by (a) choosing to participate or read about local political events or (b) initiating conflict resolution strategies in peer relationships. (Affective)

Preassessment
Informal

Students will free-write for 10 minutes about everything that comes to mind about Africa. Then they will work in groups to form lists organized around where, who, when, what, etc. A map will be provided for students to indicate where they think Zimbabwe is located and to share their knowledge about it. The teacher will collect all information and analyze it before finishing the design of the objectives and lessons.

Formal

Students will be given a pretest to see which skills and concepts (derived from the objectives) they already understand. This will include lower level understandings and higher level skills (for example, research skills or classifying skills). Use of information: Those students with extensive knowledge will be distributed through the cooperative groups used for this unit. They also will be offered opportunities for leadership, peer teaching, and special enrichment projects. Students' prior knowledge (accurate or inaccurate) will be used to develop key questions and to revise objectives and culminating project.

Ancient Zimbabwe: Selected Lesson Plans with Differentiation (Adaptations)
Lesson 1: Site Map Investigation (Inductive)

Objective

After examining the site map of Great Zimbabwe (without identifying it as such) and the drawings/photographs of the items found there, students will use higher level thinking (classification and hypothesizing) to answer three questions:

1. Where is this place (continent, present-day country)?

2. When did the people who created the artifacts live? (to the exact year, century, modern time, medieval period, ancient world)
3. From the site map and artifacts, what can we infer about their lives and culture?

Set. The teacher introduces the lesson by calling attention to the site map and the key that identifies the scale and type of surrounding vegetation and sun/shade patterns. The artifacts are described and students are asked to jot down their first hunch about where this place is located.

Objective. The teacher tells students they need to use higher level thinking to discover the answers to three questions. The teacher writes them on the board or overhead. Later projects (masks, stories, etc.) will focus on this unique culture.

Purpose. The teacher tells students it is important to view these people as significant in history, because they built impressive structures and contributed valuable knowledge, as did the Mayans, Egyptians, and Chinese cultures whom they have studied .

Exploratory Activity/Find Patterns/Form Hypotheses. Each individual investigates the site map and artifacts. After five minutes, students are placed in their cooperative groups of four students and asked to share their responses and come to consensus. The teacher circulates around the room to check on progress and answer clarifying and probing questions. A group recorder is selected to report for each group. Students are told that both group consensus and individual majority/minority reports will be accepted. The teacher or a student representative records the answers to the three questions on the board.

Metacognition. The teacher has students discuss the thinking they used to reach their conclusions. The teacher saves the responses for use the next day with Lesson 2, The Lost City of Zimbabwe. The teacher informs the students that they will see an actual photographic journey around the site map. The teacher does not reveal the location, time period, or culture of the people until the next day when they are revealed in the film. (Using/Applying is saved for next day.)

Adaptations. Teacher has struggling students explain their thinking and coach them with another set of data to find patterns. Advanced students can begin to draw images or compose a song about the place they have discovered.

Lesson 2: The Lost City Of Zimbabwe (Direct and Cooperative)

Objective

After viewing The Lost City of Zimbabwe, students will describe five characteristics about the lives of the people who lived there.

Set. The teacher introduces the film by asking a few students to share their hypotheses from yesterday's site map activity of the Great Zimbabwe ruins.

Objective. The teacher tells students they will be asked later to identify five characteristics of life in Great Zimbabwe and evaluate their previous guesses about the location of the ruins and the time period when they were constructed. So they need to look for clues in the film.

Purpose. The teacher reminds students that it is important to view African people in a light that includes them with past cultures they have studied—Mayans, Egyptians, and Chinese—who have also contributed knowledge and impressive structures. The teacher explains how students will use this information to write short stories later.

Input/Modeling. The film is shown and students find 5 to 10 characteristics of everyday life in Great Zimbabwe.

Check for Understanding. Students are divided into their assigned cooperative learning groups and compare their individual guesses from the previous day to the new knowledge generated by the film. The teacher confirms the information.

Guided Practice. In the groups, students coach each other for a Teams-Games-Tournament to be played later. (More guided practice, if needed, may include drawing or making a poem/rap using the key ideas.)

Formative Assessment. The teacher conducts a game in which each member can earn group points. The teacher asks questions, waits for all to think of the answer, and selects an individual to answer, "What have we learned about the builders of Great Zimbabwe?" and "What did we learn about the way Africans were viewed by the 19th century Europeans who came upon the ruins?"

Adaptations. Struggling students receive aid from the teacher or a peer. Advanced students create some questions to use on the board for the Set tomorrow.

Lesson 3: African Folktales (Cooperative Learning)

Objectives

Students will be able to apply the principles and genre style characteristics of the African folktale genre to develop an original folktale concerning a contemporary issue, series of events, or concern.

Students will use encouraging behavior in their groups. (Affective: social skill)

Set. The teacher introduces the activity by asking pairs of students to answer questions created yesterday by advanced students. The teacher reviews characteristics of the African folktales (studied in a prior lesson) by asking students to list as many of them as they can.

Objective and Purpose. The teacher tells students they will be publishing a class booklet of the stories to be shared at the multicultural fair. The teacher conducts a class discussion to identify potential topics for the folktales and writes them on the board.

Directions. (groups are heterogeneous, 3 to 4 students per group) All members of the group must participate in the development of the folktale. Roles are 1 = artist, 2 = writer, and 3 = idea person. Each folktale must follow the format of an African folktale, but with a modern topic. The teacher gives students a direction sheet. The stories will be presented in oral form to the class, and the class will vote on which ones will be presented at the fair. Each group will have 15 minutes to present. The teacher reminds them to include ALL members and to use encouraging behavior (the teacher refers the students to the T-chart listing the desired behavior).

Constructing/Applying. As students work in their small groups the teacher circulates to provide help and monitor their performance. The teacher also monitors and notes their use of the social skill "encouraging all to participate."

Assessing. After the first day of work, the teacher leads the group in developing a rubric for grading the stories. Later, this tool is used for peer and teacher evaluation of the stories as they are read in class. At the end of the class, the teacher gives feedback on the social skill. The students present folktales and the teacher refers to principles and characteristics of African folktales to strengthen the relationship between contemporary U.S. culture and African culture.

Adaptations. Struggling students are placed in supportive groups to help with learning problems. Advanced students can create an extra rap song or play.

Lesson 4: African Masks (Direct and Independent)

Objective

At the conclusion of the unit on Zimbabwe, students will create the designs for an African mask that is consistent with the styles of art created by the people of Zimbabwe and that represent learning achieved in the unit.

Set. The teacher shows a representative set of slides of artistic creations from Zimbabwean artists. The students are asked to discuss them.

Objective. The teacher tells students about the project, the characteristics required, and how it will be graded. The teacher reminds students that the projects will be displayed in the hallway and at the fair.

Purpose. The teacher tells students it is important to appreciate the artistic contributions of African people and to use visual and creative aspects to enhance life's enjoyment.

Input/Modeling/Checking. The assignment is to have an original African mask from each student. The teacher shows the slides and photographs and asks students (using wait time) about the people, history, and culture of Zimbabwe. When completed, the teacher distributes the mask cut-outs that have been coated with white paint as an object for students to embellish. Students may also select other media, with permission from the teacher.

Practice and Feedback. As students work, the teacher circulates through the room to encourage and monitor their performance.

Formative Assessment. When completed, the African masks are displayed around the room. The masks judged by the students as extraordinary are set in the media center display case.

Adaptations. Struggling students are provided with coaching and offered a simplified version of the assignment. Advanced students are used as peer coaches.

Lesson 5: Racism Then And Now (Direct)

Objective

Students will compare and contrast the racism involved in European imperialism in Africa in the period 1850–1950 with present-day examples of racism.

Set. The teacher asks students to recall the definition of racism studied in class (uses wait time and random selection), assigns the students to bring to class a present-day example from a recent newspaper or magazine, and asks them to be ready to explain why it is an example of racism.

Objective. The teacher tells students that next week they will be asked to write an essay that analyzes racism in a given situation and compares it with that found in Africa in the imperial era.

Purpose. The teacher tells students that although racism appears in a different environment today and aims to achieve a somewhat different outcome, its essential elements have not changed over the centuries. The teacher stresses the importance of voting citizens of the U.S. recognizing this.

Input/Modeling. The teacher distributes an example that he/she has prepared to illustrate how one person, the teacher, has interpreted the task the students are expected to do. As an alternative, the teacher distributes an example generated by a student in a previous class. A grading rubric also is provided.

Check for Understanding. Students are encouraged to discuss in pairs the directions and ask questions to ensure that they are clear about what is expected.

Practice. After the time period (a week or less) allotted for the students to gather their examples, the students each present their example in a first draft of the paper and the teacher gives feedback.

Formative Assessment. The teacher assigns a two-page, double-spaced essay in which the student must explain how the example chosen is consistent with the characteristics of racism and how it differs from what was learned about European racism in Africa during the period 1850–1950.

Adaptations. Struggling students and advanced students may choose an alternative mode for presenting their information: a videotape, a newspaper report, a debate, or role-play.

Lesson 6: Modern Zimbabwe and Cultural Traditions (Direct)

Lesson Objective (To Guide the Teacher)

Students will be able to describe key elements in the culture and lifestyle of modern-day Zimbabwe citizens and compare them with traditional ways.

Set (Beginning of Lesson). Teacher holds up a map of Zimbabwe. "I want everyone to jot down a few ideas you have about how the people in Zimbabwe live—their lifestyle and culture. Be ready to read a few of your ideas to me when I call on you in a minute." The teacher walks around the room and reads what students write. After a minute he or she calls on four randomly selected students. "Well, you have some interesting ideas about this country. Remember, we studied earlier about the geography and environment of Zimbabwe, now we'll see how that impacts the way people there live."

Objective (Learning Outcome Told to Students). By the end of this lesson I want you to be able to describe to me in your own words at least five characteristics of life in Zimbabwe. We'll play a game where you must give me information on a Jeopardy-type contest. I'll also ask you to write a short essay comparing the modern and traditional lifestyles."

Purpose (Why We're Learning This). Later, we're going to be working in groups to create video reports that you will be presenting in class about life at Great Zimbabwe in the 14th and 20th centuries, so paying attention today will be very important to that project. Also, I think learning about how modern life and ancient traditions coexist in Zimbabwe might help you understand some of the current difficulties faced by many other nations currently in the news—in Africa, Asia, and even here at home."

Information/Modeling. The teacher explains ancient traditions and shows pictures, diagrams, and artifacts. He or she points to relevant areas on a large wall map. (The teacher has previously determined by content analysis the order in which these terms and concepts should be presented. This concept map is shared with students to assist with note taking.)

Check for Understanding. The teacher asks students a series of questions based on information that has been presented. Examples include "What is a key feature of courting behavior in traditional times?" and "What is the role of music?" (The teacher tells everyone to think of a response, asks the question, gives wait time, and randomly selects students to respond.)

Information/Modeling. The teacher explains and illustrates (with pictures, graphs, charts, etc.) how modern life is conducted in Zimbabwe.

Check for Understanding. The teacher asks a few oral true/false questions to which all students respond (after wait time) with an overt signal (e.g., thumbs up or down).

Information/Modeling. The teacher describes the process of comparing and contrasting two sets of information, using part of what has already been presented and filling in a chart with two columns: Similarities and Differences. The teacher "thinks aloud" to illustrate the thinking process of comparing and contrasting—metacognition.

Check for Understanding. Students are asked to fill in the next two comparisons on their own (or in pairs) and to cross their arms when they are finished. Students are randomly selected to share their answers, and the chart is completed.

Guided Practice.
  1. The teacher writes five statements on the board and gives students two minutes to work in groups of three using their books and notes to decide if the statements are true or false. Then all students vote. After each vote a few students of varied achievement levels explain their vote.

2. Students read a story about an adolescent whose family lives in modern-day Zimbabwe. In pairs, they identify the customs and cultural norms represented in the story. Finally, they must pick two events and describe how they might be different if the story occurred in a more traditional family. Each pair is asked to share their conclusions in a five-minute presentation to two other pairs (groups of six) at the end of tomorrow's class.

3. Extra guided practice is planned, but may not be necessary if students are successful. If not used here, it may be used for reteaching or review. It is a worksheet with an outline of the key ideas from the concept map, but with many empty spaces. Students work to fill in the gaps with assistance from teacher or other students.

Formative Assessment (To Make Sure Every Student has Achieved the Objective). Teacher uses the Jeopardy game to get every student to recall the key ideas, getting around to all students, and keeping note of who may need reteaching. Students are also asked to write a brief paragraph describing five ways the modern and traditional lifestyles are the same and different. The teacher provides no help at this point and uses this information to "branch" students into one of the following.

Differentiation/Adaptations (Teacher Decides Who Does What, Depending on Need).

- Reteaching (For those who did not succeed on the assessment) Teacher (or a peer) provides information, checking, and guided practice in a different learning style or different approach: for example, CD-ROM.
- Extension activity (If more practice would seem boring to some or all) In pairs, students are asked to describe how the customs presented in the lecture relate to the climate and geography studied last week.
- Independent Practice (This may be done without teacher guidance, perhaps as extension or homework) Students look for ways their own lives are following more traditional or modern ideas from their own culture. They bring in a list of at least four ideas.

This lesson will be followed up with reteaching, review, and extension on the next days. All skills, once learned, will be reviewed intermittently. Answers are checked and feedback/reteaching is provided.

Evaluation/Assessment

The unit evaluation has two parts:

1. An objective test that includes multiple-choice, short-answer, and essay questions.
2. A portfolio, which is organized as an exhibition. Students from other classes, faculty, school board members, parents, and community guests will be invited to view exhibitions of student work from the unit. African tribal masks, site maps, and scenes from short stories created by groups of students will be featured in

displays and performances in the auditorium. The assessment portfolio will include a/an:

1. drawing of a tribal mask with a brief paper explaining how the selected elements reflect Shona culture and history;
2. original short story that accurately reflects the history and culture of the Shona people who lived at Great Zimbabwe in the 14th century or in the capital of King Monomatapa's empire at the beginning of the 16th century (successive drafts are presented and commented upon);
3. graph of the population density, area of, and perimeter enclosed by the Great Zimbabwe and modern-day Harare (for display in the hallway);
4. report of the three magazine or newspaper articles that discuss some event involving racism and the reasons why racism is alleged in each event; and
5. scale drawing of Great Zimbabwe and a comparative area of students' hometown in the form of an archeological site map (for display in the hallway).

Each of the five assignments will be evaluated using a rubric (created by the teacher and students) and will become important elements in determining the summative grade for the unit. Students with special needs will have assessments tailored to their needs: more advanced students will complete higher level extensions of the projects designed in consultation with the teacher, and struggling students will be allowed to redesign projects and retake tests until they demonstrate a sufficient level of mastery.

Feedback from students will be solicited through a short questionnaire, asking students to describe what they liked the best and what they would change.

Materials and Resources

Materials are determined by each lesson.

Primary source: *Rulers of Rhodesia*, by Ransford.

Other resources the teacher has consulted include (list specific titles, etc.):

1. state and district standards for social studies and other subjects;
2. the district's textbooks, if any;
3. a collection of historical fiction from the local library;
4. assorted videos on Africa and Zimbabwe;
5. websites that provide primary source documents, paintings, and time lines (e.g., CD-ROM materials);
6. nonfiction books on Zimbabwe at diverse grade levels;
7. materials from the historical society and history museum; and
8. a variety of texts on methods for teaching social studies through an interdisciplinary approach.

Glossary

A

academic service learning Community service that helps students achieve specific learning objectives

acceleration Pursuing the regular curriculum at a faster pace; for example, working on curriculum above the grade level, grade skipping, early entrance to school, etc.

achievement Typically entails solving a problem, answering a question, or creating something new, and then presenting the results to an interested audience

active listening A response to students that summarizes both the emotional attitude and the intellectual content of what the students said

activism To promote improvements for society or groups within society

advanced organizer An activity at the beginning of a lesson designed to preview the structure of the content to be addressed

affective domain Goals that involve emotional behavior—that is, feelings, attitudes, preferences, and values

assertive discipline A specific management system designed by Lee Canter, based on a behavior management approach

assessment The process of measuring the quantity and/or quality of a behavior or the indicator of that behavior

attending behavior Verbal and nonverbal responses from a teacher that indicate that the students' response is worthy of attention; e.g., nodding, smiling, or summarizing the response

authentic assessment A performance assessment where the focus of attention is on significant tasks such as student products, exhibits, or performances rather than on right or wrong answers on objective tests

authentic learning Learning that serves a real-world function, using information for a purpose other than simply presenting it to a teacher

authentic research Inductive lesson in which students collect and analyze data to draw new conclusions; unlike traditional inquiry lessons, the data is not presented by the teacher, nor are the preferred results identified in advance

automatic memory Memory that is conditioned through repetition

B

behavior management A tradition of management based on behaviorist theory, focusing on rewarding desired behaviors and punishing undesired behaviors

benchmarks Generally, more specific outcomes than standards; e.g., content standards translated into grade-level benchmark outcomes

Bloom's Taxonomy of Educational Objectives The most widely used process for ordering cognitive learning tasks.

Bloom's Taxonomy: Analysis At this level, the task given to students consists of unfamiliar data and/or examples but requires a more complex thought process than is elicited from an application task; requires the taking apart of a complex stimulus; for example, comparing and contrasting

Bloom's Taxonomy: Application At this level (and those that follow) students are required to exhibit complex thought as well as the retrieval of information; a typical task at this level is to provide unfamiliar math or science data, an historical incident, quotation, painting, or musical selection and ask the student if it is an example of a concept that has been previously learned

Bloom's Taxonomy: Comprehension At this level students understand material and can express it in their own words or in a similar form

Bloom's Taxonomy: Evaluation In this type of task students must defend their judgments or decisions using a combination of logical argument supported by factual evidence and the application of predetermined criteria.

Bloom's Taxonomy: Knowledge Tasks at this level oblige students to recall, recognize, or reproduce what has been previously learned

Bloom's Taxonomy: Synthesis At this level, students create an original product, exhibit, or performance that involves the selection, organization, and implementation of a number of concepts and generalizations and requires substantial thought

brain-based education Educational practices based on inferences from neural psychology

C

checking for understanding   Part of continuous assessment that takes place during teaching by checking students' understanding of individual parts of a lesson

Choice Theory (Control Theory)   A theory by Glasser emphasizing individual choice and accountability for actions

cognitive domain   Such goals require students to memorize and recall information or to use their intellectual skills to perform complex tasks

compensatory instruction   Circumventing areas of weakness or lack of experience in order to carry on planned instruction

competitive learning   Students compete with others in the class to gain a limited number of high grades or rewards

concept attainment lessons   Inductive lessons in which students examine examples and nonexamples of a concept, find common characteristics, and discover the definition of the concept

concept formation lessons, concept development lessons   Inductive lessons in which students classify data or information into categories to generate concepts

concept mapping   A thought process that culminates in a visual display of relevant knowledge and relationships

concepts   Categories or classes of things that share a set of critical characteristics

congruence   A match among goals or outcomes, lesson objectives, lesson activities, and assessment

constructivism   Education based on the premise that students construct their own understanding through experience; also known as constructivist learning theory

context   The conditions that surround classroom life: social, cultural, political, and physical

contingency management   System in which teachers reward and punish students based on desired behaviors, often using concrete tokens or incentives

continuous assessment   The idea that assessment must take place before, during, and after teaching as an inherent part of the instructional process

contract learning, as assessment   Learning in which the standards for receiving a given grade are described to all students; students contract with the teacher to perform certain tasks at a given quality level in order to receive the agreed-upon grade

contracting   An agreement between the student and teacher that directs the tasks to be completed in a given time frame

controlled assessment   In this assessment, learners are always aware they are being assessed

cooperative group learning   A group where students are responsible for both their own and others' learning

cooperative social skills   In cooperative groups, students learn how to interact in ways that promote learning, consensus, and conflict resolution

creative/productive giftedness   As used by Renzulli, individuals' ability to create—rather than consume—information or art

criterion-referenced assessment   Assessment that considers each student as an individual, and the individual's performance is assessed against predetermined performance standards

critical pedagogy   Teaching practices that promote more democratic, equitable social relations, even if that means challenging the existing order

critical/ethical reflection   Reflecting from multiple perspective on the long-term impact of teaching on students' learning and their role in society; e.g., Will this child respect and be kind to others?

cultural competence   The ability to act, communicate, and care for others in a culturally appropriate way

cultural discontinuity   Experience that occurs when the culture of the school differs from the students' home culture

cultural pluralism   A model in which cultural groups maintain their own identity while adopting some aspect of a joint culture, sometimes contrasted with the "melting pot" model in which cultural identities are merged

culturally relevant teaching   Teaching that empowers students intellectually, socially, and emotionally by using cultural referents in teaching knowledge and skills

culture   The learned, shared, and transmitted social activities of a group

curriculum   The subject matter to be taught, sometimes organized by scope (content) and sequence (order). The term is sometimes used to include the context of learning and the content, methods, and assessments used to help students learn

curriculum benchmarks   Outcomes that are expressed in terms of what students are to know or do in order to demonstrate that they have achieved what is expected of them

curriculum compacting   A strategy for differentiation that involves preassessing students' prior knowledge and eliminating previously mastered material

curriculum rationale   A section of a unit that describes the content to be taught and justifies its importance

curriculum standards   Global, long-range outcomes or goals for all students

D

descriptive research   Research that summarizes evidence, trends, or characteristics

differentiated instruction   Instruction that is modified to meet differing needs of multiple students simultaneously, usually by providing varied assignments and/or instruction

direct lesson   A lesson in which the teacher directly tells students the objective and presents information, usually in a deductive manner, moving from general principles to specific examples

disability   A condition that results in a reduced competency to perform some task or behavior

discussion   An open-ended exchange of ideas designed to share information and explore ideas, rather than to seek the "right" answer

disciplined inquiry   Students investigate meaningful questions using methods similar to those used by a professional in the discipline or area

divergent question   An open-ended question that invites multiple perspectives and may be answered with a variety of correct answers

E

educational evaluation   A systematic process that leads to a judgment about the ability or achievement exhibited by a person or persons or about the success of an instructional program.

educational goal   A goal that provides general direction to the teacher in making crucial decisions about instruction; similar to a standard

electronic appearances   Format in which students communicate electronically with a subject-matter expert

emotional disabilities   Disabilities in which students display inappropriate behavior repeatedly to the extent that it affects their academic growth, social maturity, and relationships

emotional intelligence   Combination of self-awareness, independence, optimism, accountability, empathy, and the ability to manage one's feelings

emotional memory   Memory linked to emotionally powerful events or feelings

enrichment   Incorporation of activities outside the regular curriculum to provide additional challenge and/or interest

Enrichment Triad   A model including three types of enrichment: exploratory activities, group training activities, and individual or small-group projects

episodic memory   Memories encoded in spatial relationships

essentialism   An educational philosophy that argues that the purpose of schooling is to impart essential knowledge, skills, and attitudes in order to enable young people to function as fully developed human beings

evaluative (global) praise   Praise that indicates whether the student response or work is good or bad, but does not specify the aspects that are worthy of praise

exhibition   A culminating experience that requires the application of knowledge within specific conditions, usually involving some type of presentation to an audience outside the class

experimental research   Research that manipulates one or more variables to determine causal relationships

F

facts   Specific statements about particulars—people, things, places, time, or events

formative evaluation or **assessment**   Evaluation that provides information for improvement while the person or program has the opportunity to improve

G

gender bias   Conscious or unconscious differential treatment of males and females

generalizations   A statement that expresses a generally true relationship between two or more concepts

gifted   The varied definitions all reflect ability and/or performance beyond the norm in some area, although there is no consensus to the defintion of giftedness as it pertains to either students or adults.

global classrooms   Classrooms in different locations study a common topic during the same time period

graphic organizers   Visual depictions illustrating the structure of the content to be taught or task to be addressed; can be used to introduce a lesson or to structure responses, or organize information.

group alerting   The technique of keeping students' attention in a group when they have not yet been called on to respond

group investigation   A group learning strategy where students investigate a particular question of their choice in shared-interest groups

guided practice   A type of practice at the end of direct instruction in which the teacher monitors learning and adjusts accordingly

H

handicap   The disadvantage that results from the effects of a disability; may vary depending on the situation and supports available

heterogeneous grouping   Students group according to differences; e.g., mixing males and females in a group or mixing reading performance levels in a group

higher level thinking   Thinking that uses information in some way (analysis, synthesis, evaluation, problem solving solving, etc.) rather than simple recall

historical research   Research that analyzes past trends, events, characteristics

homogenous grouping   Students grouped according to similarities; e.g., groups of all males, all minorities, all low reading performance students

humanisitic approach to classroom management   An approach to classroom management focused on healthy emotional growth as a natural process

I

inclusion   A strategy that places students with severe disabilities in general education settings with appropriate supports; full-inclusion programs place all students in general education, eliminating all full-time special education placements

independent investigations   Students conduct their own investigation into an area of interest

independent practice   A type of practice in which students work without teacher monitoring

individual accountability   Cooperative groups in which each student is held accountable for achieving the essential objectives of the lesson

IEP (Individual Educational Plan)   An educational plan required for students with disabilities that outlines goals, strategies, etc.

individualized learning   Learning in which students work on their own to accomplish an objective or preset standard

Individuals with Disabilities Education Act (IDEA)   The major federal legislation mandating educational services for students with disabilities

inductive lesson or teaching   A lesson or situation in which the teacher provides data or experiences from which students draw conclusions to discover concepts or generalizations

informal instruction   Instruction that occurs as part of the daily interactions in the home, classroom, or community rather than through prepared lessons

informational feedback   Feedback that is specific about the aspects of student work that are correct or need to be corrected

inquiry lesson   Inductive lessons in which students interpret and apply data to draw conclusions, often to determine generalizations

instructional objective   A specific statement of what the student will know or be able to do after the unit or lesson ends; similar to a benchmark; includes **A**udience, **B**ehavior, **C**onditions, and **D**egree elements

information processing theory   A theory for how human memory takes in and stores information

interdisciplinary instruction   Instruction planned to use multiple disciplines. When used to investigate a topic or time period, sometimes called multidisciplinary instruction

interdisciplinary thematic instruction   Instruction planned around a theme that is meaningful across disciplines

interest-development center   A center where a child can engage in activities that stimulate interesting areas outside the regular curriculum

intrinsic motivation   Motivation that comes from within the student, rather than from outside forces

J

jigsaw   A cooperative group strategy that requires each member to become an expert on one part of the whole lesson and teach it to the other students

K

key questions   Questions that focus a unit of instruction by providing provocative or interesting areas for exploration.

knowledge work   Student activity that involves using ideas, concepts, problem-solving skills, and applying facts to achieve some end

KWL   A strategy for collecting information on what students **K**now, **W**ant to know, and **L**earn about a topic

L

learning center   A center where a student can engage in activities that introduce or reinforce a specific part of the regular curriculum

learning disabilities   Disabilities in which students demonstrate a reduced competency to perform some behaviors while performing as well or better than peers on other tasks; may be evident only in particular subject areas

learning style   Variations in individual ways of learning across all domains, include differences in taking in and processing information

Least Restrictive Environment (LRE)   From the Individuals with Disabilities Act, this clause requires that students with disabilities be placed in the educational environment appropriate to their needs that is closest to a general education setting

less is more   The principle that students will learn more if instruction focuses on fewer ideas in greater depth

lesson design   All the activities necessary to teach a specific objective, may span one or more than one day

lesson plan   Plan of activities for a single day, usually for one subject

limited materials interdependence   Cooperative groups in which each student must share with others the essential materials (e.g., one sheet of directions, one pencil)

M

macroculture   The dominant culture in a society

mainstreaming   A practice in which students with disabilities spend part or all of the school day in a general education setting; the term originated with reference to students with mild to moderate disabilities

mastery learning   An instructional approach based on the belief that all students can be successful in achieving all objectives if additional learning time is allowed for those who need it

mental disabilities   Disabilities in which students function below the norm in all areas of learning

metacognition   Awareness of one's own thinking

microculture   A smaller culture within a macroculture that how has its own unique cultural patterns

mnemonic device   A strategy for memorizing information

modeling   Instruction that is more than simply demonstrating; it requires careful explanation of the processes being demonstrated

morning meetings   Whole-class activity used to begin the day, usually containing a greeting, sharing, group activity, and news/announcements

multicultural curriculum   Curriculum designed to promote and value diverse cultures while helping students to see the commonalities among groups

multiple intelligences   A model developed by H. Gardner establishing profiles of intelligences across at least eight domains

N

National Board for Professional Teaching Standards (NBPTS)   An organization offering advanced national teacher certification in a variety of areas

natural assessment   Assessment requiring no artificially constructed testing environment; learners are not aware that they are being assessed

noncontingent reinforcement   Reinforcement that is a given without reference to any specific reinforcement behavior

norm-referenced assessment   Assessment that considers each student in relationship to every other student in the group; the evaluator examines all the scores and determines where each individual's score first within the distribution

O

open-ended question   A question with many potential correct responses

outcome   A goal for instruction describing what students should be able to understand or do; often describes broad rather than specific behaviors, and is sometimes used synonymously with goals

overlapping   Teacher's ability to attend to more than one event or activity simultaneously

P

pattern disrupters   According to Dreikurs, students who misbehave repeatedly; divided into attention-seeking, sympathy-seeking, power-seeking, and revenge-seeking behaviors

pedagogical content knowledge   Knowledge about teaching and learning that is specific to a particular discipline or body of content

pedagogy   Knowledge about teaching and learning, including knowledge of human development, learning theory, multicultural education, teaching methods, assessment, and classroom management

peer tutoring   Activities in which students assist classmates or younger students with assigned activities

perfectionism   Individuals' pursuit of excellence to the degree that it becomes debilitating and nothing short of perferection can be accepted

performance   Assessment tasks that demonstrate understanding by asking students to use information in a real or realistic context

personal progressives   The wing of the Progressive Movement that views the curriculum as a flexible menu of options that responds to the felt needs and interests of each individual child

physical or other health disabilities   Disabilities that reduce students' capability to perform psychomotor tasks and/or affect stamina, vitality, etc.

portfolio   A collection or display of student work for assessment purposes

positive interdependence   Practice in cooperative learning groups in which students are responsible for the success of each group member; they "sink or swim together"

positive moments   A management strategy in which teachers include 15 seconds of positive time with a pattern disrupters every hour and incorporate positive touch and informational feedback into their interactions with them

preassessment The process of diagnosing students' learning before designing instruction

prior knowledge All the knowledge and experiences students bring to instruction, including general cultural understandings, relevant information, and misconceptions

probe A request for more information from a student following an incomplete or unclear response

problem-based learning Learning structured around a complex problem; students learn content and processes as necessary to solve the problem, rather than being given the problem after the skills are learned

procedural memory Memory encoded in the actions of the body

professional development Growth and learning activities that enhance the professional practice of the teacher

progressivism An educational philosophy that emphasizes thinking, the child, and democratic values and processes rather than predetermined subject matter

prompt A hint or suggestion to help a student respond correctly following an incomplete or incorrect response

psychomotor domain The domain consisting of learning that is sensory in nature, ranging from involuntary, reflexive movements to complex chains of skillful, purposeful behavior

Q

quality circles A group meeting in which students discuss the problem behaviors of and with a student and possible solutions while throughout maintaining the students' anonymity

questioning Technique in which the teacher or student poses questions; the teacher is the focus of attention; usually used to review and practice information

R

RAPSD (Rational Approach to Practical School Discipline) An eclectic approach to school management developed by Gardner

rationale An introduction to a unit explaining the content and purposes of the unit

reality therapy An approach designed by Glasser based on the premise that a student's past is over and he or she must now make choices about future behavior; emphasizes the use of individual conferences and group meetings to establish a positive environment for learning

reconstructionism An educational philosophy characterized by a belief that schools should prepare the future adults of society to work for and demand societal change

reflection State of thinking about, interpreting and analyzing one's own experiences with the goal of improving one's practice and students' learning

reflection/reflective teaching The ability to make rational educational choices and take responsibility for those decisions; reflective teaching is reflection in action, carrying through the decisions made

reflective decision maker An active designer of curriculum, instruction, and assessments who makes rational educational choices and and takes responsibility for those choices by reflecting on their effects as students

reflective listening A brief summary of a student's response to indicate that it was heard and understood

reliability Idea concerned with consistency or stability from one performance to the next so that one can be confident that the performance is a representative measure

remedial approach, remediation Practice of teaching prerequisite skills before going on to new instruction

responsive classroom model A model of classroom organization designed to promote both academic and social learning

reward interdependence Technique of cooperative groups in which students strive to help each member succeed so that each member will receive a reward

role-play An activity in which students take on a role to solve a problem or act out a situation

routines, classroom Procedures for carrying on everyday classroom functions, e.g., distributing papers, working in groups

rubric A scoring guide that reveals to the student the criteria used to grade an authentic performance or product

rules, classroom A statement that informs students which behaviors are acceptable and unacceptable in the classroom

S

scaffolded instruction Strategies used to bridge gaps between students' prior experiences and content to be taught, often involving teacher guidance and gradually shifting responsibility to students

schema (singular; schemata, plural) Cognitive structures that link knowledge together in individualized patterns to establish concepts and relationships

schoolhouse giftedness A term introduced by Renzulli reflecting individuals' ability to take in and process information, as in traditional schools

semantic memory   Memory encoded in words

sensory disabilities   Disabilities in which students have reduced visual or auditory acuity

set   A type of opening used in direct instruction to focus student attention on relevant content and activate prior knowledge; sometimes called "anticipation set"

simulation   An activity in which students experience a simplified version of reality, either through complex extended role-play or through electronic "virtual" experiences

situated cognition   Thinking or learning that occurs in a meaningful context or situation

smoothness and momentum   The ability to move from one activity to the next without losing student attention

Social Progressives   The wing of the Progressive Movement that views school curriculum as providing preparation for successful adult life in a democratic society

social skills   In cooperative groups students learn how to interact in ways that promote learning, consensus, and conflict resolution

specific praise   Praise that describes the specific aspects of students' performance that are worthy of praise

speech disabilities   Disabilities in which students have reduced competency in speech, often caused by a hearing loss

standardized tests   Tests that are administered and scored in exactly the same way for all students, frequently mass-produced national tests

standards   Outcomes to be attained by students at particular levels, usually broad; at this time most states have adopted specific content standards

stations   Areas in the classroom where students can engage in differing activities simultaneously; generally contain a narrower focus of activities than a center, often a single activity

structured content analysis   A process to break down content to be taught into its components parts (i.e., generalizations, concepts, and facts) and to display the relationships among them

student needs and characteristics   Students' culture, development level, background knowledge, mood, learning styles, interests, and needs

student-teams-achievement divisions   In heterogeneous teams members prepare each other for a quiz (which may be different for various achievement levels); teams with highest gains win

subject matter   The content to be taught, usually specified by national, state, and district curriculum standards

summative evaluation   Evaluation used to make educational decisions about persons or programs after instruction terminates

T

target paper   An example of an assignment used to portray for students the various criteria for an exemplary performance

T-chart   A list, used most often in cooperative group lessons, of what a particular social skill looks like and sounds like

teacher characteristics and beliefs   Teacher philosophy, confidence, enthusiasm, cultural background, intelligence, commitment, values, beliefs, prior experiences, and attitudes

teacher consumer   A teacher who uses textbooks, units, and lessons designed by others without critically examining their quality or appropriateness for his or her students

teacher designer   A teacher who adapts and /or creates curriculum while considering a number of variables

Teams-Games-Tournaments   Strategy in which teams of heterogeneous members prepare each other for team competitions; in the tournament students are grouped with others of similar achievement levels from different teams

technical reflection   Reflection on the short-term impact of teaching and learning strategies; e.g., Did I use this technique correctly?

technology gap   The gap between those with access to computers or other technology and those without access

telefieldtrips   Visiting locations around the world through electronic communications

telementoring   Mentoring through electronic means

thematic instruction   Instruction planned around a theme that is meaningful across disciplines

three-ring conception of giftedness   A model of creative/productive giftedness comprising above-average ability, creativity, and task commitment

tiered activities   Activities in which all students work on similar activities and content but at different levels of difficulty

transmitted knowledge   Knowledge gained from courses, discussions with teachers, observations, textbooks, and research

Triarchic Theory   A theory of intelligence developed by Sternberg including the ability to process information, response to novelty, and ability to respond to the environment

U

understanding   Mastery of content to the extent that one can use it in a new situation

understanding performance Activities that require students to demonstrate understanding by using information in new situations, typically planned for assessment purposes

unit A coordinated series of lessons that leads to one or more broad goals

V

validity The property of an assessment that makes it an accurate gauge of what it purports to measure

verbal labeling The act of pointing out in words an idea or element the teacher wants students to notice, giving notice that something is important (during modeling)

W

wait time The wait period after a question that allows students to prepare an answer; results in more equitable student involvement and deeper thinking

with-it-ness The extent to which the teacher demonstrates an awareness of student behaviors in all situations and areas of the classroom

Z

Zone of Proximal Development Level of instruction at which information is beyond the child's current understanding but close enough to be reachable with scaffolding by a teacher

Index